# STILWELL
Publishing

KEY TO ENTRIES

Use the Ordnance Survey **grid reference** with OS maps and any atlas that uses the British or Irish National Grid. The letters (two in Great Britain, one in Ireland) refer to a 100-kilometre grid square. The first two numbers refer to an east-west co-ordinate and the last two to a north-south co-ordinate within that square.

Bellingham
NY8383

▲ **Bellingham Youth Hostel,** Woodburn Road, Bellingham, Hexham, Northumberland, NE48 2ED
Actual Grid Ref: NY843834
Tel: 01434 220313
Fax: 01434 220313
Capacity: 28
Under 18: £5.75
Adults: £8.50
Open: All year, 5.00pm
Self-catering facilities • Showers • Lounge • Cycle store • No smoking • WC • Kitchen facilities
Hostel built of red cedarwood on the Pennine Way, high above the small Borders town of Bellingham. Near Kielder Water (with forest trails and watersports) and Hadrian's Wall.

▲ ***Brown Rigg Caravan & Camping Park,*** Bellingham, Hexham, Northumberland, NE48 2JY
Actual Grid Ref: NY834827
AA grade: 4 Pennants
Tel: 01434 220175
Fax: 01434 220175
Email: info@northumberlandcaravanparks.com
Tent pitches: 30
Tent rate: £3.50-£8.50
Open: Apr to Oct
Last arr: 8.30pm
Facilities for disabled people • Dogs allowed • Electric hook-up • Calor Gas/Camping Gaz • Picnic/barbecue area on site • Children's play area • Showers • Laundrette on site • Public phone on site • Shop on site • Games room • Indoor swimming pool nearby • Boating/sailing/watersports nearby • Tennis courts nearby • Golf nearby • Riding nearby • Fishing nearby
A 5 acre level site situated in the beautiful Northumberland National Park half mile south of Bellingham on B6320. The Pennine Way borders the site with the Reivers Cycle Route nearby. Hadrian's Wall and Kielder Water 9 miles.

The red triangle symbol identifies the listing as a youth hostel, bunkhouse or camping barn.

The green tent symbol identifies the listing as a camping site that accepts tents.

Last arrival – the camping site does not accept arrivals after this time in the evening.

The **location heading**: every hamlet, village, town and city listed in this directory is shown on the county map at the head of each chapter.

Time of day when the hostel opens.

The **Actual Grid Reference** for the hostel or camping site provides a more precise locator than the location grid reference, by including an extra digit both in the east-west co-ordinate and in the north-south co-ordinate. It is accurate to within 100 metres.

Distributed in Great Britain, Ireland and the Commonwealth by Orca Book Services, Stanley House, 3 Fleets Lane, Poole, Dorset BH15 3AJ (Tel: 01202 665432); and in the USA by Seven Hills Distributors, 49 Central Avenue, Cincinatti, OH 45202 (Tel: 513 381 3881).
Available from all good bookshops.

ISBN 1-900861-20-8

Published by Stilwell Publishing,
59 Charlotte Road, Shoreditch, London, EC2A 3QW.
Tel: 020 7739 7179.

© Stilwell Publishing, March 2001 (unless otherwise stated).
All base map images in this publication © Stilwell Publishing from geographical data supplied by Maps in Minutes © MAPS IN MINUTES™ 2000.
Overlaid locations © Stilwell Publishing.

All rights reserved. No part of this publication may be reproduced, stored in a retrieval system, or transmitted in any form or by any means – electronic, mechanical, photocopying, or otherwise – unless the written permission of the Publisher has been given beforehand.

Publisher: Tim Stilwell
Editor: Martin Dowling
Design and Maps: Space Design and Production Services Ltd
Front Cover Design: Crush Design Associates

All the information in this directory is published in good faith on the basis of details provided to Stilwell Publishing by the owners of the premises listed. Stilwell Publishing accepts no responsibility for any consequences arising from any errors, omissions or misrepresentations from information so provided. Any liability for loss or damage caused by information so provided, or in the event of cessation of trade of any company, individual or firm mentioned, is hereby excluded.

BRITAIN & IRELAND HOSTELS & CAMPING 2002

Publisher **Tim Stilwell**
Editor **Martin Dowling**

Publishing

Contents

Introduction and
  regional maps .... vi–xiii

CHANNEL ISLANDS 1

ENGLAND

Bedfordshire 3
Berkshire 4
Bristol 6
Buckinghamshire 7
Cambridgeshire 9
Cheshire 12
Cornwall 14
Cumbria 30
Derbyshire 46
Devon 54
Dorset 68
County Durham 75
Essex 78
Gloucestershire 81
Greater Manchester &
  Merseyside 85
Hampshire 87
Herefordshire 91
Hertfordshire 94
Isle of Wight 96
Isles of Scilly 99
Kent 100
Lancashire 105
Leicestershire 110
Lincolnshire 112
London 119
Norfolk 122
Northamptonshire 129
Northumberland 131
Nottinghamshire 137
Oxfordshire 140
Rutland 144
Shropshire 145
Somerset 150
Staffordshire 158

Suffolk 162
Surrey 167
East Sussex 170
West Sussex 174
Teesside 178
Tyne & Wear 179
Warwickshire 180
West Midlands 182
Wiltshire 183
Worcestershire 186
East Yorkshire 188
North Yorkshire 192
South Yorkshire 206
West Yorkshire 208

ISLE OF MAN 212

NORTHERN IRELAND

Antrim 213
Armagh 215
Down 216
Fermanagh 218
Londonderry 220
Tyrone 222

REPUBLIC OF IRELAND

Cavan 223
Clare 224
Cork 226
Donegal 228
Dublin 230
Galway 232
Kerry 235
Kildare 238
Kilkenny 239
Laois 240
Limerick 241
Louth 242
Mayo 243
Roscommon 245

Sligo 247
Tipperary 248
Waterford 250
Westmeath 251
Wexford 252
Wicklow 254

SCOTLAND

Aberdeenshire & Moray ... 257
Angus 262
Argyll & Bute 264
Ayrshire & Arran 268
Borders 271
Dumfries & Galloway 274
Fife 280
Glasgow & District 283
Highland 285
Inner Hebrides 297
Lanarkshire 301
Lothian & Falkirk 304
Orkney 307
Perthshire & Kinross ... 309
Shetland 312
Stirling & the Trossachs ... 313
Western Isles 316

WALES

Anglesey 318
Carmarthenshire 322
Ceredigion 325
Denbigh & Flint 330
The Glamorgans 333
Monmouthshire 336
North West Wales 339
Pembrokeshire 351
Powys 358

LOCATION INDEX 364

Introduction

The aim of this book is really very simple. It sets out to list as many hostels and camping sites in as many places throughout Britain and Ireland as possible. Stilwell's has published market-leading guides to Bed & Breakfast accommodation since 1994, founded on the twin principles of affordability and ease of geographical reference – wherever you are in Britain or Ireland there is a good-value place to stay, and you can find it fast using our directories. Having achieved great success with our B&B books (as well as self-catering since 1997) we decided it was time to turn our attention to the needs of the true budget traveller – and here is the result: Stilwell's *Hostels & Camping*.

The range of accommodation listed is wide. We have published details of all hostels in the 'official' associations – the Youth Hostels Association for England and Wales, SYHA for Scotland, An Oige for the Republic of Ireland and Hostelling International Northern Ireland. Association hostels range from modern city hostels with the highest standards of comfort and facilities, through centuries-old Irish and Scottish castles, grand English country houses and traditional Welsh farmhouses to basic croft buildings in the remote islands of Scotland. Wherever you choose, you will find clean, safe and comfortable accommodation, a friendly welcome and great value. To stay at association hostels, you are required to be a member of one of the associations – you can join at most member hostels, but you should phone in advance to check. We also feature a good number of independently-run hostels, which reflect a similar range of locations and styles of accommodation – and by no means compare unfavourably with the associations on price.

Between hostel accommodation and camping lies the middle ground of bunkhouses and camping barns. Bunkhouses (often converted farm buildings) offer basic beds in dormitories, but always have both showers and kitchen facilities. Camping barns and bothies are more basic – these offer a sheltered space for putting sleeping bags down and are sometimes referred to as 'stone tents'. These forms of accommodation are particularly suited to groups taking part in outdoor activities, and sometimes only accept group bookings. All listings of hostels, bunkhouses and camping barns are based on information provided by the owners themselves.

By far the largest number of listings in this book are for camping sites, ranging from top-of-the-range holiday parks with the widest range of facilities to small farm sites. A good number of camping site listings are based on details provided by the owners – these entries have descriptions, list the facilities available and in some cases have pictures. The majority, however, give simply the basic information of address and phone number, location and when in the year the site is open to campers.

This is quite deliberately a directory not a guidebook. Its aim is that of any directory in any field: to achieve coverage as comprehensive as possible – and therefore offer the widest choice. Wherever you find yourself as a budget traveller in Britain or Ireland there is somewhere within reach, listed in this book, where you can find either a roof to sleep under or a place to pitch your tent. Where a camping site or a hostel has its listing highlighted by a pink box, this does not imply recommendation by Stilwell's – the owner has paid a little more to have their entry stand out from the page.

The book is geographically organised to make it as easy as possible to find speedily the information you need. It is arranged in alphabetical order first by country, then county and finally within each county chapter by location. The thumb-index markings at the edge of the pages delineate the four basic sections – England (preceded by the Channel Islands and followed by the Isle of Man), Ireland (Northern Ireland followed by the Republic), Scotland and Wales. Each county has its own chapter, headed by a map showing all locations where we have listings of hostels or campsites – hostels represented by a red triangle, campsites by a green tent symbol, and locations where we have both

Introduction

categories of entry by the two symbols together. Each listing is also coded by the red triangle or green tent to indicate that it is a hostel or a camping site.

The maps are intended to act as a general reference – they show where each location lies in relation to major towns and roads. For navigational purposes you should use more detailed Ordnance Survey maps – we recommend the Landranger, Discovery and Discoverer series for Britain, the Republic of Ireland and Northern Ireland respectively. We have printed an OS grid reference under the name of every location in the book (bar those in the Channel Islands, not covered by the Ordnance Survey) – used in tandem with OS maps, these make route-planning easy. In addition, the vast majority of hostel and camping site listings include a more accurate eight-figure (seven in Ireland) Actual Grid Reference – this pinpoints position to within one hundred metres.

A brief explanation of how we have organised counties into chapters is required. Counties in Ireland are straightforward – the six historic counties of Northern Ireland are followed by the twenty-six of the Republic. In Britain things are less simple. Several reorganisations over the last three decades have left England a patchwork of 'two-tier' counties (county council coexisting with subdivided districts) and 'unitary' districts outside of any county. We have grouped certain of the unitary districts created in the mid 1990s together with the counties with which they were historically associated. For example, North Lincolnshire and North East Lincolnshire are included in the Lincolnshire chapter, leaving the other two districts created by the abolition of the former county of Humberside – the City of Hull and the East Riding – in their own East Yorkshire chapter. By and large, where 'new' counties created in 1974 have been replaced by smaller districts, our policy has been to group them in chapters that best reflect 'historic' counties. One notable exception is Teesside, which contains the four districts of the former county of Cleveland, still a natural grouping around the towns at the mouth of the Tees. Greater Manchester and Merseyside have been merged into one chapter. Where a county created or enlarged in 1974 is still in existence, we have reflected this – so Westmorland remains in the Cumbria chapter, Huntingdonshire within Cambridgeshire.

The unitary districts into which Scotland and Wales have been uniformly divided are, in many cases, too small to merit their own chapter. The groupings we have used represent a compromise between historic counties and new districts (in some cases, for example Pembrokeshire, they happily coincide) – and common-sense combinations that work for our purposes (for example Glasgow & District, which includes six districts). Districts included within a given 'county' chapter are shown on the map; if you are in any doubt about which chapter you should look in for a particular location, consult the Location Index at the end of the book.

Our directory contains 3,500 listings in 2,500 locations. You will find the vast majority of the information accurate and useful. Some may be out of date – owners may have put prices up or even gone out of business since we gathered their details. It is always, in any case, a good idea to phone in advance rather than turning up unannounced: it is possible there is no space available, particularly in high-demand periods – the summer months, half term holidays and public holidays. If you are travelling as a group, it is essential to call well in advance – not only for possible lack of space, but also because some hostels and camping sites impose restrictions on size and type of groups, such as not permitting single-sex groups. And if you've made a booking and your plans change, call to let them know – it is always possible to make a bed or a pitch available to someone else.

The outbreak of foot and mouth disease has seriously affected leisure activities in the British countryside in the early part of 2001. For this reason, the launch of this book has been delayed. Now that the disease is finally and thankfully in abeyance, the countryside is opening up again. We hope our directory will prove a valuable tool as you explore it.

The Editor, May 2001

England & Wales - Regions

ENGLAND

1	Bedfordshire		31	Somerset
2	Berkshire		32	Staffordshire
3	Buckinghamshire		33	Suffolk
4	Cambridgeshire		34	Surrey
5	Cheshire		35	East Sussex
6	Cornwall		36	West Sussex
7	Cumbria		37	Tyne & Wear
8	Derbyshire		38	Warwickshire
9	Devon		39	West Midlands
10	Dorset		40	Wiltshire
11	County Durham		41	Worcestershire
12	Essex		42	East Yorkshire
13	Gloucestershire		43	North Yorkshire
14	Greater Manchester & Merseyside		44	South Yorkshire
			45	West Yorkshire
15	Hampshire			
16	Herefordshire			
17	Hertfordshire		46	Isle of Man
18	Isle of Wight			
19	Kent			
20	Lancashire			
21	Leicestershire			

WALES

22	Lincolnshire		47	Anglesey
23	London		48	Carmarthenshire
24	Norfolk		49	Ceredigon
25	Northamptonshire		50	Denbigh & Flint
26	Northumberland		51	The Glamorgans
27	Nottinghamshire		52	Monmouthshire
28	Oxfordshire		53	North West Wales
29	Rutland		54	Pembrokeshire
30	Shropshire		55	Powys

England & Wales - Regions

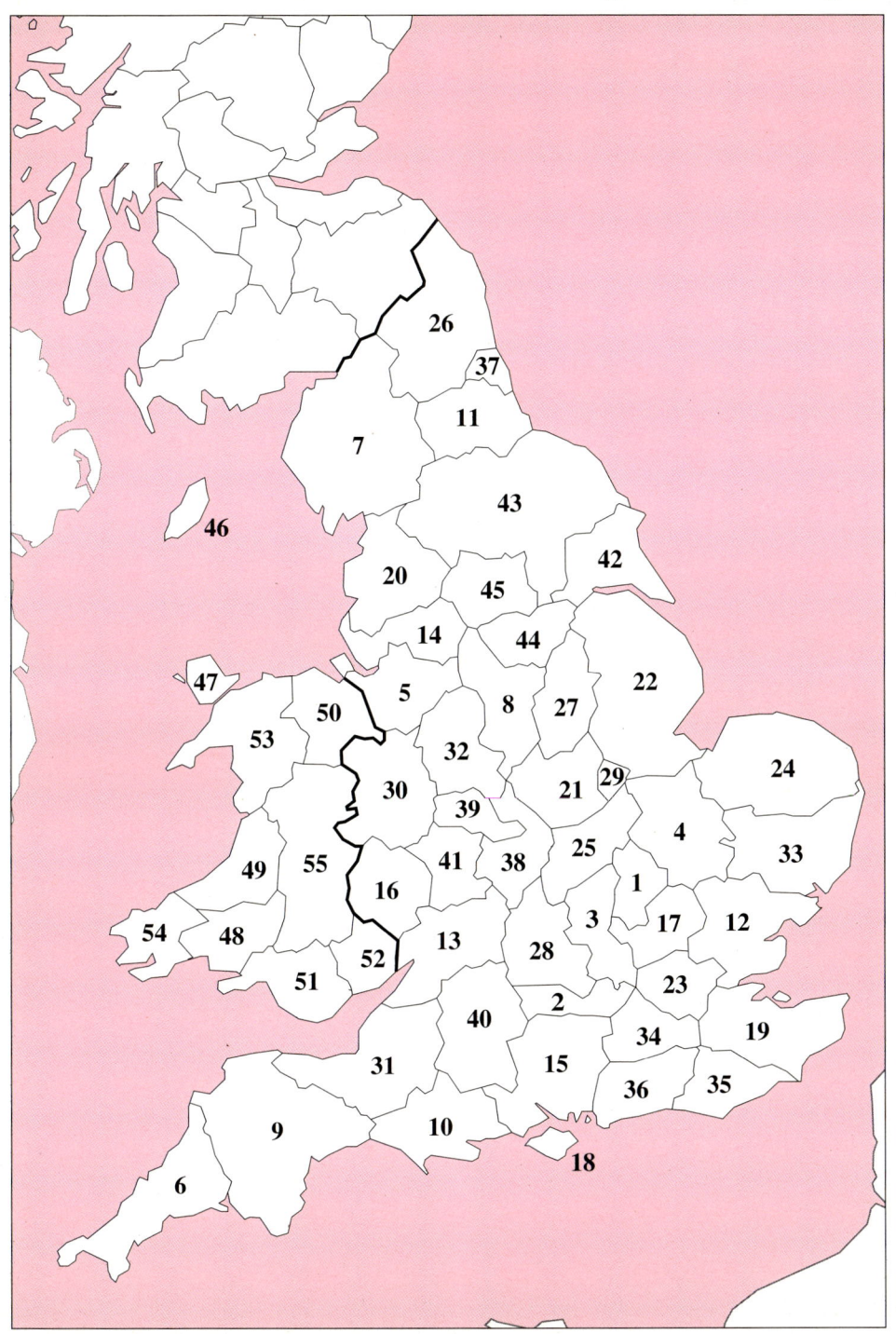

Stilwell's Hostels & Camping 2002

Scotland - Regions

56	Aberdeenshire & Moray
57	Angus
58	Argyll & Bute
59	Ayrshire & Arran
60	Borders
61	Dumfries & Galloway
62	Fife
63	Glasgow & District
64	Highland
65	Inner Hebrides
66	Lanarkshire
67	Lothian & Falkirk
68	Orkney
69	Perthshire & Kinross
70	Shetland
71	Stirling & the Trossachs
72	Western Isles

Scotland - Regions

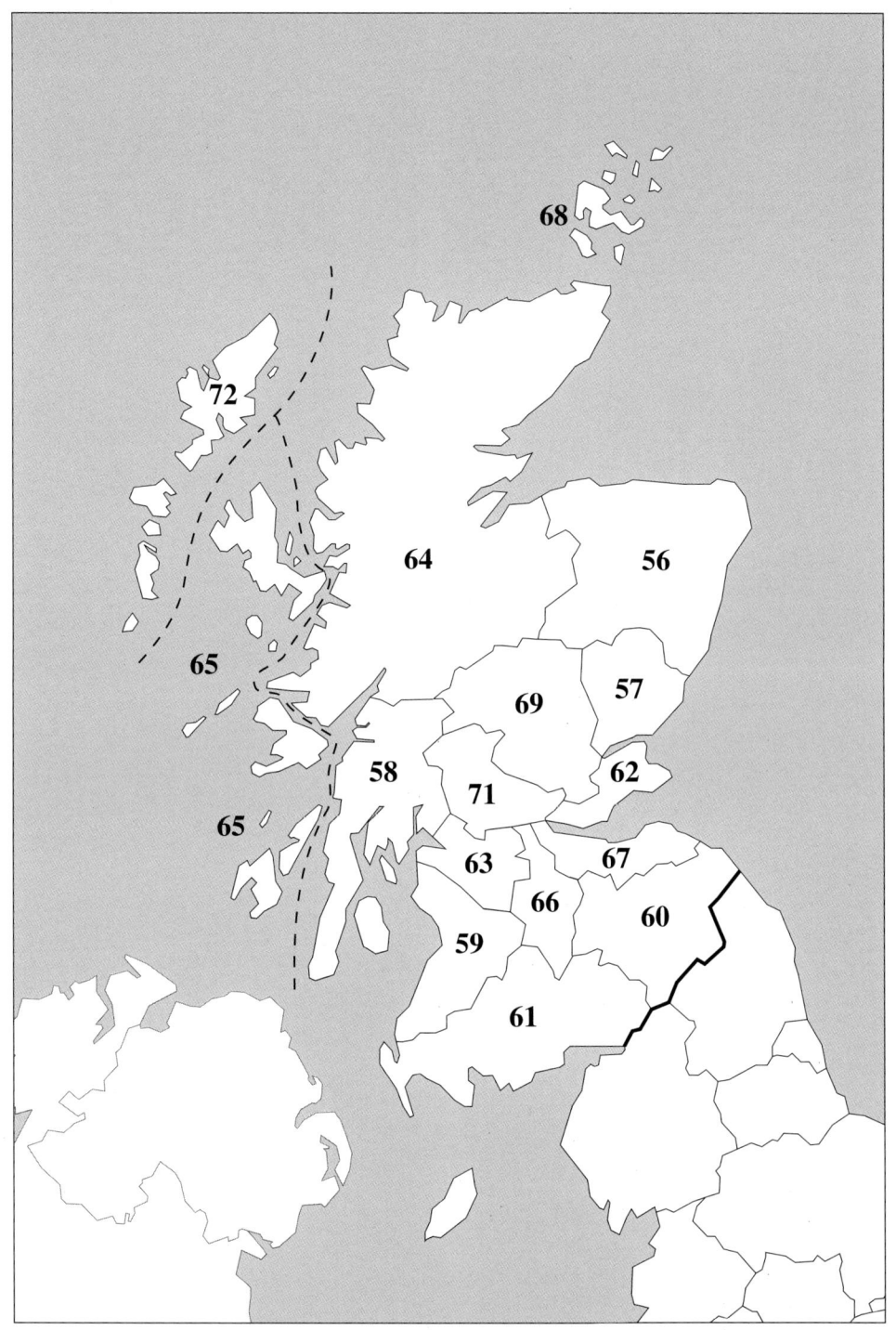

Ireland - Counties

NORTHERN IRELAND
1 County Antrim
2 County Armagh
3 County Down
4 County Fermanagh
5 County Londonderry
6 County Tyrone

REPUBLIC OF IRELAND
7 County Carlow
8 County Cavan
9 County Clare
10 County Cork
11 County Donegal
12 County Dublin
13 County Galway
14 County Kerry
15 County Kildare
16 County Kilkenny
17 County Laois
18 County Louth
19 County Limerick
20 County Longford
21 County Louth
22 County Mayo
23 County Monaghan
25 County Offaly
26 County Roscommon
27 County Sligo
28 County Tipperary
29 County Waterford
30 County Westmeath
31 County Wexford
32 County Wicklow

Ireland - Regions

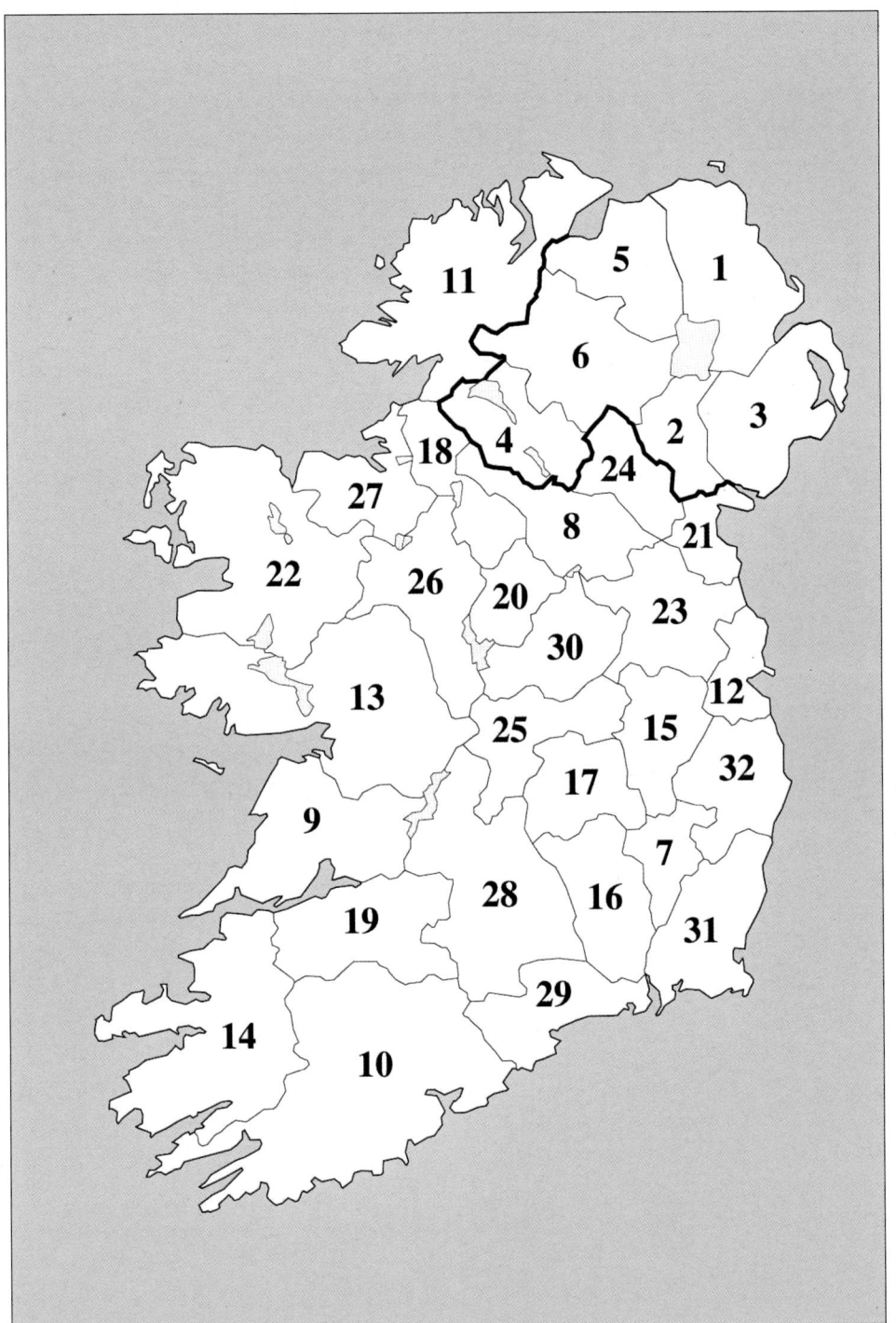

Channel Islands

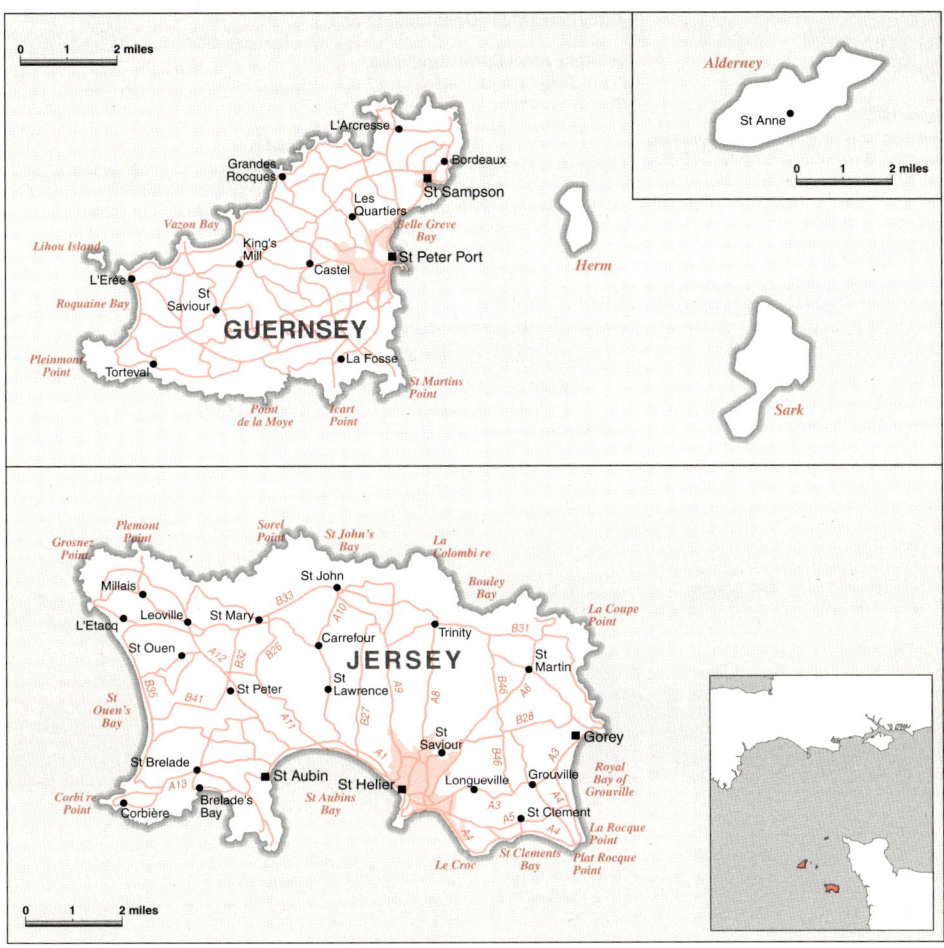

Guernsey

Castel

▲ **Fauxquets Valley Farm Campsite,** Castel, Guernsey, C.I., GY5 7QA
Tel: 01481 255460
Email: fauxquets@campguernsey.freeserve.co.uk
Open: May to Sep

Herm

▲ **Seagull Campsite,** Herm, Guernsey, C.I., GY1 3HR
Tel: 01481 722377 **Open:** May to Sep

St Sampson

▲ **Vaugrat Camping,** St Sampson, Guernsey, C.I., GY2 4TA
Tel: 01481 57468 **Fax:** 01481 51841
Open: May to Sep

▲ **Le Vaugrat Campsite,** Route de Vaugrat, St Sampson, Guernsey, C.I., GY2 4TA
Tel: 01481 257468 **Open:** May to Sep

Torteval

▲ **Laleur Camping Site,** Torteval, Guernsey, C. I., GY8 0LN
Tel: 01481 63271 **Open:** May to Sep

Channel Islands • MAP PAGE 1

Vale

▲ **La Bailloterie Camping,** La Bailloterie, Vale, Guernsey, C.I., GY3 5HA
Tel: 01481 243636
Open: May to Sep

Jersey

Leoville

▲ **Summer Lodge Camping Site,** Leoville, St Ouen, Jersey, C.I., JE3 2DB
Tel: 01534 481921
Open: May to Sep

Rozel

▲ **Rozel Camping Park,** Rozel, St Martin, Jersey, C.I., JE3 6AX
Tel: 01534 856797
Fax: 01534 856127
Open: May to Sep

St Brelade

▲ **Rose Farm,** St Brelade, Jersey, C.I., JE3 8DE
Tel: 01534 741231 **Open:** May to Sep

▲ **Rose Farm Camp Site,** Rose Farm, St Brelade, Jersey, C. I., JE3 8DF
Tel: 01534 41231
Open: May to Sep

St Martin

▲ **Beuvelande Camp Site,** Beuvelande, St Martin, Jersey, C.I., JE3 6EG
Tel: 01534 853575 / 85223
Open: May to Sep

Hostels and campsites may vary rates – be sure to check when booking.

If you have to cancel your visit to any hostel or campsite, please let them know – it is always possible to make a bed or a pitch available to someone else.

Sark

Sark

▲ **Pomme de Chien Campsite,** Sark, Guernsey, Channel Islands, GY9 0SE
Tel: 01481 832316
Open: All year

▲ **La Valette Campsite,** Sark, Guernsey, Channel Islands, GY9 0SE
Tel: 01481 832066
Open: All year

Bedfordshire

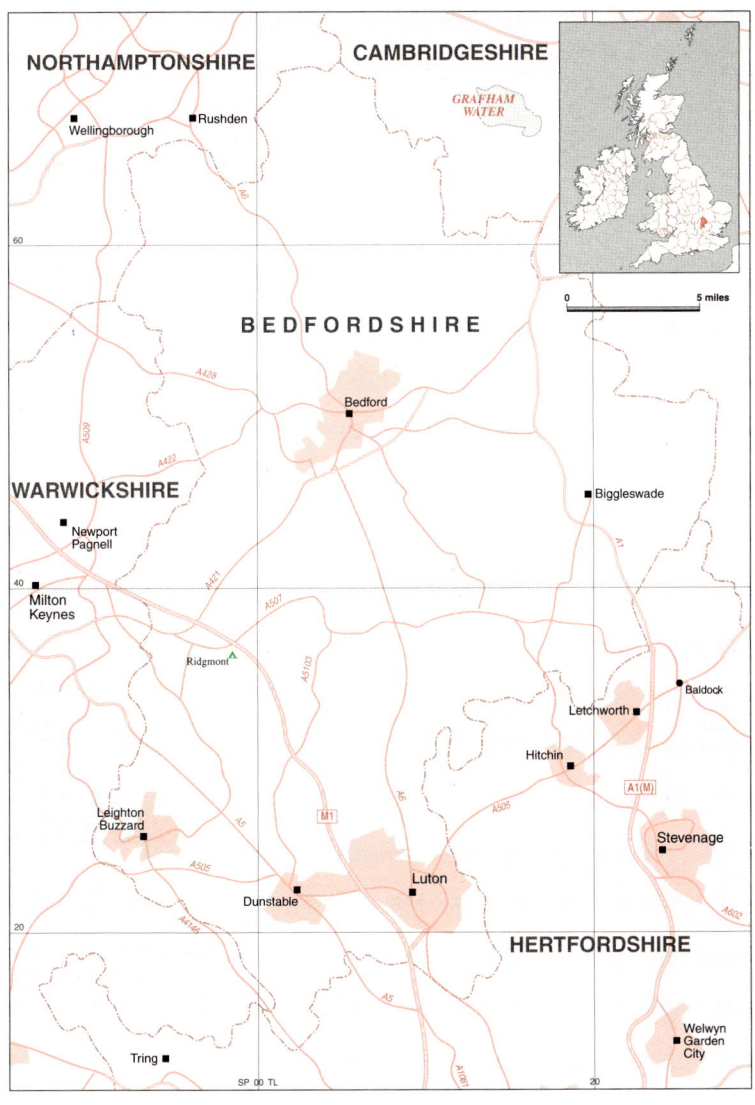

Ridgmont
SP9736

▲ *Rose & Crown Camping & Caravan Site,* 89 High Street, Ridgmont, Bedford, MK43 0TY
Tel: 01525 280245
Open: All year

Berkshire

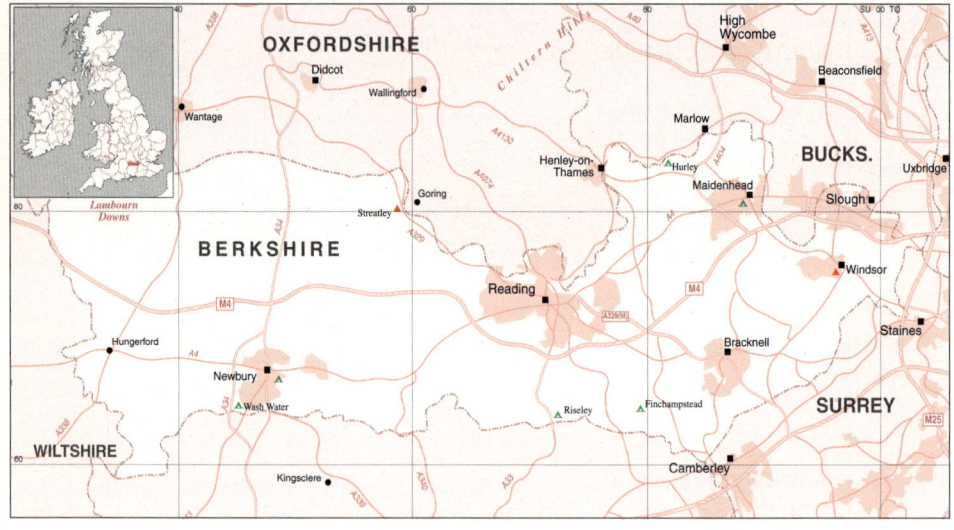

Finchampstead
SU7963

▲ **California Touring Park,** Nine Mile Ride, Finchampstead, Wokingham, Berks, RG11 3NY
Actual Grid Ref: SU787651
Tel: 0118 973 3928
Open: Mar to Oct

Hurley
SU8284

▲ **Hurley Farm Caravan & Camping Park,** Shepherds Lane, Hurley, Maidenhead, Berks, SL6 5NE
Actual Grid Ref: SU816837
Tel: 01628 823501
Fax: 01628 825533
Open: Mar to Oct

Maidenhead
SU8781

▲ **Amerden Caravan & Camping Park,** Old Marsh Lane, Dorney Reach, Maidenhead, Berks, SL6 0EE
Actual Grid Ref: SU918705
Tel: 01628 627461
Open: Apr to Oct

▲ **Harford Bridge Holiday Park,** Tavistock, Devon, PL19 9LS
Actual Grid Ref: SU504767
Tel: 01822 810349
Open: Mar to Nov

Newbury
SU4767

▲ **Bishops Green Farm,** Bishops Green, Newbury, Berks, RG20 4JP
Actual Grid Ref: SU502630
Tel: 01635 268365
Open: Apr to Oct

Riseley
SU7263

▲ **Wellington Country Park,** Riseley, Reading, Berks, RG7 1SP
Actual Grid Ref: SU734565
Tel: 0118 932 6444
Fax: 0118 932 6445
Open: Mar to Oct

Hostels and campsites may vary rates – be sure to check when booking.

Streatley
SU5980

▲ **Streatley-on-Thames Youth Hostel,** Hill House, Reading Road, Streatley, Reading, Berks, RG8 9JJ
Actual Grid Ref: SU591806
Tel: 01491 872278
Fax: 01491 873056
Email: streatley@yha.org.uk
Capacity: 51
Under 18: £7.75
Adults: £11.00
Open: Feb to Nov + New Year, 5pm
Family bunk rooms
Self-catering facilities • Television • Showers • Dining room • Drying room • Cycle store • Parking Limited • Evening meal available 7.00pm • No smoking • WC • Kitchen facilities • Breakfast available • Credit cards accepted
Homely Victorian family house, completely refurbished, in a beautiful riverside village.

MAP PAGE 4 • **Berkshire**

Wash Water

SU4563

▲ **Oakley Farm Caravan & Camping Park,** Andover Road, Wash Water, Newbury, Berks, RG20 0LP
Actual Grid Ref: SU455630
Tel: 01635 36581
Open: Mar to Oct

Windsor

SU9676

▲ **Windsor Youth Hostel,** Edgeworth House, Mill Lane, Windsor, Berks, SL4 5JE
Actual Grid Ref: SU955770
Tel: 01753 861710
Fax: 01753 832100
Email: windsor@yha.org.uk
Capacity: 67
Under 18: £7.75
Adults: £11.00
Open: All year (not Xmas/New Year), 1.00pm
Self-catering facilities • Television • Showers • Laundry facilities • Lounge • Drying room • Cycle store • Parking cars only • Kitchen facilities • Breakfast available • Luggage store • Credit cards accepted
Queen Anne residence in the old Clewer village quarter on the outskirts of historic Windsor.

Bristol

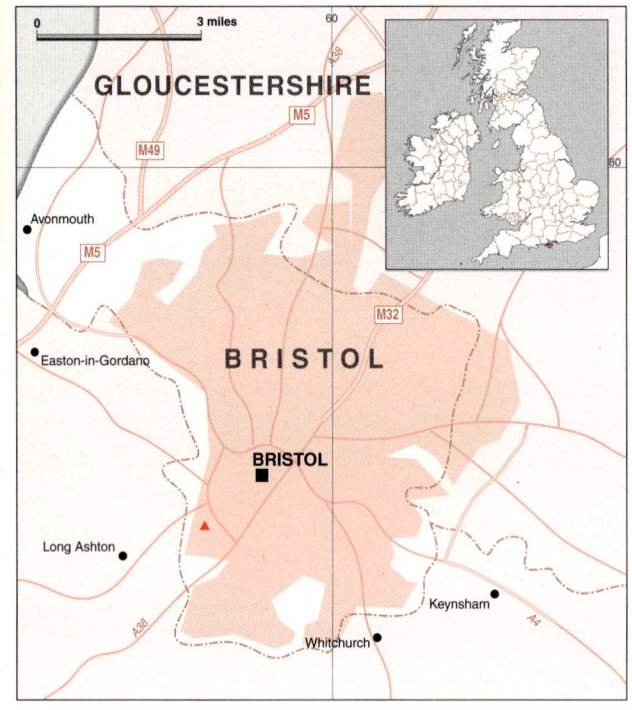

Bristol
ST6075

▲ **Bristol Youth Hostel,** Hayman House, 14 Narrow Quay, Bristol, BS1 4QA
Actual Grid Ref: ST586725
Tel: 0117 922 1659
Fax: 0117 927 3789
Email: bristol@yha.org.uk
Capacity: 92
Under 18: £8.50
Adults: £12.50
Open: All year, All day
Family bunk rooms
Self-catering facilities • Television • Showers • Laundry facilities • Lounge • Games room • Cycle store • Evening meal available 6.00-7.00pm • Kitchen facilities • Breakfast available • Luggage store • Credit cards accepted
With views over the waterways, this hostel has been sympathetically and imaginatively restored to create a relaxing yet cosmopolitan atmosphere.

Buckinghamshire

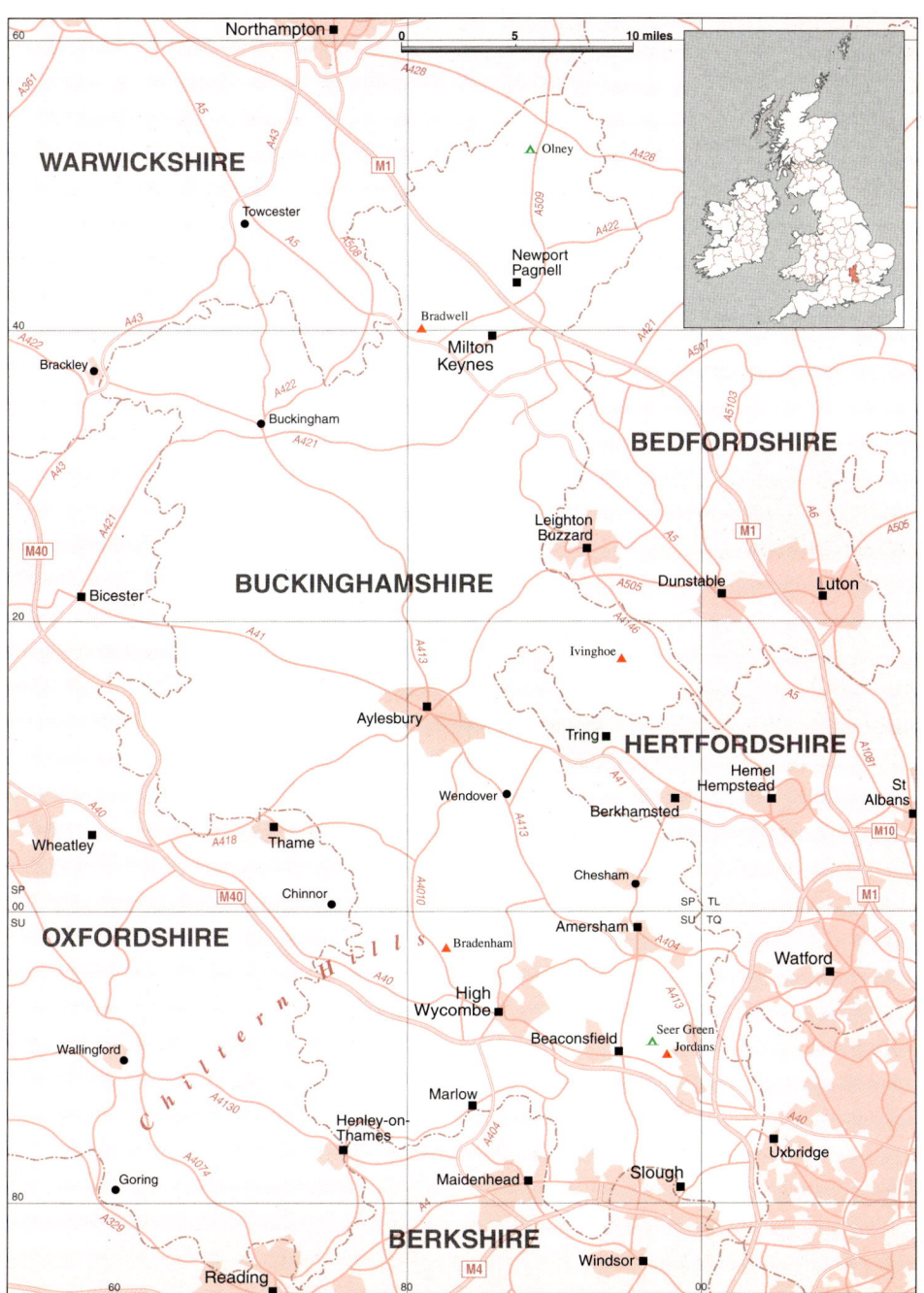

Buckinghamshire • MAP PAGE 7

Bradenham

SU8297

▲ **Bradenham Youth Hostel,** *The Village Hall, Bradenham, High Wycombe, Bucks, HP14 4HF*
Actual Grid Ref: SU828972
Tel: 01494 562929
Fax: 01494 564743
Email: bradenham@yha.org.uk
Capacity: 16 **Under 18:** £6.50
Adults: £9.15 **Open:** All year, 5.00pm
Self-catering facilities • Showers • Lounge • Drying room • Cycle store • No smoking • WC • Kitchen facilities • Credit cards accepted

Modest hostel in an old schoolhouse, with showers and WCs a short walk down the garden, in National Trust village tucked away in the Chiltern Hills.

Bradwell

SP8239

▲ **Bradwell Village (Milton Keynes) Youth Hostel,** *Manor Farm, Vicarage Road, Bradwell, Milton Keynes, Bucks, MK13 9AG*
Actual Grid Ref: SP831395
Tel: 01908 310944
Fax: 01908 310944
Capacity: 38
Under 18: £6.50
Adults: £9.15
Open: All year, 5.00pm
Self-catering facilities • Wet weather shelter • Lounge • Dining room • Drying room • Security lockers • Cycle store • Parking •

No smoking • Kitchen facilities • Breakfast available • Credit cards accepted

C17th farmhouse overlooking Norman castle earthworks in village setting close to city of Milton Keynes - a unique blend of old and new.

Ivinghoe

SP9416

▲ **Ivinghoe Youth Hostel,** *The Old Brewery House, High Street, Ivinghoe, Leighton Buzzard, LU7 9EP*
Actual Grid Ref: SP945161
Tel: 01296 668251
Fax: 01296 662903
Capacity: 50 **Under 18:** £6.90
Adults: £10.00
Open: Jan to Dec + Xmas, 5.00pm
Self-catering facilities • Television • Showers • Lounge • Drying room • Cycle store • Parking • Evening meal available 7.00pm • Kitchen facilities • Breakfast available

Georgian mansion, once home of a local brewer, next to village church in Chilterns' Area of Outstanding Natural Beauty.

Jordans

SU9791

▲ **Jordans Youth Hostel,** *Welders Lane, Jordans, Beaconsfield, Bucks, HP9 2SN*
Actual Grid Ref: SU975910
Tel: 01494 873135
Fax: 01494 875907
Capacity: 22
Under 18: £6.50
Adults: £9.15
Open: All year, 5pm
Camping
Self-catering facilities • Self-catering facilities • Showers • Showers • Showers • Wet weather shelter • Lounge • Cycle store • No smoking • WC • WC • Kitchen facilities • Credit cards accepted

Traditional purpose-built small hostel with outside washrooms and WCs, set in 2 acres of woodland. Comfortable bedrooms with central heating. The village of Jordans is closely associated with the early Quaker movement.

Olney

SP8851

▲ **Emberton Country Park,** *Olney, Bucks, MK46 5DB*
Actual Grid Ref: SP885505
Tel: 01234 711575
Fax: 01234 711575
Open: Apr to Oct

Seer Green

SU9692

▲ **Highclere Farm Country Touring Park,** *Highclere Farm, Newbarn Lane, Seer Green, Chalfont St Giles, Beaconsfield, Bucks, HP9 2QZ*
Actual Grid Ref: SU977927
Tel: 01494 874505 / 875665
Fax: 01494 875238
Email: highclere@peners.globalnet.co.uk
Open: Mar to Jan

Cambridgeshire

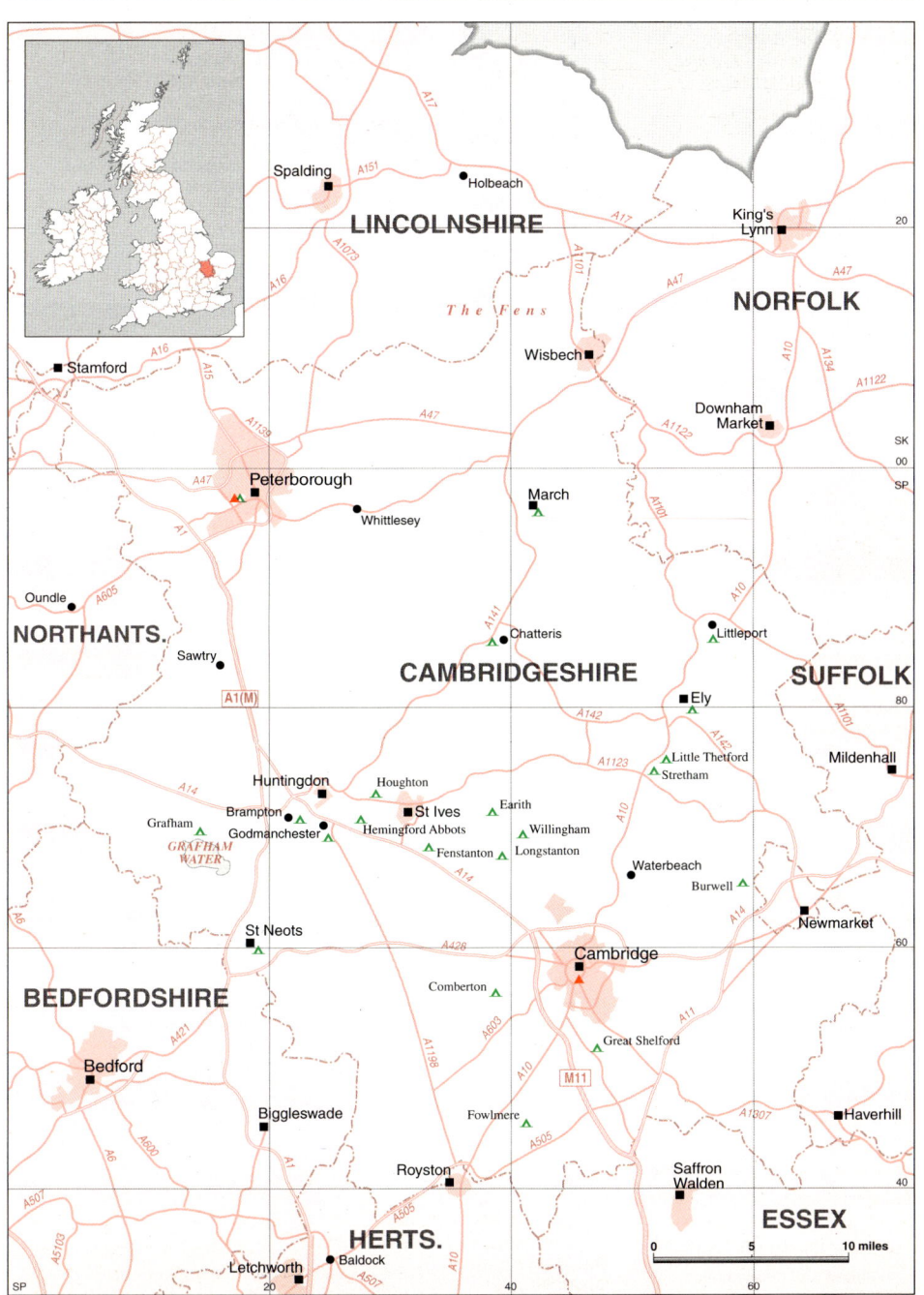

Cambridgeshire • MAP PAGE 9

ENGLAND

Brampton
TL2070

▲ **The Willows Caravan Park,** Bromholm Lane, Brampton, Huntingdon, Cambs, PE18 8NE
Actual Grid Ref: TL224708
Tel: 01480 437566
Open: Mar to Oct

Burwell
TL5866

▲ **Stanford Park,** Weirs Road, Burwell, Cambridge, CB5 0BP
Actual Grid Ref: TL585674
Tel: 01638 741547
Open: All year

Cambridge
TL4658

▲ **Cambridge Youth Hostel,** 97 Tenison Road, Cambridge, CB1 2DN
Actual Grid Ref: TL460575
Tel: 01223 354601
Fax: 01223 312780
Email: cambridge@yha.org.uk
Capacity: 100
Under 18: £8.50
Adults: £12.50
Open: All year, All day
Self-catering facilities • Showers • Licensed bar • Laundry facilities • Lounge • Games room • Cycle store • Evening meal available 6.00-7.30pm • Kitchen facilities • Breakfast available • Luggage store • Credit cards accepted
A Victorian town house convenient for the town centre and close to the train station. A perfect base to visit all the attractions of the ancient University town.

Chatteris
TL3985

▲ **Chatteris Town Football Club,** West Street, Chatteris, Cambridgeshire, PE16 6HW
Actual Grid Ref: TL386855
Tel: 01354 695764
Open: May to Oct

You are advised to book in advance for periods of high demand – the Summer months, Half Term holidays and public holidays.

Hostels and campsites may vary rates – be sure to check when booking.

Comberton
TL3856

▲ **Highfield Farm Camping Park,** Long Road, Comberton, Cambridge, CB3 7DG
Actual Grid Ref: TL389572
Tourist Board grade: 5 Star
AA grade: 4 Pennants
Tel: 01223 262308
Fax: 01223 262308
Tent pitches: 60
Tent rate: £6.50-£8.75
Open: Apr to Oct
Last arr: 10pm
Dogs allowed • Electric hook-up • Calor Gas/Camping Gaz • Children's play area • Showers • Laundrette on site • Public phone on site • Shop on site
Excellent award-winning park in attractive rural setting near Cambridge.

Earith
TL3874

▲ **Westview Marina,** High Street, Earith, Huntingdon, Cambs, PE17 3PN
Tel: 01487 841627
Open: Easter to Sep

Ely
TL5480

▲ **82 Broad Street,** Ely, Cambs, CB7 4BE
Tel: 01353 667609
Fax: 01353 667005
Open: Apr to Oct

Fenstanton
TL3168

▲ **Crystal Lakes,** Low Road, Fenstanton, Cambridgeshire, PE18 9HU
Actual Grid Ref: TL314694
Tel: 01480 497728
Open: Mar to Oct

Fowlmere
TL4145

▲ **Apple Acre Park,** London Road, Fowlmere, Royston, Cambs, SG8 7RU
Tel: 01763 208354
Open: All year

Godmanchester
TL2569

▲ **Park Lane Touring Park,** Godmanchester, Huntingdon, Cambs, PE18 8AF
Actual Grid Ref: TL245709
Tel: 01480 453740
Open: Mar to Oct

▲ **Huntingdon Boathaven & Caravan Park,** The Avenue, Godmanchester, Huntingdon, Cambs, PE18 8AF
Tel: 01480 411977
Open: Mar to Oct

Grafham
TL1668

▲ **Old Manor Caravan Park,** Church Lane, Grafham, Huntingdon, Cambs, PE28 0BB
Actual Grid Ref: TL155695
Tel: 01480 810264
Open: Feb to Nov

Great Shelford
TL4652

▲ **Camping & Caravanning Club Site,** 19 Cabbage Moor, Great Shelford, Cambridge, CB2 5NB
Actual Grid Ref: TL455539
Tel: 01223 841185
Open: Mar to Nov

Hemingford Abbots
TL2870

▲ **Quiet Waters Caravan Park,** Hemingford Abbots, Huntingdon, Cambs, PE18 9AJ
Actual Grid Ref: TL283712
Tourist Board grade: 4 Ticks
AA grade: 3 Pennants
Tel: 01480 463405
Fax: 01480 463405
Tent pitches: 20
Tent rate: £8.50-£10.00
Open: Apr to Oct **Last arr:** 8pm
Dogs allowed • Electric hook-up • Calor Gas/Camping Gaz • Showers • Laundrette on site • Public phone on site
Quiet riverside park located in centre of a picturesque village.

All details shown are as supplied by hostels and campsites in Autumn 2000.

MAP PAGE 9 • **Cambridgeshire**

Houghton

TL2872

▲ **Houghton Mill Caravan & Camping Park,** Mill Street, Houghton, Huntingdon, Cambs, PE17 2BJ
Actual Grid Ref: TL284721
Tel: 01480 462413 / 492811
Open: Apr to Sep

Little Thetford

TL5276

▲ **Two Acre Caravan Site,** Ely Road, Little Thetford, Ely, Cambridgeshire, CB6 3HH
Actual Grid Ref: TL528767
Tel: 01353 648870
Open: Mar to Oct

Littleport

TL5686

▲ **Riverside Caravan & Camping Site,** 21 New River Bank, Littleport, Ely, Cambs, CB7 4TA
Actual Grid Ref: TL577858
Tourist Board grade: 4 Star
Tel: 01353 860255
Tent rate: £5.00-£8.00
Open: Mar to Oct
Last arr: 10pm
Dogs allowed • Electric hook-up • Calor Gas/Camping Gaz • Showers • Laundrette on site • Public phone on site
Quiet, flat, fishing, hook-ups, showers, pubs 300 yards, shops nearby.

Longstanton

TL3966

▲ **Toad Acre Caravan Park,** Mills Lane, Longstanton, Cambridge, CB4 5DE
Actual Grid Ref: TL400665
Tel: 01954 780939
Open: All year

March

TL4197

▲ **Floods Ferry Touring Park,** Staffurths Bridge, Floods Ferry Road, March, Cambs, PE15 0YP
Actual Grid Ref: TL367945
Tel: 01354 677302
Open: All year

Peterborough

TL1999

▲ **Peterborough Youth Hostel,** Thorpe Meadows, Peterborough, PE3 6GA
Tel: 01629 592707
Capacity: 40
Under 18: £7.75
Adults: £11.00
Open: All year, 5.00pm
Family bunk rooms
Lounge • Parking • Evening meal available 7.00pm • WC • Breakfast available
Due to open in 2001. It is within the sculpture Park.

▲ **Northey Lodge Campsite,** North Bank, Newark Common, Peterborough, PE6 7YZ
Actual Grid Ref: TL236985
Tel: 01733 223918
Fax: 01733 223918
Tent rate: £7.50-£9.00
Open: All year
Last arr: 7pm (win)/8pm (sum) or by arrangement
Dogs allowed • Electric hook-up • Showers • Laundrette on site • Public phone on site
Immaculate campsite opposite River Nene plus security storage, boats and caravans.

▲ **Ferry Meadows Caravan Club Site,** Ham Lane, Peterborough, Cambs, PE2 0UU
Tel: 01733 233526
Open: Easter to Nov

Some hostels and campsites impose restrictions on size and type of groups they accept (e.g. not permitting single-sex groups). Always phone to enquire before booking.

St Neots

TL1860

▲ **Camping & Caravanning Club Site,** Rush Meadow, St Neots, Huntingdon, Cambs, PE19 2UD
Actual Grid Ref: TL182598
Tel: 01480 474404 / 01203 694995
Open: Mar to Nov

Stretham

TL5074

▲ **Bridge House,** Green End, Stretham, Ely, Cambs, CB6 3LF
Tel: 01353 649212
Open: All year

Willingham

TL4069

▲ **Roseberry Tourist Park,** Earith Road, Willingham, Cambridge, CB4 5LT
Actual Grid Ref: TL408728
Tel: 01954 260346
Open: Mar to Oct

▲ **Alwyn Tourist Park,** Over Road, Willingham, Cambridgeshire, CB4 5EU
Actual Grid Ref: TL397702
Tel: 01954 260977
Open: Mar to Oct

Cheshire

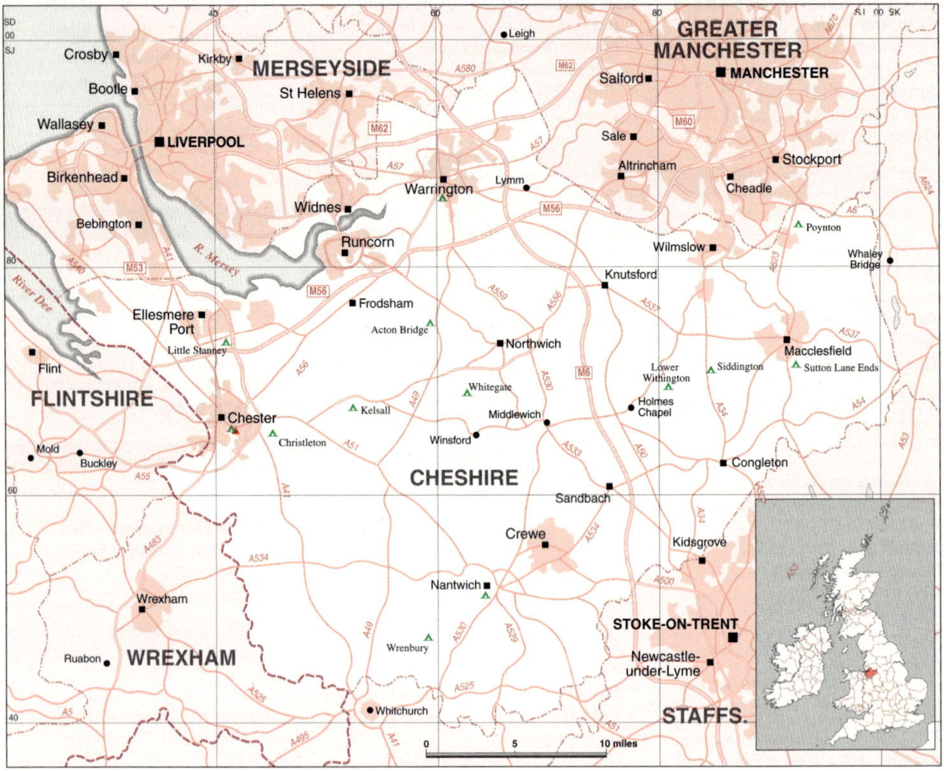

Acton Bridge

SJ5975

▲ **Manor Farm,** *Cliff Road, Acton Bridge, Northwich, Cheshire, CW8 3QP*
Tel: 01606 853181
Open: All year

▲ **Woodbine Cottage Caravan Park,** *Warrington Road, Acton Bridge, Northwich, Cheshire, CW8 3QB*
Actual Grid Ref: SJ600759
Tel: 01606 852319
Open: Mar to Oct

Chester

SJ4066

▲ **Chester Youth Hostel,** *Hough Green House, 40 Hough Green, Chester, CH4 8HD*
Actual Grid Ref: SJ397651
Tel: 01244 680056
Fax: 01244 681204
Email: chester@yha.org.uk
Capacity: 117
Under 18: £7.75 **Adults:** £11.00
Open: Jan to Dec, All day
Family bunk rooms
Self-catering facilities • Television • Showers • Shop • Laundry facilities • Lounge • Drying room • Security lockers • Parking • Evening meal available 6.00-7.30pm • Kitchen facilities • Credit cards accepted
Barely a mile from the city centre, this Victorian house and mews has comfortable accommodation for both families and singles.

▲ **Chester Southerly Caravan Park,** *Balderton Lane, Marlston-cum-Lache, Chester, CH4 9LB*
Actual Grid Ref: SJ385624
Tel: 01829 270791 / 270697
Open: Mar to Nov

12 Stilwell's Hostels & Camping 2002

MAP PAGE 12 • **Cheshire**

Christleton
SJ4465

▲ **Birch Bank Farm,** Stamford Lane, Christleton, Chester, CH3 7QD
Actual Grid Ref: SJ455663
Tel: 01244 335233
Open: May to Oct

Kelsall
SJ5268

▲ **Northwood Hall,** Dog Lane, Kelsall, Chester, Cheshire, CW6 0RP
Actual Grid Ref: SJ517680
Tel: 01829 752569 **Fax:** 01829 751157
Open: All year

Little Stanney
SJ4073

▲ **Chester Fairoaks Caravan Club Site,** Rake Lane, Little Stanney, Chester, CH2 4HS
Tel: 0151 355 1600
Open: All year

Lower Withington
SJ8169

▲ **Strawberry Wood Caravan Park,** Home Farm, Farm Lane, Lower Withington, Macclesfield, Cheshire, SK11 9DU
Actual Grid Ref: SJ804702
Tel: 01477 571407
Open: Mar to Oct

Hostels and campsites may vary rates – be sure to check when booking.

Nantwich
SJ6452

▲ **Brookfield Caravan Park,** Shrewbridge Road, Nantwich, Cheshire, CW5 7AD
Tel: 01270 69176
Fax: 01270 650736
Open: Easter to Sep

▲ **Brookfield Caravan Park,** Swimming Pool, Flag Lane, Crewe, Cheshire, CW2 7QX
Actual Grid Ref: SJ652516
Tel: 01270 569176
Open: Apr to Sep

▲ **Foxes Bank Farm,** Hunserston, Nantwich, Cheshire, CW5 7PN
Tel: 01270 520224
Open: All year

Poynton
SJ9283

▲ **Elm Beds Caravan & Camping Park,** Elm Beds Road, Higher Poynton, Stockport, Cheshire, SK12 1TG
Actual Grid Ref: SJ946827
Tel: 01625 872370
Open: Mar to Oct

Siddington
SJ8471

▲ **Capesthorne Hall Caravan Park,** Siddington, Macclesfield, Cheshire, SK11 9JY
Actual Grid Ref: SJ840727
Tel: 01625 861779
Open: Mar to Oct

Sutton Lane Ends
SJ9271

▲ **Jarman Farm,** Sutton, Macclesfield, Cheshire, SK11 0HJ
Tel: 01260 252501
Open: All year

Warrington
SJ6088

▲ **Holly Bank Caravan Park,** Warburton Bridge Road, Rixton, Warrington, Cheshire, WA3 6HU
Actual Grid Ref: SJ693904
Tel: 0161 775 2842
Open: All year

▲ **New House Farm,** Hatton Lane, Stretton, Warrington, Cheshire, WA4 4BZ
Tel: 01925 730567 **Open:** All year

Whitegate
SJ6269

▲ **Lamb Cottage,** Dalefords Lane, Whitegate, Northwich, Cheshire, CW8 2BN
Actual Grid Ref: SJ614693
Tel: 01606 882302
Open: Mar to Oct

Wrenbury
SJ5947

▲ **The Cotton Arms Public House,** Cholmondeley Road, Wrenbury, Nantwich, Cheshire, CW5 8HG
Actual Grid Ref: SJ591479
Tel: 01270 780377
Open: All year

ENGLAND

Cornwall

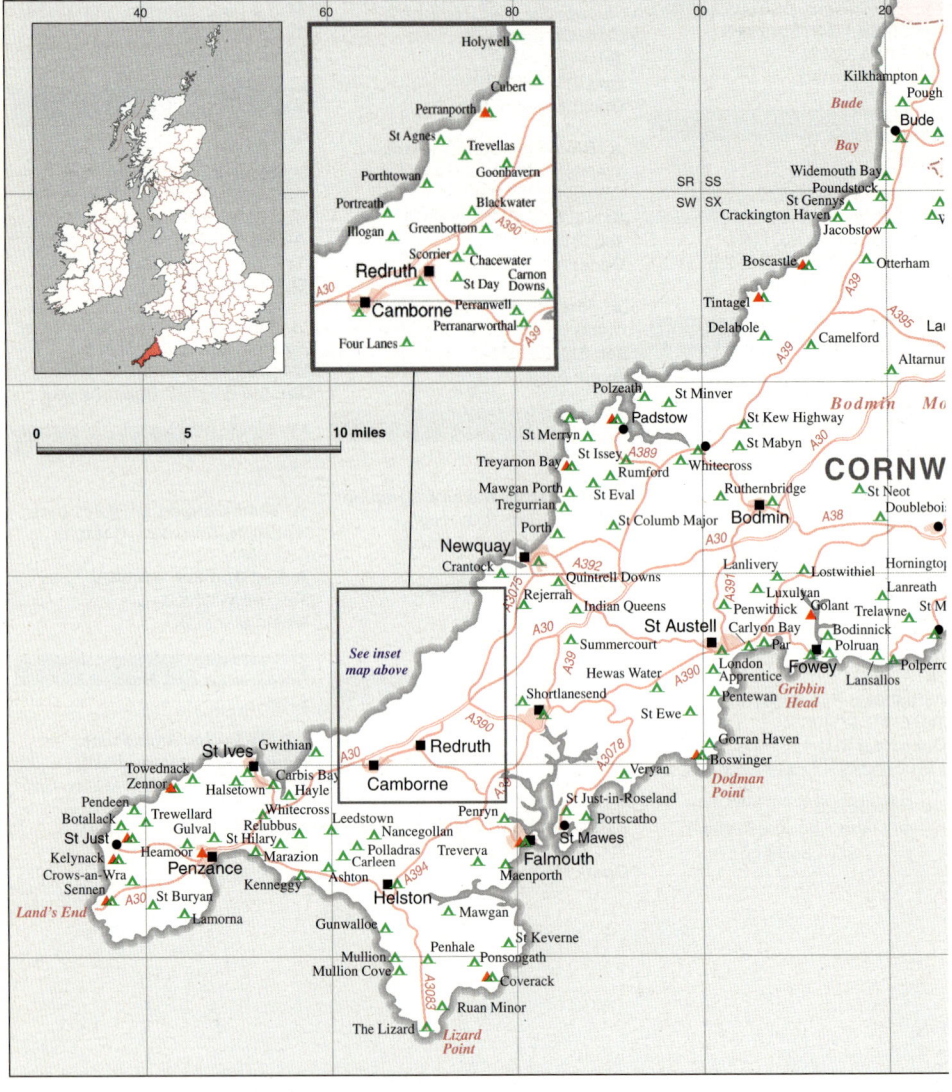

Altarnun	Ashton (Helston)	Blackwater
SX2281	SW6028	SW7346
▲ **Nathania,** Altarnun, Launceston, Cornwall, PL15 7SL **Actual Grid Ref:** SX216817 **Tel:** 01566 86426 **Open:** All year	▲ **Boscrege Caravan Park,** Ashton, Helston, Cornwall, TR13 9TG **Actual Grid Ref:** SW595305 **Tel:** 01736 762231 **Open:** Apr to Oct	▲ **Chiverton Caravan & Touring Park,** East Hill, Blackwater, Truro, Cornwall, TR4 8HS **Actual Grid Ref:** SW743468 **Tel:** 01872 560667 **Open:** Apr to Oct

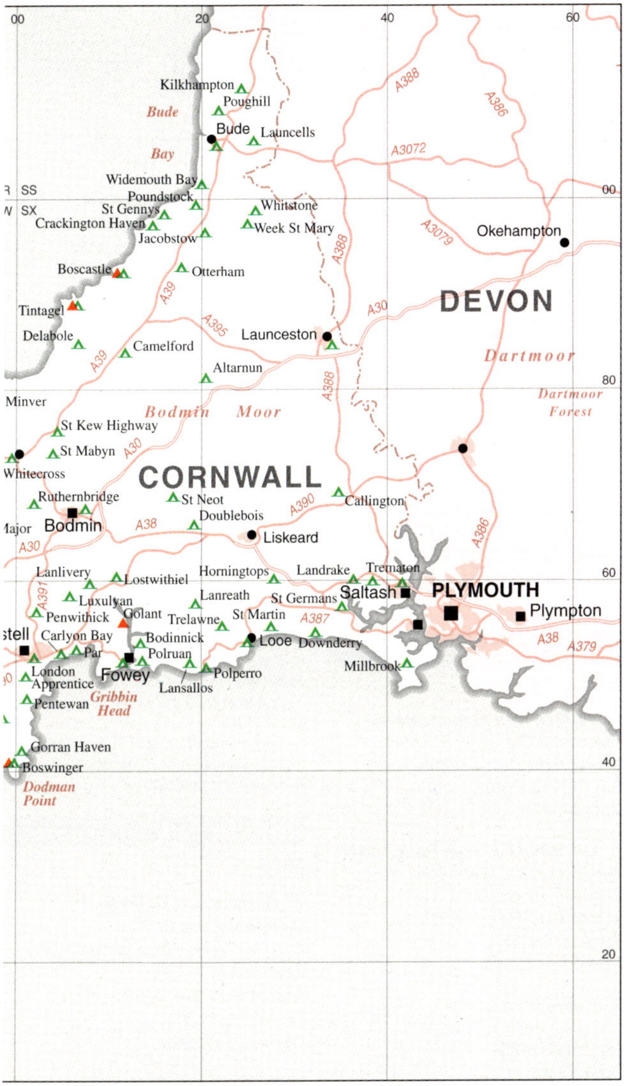

Cornwall

ENGLAND

Bodmin
SX0667

▲ **Camping & Caravanning Club Site,** Old Callywith Road, Bodmin, Cornwall, PL31 2DZ
Actual Grid Ref: SX081676
Tel: 01208 73834 / 01203 694995
Open: Mar to Nov

Boscastle
SX1090

▲ **Boscastle Harbour Youth Hostel,** Palace Stables, Boscastle, Cornwall, PL35 0HD
Actual Grid Ref: SX096915
Tel: 01840 250287
Fax: 01840 250615
Email: reservations@yha.org.uk
Capacity: 25
Under 18: £6.90
Adults: £10.00
Open: All year, 5.00pm
Self-catering facilities • Showers • Lounge • Drying room • Cycle store • Evening meal available 7.00pm • No smoking • WC • Kitchen facilities • Credit cards accepted
In superb position right on harbour edge where River Valency enters NT fishing harbour.

▲ **Lower Pennycrocker Farm,** St Juliot, Boscastle, Cornwall, PL35 0BY
Actual Grid Ref: SX125929
Tel: 01840 250257
Open: Mar to Sept

▲ **Trebyla Farm,** Minster, Boscastle, Cornwall, PL35 0HL
Actual Grid Ref: SX119922
Tel: 01840 250308
Open: Apr to Sep

▲ **Trevarth Holiday Park,** Blackwater, Truro, Cornwall, TR4 8HR
Actual Grid Ref: SW744468
Tel: 01872 560266
Open: Apr to Oct

Bodinnick
SX1352

▲ **Yeate Farm Camp & Caravan Site,** Bodinnick, Fowey, Cornwall, PL23 1LZ
Actual Grid Ref: SX133527
Tel: 01726 870256 **Open:** Apr to Oct

Some hostels and campsites impose restrictions on size and type of groups they accept (e.g. not permitting single-sex groups). Always phone to enquire before booking.

Cornwall • MAP PAGE 14

ENGLAND

Boswinger
SW9840

▲ **Boswinger Youth Hostel,** Boswinger, Gorran, St Austell, Cornwall, PL26 6LL
Actual Grid Ref: SW991411
Tel: 01726 843234
Fax: 01726 843234
Capacity: 30
Under 18: £6.90 **Adults:** £10.00
Open: All year, 5.00pm
Family bunk rooms
Self-catering facilities • Laundry facilities • Lounge • Dining room • Drying room • Cycle store • Parking • Evening meal available 7.00pm • No smoking • WC • Kitchen facilities • Breakfast available • Credit cards accepted
Stone-built cottages and a converted barn in area with outstanding coastal scenery. Sandy bathing beaches nearby.

▲ **Sea View International Caravan & Camping Park,** Boswinger, Gorran, St Austell, Cornwall, PL26 6LL
Actual Grid Ref: SW991412
Tel: 01726 843425
Open: Apr to Sep

Botallack
SW3632

▲ **Trevaylor Camping & Caravan Park,** Botallack, St Just, Penzance, Cornwall, TR19 7PY
Actual Grid Ref: SW370326
Tel: 01736 787016
Open: Mar to Oct

Bude
SS2106

▲ **Budemeadows Touring Holiday Park,** Bude, Cornwall, EX23 0NA
Actual Grid Ref: SS215012
Tel: 01288 361646
Open: All year

▲ **Sandymouth Bay Holiday Park,** Bude, Cornwall, EX23 9HW
Actual Grid Ref: SS214104
Tel: 01288 352563
Fax: 01288 352563
Open: Mar to Oct

▲ **Upper Lynstone Caravan & Camping Site,** Lynstone, Bude, Cornwall, EX23 0LP
Actual Grid Ref: SS205054
Tel: 01288 352017
Open: Easter to Sep

▲ **Willow Valley Holiday Park,** Dye House, Bush, Bude, Cornwall, EX23 9LB
Actual Grid Ref: SS236078
Tel: 01288 353104
Fax: 01288 353104
Open: Mar to Dec

▲ **Bude Holiday Park,** Maer Lane, Bude, Cornwall, EX23 9EE
Actual Grid Ref: SS206078
Tel: 01288 355955 **Open:** Apr to Oct

Callington
SX3669

▲ **Mount Pleasant Caravan Park,** St Ann's Chapel, Callington, Cornwall, PL17 8JA
Actual Grid Ref: SX414709
Tel: 01822 832325
Open: Apr to Sep

Camborne
SW6440

▲ **Magor Farm Caravan Site,** Tehidy, Camborne, Cornwall, TR14 0JF
Actual Grid Ref: SW635425
Tel: 01209 713367
Open: Mar to Oct

Camelford
SX1083

▲ **Juliot's Well Holiday Park,** Camelford, Cornwall, PL32 9RF
Actual Grid Ref: SX095829
Tel: 01840 213302
Open: Mar to Oct

▲ **Lakefield Caravan Park,** Lower Pendavey Farm, Camelford, Cornwall, PL32 9TX
Actual Grid Ref: SX095853
Tel: 01840 213279
Open: Apr to Oct

▲ **Kings Acre,** Camelford, Cornwall, PL32 9UR
Tel: 01840 213561
Open: Easter to Oct

Carbis Bay
SW5238

▲ **Carbis Bay Holiday Village,** Laity Farm, Laity Lane, Carbis Bay, St Ives, Cornwall, TR26 3HW
Actual Grid Ref: SW519388
Tel: 01736 797580
Open: May to Oct

Carleen
SW6130

▲ **Poldown Caravan Park,** Primrose Cottage, Carleen, Helston, Cornwall, TR13 9NN
Actual Grid Ref: SW631299
AA grade: 3 Pennants
Tel: 01326 574560
Email: poldown@poldown.co.uk
Tent pitches: 13
Tent rate: £6.50-£9.50
Open: Apr to Oct
Last arr: 10pm
Dogs allowed • Electric hook-up • Calor Gas/Camping Gaz • Picnic/barbecue area on site • Children's play area • Showers • Laundrette on site • Public phone on site • Baby care facilities • Indoor swimming pool nearby • Outdoor swimming pool nearby • Boating/sailing/watersports nearby • Golf nearby • Riding nearby • Fishing nearby
Small peaceful & secluded friendly site near the Lizard, nestled in woodland within easy reach of sandy beaches, very central to explore the whole of West Cornwall. Good walks nearby & also surfing, windsurfing, golf, riding. The touring area is set on flat grass, exceptionally sheltered yet very sunny.

Carlyon Bay
SX0552

▲ **Carlyon Bay Caravan & Camping Park,** Bethesda, Cypress Avenue, Carlyon Bay, St Austell, Cornwall, PL25 3RE
Actual Grid Ref: SX052526
Tel: 01726 812735
Open: Apr to Sep

Carnon Downs
SW7940

▲ **Ringwell Valley Holiday Park,** Bissoe Road, Carnon Downs, Truro, Cornwall, TR3 6LQ
Actual Grid Ref: SW794408
Tel: 01872 862194 / 865409
Fax: 01872 864343
Open: Apr to Oct

MAP PAGE 14 • **Cornwall**

▲ **Carnon Downs Caravan & Camping Park,** Carnon Downs, Truro, Cornwall, TR3 6JJ
Actual Grid Ref: SW805406
Tel: 01872 862283
Open: Apr to Oct

Chacewater
SW7444

▲ **Leverton Place,** Greenbottom, Chacewater, Truro, Cornwall, TR4 8QW
Actual Grid Ref: SW774453
Tel: 01872 560462
Open: All year

▲ **Chacewater Park,** Coxhill, Chacewater, Truro, Cornwall, TR4 8LY
Actual Grid Ref: SW740438
Tel: 01209 820762
Open: May to Sep

Coverack
SW7818

▲ **Coverack Youth Hostel,** Parc Behan, School Hill, Coverack, Helston, Cornwall, TR12 6SA
Actual Grid Ref: SW782184
Tel: 01326 280687
Fax: 01326 280119
Capacity: 38
Under 18: £6.90
Adults: £10.00
Open: All year, 5.00pm
Family bunk rooms
Camping
Self-catering facilities • Showers • Lounge • Dining room • Games room • Parking • Evening meal available 7.00pm • WC • Kitchen facilities • Breakfast available
Large country house situated above old fishing village and smugglers' haunt, with views of bay and coastline.

▲ **Little Trevothan Caravan & Camping Park,** Coverack, Helston, Cornwall, TR12 6SD
Actual Grid Ref: SW772179
Tel: 01326 280260
Open: Apr to Oct

Crackington Haven
SX1496

▲ **Hentervene Caravan & Camping Park,** Crackington Haven, Bude, Cornwall, EX23 0LZ
Actual Grid Ref: SX155944
Tel: 01840 230365
Open: All year

Crantock
SW7960

▲ **Crantock Plains Touring Park,** Crantock, Newquay, Cornwall, TR8 5PH
Actual Grid Ref: SW805589
AA grade: 3 Pennants
Tel: 01637 830955 / 831273
Tent pitches: 60
Tent rate: £2.75
Open: Apr to Sep
Last arr: 9pm
Dogs allowed • Electric hook-up • Calor Gas/Camping Gaz • Picnic/barbecue area on site • Children's play area • Showers • Laundrette on site • Public phone on site • Shop on site
Dogs allowed, showers, laundrette, Calor Gas, public phones, shop, play area.

▲ **Trevella Tourist Park,** Crantock, Newquay, Cornwall, TR8 5EW
Actual Grid Ref: SW801599
Tel: 01637 830308
Open: Apr to Oct

▲ **Treago Farm Caravan Site,** Crantock, Newquay, Cornwall, TR8 5QS
Actual Grid Ref: SW782601
Tel: 01637 830277
Open: Mar to Oct

▲ **Quarryfield Caravan & Camping Park,** Tretherras, Newquay, Cornwall, TR7 2RE
Actual Grid Ref: SW794606
Tel: 01637 872792
Open: Apr to Oct

▲ **Porth Joke Camping Site,** Treago Mill, Crantock, Newquay, Cornwall, TR8 5QS
Actual Grid Ref: SW776600
Tel: 01637 830213
Open: Apr to Oct

Crows-an-Wra
SW3927

▲ **Cardinney Caravan & Camping Park,** Crows-an-Wra, St Buryan, Penzance, Cornwall, TR19 6HX
Actual Grid Ref: SW399279
Tel: 01736 810880
Open: Feb to Nov

▲ **Lower Treave Caravan Park,** Crows-an-Wra, St Buryan, Penzance, Cornwall, TR19 6HZ
Actual Grid Ref: SW388272
Tel: 01736 810559
Open: Apr to Oct

Cubert
SW7857

▲ **Cottage Farm,** Treworgans, Cubert, Newquay, Cornwall, TR8 5WW
Actual Grid Ref: SW786589
Tel: 01637 831083
Open: Mar to Oct

▲ **Trebellan Park,** Cubert, Newquay, Cornwall, TR8 5PY
Actual Grid Ref: SW790571
Tel: 01637 830522
Open: May to Oct

Delabole
SX0784

▲ **Planet Park,** Westdown Road, Delabole, Plymouth, Devon, PL33 9DT
Actual Grid Ref: SX064834
Tel: 01840 213361
Fax: 01840 212795
Open: All year

Doublebois
SX1965

▲ **Pine Green Caravan & Camping Site,** Doublebois, Liskeard, Cornwall, PL14 6LE
Actual Grid Ref: SX195646
Tel: 01579 320183 / 01271 328981
Open: Apr to Oct

Downderry
SX3254

▲ **Carbeil Caravan & Camping Park,** Treliddon Lane, Downderry, Torpoint, Cornwall, PL11 3LS
Actual Grid Ref: SX318544
Tel: 01503 250636
Open: Mar to Oct

Falmouth
SW8032

▲ **Pendennis Castle Youth Hostel,** Falmouth, Cornwall, TR11 4LP
Actual Grid Ref: SW823319
Tel: 01326 311435
Fax: 01326 315473
Capacity: 76
Under 18: £6.20
Adults: £9.15
Open: Feb to Nov + Xmas
Evening meal available 7.00pm
Victorian barracks building, floodlit at night, in grounds of a C16th castle on the promontory beyond Falmouth town.

Stilwell's Hostels & Camping 2002

Cornwall • MAP PAGE 14

ENGLAND

To stay in a Youth Hostel affiliated to one of the Youth Hostel associations, you need to be a member. You can join at most hostels – phone in advance to check.

▲ **Maen Valley Holiday Park,** Roscarrick Road, Falmouth, Cornwall, TR11 5BJ
Actual Grid Ref: SW789311
Tel: 01326 312190
Open: Apr to Oct

▲ **Tremorvah Camping Site,** Tremorvah, Swanpool, Falmouth, Cornwall, TR11 5BA
Actual Grid Ref: SW798313
Tel: 01326 312103
Open: Mar to Oct

Four Lanes
SW6838

▲ **Lanyon Park,** Loscombe Lane, Four Lanes, Redruth, Cornwall, TR16 6LP
Actual Grid Ref: SW685389
Tourist Board grade: 4 Ticks
Tel: 01209 313474
Fax: 01209 313 422
Tent pitches: 25
Tent rate: £4.50-£12.00
Open: Mar to Oct
Last arr: 9pm
Dogs allowed • Electric hook-up • Baths • Cafe or Takeaway on site • Picnic/barbecue area on site • Children's play area • Showers • Laundrette on site • Public phone on site • Licensed bar on site
Family park in open countryside ideal touring base for Falmouth, Truro, St Ives.

Fowey
SX1251

▲ **Penhale Camping & Caravan Park,** Fowey, Cornwall, PL23 1JU
Actual Grid Ref: SX104526
Tel: 01726 833425
Open: Apr to Oct

If you have to cancel your visit to any hostel or campsite, please let them know – it is always possible to make a bed or a pitch available to someone else.

Some hostels and campsites impose restrictions on size and type of groups they accept (e.g. not permitting single-sex groups). Always phone to enquire before booking.

Golant
SX1254

▲ **Golant Youth Hostel,** Penquite House, Golant, Fowey, Cornwall, PL23 1LA
Tel: 01726 833507
Fax: 01726 832947
Email: golant@yha.org.uk
Capacity: 94
Under 18: £7.75
Adults: £11.00
Open: Feb to Oct and Xmas, 5.00pm
Family bunk rooms
Self-catering facilities • Television • Licensed bar • Shop • Laundry facilities • Lounge • Dining room • Games room • Drying room • Cycle store • Parking • Evening meal available 7.00 • WC • Kitchen facilities • Breakfast available • Credit cards accepted
Large Georgian residence, with large gardens, perfect for small children. Close to Fowey, with woods, cycle ways and watersports.

Goonhavern
SW7853

▲ **Perran Springs Touring Park,** Bodmin Road, Goonhavern, Truro, Cornwall, TR4 9QG
Actual Grid Ref: SW796535
Tel: 01872 540568
Open: Apr to Oct

▲ **Rosehill Farm Tourist Park,** Goonhavern, Truro, Cornwall, TR4 9LA
Actual Grid Ref: SW784540
Tel: 01872 572448
Open: Mar to Oct

▲ **Penrose Farm Touring Park,** Goonhavern, Truro, Cornwall, TR4 9QF
Actual Grid Ref: SW795534
Tel: 01872 573185
Open: Apr to Oct

Gorran Haven
SX0041

▲ **Trelispen Caravan & Camping Park,** Gorran Haven, St Austell, Cornwall, PL26 6HT
Actual Grid Ref: SX008421
Tourist Board grade: 2 Ticks
AA grade: Pennant Park
Tel: 01726 843501 **Fax:** 01726 843501
Tent pitches: 40
Tent rate: £7.00-£15.00
Open: Apr to Oct
Last arr: 10pm
Dogs allowed • Electric hook-up • Showers
Well sheltered level site near several beaches and fine cliffs.

▲ **Tragarton Park,** Gorran Haven, St Austell, Cornwall, PL26 6NF
Actual Grid Ref: SW984437
Tel: 01726 843666
Open: Apr to Sep

▲ **Treveor Farm,** Caravan & Camping Site, Gorran Haven, St Austell, Cornwall, PL26 6LW
Actual Grid Ref: SW988418
Tel: 01726 842387
Open: Apr to Oct

Greenbottom
SW7645

▲ **Liskey Touring Park,** Greenbottom, Truro, Cornwall, TR4 8QN
Actual Grid Ref: SW772452
Tel: 01872 560274
Open: Apr to Sep

Gulval
SW4831

▲ **Garris Farm,** Gulval, Penzance, Cornwall, TR20 8XD
Actual Grid Ref: SW484337
Tel: 01736 365806
Open: Mar to Oct

Gunwalloe
SW6522

▲ **Gunwalloe Caravan Park,** Gunwalloe, Helston, Cornwall, TR12 7QP
Actual Grid Ref: SW669240
Tel: 01326 572668
Open: Apr to Oct

MAP PAGE **14** • **Cornwall**

Gwithian

SW5841

▲ **Churchtown Farm Caravan & Camping Site,** Gwithian, Hayle, Cornwall, TR27 5BX
Actual Grid Ref: SW585414
Tel: 01736 753188
Open: Apr to Sep

Halsetown

SW5038

▲ **Polmanter Tourist Park,** Halsetown, St Ives, Cornwall, TR26 3LX
Actual Grid Ref: SW510388
Tel: 01736 795640
Open: Mar to Oct

▲ **Balnoon Camp Site,** Halsetown, St Ives, Cornwall, TR26 3JA
Actual Grid Ref: SW509382
Tel: 01736 795431
Open: Apr to Oct

Hayle

SW5537

▲ **St Ives Bay Holiday Park,** 73 Loggans Road, Upton Towans, Hayle, Cornwall, TR27 5BH
Actual Grid Ref: SW573388
Tel: 01736 752274
Open: May to Sep

▲ **Higher Trevaskis Caravan Park,** Gwinear Road, Conner Downs, Hayle, Cornwall, TR27 5JQ
Actual Grid Ref: SW611381
Tel: 01209 831736
Open: Apr to Oct

▲ **Parbola Holiday Park,** Wall, Gwinear, Hayle, Cornwall, TR27 5LE
Actual Grid Ref: SW608366
Tel: 01209 831503
Open: Mar to Sept

▲ **Beachside Holiday Park,** Hayle, Cornwall, TR27 5AW
Actual Grid Ref: SW558388
Tel: 01736 753080
Open: Mar to Sept

▲ **Treglission Farm,** Wheal Alfred Road, Hayle, Cornwall, TR27 5JT
Actual Grid Ref: SW581367
Tel: 01736 753141
Open: Apr to Oct.

▲ **Atlantic Coast Caravan Park,** 53 Upton Towans, Hayle, Cornwall, TR27 5BL
Actual Grid Ref: SW580400
Tel: 01736 752071
Open: Apr to Oct

▲ **Sunny Meadow Holiday Park,** Lelant Downs, Hayle, Cornwall, TR27 6LL
Actual Grid Ref: SW532368
Tel: 01736 752243
Open: Mar to Nov

Heamoor

SW4531

▲ **Bone Valley Caravan Park,** Heamoor, Penzance, Cornwall, TR20 8UJ
Actual Grid Ref: SW463317
Tel: 01736 60313
Open: Mar to Dec

Helston

SW6627

▲ **Silver Sands Holiday Park,** Gwendreath, Kennack Sands, Helston, Cornwall, TR12 7LZ
Actual Grid Ref: SW732170
AA grade: 3 Pennants
Tel: 01326 290631
Fax: 01326 290631
Email: silversnds@aol.com
Tent pitches: 21
Tent rate: £6.00-£7.50
Open: May to Sep **Last arr:** 9pm
Dogs allowed • Electric hook-up • Calor Gas/Camping Gaz • Picnic/barbecue area on site • Children's play area • Showers • Laundrette on site • Public phone on site • Indoor swimming pool nearby • Boating/sailing/watersports nearby • Golf nearby • Riding nearby • Fishing nearby
Come and relax in tranquil surroundings and explore the coves, coastal paths and unique countryside of the Lizard Peninsula. David Bellamy Silver Award winning park. Beautifully landscaped large individual pitches. Short woodland walk through the Lizard National Nature Reserve brings you to the award winning beaches of Kennack Sands.

▲ **Retanna Holiday Park,** Underlane, Helston, Cornwall, TR13 0EJ
Actual Grid Ref: SW711327
Tel: 01326 340643
Open: Apr to Sep

▲ **Gwendreath Farm Caravan Park,** Kennack Sands, Helston, Cornwall, TR12 7LZ
Actual Grid Ref: SW735168
Tel: 01326 290666
Open: Apr to Oct

▲ **Pinetrees,** Goonhilly Downs, Helston, Cornwall, TR12 6LQ
Actual Grid Ref: SW720224
Tel: 01326 221310
Open: Apr to Oct

▲ **Chy Carne Camping,** Kennack Sands, Helston, Cornwall, TR12 7LX
Actual Grid Ref: SW725164
Tel: 01326 290200
Open: Mar to Sept

Hewas Water

SW9649

▲ **Trencreek Farm Holiday Park,** Hewas Water, St Austell, Cornwall, PL26 7JG
Actual Grid Ref: SW966485
Tel: 01726 882540
Open: Apr to Sep

Holywell

SW7659

▲ **Trevornick Holiday Park,** Holywell Bay, Holywell, Newquay, Cornwall, TR8 5PW
Actual Grid Ref: SW776586
Tel: 01637 830531
Open: May to Sep

▲ **Holywell Bay Holiday Park,** Holywell Bay, Holywell, Newquay, Cornwall, TR8 5PR
Actual Grid Ref: SW773582
Tel: 01637 871111
Open: May to Sep

Horningtops

SX2761

▲ **Great Trethew Manor,** Horningtops, Liskeard, Cornwall, PL14 3PY
Actual Grid Ref: SX289600
Tel: 01503 240663
Fax: 01503 240695
Open: Apr to Oct

Cornwall • MAP PAGE 14

ENGLAND

Illogan
SW6744

▲ **Tehidy Holiday Park,** Harris Mill, Illogan, Portreath, Cornwall, TR16 4JQ
Actual Grid Ref: SW682434
Tel: 01209 216489
Open: Apr to Oct

Indian Queens
SW9159

▲ **Gnome World Touring Park,** Moorland Road, Indian Queens, St Columb Major, Cornwall, TR9 6HN
Tel: 01726 860812
Open: Easter to Oct

Jacobstow
SX1995

▲ **Edmore Tourist Park,** Edgar Road, Wainhouse Corner, Jacobstow, Bude, Cornwall, EX23 0BJ
Actual Grid Ref: SX184955
Tel: 01840 230467
Open: Mar to Oct

▲ **Lower Poulza Post,** Jacobstow, Bude, Cornwall, EX23 0BX
Actual Grid Ref: SX209948
Tel: 01566 781520
Open: Apr to Oct

Kelynack
SW3630

▲ **Kelynack Caravan & Camping Park Hostel,** Kelynack, St Just, Penzance, Cornwall, TR19 7RE
Actual Grid Ref: SW373301
Tel: 01736 787633
Fax: 01736 787633
Email: steve@kelynackholidays.co.uk
Capacity: 8
Under 18: £4.00
Adults: £7.00
Open: All year, 8am-10pm
Family bunk rooms: £20.00
Camping for 15 tents: £6.00
Self-catering facilities • Showers • Shop • Laundry facilities • Wet weather shelter • Grounds available for games • Drying room • Cycle store • Parking • No smoking
In beautiful valley near coast. Ideal for exploring West Cornwall.

▲ **Kelynack Caravan & Camping Park,** Kelynack, St Just, Penzance, Cornwall, TR19 7RE
Actual Grid Ref: SW373301
Tel: 01736 787633
Open: Mar to Oct

Kenneggy
SW5628

▲ **Kenneggy Cove Holiday Park,** Higher Kenneggy, Kenneggy, Rosudgeon, Penzance, Cornwall, TR20 9AU
Actual Grid Ref: SW562287
Tourist Board grade: 3 Star
AA grade: 3 Pennants
Tel: 01736 763453
Fax: 01736 763453
Email: enquiries@kenneggycove.co.uk
Tent pitches: 60
Tent rate: £5.00-£8.50
Open: Mar to Oct
Last arr: 9pm
Dogs allowed • Electric hook-up • Calor Gas/Camping Gaz • Cafe or Takeaway on site • Children's play area • Showers • Laundrette on site • Public phone on site • Shop on site
Quiet park with sea views. Short walk to coastal path.

Kilkhampton
SS2511

▲ **East Thorne Caravan & Camping Park,** Kilkhampton, Bude, Cornwall, EX23 9RY
Actual Grid Ref: SS260110
Tel: 01288 321618
Open: Apr to Oct

▲ **Tamar Lake Farm,** Thurdon, Kilkhampton, Bude, Cornwall, EX23 9SA
Actual Grid Ref: SS287108
Tel: 01288 321426
Open: Apr to Oct

Lamorna
SW4425

▲ **Boleigh Farm Caravan & Campsite,** Lamorna, Penzance, Cornwall, TR19 6BN
Actual Grid Ref: SW434249
Tel: 01736 810305
Open: Mar to Oct

Landrake
SX3760

▲ **Dolbeare Caravan & Camping Park,** St Ive Road, Landrake, Saltash, Cornwall, PL12 5AF
Actual Grid Ref: SX363616
Tel: 01752 851332
Email: dolbeare@compuserve.com
Open: All year

Lanlivery
SX0759

▲ **Powderham Castle Tourist Park,** Lanlivery, Bodmin, Cornwall, PL30 5BU
Actual Grid Ref: SX083593
Tel: 01208 872277
Open: Apr to Oct

Lanreath
SX1856

▲ **Shillamill Lakes,** Lanreath, Looe, Cornwall, PL13 2PE
Actual Grid Ref: SX170590
Tel: 01503 220886
Open: All year

Lansallos
SX1751

▲ **Great Kellow Farm,** Lansallos, Polperro, Cornwall, PL13 2QL
Actual Grid Ref: SX201522
Tel: 01503 272387
Open: Apr to Oct

Launcells
SS2405

▲ **Red Post Holiday Park,** Launcells, Bude, Cornwall, EX23 9NW
Actual Grid Ref: SS264052
Tel: 01288 381305
Open: Mar to Oct

Launceston
SX3384

▲ **Launceston Rugby Football Club,** Polson Bridge, Launceston, Cornwall, PL15 7AG
Actual Grid Ref: SX357849
Tel: 01566 77287
Fax: 01208 73744
Open: Apr to Sep

MAP PAGE **14** • **Cornwall**

Leedstown
SW6034

▲ **Calloose Caravan & Camping Park,** Leedstown, Hayle, Cornwall, TR27 5ET
Actual Grid Ref: SW600352
Tel: 01736 850431
Open: Mar to Oct

London Apprentice
SX0050

▲ **River Valley Holiday Park,** Pentewan Road, London Apprentice, St Austell, Cornwall, PL26 7AP
Actual Grid Ref: SX008504
Tel: 01726 73533
Open: Apr to Sep

Looe
SX2553

▲ **Polborder House Caravan & Camping Park,** Bucklawren Road, St Martin, Looe, Cornwall, PL13 1QR
Actual Grid Ref: SX283555
AA grade: 3 Pennants
Tel: 01503 240265
Fax: 01503 240700
Email: rlf.polborder@virgin.net
Tent pitches: 31
Tent rate: £6.00-£9.50
Open: Apr to Oct **Last arr:** 10pm
Facilities for disabled people • Dogs allowed • Electric hook-up • Calor Gas/Camping Gaz • Picnic/barbecue area on site • Children's play area • Showers • Laundrette on site • Public phone on site • Shop on site • Baby care facilities
2.5 miles from Looe, 1.25 mile from South West Coast Path.

▲ **Trelay Farmpark,** Pelynt, Looe, Cornwall, PL13 2JX
Actual Grid Ref: SX210545
Tourist Board grade: 4 Star
Tel: 01503 220900
Fax: 01503 220900
Tent pitches: 30 **Tent rate:** £5.00
Open: Mar to Oct
Last arr: 10.30pm
Facilities for disabled people • Dogs allowed • Electric hook-up • Calor Gas/Camping Gaz • Picnic/barbecue area on site • Showers • Laundrette on site • Public phone on site
Uncommercialised with immaculate facilities. Generous pitches. Also four holiday caravans.

▲ **Tencreek Caravan & Camping Park,** Looe, Cornwall, PL13 2JR
Actual Grid Ref: SX233525
Tel: 01503 262447 / 01831 411843
Fax: 01503 262447
Open: Mar to Jan

▲ **Looe Valley Touring Park,** Polperro Road, Looe, Cornwall, PL13 2JS
Actual Grid Ref: SX228536
Tel: 01503 262425
Fax: 01503 262425
Open: May to Sep

▲ **Talland Bay Caravan Park,** Talland Bay, Looe, Cornwall, PL13 2JA
Actual Grid Ref: SX228517
Tel: 01503 272715
Open: Mar to Oct

▲ **West Wayland Caravan & Touring Park,** Looe, Cornwall, PL13 2JS
Actual Grid Ref: SX224533
Tel: 01503 262418
Open: Apr to Oct

▲ **Trelawne Manor Holiday Village,** Looe, Cornwall, PL13 2NA
Actual Grid Ref: SX220542
Tel: 01503 272151
Open: Easter to Oct

Lostwithiel
SX1059

▲ **Downend Garage,** Downend, Lostwithiel, Cornwall, PL22 0RB
Actual Grid Ref: SX117597
Tel: 01208 872363
Open: Mar to Oct

Luxulyan
SX0558

▲ **Croft Farm Touring Park,** Luxulyan, Bodmin, Cornwall, PL30 5EQ
Actual Grid Ref: SX044568
Tel: 01726 850228
Fax: 01726 850498
Open: Apr to Oct

Maenporth
SW7929

▲ **Pennance Mill Touring,** Maenporth, Falmouth, Cornwall, TR11 5HJ
Actual Grid Ref: SW792307
Tel: 01326 312616
Open: Mar to Oct

▲ **Tregedna Farm Campsite,** Maenporth, Falmouth, Cornwall, TR11 5HL
Actual Grid Ref: SW785305
Tel: 01326 250529
Open: May to Sep

Marazion
SW5130

▲ **Wayfarers Caravan & Camping Park,** Relebbus Lane, St Hilary, Penzance, Cornwall, TR20 9EF
Actual Grid Ref: SW558314
AA grade: 3 Pennants
Tel: 01736 763326
Tent pitches: 60
Tent rate: £3.00-£4.25
Open: Mar to Oct
Last arr: 9.30pm
Dogs allowed • Electric hook-up • Calor Gas/Camping Gaz • Cafe or Takeaway on site • Picnic/barbecue area on site • Children's play area • Showers • Laundrette on site • Public phone on site • Shop on site • Baby care facilities
Award-winning select park. Couples discounts. Spacious, level, sheltered pitches.

▲ **Wheal Rodney,** Gwallon, Marazion, Cornwall, TR17 0HL
Actual Grid Ref: SW525315
Tel: 01736 710605
Open: Apr to Oct

Mawgan
SW7025

▲ **Trelowarren Chateau Park,** Mawgan, Helston, Cornwall, TR12 6AF
Actual Grid Ref: SW723242
Tel: 01326 221637
Open: Apr to Sep

Mawgan Porth
SW8567

▲ **Sun Haven Valley,** Caravan & Camping Site, Mawgan Porth, Newquay, Cornwall, TR8 4BQ
Actual Grid Ref: SW861669
Tel: 01637 860373
Open: Mar to Oct

▲ **Trevarrian Holiday Park,** Mawgan Porth, Newquay, Cornwall, TR8 4AQ
Actual Grid Ref: SW850663
Tel: 01637 860381
Open: Apr to Sep

ENGLAND

Stilwell's Hostels & Camping 2002

Cornwall • MAP PAGE 14

Magic Cove Touring Park,
Mawgan Porth, Newquay, Cornwall, TR8 4BZ
Actual Grid Ref: SW852672
Tel: 01637 860263
Open: Mar to Oct

Millbrook
SX4252

Ruda Holiday Park, P O Box 3,
Croyde Bay, Braunton, Devon, EX33 1NY
Actual Grid Ref: SX438397
Tel: 01271 890671
Open: Apr to Sep

Whitsand Bay Holiday Park,
Millbrook, Torpoint, Cornwall, PL10 1JZ
Actual Grid Ref: SX410515
Tel: 01752 822597
Open: Apr to Oct

Mullion
SW6719

'Franchis' Holiday Park, Cury
Cross Lanes, Mullion, Helston, Cornwall, TR12 7AZ
Actual Grid Ref: SW698203
Tourist Board grade: 4 Ticks
AA grade: 3 Pennants
Tel: 01326 240301
Tent pitches: 70
Tent rate: £7.50-£8.50
Open: Apr to Sep
Last arr: 10pm
Facilities for disabled people • Dogs allowed • Electric hook-up • Calor Gas/Camping Gaz • Showers • Public phone on site • Shop on site
A welcoming and peaceful clean, family-run site. Beaches nearby.

Teneriffe Farm, Predannack,
Mullion, Helston, Cornwall, TR12 7EZ
Actual Grid Ref: SW672166
Tel: 01326 240293
Open: Mar to Oct

Mullion Cove
SW6617

Criggan Mill, Mullion Cove,
Helston, Cornwall, TR12 7EU
Actual Grid Ref: SW669179
Tel: 01326 240496
Open: Apr to Oct

Nancegollan
SW6332

Pengoon Farm, Nancegollan,
Helston, Cornwall, TR13 0BH
Actual Grid Ref: SW632309
Tel: 01326 561219
Open: All year

Newquay
SW8161

Hendra Holiday Park,
Newquay, Cornwall, TR8 4NY
Actual Grid Ref: SW833601
Tel: 01637 875778
Open: Apr to Oct

Newquay Holiday Park,
Newquay, Cornwall, TR8 4HS
Actual Grid Ref: SW853626
Tel: 01637 871111
Open: May to Oct

Rosecliston Park, Trevemper,
Newquay, Cornwall, TR8 5JT
Actual Grid Ref: SW815594
Tel: 01637 830326
Open: Apr to Sep

Trencreek Holiday Park, Higher
Trencreek, Newquay, Cornwall, TR8 4NS
Actual Grid Ref: SW828609
Tel: 01637 874210
Open: Apr to Sep

Gwills Holiday Park, Newquay,
Cornwall, TR8 4PE
Actual Grid Ref: SW829592
Tel: 01637 873617
Open: Mar to Oct

Treloy Tourist Park, Newquay,
Cornwall, TR8 4JN
Actual Grid Ref: SW858635
Tel: 01637 872063 / 876279
Open: Apr to Sep

Trenance Caravan & Chalet Park, Edgcumbe Avenue, Newquay,
Cornwall, TR7 2JY
Actual Grid Ref: SW818612
Tel: 01637 873447
Open: Apr to Oct

Trekenning Tourist Park,
Newquay, Cornwall, TR8 4JF
Actual Grid Ref: SW910620
Tel: 01637 880462
Fax: 01637 880462
Open: Apr to Sep

Otterham
SX1690

St Tinney Farm Holidays,
Otterham, Camelford, Cornwall, PL32 9TA
Actual Grid Ref: SX169906
Tel: 01840 261274
Open: Mar to Oct

Padstow
SW9175

National Trust Cornish Basecamps, National Trust in
Cornwall Regional Office, Lanhydrock, Bodmin, Cornwall, PL30 4DE
Actual Grid Ref: SW852708
Tel: 01208 74281
Fax: 01208 862805
Email: cncsjf@smtp.ntrust.org.uk
Capacity: 14 *Groups only*
Open: Sep to June
Self-catering facilities • Showers • Laundry facilities • Wet weather shelter • Lounge • Drying room • Parking • No smoking
Basecamp is situated on the North Cornish coast, 8 miles north of Newquay, and has spectacular views. There are 2 dormitories (each with 6 bunk beds and leader's cabin), washrooms with showers, common room with easy chairs and large dining table, modern well equipped kitchen and laundry.

Dennis Cove Camping, Dennis
Farm, Dennis Cove, Padstow, Cornwall, PL28 8DR
Actual Grid Ref: SW920745
Tel: 01841 532349
Open: Mar to Sept

Trerethern Touring Park,
Padstow, Cornwall, PL28 8LE
Actual Grid Ref: SW913738
Tel: 01841 532061 **Open:** Mar to Oct

Par
SX0753

Par Sands Holiday Park, Par
Beach, Par, Cornwall, PL24 2AS
Actual Grid Ref: SX083535
Tel: 01726 812868 **Fax:** 01726 817899
Email: holidays@parsands.co.uk
Tent pitches: 150
Tent rate: £6.00-£14.00
Open: Easter to Oct **Last arr:** 10pm
Dogs allowed • Electric hook-up • Calor Gas/Camping Gaz • Children's play area • Showers • Laundrette on site • Public phone on site
Alongside large, sandy beach. On coastal footpath. Half-price for walkers and cyclists.

MAP PAGE **14** • **Cornwall**

Medros Farm Caravan & Camping Club, Par, Cornwall, PL24 2SX
Tel: 01726 812923
Open: Easter to Oct

Pendeen
SW3834

Manor Farm, Pendeen, Penzance, Cornwall, TR19 7ED
Tel: 01736 788753
Fax: 01736 788753 **Open:** All year

Penhale
SW6918

The Friendly Camping & Caravan Park, Tregullas Farm, Penhale, Ruan Minor, Helston, Cornwall, TR12 7LJ
Actual Grid Ref: SW698185
Tel: 01326 240387
Open: Apr to Oct

Penryn
SW7734

Calamankey Farm, Longdowns, Penryn, Cornwall, TR10 9DL
Actual Grid Ref: SW745342
Tel: 01209 860314
Open: Apr to Oct

Pentewan
SX0147

Penhaven Touring Park, Pentewan, St Austell, Cornwall, PL26 6DL
Actual Grid Ref: SX008481
Tel: 01726 843687
Open: Apr to Oct

Sun Valley Holiday Park, Pentewan Road, Pentewan, St Austell, Cornwall, PL26 6DJ
Actual Grid Ref: SX006483
Tel: 01726 843266
Open: Apr to Oct

Pentewan Sands Holiday Park, Pentewan Sands, Pentewan, Cornwall, PL26 6BT
Actual Grid Ref: SX018466
Tel: 01726 843485
Open: Apr to Oct

Polrudden Farm, Pentewan, Mevagissey, St Austell, Cornwall, PL26 6BJ
Tel: 01726 843213
Open: All year

Penwithick
SX0256

Innis Country Club Campsite, Innis Moor, Penwithick, St Austell, Cornwall, PL26 8YH
Actual Grid Ref: SX034568
Tel: 01726 851162
Open: Apr to Oct

Penzance
SW467299

Penzance Youth Hostel, Castle Horneck, Alverton, Penzance, Cornwall, TR20 8TF
Actual Grid Ref: SW457302
Tel: 01736 362666
Fax: 01736 362663
Email: penzance@yha.org.uk
Capacity: 80
Under 18: £7.75
Adults: £11.00
Open: Feb to December (not Xmas), 3.00pm
Camping
Self-catering facilities • Television • Showers • Laundry facilities • Lounge • Drying room • Security lockers • Security lockers • Cycle store • Parking • Evening meal available 5.30pm to 7.45pm • Breakfast available • Credit cards accepted
Early Georgian manor house in landscaped gardens, with extensive views of Mount's Bay and the Lizard Peninsula.

Penzance Backpackers - The Blue Dolphin, The Blue Dolphin, Alexandra Road, Penzance, Cornwall, TR18 4LZ
Tel: 01736 363836
Fax: 01736 363844
Email: pzbackpack@ndirect.co.uk
Capacity: 30
Adults: £9.00-£10.00
Open: All year
Self-catering facilities • Television • Showers • Central heating • Shop • Laundry facilities • Lounge • Dining room • Cycle store • No smoking
Victorian house near town centre and close to sea front.

Please respect hostels' policy on smoking. Some hostels do not allow smoking anywhere, some restrict smoking to certain areas.

Perranarworthal
SW7738

Cosawes Caravan Park, Perranarworthal, Truro, Cornwall, TR3 7QS
Actual Grid Ref: SW768376
AA grade: 3 Pennants
Tel: 01872 863724 / 863717
Fax: 01872 870268
Email: cosawes@yahoo.com
Tent pitches: 50
Tent rate: £6.50-£7.50
Open: All year **Last arr:** 11pm
Dogs allowed • Electric hook-up • Calor Gas/Camping Gaz • Picnic/barbecue area on site • Showers • Laundrette on site • Public phone on site
Situated in 100 acre wooded valley between Truro and Falmouth.

Perranporth
SW7554

Perranporth Youth Hostel, Droskyn Point, Perranporth, Cornwall, TR6 0DS
Actual Grid Ref: SW752544
Tel: 01872 573812 **Fax:** 01872 573312
Capacity: 26
Under 18: £6.50 **Adults:** £9.25
Open: All year, 5.00pm
Self-catering facilities • Showers • Lounge • Drying room • Cycle store • No smoking • WC • Kitchen facilities • Credit cards accepted
Single-storey hostel high up on the cliffs, with spectacular views along 3 miles of surf beach, looking across to Ligger Point. The hostel has a surfboard store, and the drying room is wetsuit friendly.

Perranporth Camping & Touring Site, Budnick Road, Perranporth, Cornwall, TR6 0DB
Actual Grid Ref: SW765542
Tel: 01872 572174
Open: Mar to Sept

Tollgate, Perranporth, Truro, Cornwall, TR6 0AD
Actual Grid Ref: SW768547
Tel: 01872 572130
Open: Apr to Sep

ENGLAND

Stilwell's Hostels & Camping 2002   23

Cornwall • MAP PAGE 14

Perran Sands Holiday Park,
Perranporth, Cornwall, TR6 0AQ
Actual Grid Ref: SW767554
Tel: 01872 573551
Open: May to Sep

Perranwell
SW7839

Silverbow Park, Perranwell,
Goonhavern, Truro, Cornwall, TR4 9NX
Actual Grid Ref: SW782531
Tel: 01872 572347
Open: May to Oct

Polladras
SW6130

Lower Polladras Camping,
Carleen, Polladras, Helston, Cornwall, TR13 9NX
Actual Grid Ref: SW617288
Tel: 01736 762220
Open: Apr to Oct

Polperro
SX2050

Killigarth Manor Holiday Estate, Polperro, Looe, Cornwall, PL13 2JQ
Actual Grid Ref: SX214519
Tel: 01503 272216 / 272409
Fax: 01503 272216
Open: Mar to Oct

Polruan
SX1250

Polruan Holiday Centre,
Polruan, Fowey, Cornwall, PL23 1QH
Actual Grid Ref: SX133509
Tel: 01726 870263 **Open:** Apr to Sep

Polzeath
SW9378

South Winds Caravan & Camping Park, Polzeath Road, Polzeath, Wadebridge, Cornwall, PL27 6QU
Actual Grid Ref: SW948790
Tel: 01208 863267 / 862646
Open: Apr to Oct

Tristram Camping & Caravan Park, Polzeath, Wadebridge, Cornwall, PL27 6SR
Actual Grid Ref: SW936790
Tel: 01208 862215 / 863267
Fax: 01208 862080
Open: Apr to Oct

You are advised to book in advance for periods of high demand – the Summer months, Half Term holidays and public holidays.

Ponsongath
SW7517

Wych Elm, Ponsongath, Helston, Cornwall, TR12 6SQ
Actual Grid Ref: SW755179
Tel: 01326 280576
Open: Apr to Dec

Porth
SW8362

Porth Beach Tourist Park,
Porth, Newquay, Cornwall, TR7 3NH
Actual Grid Ref: SW834629
Tel: 01637 876531
Open: Apr to Oct

Trevelgue Caravan & Camping Park, Porth, Newquay, Cornwall, TR8 4AS
Actual Grid Ref: SW837634
Tel: 01637 851851
Fax: 01637 872343
Open: Apr to Oct

Tregustick Holiday Park, Porth, Newquay, Cornwall, TR8 4AR
Actual Grid Ref: SW845631
Tel: 01637 872478
Open: Easter to Oct

Porthtowan
SW6847

Porthtowan Tourist Park, Mile Hill, Porthtowan, Truro, Cornwall, TR4 8TY
Actual Grid Ref: SW694465
Tel: 01209 890256
Open: Mar to Oct

Rose Hill Park, Rose Hill, Porthtowan, Truro, Cornwall, TR4 8AR
Actual Grid Ref: SW694474
Tel: 01209 890802
Open: Mar to Oct

Hostels and campsites may vary rates – be sure to check when booking.

Portreath
SW6545

Cambrose Touring Park,
Portreath Road, Redruth, Cornwall, TR16 4HT
Actual Grid Ref: SW684451
Tourist Board grade: 3 Ticks
AA grade: 3 Pennants
Tel: 01209 890747
Fax: 01209 891665
Tent pitches: 60
Tent rate: £7.50-£11.00
Open: Apr to Oct **Last arr:** 9pm
Facilities for disabled people • Dogs allowed • Electric hook-up • Calor Gas/Camping Gaz • Cafe or Takeaway on site • Children's play area • Showers • Laundrette on site • Public phone on site • Shop on site • Baby care facilities • TV room • Games room • Indoor swimming pool nearby • Outdoor swimming pool on site • Boating/sailing/watersports nearby • Tennis courts nearby • Golf nearby • Riding nearby
Cambrose is a small, friendly, family-run site in a level sun trap valley. We are ideally situated for touring both the north and south coasts. Nearby is part of the Mineral Tramway for walks and cycle rides.

Portscatho
SW8735

Trewince Manor, Portscatho, Truro, Cornwall, TR2 5ET
Actual Grid Ref: SW868339
Tel: 01872 580289
Open: Apr to Oct

Poughill
SS2207

Wooda Farm Park, Poughill, Bude, Cornwall, EX23 9HJ
Actual Grid Ref: SS229080
Tel: 01288 352069
Open: Apr to Oct

All details shown are as supplied by hostels and campsites in Autumn 2000.

MAP PAGE **14** • **Cornwall**

Poundstock
SX2099

▲ **Cornish Coasts Caravan Park,** Middle Penlean, Poundstock, Widemouth Bay, Bude, Cornwall, EX23 0EE
Actual Grid Ref: SX203983
Tel: 01288 361380
Open: Apr to Oct

Quintrell Downs
SW8460

▲ **Trethiggey Touring Park,** Quintrell Downs, Newquay, Cornwall, TR8 4LG
Actual Grid Ref: SW849585
Tel: 01637 877672
Open: Mar to Dec

▲ **Sunnyside Holiday Park,** Quintrell Downs, Newquay, Cornwall, TR8 4PD
Actual Grid Ref: SW855598
Tel: 01673 873338
Open: Apr to Oct

Redruth
SW6942

▲ **Caddys Corner Farm,** Carnmenellis, Redruth, Cornwall, TR16 6PH
Actual Grid Ref: SW703348
Tel: 01209 860275
Open: Apr to Oct

▲ **Globe Vale Caravan Park,** Radnor, Redruth, Cornwall, TR16 4BH
Actual Grid Ref: SW708447
Tel: 01209 891183
Fax: 01209 890160
Open: Feb to Nov

Rejerrah
SW8056

▲ **Monkey Tree Touring Park,** Rejerrah, Newquay, Cornwall, TR8 5QL
Actual Grid Ref: SW803545
Tel: 01872 572032
Open: Mar to Oct

▲ **Newperran Tourist Park,** Rejerrah, Newquay, Cornwall, TR8 5QJ
Actual Grid Ref: SW795545
Tel: 01872 572407 / 01637 830308
Open: May to Sep

▲ **Perren Quay Tourist Park,** Hendra Croft, Rejerrah, Newquay, Cornwall, TR8 5QP
Actual Grid Ref: SW800554
Tel: 01872 572561
Open: Mar to Dec

Relubbus
SW5632

▲ **River Valley Country Park,** Relubbus, Penzance, Cornwall, TR20 9ER
Actual Grid Ref: SW566320
Tel: 01736 763398
Fax: 01736 763398
Open: Mar to Jan

Ruan Minor
SW7115

▲ **Mullion Holiday Park,** Penhale Cross, Ruan Minor, Helston, Cornwall, TR12 7LJ
Actual Grid Ref: SW699185
Tel: 01326 240000 / 240428
Fax: 01326 241141
Open: May to Sep

Rumford
SW8970

▲ **Music Water Touring Site,** Rumford, Wadebridge, Cornwall, PL27 7SJ
Actual Grid Ref: SW906685
Tel: 01841 540257
Open: Mar to Oct

Ruthernbridge
SX0167

▲ **Ruthern Valley Holidays,** Ruthernbridge, Bodmin, Cornwall, PL30 5LU
Actual Grid Ref: SX013667
AA grade: 3 Pennants
Tel: 01208 831395
Fax: 01208 832324
Email: ruthernvalley@talk21.com
Tent pitches: 29
Tent rate: £7.25-£8.75
Open: Mar to Oct
Last arr: 9pm
Dogs allowed • Electric hook-up • Calor Gas/Camping Gaz • Children's play area • Showers • Laundrette on site • Public phone on site • Shop on site
Beautiful rural site. No bar, no bingo, no disco - tranquil!

Saltash
SX4259

▲ **Notter Bridge Caravan & Camping Park,** Notter Bridge, Saltash, Devon, PL12 4RW
Actual Grid Ref: SX385608
Tel: 01752 842318
Open: Apr to Sep

Scorrier
SW7244

▲ **Wheal Rose Caravan & Camping Park,** Scorrier, Redruth, Cornwall, TR16 5DD
Actual Grid Ref: SW717449
Tel: 01209 891496
Open: Mar to Nov

Sennen
SW3525

▲ **Land's End Backpackers' Hostel,** Whitesands Lodge, Sennen, Penzance, Cornwall, TR19 7AR
Actual Grid Ref: SW366264
Tel: 01736 871776
Email: info@whitesandslodge.co.uk
Capacity: 25
Under 18: £10.00
Adults: £10.00
Open: All year, 9am-9pm
Family bunk rooms: £30.00
Camping for 8 tents: £6.00
Self-catering facilities • Television • Showers • Licensed bar • Laundry facilities • Lounge • Dining room • Games room • Grounds available for games • Drying room • Cycle store • Parking • Evening meal available
Colourful, friendly hostel close to stunning coast, great beaches and much more.

▲ **Sea View Caravan Park,** Sennen, Penzance, Cornwall, TR19 7AD
Actual Grid Ref: SW357253
Tel: 01736 871266
Open: Mar to Oct

Shortlanesend
SW8245

▲ **Summer Valley,** Shortlanesend, Truro, Cornwall, TR4 9DW
Actual Grid Ref: SW800479
Tel: 01872 277878
Open: Apr to Oct

ENGLAND

Stilwell's Hostels & Camping 2002

Cornwall • MAP PAGE 14

St Agnes
SW7250

▲ **Beacon Cottage Farm Touring Park,** Beacon Drive, St Agnes, Cornwall, TR5 0NU
Actual Grid Ref: SW705502
Tel: 01872 552347
Open: May to Oct

▲ **Trevellas Porth Touring Park,** Crosscombe, St Agnes, Cornwall, TR5 0XP
Actual Grid Ref: SW732521
Tel: 01872 552999
Open: Apr to Oct

▲ **Presingoll Farm,** St Agnes, Cornwall, TR5 0PB
Actual Grid Ref: SW721494
Tel: 01872 552333
Open: Apr to Oct

St Austell
SX0252

▲ **Trewhiddle Holiday Estate,** Trewhiddle, St Austell, Cornwall, PL26 7AD
Actual Grid Ref: SX005512
Tel: 01726 67011
Open: All year

▲ **East Crinnis Farm,** Par Moor Road, Par, Cornwall, PL24 2SQ
Actual Grid Ref: SX062528
Tel: 01726 813023
Open: Apr to Oct

▲ **The Meadows Caravan & Camping Club,** Pentewan Road, St Austell, Cornwall, PL26 6DL
Tel: 01726 842547
Open: All year

▲ **Treveague Farm Campsite,** Gorran, St Austell, Cornwall, PL26 6NY
Actual Grid Ref: SX004413
Tel: 01726 843197
Open: Jul to Aug

St Buryan
SW4026

▲ **Camping & Caravanning Club Site,** Higher Tregiffian Farm, St Buryan, Penzance, Cornwall, TR19 6JB
Actual Grid Ref: SW378276
Tel: 01736 871588 / 01203 694995
Open: Mar to Sep

▲ **Tower Park Caravans & Parking,** St Buryan, Penzance, Cornwall, TR19 6BZ
Actual Grid Ref: SW408260
Tel: 01736 810286
Open: Mar to Oct

▲ **Treverven Touring Caravan & Camping Site,** Treverven Farm, St Buryan, Penzance, Cornwall, TR19 6DL
Actual Grid Ref: SW410237
Tel: 01736 810221
Open: Apr to Oct

St Columb Major
SW9163

▲ **Southleigh Manor Tourist Park,** St Columb Major, Cornwall, TR9 6HY
Actual Grid Ref: SW918623
Tel: 01637 880938
Open: Apr to Sep

▲ **Camping & Caravanning Club Site,** Trewan Hall, St Columb, Cornwall, TR9 6DB
Actual Grid Ref: SW910646
Tel: 01637 880261
Fax: 01637 880484
Open: May to Sep

St Day
SW7342

▲ **Tresaddern Holiday Park,** St Day, Redruth, Cornwall, TR16 5JR
Actual Grid Ref: SW733422
Tel: 01209 820459
Open: Apr to Oct

St Eval
SW8769

▲ **Atlantic View Caravan & Camping Park,** Trevemedar Farm, St Eval, Wadebridge, Cornwall, PL27 7UT
Actual Grid Ref: SW856712
Tel: 01841 520431
Open: Apr to Oct

St Ewe
SW9746

▲ **Pengrugla Caravan & Camping Park,** St Ewe, Mevagissey, St Austell, Cornwall, PL26 6EL
Actual Grid Ref: SW998470
Tel: 01726 842714
Open: All year

St Gennys
SX1497

▲ **Camping & Caravanning Club Site,** Gillards Moor, St Gennys, Bude, Cornwall, EX23 0BG
Actual Grid Ref: SX176943
Tel: 01840 230650 / 01203 694995
Open: Mar to Sep

St Germans
SX3657

▲ **Fox Cottage,** St Germans, Saltash, Cornwall, PL12 5LN
Tel: 01503 230296
Open: All year

St Hilary
SW5531

▲ **Trevair Touring Site,** South Treveneague, St Hilary, Goldsithney, Penzance, Cornwall, TR20 9BY
Actual Grid Ref: SW548326
Tel: 01736 740647
Open: Mar to Oct

St Issey
SW9271

▲ **Trewince Farm Holiday Park,** St Issey, Wadebridge, Cornwall, PL27 7RL
Actual Grid Ref: SW937715
Tel: 01208 812830
Open: Easter to Oct

▲ **Pickwick Camping & Caravan Site,** Burgois, St Issey, Wadebridge, Cornwall, PL27 7QQ
Tel: 01841 540361
Open: Easter to Oct

▲ **Ponderosa Caravan Park,** St Issey, Wadebridge, Cornwall, PL27 7QA
Actual Grid Ref: SW927719
Tel: 01841 540359 **Open:** Mar to Oct

St Ives
SW5140

▲ **Ayr Holiday Park,** Higher Ayr, St Ives, Cornwall, TR26 1EJ
Actual Grid Ref: SW512405
Tel: 01736 795855
Open: Apr to Oct

▲ **Trevalgan Family Camping Park,** St Ives, Cornwall, TR26 3BJ
Actual Grid Ref: SW490400
Tel: 01736 796433
Open: May to Sep

MAP PAGE **14** • **Cornwall**

▲ **Hellesveor Farm,** *St Ives, Cornwall, TR26 3AD*
Actual Grid Ref: SW503401
Tel: 01736 795738
Open: Mar to Oct

St Just-in-Penwith

SW3631

▲ **Land's End Youth Hostel,** *Letcha Vean, St Just, Penzance, Cornwall, TR19 7NT*
Actual Grid Ref: SW364305
Tel: 01736 788437
Fax: 01736 787337
Capacity: 43
Under 18: £6.90
Adults: £10.00
Open: All year, 5.00pm
Family bunk rooms
Camping
Self-catering facilities • Showers • Lounge • Cycle store • Evening meal available 7.00pm • No smoking • WC • Kitchen facilities • Breakfast available • Credit cards accepted
House with sea views in the peaceful Cot Valley, with a path leading to the cove.

▲ **Roselands Caravan Park,** *Dowran, St Just-in-Penwith, Penzance, Cornwall, TR19 7RS*
Actual Grid Ref: SW387305
Tel: 01736 788571
Open: Feb to Oct

▲ **Bosavern House,** *St Just-in-Penwith, Penzance, Cornwall, TR19 7RD*
Actual Grid Ref: SW370305
Tel: 01736 788301
Fax: 01736 788301
Open: Mar to Oct

St Just-in-Roseland

SW8435

▲ **Trethem Mill Touring Park,** *St Just-in-Roseland, Truro, Cornwall, TR2 5JF*
Actual Grid Ref: SW857366
Tel: 01872 580504
Open: Apr to Oct

St Keverne

SW7921

▲ **Penmarth Farm,** *Coverack, Helston, Cornwall, TR12 6SB*
Actual Grid Ref: SW775179
Tel: 01326 280389
Open: Mar to Oct

St Kew Highway

SX0375

▲ **Lanarth Hotel & Caravan Park,** *St Kew Highway, Bodmin, Cornwall, PL30 3EE*
Actual Grid Ref: SX027749
Tel: 01208 841215
Open: Apr to Oct

St Mabyn

SX0473

▲ **Glenmorris Park,** *Longstone Road, St Mabyn, Bodmin, Cornwall, PL30 3BY*
Actual Grid Ref: SX055733
Tel: 01208 841677
Fax: 01208 841677
Open: Easter to Oct

St Martin

SX2655

▲ **Tregoad Farm Touring Caravan & Camping Park,** *St Martin , Looe, Cornwall, PL13 1PB*
Actual Grid Ref: SX272560
Tel: 01503 262718
Open: Apr to Oct

St Merryn

SW8874

▲ **Trevean Caravan & Camping Park,** *Trevean Lane, St Merryn, Padstow, Cornwall, PL28 8PR*
Actual Grid Ref: SW875724
Tel: 01841 520772
Open: Apr to Oct

▲ **Maribou Holidays,** *St Merryn, Padstow, Cornwall, PL28 8QA*
Tel: 01841 520520
Fax: 01841 521154
Open: Easter to Oct

▲ **Tregavone Touring Park,** *St Merryn, Padstow, Cornwall, PL28 8J*
Actual Grid Ref: SW897732
Tel: 01841 520148
Open: Mar to Oct

▲ **Carnevas Farm Holiday Park,** *St Merryn, Padstow, Cornwall, PL28 5PN*
Actual Grid Ref: SW862728
Tel: 01841 520230
Open: Apr to Oct

▲ **Higher Harlyn Park,** *St Merryn, Padstow, Cornwall, PL28 8SG*
Actual Grid Ref: SW877744
Tel: 01841 520022
Open: Mar to Sept

▲ **Seagull Tourist Park,** *Treginegar, St Merryn, Padstow, Cornwall, PL28 8PT*
Actual Grid Ref: SW883713
Tel: 01841 520117
Open: Apr to Oct

St Minver

SW9677

▲ **Gunvenna Touring Caravan & Camping Park,** *St Minver, Wadebridge, Cornwall, PL27 6QN*
Actual Grid Ref: SW969782
Tel: 01208 862405
Open: Mar to Oct

▲ **St Minver Holiday Park,** *St Minver, Wadebridge, Cornwall, PL27 6RR*
Actual Grid Ref: SW967768
Tel: 01208 862305
Open: Apr to Oct

▲ **Dinham Farm Caravan & Camping Park,** *St Minver, Wadebridge, Cornwall, PL27 6RH*
Actual Grid Ref: SW972750
Tel: 01208 812878
Open: Apr to Oct

▲ **Lundynant Caravan Site,** *St Minver, Wadebridge, Cornwall, PL27 6QX*
Actual Grid Ref: SW945793
Tel: 01208 862268
Open: Apr to Oct

▲ **Carlyon Farm,** *St Minver, Wadebridge, Cornwall, PL27 6RJ*
Actual Grid Ref: SW955753
Tel: 01208 863429
Open: Apr to Oct

▲ **Trewiston Farm,** *Trewiston Lane, Rock, Wadebridge, Cornwall, PL27 6PX*
Actual Grid Ref: SW945773
Tel: 01208 863205
Open: Apr to Oct

Please respect hostels' policy on smoking. Some hostels do not allow smoking anywhere, some restrict smoking to certain areas.

Cornwall • MAP PAGE 14

St Neot
SX1867

▲ **Colliford Tavern Campsite,** Colliford Lake, St Neot, Liskeard, Cornwall, PL14 6PZ
Actual Grid Ref: SX171740
Tel: 01208 821335
Open: Apr to Oct

▲ **Trenant Caravan Park,** St Neot, Liskeard, Cornwall, PL14 6RZ
Actual Grid Ref: SX209684
Tel: 01579 320896
Open: Apr to Oct

Summercourt
SW8856

▲ **Resparva House Caravan & Camping,** Summercourt, Newquay, Cornwall, TR8 5AH
Actual Grid Ref: SW880556
Tel: 01872 510332
Open: May to Sep

The Lizard
SW7012

▲ **Sea Acres Holiday Park,** Kennack Sands, The Lizard, Helston, Cornwall, TR12 7LT
Actual Grid Ref: SW730164
Tel: 01326 290064
Open: Apr to Oct

Tintagel
SX0588

▲ **Tintagel Youth Hostel,** Dunderhole Point, Tintagel, Cornwall, PL34 0DW
Actual Grid Ref: SX047881
Tel: 01840 770334
Fax: 01840 770733
Email: reservations@yha.org.uk
Capacity: 24
Under 18: £6.90 **Adults:** £10.00
Open: All year, 5.00pm
Self-catering facilities • Showers • Lounge • Cycle store • Parking Limited • No smoking • Kitchen facilities
150-year-old slate quarry cottage now owned by NT, in spectacular clifftop setting, with extensive views across Port Isaac Bay.

▲ **Headland Caravan & Camping Park,** Dept NC, Atlantic Road, Tintagel, Cornwall, PL34 0DE
Actual Grid Ref: SX056887
Tel: 01840 770239 **Fax:** 01840 770239
Open: Easter to Oct

▲ **Trewethett Farm Caravan Club Site,** Trevethy, Tintagel, Cornwall, PL34 0BQ
Actual Grid Ref: SX074895
Tel: 01840 770222
Open: Mar to Sept

▲ **Bossiney Farm Caravan Park,** Bossiney, Tintagel, Cornwall, PL34 0AY
Actual Grid Ref: SX066888
Tel: 01840 770481
Open: Apr to Oct

Towednack
SW4838

▲ **Penderleath Caravan & Camping Park,** Towednack, St Ives, Cornwall, TR26 3AF
Actual Grid Ref: SW496375
Tel: 01736 798403
Open: Apr to Oct

Tregurrian
SW8565

▲ **Camping & Caravanning Club Site,** Tregurrian, Newquay, Cornwall, TR8 4AE
Actual Grid Ref: SW853654
Tel: 01637 860448 / 01203 694995
Open: Mar to Sep

▲ **Watergate Bay Tourist Park,** Tregurrian, Watergate Bay, Newquay, Cornwall, TR8 4AD
Actual Grid Ref: SW850653
Tel: 01637 860387
Open: Mar to Nov

Trelawne
SX2154

▲ **Camping Caradon,** Trelawne Gardens, Trelawne, Looe, Cornwall, PL13 2TR
Actual Grid Ref: SX220542
Tel: 01503 272388
Open: Mar to Oct

Trematon
SX3959

▲ **Stoketon Caravan & Camping Park,** The Crooked Inn, Stoketon Cross, Trematon, Saltash, Cornwall, PL12 4RZ
Actual Grid Ref: SX392604
Tel: 01752 848177
Fax: 01752 843203
Open: Apr to Oct

You are advised to book in advance for periods of high demand – the Summer months, Half Term holidays and public holidays.

Trevellas
SW7352

▲ **Deep Meadows,** Trevellas, St Agnes, Cornwall, TR5 0XX
Actual Grid Ref: SW741516
Tel: 01872 552236
Open: All year

Treverva
SW7531

▲ **Menallack Farm Caravan & Camping SIte,** Treverva, Penryn, Falmouth, Cornwall, TR10 9BP
Actual Grid Ref: SW750312
Tel: 01326 340333
Open: Mar to Oct

Trevose Head
SW8576

▲ **Harlyn Sands Holiday Park,** Lighthouse Road, Trevose Head, St Merryn, Padstow, Cornwall, PL28 8SQ
Actual Grid Ref: SW880756
Tel: 01841 520720
Open: Apr to Nov

▲ **Mother Ivey's Bay Caravan Park,** Trevose Head, Padstow, Cornwall, PL28 2SL
Actual Grid Ref: SW865755
Tel: 01841 520990
Open: Mar to Oct

Trewellard
SW3734

▲ **Levant Caravan & Camping,** Levant Road, Trewellard, Pendeen, Penzance, Cornwall, TR19 7SX
Actual Grid Ref: SW375337
Tel: 01736 788795
Open: Apr to Oct

To stay in a Youth Hostel affiliated to one of the Youth Hostel associations, you need to be a member. You can join at most hostels – phone in advance to check.

MAP PAGE **14** • **Cornwall**

Treyarnon Bay

SW8674

▲ **Treyarnon Bay Youth Hostel,** Tregonnan, Treyarnon, Padstow, Cornwall, PL28 8JR
Actual Grid Ref: SW859741
Tel: 01841 520322
Fax: 01841 520464
Capacity: 41
Under 18: £6.90
Adults: £10.00
Open: All year, 5.00pm
Family bunk rooms
Self-catering facilities • Showers • Lounge • Drying room • Cycle store • Parking • Evening meal available 7.00pm • No smoking • WC • Kitchen facilities • Breakfast available • Credit cards accepted
Overlooking sandy cove in designated Area of Outstanding Natural Beauty.

▲ **Treyarnon Bay Caravan & Camping Park,** Treyarnon Bay, Padstow, Cornwall, PL28 8JR
Actual Grid Ref: SW858741
Tel: 01841 520681
Open: Mar to Sept

▲ **Trethias Farm Caravan Park,** Treyarnon Bay, Padstow, Cornwall, PL28 8PL
Actual Grid Ref: SW864734
Tel: 01841 520323 **Fax:** 01841 520055
Open: Apr to Sep

Truro

SW8244

▲ **Treloan Coastal Farm Holidays,** Treloan Coastal Farm, Porthscatho, Truro, Cornwall, TR2 2EF
Actual Grid Ref: SW875247
AA grade: 2 Pennants
Tel: 01872 580989 or 580899
Fax: 01872 580989
Email: holidays@treloan.freeserve.co.uk
Tent pitches: 57
Tent rate: £5.50-£11.35
Open: All year
Last arr: any time

Facilities for disabled people • Dogs allowed • Electric hook-up • Calor Gas/Camping Gaz • Picnic/barbecue area on site • Children's play area • Showers • Laundrette on site • Public phone on site • Boating/sailing/watersports nearby • Riding nearby • Fishing on site
Idyllic site on coastal footpath. Private access to 3 beautiful, clean and safe coves. Developing organic working farm museum with shires. Self-catering, touring vans and tents, hot showers, laundry, play area, river moorings, sea fishing etc. 3 minutes' walk to Portscatho, church, shops, pubs, restaurants, galleries, etc. Pets welcome.

Veryan

SW9139

▲ **Camping & Caravanning Club Site,** Tretheake Manor, Veryan, Truro, Cornwall, TR2 5PP
Actual Grid Ref: SW934414
Tel: 01872 501658
Open: Mar to Oct

Wadebridge

SW9872

▲ **Little Bodieve Holiday Park,** Bodieve Road, Wadebridge, Cornwall, PL27 6EG
Actual Grid Ref: SW995734
Tel: 01208 812323
Open: Apr to Oct

Week St Mary

SX2397

▲ **Penhallym Farm,** Week St Mary, Holsworthy, Devon, EX22 6XR
Tel: 01288 341274
Open: All year

Whitecross (Penzance)

SW5234

▲ **White Acres Holiday Park,** Whitecross, Newquay, Cornwall, TR8 4LW
Actual Grid Ref: SW890599
Tel: 01726 860220 / 860999
Open: Mar to Oct

▲ **Summer Lodge Holiday Park,** Newquay, Cornwall, TR8 4LW
Actual Grid Ref: SW889597
Tel: 01726 860415
Open: Mar to Sept

Whitecross (Wadebridge)

SW9672

▲ **The Laurels,** Whitecross, Wadebridge, Cornwall, PL27 7JQ
Actual Grid Ref: SW957715
Tel: 01208 813341
Open: Easter to Oct

Whitstone

SX2698

▲ **Keywood Caravan Park Ltd,** Keywood Park, Whitstone, Holsworthy, Cornwall, EX22 6TW
Actual Grid Ref: SX253997
Tel: 01288 341338
Open: Mar to Oct

Widemouth Bay

SS2002

▲ **Widemouth Bay Caravan Park,** Widemouth Bay, Bude, Cornwall, EX23 0DF
Actual Grid Ref: SS199008
Tel: 01288 361208
Open: Mar to Oct

▲ **Penhalt Farm Holiday Park,** Widemouth Bay, Bude, Cornwall, EX23 0DF
Actual Grid Ref: SS194003
Tel: 01288 361210
Open: Mar to Oct

Zennor

SW4538

▲ **The Old Chapel Backpackers,** Zennor, St Ives, Cornwall, TR26 3BY
Tel: 01736 798307
Fax: 01736 798307
Email: zennorbackpackers@btinternet.com
Capacity: 32
Under 18: £10.00
Adults: £10.00
Open: All year, any time
Family bunk rooms: £30.00
Camping for 20 tents: £3.50
Television • Showers • Licensed bar • Central heating • Shop • Laundry facilities • Dining room • Grounds available for games • Drying room • Parking • Evening meal available • No smoking
Converted chapel with clear views over sea and Moorlands.

▲ **The Old Chapel Backpackers,** Zennor, St Ives, Cornwall, TR26 3BY
Tel: 01736 798307
Open: All year

Cumbria

Cumbria

Ainstable
NY5346

▲ **Eden Valley Centre,** Ainstable, Carlisle, Cumbria, CA4 9QA
Actual Grid Ref: NY529463
Tel: 01768 896202
Fax: 01768 896202
Email: eden.valley@outdoor-pursuits.com
Capacity: 37
Under 18: £8.00
Adults: £8.00
Open: All year, all day
Self-catering facilities • Television • Showers • Central heating • Wet weather shelter • Lounge • Dining room • Grounds available for games • Drying room • Cycle store • Parking • Evening meal available 6pm • No smoking
Near Cumbria cycle way, Eden Way and River Eden.

Allonby
NY0743

▲ **Spring Lea Caravan Park,** Allonby, Maryport, Cumbria, CA15 6QF
Actual Grid Ref: NY084434
Tel: 01900 881331
Open: Mar to Oct

▲ **Manor House Caravan Park,** Edderside Road, Allonby, Maryport, Cumbria, CA15 6RA
Actual Grid Ref: NY093450
Tel: 01900 881236
Open: Mar to Nov

Alston
NY7146

▲ **Alston Youth Hostel,** The Firs, Alston, Cumbria, CA9 3RW
Actual Grid Ref: NY717461
Tel: 01434 381509
Fax: 01434 382401
Capacity: 30
Under 18: £6.50
Adults: £9.25
Open: All year, 5.00pm
Camping
Self-catering facilities • Showers • Lounge • Dining room • Drying room • Cycle store • Parking • Evening meal available 7.00pm • No smoking • WC • Kitchen facilities • Breakfast available • Credit cards accepted
Purpose-built hostel overlooking River South Tyne, on outskirts of Alston, the highest market town in England.

Appleby-in-Westmorland
NY6820

▲ **Wild Rose Park,** Ormside, Appleby-in-Westmorland, Cumbria, CA16 6EJ
Actual Grid Ref: NY697165
Tel: 017683 51077
Fax: 017683 52551
Email: broch@wildrose.co.uk
Open: All year

▲ **Roman Road Campsite,** Appleby-in-Westmorland, Cumbria, CA16 6JH
Tel: 01768 351681
Open: Easter to Sep

Arnside
SD4578

▲ **Arnside Youth Hostel,** Oakfield Lodge, Redhills Road, Arnside, Carnforth, Lancashire, LA5 0AT
Actual Grid Ref: SD452783
Tel: 01524 761781
Fax: 01524 762589
Email: arnside@yha.org.uk
Capacity: 72
Under 18: £6.90 **Adults:** £10.00
Open: Feb to Nov + New Year, 5.00pm
Family bunk rooms
Self-catering facilities • Television • Showers • Laundry facilities • Lounge • Games room • Drying room • Cycle store • Parking • Evening meal available 7.00pm • WC • Kitchen facilities • Breakfast available • Credit cards accepted
A few minutes' walk from the shore with views across Morecambe Bay to the Lakeland Fells. A mellow stone house on the edge of a coastal village on the Kent estuary. RSPB reserve nearby.

Askam-in-Furness
SD2177

▲ **Marsh Farm Caravan Site,** Askam-in-Furness, Cumbria, LA16 7AW
Actual Grid Ref: SD212784
Tel: 01229 462321
Open: Mar to Oct

Hostels and campsites may vary rates – be sure to check when booking.

All details shown are as supplied by hostels and campsites in Autumn 2000.

Aspatria
NY1441

▲ **Manor House Guest House,** Oughterside, Aspatria, Carlisle, Cumbria, CA7 2PT
Tel: 01697 322420
Fax: 01697 322420
Open: All year

Ayside
SD3983

▲ **Oak Head Caravan Park,** Ayside, Grange-over-Sands, Cumbria, LA11 6JA
Actual Grid Ref: SD389839
Tel: 015395 31475
Open: Mar to Oct

Bailey Mill
NY5179

▲ **Folly,** Bailey Mill, Bailey, Newcastleton, Roxburghshire, TD9 0TR
Tel: 016977 48617 **Fax:** 016977 48074
Capacity: 22
Under 18: £8.00 **Adults:** £10.00
Open: All year, until 10pm
Family bunk rooms: £30.00
Camping for 10 tents: £5.00
Self-catering facilities • Television • Showers • Licensed bar • Central heating • Shop • Laundry facilities • Wet weather shelter • Lounge • Dining room • Games room • Grounds available for games • Drying room • Cycle store • Parking • Evening meal available • Facilities for disabled people
Courtyard Apartments on site; Pony trekking, jacuzzi, sauna, bar and mountain bike hire.

▲ **Bailey Mill,** Bailey, Newcastleton, Roxburghshire, TD9 0TR
Tel: 016977 48617
Fax: 016977 48074
Open: All year

▲ **Garden Lodge,** 324 Canterbury Road, Densole, Folkestone, Kent, CT18 7BB
Tel: 01303 893147
Fax: 01303 893147
Open: Mar to Oct

Stilwell's Hostels & Camping 2002

Cumbria • MAP PAGE 30

ENGLAND

Barrow-in-Furness
SD1969

▲ **South End Caravan Park,** Walney Island, Barrow-in-Furness, Cumbria, LA14 3YQ
Actual Grid Ref: SD208628
Tel: 01229 472823 / 471556
Open: Mar to Oct

Bassenthwaite
NY2332

▲ **Robin Hood Caravan Park,** Bassenthwaite, Keswick, Cumbria, CA12 4RJ
Actual Grid Ref: NY229329
Tel: 01768 776334
Open: Mar to Oct

▲ **Traffords Caravan Park,** Bassenthwaite, Keswick, Cumbria, CA12 4QH
Tel: 017687 76298
Open: Easter to Oct

Beckermet
NY0207

▲ **Tarnside Caravan Park,** Braystones, Beckermet, Cumbria, CA21 2YL
Tel: 01946 841308 **Open:** All year

Beckfoot (Carlisle)
NY0849

▲ **Rowanbank Caravan Park,** Beckfoot, Silloth-on-Solway, Carlisle, Cumbria, CA5 4LA
Actual Grid Ref: NY095498
Tel: 01697 331653
Open: Mar to Oct

Berrier
NY4029

▲ **Whitbarrow Hall Caravan Park,** Whitbarrow Hall, Caravan Park, Berrier, Greystoke, Penrith, Cumbria, CA11 0XB
Actual Grid Ref: NY404288
Tel: 01768 483456
Open: Mar to Oct

You are advised to book in advance for periods of high demand – the Summer months, Half Term holidays and public holidays.

Bewaldeth
NY2034

▲ **North Lakes Caravan & Camp Park,** Bewaldeth, Cockermouth, Cumbria, CA13 9SY
Actual Grid Ref: NY207354
Tel: 017687 76510
Open: Mar to Nov

Black Sail
NY1912

▲ **Black Sail Youth Hostel,** Black Sail Hut, Black Sail, Ennerdale, Cleator, Cumbria, CA23 3AY
Actual Grid Ref: NY194124
Tel: 07711 108450
Fax: 07711 159473
Capacity: 16 **Under 18:** £6.50
Adults: £9.25 **Open:** All year, 5.00pm
Self-catering facilities • Showers • Lounge • Evening meal available 7.00pm • No smoking • WC • Kitchen facilities • Breakfast available • Credit cards accepted
A former shepherd's bothy, this is the most isolated, excitingly situated hostel in England!

Blackford
NY3962

▲ **Dandy Dinmont Caravan & Camping Park,** Blackford, Carlisle, Cumbria, CA6 4EA
Actual Grid Ref: NY399620
Tel: 01228 574611
Open: Easter to Oct

▲ **Dandy Dinmont Caravan & Camping Site,** Blackford, Carlisle, Cumbria, CA6 4EA
Actual Grid Ref: NY398622
Tel: 01228 674611
Open: Mar to Oct

Blawith
SD2988

▲ **Birch Bank Farm,** Blawith, Ulverston, Cumbria, LA12 8EW
Actual Grid Ref: SD262875
Tel: 01229 885277
Open: May to Oct

Blencow
NY4532

▲ **Little Blencow Farm,** Blencow, Penrith, Cumbria, CA11 0DG
Tel: 017684 83338 **Fax:** 017684 83054
Open: Easter to Nov

Blitterlees
NY1052

▲ **Moordale Park,** Blitterlees, Silloth-on-Solway, Carlisle, Cumbria, CA5 4JZ
Tel: 016973 31375
Open: Mar to Oct

Bonningate
SD4895

▲ **Ratherheath Lane Camping & Caravan Park,** Chain House, Bonningate, Kendal, Cumbria, LA8 8JU
Tel: 01539 821154
Email: djwilson@ndirect.co.uk
Open: Mar to Nov

Boot
NY1701

▲ **Eskdale Youth Hostel,** Boot, Holmrook, Cumbria, CA19 1TH
Actual Grid Ref: NY195010
Tel: 019467 23219
Fax: 019467 23163
Email: reservations@yha.org.uk
Capacity: 50
Under 18: £6.90
Adults: £10.00
Open: All year, 5.00pm
Family bunk rooms
Television • Showers • Licensed bar • Laundry facilities • Lounge • Games room • Drying room • Cycle store • Parking • Evening meal available 7.00pm • No smoking • WC • Kitchen facilities • Breakfast available • Credit cards accepted
In the south west of the Lakeland fells, this purpose-built hostel popular with families. All standards of walkers will find routes suitable for their ability.

▲ **Hollins Farm,** Boot, Holmrook, Cumbria, CA19 1TH
Tel: 01946 723253
Open: All year

▲ **Hollins Farm,** Boot, Holmrook, Cumbria, CA19 1TH
Actual Grid Ref: NY179011
Tel: 01946 723253
Open: Apr to Nov

Bootle
SD1188

▲ **The Stables,** Bootle, Millom, Cumbria, LA19 5TJ
Tel: 01229 718644
Open: All year

MAP PAGE **30** • **Cumbria**

Borrowdale

NY2417

▲ **Ashness Farm,** *Borrowdale, Keswick, Cumbria, CA12 5UN*
Actual Grid Ref: NY272194
Tel: 017687 77361
Open: Mar to Nov

▲ **Chapel House Farm Campsite,** *Borrowdale, Keswick, Cumbria, CA12 5XG*
Actual Grid Ref: NY256140
Tel: 017687 77602
Open: Mar to Oct

Bothel

NY1838

▲ **Skiddaw View Caravan Park,** *Bothel, Carlisle, Cumbria, CA5 2JG*
Actual Grid Ref: NY180366
Tel: 016973 20919
Open: Mar to Oct

Bouth

SD3385

▲ **Black Beck Caravan Park,** *Bouth, Ulverston, Cumbria, LA12 8JN*
Actual Grid Ref: SD335855
Tel: 01229 861274
Open: Mar to Oct

Bowness (Ennerdale)

NY1015

▲ **Fallbarrow Park,** *Rayrigg Road, Bowness-on-Windermere, Windermere, Cumbria, LA23 3DL*
Actual Grid Ref: SD401973
Tel: 015394 44422
Open: Mar to Oct

Braithwaite

NY2323

▲ **Scotgate Caravan Park,** *Braithwaite, Keswick, Cumbria, CA12 5TJ*
Actual Grid Ref: NY235235
Tel: 017687 78343
Fax: 017687 78079
Open: Mar to Oct

▲ **Scotgate Holiday Park,** *Braithwaite, Keswick, Cumbria, CA12 5TF*
Actual Grid Ref: NY236236
Tel: 01768 778343
Open: Mar to Oct

Brampton (Carlisle)

NY5360

▲ **Irthing Vale Holiday Park,** *Old Church Lane, Brampton, Cumbria, CA8 2AA*
Actual Grid Ref: NY523614
Tel: 01697 73600
Open: Mar to Oct

▲ **Talkin Tarn Country Park,** *Brampton, Cumbria, CA8 1HN*
Actual Grid Ref: NY545591
Tel: 016977 3129
Open: Apr to Oct

Buttermere

NY1717

▲ **Buttermere Youth Hostel,** *King George VI Memorial Hostel, Buttermere, Cockermouth, Cumbria, CA13 9XA*
Actual Grid Ref: NT178168
Tel: 017687 70245
Fax: 017687 70231
Email: buttermere@yha.org.uk
Capacity: 70
Under 18: £7.75
Adults: £11.00
Open: All year (not Xmas/New Year), 1.00pm
Family bunk rooms
Self-catering facilities • Television • Showers • Licensed bar • Lounge • Dining room • Drying room • Cycle store • Parking • Evening meal available 7.00pm • Kitchen facilities • Credit cards accepted
Traditional Lakeland slate building in its own grounds overlooking Buttermere and Crummock Water to the high ridges beyond, particularly popular with families.

▲ **Cragg Camping Barn,** *Crag Houses, Buttermere, Cockermouth, Cumbria, CA13 9XA*
Actual Grid Ref: NY174172
Tel: 017687 72645
Adults: £3.35
Part of traditional buildings in farmyard of typical hill farm. ADVANCE BOOKING ESSENTIAL.

▲ **Dalegarth,** *Buttermere, Cockermouth, Cumbria, CA13 9XA*
Tel: 017687 70233
Open: Apr to Oct

Please respect hostels' policy on smoking. Some hostels do not allow smoking anywhere, some restrict smoking to certain areas.

Carlisle

NY3955

▲ **Carlisle Youth Hostel,** *University of Northumbria, The Old Brewery Residences, Bridge Lane, Caldewgate, Carlisle, Cumbria, CA2 5SR*
Actual Grid Ref: NY394560
Tel: 01228 597352
Fax: 01228 597352
Email: dee.carruthers@unn.ac.uk
Capacity: 56
Under 18: £8.75
Adults: £13.00
Open: July to Sep, 5.00pm
Self-catering facilities • Showers • Cycle store • Parking • Facilities for disabled people • No smoking • WC • Kitchen facilities
University accommodation in an award-winning conversion of the former Theakston's brewery. Single study bedrooms with shared kitchen and bathroom in flats for up to 7 people.

▲ **Orton Grange Caravan & Camping Park,** *Orton Grange, Wigton Road, Carlisle, Cumbria, CA5 6LA*
Actual Grid Ref: NY354520
Tel: 01228 710252
Fax: 01228 710252
Open: All year

▲ **Dalston Hall Caravan Park,** *Dalston Hall Estate, Carlisle, Cumbria, CA5 7JX*
Actual Grid Ref: NY389519
Tel: 01228 710165 / 25014
Open: Mar to Oct

Casterton

SD6279

▲ **Woodclose Caravan Park,** *Casterton, Kirkby Lonsdale, Carnforth, Lancashire, LA6 3SE*
Actual Grid Ref: SD618786
AA grade: 4 Pennants
Tel: 01524 271597
Fax: 015242 72301
Tent pitches: 15
Tent rate: £4.00
Open: Mar to Oct
Last arr: 9pm
Facilities for disabled people • Dogs allowed • Electric hook-up • Calor Gas/Camping Gaz • Picnic/barbecue area on site • Children's play area • Showers • Laundrette on site • Public phone on site • Shop on site
A privileged location in an Area of Outstanding Natural Beauty.

ENGLAND

Stilwell's Hostels & Camping 2002   33

Cumbria • MAP PAGE 30

ENGLAND

Causewayhead
NY1253

▲ **Tanglewood Caravan Park,** Causewayhead, Silloth-on-Solway, Carlisle, Cumbria, CA5 4PE
Actual Grid Ref: NY130533
Tel: 016973 31253
Open: Apr to Oct

Cautley
SD6995

▲ **Cross Hall Caravan Park,** Cautley, Sedbergh, Cumbria, LA10 5LY
Tel: 01539 620668
Open: Apr to Oct

Cockermouth
NY1230

▲ **Cockermouth Youth Hostel,** Double Mills, Cockermouth, Cumbria, CA13 0DS
Actual Grid Ref: NY118298
Tel: 01900 822561
Fax: 01900 822561
Email: reservations@yha.org.uk
Capacity: 26
Under 18: £5.75 **Adults:** £8.50
Open: All year, 5.00pm
Self-catering facilities • Showers • Wet weather shelter • Lounge • Drying room • Cycle store • Parking • Evening meal available 7.00pm • No smoking • WC • Kitchen facilities • Credit cards accepted
Simple accommodation in restored C17th watermill, convenient for northern and western fells and Cumbrian coastline.

▲ **Wyndham Hall Caravan Park,** Old Keswick Road, Cockermouth, Cumbria, CA13 9SR
Actual Grid Ref: NY130320
Tel: 01900 822571 / 825238
Fax: 01900 82 1152
Email: wyndham@amserve.net
Tent pitches: 21
Tent rate: £7.50
Open: Mar to Nov
Last arr: 10.30pm
Dogs allowed • Electric hook-up • Calor Gas/Camping Gaz • Cafe or Takeaway on site • Children's play area • Showers • Laundrette on site • Public phone on site • Licensed bar on site • Shop on site
Log cabin and caravans on A66. Take road to Embleton.

▲ **Violet Bank Holiday Home Park,** Simonscales Lane, Lorton Road, Cockermouth, Cumbria, CA13 9TG
Actual Grid Ref: NY128294
Tel: 01900 822169
Open: Mar to Nov

▲ **Grayonside Farm,** Lorton Road, Cockermouth, Cumbria, CA13 9TQ
Tel: 01900 826972
Open: Mar to Nov

Colby
NY6620

▲ **Hawkrigg Farm,** Colby, Appleby-in-Westmorland, Cumbria, CA16 6BB
Actual Grid Ref: NY659203
Tel: 017683 51046
Open: All year

Coniston
SD3097

▲ **Coniston (Holly How) Youth Hostel,** Holly How, Far End, Coniston, Cumbria, LA21 8DD
Actual Grid Ref: SD302980
Tel: 015394 41323
Fax: 015394 41803
Email: conistonhh@yha.org.uk
Capacity: 60
Under 18: £6.90
Adults: £10.00
Open: Jan to Nov, 5.00pm
Family bunk rooms
Self-catering facilities • Television • Showers • Laundry facilities • Lounge • Games room • Drying room • Cycle store • Parking • Evening meal available 7.00pm • No smoking • WC • Kitchen facilities • Breakfast available • Credit cards accepted
Traditional Lakeland slate building in its own attractive gardens, dominated in the distance by the 'Old Man of Coniston'.

If you have to cancel your visit to any hostel or campsite, please let them know – it is always possible to make a bed or a pitch available to someone else.

▲ **Coniston Coppermines Youth Hostel,** Coppermine House, Coniston, Cumbria, LA21 8HP
Actual Grid Ref: SD289986
Tel: 015394 41261 **Fax:** 015394 41261
Capacity: 28 **Under 18:** £6.50
Adults: £9.25
Open: All year, 5.00pm
Self-catering facilities • Lounge • Drying room • Parking • Evening meal available 7.00pm • No smoking • WC • Kitchen facilities • Breakfast available • Credit cards accepted
Small hostel close to Coniston yet distant enough to feel isolated, surrounded by Coniston Fells, and once the home of the manager of the old copper mines.

▲ **Coniston Hall,** Haws Bank, Coniston, Cumbria, LA21 8AS
Actual Grid Ref: SD304964
Tel: 01539 441223
Open: Mar to Oct

▲ **Park Coppice Caravan Club Site,** Coniston, Cumbria, LA21 8AU
Actual Grid Ref: SD295955
Tel: 015394 41555 **Open:** Apr to Oct

Cowgill
SD7587

▲ **Ewegales Farm,** Cowgill, Dent, Sedbergh, Cumbria, LA10 5RH
Actual Grid Ref: SD756868
Tel: 01539 625440
Open: All year

Crook
SD4695

▲ **Pound Farm Caravan Park,** Crook, Kendal, Cumbria, LA8 8JZ
Tel: 01539 821220
Open: Mar to Oct

Crooklands
SD5383

▲ **Water's Edge Caravan Park,** Crooklands, Milnthorpe, Cumbria, LA7 7NN
Actual Grid Ref: SD533838
Tel: 015395 67708 / 67414
Fax: 015395 67610
Open: Mar to Nov

▲ **Millness Hill Park,** Crooklands, Milnthorpe, Cumbria, LA7 7NU
Actual Grid Ref: SD537826
Tel: 015395 67306 **Fax:** 015395 67306
Email: holidays@millness.demon.co.uk
Open: Mar to Nov

MAP PAGE 30 • **Cumbria**

To stay in a Youth Hostel affiliated to one of the Youth Hostel associations, you need to be a member. You can join at most hostels – phone in advance to check.

Crosthwaite
SD4491

▲ **Lambhowe Caravan Park**, Crosthwaite, Kendal, Cumbria, LA8 8JE
Actual Grid Ref: SD422914
Tel: 015395 68483
Fax: 01539 723339
Open: Mar to Nov

Cumwhitton
NY5052

▲ **Cairndale Caravan Park**, Cumwhitton, Carlisle, CA4 9BZ
Actual Grid Ref: NY518520
Tel: 01768 896280
Open: Mar to Oct

Dent
SD7086

▲ **Whernside Manor**, Dent, Sedbergh, Cumbria, LA10 5RE
Actual Grid Ref: SD725858
Tel: 015396 25213
Email: whernside@21.com
Capacity: 12
Under 18: £5.00
Adults: £5.00
Open: All year, 9am-9pm
Camping for 8 tents: £3.50
Self-catering facilities • Television • Showers • Grounds available for games • Drying room • Cycle store • Parking
Set in the grounds of a historic house - excellent situation.

▲ **Conder Farm Camp Site**, Dent, Sedbergh, Cumbria, LA10 5QT
Actual Grid Ref: SD706868
Tel: 01539 625277
Open: All year

▲ **High Laning Farm Caravan & Camping Park**, Laning, Dent, Sedbergh, Cumbria, LA10 5QJ
Actual Grid Ref: SD702870
Tel: 01539 625139
Open: All year

Dent Head
SD7587

▲ **Dentdale Youth Hostel**, Dent Head, Cowgill, Sedbergh, Cumbria, LA10 5RN
Actual Grid Ref: SD773850
Tel: 015396 25251
Fax: 015396 25068
Capacity: 38
Under 18: £6.50
Adults: £9.25
Open: All year (not Xmas/New Year), 5.00pm
Showers • Lounge • Dining room • Drying room • Cycle store • Parking • Evening meal available 7.00pm • No smoking • WC • Kitchen facilities • Breakfast available • Credit cards accepted
A listed former shooting lodge, beside the River Dee in the upper reaches of magnificent Dentdale.

Derwent Water
NY2521

▲ **Camping & Caravanning Club Site**, Derwent Water, Keswick, Cumbria, CA12 5EP
Actual Grid Ref: NY258234
Tel: 01768 772392 / 01203 694995
Open: Feb to Nov

Dufton
NY6825

▲ **Dufton Youth Hostel**, Redstones, Dufton, Appleby-in-Westmorland, Cumbria, CA16 6DB
Actual Grid Ref: NY688251
Tel: 017683 51236
Fax: 017683 51236
Capacity: 36
Under 18: £6.50
Adults: £9.25
Open: All year, 5.pm
Showers • Shop • Lounge • Dining room 2 • Drying room • Parking • Evening meal available 7.00pm • No smoking • Kitchen facilities • Breakfast available • Luggage store • Credit cards accepted
Large stone-built house with log fire in attractive C18th village surrounded by fine scenery of the Eden Valley.

Hostels and campsites may vary rates – be sure to check when booking.

Eamont Bridge
NY5228

▲ **Lowther Caravan Park**, Eamont Bridge, Penrith, Cumbria, CA10 2JB
Actual Grid Ref: NY528264
Tel: 01768 863631 **Fax:** 01768 868126
Email: lowtherhols@hotmail.com
Open: Mar to Oct

Elterwater
NY3204

▲ **Elterwater (Langdale) Youth Hostel**, Elterwater, Ambleside, Cumbria, LA22 9HX
Actual Grid Ref: NY327046
Tel: 015394 37245
Fax: 015394 37120
Capacity: 45 **Under 18:** £6.50
Adults: £9.25
Open: All year, 5.00pm
Showers • Lounge • Drying room • Cycle store • Evening meal available 7.00pm • No smoking • WC • Kitchen facilities • Breakfast available • Credit cards accepted
Converted farmhouse and barn on the edge of the hamlet of Elterwater. Close to the fells at the head of Langdale, at the heart of classic Lakeland scenery - a favourite with walkers and climbers.

Eskdale
NY1500

▲ **Fisherground Campsite**, Eskdale, Holmrook, Cumbria, CA19 1TF
Actual Grid Ref: NY152002
Tel: 019467 23319
Email: camping@fisherground.co.uk
Tent pitches: 120
Tent rate: £8.00-£12.00
Open: Mar to Nov
Last arr: 11pm
Dogs allowed • Electric hook-up • Children's play area • Showers • Launderette on site • Public phone on site
Camp fires welcome! Quiet, family site. Adventure playground and raft pool. We have our own station on the Ravenglass and Eskdale Miniature Railway. Laundry. Showers. Ideal for children and pets. AA Award for excellence. 'Camping' magazine - top ten sites in Britain, 'Trail' magazine - top northern family site.

ENGLAND

Cumbria • MAP PAGE 30

ENGLAND

Field Broughton
SD3881

▲ **Greaves Farm Caravan Park,** Field Broughton, Grange-over-Sands, Cumbria, LA11 6HU
Tel: 015395 36329 / 36587
Open: Mar to Oct

Firbank
SD6294

▲ **Lincolns Inn Campsite,** Firbank, Sedbergh, Cumbria, LA10 5EE
Tel: 01539 620567 **Open:** Mar to Oct

Flookburgh
SD3675

▲ **Lakeland Leisure Park,** Moor Lane, Flookburgh, Grange-over-Sands, Cumbria, LA11 7LT
Actual Grid Ref: SD372743
Tel: 01442 248668 / 015395 58556
Fax: 01442 232459
Open: Mar to Nov

▲ **Lakeland Caravan Park,** Moor Lane, Flookburgh, Grange-over-Sands, Cumbria, LA11 7LT
Actual Grid Ref: SD371740
Tel: 015395 58556
Open: Apr to Oct

Garsdale
SD7389

▲ **Fawcetts Farm,** Garsdale, Sedbergh, Cumbria, LA10 5PB
Tel: 01539 620502
Open: Easter to Oct

Garsdale Head
SD7892

▲ **Yore House Farm Caravan & Camping Park,** Lunds, Sedbergh, Cumbria, LA10 5PX
Tel: 01969 667358 **Open:** Apr to Oct

Gillerthwaite
NY1314

▲ **Ennerdale Youth Hostel,** Cat Crag, Gillerthwaite, Ennerdale, Cleator, Cumbria, CA23 2AX
Actual Grid Ref: NY142141
Tel: 01946 861237 **Capacity:** 24
Under 18: £6.50
Adults: £9.15
Open: All year, 5.00pm

Shop • Lounge • Drying room • Parking limited • Evening meal available 7.00pm • No smoking • WC • Kitchen facilities • Breakfast available • Credit cards accepted
Two converted forest cottages, with real log fires and no electricity, dramatically situated in peaceful valley, 1 mile east of Ennerdale Water.

Glenridding
NY3816

▲ **Helvellyn Youth Hostel,** Greenside, Glenridding, Penrith, Cumbria, CA11 0QR
Actual Grid Ref: NY366173
Tel: 017684 82269
Fax: 017684 82269
Email: helvellyn@yha.org.uk
Capacity: 64
Under 18: £6.90
Adults: £10.00
Open: New Year to Nov, 5.00pm
Family bunk rooms
Self-catering facilities • Showers • Lounge • Dining room • Games room • Drying room • Cycle store • Parking • Evening meal available 7.00pm • No smoking • WC • Kitchen facilities • Breakfast available • Credit cards accepted
Isolated, peaceful hostel 900 ft above sea level beneath the towering mass of the Helvellyn range. Steam boat trips on Ullswater.

▲ **Swirral Camping Barn,** Greenside, Glenridding, Penrith, Cumbria, CA11 0PL
Actual Grid Ref: NY364174
Tel: 017687 72645
Adults: £3.35
One of group of mine buildings at 1,000 ft on the flank of the Helvellyn range.
ADVANCE BOOKING ESSENTIAL.

▲ **Striding Edge Hostel,** Greenside, Glenridding, Penrith, Cumbria, CA11 0PL
Actual Grid Ref: NY364174
Tel: 017687 72803
Fax: 017687 75043
Email: keswicktic@lake-district.gov.uk
Capacity: 18
Adults: £6.00
Open: All year, 9.30am
Self-catering facilities • Showers • Wet weather shelter • Lounge • Drying room • Drying room • No smoking
Located on the slopes of Helvellyn. Ideal walking/cycling base.

To stay in a Youth Hostel affiliated to one of the Youth Hostel associations, you need to be a member. You can join at most hostels – phone in advance to check.

Grange-in-Borrowdale
NY2517

▲ **Hollows Farm,** Grange-in-Borrowdale, Keswick, Cumbria, CA12 5UQ
Actual Grid Ref: NY247171
Tel: 017687 77298
Open: All year

Grange-over-Sands
SD4077

▲ **Low Fell Gate Farm,** Cartmel Road, Grange-over-Sands, Cumbria, LA11 7EG
Actual Grid Ref: SD398770
Tel: 015395 33149
Open: Mar to Oct

Grasmere
NY3307

▲ **Grasmere (Thorney How) Youth Hostel,** Thorney How, Grasmere, Ambleside, Cumbria, LA22 9QW
Actual Grid Ref: NY332084
Tel: 015394 35591
Fax: 015394 35866
Email: grasmere@yha.prg.uk
Capacity: 48
Under 18: £6.90
Adults: £10.00
Open: All year
Self-catering facilities • Showers • Lounge • Dining room • Drying room • Parking • Evening meal available 7.00pm • No smoking • Kitchen facilities
An old Lakeland farmhouse, full of character, open as a hostel since 1932 - 1m from centre of Grasmere, and very popular with walkers.

Please respect hostels' policy on smoking. Some hostels do not allow smoking anywhere, some restrict smoking to certain areas.

MAP PAGE 30 • **Cumbria**

▲ *Grasmere (Butterlip How) Youth Hostel,* Butterlip How, Grasmere, Ambleside, Cumbria, LA22 9QG
Actual Grid Ref: NY336077
Tel: 015394 35316
Fax: 015394 35798
Email: grasmere@yha.org.uk
Capacity: 82
Under 18: £8.50
Adults: £12.50
Open: Dec to Oct + New Year, All day
Family bunk rooms
Self-catering facilities • Television • Showers • Licensed bar • Laundry facilities • Lounge • Dining room • Games room • Drying room • Cycle store • Parking • Evening meal available 6.45-7.30pm • Kitchen facilities • Breakfast available • Credit cards accepted
Victorian Lakeland stone house in large grounds with rhododendrons & azaleas. Impressive views of the surrounding fells.

Great Langdale

NY3006

▲ *National Trust Campsite,* Great Langdale, Ambleside, Cumbria, LA22 9JU
Actual Grid Ref: NY286059
Tel: 01539 437668
Open: All year

▲ *Chapel Stile Campsite,* Great Langdale, Ambleside, Cumbria, LA22 9JZ
Tel: 015394 37300
Open: Feb to Nov

Greystoke

NY4430

▲ *Thanet Well Caravan Park,* Greystoke, Penrith, Cumbria, CA11 0XX
Actual Grid Ref: NY397252
Tel: 017684 84262 **Open:** Mar to Oct

Hale

SD5078

▲ *Fell End Caravan Park,* Slackhead Road, Hale, Milnthorpe, Cumbria, LA7 7BS
Actual Grid Ref: SD503778
Tel: 015395 62122
Fax: 015395 63810
Open: All year

▲ *Hall More Farm,* Hale, Milnthorpe, Cumbria, LA7 7BP
Actual Grid Ref: SD502771
Tel: 01539 562375
Open: Mar to Oct

Haltcliff Bridge

NY3636

▲ *Carrock Fell Youth Hostel,* High Row, Haltcliff Bridge, Hesket Newmarket, Wigton, Cumbria, CA7 8JT
Actual Grid Ref: NY358355
Tel: 016974 78325
Fax: 016974 78325
Capacity: 20
Under 18: £6.50
Adults: £9.25
Open: All year, 5.00pm
Self-catering facilities • Showers • Lounge • Drying room • Parking Limited • No smoking • Kitchen facilities • Breakfast available • Credit cards accepted
An old farmhouse, simple in character, in a peaceful hamlet on the edge of the Caldbeck Fells. Area of interest to archaeologists and geologists.

Hawkshead

SD3597

▲ *Hawkshead Youth Hostel,* Esthwaite Lodge, Hawkshead, Ambleside, Cumbria, LA22 0QD
Actual Grid Ref: SD354966
Tel: 015394 36293
Fax: 015394 36720
Email: hawkshead@yha.org.uk
Capacity: 109
Under 18: £7.75
Adults: £11.00
Open: All year, 1.00pm
Family bunk rooms
Self-catering facilities • Television • Showers • Licensed bar • Shop • Laundry facilities • Lounge • Games room • Drying room 2 • Cycle store • Parking • Evening meal available 7.00pm • WC • Kitchen facilities • Breakfast available • Credit cards accepted
A Regency mansion, which has its own grounds, about a mile from Hawkshead. Families are accommodated around the courtyard. The hostel is closeby Beatrix Potter's Hill Top Farm.

▲ *Camping & Caravanning Club Site,* Grizedale Hall, Hawkshead, Ambleside, Cumbria, LA22 0GL
Actual Grid Ref: SD337943
Tel: 01229 860257
Open: Mar to Sep

▲ *Hawkshead Hall Farm,* Hawkshead, Ambleside, Cumbria, LA22 0NN
Actual Grid Ref: SD351988
Tel: 01539 436221
Open: Mar to Oct

▲ *The Croft Caravan and Camp Site,* The Croft, North Lonsdale Road, Hawkshead, Ambleside, Cumbria , LA22 0NX
Actual Grid Ref: SD353982
Tel: 015394 36374
Open: Mar to Oct

Hesket Newmarket

NY3338

▲ *Hudscales Camping Barn,* Hudscales, Hesket Newmarket, Wigton, Cumbria, CA7 8JY
Actual Grid Ref: NY332375
Tel: 017687 72645
Adults: £3.35
Part of group of traditional farm buildings situated at 1,000 ft on northernmost edge of Lakeland Fells. ADVANCE BOOKING ESSENTIAL.

High Harrington

NY0025

▲ *West Ghyll End Farm Caravan Park,* High Harrington, Workington, Cumbria, CA14 5RT
Tel: 01946 832062
Open: All year

Holker

SD3677

▲ *Old Park Wood Caravan Park,* Holker, Cark-in-Cartmel, Grange-over-Sands, Cumbria, LA11 7PP
Actual Grid Ref: SD335784
Tel: 015395 58266
Fax: 015395 58101
Open: Mar to Oct

Holmrook

SD0799

▲ *Seven Acres Caravan Park,* Children's Animal Park, Holmrook, Cumbria, CA19 1YD
Actual Grid Ref: NY073019
Tel: 01946 725480
Open: Mar to Nov

Cumbria • MAP PAGE 30

ENGLAND

Honister Pass
NY2213

▲ **Honister Pass Youth Hostel,** Honister House, Honister Pass, Seatoller, Keswick, Cumbria, CA12 5XN
Actual Grid Ref: NY224133
Tel: 017687 77267
Fax: 017687 77267
Capacity: 26
Under 18: £6.50 **Adults:** £9.25
Open: Jan to Oct, 5.00pm
Self-catering facilities • Showers • Wet weather shelter • Lounge • Drying room • Parking Limited • Evening meal available 7.00pm • No smoking • WC • Kitchen facilities • Breakfast available • Credit cards accepted
A purpose-built youth hostel dramatically situated at the summit of Honister Pass, with superb views of Honister Crag. Hearty and substantial food.

Houghton
NY4059

▲ **Green Acres Caravan Park,** High Knells, Houghton, Carlisle, Cumbria, CA6 4JW
Actual Grid Ref: NY418615
Tel: 01228 577403
Open: Mar to Oct

Hutton Roof (Kirkby Lonsdale)
SD5778

▲ **Cragside,** Hutton Roof, Kirkby Lonsdale, Carnforth, Lancashire, LA6 2PG
Tel: 01524 271415
Open: All year

Kendal
SD5192

▲ **Kendal Youth Hostel,** 118 Highgate, Kendal, Cumbria, LA9 4HE
Actual Grid Ref: SD515924
Tel: 015397 24066
Fax: 015397 24906
Email: kendal@yha.org.uk
Capacity: 54
Under 18: £10.00 **Adults:** £13.00
Open: All year, 1.00pm
Family bunk rooms
Television • Showers • Lounge • Dining room 2 • Drying room • Cycle store • Evening meal available pre-booked • Kitchen facilities
Converted Georgian town house, adjoining Brewery Arts Centre in the centre of Kendal.

Kentmere
NY4504

▲ **Maggs Howe Barn,** Maggs Howe, Kentmere, Kendal, Cumbria, LA8 9JP
Tel: 01539 821689
Capacity: 12
Under 18: £6.00
Adults: £6.00
Open: All year, until 10pm
Self-catering facilities • Showers • Cycle store • Parking • Evening meal available 7pm • No smoking
Excellent walking and mountain bikers base. Horse and riders welcome.

Keswick
NY2623

▲ **Keswick Youth Hostel,** Station Road, Keswick, Cumbria, CA12 5LH
Actual Grid Ref: NY267235
Tel: 017687 72484
Fax: 017687 74129
Email: keswick@yha.org.uk
Capacity: 91
Under 18: £7.75 **Adults:** £11.00
Open: All year
Self-catering facilities • Television • Showers • Laundry facilities • Lounge • Dining room • Drying room • Cycle store • Evening meal available 7.00pm • Kitchen facilities • Breakfast available • Credit cards accepted
Standing above the River Greta, this hostel is ideally placed in Keswick - the northern hub of the Lake District - for superb views across the park to Skiddaw.

▲ **Castlerigg Hall Caravan & Camping Park,** Castlerigg Hall, Keswick, Cumbria, CA12 4TE
Actual Grid Ref: NY282227
Tel: 017687 72437 **Fax:** 017687 72437
Open: Apr to Nov

▲ **Castlerigg Farm Campsite,** Keswick, Cumbria, CA12 4TE
Actual Grid Ref: NY282227
Tel: 017687 72479
Email: doris@castleriggfarm.freeserve.co.uk
Open: Easter to Nov

▲ **Dale Bottom Farm,** Keswick, Cumbria, CA12 4TF
Actual Grid Ref: NY297217
Tel: 017687 72176
Open: Mar to Oct

Kirkby Lonsdale
SD6178

▲ **New House Caravan Park,** New House, Kirkby Lonsdale, Carnforth, LA6 2HR
Actual Grid Ref: SD628774
Tel: 015242 71590
Open: Mar to Oct

▲ **Whoop Hall Inn Camping & Caravanning,** Kirkby Lonsdale, Carnforth, Lancs, LA6 2HP
Tel: 015242 71284
Open: All year

▲ **New House Caravan Park,** Kirkby Lonsdale, Carnforth, Lancashire, LA6 2HR
Actual Grid Ref: SD625774
Tel: 01524 271590
Open: Mar to Oct

Kirkby Stephen
NY7708

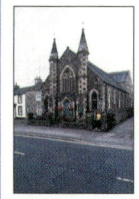

▲ **Kirkby Stephen Youth Hostel,** Fletcher Hill, Market Street, Kirkby Stephen, Cumbria, CA17 7QQ
Actual Grid Ref: NY774085
Tel: 017683 71793
Fax: 017683 72236
Capacity: 44
Under 18: £6.90
Adults: £10.00
Open: All year, 5.00pm
Self-catering facilities • Showers • Laundry facilities • Lounge • Dining room • Drying room • Cycle store • Parking • Evening meal available 7.00pm • No smoking • WC • Kitchen facilities • Breakfast available • Luggage store • Credit cards accepted
Attractive converted chapel, just south of the town square in this interesting old market town in the Upper Eden Valley.

▲ **Pennine View Caravan & Camping Park,** Pennine View, Station Road, Kirkby Stephen, Cumbria, CA17 4SZ
Actual Grid Ref: NY772076
Tel: 01768 371717
Open: Mar to Nov

MAP PAGE 30 • **Cumbria**

ENGLAND

Kirkby Thore

NY6326

▲ **Low Moor Caravan Site,** Kirkby Thore, Appleby-in-Westmorland, Cumbria, CA10 1XQ
Actual Grid Ref: NY625259
Tel: 017683 61231
Open: Apr to Oct

Lamplugh

NY0820

▲ **Inglenook Caravan Park,** Fitzbridge, Lamplugh, Workington, Cumbria, CA14 4SH
Actual Grid Ref: NY084205
Tel: 01946 861240
Open: All year

Legburthwaite

NY3119

▲ **Thirlmere Youth Hostel,** The Old School, Stanah Cross, Legburthwaite, Keswick, Cumbria, CA12 4TH
Actual Grid Ref: NY318190
Tel: 017687 73224
Fax: 017687 73224
Capacity: 28
Under 18: £4.75
Adults: £6.75
Open: Apr to Sep, 5.00pm
Self-catering facilities • Showers • Lounge • Drying room • Cycle store • Parking Limited • Evening meal available 7.00pm • No smoking • Kitchen facilities • Breakfast available
A woodburning stove heats the lounge in this basic hostel at the heart of the Lake District. It is convenient for Keswick or Helvellyn and other climbers' haunts.

Longthwaite

NY2514

▲ **Borrowdale Youth Hostel,** Longthwaite, Borrowdale, Keswick, Cumbria, CA12 5XE
Actual Grid Ref: NY254142
Tel: 017687 77257
Fax: 017687 77393
Email: borrowdale@yha.org.uk
Capacity: 88
Under 18: £7.75
Adults: £11.00
Open: All year (not New Year), 1.00pm
Family bunk rooms
Self-catering facilities • Showers • Shop • Laundry facilities • Lounge • Dining room • Drying room • Cycle store • Parking • Evening meal available 7.00pm • No smoking • Kitchen facilities • Breakfast available • Credit cards accepted
Purpose-built hostel constructed from Canadian Red cedar wood in extensive riverside grounds in the beautiful Borrowdale valley.

Longtown

NY3868

▲ **Camelot Caravan Park,** Longtown, Carlisle, Cumbria, CA6 5SZ
Actual Grid Ref: NY390667
Tel: 01228 791248
Open: Mar to Oct

▲ **Oakbank Lakes Country Park,** Longtown, Carlisle, Cumbria, CA6 5NA
Actual Grid Ref: NY369700
Tel: 01228 791108
Open: All year

▲ **High Gaitle Caravan Park,** High Gaitle Bridge, Longtown, Cumbria, CA6 5LU
Actual Grid Ref: NY365685
Tel: 01228 791819
Open: All year

Low Lorton

NY1525

▲ **Whinfell Hall Farm,** Low Lorton, Cockermouth, Cumbria, CA13 0RQ
Actual Grid Ref: NY151255
Tel: 01900 85260
Open: Mar to Oct

Low Wray

NY3701

▲ **Low Wray National Trust Campsite,** Low Wray, Ambleside, Cumbria, LA22 0JA
Actual Grid Ref: NY372018
Tel: 015394 32810
Open: Apr to Oct

Lowgill

SD6297

▲ **Cowperthwaite Farm,** Lowgill, Kendal, Cumbria, LA8 9BZ
Tel: 01539 824240
Open: All year

Lupton

SD5581

▲ **Crabtree Farm,** Lupton, Cow Brow, Carnforth, Lancashire, LA6 1PJ
Actual Grid Ref: SD557817
Tel: 015395 67288
Open: Mar to Oct

Mary Mount

NY2619

▲ **Derwentwater Youth Hostel,** Barrow House, Mary Mount, Borrowdale, Keswick, Cumbria, CA12 5UR
Actual Grid Ref: NY268200
Tel: 017687 77246
Fax: 017687 77396
Email: derwentwater@yha.org.uk
Capacity: 88
Under 18: £7.75
Adults: £11.00
Open: New Year to Nov, All day
Family bunk rooms
Television • Showers • Licensed bar • Laundry facilities • Lounge • Games room • Drying room • Parking • Evening meal available 7.00pm • WC • Kitchen facilities • Breakfast available • Credit cards accepted
Magnificent 200-year-old mansion overlooking beautiful Derwent Water in lovely Borrowdale.

Mealsgate

NY2041

▲ **Larches Caravan Park,** Mealsgate, Carlisle, Cumbria, CA5 1LQ
Actual Grid Ref: NY206415
Tel: 016973 71379
Open: Mar to Oct

If you have to cancel your visit to any hostel or campsite, please let them know – it is always possible to make a bed or a pitch available to someone else.

Cumbria • MAP PAGE 30

Millom
SD1780

▲ **Duddon Estuary Youth Hostel,** Borwick Rails, Millom, Cumbria, LA18 4JU
Tel: 01229 773937
Fax: 01629 581062
Capacity: 18
Under 18: £5.75
Adults: £8.50
Open: All year
Self-catering facilities • Showers • Laundry facilities • Lounge • Parking • Facilities for disabled people • No smoking • Kitchen facilities
The hostel overlooks the estuary, and has fine views in all directions. Handy for the RSPB reserve.

▲ **Butterflowers Holiday Homes,** Port Hverigg, Millom, Cumbria, LA18 4EY
Actual Grid Ref: SD159785
Tel: 01229 772880
Open: All year

Milnthorpe
SD4981

▲ **Hazelslack Caravan Site,** Milnthorpe, Cumbria, LA7 7LG
Actual Grid Ref: SD476785
Tel: 01524 701482
Open: Mar to Oct

Mockerkin
NY0923

▲ **Swallow Camping Barn,** Waterend, Mockerkin, Cockermouth, Cumbria, CA13 0ST
Actual Grid Ref: NY116226
Tel: 017687 72645
Adults: £3.35
In picturesque valley of Loweswater, on a 200-acre working farm. Permits for fishing and boat hire on Loweswater available. ADVANCE BOOKING ESSENTIAL.

Nentsberry
NY7545

▲ **Horse & Wagon Caravan Park,** Nentsberry, Alston, Cumbria, CA9 3LH
Actual Grid Ref: NY764452
Tel: 01434 382805
Open: Mar to Oct

Newbiggin (Stainton)
NY4629

▲ **Stonefolds,** Newbiggin, Stainton, Penrith, Cumbria, CA11 0HP
Actual Grid Ref: NY475285
Tel: 01768 866383
Open: All year

Newbiggin-on-Lune
NY7005

▲ **Bents Camping Barn,** Bents Farm, Newbiggin-on-Lune, Kirkby Stephen, Cumbria, CA17 4NX
Actual Grid Ref: NY708065
Tel: 017687 72645 / 015396 23681
Adults: £3.35
Converted farm building close to the Howgill Fells. ADVANCE BOOKING ESSENTIAL.

Newby Bridge
SD3786

▲ **Newby Bridge Caravan Park,** Newby Bridge, Ulverston, Cumbria, LA12 8NF
Tel: 015395 31030
Open: Mar to Oct

Newlands
NY2420

▲ **Catbells Camping Barn,** Low Skell Gill, Newlands, Keswick, Cumbria, CA12 5TU
Actual Grid Ref: NY243208
Tel: 017687 72645
Adults: £3.35
Part of a traditional set of farm buildings dating back to C14th. ADVANCE BOOKING ESSENTIAL.

Ousby
NY6135

▲ **Fox Inn Caravan Park,** Ousby, Penrith, Cumbria, CA10 1QA
Tel: 01768 881374
Open: Mar to Jan

Outgate
SD3599

▲ **Waterson Ground Farm,** Outgate, Ambleside, Cumbria, LA22 0NJ
Actual Grid Ref: SD351994
Tel: 015394 36225
Open: Mar to Oct

Patterdale
NY3915

▲ **Patterdale Youth Hostel,** Goldrill House, Patterdale, Penrith, Cumbria, CA11 0NW
Actual Grid Ref: NY399156
Tel: 017684 82394
Fax: 017684 82034
Email: patterdale@yha.org.uk
Capacity: 82
Under 18: £7.75 **Adults:** £11.00
Open: Feb to Dec, All day
Self-catering facilities • Showers • Laundry facilities • Lounge • Dining room • Drying room • Cycle store • Parking • Evening meal available 7.00pm • Kitchen facilities • Breakfast available • Credit cards accepted
Purpose-built hostel open all day, to the south of Ullswater. On the Coast to Coast Path, and a good base for those who want to climb Helvellyn.

▲ **Skyeside Camping Park,** Brotherswater Inn, Brotherswater, Patterdale, Penrith, Cumbria, CA11 0NZ
Actual Grid Ref: NY402118
Tel: 017684 82239
Open: All year

▲ **Side Farm Camp Site & Pony Trekking,** Patterdale, Penrith, Cumbria, CA11 0NP
Actual Grid Ref: NY399161
Tel: 01768 482337
Open: All year

Penrith
NY5130

▲ **Corney House,** 1 Corney Place, Penrith, Cumbria, CA11 7PY
Actual Grid Ref: NY515303
Tel: 01768 867627
Email: kimrose@talk21.com
Capacity: 6
Under 18: £8.00
Adults: £10.00
Open: All year, 10am
Self-catering facilities • Television • Showers • Central heating • Laundry facilities • Lounge • Dining room • Cycle store • Evening meal available by arrangement • Facilities for disabled people • No smoking
Listed Georgian townhouse. Friendly welcome. Interestingly located. Private unit available.

▲ **Thacka Lea Caravan Site,** Penrith, Cumbria, CA11 9HX
Actual Grid Ref: NY509310
Tel: 01768 863319
Open: Mar to Oct

MAP PAGE 30 • **Cumbria**

Penruddock

NY4227

▲ **Beckses Caravan Park,** Penruddock, Penrith, Cumbria, CA11 0RX
Actual Grid Ref: NY416277
Tel: 01768 483224
Open: Apr to Oct

Pooley Bridge

NY4724

▲ **Hillcroft Caravan & Camping Site,** Roe Head Lane, Pooley Bridge, Penrith, Cumbria, CA10 2LT
Actual Grid Ref: NY476243
Tel: 017684 86363
Fax: 017684 86010
Open: Mar to Oct

▲ **Waterside House,** Howtown Road, Pooley Bridge, Penrith, Cumbria, CA10 2NA
Tel: 01768 486332
Open: Mar to Oct

▲ **Park Foot Caravan & Camping Park,** Parkfoot Caravan Park, Howtown Road, Pooley Bridge, Penrith, Cumbria, CA10 2NA
Actual Grid Ref: NY469235
Tel: 017684 86309
Open: Mar to Oct

Port Carlisle

NY2461

▲ **Cottage Caravan Park,** Port Carlisle, Carlisle, Cumbria, CA5 5DJ
Tel: 01697 351317
Open: Mar to Nov

Raisbeck

NY6407

▲ **New House Farm,** Raisbeck, Orton, Penrith, Cumbria, CA10 3SD
Tel: 015396 24324
Open: All year

Ravenglass

SD0896

▲ **Walls Caravan & Camping Park,** Ravenglass, Whitehaven, Cumbria, CA18 1SR
Actual Grid Ref: SD087964
Tel: 01229 717150
Open: Mar to Nov

Ravenstonedale

NY7203

▲ **Bowber Head Camping Site,** Ravenstonedale, Kirkby Stephen, Cumbria, CA17 4NL
Actual Grid Ref: NY740032
Tel: 015396 23254
Open: All year

Rosthwaite (Borrowdale)

NY2514

▲ **Dinah Hoggus Camping Barn,** Hazel Bank, Rosthwaite, Keswick, Cumbria, CA12 5XB
Actual Grid Ref: NY259151
Tel: 017687 72645
Adults: £3.35
Camping
Traditional Lakeland field barn or Hogghouse. ADVANCE BOOKING ESSENTIAL.

Sandwith

NX9614

▲ **Tarn Flatt Camping Barn,** Tarnflat Hall, Sandwith, Whitehaven, Cumbria, CA28 9UX
Actual Grid Ref: NX947146
Tel: 017687 72645
Adults: £3.35
Situated on St Bees Head overlooking Scottish coastline and the Isle of Man. RSPB seabird reserve and lighthouse nearby. ADVANCE BOOKING ESSENTIAL.

Seatoller

NY2413

▲ **Seatoller Farm,** Borrowdale, Keswick, Cumbria, CA12 5XN
Tel: 01596 84232
Open: All year

Sedbergh

SD6592

▲ **Pinfold Caravan Park,** Garsdale Road, Sedbergh, Cumbria, LA10 5JL
Actual Grid Ref: SD667919
Tel: 01539 620576
Open: Mar to Oct

▲ **Bank Cottage Farm,** Frostrow Lane, Sedbergh, Cumbria, LA10 5JU
Tel: 01539 620429
Open: All year

▲ **Borrett Farm,** Sedbergh, Cumbria, LA10 5HL
Tel: 01539 620440
Open: May to Oct

▲ **Bowers Farm,** Garsdale Road, Sedbergh, Cumbria, LA10 5JP
Tel: 01587 20249
Open: All year

▲ **Mill Beck Farm Camp Site,** Mill Beck Farm, Sedbergh, Cumbria, LA10 5TB
Tel: 01539 625272
Open: Apr to Oct

Silecroft

SD1381

▲ **Silecroft Caravan Site,** Silecroft, Millom, Cumbria, LA18 4NX
Actual Grid Ref: SD124811
Tel: 01229 772659
Open: Mar to Oct

Silloth

NY1053

▲ **Stanwix Park Holiday Centre,** Green Row, Silloth, Carlisle, Cumbria, CA5 4HH
Actual Grid Ref: NY108527
Tel: 016973 32666 / 31671
Fax: 016973 32555
Email: stanwix.park@btinternet.com
Open: Mar to Oct

▲ **Hylton Park Holiday Centre,** Eden Street, Silloth, Carlisle, Cumbria, CA5 4AY
Actual Grid Ref: NY113533
Tel: 01697 331707
Open: Apr to Sep

▲ **Solway Holiday Village,** Skinburness Drive, Silloth-on-Solway, Carlisle, Cumbria, CA5 4QQ
Actual Grid Ref: NY117547
Tel: 016973 31236
Open: All year

Skelsmergh

SD5395

▲ **Camping & Caravanning Club Site,** Millcrest, Skelsmergh, Kendal, Cumbria, LA9 6NY
Actual Grid Ref: SD526948
Tel: 01539 741363 / 01203 694995
Open: Mar to Nov

Cumbria • MAP PAGE 30

All details shown are as supplied by hostels and campsites in Autumn 2000.

Skiddaw
NY2629

▲ **Skiddaw House Youth Hostel,** Skiddaw, Bassenthwaite, Keswick, Cumbria, CA12 4QX
Actual Grid Ref: NY288291
Tel: 016974 78325
Fax: 016974 78325 (enquiries)
Capacity: 20
Under 18: £5.25 **Adults:** £7.50
Open: Apr to Oct, 5.00pm
Self-catering facilities • Showers • Games room • Drying room • Cycle store • No smoking • WC • Kitchen facilities • Breakfast available
At 1550 ft this is one of the highest, most remote and isolated hostels in the UK, with no sign of civilisation in any direction, beneath the summit of Skiddaw. A torch is a necessity.

St Bees
NX9711

▲ **Seacote Holiday Park,** Beach Road, St Bees, Cumbria, CA27 0ES
Tel: 01946 822177
Open: All year

St Johns-in-the-Vale
NY3122

▲ **Low Bridge End,** Low Bridge End Farm, St John's-in-the-Vale, Keswick, Cumbria, CA12 4TS
Actual Grid Ref: NY317205
Tel: 017687 79242
Email: lbe@sjitv.freeserve.co.uk
Capacity: 8
Under 18: £3.50
Adults: £3.50
Open: All year, 2pm
Showers • Wet weather shelter • Cycle store • Parking • No smoking
Stunning, peaceful riverside location. Walking and climbing from the door.

▲ **Burns Farm Caravan & Camping Site,** St Johns-in-the-Vale, Keswick, Cumbria, CA12 4RR
Actual Grid Ref: NY306243
Tel: 01768 779225
Open: Mar to Nov

Stonethwaite
NY2613

▲ **Stonethwaite Farm,** Borrowdale, Keswick, Cumbria, CA12 5XG
Tel: 01768 777234
Open: All year

Tebay
NY6104

▲ **Tebay Caravan Park,** Tebay, Penrith, Cumbria, CA10 3SB
Actual Grid Ref: NY609060
Tel: 015396 24511
Fax: 015396 24511
Open: Mar to Oct

Thornthwaite
NY2225

▲ **Lanefoot Farm,** Thornthwaite, Keswick, Cumbria, CA12 5RZ
Tel: 01768 778315
Open: Apr to Oct

Torver
SD2894

▲ **Scarr Head Farm ,** Torver, Coniston, Cumbria, LA21 8BP
Tel: 015394 41328
Email: scarr.head@virgin.net
Tent pitches: 15
Tent rate: £4.00-£8.00
Open: Mar to Oct **Last arr:** 10pm
Dogs allowed • Electric hook-up • Showers • Boating/sailing/watersports nearby • Riding nearby • Fishing nearby
Small working farm at foot of Coniston Mountains. 3 miles south of Coniston village. Quiet family-run site. Many spectacular walks straight off campsite - Coniston Old Man, Walna Scar and surrounding fells. Pony trekking 500 yards. 2 pubs in Torver, 5 minutes' walk. Coniston Lake by footpath in 30 minutes. Come and see us soon.

▲ **Hoathwaite Farm,** Torver, Coniston, Cumbria, LA21 8AX
Actual Grid Ref: SD296949
Tel: 01539 441349
Open: All year

▲ **Cook Farm Camping Site,** Torver, Coniston, Cumbria, LA21 8BP
Tel: 015394 41453
Open: All year

Troutbeck (Penrith)
NY3826

▲ **Blake Beck Camping Barn,** Blakebeck, Troutbeck, Penruddock, Penrith, Cumbria, CA11 0SZ
Actual Grid Ref: NY367278
Tel: 017687 72645
Adults: £3.35
On the edge of the northern fells close to Blencathra. ADVANCE BOOKING ESSENTIAL.

▲ **Gill Head Farm,** Troutbeck, Penrith, Cumbria, CA11 0ST
Actual Grid Ref: NY380269
Tel: 017687 79652
Open: Apr to Oct

▲ **Hutton Moor End Caravan & Camping Site,** Troutbeck, Penrith, Cumbria, CA11 0SX
Actual Grid Ref: NY365271
Tel: 01768 779615
Open: Apr to Oct

Troutbeck (Windermere)
NY4002

▲ **Windermere Youth Hostel,** High Cross, Bridge Lane, Troutbeck, Windermere, Cumbria, LA23 1LA
Actual Grid Ref: NY405013
Tel: 015394 43543
Fax: 015394 47165
Email: windermere@yha.org.uk
Capacity: 73
Under 18: £6.20
Adults: £9.15
Open: All year (not New Year), All day (not 12.00 - 13.00hrs)
Family bunk rooms
Self-catering facilities • Television • Showers • Laundry facilities • Lounge • Drying room • Cycle store • Parking • Evening meal available 7.00pm • Kitchen facilities • Breakfast available • Credit cards accepted
2 miles outside Windermere, above the village of Troutbeck. The hostel is a large house, with extensive views, and is popular with walkers of all levels.

MAP PAGE 30 • **Cumbria**

Ulverston

SD2878

▲ **Bardsea Leisure Park,** Priory Road, Ulverston, Cumbria, LA12 9QE
Actual Grid Ref: SD292765
Tel: 01229 584712
Open: All year

Under Loughrigg

NY3404

▲ **Langdale (High Close) Youth Hostel,** High Close, Under Loughrigg, Ambleside, Cumbria, LA22 9HJ
Actual Grid Ref: NY338052
Tel: 015394 32304
Fax: 015394 34408
Capacity: 96
Under 18: £6.90
Adults: £10.00
Open: March to Oct, 5.00pm
Self-catering facilities • Self-catering facilities • Television • Showers • Wet weather shelter • Lounge • Dining room • Games room • Drying room • Cycle store • Parking • Evening meal available 6.30pm • WC • Kitchen facilities • Breakfast available • Credit cards accepted • Credit cards accepted
Victorian mansion set in extensive grounds between Elterwater and Grasmere, owned by National Trust. Close to Langdale Pikes.

Underskiddaw

NY2328

▲ **Burnside Caravan Park,** Underskiddaw, Keswick, Cumbria, CA12 4PF
Tel: 017687 72950
Open: Mar to Dec

Wasdale Head

NY1808

▲ **Church Stile Farm,** Wasdale Head, Seascale, Cumbria, CA20 1ED
Actual Grid Ref: NY124040
Tel: 01946 726388
Open: Mar to Oct

▲ **National Trust Campsite,** Wasdale Head, Seascale, Cumbria, CA20 1EX
Actual Grid Ref: NY183076
Tel: 01946 726220 **Open:** Apr to Oct

Wasdale (Nether Wasdale)

NY1204

▲ **Wastwater Youth Hostel,** Wasdale Hall, Nether Wasdale, Seascale, Cumbria, CA20 1ET
Actual Grid Ref: NY145045
Tel: 019467 26222
Fax: 019467 26056
Email: wastwater@yha.org.uk
Capacity: 50
Under 18: £6.90 **Adults:** £10.00
Open: All year (not Xmas), 5.00pm
Self-catering facilities • Showers • Licensed bar • Shop • Lounge • Dining room • Games room • Drying room • Cycle store • Parking • Evening meal available 7.00pm • No smoking • WC • Kitchen facilities • Breakfast available • Credit cards accepted
A National Trust early C19th house, in a beautiful setting, with grounds leading down to Wastwater. Popular with walkers and climbers of all levels.

Waterhead

NY3803

▲ **Ambleside Youth Hostel,** Waterhead, Ambleside, Cumbria, LA22 0EU
Actual Grid Ref: NY377031
Tel: 015394 32304
Fax: 015394 34408
Email: ambleside@yha.org.uk
Capacity: 245
Under 18: £9.50 **Adults:** £13.50
Open: All year, All day
Family bunk rooms
Self-catering facilities • Television • Showers • Licensed bar • Laundry facilities • Lounge • Games room • Drying room • Cycle store • Parking • Evening meal available 5.30-7.30pm • Kitchen facilities • Breakfast available • Luggage store • Credit cards accepted
Former hotel refurbished to a high standard of comfort with many small rooms and lake views. Hostel has its own waterfront and jetty.

Watermillock

NY4422

▲ **Cove Caravan & Camping Park,** Ullswater, Watermillock, Penrith, Cumbria, CA11 0LS
Actual Grid Ref: NY431236
Tel: 017684 86549
Open: Mar to Oct

▲ **The Quiet Site,** Ullswater, Watermillock, Penrith, Cumbria, CA11 0LS
Actual Grid Ref: NY432236
Tel: 01768 486337
Open: Mar to Oct

▲ **Ullswater Caravan & Camping Site & Marine Park,** High Longthwaite, Watermillock, Penrith, Cumbria, CA11 0LR
Actual Grid Ref: NY438230
Tel: 01768 486666
Open: Mar to Nov

Wellington

NY0804

▲ **Mill House Camping Barn,** Wellington, Gosforth, Seascale, Cumbria, CA20 1BH
Actual Grid Ref: NY075043
Tel: 017687 72645
Capacity: 12
Under 18: £3.50 **Adults:** £3.50
Open: All year, any time
Camping for 5 tents: £5.00
Wet weather shelter • Games room • Grounds available for games • Cycle store • Parking
Situated in a secluded valley between Gosforth and Nether Wasdale.

Westward

NY2744

▲ **Clea Hall Holiday Park,** Westward, Wigton, Cumbria, CA7 8NQ
Actual Grid Ref: NY279425
AA grade: 4 Pennants
Tel: 016973 42880 **Fax:** 016973 42880
Email: nedyken@aol.com
Tent pitches: 16
Tent rate: £8.00-£10.00
Open: All year **Last arr:** 10.30pm
Facilities for disabled people • Dogs allowed • Electric hook-up • Baths • Calor Gas/Camping Gaz • Picnic/barbecue area on site • Children's play area • Showers • Laundrette on site • Public phone on site • Licensed bar on site • Shop on site
Immaculate North Lakeland park, heated pool, bar, gym. Friendly hosts!

Stilwell's Hostels & Camping 2002 — 43

Cumbria • MAP PAGE 30

Windermere

SD4198

▲ **Limefitt Park,** Patterdale Road, Windermere, Cumbria, LA23 1PA
Actual Grid Ref: NY416030
Tel: 015394 32300 ext 41
Open: Mar to Oct

▲ **Ashes Lane Caravan & Camping Park,** Ashes Lane, Staveley, Kendal, Cumbria, LA8 9JS
Actual Grid Ref: SD478962
Tel: 01539 821119 **Open:** Mar to Jan

▲ **Park Cliffe Farm Camping & Caravan Estate,** Birks Road, Windermere, Cumbria, LA23 3PG
Actual Grid Ref: SD391912
Tel: 015395 31344 **Fax:** 015395 31971
Email: parkcliffe@btinternet.com
Open: Mar to Oct

▲ **White Cross Bay Leisure Park & Marina,** Ambleside Road, Windermere, Cumbria, LA23 1LF
Tel: 015394 43937
Email: wxb@windermere.uk.com
Open: Mar to Nov

Woodland

SD2489

▲ **Fell End Camping Barn,** Fell End, Woodland, Broughton in Furness, Cumbria, LA20 6DF
Actual Grid Ref: SD239881
Tel: 017687 72645
Adults: £3.35
Redundant 'Bank Barn' a third of a mile from working farm in South Western fells.
ADVANCE BOOKING ESSENTIAL.

Britain: Bed & Breakfast

The essential guide to B&Bs in England, Scotland & Wales

The Bed & Breakfast is one of the great British institutions. Like Fish & Chips, it's known by people around the world. But you don't have to be a tourist to enjoy this traditional accommodation. Whether you're travelling, on holiday, away on business or just escaping from it all, the B&B is a great value alternative to expensive hotels and a world away from camping and caravanning.

Stilwell's Britain: Bed & Breakfast 2001 is the most comprehensive guide of its kind, containing over 7,750 entries listed by country, county and location, in England, Scotland and Wales. Each entry includes room rates, facilities, Tourist Board grades and a brief description of the B&B and its location and surroundings.

Stilwell's Britain: Bed & Breakfast 2001: The indispensable guide to great value accommodation:

- Private houses, country halls, farms, cottages, inns, small hotels and guest houses
- Over 7,750 entries
- Average price £19 per person per night
- All official grades shown
- Local maps
- Pubs serving hot evening meals shown
- Tourist Information Centres listed
- Handy size for easy packing

£9.95 from all good bookstores (ISBN 1-900861-22-4) or £11.95 (inc p&p) from Stilwell Publishing, 59 Charlotte Road, London EC2A 3QW (020 7739 7179)

Derbyshire

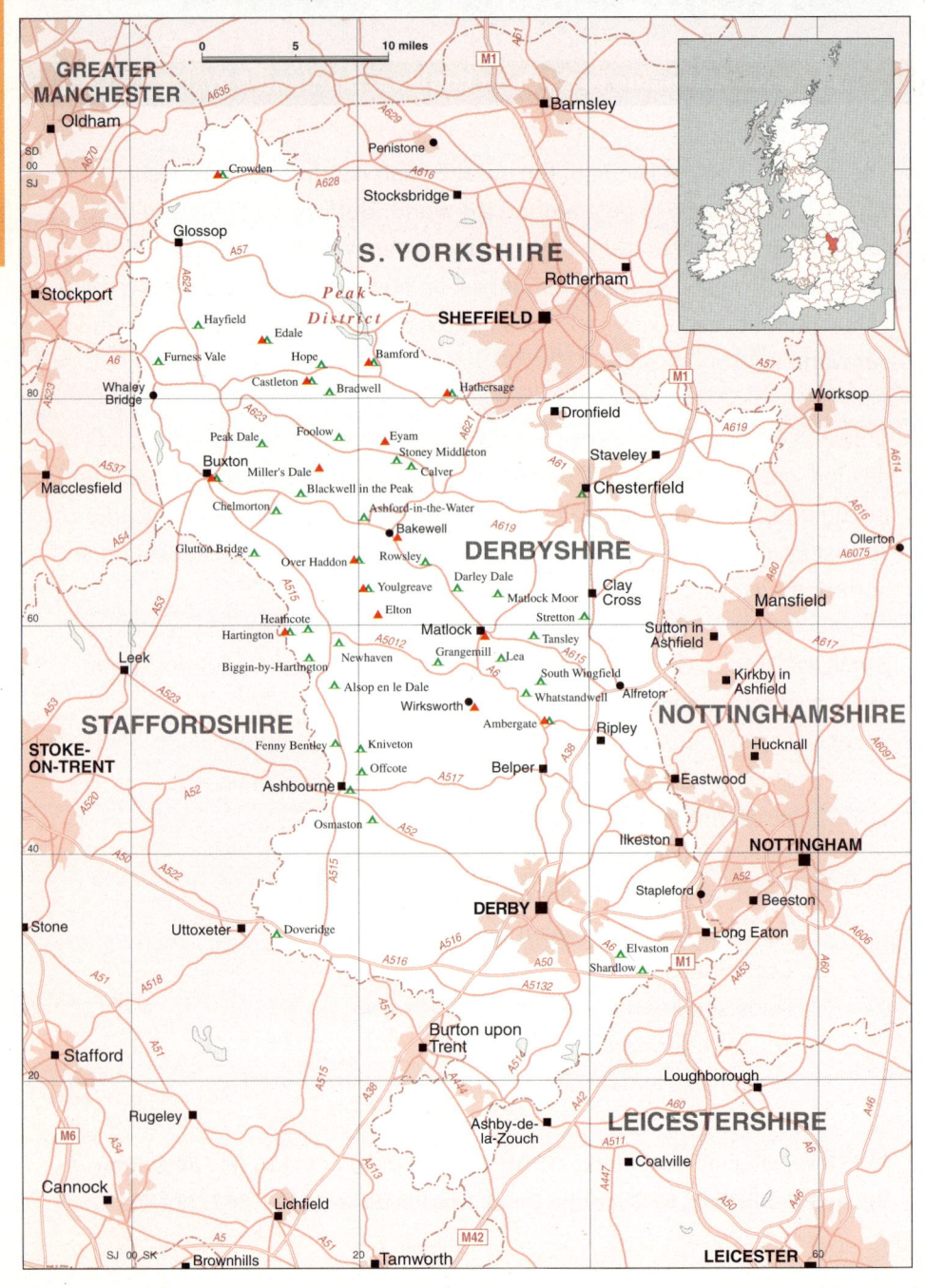

Derbyshire

Alsop en le Dale
SK1655

▲ **Rivendale Caravan and Leisure Park,** Buxton Road, Alsop en le Dale, Ashbourne, Derbyshire, DE6 1QU
Actual Grid Ref: SK159548
Tel: 01332 843000
Open: Mar to Jan

Ambergate
SK3451

▲ **Shining Cliff Youth Hostel,** Shining Cliff Woods, Jackass Lane, Ambergate, Belper, Derbyshire, DE56 2HF
Actual Grid Ref: SK335522
Tel: 01629 760827 / 01629 825893
Email: reservations@yha.org.uk
Capacity: 20
Under 18: £5.75
Adults: £8.50
Open: All year, 5.00pm
Self-catering facilities • Lounge • Cycle store • No smoking • Kitchen facilities
Very secluded little building in the middle of a wood, offering basic accommodation with outside toilets and no showers. A torch is advisable

▲ **The Firs Farm Caravan and Camping,** Crich Lane, Nether Heage, Ambergate, Belper, Derbyshire, DE56 2JH
Actual Grid Ref: SK354504
Tourist Board grade: 4 Star
Tel: 01773 852913
Tent pitches: 60
Tent rate: £8.00
Open: All year
Last arr: 10pm
Dogs allowed • Electric hook-up • Calor Gas/Camping Gaz nearby • Picnic/barbecue area on site • Showers • Public phone on site
Award-winning park with magnificent views. Friendly service; immaculate loos. Adults only.

Ashbourne
SK1846

▲ **Sandybrook Country Park,** Buxton Rd, Ashbourne, Derbyshire, DE6 2AQ
Actual Grid Ref: SK178484
Tel: 01335 300000
Fax: 01335 342679
Email: admin@sandybrook.co.uk
Tent pitches: 30
Tent rate: £6.00-£9.00
Open: Apr to Oct
Last arr: 10pm
Dogs allowed • Electric hook-up • Calor Gas/Camping Gaz • Showers • Public phone on site
Quiet park in grounds of Sandybrook Hall, delightful views across countryside.

▲ **Callow Top Holiday Park,** Buxton Road, Ashbourne, Derbyshire, DE6 2AQ
Actual Grid Ref: SK172477
Tel: 01335 344020
Fax: 01335 343726
Open: Apr to Nov

▲ **Sandybrook Hall,** Ashbourne, Derbyshire, DE6 2AQ
Actual Grid Ref: SK179482
Tel: 01335 342679
Open: Apr to Oct

Ashford-in-the-Water
SK1969

▲ **Greenhills Caravan Park,** Crow Hill Lane, Ashford Road, Ashford-in-the-Water, Bakewell, Derbyshire, DE45 1PX
Actual Grid Ref: SK201693
Tel: 01629 813467
Fax: 01629 815131
Open: All year

Bakewell
SK2168

▲ **Bakewell Youth Hostel,** Fly Hill, Bakewell, Derbyshire, DE45 1DN
Actual Grid Ref: SK215685
Tel: 01629 812313
Fax: 01629 812313
Email: bakewell@yha.org.uk
Capacity: 28
Under 18: £6.90
Adults: £10.00
Open: All year (not New Year), 5.00pm
Self-catering facilities • Showers • Shop • Lounge • Drying room • Parking • Evening meal available 6.30pm • No smoking • WC • Kitchen facilities • Breakfast available • Credit cards accepted
Modern building close to town centre, with views across valley of Derbyshire's River Wye. Excellent walks in limestone dales and along gritstone edges. Chatsworth House is nearby.

Hostels and campsites may vary rates – be sure to check when booking.

Bamford
SK2083

▲ **Lockerbrook Outdoor Activities & Environmental Education Centre,** Snake Road, Bamford, Hope Valley, Derbyshire, S33 0BJ
Actual Grid Ref: SK165894
Tel: 01433 651412
Fax: 01433 651412
Email: enquiries@lockerbrook.org.uk
Capacity: 36
Under 18: £6.60 **Adults:** £10.50
Open: All year, any time
Self-catering facilities • Showers • Central heating • Wet weather shelter • Lounge • Dining room • Games room • Grounds available for games • Drying room • Parking • Evening meal available as required • Facilities for disabled people • No smoking
Set in open countryside above the Ladybower Reservoir overlooking Derwent Edge, Lockerbrook provides an excellent base for schools/youth groups, special needs and family groups to explore and discover the northern reaches of the Peak District National Park. Activities and courses are tailored to suit the needs of individual groups.

▲ **Swallow Holme Caravan Park,** Station Road, Bamford, Hope Valley, Derbyshire, S33 0BN
Actual Grid Ref: SK207827
Tel: 01433 650981
Open: Apr to Oct

Biggin-by-Hartington
SK1559

▲ **The Waterloo Inn,** Biggin-by-Hartington, Buxton, Derbyshire, SK17 0DH
Actual Grid Ref: SK152595
Tel: 01298 84284
Open: Apr to Oct

Blackwell in the Peak
SK1272

▲ **Cottage Farm Caravan Park,** Blackwell in the Peak, Taddington, Buxton, Derbyshire, SK17 9TQ
Actual Grid Ref: SK126717
Tel: 01298 85330
Open: Mar to Oct

ENGLAND

Stilwell's Hostels & Camping 2002   47

Derbyshire • MAP PAGE 46

ENGLAND

Bradwell
SK1781

▲ **Eden Tree Caravan Park,** Bradwell, Hope Valley, Derbyshire, S33 9JT
Actual Grid Ref: SK174820
Tel: 01433 620873
Open: Mar to Oct

Buxton
SK0573

▲ **Buxton Youth Hostel,** Sherbrook Lodge, Harpur Hill Road, Buxton, Derbyshire, SK17 9NB
Actual Grid Ref: SK062722
Tel: 01298 22287
Fax: 01298 22287
Email: buxton@yha.org.uk
Capacity: 56
Under 18: £5.75
Adults: £8.50
Open: Feb to Dec (not New Year), 5.00pm
Self-catering facilities • Showers • Lounge • Dining room • Drying room • Parking • Evening meal available 7.00pm • No smoking • WC • Kitchen facilities • Breakfast available • Luggage store • Credit cards accepted
Victorian house in wooded grounds close to the railway station, Opera House and Buxton's varied shops. Days out could take in Granada Studios, Alton Towers, as well as the Peak District.

▲ **Limetree Holiday Park,** Dukes Drive, Buxton, Derbyshire, SK17 9RP
Actual Grid Ref: SK068725
Tel: 01298 22988
Open: Mar to Oct

▲ **Cold Springs Farm,** Manchester Road, Buxton, Derbyshire, SK17 6SS
Tel: 01298 72762
Open: Mar to Nov

▲ **Cold Springs Farm,** Buxton, Derbyshire, SK17 6ST
Actual Grid Ref: SK044747
Tel: 01298 22762
Open: May to Nov

All details shown are as supplied by hostels and campsites in Autumn 2000.

Calver
SK2374

▲ **Stocking Farm Caravan Site,** Calver, Hope Valley, Derbyshire, S32 3XA
Actual Grid Ref: SK247747
Tel: 01433 630516
Open: Apr to Oct

Castleton
SK1582

▲ **Castleton Youth Hostel,** Castleton Hall, Castleton, Hope Valley, S33 8WG
Actual Grid Ref: SK150828
Tel: 01433 620235
Fax: 01433 621767
Email: castleton@yha.org.uk
Capacity: 150
Under 18: £7.75 **Adults:** £11.00
Open: All year, All day
Family bunk rooms
Self-catering facilities • Television • Showers • Licensed bar • Lounge • Games room • Drying room • Cycle store • Evening meal available 6.00-7.00pm • Kitchen facilities • Breakfast available • Luggage store • Credit cards accepted
Comprising an C18th hall and C19th vicarage, this centrally-placed hostel is ideal for families and perfect for exploring the Peak District National Park.

▲ **Rowter Farm ,** Castleton, Hope Valley, Derbyshire, S33 8WA
Actual Grid Ref: SK132822
Tel: 01433 620271
Open: Apr to Oct

Chelmorton
SK1169

▲ **Shallow Grange,** Chelmorton, Buxton, Derbyshire, SK17 9SG
Actual Grid Ref: SK094702
Tel: 01298 23578 **Fax:** 01298 78242
Open: All year

Chesterfield
SK3871

▲ **Millfield Mobile Home Park,** Old Tupon, Chesterfield, Derbyshire, S42 6AE
Actual Grid Ref: SK376646
Tel: 01246 862296
Open: All year

Crowden
SK0799

▲ **Crowden Youth Hostel,** Crowden, Glossop, Derbyshire, SK14 7HZ
Actual Grid Ref: SJ073995
Tel: 01457 852135
Fax: 01457 852135
Capacity: 38
Under 18: £6.50
Adults: £9.25
Open: All year, 5.0pm
Family bunk rooms
Self-catering facilities • Showers • Lounge • Dining room • Drying room • Cycle store • Evening meal available 7.30pm • No smoking • WC • Kitchen facilities • Breakfast available • Credit cards accepted
Formerly a row of railwaymen's cottages, right on the Pennine Way in a remote part of Longdendale.

▲ **Camping & Caravanning Club Site,** Crowden, Glossop, Derbyshire, SK13 1HZ
Actual Grid Ref: SK072992
Tel: 01457 866057
Open: Mar to Nov

Darley Dale
SK2862

▲ **Darwin Forest Country Park,** Two Dales, Matlock, Derbyshire, DE4 5LN
Actual Grid Ref: SK302649
Tel: 01629 732428
Email: admin@darwinforest.co.uk
Open: Mar to Dec

Doveridge
SK1134

▲ **Cavendish Caravan & Camping Site,** Derby Road, Doveridge, Ashbourne, Derbyshire, DE6 5JR
Actual Grid Ref: SK118344
Tel: 01889 562092
Open: Apr to Oct

To stay in a Youth Hostel affiliated to one of the Youth Hostel associations, you need to be a member. You can join at most hostels – phone in advance to check.

MAP PAGE 46 • **Derbyshire**

ENGLAND

Edale

SK1285

▲ **Edale Youth Hostel,** Rowland Cote, Nether Booth, Edale, Hope Valley, Derbyshire, S33 7ZH
Actual Grid Ref: SJ139865
Tel: 01433 670302
Fax: 01433 670243
Email: edale@yha.org.uk
Capacity: 141
Under 18: £7.75
Adults: £11.00
Open: All year
Showers • Licensed bar • Laundry facilities • Lounge • Games room • Grounds available for games • Drying room • Parking • Evening meal available 5.30-7.15pm • Kitchen facilities • Breakfast available • Credit cards accepted
Large former private house set in extensive grounds on hillside below Kinder Scout Plateau.

▲ **Coopers Caravan Site,** Newfold Farm, Edale, Hope Valley, Derbyshire, S33 7ZD
Actual Grid Ref: SK122859
Tel: 01433 670372
Open: Easter to Dec

▲ **Fieldhead Camp Site,** Hope Road, Edale, Hope Valley, Derbyshire, S33 7ZF
Tel: 01433 70386
Open: All year

▲ **Highfield Farm,** Upper Booth, Edale, Hope Valley, Derbyshire, S33 7ZJ
Tel: 01433 670245
Open: Easter to Oct

▲ **Upper Booth Farm,** Edale, Hope Valley, Derbyshire, S33 7ZJ
Tel: 01433 670250
Open: Feb to Oct

▲ **Waterside Farm,** Barber Booth Road, Edale, Hope Valley, Derbyshire, S33 7ZL
Actual Grid Ref: SK118850
Tel: 01433 670215
Open: Mar to Oct

▲ **Fieldhead Campsite,** Edale, Hope Valley, Derbyshire, S30 2ZE
Actual Grid Ref: SK124856
Tel: 01433 670386
Open: Apr to Oct

Elton

SK2261

▲ **Elton Youth Hostel,** Elton Old Hall, Main Street, Elton, Matlock, Derbyshire, DE4 2BW
Actual Grid Ref: SK224608
Tel: 01629 650394
Fax: 01629 650394
Capacity: 32
Under 18: £5.75
Adults: £8.50
Open: All year, 5.00pm
Self-catering facilities • Showers • Shop • Lounge • Drying room • Cycle store • No smoking • Kitchen facilities • Luggage store • Credit cards accepted
A C17th listed building in a village inside the Peak District National Park. Popular with both walkers and cyclists, it is convenient for the historic houses and for Bakewell and Matlock.

Elvaston

SK4132

▲ **Elvaston Castle Country Park,** Borrowash Road, Elvaston, Derby, DE72 3EP
Actual Grid Ref: SK412332
Tel: 01332 573735
Open: Apr to Oct

▲ **Turnberry House Caravan Park,** Main Road, Elvaston, Derby, DE7 3EQ
Actual Grid Ref: SK413328
Tel: 01332 751938
Open: All year

Eyam

SK2176

▲ **Bretton Youth Hostel,** Bretton, Eyam, Hope Valley, Derbyshire, S32 5QD
Actual Grid Ref: SK200780
Tel: 0114 288 4541 (bookings)
Email: reservations@yha.org.uk
Capacity: 18
Under 18: £5.75
Adults: £8.50
Open: All year, 5.00pm
Self-catering facilities • Showers • Lounge • Drying room • Cycle store • Parking • No smoking • Credit cards accepted Advance bookings
Small simple hostel ideal for groups of friends and families, near a tiny hamlet high on Eyam Edge and enjoying superb views across unspoilt countryside.

▲ **Eyam Youth Hostel,** Hawkhill Road, Eyam, Hope Valley, S32 5QX
Actual Grid Ref: SK219769
Tel: 01433 630335
Fax: 01433 639202
Email: eyam@yha.org.uk
Capacity: 60
Under 18: £7.75
Adults: £11.00
Open: Feb to Nov + New Year, 5.00pm
Family bunk rooms
Wet weather shelter • Lounge • Games room • Drying room • Cycle store • Parking • Evening meal available 6.30pm • No smoking • Breakfast available • Credit cards accepted
A spacious Victorian house (with a turret) and grounds which overlook the Plague village of Eyam. Highly convenient for the Peak District as well as the historic houses of Chatsworth and Haddon Hall.

Fenny Bentley

SK1750

▲ **Bank Top Farm,** Fenny Bentley, Ashbourne, Derbyshire, DE6 1LF
Actual Grid Ref: SK182498
Tel: 01335 350250
Open: Apr to Sep

▲ **Highfields Camping & Caravan Park,** Fenny Bentley, Ashbourne, Derbyshire, DE6 1LE
Actual Grid Ref: SK170510
Tel: 01335 350228
Fax: 01335 350253
Open: Mar to Oct

Flagg

SK1368

▲ **Pomeroy Caravan & Camping Park,** Street House Farm, Pomeroy, Flagg, Buxton, Derbyshire, SK17 9QG
Actual Grid Ref: SK116675
Tel: 01298 83259
Open: Apr to Oct

Stilwell's Hostels & Camping 2002   49

Derbyshire • MAP PAGE 46

Foolow
SK1976

▲ **Brosterfield Farm,** Foolow, Eyam, Hope Valley, Derbyshire, S32 5QB
Tel: 01433 630958
Open: Mar to Oct

Furness Vale
SK0183

▲ **Ringstones Caravan Park,** Yeardsley Lane, Furness Vale, High Peak, Derbyshire, SK23 7EB
Actual Grid Ref: SK005825
Tel: 01663 732152
Open: Mar to Oct

Glutton Bridge
SK0866

▲ **Dowall Hall Farm,** Glutton Bridge, Buxton, Derbyshire, SK17 0RW
Actual Grid Ref: SK076675
Tel: 01298 83297
Open: Apr to Oct

Grangemill
SK2457

▲ **Middle Hills Farm,** Grangemill, Matlock, Derbyshire, DE4 4HY
Actual Grid Ref: SK236577
Tel: 01629 650368
Fax: 01629 650368
Email: l.lomas@btinternet.com
Open: All year

Hartington
SK1260

▲ **Hartington Hall Youth Hostel,** Hartington, Buxton, Derbyshire, SK17 0AT
Actual Grid Ref: SK131603
Tel: 01298 84223
Fax: 01298 84415
Email: hartington@yha.org.uk
Capacity: 122

Under 18: £9.50
Adults: £13.50
Open: All year, All day
Family bunk rooms
Self-catering facilities • Television • Showers • Licensed bar • Shop • Laundry facilities • Dining room • Games room • Drying room • Cycle store • Parking Limited • Evening meal available 5.30-7.00pm • WC • Kitchen facilities • Breakfast available • Credit cards accepted
Sleep where Bonnie Prince Charlie once slept, in a C17th Hall, with oak panels and log fires. Bikes can be hired to explore Dovedale or attempt the Tissington Trail. Families are welcome.

▲ **Barracks Farm,** Beresford Dale, Hartington, Buxton, Derbyshire, SK17 0HQ
Actual Grid Ref: SK112588
Tel: 01298 84261
Open: Apr to Oct

Hathersage
SK2381

▲ **Hathersage Youth Hostel,** Castleton Road, Hathersage, Hope Valley, Derbyshire, S32 1EH
Actual Grid Ref: SK226814
Tel: 01433 650493
Fax: 01433 650493
Capacity: 40
Under 18: £5.65
Adults: £8.35
Open: All year, 5.00pm
Showers • Lounge • Dining room • Cycle store • Parking 6 cars • Evening meal available 7.00pm • No smoking • WC • Kitchen facilities • Breakfast available • Credit cards accepted
Popular with walkers and climbers of all abilities, wanting to try Stanage Edge the White Peak Way. The village has strong connections with Charlotte Bronte, and also with Robin Hood, in that Little John's grave is here. The hostel, in a Victorian house, is on the way into the village

▲ **North Lees Campsite,** Birley Lane, Hathersage, South Yorkshire, S30 1BR
Actual Grid Ref: SK235832
Tel: 01433 650838
Open: Easter to Dec

All details shown are as supplied by hostels and campsites in Autumn 2000.

Hayfield
SK0386

▲ **Hayfield Camping & Caravanning Club Site,** Kinder Road, Hayfield, High Peak, Derbyshire, SK22 5LE
Actual Grid Ref: SK048868
Tel: 01663 745394 / 01203 694995
Open: Mar to Nov

Heathcote
SK1460

▲ **Chapel Farm,** Heathcote, Hartington, Buxton, Derbyshire, SK17 0AY
Actual Grid Ref: SK147602
Tel: 01298 84312
Open: Mar to Oct

Hope
SK1683

▲ **Hardhurst Farm,** Borough Lane Ends, Hope, Hope Valley, Derbyshire, S33 6RB
Actual Grid Ref: SK185827
Tel: 01433 620001
Open: All year

▲ **Laneside Caravan Park,** Hope, Hope Valley, Derbyshire, S33 6RR
Actual Grid Ref: SK177832
Tel: 01433 620215
Open: Apr to Oct

▲ **Laneside Farm Caravan,** Hope, Hope Valley, Derbyshire, S33 6RR
Tel: 01433 620214
Open: Easter to Oct

Kniveton
SK2050

▲ **The Closes Caravan Park,** Ostrich Lane, Kniveton, Ashbourne, Derbyshire, DE6 1JL
Tel: 01335 343191
Open: Easter to Oct

▲ **Rowfields Hall Farm Caravan,** Kniveton, Ashbourne, Derbyshire, DE6 1JF
Tel: 01335 342805
Email: emcress@aol.com
Open: May to Oct

Hostels and campsites may vary rates – be sure to check when booking.

MAP PAGE 46 • **Derbyshire**

Lea

SK3257

▲ **Lea Gardens Caravan and Camping Site,** Lea, Matlock, Derbyshire, DE4 5GH
Tel: 01629 534380
Open: June to April

Matlock

SK3060

▲ **Matlock Youth Hostel & Training Centre,** 40 Bank Road, Matlock, Derbyshire, DE4 3NF
Actual Grid Ref: SK300603
Tel: 01629 582983
Fax: 01629 583484
Email: matlock@yha.org.uk
Capacity: 53
Under 18: £7.75
Adults: £11.00
Open: Jan to Dec (not New Year), 1.00pm
Self-catering facilities • Television • Showers • Licensed bar • Laundry facilities • Lounge • Games room • Drying room • Cycle store • Evening meal available 6.30 to 7.00pm • Kitchen facilities • Credit cards accepted
A Victorian building, but with modern facilities, meeting & conference rooms. It is located at the edge of the Peak District National Park.

Matlock Moor

SK3062

▲ **Sycamore Caravan & Camping Park,** Lant Lane, Matlock Moor, Matlock, Derbyshire, DE4 5LF
Actual Grid Ref: SK326617
Tel: 01629 55760
Email: info@sycamore-park.co.uk
Open: Mar to Oct

▲ **Wayside Farm Caravans,** Matlock Moor, Matlock, Derbyshire, DE4 5LF
Actual Grid Ref: SK321620
Tel: 01629 582967
Open: All year

You are advised to book in advance for periods of high demand – the Summer months, Half Term holidays and public holidays.

Miller's Dale

SK1473

▲ **Ravenstor Youth Hostel,** Miller's Dale, Buxton, Derbyshire, SK17 8SS
Actual Grid Ref: SK152732
Tel: 01298 871826
Fax: 01298 871275
Email: ravenstor@yha.org.uk
Capacity: 83
Under 18: £7.75 **Adults:** £10.00
Open: Feb to Nov + Xmas/New Year, 1.00pm
Self-catering facilities • Television • Showers • Licensed bar • Shop • Lounge • Dining room • Cycle store • Parking • Evening meal available 7.00pm • Kitchen facilities • Breakfast available • Credit cards accepted
Set among the limestone scenery of the River Wye and the White Peak, this is a National Trust property. It is a good area for walking.

Newhaven

SK1660

▲ **Newhaven Holiday Camping & Caravan Park,** Newhaven, Buxton, Derbyshire, SK17 0DT
Actual Grid Ref: SK166603
Tourist Board grade: 3 Star
AA grade: 3 Pennants
Tel: 01298 84300
Tent pitches: 30
Tent rate: £7.25-£8.50
Open: Mar to Oct **Last arr:** 10pm
Dogs allowed • Electric hook-up • Calor Gas/Camping Gaz • Cafe or Takeaway on site • Picnic/barbecue area on site • Children's play area • Showers • Laundrette on site • Public phone on site • Licensed bar on site • Shop on site • Games room • Indoor swimming pool nearby • Outdoor swimming pool nearby • Boating/sailing/watersports nearby • Golf nearby • Riding nearby • Fishing nearby
Situated between Ashbourne/Buxton, entrance from A5012. Ideal location for exploring Derbyshire Dales, historic houses and villages of the Peak National Park. Close to High Peak/Tissington Trails, the park is immaculately kept, with tarmacked road, two toilet blocks and woods.

Offcote

SK2048

▲ **Offcote Grange,** Offcote, Kniveton, Ashbourne, Derbyshire, DE6 1JQ
Tel: 01335 344795
Fax: 01335 348458
Open: All year

Osmaston (Ashbourne)

SK1944

▲ **Gateway Caravan Park,** Osmaston, Ashbourne, Derbyshire, DE6 1NA
Actual Grid Ref: SK194449
Tel: 01335 344643
Open: All year

Over Haddon

SK2066

▲ **Reckoning House,** Mandale House, Haddon Grove, Over Haddon, Bakewell, Derbyshire, DE45 1JF
Tel: 01629 812416
Email: julia.finney@virgin.net
Capacity: 12
Under 18: £4.50
Adults: £4.50
Open: All year, 4pm
Camping for 20 tents: £6.00
Self-catering facilities • Dining room • Grounds available for games • Parking
Superb historic camping barn in quiet location, near Lathkill Dale.

▲ **Mandale,** Haddon Grove, Over Haddon, Bakewell, Derbyshire, DE45 1JF
Actual Grid Ref: SK182665
Tel: 01629 812416
Fax: 01629 812416
Email: julia.finney@virgin.net
Tent pitches: 20
Tent rate: £1.50-£6.00
Open: All year
Last arr: 10pm
Cafe or Takeaway on site
Small campsite specialising in small groups and DOE, basic facilities.

▲ **Haddon Grove,** Over Haddon, Bakewell, Derbyshire, DE45 1JE
Actual Grid Ref: SK177662
Tel: 01629 812343
Open: Mar to Oct

Peak Dale

SK0976

▲ **Thornheyes Farm Campsite,** Thornheyes Farm, Longridge Ln, Peak Dale, Buxton, Derbyshire, SK17 8AD
Actual Grid Ref: SK083761
Tel: 01298 26421
Open: Apr to Oct

ENGLAND

Stilwell's Hostels & Camping 2002   51

Derbyshire • MAP PAGE 46

Rowsley
SK2565

▲ **Grouse & Claret,** Station Rd, Rowsley, Matlock, Derbyshire, DE4 2EL
Actual Grid Ref: SK258660
Tel: 01629 733233
Open: All year

Shardlow
SK4330

▲ **Shardlow Marina Caravan Park,** London Rd, Shardlow, Derby, DE72 2GL
Actual Grid Ref: SK444303
Tel: 01332 792832
Open: Mar to Oct

South Wingfield
SK3755

▲ **Wingfield Manor Caravan Site,** South Wingfield, Alfreton, Derbyshire, DE55 7NH
Actual Grid Ref: SK375547
Tel: 01773 833166
Open: All year

Stoney Middleton
SK2275

▲ **Peakland Caravans,** High Street, Stoney Middleton, Hope Valley, Derbyshire, S32 4TL
Tel: 01433 631414
Open: Apr to Oct

Stretton
SK3961

▲ **Alnmoor Caravan and Camping Park,** Mickley Lane, Stretton, Alfreton, Derbyshire, DE55 6ES
Actual Grid Ref: SK394605
Tel: 01773 833607
Open: All year

Tansley
SK3259

▲ **Pinegroves Caravan Park,** High Lane, Tansley, Matlock, Derbyshire, DE4 5GS
Actual Grid Ref: SK343586
Tel: 01629 534815 / 534670
Open: Apr to Oct

▲ **Packhorse Farm,** Tansley, Matlock, Derbyshire, DE4 5LF
Actual Grid Ref: SK323617
Tel: 01629 580950
Fax: 01629 580950
Open: All year

Whatstandwell
SK3354

▲ **Merebrook Caravan Park,** Matlock Road, Whatstandwell, Matlock, Derbyshire, DE4 5HH
Actual Grid Ref: SK332555
Tel: 01773 852154
Open: All year

▲ **Haytop Farm Caravanserai Ltd,** Whatstandwell, Matlock, Derbyshire, DE4 5HP
Tel: 01773 852063
Open: All year

▲ **Birchwood Farm Caravan Park,** Wirksworth Road, Whatstandwell, Matlock, Derbyshire, DE4 5HS
Actual Grid Ref: SK315551
Tel: 01629 822280
Open: Mar to Oct

▲ **Meerbrook Farm,** Wirksworth Road, Whatstandwell, Matlock, Derbyshire, DE4 5HU
Tel: 01629 824180
Open: All year

Wirksworth
SK2853

▲ **New Buildings Farm Bunk Barn,** New Buildings Farm, Ashleyhay, Wirksworth, Derbyshire, DE4 4AH
Actual Grid Ref: SK296518
Tel: 01629 823191
Fax: 01629 823191
Capacity: 122
Under 18: £8.00
Adults: £8.00
Open: All year (not Xmas/New Year)

Self-catering facilities • Showers • Central heating • Wet weather shelter • Grounds available for games • Cycle store • Parking
Converted barn on working sheep farm 2 miles from the historic market town of Wirksworth. Accommodation in 2 rooms each sleeping 6 + 2 in large living room with fitted kitchen and wood burner. Electricity included. Excellent walking and cycling locally. Easy access to the White Peak and Derbyshire tourist attractions.

Youlgreave
SK2164

▲ **Youlgreave Youth Hostel,** Fountain Square, Youlgreave, Bakewell, Derbyshire, DE45 1UR
Actual Grid Ref: SK210641
Tel: 01629 636518
Fax: 01629 636518
Capacity: 42
Under 18: £7.35
Adults: £11.00
Open: Feb to Dec + New Year, 5.00pm
Family bunk rooms
Self-catering facilities • Showers • Lounge • Drying room • Cycle store • Evening meal available 7.00pm • No smoking • WC • Kitchen facilities • Breakfast available
Unique Co-op building offering excellent accommodation. It is located in the centre of the town, but is convenient for walkers and cyclists.

▲ **Camping & Caravanning Club Site,** Hopping Farm, Youlgreave, Bakewell, Derbyshire, DE45 1NA
Tel: 01629 636555
Open: Mar to Sep

▲ **Hopping Farn,** Mawstone Lane, Youlgreave, Bakewell, Derbyshire, DE45 1NA
Actual Grid Ref: SK209631
Tel: 01629 636302
Open: Apr to Sep

To stay in a Youth Hostel affiliated to one of the Youth Hostel associations, you need to be a member. You can join at most hostels – phone in advance to check.

Stilwell's Hostels & Camping 2002

Stilwell's Britain Cycleway Companion

23 Long Distance Cycleways • Where to Stay • Where to Eat

ENGLAND

County Cycleways – Sustrans Routes

The first guide of its kind, Stilwell's Britain Cycleway Companion makes planning accommodation for your cycling trip easy. It lists B&Bs, hostels, campsites and pubs– in the order they appear along the selected cycleways – allowing the cyclist to book ahead. No more hunting for a room, a hot meal or a cold drink after a long day in the saddle. Stilwell's gives descriptions of the featured routes and includes such relevant information as maps, grid references and distance from route; Tourist Board ratings; and the availability of drying facilities and packed lunches. No matter which route – or part of a route – you decide to ride, let the Cycleway Companion show you where to sleep and eat.

As essential as your tyre pump – the perfect cycling companion:
Stilwell's Britain Cycleway Companion.

Cycleways – Sustrans
Carlisle to Inverness – Clyde to Forth - Devon Coast to Coast - Hull to Harwich – Kingfisher Cycle Trail - Lon Las Cymru – Sea to Sea (C2C) – Severn and Thames - West Country Way – White Rose Cycle Route

Cycleways – County
Round Berkshire Cycle Route – Cheshire Cycleway – Cumbria Cycleway – Essex Cycle Route – Icknield Way - Lancashire Cycleway – Leicestershire County Cycleway – Oxfordshire Cycleway – Reivers Cycle Route – South Downs Way - Surrey Cycleway – Wiltshire Cycleway – Yorkshire Dales Cycleway

£9.95 from all good bookstores (ISBN 1-900861-26-7) or £10.95 (inc p&p) from Stilwell Publishing, 59 Charlotte Road, London EC2A 3QW (020 7739 7179)

Devon

Devon

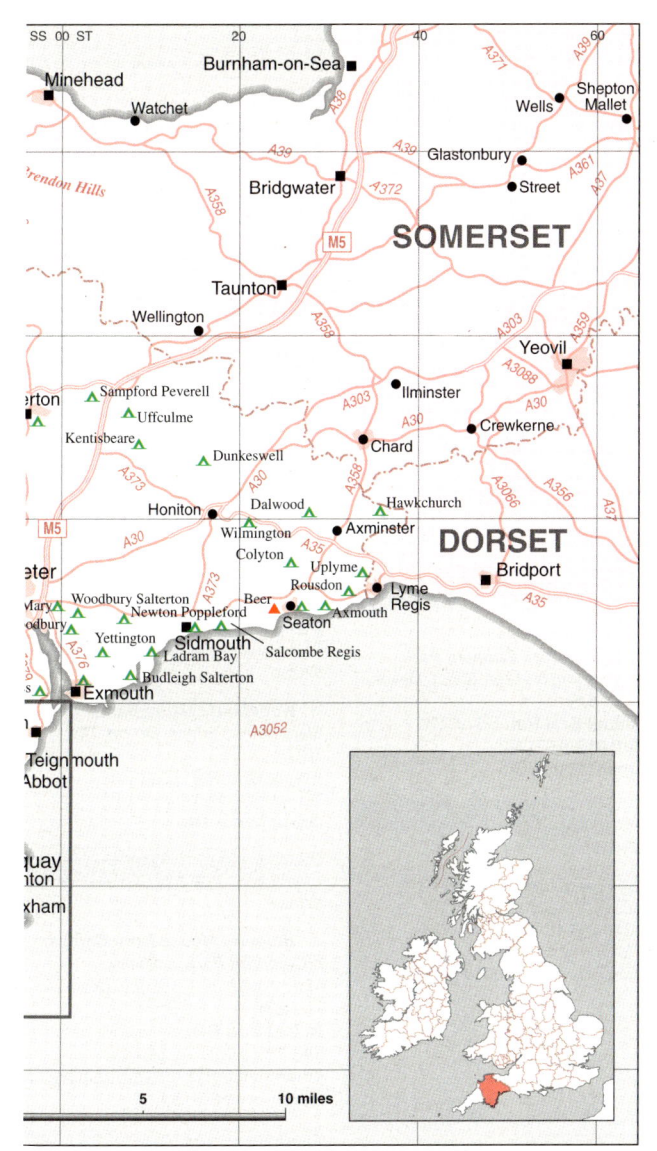

Ashburton
SX7570

▲ **Landscove Camping Site,** Wolston Green, Lanscove, Ashburton, Newton Abbot, Devon, TQ13 7LZ
Actual Grid Ref: SX777661
Tel: 01803 762225
Open: Apr to Sep

▲ **Ashburton Caravan Park,** Waterleat, Ashburton, Newton Abbot, Devon, TQ13 7HU
Actual Grid Ref: SX753718
Tel: 01364 652552
Open: Mar to Oct

▲ **Parkers Farm Holiday Park,** Higher Mead Farm, Ashburton, Newton Abbot, Devon, TQ13 7LJ
Actual Grid Ref: SX779713
Tel: 01364 652598
Open: Apr to Oct

Avonwick
SX7158

▲ **Webland Farm Holiday Park,** Avonwick, South Brent, Devon, TQ10 9EX
Actual Grid Ref: SX714592
Tel: 01364 73273
Open: Mar to Nov

Axmouth
SY2591

▲ **Axmouth Camping Site,** Axe Farm, Axmouth, Seaton, Devon, EX12 4BG
Actual Grid Ref: SY256912
Tel: 01297 24707
Open: Mar to Nov

Barnstaple
SS5633

▲ **Brightlycott Farm Camping Site,** Barnstaple, Devon, EX31 4JJ
Actual Grid Ref: SS580354
Tel: 01271 850330
Email: friend.brightlycott@virgin.net
Tent pitches: 20
Tent rate: £5.00-£8.00
Open: May to Sep
Dogs allowed • Electric hook-up • Showers
Peaceful situation, panoramic views. Close to Exmoor and wonderful beaches.

Stilwell's Hostels & Camping 2002

Devon • MAP PAGE 54

ENGLAND

▲ **Midland Caravan Park,** Braunton Road, Barnstaple, Devon, EX31 4AU
Actual Grid Ref: SS533346
Tel: 01271 43691
Fax: 01271 43691
Open: Apr to Sep

▲ **Chivenor Caravan Park,** Chivenor, Barnstaple, Devon, EX31 4BN
Actual Grid Ref: SS505350
Tel: 01271 812217
Open: Mar to Nov

Beer
SY2289

▲ **Beer Youth Hostel,** Bovey Combe, Beer, Seaton, Devon, EX12 3LL
Actual Grid Ref: SY223896
Tel: 01297 20296
Fax: 01297 23690
Email: beer@yha.org.uk
Capacity: 40
Under 18: £7.75
Adults: £11.00
Open: All year, 5.00pm
Family bunk rooms
Self-catering facilities • Showers • Lounge • Dining room • Drying room • Cycle store • Parking • Evening meal available 6.45 to 7.15pm • No smoking • WC • Kitchen facilities • Credit cards accepted
Large house standing in landscaped grounds on hillside to the west of a picturesque 'old world' fishing village.

Bellever
SX6577

▲ **Bellever Youth Hostel,** Bellever, Postbridge, Yelverton, Devon, PL20 6TU
Actual Grid Ref: SX654773
Tel: 01822 880227
Fax: 01822 880302
Capacity: 38
Under 18: £6.90 **Adults:** £10.00
Open: All year, 5.00pm
Family bunk rooms
Self-catering facilities • Lounge • Dining room • Drying room • Cycle store • Parking Limited • Evening meal available 7.00pm • No smoking • Kitchen facilities • Breakfast available • Credit cards accepted
Recently refurbished converted barn, idyllically situated at the heart of Dartmoor National Park.

Berrynarbor
SS5646

▲ **Napps Camping Site,** Old Coast Rd, Berrynarbor, Ilfracombe, Devon, EX34 9SW
Actual Grid Ref: SS561474
Tel: 01271 882557
Open: Mar to Nov

▲ **Watermouth Cove Holiday Park,** Berrynarbor, Ilfracombe, Devon, EX34 9SJ
Actual Grid Ref: SS558477
Tel: 01271 862504
Open: Easter to Oct

▲ **Sandaway Holiday Park,** Berrynarbor, Ilfracombe, Devon, EX34 9ST
Actual Grid Ref: SS575470
Tel: 01271 883155 **Open:** Mar to Oct

▲ **Mill Park Touring Site,** Mill Park Guest House, Berrynarbor, Ilfracombe, Devon, EX34 9SH
Actual Grid Ref: SS559471
Tel: 01271 882647 **Open:** Mar to Nov

Bickington (Barnstaple)
SS5232

▲ **Lemonford Caravan Park,** Bickington, Newton Abbot, Devon, TQ12 6JR
Actual Grid Ref: SS793723
Tel: 01626 821242
Open: Mar to Oct

Bideford
SS4526

▲ **Steart Farm Touring Park,** Bideford, Devon, EX39 5DW
Actual Grid Ref: SS356228
Tel: 01237 431836
Tent pitches: 25 **Tent rate:** £2.50-£5.00
Open: Easter to Oct **Last arr:** 10.30pm
Dogs allowed • Electric hook-up • Calor Gas/Camping Gaz • Picnic/barbecue area on site • Children's play area • Showers • Laundrette on site • Public phone on site • Indoor swimming pool nearby • Golf nearby • Boating/sailing/watersports nearby • Riding nearby • Fishing nearby
Quiet family-run site set in 17 acres of former farmland within designated Area of Outstanding Natural Beauty overlooking Bideford Bay. Majority of tent pitches on terraces providing some privacy with easy access to neighbouring Woodland Trust Land linking to coastal path. Dedicated dog exercise field and day kennelling facility.

▲ **Pusehill Farm,** Westward Ho, Bideford, Devon, EX29 5AH
Tel: 01237 47295
Open: Easter to Sep

Bigbury on Sea
SX6544

▲ **Mount Folly Farm,** Folly Hill, Bigbury-on-Sea, Kingsbridge, Devon, TQ7 4AR
Actual Grid Ref: SX662446
Tel: 01548 810267
Tent pitches: 30
Tent rate: £3.50-£4.50
Open: All year
Last arr: 10pm
Dogs allowed
Basic campsite with tremendous views. Sandy beaches within walking distance.

Bishopsteignton
SX9073

▲ **Wear Farm,** Newton Road, Bishopsteignton, Teignmouth, Devon, TQ14 9PT
Actual Grid Ref: SX890371
Tel: 01626 775249
Open: Mar to Oct

Blackawton
SX8050

▲ **Woodland Leisure Park,** Blackawton, Totnes, Devon, TQ9 7DQ
Actual Grid Ref: SX813522
Tel: 01803 712598
Open: Mar to Nov

Bolberry
SX6939

▲ **Bolberry House Farm Caravan & Camping Park,** Bolberry, Malborough, Kingsbridge, Devon, TQ7 3DY
Actual Grid Ref: SX693394
Tel: 01548 561251 / 560926
Email: bolberry.house@virgin.net
Open: Easter to Oct

Braunton
SS4936

▲ **Lobb Fields** Caravan & Camping Park, Saunton Rd, Braunton, Devon, EX33 1EB
Actual Grid Ref: SS473371
Tel: 01271 812090 **Fax:** 01271 812090
Open: May to Sep

MAP PAGE 54 • Devon

▲ **Bay View Farm,** Braunton, Devon, EX33 1PN
Actual Grid Ref: SS443388
Tel: 01271 890501
Open: Mar to Oct

Brendon (Lynmouth)
SS7647

▲ **Millslade House,** Brendon, Lynton, Devon, EX35 6PS
Actual Grid Ref: SS768482
Tel: 01598 741322
Open: All year

▲ **Southernwood Farm,** Brendon, Lynton, Devon, EX35 6NU
Actual Grid Ref: SS786485
Tel: 01598 741277
Open: May to Sep

▲ **Leeford Farm,** Brendon, Lynton, Devon, EX35 6NU
Actual Grid Ref: SS775482
Tel: 01598 741231
Open: All year

Bridestowe
SX5189

▲ **Bridestowe Caravan Park,** Bridestowe, Okehampton, Devon, EX20 4ER
Actual Grid Ref: SX520892
Tel: 01837 861261
Open: Mar to Dec

Bridgerule
SS2702

▲ **Hedleywood Caravan and Camping Park,** Bridgerule, Holsworthy, Devon, EX22 7ED
Actual Grid Ref: SS262015
Tel: 01288 381404
Open: All year

Brixham
SX9255

▲ **Galmpton Touring Park,** Greenway Road, Brixham, Devon, TQ5 0EP
Actual Grid Ref: SX885558
Tel: 01803 842066
Open: Mar to Sept

▲ **Hillhead Holiday Camp,** Brixham, Devon, TQ5 0HH
Actual Grid Ref: SX903538
Tel: 01803 853204
Open: Apr to Oct

▲ **Upton Manor Farm Camping Site,** St Mary's Road, Brixham, Devon, TQ5 9QH
Actual Grid Ref: SX925548
Tel: 01803 882384
Fax: 01803 882384
Open: May to Sep

▲ **Southdown Farm,** Brixham, Devon, TQ5 0AJ
Tel: 01803 857991
Open: July to Oct

▲ **Centry Touring Caravan & Camping Site,** Gillard Road, Brixham, Devon, TQ5 9EY
Actual Grid Ref: SX932558
Tel: 01803 353215
Open: Mar to Oct

Brixton
SX5551

▲ **Brixton Caravan & Camping Park,** Venn Farm, Brixton, Plymouth, Devon, PL8 2AX
Actual Grid Ref: SX548520
Tel: 01752 880378
Open: Mar to Oct

Buckfastleigh
SX7366

▲ **Beara Farm Caravan & Camping Site,** Colston Rd, Buckfastleigh, Devon, TQ11 0LW
Actual Grid Ref: SX751645
Tel: 01364 642234
Open: All year

▲ **Churchill Farm Campsite,** Buckfastleigh, Devon, TQ11 0EZ
Actual Grid Ref: SX743664
Tel: 01364 642844
Open: Easter to Oct

▲ **Bowden Farm Campsite,** Bowden Farm, Buckfastleigh, Devon, TQ11 0JG
Actual Grid Ref: SX701672
Tel: 01364 643219
Open: All year

Budleigh Salterton
SY0682

▲ **Pooh Cottage,** Bear Lane, Budleigh Salterton, Devon, EX9 7AQ
Tel: 01395 442354
Open: Apr to Oct

Capton
SX8453

▲ **Dittisham Fruit Farm Caravan Hook-ups,** Capton, Dartmouth, Devon, TQ6 0JE
Tel: 01803 712452
Open: All year

Chudleigh
SX8679

▲ **Finlake Holiday Park,** Chudleigh, Newton Abbot, Devon, TQ13 0EJ
Actual Grid Ref: SX855786
Tel: 01626 853933
Open: Easter to Oct

▲ **Finlake Holiday Park,** Chudleigh, Newton Abbot, Devon, TQ13 0EJ
Actual Grid Ref: SX846775
Tel: 01626 853833
Open: All year

Clifford Bridge
SX7889

▲ **Clifford Bridge Park,** Clifford Bridge, Drewsteignton, Exeter, Devon, EX6 6QE
Actual Grid Ref: SX780897
Tel: 01647 24226
Open: Apr to Sep

Clyst St Mary
SX9791

▲ **Hill Pond Camping Site,** Sidmouth Road, Clyst St Mary, Exeter, Devon, EX5 1DP
Actual Grid Ref: SX997907
Tel: 01395 232483
Open: All year

Colyton
SY2493

▲ **Leacroft Touring Park,** Colyton Hill, Colyton, Axminster, Devon, EX13 6HY
Actual Grid Ref: SY219923
Tel: 01297 552823
Open: Mar to Oct

All details shown are as supplied by hostels and campsites in Autumn 2000.

Devon • MAP PAGE 54

Combe Martin
SS5846

▲ **Newberry Farm Touring Caravan & Camping Site,** Combe Martin, Ilfracombe, Devon, EX34 0AT
Actual Grid Ref: SS576473
Tel: 01271 882333 **Fax:** 01271 882880
Tent pitches: 85
Tent rate: £6.50-£8.00
Open: Apr to Oct **Last arr:** 8pm
Facilities for disabled people • Electric hook-up • Children's play area • Showers • Laundrette on site
Quiet and peaceful location. Level pitches in secluded countryside valley.

▲ **Stowford Farm Meadows,** Berry Down, Combe Martin, Ilfracombe, Devon, EX34 0PW
Actual Grid Ref: SS560425
Tel: 01271 882476
Open: Apr to Oct

Compton
SX8665

▲ **Widdicombe Farm Tourist Park,** Compton, Torquay, Devon, TQ3 1ST
Actual Grid Ref: SX874641
Tel: 01803 558325
Open: Mar to Oct

Creacombe
SS8219

▲ **Creacombe Parsonage Farm,** Parsonage Cross, Creacombe, Rackenford, Tiverton, Devon, EX16 8EL
Actual Grid Ref: SS820185
Tel: 01884 881441
Fax: 01884 881551
Email: creaky.parson@dial.pipex.com
Tent pitches: 6 **Tent rate:** £4.00
Open: All year
Facilities for disabled people • Dogs allowed • Cafe or Takeaway on site • Picnic/barbecue area on site • Showers • Baby care facilities
Peaceful farm site, extensive views of Mid Devon.

Crockernwell
SX7592

▲ **Barley Meadow Caravan & Camping Park,** Crockernwell, Exeter, Devon, EX6 6NR
Actual Grid Ref: SX744923
Tel: 01647 281629
Open: Mar to Nov

Croyde
SS4439

▲ **Cherry Tree Farm Campsite,** Croyde, Braunton, Devon, EX33 1NH
Actual Grid Ref: SS442399
Tel: 01237 890386
Open: May to Sep

Daccombe
SX9068

▲ **Manor Farm Campsite,** Manor Farm, Daccombe, Newton Abbott, Devon, TQ12 4ST
Actual Grid Ref: SX903678
Tel: 01803 328294
Open: May to Sep

Dalwood
ST2400

▲ **Andrewshayes Caravan Park,** Dalwood, Axminster, Devon, EX13 7DY
Actual Grid Ref: SY247988
Tel: 01404 831225
Fax: 01404 831225
Open: Apr to Oct

Dartington
SX7862

▲ **Dartington Youth Hostel,** Lownard, Dartington, Totnes, Devon, TQ9 6JJ
Actual Grid Ref: SX782622
Tel: 01803 862303
Fax: 01803 865171
Capacity: 30
Under 18: £6.50
Adults: £9.25
Open: All year, 5.00pm
Family bunk rooms
Self-catering facilities • Showers • Lounge • Drying room • Cycle store • Parking Limited • No smoking • WC • Kitchen facilities 2 • Credit cards accepted
A small traditional cottage-style hostel with a wooden cabin annexe containing the bunk rooms, in a peaceful village setting complete with its own gardens and stream. An ideal base for exploring the South Hams countryside.

Dartmouth
SX8751

▲ **Little Cotton Caravan Park,** Little Cotton, Dartmouth, Devon, TQ6 0LB
Actual Grid Ref: SX857508
Tel: 01803 832558
Open: Mar to Nov

Dawlish
SX9676

▲ **Lady's Mile Touring & Caravan Park,** Dawlish, Devon, EX7 0LX
Actual Grid Ref: SX967784
Tel: 01626 863411
Fax: 01626 888689
Open: Mar to Oct

▲ **Peppermint Park,** Warren Rd, Dawlish, Devon, EX7 0PQ
Actual Grid Ref: SX973786
Tel: 01626 863436
Open: Mar to Oct

▲ **Leadstone Camping,** Warren Road, Dawlish, Devon, EX7 0NG
Actual Grid Ref: SX974782
Tel: 01626 872239
Fax: 01626 873833
Open: Jun to Sep

Dolton
SS5712

▲ **Dolton Caravan Park,** Dolton, Winkleigh, Devon, EX19 8QF
Actual Grid Ref: SS572122
Tel: 01805 804536
Open: Apr to Oct

Dunkeswell
ST1307

▲ **Fishpond House Campsite,** Dunkeswell, Honiton, Devon, EX14 0SH
Tel: 01404 891287
Open: Apr to Nov

▲ **Fishponds House,** Dunkeswell, Honiton, Devon, EX14 4SH
Actual Grid Ref: ST152075
Tel: 01404 891358
Open: All year

Dunsford
SX8189

▲ **Steps Bridge Youth Hostel,** Steps Bridge, Dunsford, Exeter, Devon, EX6 7EQ
Actual Grid Ref: SX802882
Tel: 01647 252435
Fax: 01647 252948
Email: reservations@yha.org.uk
Capacity: 24
Under 18: £5.75
Adults: £8.50
Open: All year, 5.00pm

MAP PAGE **54** • **Devon**

Self-catering facilities • Showers • Drying room • Cycle store • No smoking • WC • Kitchen facilities • Credit cards accepted
A back-to-nature haven in secluded woodland ideal for exploring Dartmoor. This small self-catering hostel with modest facilities has a friendly atmosphere and overlooks the beautiful Teign Valley.

▲ **East Down,** Dunsford, Exeter, EX6 7AL
Tel: 01647 24041
Fax: 01626 24041
Open: All year

East Allington

SX7648

▲ **Mounts Farm,** The Mounts, East Allington, Kingsbridge, Devon, TQ9 7QJ
Actual Grid Ref: SX757488
Tel: 01548 521591
Open: Apr to Oct

East Portlemouth

SX7438

▲ **Village Farm Campsite,** East Portlemouth, Kingsbridge, Devon
Tel: 0116 244 0142
Open: June to Sept

▲ **Meadow Barn,** East Portlemouth, Salcombe, Devon, TQ8 8PN
Tel: 01548 843085
Open: All year

East Prawle

SX7836

▲ **Maelcombe House,** East Prawle, Kingsbridge, Devon, TQ7 2DE
Actual Grid Ref: SX791363
Tel: 01548 511300
Open: All year

East Worlington

SS7713

▲ **Yeatheridge Farm Caravan Park,** East Worlington, Crediton, Devon, EX17 4TN
Actual Grid Ref: SS768111
Tel: 01884 860330
Open: Mar to Sept

Hostels and campsites may vary rates – be sure to check when booking.

Elmscott

SS2321

▲ **Elmscott Youth Hostel,** Elmscott, Hartland, Bideford, Devon, EX39 6ES
Actual Grid Ref: SS231217
Tel: 01237 441367
Fax: 01237 441910
Email: reservations@yha.org.uk
Capacity: 38
Under 18: £6.90
Adults: £10.00
Open: All year, 5.00pm
Self-catering facilities • Showers • Wet weather shelter • Lounge • Dining room • Cycle store • No smoking • WC • Credit cards accepted
Former Victorian schoolhouse and enclosed garden in a remote Area of Outstanding Natural Beauty with views of Lundy island.

Exeter

SX9192

▲ **Exeter Youth Hostel,** 47 Countess Wear Road, Exeter, Devon, EX2 6LR
Actual Grid Ref: SX941897
Tel: 01392 873329
Fax: 01392 876939
Email: exeter@yha.org.uk
Capacity: 88
Under 18: £7.75
Adults: £11.00
Open: All year (not New Year), 5.00pm
Camping
Self-catering facilities • Television • Showers • Laundry facilities • Lounge • Drying room • Security lockers • Cycle store • Parking • Evening meal available 7pm • WC • Kitchen facilities • Breakfast available • Luggage store • Credit cards accepted
A comfortable hostel with modern facilities on the outskirts of the city.

Exmouth

SY0081

▲ **Devon Cliffs Holiday Centre,** Sandy Bay, Exmouth, Devon, EX8 5BT
Actual Grid Ref: SY036807
Tel: 01395 226226
Open: Apr to Oct

Filham

SX6455

▲ **Whiteoaks of Ivybridge Camp Site,** Davey Cross, Filham, Ivybridge, Devon, PL21 0DW
Actual Grid Ref: SX650563
Tel: 01752 892340
Open: Mar to Oct

Goodrington

SX8958

▲ **Grange Court Holiday Centre,** Grange Road, Goodrington, Paignton, Devon, TQ4 7JP
Actual Grid Ref: SX888583
Tel: 01803 558010
Fax: 01803 66336
Open: All year

Great Torrington

SS4919

▲ **Greenways Valley,** Great Torrington, Devon, EX38 7EW
Actual Grid Ref: SS505185
Tel: 01805 622153
Open: Mar to Oct

Haccombe

SX8970

▲ **Holmans Wood Tourist Park,** Haccombe Cross, Haccombe, Newton Abbot, Devon, TQ12 5TX
Actual Grid Ref: SX882810
Tel: 01626 853785
Open: Mar to Oct

Hartland

SS2624

▲ **South Lane,** Hartland, Devon, EX39 6AB
Actual Grid Ref: SS263243
Tel: 01237 441242
Open: All year

Hawkchurch

ST3300

▲ **Hunters Moon Touring Park,** Hawkchurch, Axminster, Devon, EX13 5UL
Actual Grid Ref: SY345990
Tel: 01297 678402
Open: Mar to Oct

Devon • MAP PAGE 54

ENGLAND

Hele (Ilfracombe)
SS5347

▲ **Hele Valley Holiday Park,** Hele Bay, Hele, Ilfracombe, Devon, EX34 9RD
Actual Grid Ref: SS536474
Tel: 01271 862460
Fax: 01271 862460
Open: Apr to Oct

Higher Clovelly
SS3124

▲ **Dyke Green Farm,** Higher Clovelly, Bideford, Devon, EX39 5RU
Actual Grid Ref: SS313233
Tel: 01237 431699
Fax: 01237 431699
Open: All year

Holne
SX7069

▲ **River Dart Country Park,** Holne Park, Holne, Ashburton, Newton Abbot, Devon, TQ13 7NP
Actual Grid Ref: SX733701
Tel: 01364 652511
Fax: 01364 652020
Open: Mar to Sept

Holsworthy
SS3403

▲ **New Buildings,** Brandis Corner, Holsworthy, Devon, EX22 7VQ
Tel: 01409 221305
Open: All year

▲ **Noteworthy,** Bude Road, Holsworthy, Devon, EX22 7JB
Actual Grid Ref: SS306050
Tel: 01409 253731
Open: Jul to Dec

Horrabridge
SX5169

▲ **Magpie Leisure Park,** Bedford Bridge, Horrabridge, Yelverton, Devon, PL20 7RY
Actual Grid Ref: SX505703
Tel: 01822 852651
Open: Mar to Oct

▲ **The Old Mine House,** Sortridge, Horrabridge, Yelverton, Devon, PL20 7UA
Tel: 01822 855586
Fax: 01822 855586
Open: All year

All details shown are as supplied by hostels and campsites in Autumn 2000.

Ilfracombe
SS5147

▲ **Ilfracombe Youth Hostel,** Ashmour House, 1 Hillsborough Terrace, Ilfracombe, Devon, EX34 9NR
Actual Grid Ref: SS524476
Tel: 01271 865337
Fax: 01271 862652
Email: ilfracombe@yha.org.uk
Capacity: 50
Under 18: £6.90
Adults: £10.00
Open: Feb to Oct + New Year, 5.00pm
Family bunk rooms
Self-catering facilities • Showers • Licensed bar • Drying room • Cycle store • Evening meal available 7.00pm • No smoking • Kitchen facilities • Breakfast available • Credit cards accepted
End house on a fine Georgian terrace, overlooking the picturesque harbour and the Bristol Channel.

▲ **Little Meadow,** Lydford Farm, Watermouth, Berrynarbour, Ilfracombe, Devon, EX34 9SJ
Actual Grid Ref: SS500409
Tel: 01271 862222
Email: info@littlemeadow.co.uk
Tent pitches: 50
Tent rate: £5.00-£8.00
Open: Mar to Nov
Last arr: 10pm
Dogs allowed • Electric hook-up • Calor Gas/Camping Gaz • Picnic/barbecue area on site • Children's play area • Showers • Public phone on site • Shop on site
Small uncommercialised site with one of the most spectacular views of the Bristol Channel.

▲ **Mullacott Cross Caravan Park,** Ilfracombe, Devon, EX34 8NB
Actual Grid Ref: SS512445
Tel: 01271 862212
Fax: 01271 862979
Open: Apr to Oct

▲ **Little Shelfin Farm,** Ilfracombe, Devon, EX34 8NZ
Actual Grid Ref: SS507445
Tel: 01271 862449
Open: Mar to Oct

Ipplepen
SX8366

▲ **Ross Park,** Park Hill Farm, Ipplepen, Newton Abbot, Devon, TQ12 5TT
Actual Grid Ref: SX845671
Tel: 01803 812983
Fax: 01803 812983
Open: All year

Kennford
SX9186

▲ **Exeter Racecourse Caravan Club Site,** Haldon Racecourse, Kennford, Exeter, Devon, EX6 7XS
Actual Grid Ref: SX897836
Tel: 01392 832107
Open: Mar to Oct

▲ **Haldon Lodge Farm Caravan & Camping Park,** Kennford, Exeter, Devon, EX6 7XW
Actual Grid Ref: SX894868
Tel: 01392 832312
Open: All year

▲ **Kennford International Caravan Park,** Kennford, Exeter, Devon, EX6 7YN
Actual Grid Ref: SX911856
Tel: 01392 833046
Open: All year

Kentisbeare
ST0607

▲ **Forest Glade Holiday Park,** Kentisbeare, Cullompton, Devon, EX15 2DT
Actual Grid Ref: ST100075
Tel: 01404 841381
Fax: 01404 841593
Open: Mar to Nov

Kingsbridge
SX7344

▲ **Island Lodge,** Stumpy Post Cross, Kingsbridge, Devon, TQ7 4BL
Actual Grid Ref: SX741472
Tel: 01548 852956
Open: Jan to Nov

▲ **Parkland Caravan & Camping Site,** Sorley Green Cross, Kingsbridge, Devon, TQ7 4AF
Actual Grid Ref: SX728462
Tel: 01548 852723
Open: All year

MAP PAGE 54 • **Devon**

Kingsteignton

SX8673

▲ **Ware Burton,** Kingsteignton, Newton Abbot, Devon, TQ12 3QQ
Actual Grid Ref: SX885729
Tel: 01626 54025
Open: May to Sep

Ladram Bay

SY0985

▲ **Ladram Bay Holiday Centre,** Ladram Bay, Otterton, Budleigh Salterton, Devon, EX9 7BX
Actual Grid Ref: SY096851
Tel: 01395 568398
Open: Mar to Sept

Landkey

SS5930

▲ **Crossway Caravan Park,** Landkey, Barnstaple, Devon, EX32 0NN
Actual Grid Ref: SS610305
Tel: 01271 830352
Open: Mar to Nov

Little Torrington

SS4916

▲ **Smytham Holiday Park,** Smytham Manor, Little Torrington, Torrington, Devon, EX38 8PU
Actual Grid Ref: SS485162
Tel: 01805 622110
Fax: 01805 625451
Tent pitches: 30
Tent rate: £6.50-£12.50
Open: Mar to Oct
Last arr: 10pm
Dogs allowed • Electric hook-up • Calor Gas/Camping Gaz • Cafe or Takeaway on site • Picnic/barbecue area on site • Children's play area • Showers • Laundrette on site • Public phone on site • Licensed bar on site • Shop on site • Games room • Indoor swimming pool nearby • Outdoor swimming pool on site • Boating/sailing/watersports nearby • Golf on site • Riding nearby • Fishing nearby
Set in 25 acres of leafy tranquil grounds of C17th Manor House, direct access to Tarka Trail. Easy reach of moors and beaches. Friendly family-run park. Restaurant and olde world bar, outdoor heated pool, pitch and putt golf, centrally located for Devon attractions, fishing, horseriding close by.

Liverton

SX8075

▲ **Green Gables,** Exeter Cross, Liverton, Newton Abbott, Devon, TQ12 6EY
Actual Grid Ref: SX822747
Tel: 01626 821421
Open: Mar to Oct

Lundy

SS1344

▲ **The Landmark Trust,** Lundy, Bideford, Devon, EX39 2LY
Actual Grid Ref: SS136442
Tel: 01237 431831
Open: All year

Lydford

SX5184

▲ **Camping & Caravanning Club Site,** Lydford, Okehampton, Devon, EX20 4BE
Actual Grid Ref: SX512853
Tel: 01822 820275
Open: Mar to Oct

Lynbridge

SS7248

▲ **Lynton Youth Hostel,** Lynbridge, Lynton, Devon, EX35 6BE
Actual Grid Ref: SS720487
Tel: 01598 753237
Fax: 01598 753305
Capacity: 36
Under 18: £6.90
Adults: £10.00
Open: All year, 5.00pm
Family bunk rooms
Self-catering facilities • Showers • Shop • Laundry facilities • Lounge • Dining room • Drying room • Cycle store • Parking Limited • Evening meal available 7.00pm • No smoking • WC • Kitchen facilities • Breakfast available • Credit cards accepted
Victorian house in the steep wooded gorge of the West Lyn River, where Exmoor reaches the sea, with opportunities to explore the National Park, the sea shore and the river valley.

▲ **Sunny Lyn Holiday Park,** Lynbridge, Lynton, Devon, EX35 6NS
Actual Grid Ref: SS719485
Tel: 01598 753384
Open: Mar to Oct

Lynton

SS7149

▲ **Camping & Caravanning Club Site,** Caffyns Cross, Lynton, Devon, EX35 6JS
Actual Grid Ref: SS700484
Tel: 01598 752379
Open: Mar to Sept

▲ **Channel View Caravan Park,** Manor Farm, Lynton, Devon, EX35 6LD
Actual Grid Ref: SS723481
Tel: 01598 753349
Open: Mar to Oct

▲ **Hillsford Camping Site,** Hillsford, Lynton, Devon, EX35 6LF
Tel: 01598 753411
Open: Mar to Oct

Malborough

SX7039

▲ **Alston Farm Caravan Site,** Malborough, Kingsbridge, Devon, TQ7 3BJ
Actual Grid Ref: SX717407
Tel: 01548 561260 **Fax:** 01548 561260
Tent pitches: 120
Tent rate: £6.00-£10.00
Open: Apr to Oct
Dogs allowed • Electric hook-up • Calor Gas/Camping Gaz • Children's play area • Showers • Laundrette on site • Public phone on site
Sheltered site in secluded valley adjoining Salcombe Estuary. Family-run site.

▲ **Higher Rew Caravan & Camping Park,** Middle Rew, Malborough, Kingsbridge, Devon, TQ7 3DW
Actual Grid Ref: SX714383
Tel: 01548 842681 / 843681
Open: Apr to Oct

▲ **Karrageen Caravan & Camping Park,** Malborough, Kingsbridge, Devon, TQ7 3EN
Actual Grid Ref: SX689394
Tel: 01548 561230
Email: phil@karrageen.co.uk
Open: Mar to Nov

Marldon

SX8663

▲ **Widend Touring Park,** Berry Pomeroy Road, Marldon, Paignton, Devon, TQ3 1RT
Actual Grid Ref: SX855620
Tel: 01803 550116 **Open:** Apr to Oct

Devon • MAP PAGE 54

Maypool

SX8754

▲ **Maypool Youth Hostel,** Maypool, Galmpton, Brixham, Devon, TQ5 0ET
Actual Grid Ref: SX877546
Tel: 01803 842444
Fax: 01803 845939
Capacity: 65
Under 18: £6.90
Adults: £10.00
Open: All year, 5.00pm
Family bunk rooms
Camping
Self-catering facilities • Television • Showers • Lounge • Dining room • Games room • Drying room • Cycle store • Parking • Evening meal available 7.00pm • WC • Kitchen facilities • Breakfast available • Credit cards accepted
Victorian house set in 4-acre grounds, originally built for local boatyard owner, with views of Kingswear, Dartmouth and the Dart Estuary.

Meshaw

SS7519

▲ **Bournebridge Farm,** Meshaw, South Molton, Devon, EX36 4NL
Tel: 01884 860002
Open: Easter to Sep

Modbury

SX6551

▲ **Camping & Caravanning Club Site,** California Cross, Modbury, Ivybridge, Devon, PL21 0SG
Actual Grid Ref: SX705530
Tel: 01548 821297
Open: Mar to Oct

▲ **Moor View Touring Park,** California Cross, Modbury, Ivybridge, Devon, PL21 0SG
Actual Grid Ref: SX702525
Tel: 01548 821485
Open: Apr to Sep

▲ **Southleigh Caravan & Camping Park,** Modbury, Ivybridge, Devon, PL21 0SB
Actual Grid Ref: SX680516
Tel: 01548 830346
Open: Mar to Nov

▲ **Pennymoor Caravan Park,** Modbury, Ivybridge, Devon, PL21 0SB
Actual Grid Ref: SX685516
Tel: 01548 830542
Open: Mar to Nov

Molland

SS8028

▲ **Blackcock Inn & Camping Park,** Molland, South Molton, Devon, EX36 3NW
Actual Grid Ref: SS788262
Tel: 01769 550297
Fax: 01769 550297
Open: All year

Mortehoe

SS4545

▲ **North Morte Farm Caravan & Camping Park,** Mortehoe, Woolacombe, Devon, EX34 7EG
Actual Grid Ref: SS462455
Tourist Board grade: 3 Star
Tel: 01271 870381
Fax: 01271 870381
Email: north.morte.farm@talk21.com
Tent pitches: 150
Tent rate: £4.00-£18.00
Open: Mar to Sept
Last arr: 11.45pm
Facilities for disabled people • Dogs allowed • Electric hook-up • Calor Gas/Camping Gaz • Children's play area • Showers • Launderette on site • Public phone on site • Shop on site
Family-run park set in beautiful countryside overlooking Rockham Bay.

▲ **Easewell Farm Coastal Holiday Park,** Easewell Farm, Mortehoe, Woolacombe, Devon, EX34 7EH
Actual Grid Ref: SS465455
Tel: 01271 870225
Open: Apr to Oct

▲ **Twitchen Park,** Mortehoe, Woolacombe, Devon, EX34 7ES
Actual Grid Ref: SS465450
Tel: 01271 870476
Open: Mar to Oct

▲ **Warcombe Farm Camping Park,** Station Rd, Mortehoe, Woolacombe, Devon, EX34 7EJ
Actual Grid Ref: SS477447
Tel: 01271 870690
Open: Mar to Oct

▲ **Camping & Caravanning Club Site,** Damage Barton, Mortehoe, Mortehoe, Woolacombe, Devon, EX34 7EJ
Actual Grid Ref: SS471451
Tel: 01271 870502
Fax: 01271 870712
Open: Mar to Oct

Newton Abbot

SX8671

▲ **Dornafield Farm Caravan Park,** Dornafield Farm, Two Mile Oak, Newton Abbot, Devon, TQ12 6DD
Actual Grid Ref: SX839683
Tel: 01803 812732
Open: Mar to Oct

▲ **Milber Down Farm Camping,** St Marychurch Road, Newton Abbot, Devon, TQ12 4SZ
Tel: 01803 873951
Open: May to Sep

▲ **Stover International Caravan Park,** Lower Staple Hill, Newton Abbott, Devon, TQ12 6JD
Actual Grid Ref: SX823742
Tel: 01626 821446
Fax: 01626 821606
Open: Easter to Oct

Newton Poppleford

SY0889

▲ **Popplefords,** Newton Poppleford, Devon, EX10 0DE
Actual Grid Ref: SY064895
Tel: 01395 568672
Open: All year

Nomansland

SS8313

▲ **West Middlewick Farm,** Nomansland, Tiverton, Devon, EX16 8NP
Actual Grid Ref: SS825138
Tel: 01884 860286
Open: All year

Northam

SS4429

▲ **Knapp House,** Churchill Way, Northam, Bideford, Devon, EX39 1NT
Actual Grid Ref: SS458294
Tel: 01237 474804
Open: Mar to Oct

MAP PAGE **54** • **Devon**

Okehampton

SX5895

▲ **Okehampton Youth Hostel,** The Goods Yard, Okehampton Station, Okehampton, Devon, EX20 1EJ
Actual Grid Ref: SX591942
Tel: 01837 53916 **Fax:** 01837 53965
Email: okehampton@yha.org.uk
Capacity: 102
Under 18: £7.75
Adults: £11.00
Open: All year, 5.00pm
Family bunk rooms Camping
Self-catering facilities • Showers • Showers • Licensed bar • Laundry facilities • Laundry facilities • Lounge • Lounge • Parking • Evening meal available 7.00pm • No smoking • WC • WC • Kitchen facilities • Kitchen facilities • Credit cards accepted
Converted Victorian railway goods shed on northern edge of Dartmoor National Park.

▲ **Yertiz Caravan & Camping Park,** Exeter Road, Okehampton, Devon, EX20 1QF
Actual Grid Ref: SX601954
AA grade: 3 Pennants
Tel: 01837 52281
Email: yertiz@dial.pipex.com
Tent pitches: 15
Tent rate: £3.50-£6.50
Open: All year
Last arr: 11pm
Facilities for disabled people • Dogs allowed • Electric hook-up • Calor Gas/Camping Gaz • Picnic/barbecue area on site • Children's play area • Showers • Laundrette on site • Public phone on site
Small friendly site. Good views, local walks. Holiday vans available.

▲ **Moorcroft Leisure Park,** Exeter Road, Okehampton, Devon, EX20 1QF
Actual Grid Ref: SX603954
Tel: 01837 55116
Open: All year

▲ **Bundu Camping & Caravan Park,** Stourton Cross, Okehampton, Devon, EX20 4HT
Actual Grid Ref: SX546916
Tel: 01837 831611
Open: Mar to Nov

Paignton

SX8960

▲ **Marine Park Caravan & Camping Park,** Goodrington Road, Paignton, Devon, TQ4 7JE
Actual Grid Ref: SX888582
Tel: 01803 843887
Open: Mar to Oct

▲ **Byslades Camping Park,** Totnes Rd, Paignton, Devon, TQ4 7PY
Actual Grid Ref: SX846603
Tel: 01803 555072
Open: Mar to Oct

▲ **Holly Gruit Camp,** Brixham Road, Paignton, Devon, TQ4 7BA
Actual Grid Ref: SX876586
Tel: 01803 550763
Open: Jun to Sep

▲ **Lower Yalberton Holiday Park,** Long Road, Lower Yalberton, Paignton, Devon, TQ4 7PQ
Actual Grid Ref: SX863586
Tel: 01803 558127
Fax: 01803 558127
Open: May to Sep

▲ **Whitehill Farm Holiday Park,** Stoke Road, Paignton, Devon, TQ4 7PF
Actual Grid Ref: SX857588
Tel: 01803 782338
Fax: 01803 782722
Open: May to Sep

▲ **Barton Pines Inn,** Blagdon Road, Paignton, Devon, TQ3 3YG
Actual Grid Ref: SX846614
Tel: 01803 553350
Open: Mar to Sept

▲ **Paignton Holiday Park,** Totnes Road, Paignton, Devon, TQ4 7PW
Actual Grid Ref: SX855601
Tel: 01803 550504
Open: Mar to Oct

Parracombe

SS6644

▲ **Lorna Doone Farm,** Parracombe, Barnstaple, Devon, EX31 4RJ
Tel: 01598 763262
Open: Mar to Oct

Plymouth

SX4756

▲ **Plymouth Youth Hostel,** Belmont House, Devonport Road, Stoke, Plymouth, Devon, PL3 4DW
Actual Grid Ref: SX461555
Tel: 01752 562189
Fax: 01752 605360
Email: plymouth@yha.org.uk
Capacity: 62

Under 18: £7.75
Adults: £11.00
Open: Jan to Dec (not New Year), 5.00pm
Self-catering facilities • Television • Showers • Wet weather shelter • Lounge • Games room • Drying room • Cycle store • Parking • Evening meal available 7.00pm • Kitchen facilities • Breakfast available • Luggage store • Credit cards accepted
Classical Greek-style house built in 1820 for a wealthy banker, set in own grounds, within easy walking distance of the city centre.

Plympton

SX5455

▲ **Riverside Caravan Park,** Longbridge Rd, Marsh Mills, Plympton, Plymouth, Devon, PL6 8LD
Actual Grid Ref: SX517575
Tel: 01752 344122
Open: All year

▲ **Smithaleigh Caravan & Camping Park,** Smithaleigh, Plympton, Plymouth, Devon, PL7 5AX
Tel: 01752 893194
Open: All year

Poundsgate

SX7072

▲ **Lower Aish Guest House,** Poundsgate, Ashburton, Newton Abbot, Devon, TQ13 7NY
Actual Grid Ref: SX705722
Tel: 01364 631229
Open: Mar to Oct

Princetown

SX5873

▲ **The Plume of Feathers Inn,** Princetown, Yelverton, Devon, PL20 6QG
Actual Grid Ref: SX591734
Tel: 01822 890240
Open: All year

Pyworthy

SS3103

▲ **Little Knowle Farm,** Pyworthy, Holsworthy, Devon, EX22 6JY
Tel: 01409 254642
Open: All year

Stilwell's Hostels & Camping 2002

Devon • MAP PAGE 54

ENGLAND

Rattery
SX7461

▲ **Edeswell Farm Country Caravan Park,** Edeswell Farm, Rattery, South Brent, Devon, TQ10 9LN
Actual Grid Ref: SX729607
Tel: 01364 72177 **Open:** Mar to Oct

Rewe
SX9499

▲ **Heazillie Barton,** Rewe, Exeter, Devon, EX5 4HB
Actual Grid Ref: SS954004
Tel: 01392 860253
Open: Apr to Oct

Romansleigh
SS7220

▲ **Romansleigh Holiday Park,** Odam Hill, Romansleigh, South Molton, Devon, EX36 4NB
Actual Grid Ref: SS740199
Tel: 01769 550259
Open: Mar to Oct

Rousdon
SY2991

▲ **Shrubbery Caravan Park,** Rousdon, Lyme Regis, Dorset, DT7 3XW
Actual Grid Ref: SY296914
Tel: 01297 442227
Open: Mar to Nov

▲ **West Hayes Caravan Park,** Rousdon, Lyme Regis, Dorset, DT7 3RD
Actual Grid Ref: SY285919
Tel: 01297 23456
Open: All year

Salcombe Regis
SY1589

▲ **Kings Down Tail Caravan & Camping Park,** Salcombe Regis, Sidmouth, Devon, EX10 0PD
Actual Grid Ref: SY172908
Tel: 01297 680313
Open: Mar to Nov

▲ **Salcombe Regis Caravan & Camping Park,** Salcombe Regis, Sidmouth, Devon, EX10 0JH
Actual Grid Ref: SY149892
Tel: 01395 514303
Open: Apr to Oct

Sampford Courtenay
SS6301

▲ **Culverhayes Caravan & Camping Site,** Sampford Courtenay, Okehampton, Devon, EX20 2TG
Actual Grid Ref: SS629010
Tel: 01837 82431
Open: Mar to Oct

Sampford Peverell
ST0314

▲ **Minnows Camping & Caravan Park,** Sampford Peverell, Tiverton, Devon, EX16 7EN
Actual Grid Ref: ST042148
Tel: 01884 821770
Open: Mar to Jan

Seaton
SY2490

▲ **Manor Farm Camping & Caravan Site,** Seaton Down Hill, Seaton, Devon, EX12 2JA
Actual Grid Ref: SY236917
Tel: 01297 21524
Open: Mar to Oct

Shaldon
SX9372

▲ **Coast View Holiday Park,** Torquay Road, Shaldon, Teignmouth, Devon, TQ14 0BG
Actual Grid Ref: SX932720
Tel: 01626 872392
Fax: 01626 872719
Open: Mar to Oct

Sharpitor
SX7237

▲ **Salcombe Youth Hostel,** Overbecks, Sharpitor, Salcombe, Devon, TQ8 8LW
Actual Grid Ref: SX728374
Tel: 01548 842856
Fax: 01548 843865
Capacity: 51

Under 18: £6.20
Adults: £9.15
Open: Apr to Oct, 5.00pm
Family bunk rooms
Self-catering facilities • Television • Showers • Lounge • Drying room • Cycle store • Evening meal available 7.00pm • No smoking • Kitchen facilities • Breakfast available • Credit cards accepted
Large house in NT semi-tropical gardens on the cliff just before Sharpitor Rocks, overlooking estuary and sea.

Shaugh Prior
SX5462

▲ **Huxton Farm,** Shaugh Prior, Plymouth, Devon, PL7 5EQ
Actual Grid Ref: SX546629
Tel: 01752 839484
Open: All year

Sidmouth
SY1287

▲ **Oakdown Touring & Holiday Home Park,** Sidmouth, Devon, EX10 0PH
Actual Grid Ref: SY167903
Tel: 01297 680387
Open: Apr to Oct

Slapton
SX8245

▲ **Camping & Caravanning Club Site,** Middle Grounds, Slapton, Kingsbridge, Devon, TQ7 1QW
Actual Grid Ref: SX825450
Tel: 01548 580538
Open: Mar to Oct

▲ **Newlands Farm Camp Site,** Slapton, Kingsbridge, Devon, TQ7 2RB
Tel: 01548 580366
Open: May to Sep

Soar
SX7137

▲ **Sun Park Caravan & Camping Park,** Soar Mill Cove, Soar, Malborough, Kingsbridge, Devon, TQ7 3DS
Actual Grid Ref: SX708378
Tel: 01548 561378
Open: Apr to Oct

Hostels and campsites may vary rates – be sure to check when booking.

MAP PAGE 54 • **Devon**

South Brent

SX6960

Cheston Caravan Park , Wrangaton Road, South Brent, Devon, TQ10 9HF
Actual Grid Ref: SX684585
Tel: 01364 72586
Open: Mar to Nov

Great Palstone Caravan Park, South Brent, Devon, TA19 9JP
Actual Grid Ref: SX705601
Tel: 01364 72227
Open: Mar to Nov

St Giles on the Heath

SX3590

Chapmanswell Caravan Park, St Giles-on-the-Heath, Launceston, Cornwall, PL15 9SG
Actual Grid Ref: SX354931
Tel: 01409 211382
Open: Mar to Oct

Starcross

SX9781

Cofton Country Holiday Park, Starcross, Dawlish, Devon, EX6 8RP
Actual Grid Ref: SX968804
Tel: 01626 890111
Fax: 01626 891572
Open: Apr to Oct

Sticklepath

SX6394

Olditch Caravan & Camping Park, Sticklepath, Okehampton, Devon, EX20 2NT
Actual Grid Ref: SX645934
Tourist Board grade: 3 Star
AA grade: 3 Pennants
Tel: 01837 840734
Fax: 01837 840877
Email: info@olditch.co.uk
Tent pitches: 35
Tent rate: £7.00-£9.00
Open: Mar to Nov
Last arr: 9pm
Dogs allowed • Electric hook-up • Calor Gas/Camping Gaz • Cafe or Takeaway on site • Picnic/barbecue area on site • Children's play area • Showers • Laundrette on site • Public phone on site Quiet site in Dartmoor National Park - static vans for hire.

Stoke Fleming

SX8648

Deer Park Holiday Estate, Stoke Fleming, Dartmouth, Devon, TQ6 0RF
Actual Grid Ref: SX865492
Tel: 01803 770253
Open: Mar to Oct

Leonards Cove Holiday Park, Stoke Fleming, Dartmouth, Devon, TQ6 0NR
Actual Grid Ref: SX863482
Tel: 01803 770206
Open: Mar to Oct

Stoke Gabriel

SX8457

Ramslade Touring Park, Stoke Rd, Stoke Gabriel, Totnes, Devon, TQ9 6QB
Actual Grid Ref: SX856583
Tel: 01803 782575
Open: Mar to Oct

Higher Well Farm Holiday Park, Stoke Gabriel, Totnes, Devon, TQ9 6RN
Actual Grid Ref: SX857577
Tel: 01803 782289
Open: Mar to Oct

Stokenham

SX8042

Old Cotmore Touring Caravan & Touring Camping Park, Stokenham, Kingsbridge, Devon, TQ7 2LR
Actual Grid Ref: SX804417
Tel: 01548 580240
Open: Mar to Nov

Tavistock

SX4874

Langstone Manor Camping & Caravan Park, Moortown, Tavistock, Devon, PL19 9JZ
Actual Grid Ref: SX524738
Tel: 01922 613371
Open: Mar to Nov

Woodovis Holiday Park, Tavistock, Devon, PL19 8NY
Actual Grid Ref: SX432744
Tel: 01822 832968
Open: Mar to Dec

Higher Longford Farm, Moorshop, Tavistock, Devon, PL19 9JY
Actual Grid Ref: SX518747
Tel: 01822 613360
Fax: 01822 618722
Open: All year

Langstone Manor Caravan & Camping Park, Moortown, Tavistock, Devon, PL11 9TZ
Actual Grid Ref: SX525738
Tel: 01822 613371
Open: Mar to Nov

Tedburn St Mary

SX8194

Springfield Holiday Park, Tedburn Rd, Tedburn St Mary, Exeter, Devon, EX6 6EW
Actual Grid Ref: SX788937
Tel: 01647 24242
Open: Mar to Oct

Teigngrace

SX8473

Compass Caravans, Higher Brock Plantation, Teigngrace, Newton Abbot, Devon, TQ12 6QZ
Actual Grid Ref: SX836756
Tel: 01626 832792
Open: All year

Twelve Oaks Farm, Teigngrace, Newton Abbot, Devon, TQ12 6QT
Actual Grid Ref: SX852737
Tel: 01626 352769
Open: All year

Tiverton

SS9512

Zeacombe House Caravan Site, East Ansley, Tiverton, Devon, EX16 9JU
Actual Grid Ref: SS860240
Tel: 01398 341279
Open: Mar to Nov

Topsham Bridge

SX7651

Yeo Farm, Topsham Bridge, Woodleigh, Kingsbridge, Devon, TQ7 4DR
Actual Grid Ref: SX733513
Tel: 01548 550586
Open: Apr to Oct

ENGLAND

Stilwell's Hostels & Camping 2002   65

Devon • MAP PAGE 54

ENGLAND

Torquay
SX9165

▲ **Torquay International Backpackers Hostel,** Torquay International Backpackers, 119 Abbey Road, Torquay, Devon, TQ2 5NP
Tel: 01803 299924
Fax: 01803 213479
Email: torquay.backpackers@btinternet.com
Capacity: 46
Under 18: £6.50-£8.00
Adults: £6.50-£9.00
Open: All year, 9am
Family bunk rooms: £28.00
Self-catering facilities • Television • Central heating • Shop • Laundry facilities • Wet weather shelter • Lounge • Dining room • Security lockers • Cycle store • Parking
Centrally located less than 10 minutes from beach and harbour.

Uffculme
ST0612

▲ **Waterloo Inn Caravan & Camping Site,** Waterloo Cross, Uffculme, Cullompton, Devon, EX15 3ES
Actual Grid Ref: ST055139
Tel: 01884 841342
Open: Mar to Jan

Umberleigh
SS6123

▲ **Camping & Caravanning Club Site,** Over Weir, Umberleigh, Devon, EX37 9DU
Actual Grid Ref: SS606242
Tel: 01769 560009
Open: Mar to Sept

Uplyme
SY3293

▲ **Uplyme Touring Park,** Gole Lane, Uplyme, Lyme Regis, Dorset, DT7 3UU
Actual Grid Ref: SY322929
Tel: 01297 442801 **Fax:** 01297 442801
Tent pitches: 100
Tent rate: £7.00-£9.00
Open: All year
Facilities for disabled people • Dogs allowed • Electric hook-up • Calor Gas/Camping Gaz • Children's play area • Showers • Laundrette on site • Public phone on site • Shop on site
Quiet campsite set in an Area of Outstanding Natural Beauty.

▲ **Cannington Farm,** Cannington Lane, Uplyme, Lyme Regis, Dorset, DT7 3SW
Tel: 01297 443172 **Fax:** 01297 445005
Open: All year

Uton
SX8298

▲ **Salmonhutch Fishery,** Uton, Crediton, Devon, EX17 3QL
Actual Grid Ref: SX827989
Tel: 01363 772749
Open: All year

Venton (Whiddon Down)
SX6991

▲ **Woodland Springs Touring Park,** Venton, Drewsteignton, Exeter, Devon, EX6 6PG
Actual Grid Ref: SX694912
Tel: 01647 231695
Open: Mar to Nov

Watermouth
SS5547

▲ **Big Meadow Caravan & Camping Park,** Watermouth, Ilfracombe, Devon, EX34 9SJ
Actual Grid Ref: SS559478
Tel: 01271 862282
Open: Easter to Nov

Weare Giffard
SS4721

▲ **Sea Lock Camping Barn & Tent Site,** Vale Cottage, 7 Annery Kiln, Weare Giffard, Bideford, Devon, EX39 5JE
Tel: 01237 477705 / 07866 026194
Email: ahwills@annerykiln.freeserve.co.uk
Capacity: 16
Under 18: £5.00
Adults: £5.00
Open: All year
Family bunk rooms: £25.00
Camping for 12 tents: £6.50
Self-catering facilities • Showers • Parking • Facilities for disabled people
Newly converted barn, offering basic accommodation, in beautiful, tranquil wooded valley overlooking River Torridge, between Bideford and Torrington. Private access to Tarka Trail (NCN 3) and conservation area. Superb walking, cycling, canoeing, fishing, birdwatching. Pubs/shops within 2.5 miles. Book individual beds/family rooms (sharing facilities) or sole use.

▲ **Vale Cottage,** Weare Giffard, Bideford, Devon, EX39 5JE
Tel: 01237 477705
Open: All year

West Down
SS5142

▲ **Hidden Valley Coast & Country Park,** West Down, Ilfracombe, Devon, EX34 8NU
Actual Grid Ref: SS499408
Tel: 01271 813837
Open: Mar to Nov

▲ **Twitchen Farm,** West Down, Ilfracombe, Devon, EX34 8NP
Actual Grid Ref: SS509439
Tel: 01271 862720
Open: All year

Whiddon Down
SX6892

▲ **Dartmoor View Holiday Park,** Whiddon Down, Okehampton, Devon, EX20 2QL
Actual Grid Ref: SX683926
Tourist Board grade: 5 Star
AA grade: 5 Pennants
Tel: 01647 231545
Fax: 01647 231654
Email: jo@dartmoorview.co.uk
Tent pitches: 30
Tent rate: £4.75-£9.50
Open: Mar to Nov
Last arr: 10pm
Dogs allowed • Electric hook-up • Calor Gas/Camping Gaz • Picnic/barbecue area on site • Children's play area • Showers • Laundrette on site • Public phone on site • Licensed bar on site • Shop on site • Baby care facilities • TV room • Games room • Outdoor swimming pool on site • Boating/sailing/watersports nearby • Tennis courts nearby • Golf nearby • Riding nearby • Fishing nearby
Superb 5 Star family-run park located on the northern edge of Dartmoor National Park. Good base for exploring Devon and Cornwall. Excellent pubs and restaurants close by. Riding, cycling, fishing and walking on Dartmoor. Easy access from M5 via A30. Pets welcome.

Some hostels and campsites impose restrictions on size and type of groups they accept (e.g. not permitting single-sex groups). Always phone to enquire before booking.

MAP PAGE 54 • **Devon**

Widecombe in the Moor

SX7176

▲ **Dartmoor Expedition Centre,** Rowden Farm, Widecombe in the Moor, Newton Abbot, Devon, TQ13 7TX
Actual Grid Ref: SX699764
Tel: 01364 621249
Fax: 01364621249
Email: earle@clara.co.uk
Capacity: 35
Under 18: £7.00
Adults: £7.00
Open: All year, 7am-11pm
Family bunk rooms: £8.00
Camping for 10 tents: £5.00
Self-catering facilities • Showers • Central heating • Dining room • Drying room • Parking • Evening meal available 6.30 pm • No smoking
Bunkhouses on Dartmoor Farm at 1,000 feet in remote moorland.

▲ **Cockingford Farm,** Widecombe-in-the-Moor, Newton Abbott, Devon, TQ13 7TG
Actual Grid Ref: SX718751
Tel: 01364 621258
Open: Apr to Oct

Wilmington

ST2000

▲ **The Crest Guest House,** Moorcox Lane, Wilmington, Honiton, Devon, EX14 9JU
Tel: 01404 831419
Open: Mar to Oct

Winkleigh

SS6307

▲ **Wagon Wheels Holiday Park,** Winkleigh, Devon, EX19 8DP
Actual Grid Ref: SS624089
Tel: 01837 83456
Open: Mar to Sept

Please respect hostels' policy on smoking. Some hostels do not allow smoking anywhere, some restrict smoking to certain areas.

Woodbury

SY0187

▲ **Webbers Farm Caravan & Camping Site,** Castle Lane, Woodbury, Exeter, Devon, EX5 1EA
Actual Grid Ref: SY018874
Tourist Board grade: 5 Star
AA grade: 3 Pennants
Tel: 01395 232276
Fax: 01395 233389
Email: reception@webbersfarm.co.uk
Tent pitches: 115
Tent rate: £8.00-£11.00
Open: Apr to Sep
Last arr: 9pm
Facilities for disabled people • Dogs allowed • Electric hook-up • Baths • Picnic/barbecue area on site • Children's play area • Showers • Laundrette on site • Public phone on site • Shop on site • Baby care facilities
Space to relax. Friendly natives. Short stroll to village pubs.

▲ **Castle Brake Holiday Park,** Woodbury, Exeter, Devon, Ex5 1HA
Actual Grid Ref: SY028879
Tel: 01395 232431
Open: Mar to Oct

Woodbury Salterton

SY0189

▲ **Browns Farm,** Woodbury Salterton, Exeter, Devon, EX5 1PS
Actual Grid Ref: SY014884
Tel: 01395 232895
Open: All year

Woolacombe

SS4543

▲ **Golden Coast Holiday Village,** Station Rd, Woolacombe, Devon, EX34 7HW
Actual Grid Ref: SS481373
Tel: 01271 870343
Email: goodtimes@woolacombe-bay.co.uk
Open: Mar to Oct

▲ **Woolacombe Sands Holiday Park,** Beach Rd, Woolacombe, Devon, EX34 7AF
Actual Grid Ref: SS463438
Tel: 01271 870569
Email: lifesabeach@woolacombe-sands.co.uk
Open: Mar to Oct

▲ **Europa Park,** Station Road, Woolacombe, Devon, EX34 7AN
Actual Grid Ref: SS464438
Tel: 01271 870159
Open: Apr to Oct

▲ **Little Roadway Farm Camping Park,** Woolacombe, Devon, EX34 7HL
Tel: 01271 870313
Open: Mar to Oct

▲ **Woolacombe Bay Holiday Village,** Sandy Lane, Woolacombe, Devon, EX34 7AH
Tel: 01271 870221
Open: Easter to Oct

Yettington

SY0585

▲ **St Johns Farm,** Yettington, Budleigh Salterton, Devon, EX9 7BP
Tel: 01395 263170
Open: All year

ENGLAND

Dorset

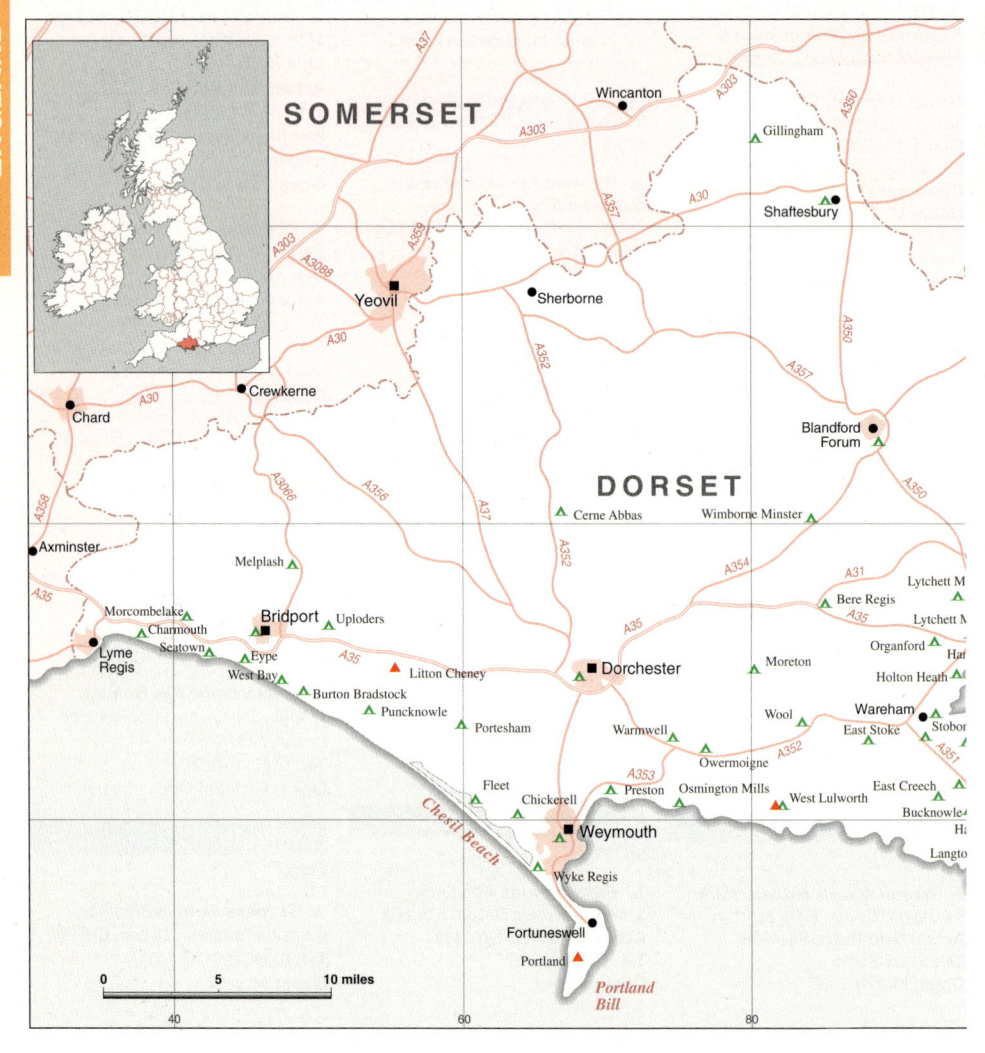

Bere Regis

SY8494

▲ **Rowlands Wait Touring Park,** Rye Hill, Bere Regis, Wareham, Dorset, BH20 7LP
Actual Grid Ref: SY845937
Tel: 01929 471958
Email: rwtp@btinternet.com
Open: Mar to Jan

Blandford Forum

ST8806

▲ **Inside Park Caravan & Camping,** Blandford Forum, Dorset, DT11 9AP
Actual Grid Ref: ST864045
Tel: 01258 453719 **Fax:** 01258 459921
Email: inspark@aol.com
Open: Apr to Oct

Bridport

SY4693

▲ **The Traveller's Rest Inn,** Dorchester Road, Bridport, Dorset, DT6 4PJ
Tel: 01308 423270
Open: Mar to Oct

Dorset

▲ **Freshwater Beach Holiday Park,** Burton Bradstock, Bridport, Dorset, DT6 4PT
Actual Grid Ref: SY480898
Tel: 01308 897317
Fax: 01308 897336
Open: Mar to Oct

Cerne Abbas

ST6601

▲ **Giant's Head Caravan & Camping Park,** Giant's Head Farm, Old Sherborne Rd, Cerne Abbas, Dorchester, Dorset, DT2 7TR
Actual Grid Ref: ST675029
Tel: 01300 341242
Open: Apr to Oct

▲ **Lyons Gate Caravan & Camping Park,** Lyons Gate, Cerne Abbas, Dorchester, Dorset, DT2 7AZ
Actual Grid Ref: ST663064
Tel: 01300 345260
Open: Mar to Oct

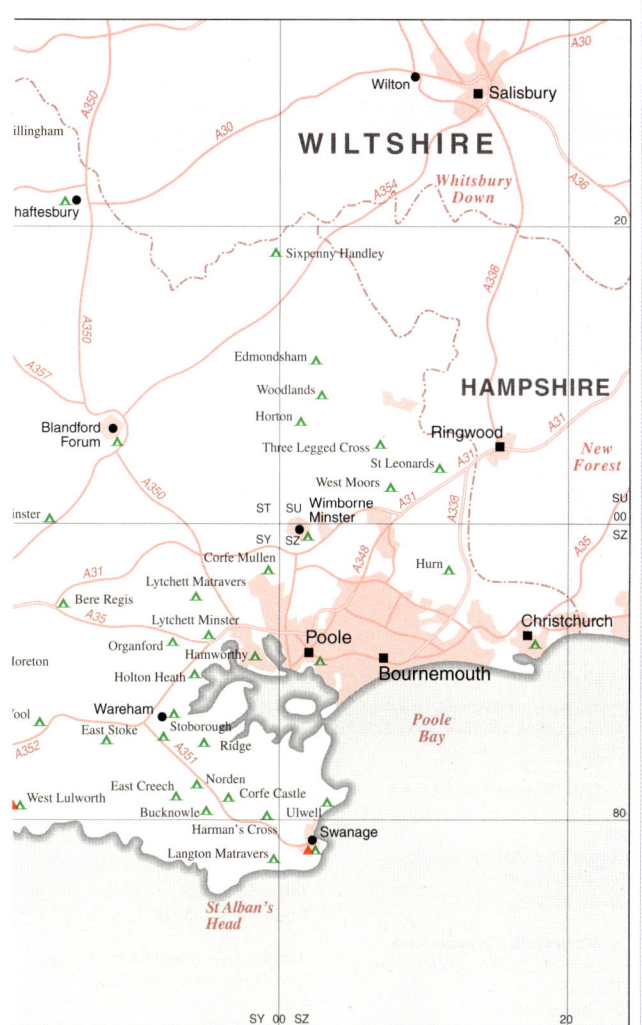

Charmouth

SY3693

▲ **Manor Farm Holiday Centre,** Charmouth, Bridport, Dorset, DT6 6QL
Actual Grid Ref: SY368937
Tel: 01297 560226
Fax: 01297 560429
Tent pitches: 300
Tent rate: £8.00-£11.00
Open: All year
Last arr: 10pm
Facilities for disabled people • Dogs allowed • Electric hook-up • Calor Gas/Camping Gaz • Cafe or Takeaway on site • Children's play area • Showers • Laundrette on site • Public phone on site • Licensed bar on site • Shop on site • Baby care facilities
10 minutes' level walk from beach, groups catered for.

▲ **Wood Farm Caravan & Camping Park,** Axminster Rd, Charmouth, Bridport, Dorset, DT6 6BT
Actual Grid Ref: SY354942
Tel: 01297 560697 **Fax:** 01297 560697
Email: i.pointing@zetnet.co.uk
Open: Apr to Oct

▲ **Camping & Caravanning Club Site,** Monkton Wylde Farm, Charmouth, Bridport, Dorset, DT6 6DB
Tel: 01297 32965
Open: Mar to Oct

Bucknowle

SY9481

▲ **Woodland Caravan & Camping Park,** Glebe Farm, Bucknowle, Wareham, Dorset, BH20 5NS
Actual Grid Ref: SY950819
Tel: 01929 480280
Open: Easter to Oct

Burton Bradstock

SY4889

▲ **Coastal Caravans,** Annings Lane, Burton Bradstock, Bridport, Dorset, DT6 4QP
Tel: 01308 897361
Open: May to Oct

Dorset • MAP PAGE 68

ENGLAND

▲ **Newlands Camping & Caravan Park,** Charmouth, Bridport, Dorset, DT6 6RB
Actual Grid Ref: SY375935
Tel: 01297 560787
Open: All year

Chickerell
SY6480

▲ **Bagwell Farm Touring Park,** Chickerell, Weymouth, Dorset, DT3 4EA
Actual Grid Ref: SY623815
Tel: 01305 782575
Open: All year

▲ **East Fleet Farm Touring Park,** Chickerell, Weymouth, Dorset, DT3 4DW
Actual Grid Ref: SY640797
Tel: 01305 785768
Email: camping@easfleet.abel.co.uk
Open: Mar to Jan

Christchurch
SZ1693

▲ **Grove Farm Meadow,** Holiday Park, Christchurch, Dorset, BH23 2PQ
Actual Grid Ref: SZ136946
Tel: 01202 483597 **Fax:** 01202 483878
Open: Mar to Oct

▲ **Hoburne Park,** Hoburne Lane, Christchurch, BH23 4HU
Actual Grid Ref: SZ194936
Tel: 01425 273379
Email: enquiries@hoburne.co.uk
Open: Mar to Oct

Corfe Castle
SY9682

▲ **Knitson Tourers Site,** Knitson Farm, Corfe Castle, Wareham, Dorset, BH20 5JB
Actual Grid Ref: SZ010801
Tel: 01929 425121 **Open:** Apr to Oct

▲ **Burnbake Campsite,** Rempstone, Corfe Castle, Wareham, Dorset, BH20 5JJ
Tel: 01929 480570
Open: Apr to Sep

▲ **Downshay Farm,** Haycrafts Lane, Harmans Cross, Corfe Castle, Wareham, Dorset, BH19 3EB
Tel: 01929 480316
Open: July to Aug

▲ **Norden Farm,** Corfe Castle, Wareham, Dorset, BH20 5DS
Tel: 01929 480348
Open: Mar to Oct

▲ **Burnbake Campsite,** Old Farm House, Rempstone, Corfe Castle, Dorset, BH20 5JH
Actual Grid Ref: SY994833
Tel: 01929 480317
Open: Apr to Sep

▲ **Woodhyde Farm,** Corfe Castle, Wareham, Dorset, BH20 5HT
Actual Grid Ref: SY974804
Tel: 01929 480274
Open: Apr to Oct

Corfe Mullen
SY9897

▲ **Charris Camping & Caravan Park,** Candy's Lane, Corfe Mullen, Wimborne Minster, Dorset, BH21 3EF
Actual Grid Ref: SY992988
Tel: 01202 885970
Open: Mar to Oct

▲ **Springfield Touring Park,** Candy's Lane, Corfe Mullen, Wimborne Minster, Dorset, BH21 3EF
Actual Grid Ref: SY991988
Tel: 01202 881719
Open: Mar to Oct

Dorchester
SY6890

▲ **Clay Pigeon Tourist Park,** Wardon Hill, Dorchester, Dorset, DT2 9PW
Actual Grid Ref: ST608028
Tel: 01935 83492
Open: All year

▲ **Morn Gate Caravan Park,** Bridport Road, Dorchester, Dorset, DT2 9DS
Tel: 01305 889284
Open: Mar to Jan

▲ **Maiden Castle Farm,** Dorchester, Dorset, DT2 9PR
Tel: 01305 262356
Fax: 01305 251085
Open: All year

You are advised to book in advance for periods of high demand – the Summer months, Half Term holidays and public holidays.

East Creech
SY9282

▲ **East Creech Farm Caravan & Camping Site,** East Creech, Wareham, Dorset, BH20 5AP
Actual Grid Ref: SY928827
Tel: 01929 480519
Open: Mar to Oct

East Stoke
SY8786

▲ **Woodlands Camping Park,** Bindon Lane, East Stoke, Wareham, Dorset, BH20 6AS
Actual Grid Ref: SY867861
Tel: 01929 462327
Fax: 01929 462 327
Tent pitches: 40
Tent rate: £4.00
Open: Mar to Sept
Last arr: 9pm
Facilities for disabled people • Dogs allowed • Calor Gas/Camping Gaz • Showers • Laundrette on site • Shop on site • Indoor swimming pool nearby • Boating/sailing/watersports nearby • Golf nearby • Riding nearby • Fishing nearby
Essentially a quiet family site in a secluded woodland setting, well-drained, level pitches. Ideally situated for touring the Purbecks. Positioned along a quiet country lane which is part of Purbeck cycleway. Lulworth Cove and Durdle Door within 15 minutes' drive.

▲ **Manor Farm Caravan Park,** 1 Manor Farm Cottage, East Stoke, Wareham, Dorset, BH20 6AW
Actual Grid Ref: SY870865
Tel: 01929 462870
Open: Mar to Sept

▲ **Luckford Wood Farm House,** East Stoke, Wareham, Dorset, BH20 6AW
Tel: 01929 463098
Fax: 01929 405715
Open: Easter to Oct

Edmondsham
SU0611

▲ **Hillside Camping & Caravan Site,** Hillside, Nellys Lane, Edmondsham, Verwwod, Dorset, BH21 5QY
Tel: 01202 824460
Open: Easter to Nov

MAP PAGE 68 • **Dorset**

Eype

SY4491

▲ **Eype House Caravan & Camping Park,** Eype, Bridport, Dorset, DT6 6AL
Actual Grid Ref: SY446912
Tel: 01308 424903
Open: Apr to Oct

▲ **Highlands End Farm Caravan Park,** Seatown, Chideock, Bridport, Dorset, DT6 6JX
Actual Grid Ref: SY453915
Tel: 01308 422139 **Fax:** 01308 425672
Open: Mar to Oct

Fleet

SY6380

▲ **West Fleet Holiday Farm,** Fleet, Weymouth, Dorset, DT3 4EF
Actual Grid Ref: SY625810
Tel: 01305 782218
Open: Mar to Oct

▲ **Sea Barn Farm Campsite,** Fleet, Weymouth, Dorset, DT3 4EF
Actual Grid Ref: SY626806
Tel: 01305 782218
Open: Mar to Oct

Gillingham

ST8026

▲ **Thorngrove Caravan & Camping Park,** Common Mead Lane, Gillingham, Dorset, SP8 4RE
Actual Grid Ref: ST794258
Tel: 01747 822242
Open: All year

Hamworthy

SY9991

▲ **Rockley Park,** Hamworthy, Poole, Dorset, BH15 4LZ
Actual Grid Ref: SY980913
Tel: 01202 679393
Open: Mar to Oct

Harman's Cross

SY9880

▲ **Flower Meadow Caravan & Camping Park,** Haycrafts Lane, Harman's Cross, Swanage, Dorset, BH19 3EB
Actual Grid Ref: SY983802
Tel: 01929 480035
Open: Apr to Oct

▲ **Haycrafts Caravan & Camping Park,** Haycrafts Lane, Harman's Cross, Swanage, Dorset, BH19 3EB
Tel: 01929 480572
Open: Easter to Sep

Holton Heath

SY9490

▲ **Sandfor Holiday Park,** Holton Heath, Poole, Dorset, BH16 6JZ
Actual Grid Ref: SY940912
Tel: 01202 631600 **Open:** Mar to Jan

▲ **Holton Lee,** East Holton, Holton Heath, Poole, Dorset, BH16 6JN
Tel: 01202 631063 **Fax:** 01202 631063
Open: All year

Horton

SU0307

▲ **Meadow View Touring Caravan Park,** Wigbeth, Horton, Wimborne, Dorset, BH21 7JH
Actual Grid Ref: SU044073
Tel: 01258 840536
Open: All year

Hurn

SZ1397

▲ **Mount Pleasant Touring Park,** Matchams Lane, Hurn, Christchurch, Dorset, BH23 6AW
Actual Grid Ref: SZ129987
Tel: 01202 475474 **Open:** Mar to Oct

▲ **Port View Caravan & Camping Park,** Matchams Lane, Hurn, Christchurch, Dorset, BH23 6AW
Actual Grid Ref: SZ129991
Tel: 01202 474214
Open: Mar to Oct

▲ **Heathfield,** Avon Causeway, Hurn, Christchurch, Dorset, BH23 6AS
Actual Grid Ref: SZ137975
Tel: 01202 485208
Open: Mar to Oct

Langton Matravers

SY9978

▲ **Tom's Field Camping,** Tom's Field Road, Langton Matravers, Swanage, Dorset, BH19 3HN
Actual Grid Ref: SY995786
Tel: 01929 427110
Open: Mar to Oct

▲ **Acton Field Camping Site,** Acton Field, Langton Matravers, Swanage, Dorset, BH19 3JA
Actual Grid Ref: SY994786
Tel: 01929 424184
Open: Jul to Aug

Litton Cheney

SY5590

▲ **Litton Cheney Youth Hostel,** Litton Cheney, Dorchester, Dorset, DT2 9AT
Actual Grid Ref: SY548900
Tel: 01308 482340
Fax: 01308 482636
Email: reservations@yha.org.uk
Capacity: 22
Under 18: £6.90
Adults: £10.00
Open: All year, 5.00pm
Family bunk rooms
Self-catering facilities • Showers • Lounge • Drying room • Cycle store • Parking Limited • No smoking • Kitchen facilities • Credit cards accepted
Traditional Dutch barn in the Bride Valley, once a cheese factory. This is an Area of Outstanding Natural Beauty.

Lytchett Matravers

SY9495

▲ **Huntick Farm,** Huntick Road, Lytchett Matravers, Poole, Dorset, BH16 6BB
Actual Grid Ref: SY956949
Tel: 01202 622222
Open: Apr to Sep

Lytchett Minster

SY9693

▲ **South Lychett Manor Caravan Park,** Lytchett Minster, Poole, Dorset, BH16 6JB
Actual Grid Ref: SY964935
Tel: 01202 622577
Open: Apr to Oct

Melplash

SY4898

▲ **Binghams Farm Touring Caravan Park,** Melplash, Bridport, Dorset, DT6 3TT
Actual Grid Ref: SY478963
Tel: 01308 488234
Email: royphilpott@msn.com
Open: All year

Dorset • MAP PAGE 68

ENGLAND

Morcombelake
SY3994

▲ **St Gabriel Camping Site,** Golden Cap Estate, Morcombelake, Bridport, Dorset, DT6 6EP
Tel: 01297 489628
Open: Apr to Sep

Moreton
SY8089

▲ **Camping & Caravanning Club Site,** Station Road, Moreton, Dorchester, Dorset, DT2 8BB
Actual Grid Ref: SY782892
Tel: 01305 853801
Open: Mar to Nov

Norden
SY9483

▲ **Catseye Cottage,** Norden, Corfe Castle, Dorset, BH20 5BT
Actual Grid Ref: SY942838
Tel: 01929 481076
Open: Apr to Sep

Organford
SY9392

▲ **Pear Tree Caravan Park,** Organford, Poole, Dorset, BH16 6LA
Actual Grid Ref: SY940915
Tel: 01202 622434
Email: enquiries@peartree-touringpark.freeserve.co.uk
Open: Apr to Oct

Osmington Mills
SY7381

▲ **Osmington Mills Holidays Ltd,** The Ranch House, Osmington Mills, Weymouth, Dorset, DT3 6HB
Actual Grid Ref: SY733822
Tel: 01305 832311
Open: Mar to Oct

Owermoigne
SY7685

▲ **Sandyholme Caravan Park,** Moreton Rd, Owermoigne, Dorchester, Dorset, DT2 8HZ
Actual Grid Ref: SY768867
Tel: 01305 852677
Open: Apr to Oct

Poole
SZ0191

▲ **Beacon Hill Touring Park,** Blandford Road North, Poole, Dorset, BH16 6AB
Actual Grid Ref: SY975940
Tel: 01202 631631
Open: Apr to Sep

▲ **Organford Manor Caravans & Holidays,** Poole, Dorset, BH16 6ES
Actual Grid Ref: SY945925
Tel: 01202 622202
Open: Mar to Oct

Portesham
SY6085

▲ **Portesham Dairy Farm Campsite,** Bramdon Laane, Portesham, Weymouth, Dorset, DT3 4HG
Actual Grid Ref: SY603855
Tel: 01305 871297
Open: Apr to Oct

Portland
SY6874

▲ **Portland Bird Observatory,** Old Lower Light, Portland, Dorset, DT5 2JT
Actual Grid Ref: SY681690
Tel: 01305 820553
Email: obs@btinternet.com
Capacity: 26
Under 18: £9.00
Adults: £9.00
Open: Mar to Oct
Self-catering facilities • Showers • Lounge • Parking • No smoking
Superb situation in restored lighthouse at Portland Bill.

▲ **Portland Youth Hostel,** Hardy House, Castletown, Portland, Dorset, DT5 1BJ
Tel: 01305 861368
Fax: 01305 861568
Email: portland@yha.org.uk
Capacity: 28
Under 18: £7.75
Adults: £11.00
Open: All year, 5.00pm
Self-catering facilities • No smoking
Due to open at Easter 2001, this former provost's house provides a good base for Chesil Beach, Portland Bill and exploring Dorset.

Preston
SY7083

▲ **Seaview Holiday Park,** Preston, Weymouth, Dorset, DT3 6DZ
Actual Grid Ref: SY710831
Tel: 01305 833037
Open: Apr to Oct

▲ **Weymouth Bay Holiday Park,** Preston, Weymouth, Dorset, DT3 6BQ
Tel: 01305 822271
Open: Easter to Oct

Puncknowle
SY5388

▲ **Home Farm Camping & Caravan Site,** Puncknowle, Dorchester, DT2 9BW
Actual Grid Ref: SY535888
Tel: 01308 897258
Tent pitches: 22
Tent rate: £4.00-£7.00
Open: Apr to Oct
Last arr: 9.30pm
Dogs allowed • Electric hook-up • Calor Gas/Camping Gaz • Children's play area • Showers • Public phone on site
Near Heritage Coast. Good touring and walking area. Sea fishing.

Ridge
SY9386

▲ **Ridge Farm Camping & Caravan Park,** Barnhill Road, Ridge, Wareham, Dorset, BH20 5BG
Actual Grid Ref: SY939867
Tel: 01929 556444
Open: Mar to Oct

▲ **Redcliffe Farm,** Ridge, Wareham, Dorset, BH20 5BE
Actual Grid Ref: SY931867
Tel: 01929 552225
Open: Mar to Oct

Seatown
SY4291

▲ **Golden Cap Caravan Park,** Eype, Bridport, Dorset, DT6 6AR
Actual Grid Ref: SY423920
Tel: 01308 422139
Fax: 01308 425672
Email: highlands@wdlh.co.uk
Open: Mar to Oct

MAP PAGE 68 • Dorset

▲ **Golden Cap Caravan Park**, Seatown, Chideock, Bridport, Dorset, DT6 6JX
Actual Grid Ref: SY422919
Tel: 01297 489341
Open: Mar to Nov

Shaftesbury
ST8622

▲ **Blackmore Vale Caravan & Camping Park**, Sherborne Causeway, Shaftesbury, Dorset, SP7 9PX
Actual Grid Ref: ST835233
Tel: 01747 85257
Open: All year

▲ **Shaftesbury Football Club**, Coppice Street, Shaftesbury, Dorset, SP7 8PE
Actual Grid Ref: ST867231
Tel: 01747 853990
Open: May to Sep

Sixpenny Handley
ST9918

▲ **Church Farm Caravan and Camping Park**, Church Farm, Sixpenny Handley, Salisbury, Wiltshire, SP5 5ND
Actual Grid Ref: ST996174
Tel: 01725 552563
Fax: 01725 552563
Tent pitches: 20
Tent rate: £3.00-£8.00
Open: All year
Last arr: 11pm
Facilities for disabled people • Dogs allowed • Electric hook-up • Calor Gas/Camping Gaz • Picnic/barbecue area on site • Children's play area • Showers
Family site, working farm, new amenity block. Excellent for touring.

St Leonards
SU1103

▲ **Camping International Holiday Park**, Atholl Lodge, 229 Ringwood Rd, St Leonards, Ringwood, Hampshire, BH24 2SD
Actual Grid Ref: SU104023
Tel: 01202 872817
Fax: 01202 861292
Open: Mar to Oct

▲ **Oakdene**, St Leonards, Ringwood, Hampshire, BH24 2RZ
Actual Grid Ref: SZ095023
Tel: 01202 875422
Open: Mar to Dec

▲ **Shamba Holiday Park**, 230 Ringwood Road, St Leonards, Ringwood, Dorset, BH24 2SB
Actual Grid Ref: SU104026
Tel: 01202 873302
Open: Mar to Oct

▲ **Oakhill Farm**, St Leonards, Ringwood, Hampshire, BH24 2SB
Tel: 01202 876968
Open: Apr to Oct

▲ **Redcote Holiday Park**, Boundary Lane, St Leonards, Ringwood, Hampshire, BH24 2SB
Tel: 01202 872742
Open: Mar to Oct

▲ **Oakdene Holiday Park**, St Leonards, Ringwood, Hampshire, BH24 2RZ
Actual Grid Ref: SU097015
Tel: 01202 648331
Email: holidays@shorefield.co.uk
Open: Mar to Jan

Stoborough
SY9286

▲ **Lookout Holiday Park**, Stoborough, Wareham, Dorset, BH20 5AZ
Actual Grid Ref: SY928855
Tel: 01929 552546
Open: Apr to Oct

Swanage
SZ0278

▲ **Swanage Youth Hostel**, Cluny, Cluny Crescent, Swanage, Dorset, BH19 2BS
Actual Grid Ref: SZ031785
Tel: 01929 422113
Fax: 01929 426327
Email: swanage@yha.org.uk
Capacity: 104
Under 18: £7.75
Adults: £11.00
Open: Feb to Oct, All day
Family bunk rooms
Self-catering facilities • Television • Showers • Laundry facilities • Lounge • Games room • Drying room • Cycle store • Parking • Evening meal available 6.15-7.15pm • Kitchen facilities • Breakfast available • Credit cards accepted
Large refurbished house built on the site of a Cluny monastery in the well-known seaside resort of the Isle of Purbeck.

▲ **Priestway Holiday Park**, Priestway, Swanage, Dorset, BH19 2RS
Tel: 01929 422747
Open: Apr to Oct

▲ **Herston Yards Farm**, Washpond Lane, Swanage, Dorset, BH19 3DJ
Tel: 01929 422932
Open: Apr to Oct

Three Legged Cross
SU0806

▲ **Woolsbridge Manor Farm Caravan Park**, Three Legged Cross, Wimborne, Dorset, BH21 6RA
Actual Grid Ref: SU099052
Tel: 01202 826369
Open: Mar to Oct

▲ **Haddons Farm Camping**, Haddons Drive, Three Legged Cross, Wimborne, Dorset, BH21 6QU
Actual Grid Ref: SU077053
Tel: 01202 822582
Open: Apr to Oct

Ulwell
SZ0281

▲ **Ulwell Cottage Caravan Park**, Ulwell Cottage, Ulwell, Swanage, Dorset, BH19 3DG
Actual Grid Ref: SZ018809
Tel: 01929 422823
Fax: 01929 421500
Open: Mar to Jan

▲ **Ulwell Farm Caravan Park**, Ulwell, Swanage, Dorset, BH19 3DG
Actual Grid Ref: SZ019809
Tel: 01929 422825
Open: Mar to Dec

Uploders
SY5093

▲ **Uploders Farm**, Uploders, Bridport, Dorset, DT6 4NZ
Tel: 01308 423380
Open: July to Aug

Some hostels and campsites impose restrictions on size and type of groups they accept (e.g. not permitting single-sex groups). Always phone to enquire before booking.

Stilwell's Hostels & Camping 2002

Dorset • MAP PAGE 68

Wareham
SY9287

▲ Wareham Forest Tourist Park,
North Trigon, Wareham, Dorset, BH20 7NZ
Actual Grid Ref: SY894913
Tourist Board grade: 5 Ticks
Tel: 01929 551393
Email: holiday@wareham-forest.co.uk
Tent rate: £6.50-£12.00
Open: All year **Last arr:** 10pm
Facilities for disabled people • Dogs allowed • Electric hook-up • Showers • Children's play area • Shop on site • Cafe or Takeaway on site
Wareham Forest Tourist Park. Open all year. 5 Tick graded. Family operated. Direct forest access. Level F/serviced. Grass/hard standing pitches. Toilets/Showers. Heated toilet block during winter. Disabled facilities. Children's adventure play area. High season: shop/cafe, heated pools. Long/short term storage. Free colour brochure.

▲ Birchwood Tourist Park,
Bere Rd, North Trigon, Wareham, Dorset, BH20 7PA
Actual Grid Ref: SY897910
Tel: 01929 554763
Open: Mar to Oct

Warmwell
SY7586

▲ Warmwell Country Touring Park,
Warmwell, Dorchester, Dorset, DT2 8JD
Actual Grid Ref: SY764878
Tel: 01305 852313
Open: Mar to Jan

West Bay
SY4690

▲ West Bay Holiday Park,
West Bay, Bridport, Dorset, DT6 4HB
Actual Grid Ref: SY461290
Tel: 01308 422424
Open: Mar to Oct

West Lulworth
SY8280

▲ Lulworth Cove Youth Hostel,
School Lane, West Lulworth, Wareham, Dorset, BH20 5SA
Actual Grid Ref: SY832806
Tel: 01929 400564
Fax: 01929 400640
Capacity: 34

Under 18: £6.90
Adults: £10.00
Open: All year, 5.00pm
Family bunk rooms
Showers • Wet weather shelter • Lounge • Drying room • Cycle store • Parking • Evening meal available 7.00pm • No smoking • Kitchen facilities • Luggage store • Credit cards accepted
Purpose-built cedarwood hostel, recently refurbished. In an Area of Outstanding Natural Beauty.

▲ Durdle Door Holiday Park,
West Lulworth, Wareham, Dorset, BH20 5PU
Actual Grid Ref: SY812809
Tel: 01929 400200
Fax: 01929 400260
Open: Mar to Oct

West Moors
SU0803

▲ St Leonards Farm Camping & Caravan Park,
West Moors, Bournemouth, Dorset, BH22 0AQ
Actual Grid Ref: SU093015
Tel: 01202 872637
Open: Apr to Sep

Weymouth
SY6779

▲ Waterside Holiday Park,
Bowleaze Cove, Weymouth, Dorset, DT3 6PP
Actual Grid Ref: SY702821
Tel: 01305 833103
Fax: 01305 832830
Open: Mar to Oct

▲ Littlesea Holiday Park,
Lynch Lane, Weymouth, Dorset, DT4 9DT
Actual Grid Ref: SY654785
Tel: 01305 774414
Open: Mar to Nov

▲ Goldcroft Guest House,
6 Goldcroft Avenue, Weymouth, Dorset, DT4 0ET
Tel: 01305 789953
Open: All year

Wimborne Minster
SU0100

▲ Merley Court Touring Park,
Merley House Lane, Merley Park, Wimborne Minster, Dorset, BH21 3AA
Actual Grid Ref: SU013983
Tel: 01202 881488
Open: Mar to Jan

▲ Wilksworth Farm Caravan Park,
Cranborne Rd, Wimborne Minster, Dorset, BH21 4HW
Actual Grid Ref: SU008018
Tel: 01202 885467
Open: Mar to Oct

Winterborne Whitechurch
ST8300

▲ Lady Bailey Caravan Park,
Winterborne Whitechurch, Blandford Forum, Dorset, DT11 0HS
Actual Grid Ref: SY835998
Tel: 01258 880786
Open: Mar to Oct

Woodlands
SU0509

▲ Camping & Caravanning Club Site,
Sutton Hill Woodlands, Verwood, Wimborne, Dorset, BH21 6LF
Actual Grid Ref: SU069098
Tel: 01202 822763
Open: Mar to Oct

Wool
SY8486

▲ Whitemead Caravan Park,
Frome Cottage, East Burton Road, Wool, Wareham, Dorset, BH20 6HG
Actual Grid Ref: SY840869
Tel: 01929 462241
Open: Apr to Oct

Wyke Regis
SY6677

▲ Pebble Bank Caravan Park,
Camp Rd, Wyke Regis, Weymouth, Dorset, DT4 9HF
Actual Grid Ref: SY657776
Tourist Board grade: 3 Star
AA grade: 2 Pennants
Tel: 01305 774844
Fax: 01305 774844
Email: ian@pebbank.freeserve.co.uk
Tent pitches: 40
Tent rate: £6.00-£11.50
Open: Apr to Oct
Last arr: 9pm
Dogs allowed • Electric hook-up • Calor Gas/Camping Gaz • Children's play area • Showers • Laundrette on site • Public phone on site • Licensed bar on site
Quiet family park close to Weymouth. Good sea views.

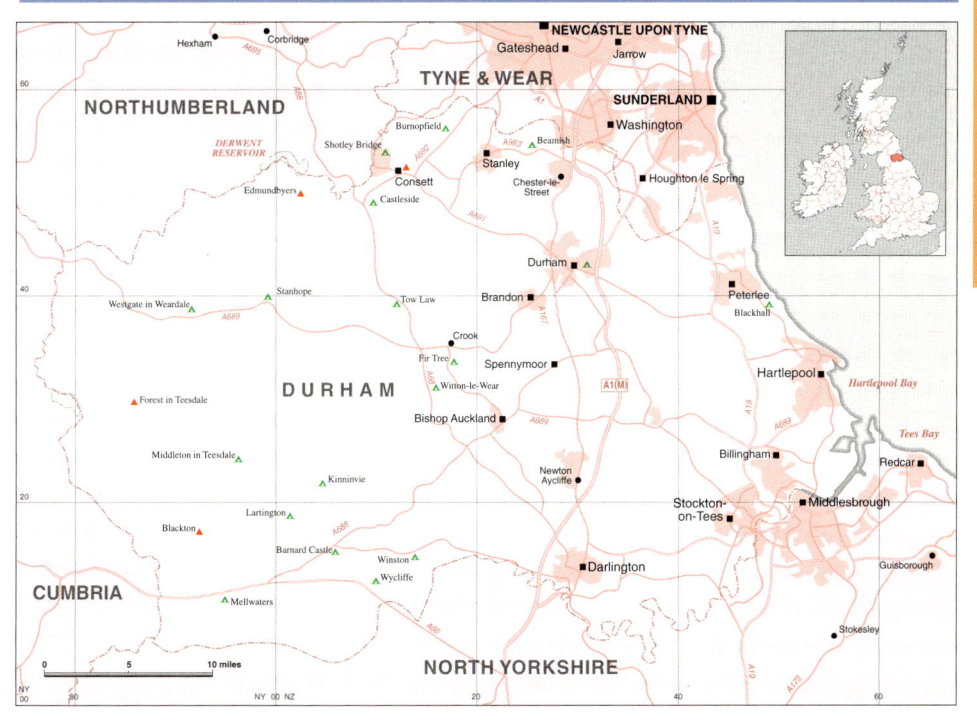

County Durham

Barnard Castle
NZ0516

▲ **East Lendings Caravan Park,** Abbey Lane, Barnard Castle, Co Durham, DL12 9TJ
Tel: 01883 37271
Open: Mar to Oct

▲ **Daleview Caravan Park,** Middleton-in-Teesdale, Barnard Castle, County Durham, DL12 0NG
Actual Grid Ref: NY948248
Tel: 01833 640233
Open: Mar to Oct

Beamish
NZ2253

▲ **Bobby Shafto Caravan Park,** Cranberry Plantation, Beamish, Stanley, Co Durham, DH9 0RY
Actual Grid Ref: NZ232545
Tel: 0191 370 1776
Open: Mar to Oct

Blackhall
NZ4638

▲ **Crimdon Park,** Coast Road, Blackhall, Hartlepool, TS27 4BL
Tel: 01429 267801 **Open:** Mar to Oct

Blackton
NY9317

▲ **Baldersdale Youth Hostel,** Blackton, Baldersdale, Barnard Castle, County Durham, DL12 9UP
Actual Grid Ref: NY931179
Tel: 01833 650629 **Fax:** 01833 650513
Capacity: 40
Under 18: £6.50 **Adults:** £9.25
Open: Apr to Sep, 5.00pm
Camping
Self-catering facilities • Television • Showers • Shop • Dining room • Games room • Drying room • Cycle store • Evening meal available 7.00pm • No smoking • WC • Kitchen facilities • Breakfast available • Credit cards accepted
Fully modernised farmhouse at mid-point of the Pennine Way.

Burnopfield
NZ1656

▲ **Cut Thorn Farm,** OS Field 4847, Gibside, Burnopfield, Tyne & Wear, NE16
Actual Grid Ref: NZ182583
Tel: 01207 270230
Open: All year

Castleside
NZ0849

▲ **Allensford Caravan & Camping Park,** Castleside, Consett, Co Durham, DH8 9BA
Actual Grid Ref: NZ082504
Tel: 01207 505572 **Open:** May to Sep

▲ **Manor Park Caravan Park,** Manor Park, Broadmeadows, Rippon Burn, Castleside, Consett, County Durham, DH8 9HD
Actual Grid Ref: NZ103464
Tel: 01207 501000
Open: Apr to Oct

Stilwell's Hostels & Camping 2002

County Durham • MAP PAGE 75

Consett
NZ1151

▲ **Consett YMCA,** Parliament Street, Consett, County Durham, DH8 5DH
Tel: 01207 502680
Fax: 01207 501578
Email: ymca@derwentside.org.uk
Capacity: 50
Under 18: £12.50
Adults: £12.50
Open: All year, 9am
Family bunk rooms: £12.50
Television • Showers • Central heating • Lounge • Dining room • Games room • Drying room • Cycle store • Parking • Facilities for disabled people • No smoking
In town centre. Close to C2C route.

Durham
NZ2742

▲ **Finchale Abbey Caravan Park,** Finchale Abbey Farm, Durham, DH1 5SH
Actual Grid Ref: NZ295468
Tel: 0191 386 6528
Open: All year

▲ **Grange Caravan Club Site,** Meadow Lane, Carville, Durham, DH1 1TL
Actual Grid Ref: NZ303446
Tel: 0191 384 4778
Open: All year

Edmundbyers
NZ0250

▲ **Edmundbyers Youth Hostel,** Low House, Edmundbyers, Consett, County Durham, DH8 9NL
Actual Grid Ref: NZ017500
Tel: 01207 255651
Fax: 01207 255345
Capacity: 29
Under 18: £5.75
Adults: £8.50
Open: All year, 5.00pm
Showers • Wet weather shelter • Drying room • Cycle store • No smoking • Kitchen facilities • Credit cards accepted
A simple hostel in a C17th inn, ideal for walkers and cyclists exploring this Area of Outstanding Natural Beauty.

Hostels and campsites may vary rates – be sure to check when booking.

Fir Tree
NZ1434

▲ **Greenhead Country Caravan Park,** Fir Tree, Crook, Co Durham, DL15 8BL
Actual Grid Ref: NZ147343
Tel: 01388 763143
Open: All year

Forest in Teesdale
NY8629

▲ **Langdon Beck Youth Hostel,** Forest in Teesdale, Barnard Castle, County Durham, DL12 0XN
Actual Grid Ref: NY860304
Tel: 01833 622228
Fax: 01833 622372
Email: langdonbeck@yha.org.uk
Capacity: 34
Under 18: £6.90
Adults: £10.00
Open: All year, 5.00pm
Family bunk rooms
Self-catering facilities • Showers • Laundry facilities • Wet weather shelter • Lounge • Drying room • Cycle store • Parking • Evening meal available 7.00pm • No smoking • Kitchen facilities • Breakfast available • Credit cards accepted
Purpose-built hostel in Upper Teesdale with an excellent standard of accommodation.

Kinninvie
NZ0522

▲ **Hetherick Caravan Park,** Kinninvie, Barnard Castle, Co Durham, DL12 8QX
Actual Grid Ref: NZ056211
Tel: 01833 631170
Open: Mar to Oct

Lartington
NZ0118

▲ **Camping & Caravanning Club Site,** Dockenflatts Lane, Lartington, Barnard Castle, County Durham, DL12 9DG
Tel: 01833 630228
Open: Mar to Nov

▲ **Pecknell Farm,** Lartington, Barnard Castle, County Durham, DL12 9DF
Actual Grid Ref: NZ029177
Tel: 01833 638357
Open: Mar to Oct

Mellwaters
NY9612

▲ **East Mellwaters,** Mellwaters, Bowes, Barnard Castle, Co Durham, DL12 9RH
Actual Grid Ref: NY968127
Tel: 01833 628269
Open: Mar to Oct

Middleton in Teesdale
NY9425

▲ **Kingsway Adventure Centre,** Alston Road, Middleton in Teesdale, Barnard Castle, Co Durham, DL12 0UU
Tel: 01833 640881
Fax: 01833 640155
Open: All year

Shotley Bridge
NZ0852

▲ **Redwell Hall Farm,** Shotley Bridge, Consett, Co Durham, DH8 9TS
Tel: 01207 255216
Open: All year

Stanhope
NY9939

▲ **Heather View Caravan Park,** Stanhope, Weardale, North Yorkshire, DL13 2PS
Actual Grid Ref: NY998383
Tel: 01388 528728
Open: Mar to Oct

Tow Law
NZ1138

▲ **Viewley Hill Farm,** Tow Law, Bishop Auckland, Co Durham, DL13 4HH
Tel: 01388 730308
Open: Apr to Sep

Westgate in Weardale
NY9038

▲ **Westgate Camping Site,** Westgate in Weardale, Bishop Auckland, Co Durham, DL13 1LJ
Tel: 01388 517309
Open: Mar to Oct

MAP PAGE 75 • **County Durham**

Winston

NZ1316

▲ ***Winston Caravan Park,*** The Old Forge, Winston, Darlington, County Durham, DL2 3RH
Actual Grid Ref: NZ139168
Tel: 01325 730228
Open: Mar to Oct

To stay in a Youth Hostel affiliated to one of the Youth Hostel associations, you need to be a member. You can join at most hostels – phone in advance to check.

Witton-le-Wear

NZ1431

▲ ***Witton Castle Caravan and Camping Site,*** Witton-le-Wear, Bishop Auckland, Co Durham, DL14 0DE
Actual Grid Ref: NZ155305
Tel: 01388 488230 **Fax:** 01388 488008
Tent pitches: 280
Tent rate: £6.75-£12.00
Open: Mar to Oct **Last arr:** 10pm
Dogs allowed • Electric hook-up • Calor Gas/Camping Gaz • Cafe or Takeaway on site • Picnic/barbecue area on site • Children's play area • Showers • Laundrette on site • Public phone on site • Licensed bar on site • Shop on site
In grounds of C15th castle, parkland views and glorious Weardale.

If you have to cancel your visit to any hostel or campsite, please let them know – it is always possible to make a bed or a pitch available to someone else.

Wycliffe

NZ1114

▲ ***Thorpe Hall,*** Wycliffe, Barnard Castle, Co Durham, DL12 9TW
Actual Grid Ref: NZ105141
Tel: 01833 627230
Open: Mar to Oct

Essex

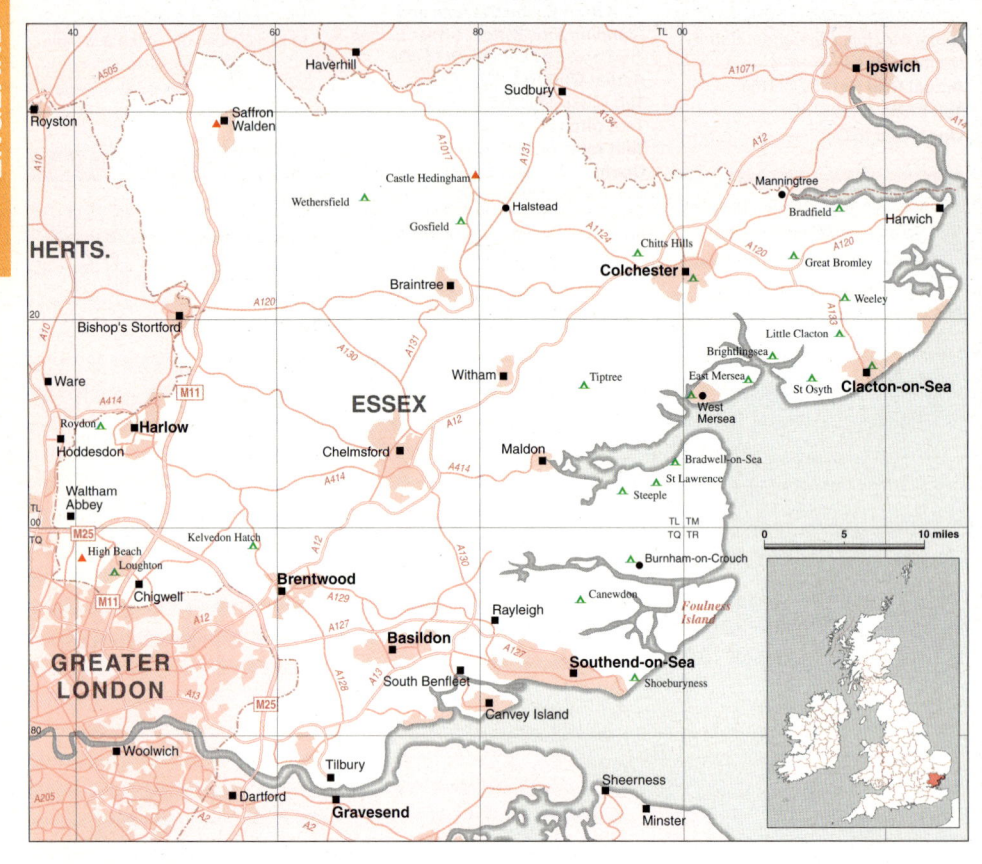

Bradfield

TM1430

⚑ **Strangers Home Public House,** Bradfield, Manningtree, Essex, CO11 2US
Actual Grid Ref: TM143308
Tel: 01255 870304
Open: Mar to Oct

Bradwell-on-Sea

TL9906

⚑ **Eastland Caravan Park,** East End Road, Bradwell-on-Sea, Southminster, CM0 7PP
Tel: 01621 776571
Open: Apr to Oct

Brightlingsea

TM0817

⚑ **Lakeside Touring Caravan & Tent Site,** Promenade Way, Brightlingsea, Essex, CO16 8NA
Actual Grid Ref: TM084164
Tel: 01206 303421
Open: Mar to Oct

Burnham-on-Crouch

TQ9596

⚑ **Silver Road Caravan Park,** 5 Silver Road, Burnham-on-Crouch, Essex, CM0 8LA
Actual Grid Ref: TQ956957
Tel: 01621 782934
Open: Mar to Sept

Canewdon

TQ8994

⚑ **Riverside Village Holiday Park,** Creeksea Ferry Rd, Wallasea Island, Canewdon, Rochford, Essex, SS4 2EY
Actual Grid Ref: TQ929951
Tel: 01702 258297
Open: Mar to Oct

If you have to cancel your visit to any hostel or campsite, please let them know – it is always possible to make a bed or a pitch available to someone else.

Castle Hedingham

TL7835

▲ **Castle Hedingham Youth Hostel,** 7 Falcon Square, Castle Hedingham, Halstead, Essex, CO9 3BU
Actual Grid Ref: TL786355
Tel: 01787 460799
Fax: 01787 461302
Email: castlehed@yha.org.uk
Capacity: 50
Under 18: £6.90
Adults: £10.00
Open: Feb to Nov, 5.00pm
Self-catering facilities • Television • Showers • Wet weather shelter • Lounge • Drying room • Cycle store • Evening meal available 7.00pm • No smoking • WC • Kitchen facilities • Breakfast available • Credit cards accepted
C16th building with modern annexe and large lawned garden, closeby the Norman Castle and half-timbered houses of this medieval town.

Chitts Hills

TL9525

▲ **Seven Arches Farm,** Chitts Hills, Lexden, Colchester, Essex, CO3 5SX
Tel: 01206 574896
Fax: 01206 574896
Open: All year

Clacton-on-Sea

TM1715

▲ **Sackett's Grove Caravan Park,** Jaywick Lane, Clacton-on-Sea, Essex, CO16 9DH
Tel: 01255 427765
Open: Easter to Oct

Colchester

TL9925

▲ **Colchester Camping Caravan Park,** Cymbeline Way, Lexden, Colchester, Essex, CO3 4AG
Actual Grid Ref: TL971252
Tel: 01206 545551
Email: enquiries@colchestercamping.co.uk
Open: All year

All details shown are as supplied by hostels and campsites in Autumn 2000.

East Mersea

TM0514

▲ **Fen Farm Campsite,** East Mersea, Colchester, Essex, CO5 8UA
Actual Grid Ref: TM058144
Tel: 01206 383275
Open: Apr to Oct

Gosfield

TL7829

▲ **Gosfield Lake Touring Park,** Church Road, Gosfield, Halstead, Essex, CO9 1UG
Actual Grid Ref: TL777294
Tel: 01787 475043
Email: turps@gosfieldlake.ndo.co.uk
Open: All year

Great Bromley

TM0724

▲ **Mill Farm Camp Site,** Harwich Road, Great Bromley, Colchester, Essex, CO7 7JQ
Tel: 01206 250485
Open: May to Sep

High Beach

TQ4097

▲ **Epping Forest Youth Hostel,** Wellington Hall, High Beach, Loughton, Essex, IG10 4AG
Actual Grid Ref: TQ408983
Tel: 020 8508 5971
Fax: 020 8508 5161
Capacity: 36
Under 18: £6.90
Adults: £10.00
Open: All year, 5pm
Family bunk rooms Camping
Self-catering facilities • Television • Showers • Showers • Shop • Wet weather shelter • Lounge • Cycle store • Parking • No smoking • WC • WC • Kitchen facilities • Credit cards accepted
In the heart of the former royal forest, but a mere 10 miles from the centre of London. Ideal also for visiting historical sites such as the Loughton Iron Age Camp, Waltham Abbey and Queen Elizabeth's Hunting Lodge.

MAP PAGE 78 • **Essex**

Hostels and campsites may vary rates – be sure to check when booking.

Kelvedon Hatch

TQ5799

▲ **Camping & Caravanning Club Site,** Warren Lane, Frog Street, Kelvedon Hatch, Brentwood, Essex, CM15 0JG
Actual Grid Ref: TQ577976
Tel: 01277 372773 **Open:** Mar to Oct

Little Clacton

TM1617

▲ **Crackstakes Farm,** Tan Lane, Little Clacton, Essex, CO16 9PS
Actual Grid Ref: TM150147
Tel: 01255 474472
Open: All year

Loughton

TQ4396

▲ **The Elms Caravan Park,** Lippitts Hill, High Beech, Loughton, Essex, IG10 4AW
Actual Grid Ref: TQ399971
Tel: 0181 508 3749 / 508 1000
Fax: 0181 508 3749
Email: elmscar@aol.com
Open: Mar to Oct

▲ **Debden House Camp Site,** Debden Green, Loughton, Essex, IG10 2PA
Actual Grid Ref: TQ438982
Tel: 0181 508 3008
Open: Apr to Oct

Roydon

TL4010

▲ **Roydon Mill Leisure Park,** Roydon, Harlow, Essex, CM19 5EJ
Actual Grid Ref: TL405104
Tel: 01279 792777 **Open:** All year

Some hostels and campsites impose restrictions on size and type of groups they accept (e.g. not permitting single-sex groups). Always phone to enquire before booking.

Essex • MAP PAGE 78

Saffron Walden
TL5438

▲ **Saffron Walden Youth Hostel,** 1 Myddylton Place, Saffron Walden, Essex, CB10 1BB
Actual Grid Ref: TL535386
Tel: 01799 523117
Fax: 01799 520840
Capacity: 40
Under 18: £6.50
Adults: £9.25
Open: All year, 5.00pm
Lounge • Dining room • Drying room • Evening meal available 7.00pm • No smoking • Breakfast available • Credit cards accepted
500-year-old oak-beamed former maltings with oak beams and uneven floors, and courtyard garden, a stone's throw from the town centre.

Shoeburyness
TQ9385

▲ **East Beach Caravan Park,** East Beach, Shoeburyness, Southend-on-Sea, Essex, SS3 9SG
Tel: 01702 292466
Open: Mar to Oct

Some hostels and campsites impose restrictions on size and type of groups they accept (e.g. not permitting single-sex groups). Always phone to enquire before booking.

Please respect hostels' policy on smoking. Some hostels do not allow smoking anywhere, some restrict smoking to certain areas.

St Lawrence
TL9603

▲ **Beacon Hill Holiday Village,** St Lawrence Bay, St Lawrence, Southminster, Essex, CM0 7LS
Actual Grid Ref: TL961049
Tel: 01621 779248
Open: Apr to Oct

St Osyth
TM1114

▲ **Orchards Holiday Park,** Point Clear, St Osyth, Clacton-on-Sea, Essex, CO16 8LJ
Tel: 01255 820651
Open: Mar to Oct

Steeple
TL9202

▲ **Steeple Bay Holiday Park,** Steeple, Southminster, Essex, CM0 7RS
Actual Grid Ref: TL929027
Tel: 01621 773991
Open: Mar to Oct

▲ **The Sun & Anchor Public House,** The Street, Steeple, Southminster, Essex, CM0 7RH
Actual Grid Ref: TL935030
Tel: 01621 772700
Open: May to Oct

Tiptree
TL8916

▲ **Villa Farm,** West End Road, Tiptree, Colchester, Essex, CO5 9QN
Actual Grid Ref: TL881155
Tel: 01621 815217
Open: May to Oct

Weeley
TM1421

▲ **Weeley Bridge Holiday Park,** Weeley, Clacton-on-Sea, Essex, O16 9DH
Tel: 01255 830403
Fax: 01255 831544
Open: Mar to Oct

West Mersea
TM0112

▲ **Waldegraves Holiday Park,** West Mersea, Colchester, Essex, CO5 8SE
Actual Grid Ref: TM034132
Tel: 01206 382898
Email: holidays@walde.co.uk
Open: Mar to Nov

▲ **Seaview Holiday Park,** Seaview Avenue, West Mersea, Colchester, Essex, CO5 8DA
Actual Grid Ref: TM027126
Tel: 01206 382534
Open: Mar to Oct

Wethersfield
TL7131

▲ **Brook Farm,** Wethersfield, Braintree, Essex, CM7 4BX
Tel: 01371 850284
Open: All year

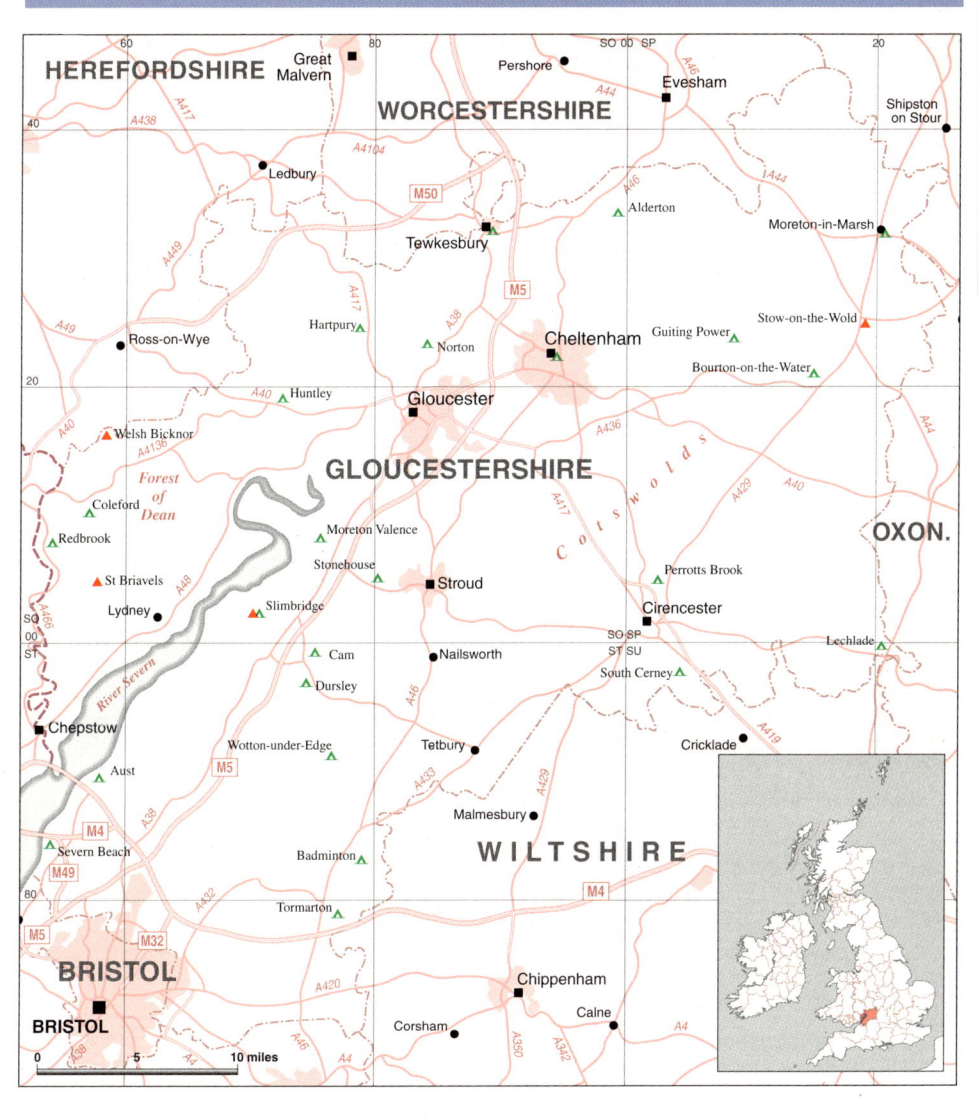

Gloucestershire

Alderton
SO9933

▲ **Camping & Caravanning Club Site,** Brooklands Farm, Alderton, Tewkesbury, Gloucestershire, GL20 8NX
Actual Grid Ref: SP007324
Tel: 01242 620259
Open: Mar to Jan

▲ **Corner Cottage,** Alderton, Tewkesbury, Glos, GL20 8NH
Tel: 01242 620630
Open: Mar to Sep

Hostels and campsites may vary rates – be sure to check when booking.

Aust
ST5789

▲ **Boars Head Camping Site,** Aust, Bristol, BS35 4AX
Tel: 01454 52278
Open: Mar to Oct

Gloucestershire • MAP PAGE 81

ENGLAND

Badminton

ST8082

▲ **Petty France Farm,** Dunkirk, Badminton, Gloucestershire, GL9 1AF
Actual Grid Ref: ST785855
Tel: 01454 238665
Open: Apr to Sep

Bourton-on-the-Water

SP1620

▲ **Folly Farm,** Bourton-on-the-Water, Cheltenham, Gloucestershire, GL54 3BY
Actual Grid Ref: SP124206
Tel: 01451 820285
Open: All year

Cam

ST7499

▲ **16 Field Lane,** Cam, Dursley, Glos, GL11 0JE
Tel: 01453 544222
Open: All year

Cheltenham

SO9422

▲ **Briarfields Touring Park,** Gloucester Road, Cheltenham, Gloucestershire, GL51 0SX
Actual Grid Ref: SO909218
Tel: 01242 235324
Open: All year

▲ **Stansby Caravan & Camping Park,** The Reddings, Cheltenham, Gloucestershire, GL51 6RS
Actual Grid Ref: SO908208
Tel: 01452 712168
Open: Feb to Dec

▲ **Freedom Camping & RV Park,** Bamfurlong Lane, Bamfurlong, Cheltenham, Gloucestershire, GL51 6SL
Actual Grid Ref: SO901216
Tel: 01452 712705
Open: All year

Coleford

SO5710

▲ **Christchurch Caravan & Camping Site,** Christchurch Campsite Office, Bracelands Drive, Coleford, Gloucestershire, GL16 7NN
Actual Grid Ref: SO569129
Tel: 01594 833376
Open: Mar to Dec

▲ **Woodlands View Caravan & Camping Site,** Sling, Coleford, Gloucestershire, GL16 8JA
Actual Grid Ref: SO582085
Tel: 01594 835127
Open: All year

▲ **Braceland Caravan & Camping Site,** Bracelands Drive, Coleford, Gloucestershire, GL16 7NN
Actual Grid Ref: SO569129
Tel: 01594 833376
Open: Mar to Nov

Dursley

ST7698

▲ **Hogsdown Farm,** Lower Wick, Dursley, Gloucestershire, GL11 6DS
Actual Grid Ref: ST711974
Tel: 01453 810224
Open: All year

Guiting Power

SP0924

▲ **Cotswold Farm Park,** Guiting Power, Cheltenham, Gloucestershire, GL54 5UG
Actual Grid Ref: SP112270
Tel: 01451 850307
Open: Mar to Oct

Hartpury

SO7925

▲ **Stone End Farm,** Corse Church Lane, Hartpury, Gloucestershire, GL19 3BX
Actual Grid Ref: SO790269
Tel: 01452 700254
Open: All year

Huntley

SO7219

▲ **Forest Gate Campsite,** Huntley, Gloucester, GL19 3EU
Actual Grid Ref: SO717194
Tel: 01452 831192
Fax: 01452 831192
Email: forest.gate@huntley-glos.demon.co.uk
Tent pitches:
Tent rate: £4.60
Open: Mar to Oct
Last arr: 10.30pm
Dogs allowed • Electric hook-up • Calor Gas/Camping Gaz • Picnic/barbecue area on site • Showers • Public phone on site • Shop on site
Small peaceful sheltered site in grounds of Victorian rectory.

Lechlade

SU2199

▲ **St John's Priory Parks,** Faringdon Road, Lechlade, Gloucestershire, GL7 3EZ
Actual Grid Ref: SU223992
Tel: 01367 252360
Open: Mar to Oct

▲ **Bridge House Campsite,** Lechlade, Gloucestershire, GL7 3AG
Actual Grid Ref: SU213992
Tel: 01367 252348
Open: Mar to Oct

Moreton Valence

SO7809

▲ **Gables Farm,** Moreton Valence, Gloucester, GL2 7ND
Actual Grid Ref: SO787100
Tel: 01452 720331
Open: All year

Moreton-in-Marsh

SP2032

▲ **Cross Hands Inn,** Moreton-in-Marsh, Gloucestershire, GL56 0SP
Actual Grid Ref: SP271289
Tel: 01608 643106
Open: All year

Norton

SO8524

▲ **Red Lion Camping & Caravan Park,** Wainlode Hill, Norton, Gloucester, GL2 9LW
Actual Grid Ref: SO848258
Tel: 01452 730251
Open: All year

Perrotts Brook

SP0106

▲ **Mayfield House Touring Park,** Cheltenham Road, Perrotts Brook, Cirencester, Glos, GL7 7BH
Actual Grid Ref: SP021054
Tourist Board grade: 4 Ticks
AA grade: 3 Pennants
Tel: 01285 831301
Fax: 01285 831301
Tent pitches: 36
Tent rate: £6.10-£9.85
Open: All year
Last arr: 10pm
Facilities for disabled people • Running water • WC • Drying facilities • Showers • Washing facilities • Camper vans accepted

MAP PAGE 81 • **Gloucestershire**

- Cars accepted • Motorcycles accepted • Adjacent parking • Electric hook-up • Calor Gas/Camping Gaz • Picnic/barbecue area on site • Showers • Laundrette on site • Public phone on site • Shop on site
Free showers, laudrette, chemical disposal, phone, shop, gas, local pub.

Redbrook
SO5310

▲ **Tresco,** Redbrook, Monmouth, NP5 4LY
Tel: 01600 712325
Open: All year

Severn Beach
ST5385

▲ **Salthouse Farm Caravan & Camping Park,** Severn Beach, Bristol, South Gloucestershire, BS12 3NH
Actual Grid Ref: ST542855
Tel: 01454 632274
Open: Apr to Oct

Slimbridge
SO7303

▲ **Slimbridge Youth Hostel,** Shepherd's Patch, Slimbridge, Gloucester, GL2 7BP
Actual Grid Ref: ST730043
Tel: 01453 890275
Fax: 01453 890625
Email: slimbridge@yha.org.uk
Capacity: 56
Under 18: £6.90
Adults: £10.00
Open: Feb to Nov
Family bunk rooms
Self-catering facilities • Showers • Shop • Laundry facilities • Lounge • Games room • Drying room • Cycle store • Parking • Evening meal available 7.00pm • No smoking • Kitchen facilities • Breakfast available • Credit cards accepted
Purpose-built youth hostel, with its own pond & wildfowl collection, next to the Sharpness Canal and Sir Peter Scott's famous wildfowl reserve.

▲ **Tudor Caravan & Camping,** Shepherds Patch, Slimbridge, Gloucester, GL2 7BP
Actual Grid Ref: SO728041
Tel: 01453 890483
Open: All year

Hostels and campsites may vary rates – be sure to check when booking.

South Cerney
SU0497

▲ **Cotswold Hoburne,** Broadway Lane, South Cerney, Cirencester, Gloucestershire, GL7 5UQ
Actual Grid Ref: SU055958
Tel: 01285 860216
Open: Easter to Oct

St Briavels
SO5604

▲ **St Briavels Castle Youth Hostel,** The Castle, St Briavels, Lydney, Gloucestershire, GL15 6RG
Actual Grid Ref: SO558045
Tel: 01594 530272
Fax: 01594 530849
Email: stbriavels@yha.org.uk
Capacity: 70
Under 18: £7.75
Adults: £11.00
Open: Apr to Oct, 5.00pm
Self-catering facilities • Showers • Licensed bar • Shop • Lounge • Dining room • Drying room • Cycle store • Parking • Evening meal available 7.00pm • No smoking • WC • Breakfast available • Breakfast available • Credit cards accepted
800-year-old Norman castle with moat, used by King John as a hunting lodge, in the centre of a quiet village above the River Wye.

Stonehouse
SO8005

▲ **Grove Farm,** Westend, Stonehouse, Gloucestershire, GL10 3SJ
Actual Grid Ref: SO785069
Tel: 01453 822885
Open: All year

Some hostels and campsites impose restrictions on size and type of groups they accept (e.g. not permitting single-sex groups). Always phone to enquire before booking.

All details shown are as supplied by hostels and campsites in Autumn 2000.

Stow-on-the-Wold
SP1826

▲ **Stow-on-the-Wold Youth Hostel,** The Square, Stow-on-the-Wold, Cheltenham, Gloucestershire, GL54 1AF
Actual Grid Ref: SP191258
Tel: 01451 830497
Fax: 01451 870102
Capacity: 50 **Under 18:** £8.50
Adults: £12.50
Open: Feb to Dec (not Xmas) + New Year
Family bunk rooms
Self-catering facilities • Television • Laundry facilities • Lounge • Dining room • Cycle store • Parking • Evening meal available 7.00pm • No smoking • Kitchen facilities • Breakfast available • Credit cards accepted
Listed C16th building in the town centre offers traditional accommodation. Stow is a perfect base for exploring the Cotswolds, with many walks and cycle ways.

Tewkesbury
SO8933

▲ **Dawleys Caravan Park,** Owis' Lane, Shuthorpe, Tewkesbury, Gloucestershire, GL20 6EQ
Actual Grid Ref: SO883353
Tel: 01684 292622
Open: Mar to Oct

▲ **Sunset View Touring Tent & Caravan Park,** Church End Lane, Twining, Tewkesbury, Gloucestershire, GL20 6EH
Actual Grid Ref: SO889356
Tel: 01684 292145
Open: All year

Tormarton
ST7678

▲ **The Portcullis,** Tormarton, Badminton, GL9 1HZ
Tel: 01454 218263
Fax: 01454 218094
Open: All year (not Xmas)

Gloucestershire • MAP PAGE 81

Welsh Bicknor
SO5817

▲ **Welsh Bicknor Youth Hostel,**
*The Rectory, Welsh Bicknor,
Goodrich, Ross-on-Wye,
Herefordshire, HR9 6JJ*
Actual Grid Ref: SO591177
Tel: 01594 860300
Fax: 01594 861276
Email: welshbicknor@yha.org.uk
Capacity: 80
Under 18: £7.75 **Adults:** £11.00
Open: Feb to Dec (not Xmas), 5.00pm
Family bunk rooms
Camping
Self-catering facilities • Television • Showers • Laundry facilities • Wet weather shelter • Lounge • Dining room • Games room • Drying room • Cycle store • Parking • Evening meal available 7.00pm • WC • Kitchen facilities • Breakfast available • Credit cards accepted
On the banks of the River Wye, an early Victorian rectory surrounded by meadows with great views across Forest of Dean and Symonds Yat Rock.

Wotton-under-Edge
ST7692

▲ **Canons Court Caravan Park,**
*Bradley Green, Wotton-under-Edge,
Gloucestershire, GL12 7PN*
Actual Grid Ref: ST744938
Tel: 01453 843128
Open: Mar to Oct

To stay in a Youth Hostel affiliated to one of the Youth Hostel associations, you need to be a member. You can join at most hostels – phone in advance to check.

Greater Manchester & Merseyside

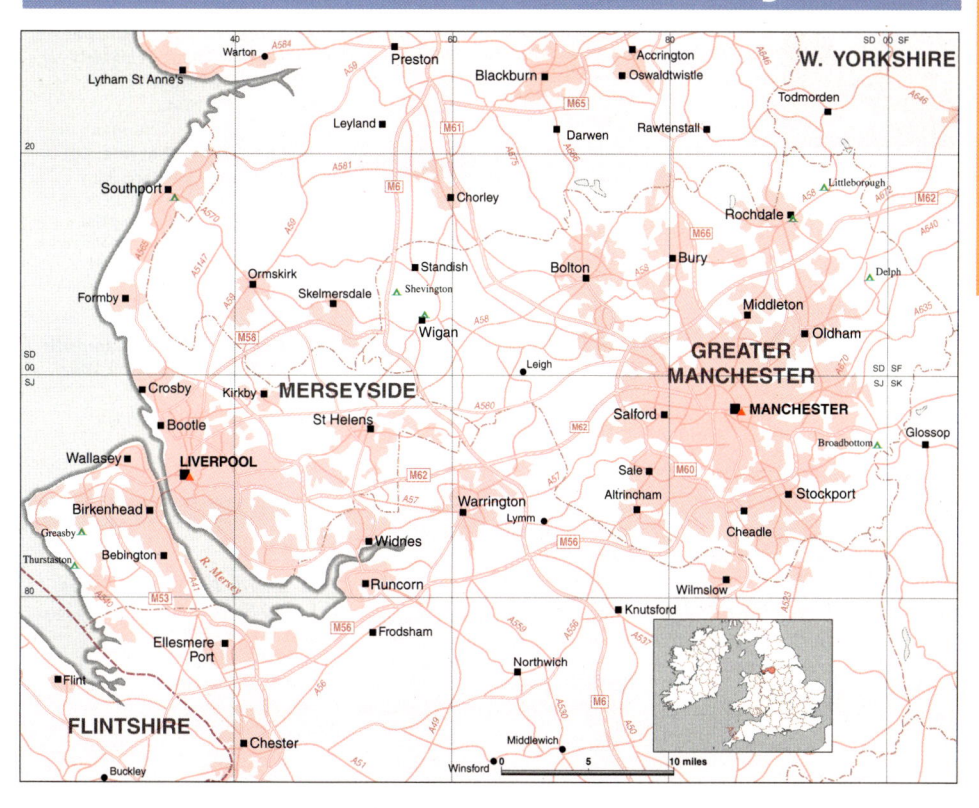

Broadbottom
SJ9993

▲ **Lymefield Campsite,** Broadbottom, Hyde, Cheshire, SK14 6AG
Tel: 01457 764094 **Open:** All year

Delph
SD9807

▲ **Globe Farm Camping,** Huddersfield Road, Standedge, Delph, Oldham, Lancashire, OL3 5LU
Tel: 01457 873040
Open: Easter to Oct

Greasby
SJ2586

▲ **Green House Farm,** Arrowe Road, Greasby, Wirral, CH49 1RY
Tel: 0151 677 1615 **Open:** All year

Littleborough
SD9316

▲ **Hollingworth Lake Caravan Park,** Rakewood, Littleborough, Rochdale, OL15 0AT
Actual Grid Ref: SD943146
Tel: 01706 378661 **Open:** All year

Liverpool Central
SJ3490

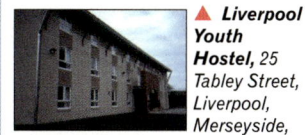

▲ **Liverpool Youth Hostel,** 25 Tabley Street, Liverpool, Merseyside, L1 8EE
Actual Grid Ref: SJ344895
Tel: 0151 709 8888
Fax: 0151 709 0417
Email: liverpool@yha.org.uk

Capacity: 100
Under 18: £13.50
Adults: £18.00
Open: All year, All day
Family bunk rooms
Self-catering facilities • Television • Showers • Licensed bar • Laundry facilities • Lounge • Games room • Cycle store • Parking • Evening meal available 5.30-8.15pm • Breakfast available • Luggage store • Luggage store • Credit cards accepted
A short walk from Albert Dock and the Pier Head. Up-to-the-minute facilities and comforts.

Some hostels and campsites impose restrictions on size and type of groups they accept (e.g. not permitting single-sex groups). Always phone to enquire before booking.

Greater Manchester & Merseyside • MAP PAGE 85

Manchester Central

SJ8397

▲ **Manchester Youth Hostel,** Potato Wharf, Castlefield, Manchester, M3 4NB
Actual Grid Ref: SJ831979
Tel: 0161 839 9960
Fax: 0161 835 2054
Email: manchester@yha.org.uk
Capacity: 144
Under 18: £9.00 **Adults:** £13.00
Open: All year, All day
Family bunk rooms
Self-catering facilities • Television • Showers • Showers • Licensed bar • Laundry facilities • Lounge • Games room • Security lockers • Cycle store • Parking • Evening meal available 6.00 to 7.30pm • Facilities for disabled people • Kitchen facilities • Luggage store • Credit cards accepted
Modern hostel a short walk away from the busy city centre, with its varied culture, clubs, shops and museums.

All details shown are as supplied by hostels and campsites in Autumn 2000.

Rochdale

SD8913

▲ **Gelder Wood Country Park,** Ashworth Road, Rochdale, OL11 5UP
Actual Grid Ref: SD852127
Tel: 01706 364858
Open: Mar to Oct

Shevington

SD5408

▲ **Gathurst Hall Farm Camp Site,** Gathurst Lane, Shevington, Wigan, Greater Manchester, WN6 8JA
Actual Grid Ref: SD538071
Tel: 01257 253464
Open: Mar to Oct

Southport

SD3317

▲ **Hurlston Hall County Caravan Park,** Southport Road, Southport, L40 8HB
Actual Grid Ref: SD398107
Tel: 01704 841064
Open: Easter to Oct

▲ **Riverside Touring & Camping Leisure Centre,** Southport New Road, Southport, Merseyside, PR9 8DF
Actual Grid Ref: SD410190
Tel: 01704 28886 **Open:** Mar to Jan

Thurstaston

SJ2483

▲ **Church Farm,** Church Lane, Thurstaston, Wirral, CH61 0HW
Tel: 0151 648 7838
Fax: 0151 648 9644
Email: sale@churchfarm.org.uk
Tent pitches: 50 **Tent rate:** £6.00
Open: All year **Last arr:** 8pm
Facilities for disabled people • Electric hook-up • Calor Gas/Camping Gaz • Picnic/barbecue area on site • Showers • Shop on site • Baby care facilities
Organic farm and shop, farm animals to see, beautiful views.

▲ **Thurstaton Family Campsite,** Station Road, Thurstaston, Wirral, L61 0HN
Actual Grid Ref: SJ241835
Tel: 0151 648 4371
Open: Apr to Sep

Wigan

SD5805

▲ **Charity Farm Caravan Park,** Smithy Brow, Wrightington, Wigan, Lancashire, WN6 9PP
Actual Grid Ref: SD520137
Tel: 01257 451326
Open: All year

Hampshire

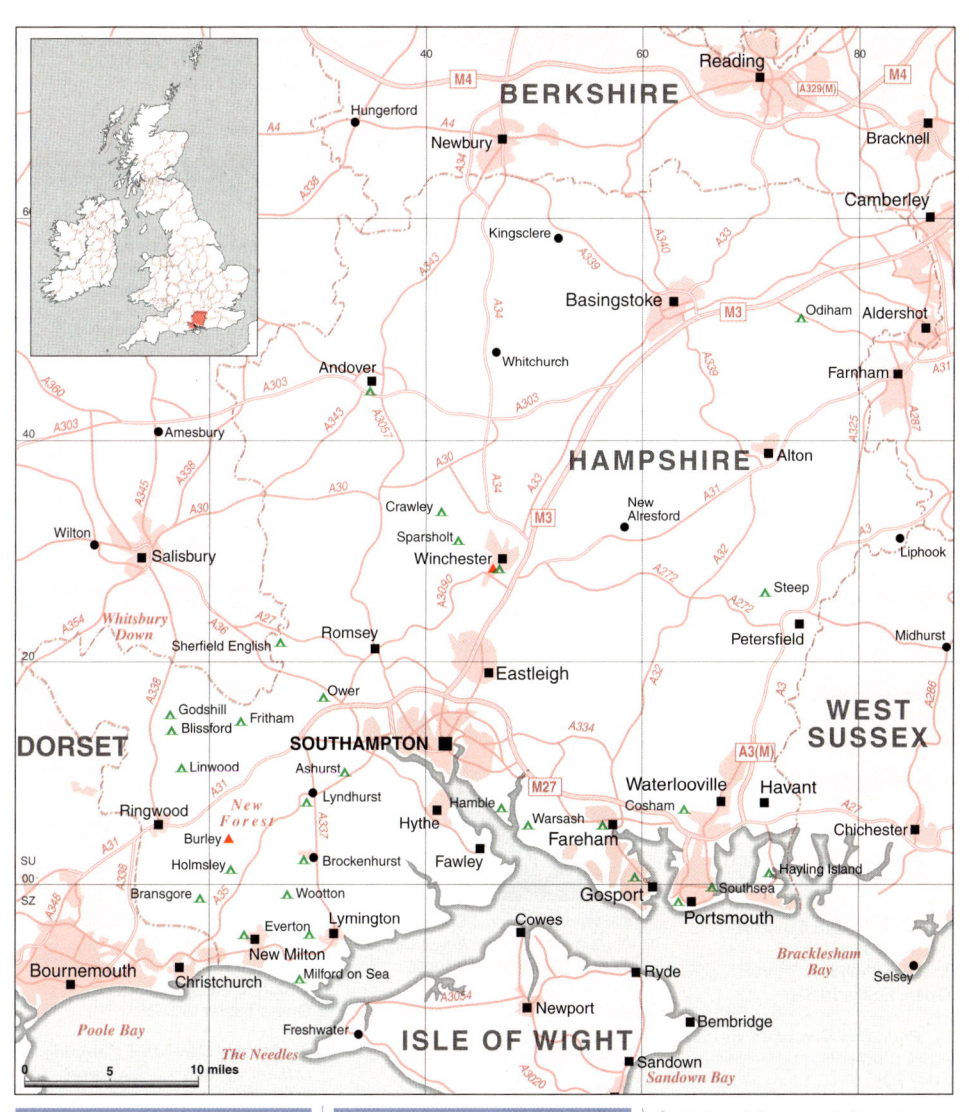

Andover
SU3645

▲ **Wyke Down Caravan & Camping Park,** Picket Piece, Andover, Hampshire, SP11 6LX
Actual Grid Ref: SU403476
Tel: 01264 352048
Fax: 01264 324661
Open: All year

Ashurst
SU3411

▲ **Ashurst Campsite,** Lyndhurst Road, Ashurst, Southampton, SO40 7AA
Actual Grid Ref: SU332099
Tel: 0131 314 6100
Email: fe.holidays@forestry.gov.uk
Open: Easter to Sep

▲ **Ashurst Caravan & Camping Site,** Ocknell Caravan & Camping, Fritham, Lyndhurst, Hampshire, SO43 7HH
Actual Grid Ref: SU332098
Tel: 0131 314 6505
Open: Mar to Sept

Hampshire • MAP PAGE 87

Blissford
SU1713

▲ **Gorse Farm,** Blissford, Fordingbridge, Hampshire, SP6 2JH
Actual Grid Ref: SU170140
Tel: 01425 653250
Open: All year

Bransgore
SZ1998

▲ **Holmsley Campsite,** Forest Road, Holmsley, Bransgore, Christchurch, Dorset, BH23 7EQ
Actual Grid Ref: SZ215991
Tel: 0131 314 6100
Email: fe.holidays@forestry.gov.uk
Open: Easter to Nov

▲ **Harrow Wood Farm Caravan Park,** Harrow Wood Farm, Poplar Lane, Bransgore, Christchurch, Hampshire, BH23 8JE
Actual Grid Ref: SZ194978
Tel: 01425 672487
Email: harrowwood@caravan.sites.co.uk
Open: Mar to Dec

▲ **Heathfield Caravan Park,** Bransgore, Christchurch, Dorset, BH23 8LA
Actual Grid Ref: SZ208985
Tel: 01425 672397
Open: Mar to Oct

Brockenhurst
SU2902

▲ **Hollands Wood Campsite,** Lyndhurst Road, Brockenhurst, Hampshire, SO42 7QH
Actual Grid Ref: SU303034
Tel: 0131 314 6100
Email: fe.holidays@forestry.gov.uk
Open: Easter to Sep

▲ **Roundhill Campsite,** Beaulieu Road, Brockenhurst, Hampshire, SO42 7QL
Actual Grid Ref: SU332021
Tel: 0131 314 6100
Email: fe.holidays@forestry.gov.uk
Open: Easter to Sep

▲ **Roundhill Campsite,** Beaulieu Road, Brockenhurst, Hampshire, SO42 7QL
Actual Grid Ref: SU335021
Tel: 0131 314 6100
Open: Easter to Sep

▲ **Hollands Wood Caravan & Camping Site,** Ocknell Caravan & Camping, Fritham, Lyndhurst, Hampshire, SO43 7HH
Actual Grid Ref: SU303038
Tel: 0131 314 6505
Open: Mar to Sept

Burley
SU2103

▲ **Burley Youth Hostel,** Cott Lane, Burley, Ringwood, Hampshire, BH24 4BB
Actual Grid Ref: SU220028
Tel: 01425 403233
Fax: 01425 403233
Capacity: 36
Under 18: £6.90
Adults: £10.00
Open: All year, 5.00pm
Camping
Self-catering facilities • Self-catering facilities • Showers • Showers • Lounge • Dining room • Drying room • Cycle store • Cycle store • Parking • Evening meal available 7.00pm • No smoking • Kitchen facilities • Breakfast available • Credit cards accepted
Former family home situated along an unmade track in extensive grounds in the heart of the New Forest. Cycling, pony trekking and watersports all within easy reach.

Cosham
SU6605

▲ **Portsmouth Youth Hostel,** Wymering Manor, Old Wymering Lane, Cosham, Portsmouth, Hampshire, PO6 3NL
Actual Grid Ref: SU649055
Tel: 023 9237 5661
Fax: 023 9221 4177
Email: portsmouth@yha.org.uk
Capacity: 64
Under 18: £6.90
Adults: £10.00
Open: Feb to Dec, 5.00pm
Self-catering facilities • Showers • Lounge • Drying room • Cycle store • Parking • Evening meal available 7.00pm • Kitchen facilities • Breakfast available • Credit cards accepted
One of the oldest manor houses in Hampshire (Tudor), with a magnificent entrance hall and Jacobean staircases. Handy for all the Naval and historical sites that Portsmouth can offer.

Crawley
SU4234

▲ **Folly Farm,** Crawley, Winchester, Hampshire, SO21 2PH
Actual Grid Ref: SU415338
Tel: 01962 776486
Fax: 01962 776724
Open: Mar to Oct

Everton
SZ2994

▲ **Lytton Lawn Camping & Caravan Park,** Shorefield Road, Everton, Lymington, Hampshire, SO41 0TX
Actual Grid Ref: SZ295932
Tel: 01590 642513 / 643339
Email: holidays@shorefield.co.uk
Open: Mar to Dec

Fareham
SU5606

▲ **Ellerslie Camping & Caravan Park,** Down End Road, Fareham, Hampshire, PO16 8TS
Tel: 01329 822248
Fax: 01329 822248
Open: Mar to Oct

Fritham
SU2314

▲ **Longbeach Campsite,** Fritham, Lyndhurst, Hampshire, SO43 7HH
Actual Grid Ref: SU251119
Tel: 0131 314 6100
Email: fe.holidays@forestry.gov.uk
Open: Easter to Sep

▲ **Ocknell Campsite,** Fritham, Lyndhurst, Hampshire, SO43 7HH
Actual Grid Ref: SU251119
Tel: 0131 314 6100
Email: fe.holidays@forestry.gov.uk
Open: Easter to Sep

▲ **Ocknell Caravan & Camping,** Fritham, Lyndhurst, Hampshire, SO43 7HH
Actual Grid Ref: SU251119
Tel: 0131 314 6505
Open: Mar to Sept

You are advised to book in advance for periods of high demand – the Summer months, Half Term holidays and public holidays.

MAP PAGE **87** • Hampshire

Godshill

SU1714

▲ **Sandy Balls Holiday Centre,**
Sandy Balls Estate Ltd, Godshill,
Fordingbridge, Hampshire, SP6 2JY
Actual Grid Ref: SU169146
Tel: 01425 653042
Fax: 01425 653067
Email: post@sandy-balls.co.uk
Open: All year

Gosport

SU5900

▲ **Kingfisher Caravan Park,**
Browndown Road, Stokes Bay,
Gosport, Hampshire, PO13 9BE
Actual Grid Ref: SZ589988
Tel: 01705 502611
Fax: 01705 583583
Open: All year

Hamble

SU4706

▲ **Riverside Park,** Satchell Lane,
Hamble, Southampton, SO31 4RH
Actual Grid Ref: SU483080
Tel: 01703 453220
Open: Mar to Oct

▲ **Riverside Park,** Satchell Lane,
Hamble, Southampton, Hampshire,
SO31 4HR
Actual Grid Ref: SU481081
Tel: 023 8045 3220
Open: Mar to Oct

Hayling Island

SU7201

▲ **Lower Tye Farm Camp Site,**
Copse Lane, Hayling Island,
Hampshire, PO11 0RQ
Actual Grid Ref: SU729020
Tel: 023 9246 2479
Fax: 023 9246 2479
Email: lowertye@euphony.net
Tent pitches:
Tent rate: £10.00
Open: Mar to Oct
Last arr: 11pm
Facilities for disabled people • Dogs allowed • Electric hook-up • Calor Gas/Camping Gaz • Cafe or Takeaway on site • Picnic/barbecue area on site • Children's play area • Showers • Laundrette on site • Public phone on site • Shop on site
Level, sheltered, unit parking, yearly parking, rallies, Blue Flag beaches.

Please respect hostels' policy on smoking. Some hostels do not allow smoking anywhere, some restrict smoking to certain areas.

▲ **The Oven Camping Site,** Manor Road, Hayling Island, Hampshire, PO11 0QX
Actual Grid Ref: SU719005
Tel: 023 9246 4695
Fax: 023 9246 2479
Email: lowertye@euphony.net
Tent pitches: 300
Tent rate: £5.00-£10.00
Open: Mar to Jan
Facilities for disabled people • Dogs allowed • Electric hook-up • Calor Gas/Camping Gaz • Cafe or Takeaway on site • Children's play area • Showers • Laundrette on site • Public phone on site • Shop on site
Hayling Island, quiet family sites, amenities nearby, Blue Flag beaches.

▲ **Fleet Farm Caravan & Camping Park,** Yew Tree Road, Hayling Island, Hampshire, PO11 0QE
Actual Grid Ref: SU724017
Tel: 01705 463684
Open: Mar to Nov

▲ **Fishery Creek Caravan & Camping Park,** 31 Fishery Lane, Hayling Island, Hampshire, PO11 9NR
Actual Grid Ref: SZ734985
Tel: 01705 462164
Email: johnadams@hay-isle.demon.co.uk
Open: Mar to Oct

Holmsley

SU2200

▲ **Holmsley Caravan & Camping Site,** Ocknell Caravan & Camping, Fritham, Lyndhurst, Hampshire, SO43 7HH
Actual Grid Ref: SZ218992
Tel: 0131 314 6505
Open: Mar to Sept

Linwood

SU1809

▲ **Red Shoot Camping Park,**
Linwood, Ringwood, Hampshire, BH24 3QT
Actual Grid Ref: SU188094
Tel: 01425 473789
Fax: 01425 471558
Open: Mar to Oct

Lyndhurst

SU2908

▲ **Denny Wood Campsite,**
Beaulieu Road, Lyndhurst, Hampshire, SO43 7FZ
Actual Grid Ref: SU334069
Tel: 0131 314 6100
Email: fe.holidays@forestry.gov.uk
Open: Easter to Sep

▲ **Matley Wood Campsite,**
Beaulieu Road, Lyndhurst, Hampshire, SO43 7FZ
Actual Grid Ref: SU332076
Tel: 0131 314 6100
Email: fe.holidays@forestry.gov.uk
Open: Easter to Sep

Milford on Sea

SZ2891

▲ **Shorefield Country Park,**
Shorefield Road, Milford on Sea, Lymington, Hampshire, SO41 0LH
Tel: 01202 648331
Email: holidays@shorefield.co.uk
Open: Mar to Dec

New Milton

SZ2395

▲ **Bashley Park,** Sway Road, New Milton, Hampshire, BH25 5QR
Actual Grid Ref: SZ245972
Tel: 01425 612340
Fax: 01425 612602
Email: enquiries@hoburne.co.uk
Open: Mar to Oct

▲ **Glen Orchard Holiday Park,**
Walkford Lane, New Milton, Hampshire, BH25 5NH
Tel: 01425 616463
Email: enquiries@glenorchard.co.uk
Open: Mar to Oct

▲ **Naish Holiday Village,** New Milton, Hampshire, BH25 7RE
Tel: 01425 273586
Email: enquiries@hoburne.co.uk
Open: Mar to Oct

Odiham

SU7451

▲ **Newlands Farm,** Odiham, Hook, Hampshire, RG29 1JD
Tel: 01256 702373
Fax: 01256 702373
Open: All year

Stilwell's Hostels & Camping 2002

Hampshire • MAP PAGE 87

Ower
SU3217

▲ **Green Pastures Farm,** Ower, Romsey, Hampshire, SO51 6AJ
Actual Grid Ref: SU323158
Tourist Board grade: 3 Star
AA grade: 3 Pennants
Tel: 023 8081 4444
Email: enquiries@greenpasturesfarm.com
Tent pitches:
Tent rate: £9.00
Open: Mar to Oct
*Facilities for disabled people • Dogs allowed • Electric hook-up • Calor Gas/Camping Gaz • Children's play area • Showers • Laundrette on site • Public phone on site • Shop on site
Family-run farm/campsite. Very good toilet facilities. Safe for children.*

Portsmouth
SU6501

▲ **Harbour Side Holiday Caravan & Camping,** Eastern Road, Portsmouth, Hampshire, PO3 6QD
Actual Grid Ref: SU676023
Tel: 01705 663867
Open: Mar to Oct

Sherfield English
SU2922

▲ **Doctors Hill Farm,** Sherfield English, Romsey, Hampshire, SO51 6JX
Actual Grid Ref: SU299230
Tel: 01794 340402
Open: Mar to Oct

Southsea
SZ6598

▲ **Southsea Leisure Park,** Melville Road, Southsea, Hampshire, PO4 9TB
Actual Grid Ref: SZ677990
Tel: 01705 735070 **Fax:** 01705 821302
Open: All year

Sparsholt
SU4331

▲ **Balldown Caravan & Camping Park,** Stockbridge Road, Sparsholt, Winchester, Hampshire, SO21 2NA
Tel: 01962 776691
Open: Mar to Oct

▲ **Balldown Caravan & Camping Park,** Stockbridge Road, Sparsholt, Winchester, Hampshire, SO21 2NA
Actual Grid Ref: SU433329
Tel: 01962 776619
Open: Mar to Oct

Steep
SU7425

▲ **The White Horse Inn,** Priors Dean, Steep, Petersfield, Hampshire, GU32 1DA
Actual Grid Ref: SU715290
Tel: 01420 588387
Open: All year

Warsash
SU4906

▲ **Dibles Park,** Dibles Road, Warsash, Southampton, SO31 9SA
Actual Grid Ref: SU505060
Tel: 01489 575232
Open: Mar to Nov

Winchester
SU4829

▲ **Winchester Youth Hostel,** The City Mill, 1 Water Lane, Winchester, Hampshire, SO23 8EJ
Actual Grid Ref: SU486293
Tel: 01962 853723
Fax: 01962 855524
Capacity: 31
Under 18: £6.50
Adults: £9.25
Open: Mar to Nov, 5.00pm
*Showers • Lounge • Cycle store • No smoking • Kitchen facilities • Breakfast available 7.00pm • Credit cards accepted
Charming C18th watermill (NT) straddling the River Itchen at East End of King Alfred's capital, a half mile from the cathedral*

▲ **Morn Hill Caravan Club Site,** Morn Hill, Winchester, Hampshire, SO21 1HL
Tel: 01962 869877
Open: Apr to Oct

Wootton
SZ2498

▲ **Sethorns Caravan & Camping Site,** Wootton, New Milton, Hampshire, BH25 5UA
Actual Grid Ref: SU262003
Tel: 0131 314 6100
Email: fe.holidays@forestry.gov.uk
Open: All year

Herefordshire

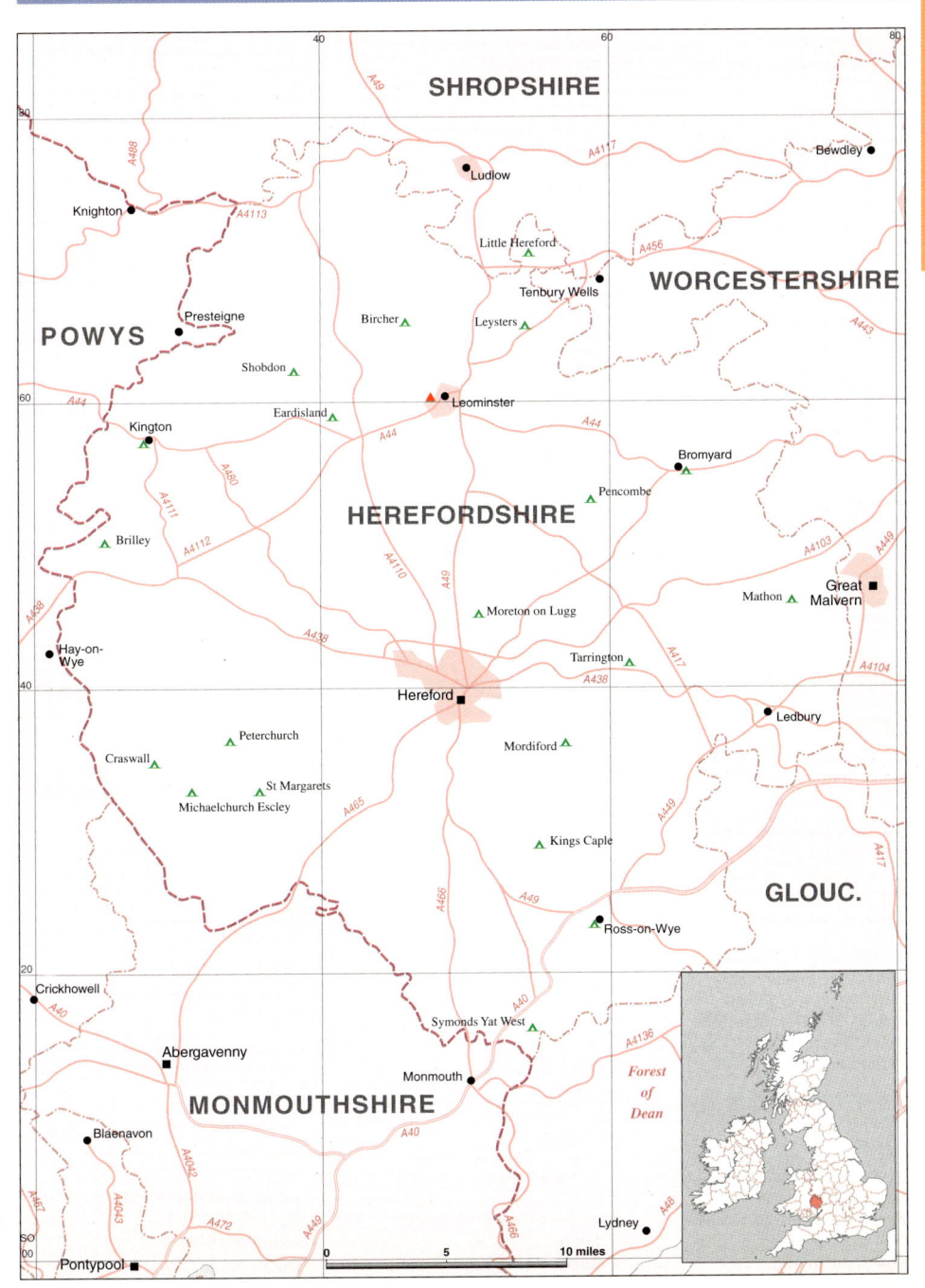

Herefordshire • MAP PAGE 91

Bircher
SO4765

▲ **Home Farm,** Bircher, Leominster, Herefordshire, HR6 0AX
Actual Grid Ref: SO477655
Tel: 01568 780525
Open: All year

Brilley
SO2649

▲ **Penlan Caravan Park,** Penlan, Brilley, Whitney, Hereford, HR3 6JW
Actual Grid Ref: SO273516
Tel: 01497 831485
Fax: 01497 831485
Email: p.joyce@btinternet.com
Open: Easter to Oct

Bromyard
SO6554

▲ **Saltmarshe Castle Caravan Site,** Bromyard, Hereford, HR7 4PN
Actual Grid Ref: SO670578
Tel: 01885 488465
Open: Mar to Oct

Craswall
SO2835

▲ **Old Mill Campsite,** Craswall, Hereford, HR2 0PN
Tel: 01981 510226
Open: Easter to Oct

Eardisland
SO4158

▲ **The Elms Camping Site,** Eardisland, Leominster, Herefordshire, HR6 9BN
Tel: 01544 388405
Open: Easter to Sep

▲ **Arrow Bank Caravan Park,** Eardisland, Leominster, Herefordshire, HR6 9BG
Actual Grid Ref: SO419589
Tel: 01544 388312
Open: Mar to Oct

Kings Caple
SO5628

▲ **Lower Ruxton Farm,** Kings Caple, Hereford, HR1 4TX
Actual Grid Ref: SO552292
Tel: 01432 840223
Open: Jul to Aug

Kington
SO2956

▲ **Harbour Farm,** Newchurch, Kington, Herefordshire, HR5 3QW
Tel: 01544 22248
Open: Mar to Oct

▲ **Cambridge Cottage,** 19 Church Street, Kington, Herefordshire, HR5 3BE
Tel: 01544 231300
Open: All year

Leominster
SO4959

▲ **Leominster Youth Hostel,** The Old Priory, Leominster, Herefordshire, HR6 8EQ
Tel: 01568 620517
Fax: 01568 620517
Capacity: 30
Under 18: £7.75 **Adults:** £11.00
Open: All year, 5.00pm
Family bunk rooms
Self-catering facilities • Showers • Laundry facilities • Lounge • Drying room • Parking • Facilities for disabled people • No smoking • Kitchen facilities
A brand new hostel, within the Old Priory monastic complex.

Leysters
SO5663

▲ **Woonton Court Farm,** Woonton, Leysters, Leominster, Herefordshire, HR6 0HL
Tel: 01568 750232
Open: All year

Little Hereford
SO5568

▲ **Westbrook Park,** Little Hereford, Ludlow, Shropshire, SY8 4AU
Tel: 01584 711280
Open: All year

Mathon
SO7346

▲ **South Hyde,** Mathon, Malvern, Hereford & Worcester, WR13 5PD
Actual Grid Ref: SO739441
Tel: 01684 540289
Open: Mar to Sept

Michaelchurch Escley
SO3134

▲ **The Bridge Inn,** Michaelchurch Escley, Hereford & Worcester, HR2 0JW
Actual Grid Ref: SO310341
Tel: 01981 510646
Open: Apr to Sep

Mordiford
SO5737

▲ **Lucksall Caravanning & Camping Park,** Mordiford, Hereford, HR1 4LP
Actual Grid Ref: SO567362
Tel: 01432 870213
Open: Mar to Oct

Moreton on Lugg
SO5045

▲ **Cuckoos Corner,** Moreton on Lugg, Hereford, HR4 8AH
Tel: 01432 760234
Open: All year

Pencombe
SO5952

▲ **Shortwood,** Pencombe, Bromyard, Herefordshire, HR7 4RP
Tel: 01885 400205
Open: May to Oct

Peterchurch
SO3438

▲ **Poston Mill Caravan & Camping Site,** Peterchurch, Hereford, HR2 0SF
Actual Grid Ref: SO356371
Tel: 01981 550225
Fax: 01981 550885
Email: enquiries@poston-mill.co.uk
Open: All year

Ross-on-Wye
SO6024

▲ **Broadmeadow Caravan Park,** Broadmeadow, Ross-on-Wye, Herefordshire, HR9 7BH
Actual Grid Ref: SO607246
Tel: 01989 768076
Fax: 01989 566030
Open: Apr to Oct

MAP PAGE 91 • **Herefordshire**

Shobdon

SO3961

▲ **Shobdon Airfield Touring Site,**
Shobdon, Leominster, HR6 9NR
Tel: 01568 708369
Fax: 01568 708935
Open: Mar to Jan

▲ **Pearl Lake Leisure Park,**
Shobdon, Leominster, HR6 9NQ
Tel: 01568 708326
Open: Mar to Nov

St Margarets

SO3533

▲ **Upper Gilvach Farm,** St Margarets, Vowchurch, Hereford, HR2 0QY
Actual Grid Ref: SO342347
Tel: 01981 510618
Open: All year

Hostels and campsites may vary rates – be sure to check when booking.

Symonds Yat West

SO5516

▲ **Doward Park Campsite,** Great Doward, Symonds Yat West, Ross-on-Wye, Herefordshire, HR9 6BP
Actual Grid Ref: SO543164
Tel: 01600 890438
Open: Mar to Oct

▲ **Symonds Yat Caravan & Camping Site,** Symonds Yat West, Ross-on-Wye, Herefordshire, HR9 6BY
Actual Grid Ref: SO556173
Tel: 01600 890883
Open: Apr to Oct

All details shown are as supplied by hostels and campsites in Autumn 2000.

Tarrington

SO6141

▲ **Little Tarrington Fishing and Leisure,** The Mill Pond, Tarrington, Hereford, HR1 4JD
Actual Grid Ref: SO626409
Tel: 01432 890243
Open: Mar to Oct

If you have to cancel your visit to any hostel or campsite, please let them know – it is always possible to make a bed or a pitch available to someone else.

ENGLAND

Hertfordshire

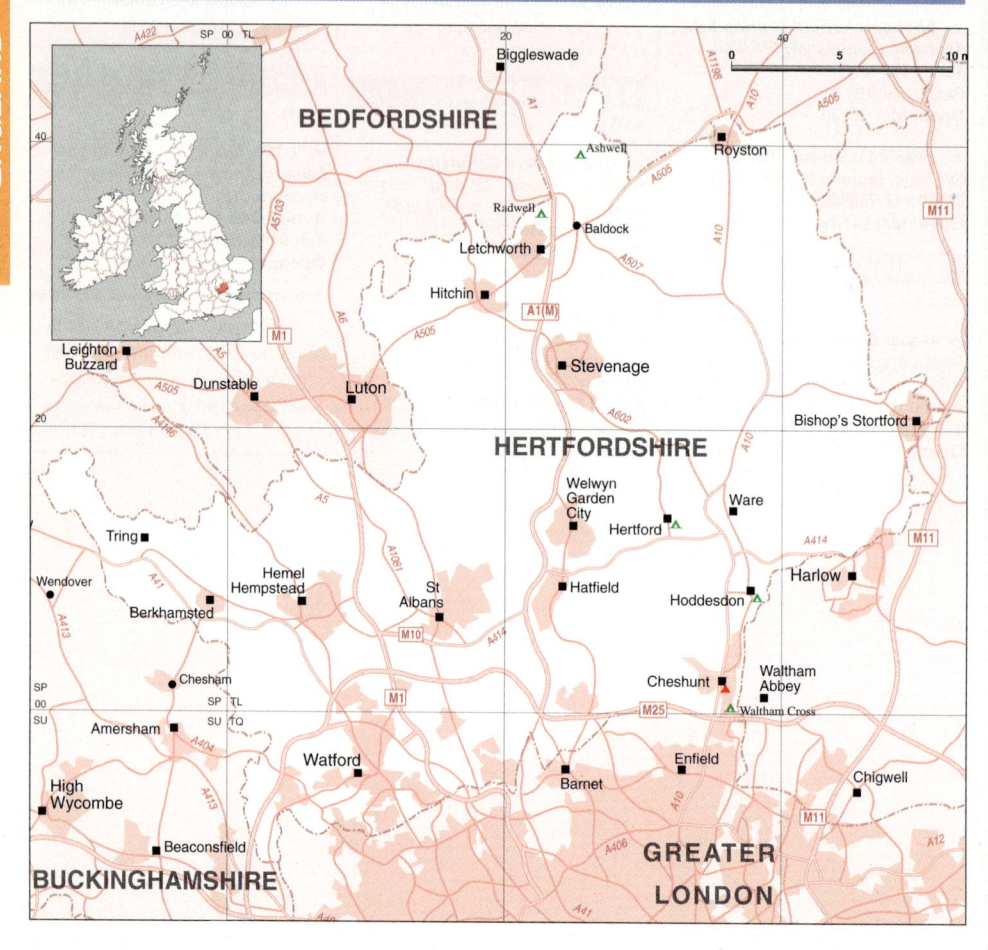

Ashwell
TL2639

▲ **Ashridge Farm Touring Caravan Park,** 1 Ahwell Street, Ashwell, Baldock, Hertfordshire, SG7 5QF
Actual Grid Ref: TL276299
Tel: 01462 742527
Open: All year

Hostels and campsites may vary rates – be sure to check when booking.

Cheshunt
TL3602

▲ **Lee Valley Youth Hostel,** Lee Valley Park, Cheshunt, Waltham Cross, Hertfordshire, EN8 0QU
Tel: 020 7373 3400
Capacity: 112
Under 18: £11.50 **Adults:** £15.50
Family bunk rooms
Evening meal available • Facilities for disabled people

A spanking new hostel, due to open in late summer 2001, in the heart of the Lee Valley, with its Country Park, nature reserves, lakes and reservoirs, as well as historical and heritage sites.

Hertford
TL3212

▲ **Camping & Caravanning Club Site,** Mangrove Lane, Hertford, SG13 8QF
Actual Grid Ref: TL334113
Tel: 01992 586696
Open: Mar to Oct

You are advised to book in advance for periods of high demand – the Summer months, Half Term holidays and public holidays.

Hertfordshire

Hoddesdon

TL3708

▲ **Lee Valley Caravan Park,** *Dobbs Weir, Essex Road, Hoddesdon, Herts, EN11 0AS*
Actual Grid Ref: TL383082
Tel: 01992 462090
Open: Mar to Oct

Radwell

TL2335

▲ **Radwell Mill Caravan Site,** *Radwell Mill, Radwell, Baldock, Hertfordshire, SG7 5ET*
Tel: 01462 730253
Open: Easter to Oct

Waltham Cross

TL3501

▲ **Camping & Caravanning Club Site,** *Theobands Park, Bulls Cross Ride, Waltham Cross, Herts, EN7 5HS*
Actual Grid Ref: TL344005
Tel: 01992 620604
Open: Mar to Oct

Isle of Wight

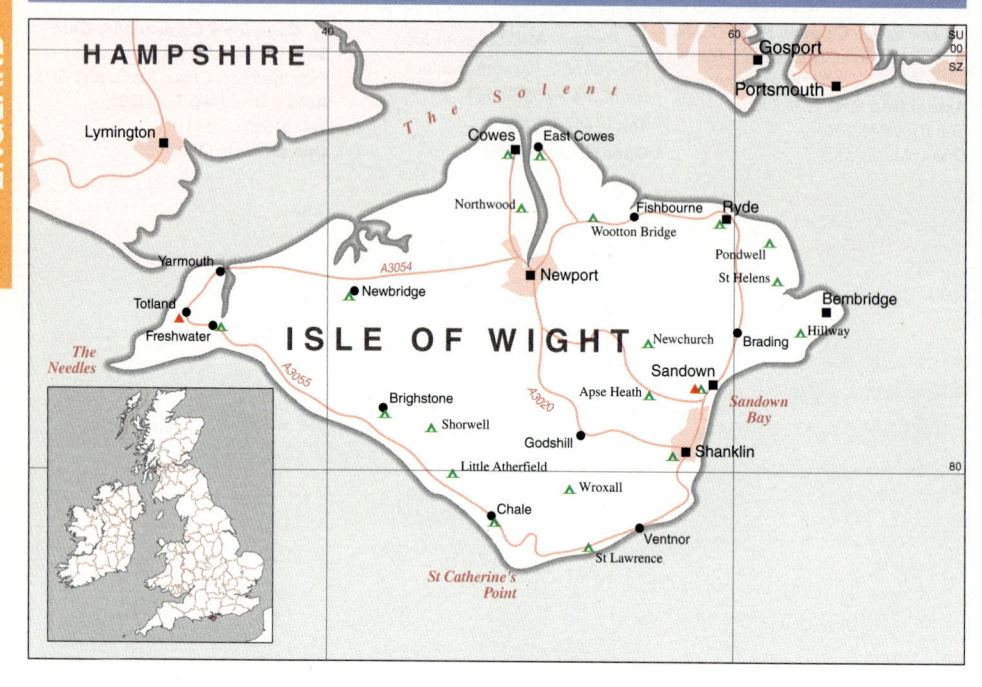

Apse Heath
SZ5683

▲ **Village Way Camping,** Newport Road, Apse Heath, Sandown, Isle of Wight, PO36 9PJ
Actual Grid Ref: SZ569834
Tel: 01983 863279
Tent rate: £2.50
Open: Mar to Oct
Last arr: any time
Dogs allowed • Electric hook-up • Calor Gas/Camping Gaz • Picnic/barbecue area on site • Showers • Laundrette on site • Public phone on site
Marvellous views, free carp fishing on site. Showers, laundrette, Calor Gas/Camping Gaz, phone.

Brighstone
SZ4382

▲ **Grange Farm Caravan & Camping Site,** Military Road, Brighstone, Newport, Isle of Wight, PO30 4DA
Actual Grid Ref: SZ421819
Tel: 01983 740296 **Open:** Mar to Nov

Chale
SZ4877

▲ **Tuttons Hill Camping,** Tuttons Hill Cottage, South Down, Chale, Ventnor, Isle of Wight, PO38 2LJ
Actual Grid Ref: SZ47684
Tel: 01983 551277
Fax: 01983 551277
Email: drdog234@aol.com
Tent pitches: 12
Tent rate: £5.00
Open: All year
Last arr: any time
Dogs allowed • Showers
Peaceful family farm with stunning sea and Downs views.

Cowes
SZ4996

▲ **Gurnard Pines Holiday Village,** Cocketon Lane, Cowes, Isle of Wight, PO31 8QE
Tel: 01983 292395
Open: Mar to Sept

▲ **Thorness Bay Holiday Park,** Thorness, Cowes, Isle of Wight, PO31 8QE
Actual Grid Ref: SZ452927
Tel: 01983 523109
Open: May to Sep

East Cowes
SZ5095

▲ **Waverley Park Holiday Centre,** 51 Old Road, East Cowes, Isle of Wight, PO32 6AW
Actual Grid Ref: SZ505958
Tourist Board grade: 2 Star
Tel: 01983 293452 **Fax:** 01983 200494
Email: waverleypark@netscapeonline.co.uk
Tent pitches: 30
Tent rate: £6.50-£10.50
Open: Mar to Oct **Last arr:** 10pm
Dogs allowed • Electric hook-up • Calor Gas/Camping Gaz • Children's play area • Showers • Laundrette on site • Public phone on site • Licensed bar on site • Shop on site
Panoramic views of the Solent - easy walking distance from Cowes.

Isle of Wight

Freshwater
SZ3486

▲ **Heathfield Farm Camping Site,** Heathfield Road, Freshwater, Isle of Wight, PO40 7SH
Actual Grid Ref: SZ335879
Tel: 01983 756756
Open: May to Sep

Hillway
SZ6486

▲ **Whitecliff Bay Holiday Park,** Hillway, Whitecliff Bay, Bembridge, Isle of Wight, PO35 5PL
Actual Grid Ref: SZ642867
Tel: 01983 872671 **Open:** Mar to Oct

Little Atherfield
SZ4679

▲ **Chine Farm Camping Site,** Military Road, Atherfield Bay, Little Atherfield, Ventnor, Isle of Wight, PO38 2JH
Tel: 01983 740228
Open: May to Sep

Newbridge
SZ4187

▲ **Orchards Holiday Caravan Park,** Newbridge, Yarmouth, Isle of Wight, PO41 0TS
Actual Grid Ref: SZ411878
Tel: 01983 531331
Email: info@orchards-holiday-park.co.uk
Open: All year

Newchurch
SZ5685

▲ **Southlands Camping Park,** Newchurch, Sandown, Isle of Wight, PO36 0LZ
Actual Grid Ref: SZ557847
Tel: 01983 865385
Email: info@southland.co.uk
Open: Apr to Sep

Northwood
SZ4894

▲ **Comforts Farm,** Pallance Road, Northwood, Cowes, Isle of Wight, PO31 8LS
Actual Grid Ref: SZ478936
Tel: 01983 293888
Open: May to Sep

Pondwell
SZ6191

▲ **Pondwell Camp Site,** Pondwell Hill, Ryde, Isle of Wight, PO33 1QA
Actual Grid Ref: SZ618913
Tel: 01983 612330
Open: May to Sep

Ryde
SZ5992

▲ **Beaper Farm,** Ryde, Isle of Wight, PO33 1QJ
Actual Grid Ref: SZ607893
Tel: 01983 615210
Open: Apr to Oct

▲ **Carpenters Farm,** Ryde, Isle of Wight, PO33 1JL
Actual Grid Ref: SZ618886
Tel: 01983 872450
Open: Jun to Sep

Sandown
SZ5984

▲ **Sandown Youth Hostel,** The Firs, Fitzroy Street, Sandown, Isle of Wight, PO36 8JH
Actual Grid Ref: SZ597843
Tel: 01983 402651
Fax: 01983 403565
Capacity: 47
Under 18: £7.75
Adults: £11.00
Open: All year, 5.00pm
Family bunk rooms
Self-catering facilities • Self-catering facilities • Television • Showers • Showers • Lounge • Drying room • Cycle store • Parking • Evening meal available 6.30pm • No smoking • Kitchen facilities • Breakfast available • Luggage store • Credit cards accepted
The hostel is just a few minutes walk from the town centre. The Isle of Wight has interests for everyone, from Osborne and other sites of historic interest, geological interests, fishing to walking, cycling and watersports of all descriptions.

▲ **Camping & Caravanning Club Site,** Cheverton Farm, Newport Road, Sandown, Isle of Wight, PO36 9PJ
Actual Grid Ref: SZ573833
Tel: 01983 866414
Open: Mar to Nov

▲ **Adgestone Camping Park,** Lower Road, Adgestone, Sandown, Isle of Wight, PO36 0HL
Actual Grid Ref: SZ590856
Tel: 01983 403432
Fax: 01983 404955
Open: Easter to Sep

▲ **Fairway Holiday Park Ltd,** Sandown, Isle of Wight, PO36 9PS
Actual Grid Ref: SZ592850
Tel: 01983 403462
Open: Mar to Oct

▲ **Cheverton Copse Holiday Park,** Newport Road, Sandown, Isle of Wight, PO36 0JP
Actual Grid Ref: SZ574838
Tel: 01983 403161
Open: May to Sep

Shanklin
SZ5881

▲ **Landguard Camping Park,** Landguard Manor Road, Shanklin, Isle of Wight, PO37 7PH
Actual Grid Ref: SZ576826
Tel: 01983 867028
Open: May to Sep

▲ **Ninham Country Holidays,** Shanklin, Isle of Wight, PO37 7PL
Actual Grid Ref: SZ572827
Tel: 01983 864243 **Fax:** 01983 868881
Open: Apr to Sep

▲ **Lower Hyde Holiday Village,** Languard Road, Shanklin, Isle of Wight, PO37 7LL
Actual Grid Ref: SZ575819
Tel: 01983 866131
Open: Apr to Oct

Shorwell
SZ4682

▲ **Tythe Barn,** Bucks Farm, Shorwell, Newport, Isle of Wight, PO30 3LP
Tel: 01983 551206
Fax: 01983 551206
Open: All year

St Helens
SZ6389

▲ **Nodes Point Holiday Park,** Nodes Road, St Helens, Ryde, Isle of Wight, PO33 1YA
Actual Grid Ref: SZ637897
Tel: 01983 872401
Open: May to Oct

ENGLAND

Stilwell's Hostels & Camping 2002   97

Isle of Wight • MAP PAGE 96

St Lawrence

SZ5376

▲ **The Orchard Estate,** St Lawrence, Ventnor, Isle of Wight, PO38 1YA
Actual Grid Ref: SZ513760
Tel: 01983 511089
Open: All year

Totland Bay

SZ3186

▲ **Totland Bay (West Wight) Youth Hostel,** Hurst Hill, Totland Bay, Isle of Wight, PO39 0HD
Actual Grid Ref: SZ324865
Tel: 01983 752165
Fax: 01983 756443
Capacity: 56
Under 18: £7.75
Adults: £11.00
Open: All year, 5.00pm
Family bunk rooms *Self-catering facilities • Self-catering facilities • Television • Showers • Shop • Wet weather shelter • Lounge • Dining room • Drying room • Cycle store • Parking • Evening meal available 6.30pm • No smoking • Kitchen facilities • Credit cards accepted* Seaside location, close to downland, cliffs, beaches and quiet country walks.

Wootton Bridge

SZ5491

▲ **Kite Hill Farm Caravan and Camping Park,** Wootton Bridge, Ryde, Isle of Wight, PO33 4LE
Actual Grid Ref: SZ551917
Tel: 01983 882543
Open: All year

Wroxall

SZ5579

▲ **Appuldurcombe Gardens Caravan & Camping Park,** Appuldurcombe Road, Wroxall, Ventnor, Isle of Wight, PO38 3EP
Actual Grid Ref: SZ548802
Tel: 01983 852597
Open: Apr to Oct

Isles of Scilly

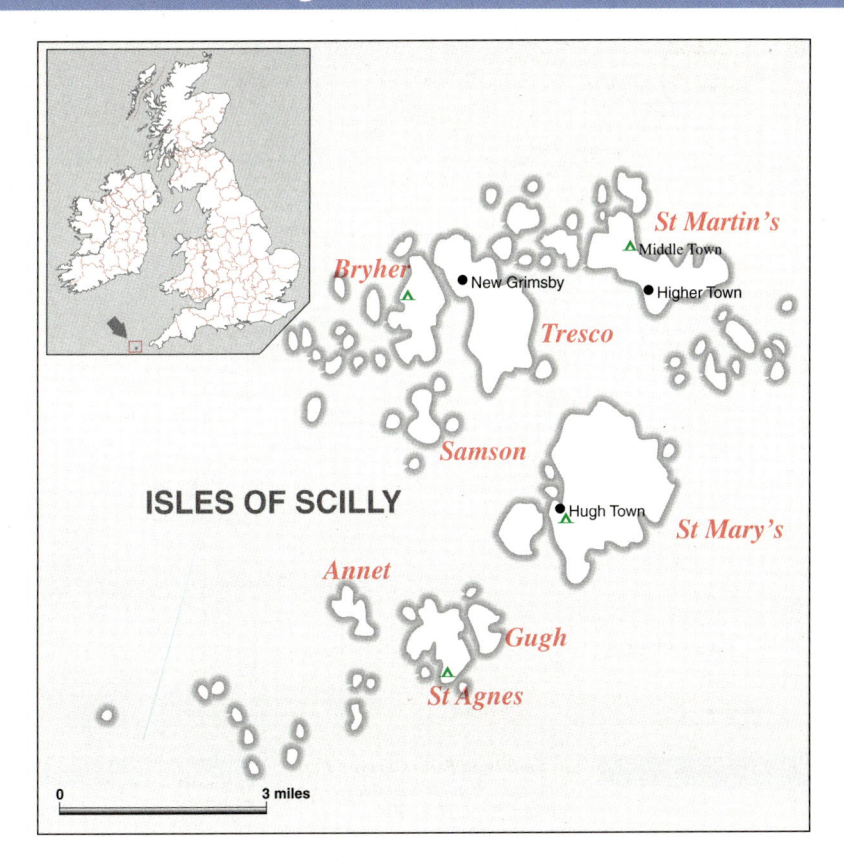

Bryher
SV8715

▲ **Jenford,** Bryher, Isles of Scilly, TR23 0PR
Actual Grid Ref: SV880155
Tel: 01720 422886
Open: Apr to Oct

Middle Town
SV9216

▲ **St Martin's Campsite,** Middle Town, St Martins, Isles of Scilly, TR25 0QN
Actual Grid Ref: SV923164
Tel: 01720 422888
Open: All year

St Agnes
SV8807

▲ **Troytown Farm,** St Agnes, Isles of Scilly, TR22 0PL
Actual Grid Ref: SV875081
Tel: 01720 422360
Open: Mar to Oct

St Mary's
SV9010

▲ **Garrison Farm Camping Site,** The Garrison, St Mary's, Isles of Scilly, TR21 0LS
Actual Grid Ref: SV898104
Tel: 01720 422670
Open: Mar to Oct

Kent

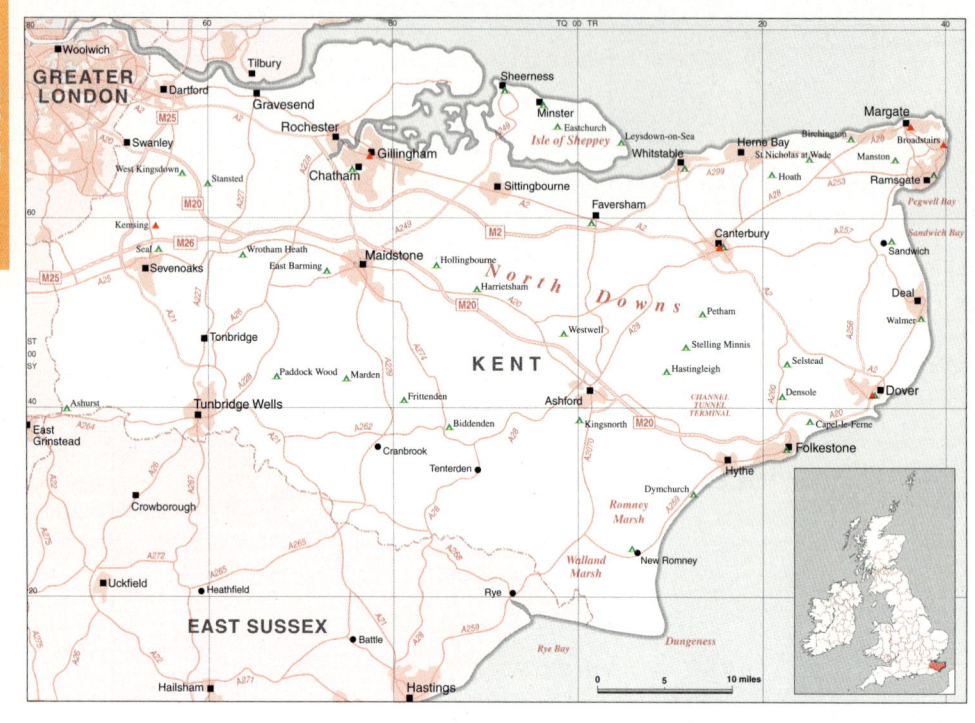

Ashurst

TQ5138

▲ **Manor Court Farm,** Ashurst, Tunbridge Wells, Kent, TN3 9TB
Tel: 01892 740279
Fax: 01892 740919
Email: jsoyke.freeserve.co.uk
Tent pitches: 5
Tent rate: £4.00-£5.00
Open: All year **Last arr:** 9pm
Dogs allowed • Electric hook-up • Showers • Public phone on site
Choose own site in garden/pond/orchard area. Lovely views.

Biddenden

TQ8438

▲ **Woodlands Park,** Tenterden Road, Biddenden, Ashford, Kent, TN27 8BT
Actual Grid Ref: TQ867372
Tel: 01580 291216
Email: woodlandsp@aol.com
Open: Mar to Oct

▲ **Spill Land Farm Caravan Park,** Benenden Road, Biddenden, Ashford, Kent, TN27 8BX
Tel: 01580 291379
Open: Mar to Oct

Birchington

TR2969

▲ **Two Chimneys Caravan Park,** Five Acres, Shottendane Road, Birchington, Kent, CT7 0HD
Actual Grid Ref: TR320684
Tel: 01843 841068 **Fax:** 01843 848099
Open: Mar to Oct

▲ **Quex Caravan Park,** Park Road, Birchington, Kent, CT7 0BL
Actual Grid Ref: TR321685
Tel: 01843 841273
Open: Mar to Nov

Hostels and campsites may vary rates – be sure to check when booking.

Broadstairs

TR3967

▲ **Broadstairs (Ramsgate) Youth Hostel,** Thistle Lodge, 3 Osborne Road, Broadstairs, Kent, CT10 2AE
Actual Grid Ref: TR390679
Tel: 01843 604121
Fax: 01843 604121
Email: broadstairs@yha.org.uk
Capacity: 34
Under 18: £6.90 **Adults:** £10.00
Open: All year, 5.00
Self-catering facilities • Television • Showers • Laundry facilities • Lounge • Dining room • Drying room • Cycle store • Evening meal available 6.30-7.30pm • No smoking • Kitchen facilities • Credit cards accepted
Victorian villa in a residential area. Near museums, coastal walks and sheltered sandy beach.

Stilwell's Hostels & Camping 2002

Kent

Canterbury
TR151560

▲ **Canterbury Youth Hostel,** Ellerslie, 54 New Dover Road, Canterbury, Kent, CT1 3DT
Actual Grid Ref: TR157570
Tel: 01227 462911
Fax: 01227 470752
Email: canterbury@yha.org
Capacity: 85
Under 18: £7.75 **Adults:** £11.00
Open: Feb to Dec, 1 pm
Self-catering facilities • Television • Showers • Laundry facilities • Lounge • Cycle store • Parking • Evening meal available 6.00pm to 7.30pm • Kitchen facilities • Breakfast available • Credit cards accepted
A Victorian villa close to centre of principal cathedral city of England.

▲ **Kipps Independent Hostel,** 40 Nunnery Fields, Canterbury, Kent, CT1 3JT
Tel: 01227 786121
Fax: 01227 766992
Email: info@kipps-hostel.com
Capacity: 33 **Adults:** £11.00
Open: All year (not Xmas), 8am
Family bunk rooms: £38.00
Camping for 2 tents: £7.50
Self-catering facilities • Television • Showers • Central heating • Shop • Laundry facilities • Lounge • Dining room • Cycle store • Parking • No smoking
100-year-old town house. Cathedral 10 minutes' walk away.

▲ **Camping & Caravanning Club Site,** Bekesbourne Lane, Canterbury, CT3 4AB
Actual Grid Ref: TR172577
Tel: 01227 463216
Open: All year

▲ **Royal Oak,** 114 Sweechgate, Broad Oak, Canterbury, CT2 0QP
Tel: 01227 710448
Open: Apr to Oct

Capel-le-Ferne
TR2538

▲ **Little Satmar Holiday Park,** Winehouse Lane, Capel-le-Ferne, Folkestone, Kent, CT18 7JF
Actual Grid Ref: TR256392
Tel: 01303 251188
Open: Apr to Oct

Chatham
TQ7665

▲ **Woolmans Wood Caravan Park,** Bridgewood, Chatham, Kent, ME5 9SB
Actual Grid Ref: TQ747637
Tel: 01634 867685
Email: woolmans.wood@currantbun.com
Open: All year

Densole
TR2141

▲ **Black Horse Farm,** 385 Canterbury Road, Densole, Folkestone, Kent, CT18 7BG
Actual Grid Ref: TR211418
Tel: 01303 892665
Open: All year

Dover
TR3141

▲ **Dover Youth Hostel,** 306 London Road, Dover, Kent, CT17 0SY
Actual Grid Ref: TR311421
Tel: 01304 201314
Fax: 01304 202236
Email: dover@yha.org.uk
Capacity: 132
Under 18: £7.75 **Adults:** £11.00
Open: All year, 1.00pm
Self-catering facilities • Television • Showers • Lounge • Games room • Evening meal available 6.30pm to 7.30pm • Kitchen facilities • Breakfast available
There are two buildings for hostel accommodation in historic Dover, both recently refurbished.

▲ **Hawthorn Farm Caravan Park,** Station Road, Martin Hill, Dover, Kent, CT15 5LA
Actual Grid Ref: TR341465
Tel: 01304 852658 / 852914
Fax: 01304 853417
Open: Mar to Oct

Dymchurch
TR1029

▲ **New Beach Holiday Village,** Hythe Road, Dymchurch, Romney Marsh, Kent, TN29 0JX
Actual Grid Ref: TR122519
Tel: 01303 872233
Fax: 01303 872939
Open: Mar to Jan

East Barming
TQ7254

▲ **Riverside Caravan Park,** Farleigh Bridge, Farleigh Lane, East Barming, Maidstone, Kent, ME16 9ND
Tel: 01622 726647
Open: Mar to Oct

Eastchurch
TQ9871

▲ **Warden Springs Caravan Park Ltd,** Warden Point, Eastchurch, Sheerness, Kent, ME12 4HF
Actual Grid Ref: TR017722
Tel: 01795 880216
Fax: 01795 880218
Open: Mar to Oct

Faversham
TR0161

▲ **Painters Farm Caravan & Camping Site,** Painters Forstal, Faversham, Kent, ME13 0EG
Actual Grid Ref: TQ990591
Tel: 01795 532995
Open: Mar to Oct

Folkestone
TR2136

▲ **Camping & Caravanning Club Site,** The Warren, Folkestone, Kent, CT19 6PT
Actual Grid Ref: TR246376
Tel: 01303 255093
Open: Mar to Sept

▲ **Little Switzerland Camping & Caravan Site,** Wear Bay Road, Folkestone, Kent, CT19 6PS
Actual Grid Ref: TR243375
Tel: 01303 252168
Open: Mar to Oct

Frittenden
TQ8141

▲ **Manor Farm,** Frittenden, Cranbrook, Kent, TN17 2EN
Actual Grid Ref: TQ41
Tel: 01580 852288
Tent pitches: 10
Tent rate: £2.50
Open: May to Sep
Last arr: 6pm
Dogs allowed
WC; hot/cold water. Coarse fishing £1 per day, pub 300 yds.

Kent • MAP PAGE 100

Gillingham
TQ7767

▲ **Medway Youth Hostel,** Capstone Road, Gillingham, Kent, ME7 3JE
Actual Grid Ref: TQ783653
Tel: 01634 400788
Fax: 01634 400794
Capacity: 40
Under 18: £7.75
Adults: £11.00
Open: Jan to Dec, 5.00pm
Family bunk rooms
Self-catering facilities • Television • Showers • Laundry facilities • Drying room • Cycle store • Parking • Evening meal available 7.00pm • Facilities for disabled people • No smoking • WC • Kitchen facilities • Breakfast available • Luggage store • Credit cards accepted
Archetypal Kentish oasthouse, fully restored and refurbished. Opposite Capstone Country Park, with nature trails & fishing lake. Rochester with its Dickens connections is closeby as are the historic Dockyards and museums at Chatham. A dry ski slope is nearby.

Harrietsham
TQ8752

▲ **Hogbarn Caravan Park,** Hogbarn Lane, Stede Mill, Harrietsham, Maidstone, Kent, ME17 1NZ
Actual Grid Ref: TQ884550
Tel: 01622 859648
Open: Apr to Oct

Hastingleigh
TR0944

▲ **Hazel Tree Farm,** Hassell Street, Hastingleigh, Ashford, Kent, TN25 5JE
Actual Grid Ref: TR091464
Tel: 01233 750234
Open: May to Oct

Hoath
TR1964

▲ **South View,** Maypole Lane, Hoath, Canterbury, CT3 4LL
Actual Grid Ref: TR202648
Tel: 01227 860280
Open: All year

Hollingbourne
TQ8455

▲ **Pine Lodge Touring Park,** Ashford Road, Hollingbourne, Maidstone, Kent, ME17 1XH
Actual Grid Ref: TQ818549
Tel: 01622 730018
Open: All year

Kemsing
TQ5558

▲ **Kemsing Youth Hostel,** Church Lane, Kemsing, Sevenoaks, Kent, TN15 6LU
Actual Grid Ref: TQ555588
Tel: 01732 761341
Fax: 01732 763044
Capacity: 50
Under 18: £6.90 **Adults:** £10.00
Open: Jan to Dec, 5.00pm
Camping
Self-catering facilities • Television • Showers • Lounge • Dining room • Drying room • Cycle store • Evening meal available 7.00pm • Kitchen facilities • Breakfast available • Credit cards accepted
Imposing Victorian vicarage in its own grounds at the foot of the North Downs.

Kingsnorth
TR0039

▲ **Broad Hembury Farm Caravan & Camping,** Steeds Lane, Kingsnorth, Ashford, Kent, TN26 1NQ
Actual Grid Ref: TR009380
Tel: 01233 620859 **Fax:** 01233 620859
Email: holidays@broadhembury.co.uk
Open: All year

Leysdown-on-Sea
TR0370

▲ **Harts Holiday Village,** Leysdown Road, Leysdown-on-Sea, Sheerness, Kent, ME12 4RL
Tel: 01795 510225
Open: Mar to Oct

▲ **Priory Hill,** Wing Road, Leysdown-on-Sea, Sheerness, Kent, ME12 4QT
Actual Grid Ref: TR038704
Tel: 01795 510267
Open: Mar to Oct

Manston
TR3366

▲ **Manston Caravan & Camping Park,** Manston Court Road, Manston, Ramsgate, Kent, CT12 5AU
Actual Grid Ref: TR344667
Tel: 01843 823442
Open: Mar to Oct

▲ **Pine Meadow Caravan Park,** Sprattling Court Farm, Sprattling Street, Manston, Ramsgate, Kent, CT12 5AN
Actual Grid Ref: TR357662
Tel: 01843 587770
Open: Apr to Sep

Marden
TQ7444

▲ **Tanner Farm Caravan & Camping Park,** Goodhurst Road, Marden, Tonbridge, Kent, TN12 9ND
Actual Grid Ref: TQ733415
Tourist Board grade: 5 Ticks
Tel: 01622 832399
Fax: 01622 832472
Email: tannerfarmpark@cs.com
Tent pitches: 100
Tent rate: £5.50-£10.80
Open: All year
Last arr: 8pm
Facilities for disabled people • Dogs allowed • Electric hook-up • Baths • Calor Gas/Camping Gaz • Children's play area • Showers • Laundrette on site • Public phone on site • Shop on site • Baby care facilities • Fishing
Secluded touring park set amidst 150 acre arable family farm. Idyllic setting with immaculate quality centrally-heated facilities. Surrounded by beautiful countryside and abundant wildlife as well as our own animals and our wonderful shire horses. An ideal location for visiting the many attractions in the Weald area.

Hostels and campsites may vary rates – be sure to check when booking.

MAP PAGE 100 • **Kent**

Margate

TR3570

▲ **Margate Youth Hostel,** 3-4 Royal Esplanade Westbrook Bay, Margate, Kent, CT9 5DL
Tel: 01843 221616
Fax: 01843 221616
Email: margate@yha.org.uk
Capacity: 54
Under 18: £7.75 **Adults:** £11.00
Open: All year, 5.00pm
Family bunk rooms
Self-catering facilities • Television • Laundry facilities • Lounge • Dining room • Cycle store • No smoking • Kitchen facilities • Credit cards accepted
Opposite the beach and a half mile from the pier, in the centre of this Victorian seaside resort.

Minster in Sheppey

TQ9573

▲ **The Plough Inn,** Kingsbury Leisure Park, Plough Road, Minster, Sheppey, Kent, ME12 4JF
Actual Grid Ref: TQ972725
Tel: 01795 872895
Open: Mar to Oct

New Romney

TR0625

▲ **Marlie Farm Caravan & Camping Site,** Dymchurch Road, New Romney, Kent, TN28 8EU
Actual Grid Ref: TR073258
Tel: 01797 363060
Open: Apr to Oct

Paddock Wood

TQ6744

▲ **Whitbread Hop Farm,** Paddock Wood, Tonbridge, Kent, TN12 6PY
Actual Grid Ref: TQ674473
Tel: 01622 872068
Open: All year

Petham

TR1351

▲ **Ashfield Farm,** Waddenhall, Petham, Canterbury, CT4 5PX
Actual Grid Ref: TR136490
Tel: 01227 700624
Open: Mar to Oct

▲ **Yew Tree Caravan Park,** Stone Street, Petham, Canterbury, CT4 5TL
Actual Grid Ref: TR137508
Tel: 01227 700306 **Fax:** 01227 700306
Open: Mar to Oct

Ramsgate

TR3864

▲ **Nethercourt Touring Park,** Nethercourt Hill, Ramsgate, Kent, CT11 0RX
Tel: 01843 595485
Open: Easter to Oct

Sandwich

TR3158

▲ **Sandwich Leisure Park,** Woodnesborough Road, Sandwich, Kent, CT13 0AA
Actual Grid Ref: TR327581
Tel: 01304 612681 / 01227 771777
Fax: 01227 273512
Open: Mar to Oct

Seal

TQ5556

▲ **Camping & Caravanning Club Site,** Styants Bottom Road, Styants Bottom, Seal, Sevenoaks, Kent, TN15 0ET
Tel: 01732 762728 **Open:** Apr to Oct

Selstead

TR2144

▲ **Chequers Inn,** 260 Canterbury Road, Selstead, Dover, Kent, CT15 7HJ
Tel: 01303 844240
Open: All year

Sheerness

TQ9175

▲ **Sheerness Holiday Park,** Halfway Road, Sheerness, Kent, ME12 3AA
Actual Grid Ref: TQ929741
Tel: 01795 662638 **Open:** Apr to Sep

St Nicholas at Wade

TR2567

▲ **St Nicholas Camping Site,** Court Road, St Nicholas at Wade, Birchington, Kent, CT7 0NH
Tel: 01483 847245
Open: Mar to Oct

▲ **St Nicholas Camping Site,** Court Road, St Nicholas at Wade, Birchington, Kent, CT7 0NH
Actual Grid Ref: TR264669
Tel: 01843 847245
Open: Mar to Oct

Stansted

TQ6062

▲ **Thriftwood Caravan & Camping Park,** Plaxdale Green Road, Stansted, Sevenoaks, Kent, TN15 7PB
Actual Grid Ref: TQ598608
Tel: 01732 822261
Fax: 01732 822261
Open: Mar to Jan

Stelling Minnis

TR1346

▲ **Rose & Crown,** Stelling Minnis, Canterbury, CT4 6AS
Tel: 01227 709265
Open: Mar to Oct

Walmer

TR3650

▲ **Clifford Park Caravans,** Thompson Close, Walmer, Deal, Kent, CT14 7PB
Actual Grid Ref: TR366499
Tel: 01304 373373
Open: Mar to Oct

West Kingsdown

TQ5762

▲ **To the Woods,** Botsam Lane, West Kingsdown, Sevenoaks, Kent, TN15 6BN
Tel: 01322 863751
Open: All year

Westwell

TQ9847

▲ **Dunn Street Farm,** Westwell, Ashford, Kent, TN25 4NJ
Actual Grid Ref: TQ992480
Tel: 01233 712537
Open: Apr to Oct

▲ **Dean Court Farm,** Challock Lane, Westwell, Ashford, Kent, TN25 4NH
Actual Grid Ref: TQ990487
Tel: 01233 712924
Open: All year

Kent • MAP PAGE 100

ENGLAND

Whitstable
TR1066

▲ **Sea View Caravan Park,** St John's Road, Whitstable, Kent, CT5 2RY
Actual Grid Ref: TR144677
Tel: 01227 792246
Open: Apr to Oct

▲ *Primrose Cottage Caravan Park,* Golden Hill, Whitstable, Kent, CT5 3AR
Tel: 01227 273694
Open: Mar to Oct

Wrotham Heath
TQ6457

▲ **Gate House Wood Touring Park,** Ford Lane, Wrotham Heath, Sevenoaks, Kent, TN15 7SD
Actual Grid Ref: TQ636583
Tel: 01732 843062
Open: All year

Lancashire

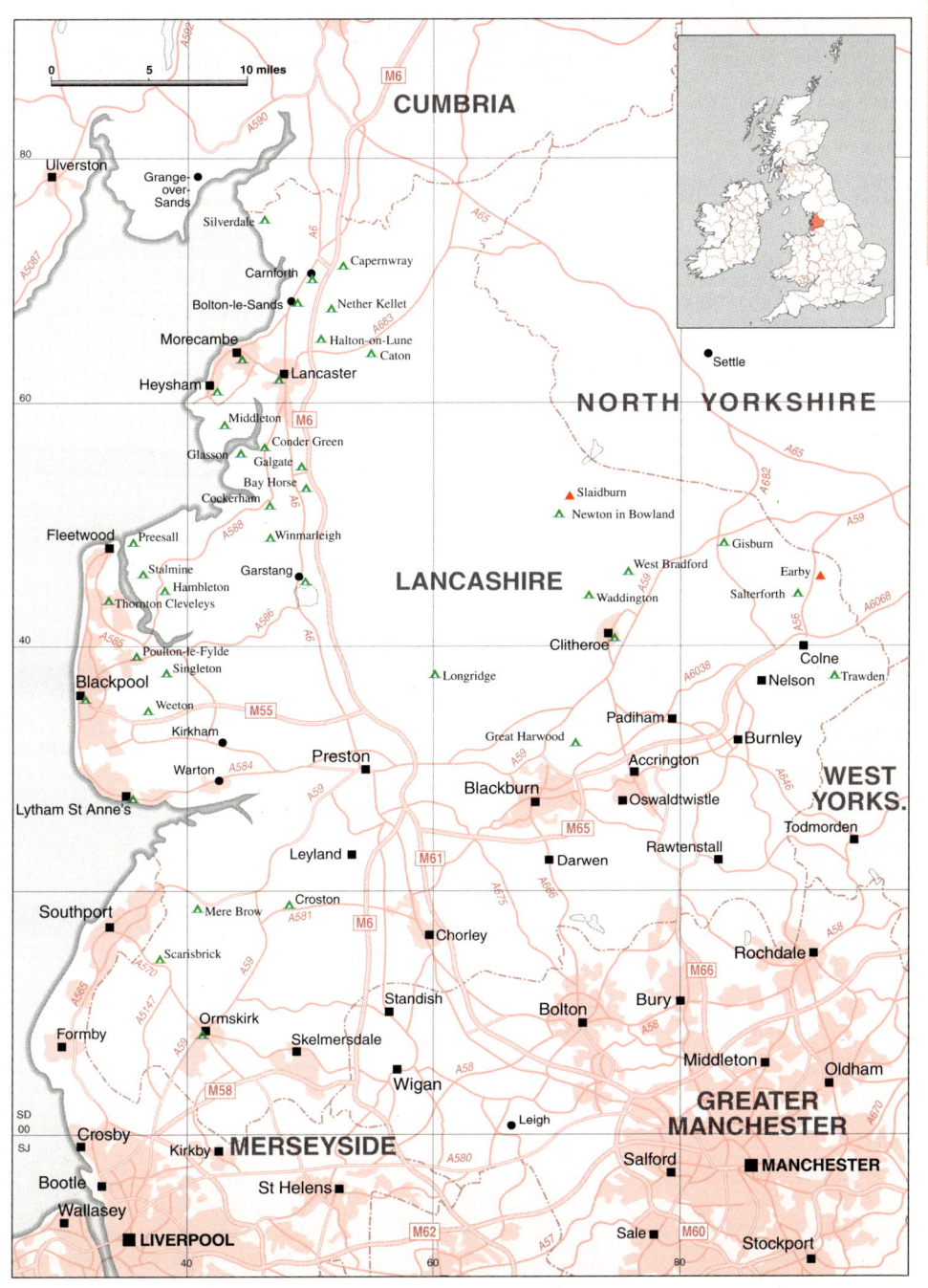

Lancashire • MAP PAGE 105

ENGLAND

Bay Horse
SD4953

▲ **Wyreside Lakes Fishery,** Sunnyside Farmhouse, Gleaves Hill Road, Bay Horse, Lancaster, Lancashire, LA2 9PG
Actual Grid Ref: SD512522
Tel: 01524 792093
Open: All year

Blackpool
SD3136

▲ **Under Hill Farm Camp Site,** Peel, Blackpool, Lancashire, FY4 5JS
Actual Grid Ref: SD360266
Tel: 01253 763107
Fax: 01953 498373
Email: hq@ilph.org
Tent pitches: 10
Open: Mar to Nov
Last arr: dusk

Dogs allowed • Electric hook-up • Cafe or Takeaway on site • Picnic/barbecue area on site • Children's play area • Showers • Laundrette on site • Public phone on site
Friendly site with panoramic views over the picturesque Fylde countryside.

▲ **Marton Mere Holiday Park,** Mythope Road, Blackpool, Lancashire, FY4 4XN
Tel: 01253 767544
Fax: 01253 767544
Open: Mar to Nov

▲ **Mariclough Hampsfield Camping Site,** Preston New Road, Peel Corner, Blackpool, Lancashire, FY4 5JR
Actual Grid Ref: SD357325
Tel: 01253 761034
Open: Mar to Nov

▲ **Gillett Farm Caravan Park,** Peel Road, Peel, Blackpool, Lancashire, FY4 5JU
Tel: 01253 761676
Open: Mar to Oct

▲ **Pipers Height Caravan & Camping Park,** Peel, Blackpool, Lancashire, FY4 5JT
Actual Grid Ref: SD355327
Tel: 01253 763767
Open: Mar to Oct

Hostels and campsites may vary rates – be sure to check when booking.

Bolton le Sands
SD4868

▲ **Sandside Caravan & Camping Park,** The Shore, Bolton-le-Sands, Carnforth, Lancashire, LA5 8JS
Actual Grid Ref: SD477684
Tel: 01524 822311
Open: Mar to Oct

▲ **Bolton Holmes Farm,** off Mill Lane, Bolton-Le-Sands, Carnforth, Lancashire, LA5 8ES
Actual Grid Ref: SD481692
Tel: 01524 732854
Open: Apr to Sep

▲ **Detron Gate Caravan Site,** Bolton-le-Sands, Carnforth, LA5 9TN
Tel: 01524 732842 / 733617
Open: Apr to Sep

Capernwray
SD5371

▲ **Old Hall Caravan Park,** Capernwray, Carnforth, LA6 1AD
Actual Grid Ref: SD533716
Tel: 01524 733276
Email: oldhall@charis.co.uk
Open: Mar to Jan

▲ **Capernwray House,** Capernwray, Carnforth, Lancs, LA6 1AE
Actual Grid Ref: SD539719
Tel: 01524 732363
Open: Mar to Oct

Carnforth
SD4970

▲ **Red Bank Farm,** Bolton-le-Sands, Carnforth, Lancashire, LA5 8JR
Actual Grid Ref: SD472681
Tel: 01524 823196
Open: Apr to Oct

▲ **Detron Gate Farm,** Bolton-le-Sands, Carnforth, Lancashire, LA5 9TN
Actual Grid Ref: SD484693
Tel: 01524 733617
Open: Apr to Oct

▲ **Marsh House Farm Caravan Park,** Crag Bank, Carnforth, Lancashire, LA5 9JA
Actual Grid Ref: SD482703
Tel: 01524 732897
Open: Mar to Oct

All details shown are as supplied by hostels and campsites in Autumn 2000.

Caton
SD5364

▲ **Crook o' Lune Caravan Park,** Caton, Lancaster, LA2 9HP
Tel: 01524 770216
Open: Feb to Nov

Clitheroe
SD7441

▲ **Camping & Caravanning Club Site,** Edisford Bridge, Edisford Road, Clitheroe, Lancashire, BB7 3LA
Actual Grid Ref: SD727413
Tel: 01200 425294
Open: Mar to Oct

Cockerham
SD4652

▲ **Mosswood Caravan Park,** Crimbles Lane, Cockerham, Lancaster, Lancs., LA2 0ES
Actual Grid Ref: SD456497
Tel: 01524 791041
Open: Mar to Oct

Conder Green
SD4656

▲ **Marina Luxury Holiday Park,** Conder Green, Glasson Dock, Lancaster, LA2 0BP
Actual Grid Ref: SD453556
Tel: 01524 751787
Fax: 01524 751436
Open: Mar to Dec

Croston
SD4819

▲ **Royal Umpire Touring Park,** Southport Road, Croston, Preston, Lancashire, PR5 7HP
Actual Grid Ref: SD504191
Tel: 01772 600257
Open: All year

To stay in a Youth Hostel affiliated to one of the Youth Hostel associations, you need to be a member. You can join at most hostels – phone in advance to check.

MAP PAGE 105 • **Lancashire**

ENGLAND

Earby

SD9046

▲ **Earby Youth Hostel,** Glen Cottage, Birch Hall Lane, Earby, Colne, Lancashire, BB8 6JX
Actual Grid Ref: SD915468
Tel: 01282 842349
Fax: 01282 842349
Capacity: 22
Under 18: £6.50
Adults: £9.25
Open: All year, 5.00pm
Self-catering facilities • Showers • Lounge 2 • Dining room • Drying room • Cycle store • Parking • No smoking • WC • Kitchen facilities • Credit cards accepted
Attractive cottage with own picturesque garden and waterfall, on NE outskirts of Earby. Convenient for Pendle.

Galgate

SD4855

▲ **Laundsfield,** Stoney Lane, Galgate, Lancaster, LA2 0JZ
Actual Grid Ref: SD485553
Tel: 01524 751763
Open: Mar to Nov

Garstang

SD4945

▲ **Claylands Caravan Park,** Cabus, Garstang, Preston, Lancashire, PR3 1AJ
Actual Grid Ref: SD496485
Tel: 01524 791242
Open: Mar to Oct

▲ **Bridge House Marina & Caravan Site,** Nateby Crossing Lane, Nateby, Garstang, Preston, Lancashire, PR3 0JJ
Actual Grid Ref: SD483457
Tel: 01995 603207
Fax: 01995 601612
Open: Mar to Dec

Gisburn

SD8248

▲ **Todber Caravan Park,** Gisburn, Clitheroe, Lancashire, BB7 4JJ
Actual Grid Ref: SD833467
Tel: 01200 445322
Open: Mar to Oct

Glasson

SD4456

▲ **Marina Caravan Park,** Conderside, Glasson Dock, Glasson, Lancaster, LA2 0BE
Actual Grid Ref: SD450561
Tel: 01524 751657
Open: Mar to Jan

Great Harwood

SD7332

▲ **Harwood Bar Caravan Park,** Mill Lane, Great Harwood, Blackburn, BB6 7UQ
Tel: 015395 64163
Open: All year

Halton-on-Lune

SD5064

▲ **Pye Nanny Hall Camping & Caravanning Site,** Pye Nanny Hall, Halton-on-Lune, Lancaster, LA2 6BH
Actual Grid Ref: SD648499
Tel: 01524 32755
Open: Mar to Oct

Hambleton

SD3742

▲ **Sunset Adventure Park,** Sower Carr Lane, Hambleton, Poulton-le-Fylde, Lancashire, FY6 9EQ
Actual Grid Ref: SD375437
Tel: 01253 700222 / 701888
Email: sunset@caravans.com
Open: Mar to Oct

Heysham

SD4161

▲ **Ocean Edge Caravan Park,** Moneyclose Lane, Heysham, Morecambe, Lancashire, LA3 2XA
Actual Grid Ref: SD407591
Tel: 01524 855657
Open: Mar to Oct

Lancaster

SD4761

▲ **New Parkside Farm Caravan Park,** Denny Beck, Caton Road, Lancaster, LA2 9HH
Actual Grid Ref: SD512643
Tel: 01524 770723
Open: Mar to Oct

Longridge

SD6037

▲ **Beacon Fell View Caravan Park,** 110 High Road, Longridge, Preston, Lancashire, PR3 2TF
Actual Grid Ref: SD618383
Tel: 01772 785434
Open: Mar to Oct

Lytham St Annes

SD3327

▲ **Eastham Hall Caravan Site,** Saltcotes Road, Lytham St Annes, Lancashire, FY8 4LS
Actual Grid Ref: SD379291
Tel: 01253 737907
Open: Mar to Oct

Mere Brow

SD4119

▲ **Leisure Lakes,** Mere Brow, Preston, Lancashire, PR4 6JX
Actual Grid Ref: SD415187
Tel: 01772 813446
Open: All year

Middleton

SD4259

▲ **Melbreak Caravan Park,** Carr Lane, Middleton, Morecambe, Lancashire, LA3 3LH
Actual Grid Ref: SD416585
Tel: 01524 852430
Open: Mar to Sept

▲ **Hawthorn Camping Site,** Carr Lane, Middleton Sands, Middleton, Morecambe , Lancashire, LA3 3LL
Tel: 01524 52074
Open: Easter to Oct

Morecambe

SD4364

▲ **Riverside Caravan Park,** Snatchems, Heaton-with-Oxcliffe, Morecambe, Lancashire, LA3 3ER
Actual Grid Ref: SD448615
Tel: 01524 844193
Open: Mar to Oct

▲ **Broadfields Camp Site,** 276 Oxcliffe Road, Morecambe, Lancashire, LA3 3EH
Actual Grid Ref: SD435626
Tel: 01524 410278
Open: Mar to Jan

Stilwell's Hostels & Camping 2002

Lancashire • MAP PAGE 105

▲ **Venture Caravan Park,**
Langridge Way, Westgate,
Morecambe, Lancashire, LA4 4TQ
Actual Grid Ref: SD436633
Tel: 01524 412986
Fax: 01524 855884
Email:
mark@venturecaravanpark.co.uk
Open: All year

▲ **Sunnyside Camping Site,**
Oxcliffe Road, Morecambe,
Lancashire, LA3 1PU
Tel: 01524 418373
Open: Mar to Oct

▲ **The Bungalow Camping &
Caravan Park,** 272 Oxcliffe Road,
Morecambe, Lancashire, LA3 3EH
Actual Grid Ref: SD434634
Tel: 01524 411273
Open: Apr to Sep

▲ **Regent Leisure Park,** Westgate,
Morecambe, Lancs, LA3 3DF
Actual Grid Ref: SD430629
Tel: 01524 413940
Open: Mar to Feb

Nether Kellet

SD5068

▲ **Hawthorns Caravan &
Camping Park,** Nether Kellet,
Carnforth, LA6 1EA
Actual Grid Ref: SD514686
Tel: 01524 732079
Open: Mar to Oct

Newton in Bowland

SD6950

▲ **Crawshaw Farm Caravan and
Campsite,** Newton in Bowland,
Clitheroe, Lancashire, BB7 3EE
Tel: 01200 446638
Open: All year

Ormskirk

SD4108

▲ **Abbey Farm Caravan Park,** Dark
Lane, Ormskirk, Lancashire, L40 5TX
Actual Grid Ref: SD433099
Tel: 01695 572686
Email: abbeyfarm@yahoo.com
Open: All year

Hostels and campsites may
vary rates – be sure to check
when booking.

Poulton-le-Fylde

SD3539

▲ **High Bank Farm,** Hardhorn,
Poulton-le-Fylde, Blackpool,
Lancashire, FY6 8DN
Actual Grid Ref: SD353375
Tel: 01253 890422
Open: Mar to Oct

Preesall

SD3647

▲ **Maaruig Caravan Park,** 71
Pilling Lane, Preesall, Blackpool,
Lancashire, FY6 0HB
Actual Grid Ref: SD360487
Tel: 01253 810404
Open: Mar to Jan

▲ **Willowgrove Caravan Park,**
Sandy Lane, Preesall, Poulton-le-
Fyld, Lancs., FY6 0EJ
Tel: 01253 811306
Open: Mar to Oct

▲ **Old Post Office,** Park Lane,
Preesall, Poulton-le-Fylde, Lancs, FY6
0NW
Tel: 01253 811261
Fax: 01253 811261
Open: All year

Salterforth

SD8945

▲ **Lower Greenhill Caravan Site,**
Salterforth, Barnoldswick,
Lancashire, BB18 3TG
Actual Grid Ref: SD893452
Tel: 01282 813067
Open: All year

Scarisbrick

SD3713

▲ **Shaw Hall Caravan Park,**
Smithy Lane, Scarisbrick, Ormskirk,
Lancashire, L40 8HJ
Actual Grid Ref: SD397119
Tel: 01704 840298 **Fax:** 01704 840539
Open: Mar to Jan

Silverdale

SD4675

▲ **Holgate's Caravan Park,** Cove
Road, Silverdale, Carnforth,
Lancashire, LA5 0SH
Actual Grid Ref: SD455758
Tel: 01524 701508
Open: Mar to Nov

▲ **Gibraltar Farm,** Silverdale,
Carnforth, Cumbria, LA5 0TH
Actual Grid Ref: SD462750
Tel: 01524 701736
Open: Apr to Oct

▲ **Hollins Farm,** Far Arnside,
Silverdale, Carnforth, Lancashire,
LA5 0SL
Actual Grid Ref: SD452766
Tel: 01524 701767
Open: Mar to Oct

Singleton

SD3838

▲ **River Wyre Holiday Camp,**
Mains Lane, Singleton, Poulton-le-
Fylde, Blackpool, Lancashire, FY6
7LG
Tel: 01253 883368
Open: Mar to Oct

▲ **Windy Harbour Holiday Centre,**
Little Singleton, Poulton le Fyld,
Blackpool, Lancashire, FY6 8NB
Actual Grid Ref: SD389403
Tel: 01253 883064
Open: Mar to Oct

Slaidburn

SD7152

▲ **Slaidburn Youth Hostel,**
King's House, Slaidburn, Clitheroe,
Lancashire, BB7 3ER
Actual Grid Ref: SD711523
Tel: 01200 446656
Capacity: 30
Under 18: £6.50
Adults: £9.25
Open: All year
Family bunk rooms
• Self-catering facilities • Television •
Showers • Shop • Lounge • Drying room •
Parking • No smoking • WC • Kitchen
facilities
Basic village accommodation for walkers
and cyclists in the middle of the Forest of
Bowland. The hostel is a C17th former
inn, with log fires as well as central
heating.

You are advised to book in advance
for periods of high demand –
the Summer months, Half Term
holidays and public holidays.

MAP PAGE 105 • **Lancashire**

Stalmine

SD3745

▲ **Grange Farm,** Grange Lane, Stalmine, Poulton-le-Fylde, Lancashire, FY6 0JQ
Actual Grid Ref: SD365454
Tel: 01253 700285
Open: Mar to Oct

Thornton Cleveleys

SD3442

▲ **Kneps Farm Holiday Park,** River Road, Thornton Cleveleys, Blackpool, Lancashire, FY5 5LR
Actual Grid Ref: SD354430
Tel: 01253 823632 **Fax:** 01253 863967
Open: Mar to Nov

▲ **Stanah House Caravan Park,** River Road, Thornton Cleveleys, Blackpool, Lancashire, FY5 5LW
Actual Grid Ref: SD357430
Tel: 01253 824000 **Fax:** 01253 863060
Open: Mar to Oct

Trawden

SD9138

▲ **Middle Beardshaw Head Farm,** Trawden, Colne, Lancs, BB8 8PP
Tel: 01282 865257
Open: All year (not Xmas)

Waddington

SD7243

▲ **Fields House Farm Caravanning,** Waddington, Clitheroe, Lancs., BB7 3LB
Tel: 01200 422693
Open: All year

Weeton

SD3835

▲ **High Moor Farm Caravan Park,** Weeton, Preston, Lancashire, PR4 3JJ
Actual Grid Ref: SD388365
Tel: 01253 836273
Open: Mar to Oct

West Bradford

SD7444

▲ **Three Rivers Woodland Park,** Eaves Hall Lane, West Bradford, Clitheroe, Lancs, BB7 3JG
Tel: 01200 423523
Open: All year

Winmarleigh

SD4748

▲ **Smithy Caravan Park,** Cabus Nook Lane, Winmarleigh, Preston, Lancashire, PR3 1AA
Actual Grid Ref: SD485484
Tel: 01995 606200
Open: Mar to Jan

You are advised to book in advance for periods of high demand – the Summer months, Half Term holidays and public holidays.

ENGLAND

Leicestershire

Isley Walton

SK4225

▲ **Donington Park Farmhouse Caravan Site,** *Melbourne Road, Isley Walton, Castle Donington, Derby, DE74 2RN*
Actual Grid Ref: SK414255
Tel: 01332 862409
Email: info@parkfarmhouse.co.uk
Open: Mar to Dec

Leicester

SK5804

▲ **Richard's Backpacker's and Student's Hostel,** *157 Wanlip Lane, Birstall, Leicester, LE4 4GL*
Actual Grid Ref: SK597095
Tel: 0116 267 3107
Capacity: 5
Under 18: £9.00 **Adults:** £9.00
Open: All year, 5pm
Television • Showers • Central heating • Laundry facilities • Wet weather shelter • Lounge • Dining room • Cycle store • Evening meal available • No smoking
Cosy hostel near Watermead Park. Convenient for National Space Centre.

Market Bosworth

SK4003

▲ **Bosworth Water Trust,** *Far Coton Lane, Market Bosworth, Nuneaton, Warwickshire, CV13 6PD*
Tel: 01455 291876
Open: All year

North Kilworth

SP6183

▲ **Kilworth Caravan Park,** *North Kilworth House, Lutterworth, Leicestershire, LE17 6JE*
Actual Grid Ref: SP605839
Tel: 01858 880597 **Open:** All year

Ullesthorpe

SP5087

▲ **Ullesthorpe Garden and Aquatic Centre,** *Lutterworth Road, Ullesthorpe, Lutterworth, Leics, LE17 5DY*
Actual Grid Ref: SP515872
Tel: 01455 202144
Open: Mar to Oct

Barrow upon Soar

SK5717

▲ **Huston Farm Marina & Touring Caravan Park,** *Huston Close, Barrow upon Soar, Loughborough, Leicestershire, LE12 8NB*
Actual Grid Ref: SK585167
Tel: 01509 816035
Open: All year

Copt Oak

SK4813

▲ **Copt Oak Youth Hostel,** *Whitwick Road, Copt Oak, Markfield, Leicestershire, LE67 9QB*
Actual Grid Ref: SK482129
Tel: 01530 242661
Fax: 01530 242661

Email: reservations@yha.org.uk
Capacity: 16
Under 18: £5.75
Adults: £8.50
Open: All year, 5.00pm
Self-catering facilities • Showers • Shop • Wet weather shelter • Lounge • Security lockers • Cycle store • Parking • No smoking • Kitchen facilities • Credit cards accepted
Converted schoolhouse in the hills of north west Leicestershire providing basic accommodation. Charnwood Forest is nearby, with superb countryside for walking and cycling.

Cotes

SK5520

▲ **Hall Farm Caravan Site,** *10 Stantford Lane, Cotes, Loughborough, Leicestershire, LE12 5TW*
Tel: 01509 266908
Open: All year

Britain: Bed & Breakfast

The essential guide to B&Bs in England, Scotland & Wales

ENGLAND

The Bed & Breakfast is one of the great British institutions. Like Fish & Chips, it's known by people around the world. But you don't have to be a tourist to enjoy this traditional accommodation. Whether you're travelling, on holiday, away on business or just escaping from it all, the B&B is a great value alternative to expensive hotels and a world away from camping and caravanning.

Stilwell's Britain: Bed & Breakfast 2001 is the most comprehensive guide of its kind, containing over 7,750 entries listed by country, county and location, in England, Scotland and Wales. Each entry includes room rates, facilities, Tourist Board grades and a brief description of the B&B and its location and surroundings.

Stilwell's Britain: Bed & Breakfast 2001: The indispensable guide to great value accommodation:

- Private houses, country halls, farms, cottages, inns, small hotels and guest houses
- Over 7,750 entries
- Average price £19 per person per night
- All official grades shown
- Local maps
- Pubs serving hot evening meals shown
- Tourist Information Centres listed
- Handy size for easy packing

£9.95 from all good bookstores (ISBN 1-900861-22-4) or £11.95 (inc p&p) from Stilwell Publishing, 59 Charlotte Road, London EC2A 3QW (020 7739 7179)

Lincolnshire

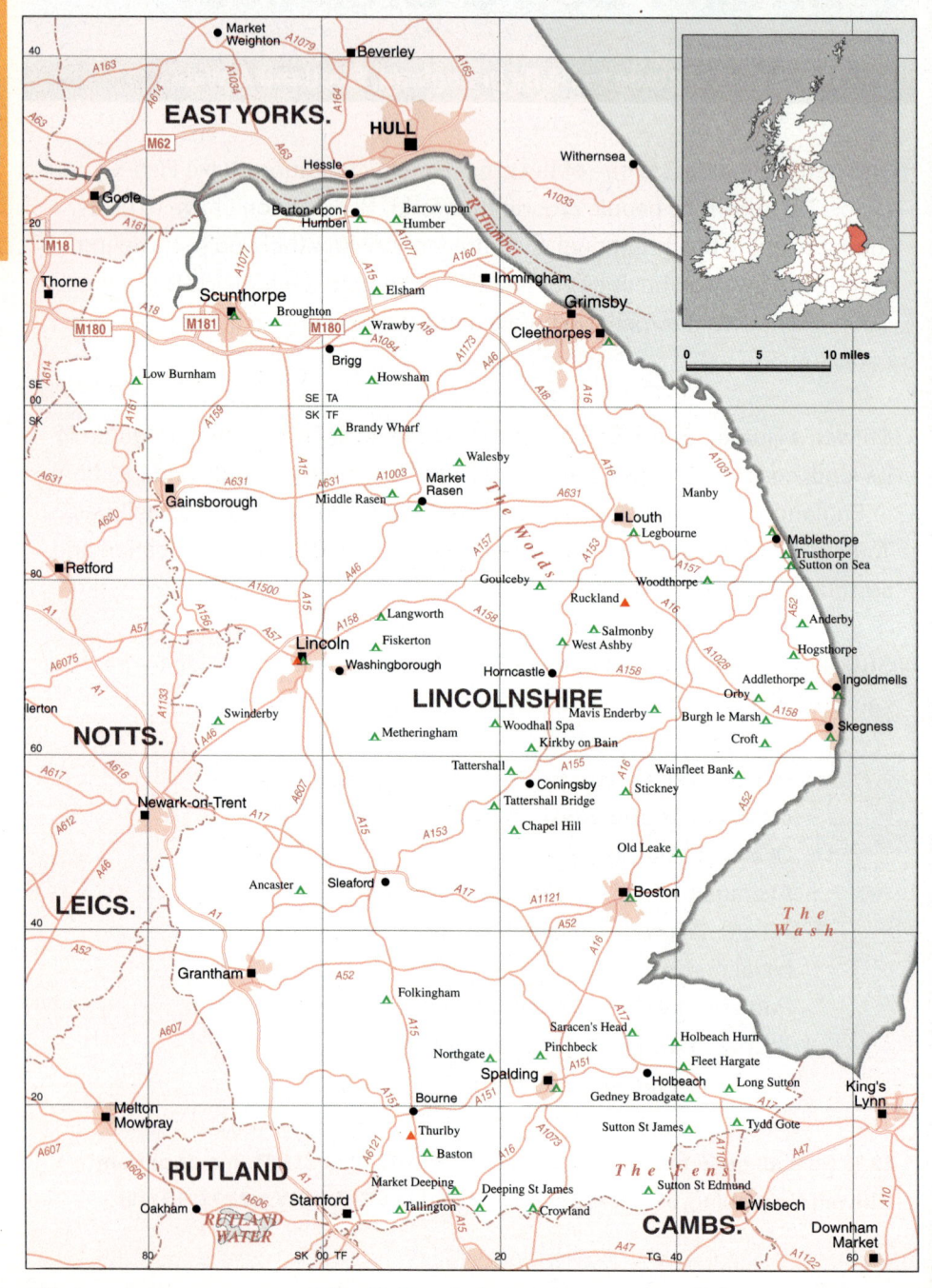

Lincolnshire

Addlethorpe
TF5468

▲ **Valetta Farm,** Mill Lane, Addlethorpe, Skegness, Lincolnshire, PE24 4TB
Actual Grid Ref: TF553674
Tel: 01754 763758
Open: Mar to Oct

Ancaster
SK9643

▲ **Woodland Waters Ltd,** Willoughby Road, Ancaster, Grantham, Lincs, NG32 3RT
Actual Grid Ref: SK984431
Tel: 01400 230888
Fax: 01400 230888
Open: All year

Anderby
TF5275

▲ **Manor Farm Caravan Park,** Sea Road, Anderby, Skegness, Lincolnshire, PE24 5YB
Actual Grid Ref: TF534762
Tel: 01507 490372
Open: Mar to Nov

Barrow upon Humber
TA0720

▲ **Greenfields Camping ,** Goxhill Road, Barrow upon Humber, North Lincs, DN19 7EE
Actual Grid Ref: TA083213
Tel: 01469 530760
Tent pitches: 15
Tent rate: £4.00
Open: All year
Last arr: 11pm
Dogs allowed • Electric hook-up • Showers
Small quiet site, pleasant gardens. Near Humber Bridge. Adults only.

Barton-upon-Humber
TA0321

▲ **Silver Birches Tourist Park,** Waterside Road, Barton-upon-Humber, Lincs, DN18 5BA
Actual Grid Ref: TA028232
Tel: 01652 632509
Open: Apr to Oct

All details shown are as supplied by hostels and campsites in Autumn 2000.

Baston
TF1114

▲ **Golden Pond Caravan Park,** Vine House, Baston, Peterborough, Lincs., PE6 9PA
Actual Grid Ref: TF138146
Tel: 01778 560607
Open: Apr to Sep

Boston
TF3344

▲ **Orchard Park,** Frampton Lane, Hubbert's Bridge, Boston, Lincolnshire, PE20 3QU
Actual Grid Ref: TF273433
Tourist Board grade: 3 Star
Tel: 01205 290328
Fax: 01205 290247
Tent pitches:
Tent rate: £4.00-£10.00
Open: All year
Last arr: 11pm
Facilities for disabled people • Dogs allowed • Electric hook-up • Calor Gas/Camping Gaz • Children's play area • Showers • Laundrette on site • Public phone on site • Licensed bar on site • Shop on site • Games room • Golf nearby • Riding nearby • Fishing on site
Level, grassy, shady & peaceful park. Only 4 miles from Boston. 35 miles from Lincoln or Stamford (all historic towns). A 9 hole golf course is only 2 miles away & an 18 hole with driving range is within walking distance. Licensed bar on site with entertainment on summer weekends.

▲ **Pilgrims Way,** Church Green Road, Boston, Lincolnshire, PE21 0QY
Actual Grid Ref: TF359432
AA grade: 4 Pennants
Tel: 01205 366616
Fax: 01205 366646
Email: pilgrimswaylincs@yahoo.co.uk
Tent pitches: 22
Tent rate: £7.50
Open: Apr to Nov
Last arr: 9pm
Facilities for disabled people • Dogs allowed • Electric hook-up • Calor Gas/Camping Gaz • Picnic/barbecue area on site • Showers • Laundrette on site • Public phone on site
Small park, showers, laundrette, set in country, close to Boston.

▲ **The Plough,** Swineshead Bridge, Boston, Lincolnshire, PE20 3PT
Tel: 01205 820300
Open: Mar to Sept

Hostels and campsites may vary rates – be sure to check when booking.

Brandy Wharf
TF0196

▲ **Brandy Wharf Leisure Park,** Brandy Wharf, Waddingham, Gainsborough, Lincolnshire, DN21 4RT
Actual Grid Ref: TF013969
Tel: 01673 818010 **Fax:** 01673 818010
Email: brandywharflp@freenetname.co.uk
Tent pitches: 50
Tent rate: £3.00-£10.00
Open: All year
Last arr: any time
Dogs allowed • Electric hook-up • Picnic/barbecue area on site • Children's play area • Showers • Laundrette on site
Level site adjacent River Ancholme, Cider Centre in Brandy Wharf.

Broughton
SE9608

▲ **Castlethorpe Carr Lodge,** Broughton, Brigg, DN20 0BZ
Tel: 01652 652840
Open: All year

Burgh le Marsh
TF5064

▲ **Sycamore Lakes Touring Site,** Skegness Road, Burgh-le-Marsh, Skegness, Lincolnshire, PE24 5LN
Actual Grid Ref: TF510648
Tel: 01754 810749
Open: Apr to Oct

Chapel Hill
TF2054

▲ **Orchard Caravans,** Witham Bank, Chapel Hill, Lincoln, LN4 4PZ
Actual Grid Ref: TF208542
Tel: 01526 342414
Open: Feb to Dec

Cleethorpes
TA3008

▲ **Thorpe Park Holiday Centre,** Cleethorpes, Lincs, DN36 4HG
Actual Grid Ref: TA321035
Tel: 01472 813395
Open: Mar to Oct

Lincolnshire • MAP PAGE 112

ENGLAND

Croft
TF5061

▲ **Retreat Farm,** Croft Bank, Croft, Skegness, Lincolnshire, PE24 4RE
Actual Grid Ref: TF538622
Tel: 01754 762092
Open: Mar to Nov

Crowland
TF2410

▲ **Alderlands Caravan Park,** Peterborough Road, Crowland, Peterborough, Cambridgeshire, PE6 0AA
Actual Grid Ref: TF239089
Tel: 01733 210438
Open: All year

Deeping St James
TF1609

▲ **Lakeside Caravan Park,** Station Road, Deeping St James, Peterborough, Cambridgeshire, PE6 8PW
Actual Grid Ref: TF178088
Tel: 01778 343785
Open: Feb to Dec

Elsham
TA0411

▲ **Elsham Country & Wildlife Park,** Elsham, Brigg, DN20 0QZ
Actual Grid Ref: TA031119
Tel: 01652 680290
Open: Apr to Oct

Fiskerton
TF0572

▲ **Shortferry Caravan Park,** Ferry Road, Fiskerton, Lincoln, LN3 4HU
Tel: 01526 398021
Email: shortferry@aol.com
Open: All year

Fleet Hargate
TF3925

▲ **Delph Bank Touring Caravan & Camping Park,** Main Street, Fleet Hargate, Spalding, Lincolnshire, PE12 8LL
Actual Grid Ref: TF398248
Tel: 01406 422910
Open: Mar to Oct

Folkingham
TF0733

▲ **Low Farm Touring Park,** Spring Lane, Folkingham, Sleaford, Lincs, NG34 0SJ
Tel: 01529 497322
Open: Easter to Oct

Gedney Broadgate
TF4022

▲ **Laurel Park Caravan & Camping Site,** Hunts Gate, Gedney, Spalding, Lincs, PE12 0DJ
Tel: 01406 364369
Open: Mar to Dec

Goulceby
TF2579

▲ **The Three Horse Shoes Public House,** Goulceby, Louth, Lincolnshire, LN11 9UR
Actual Grid Ref: TF252790
Tel: 01507 252790
Open: All year

Hogsthorpe
TF5372

▲ **Hill View Caravan & Camping Park,** Skegness Road, Hogsthorpe, Skegness, PE24 5NR
Tel: 01754 872979
Open: Mar to Oct

Holbeach Hurn
TF3927

▲ **Rose & Crown Caravan Park,** Marsh Road, Holbeach Hurn, Holbeach, Spalding, Lincs, PE12 8JN
Tel: 01406 426085
Open: Mar to Oct

Howsham
TA0403

▲ **Hamsden Garth,** Cadney Road, Howsham, Market Rasen, Lincolnshire, LN7 6LA
Tel: 01652 678703
Fax: 01652 678703
Open: All year

All details shown are as supplied by hostels and campsites in Autumn 2000.

Hostels and campsites may vary rates – be sure to check when booking.

Ingoldmells
TF5668

▲ **Countrymeadows Holiday Park,** Anchor Lane, Ingoldmells, Skegness, Lincolnshire, PE25 1LZ
Actual Grid Ref: TF565696
Tel: 01754 874455
Open: Apr to Oct

▲ **Greenacres,** Bolton Lane, Ingoldmells, Skegness, Lincolnshire, PE25 1JJ
Actual Grid Ref: TF564684
Tel: 01754 872263
Open: Apr to Oct

Kirkby on Bain
TF2462

▲ **Camping & Caravanning Club Site,** Wellsyke Lane, Kirkby on Bain, Woodhall Spa, Lincolnshire, LN10 6YU
Actual Grid Ref: TF225633
Tel: 01526 352911
Open: Mar to Oct

Langworth
TF0676

▲ **Lakeside Caravan Park,** Barlings Lane, Langworth, Lincoln, LN3 5DE
Actual Grid Ref: TF070761
Tel: 01522 753200
Fax: 01522 750758
Email: camping@lakeside-langworth.co.uk
Tent pitches: 22
Tent rate: £5.00-£10.00
Open: All year
Last arr: 7pm
Dogs allowed • Electric hook-up • Calor Gas/Camping Gaz • Picnic/barbecue area on site • Children's play area • Showers • Laundrette on site

Legbourne
TF3684

▲ **Frog Hall,** Furze Lane, Legbourne, Louth, Lincolnshire, LN11 8LR
Tel: 07931 532597
Email: pvfroghall@aol.com
Open: All year

MAP PAGE 112 • **Lincolnshire**

Lincoln

SK9771

▲ **Lincoln Youth Hostel,** 77 South Park, Lincoln, LN5 8ES
Actual Grid Ref: SK980700
Tel: 01522 522076
Fax: 01522 567424
Email: lincoln@yha.org.uk
Capacity: 46
Under 18: £6.90
Adults: £10.00
Open: All year, 5.00pm
Family bunk rooms
Self-catering facilities • Television • Laundry facilities • Lounge • Cycle store • Parking • Evening meal available 7.00pm • No smoking • Kitchen facilities • Breakfast available • Luggage store • Credit cards accepted
Victorian villa in a quiet road opposite South Common open parkland within easy reach of the centre, castle and cathedral.

▲ **Hartsholme Country Park,** Skellingthorpe Road, Lincoln, LN6 0EY
Actual Grid Ref: SK946697
Tel: 01522 686264
Open: Mar to Oct

▲ **West Lodge Farm,** Whisby Moor, Lincolnshire, LN6 9BY
Actual Grid Ref: SK922681
Tel: 01522 681720
Open: All year

Long Sutton

TF4323

▲ **Silverhill Touring & Camping Park,** Lutton Gowts, Long Sutton, Spalding, Lincs, PE12 9LQ
Actual Grid Ref: TF43245
Tel: 01406 365673
Fax: 01406 364406
Tent pitches: 50
Tent rate: £3.00-£4.00
Open: Mar to Nov

Last arr: 8pm
Facilities for disabled people • Dogs allowed • Electric hook-up • Picnic/barbecue area on site • Showers • Golf nearby • Fishing nearby
Quiet location, lots of space, within half mile of the Butterfly & Wildlife Park. One mile from Friday market and pubs, clubs and restaurants of Long Sutton. Ideal for a relaxing holiday in a small hamlet. Available for caravan rallies.

Low Burnham

SE7802

▲ **Windyridge,** Low Burnham, Doncaster, DN9 1DE
Tel: 01427 752380
Open: All year

Mablethorpe

TF5085

▲ **Camping & Caravanning Club Site,** Highfield , Church Lane, Mablethorpe, Lincolnshire, LN12 2NU
Actual Grid Ref: TF499839
Tel: 01507 472374
Open: Mar to Sept

▲ **Golden Sands Holiday Park,** Quebec Road, Mablethorpe, Lincolnshire, LN12 1QJ
Actual Grid Ref: TF497868
Tel: 01507 477871 / 472671
Open: Apr to Nov

▲ **Mermaid Caravan Site,** Seaholme Road, Mablethorpe, Lincolnshire, LN12 2NX
Actual Grid Ref: TF503841
Tel: 01507 473273
Open: Mar to Oct

▲ **Sandtoft,** Huttoft Road, Sutton-on-sea, Mablethorpe, Lincolnshire, LN12 2RU
Actual Grid Ref: TF520795
Tel: 01507 441248
Open: All year

Manby

TF3986

▲ **Manby Caravan Park,** Middlegate, Manby, Louth, Lincolnshire, LN11 8SX
Actual Grid Ref: TF392874
Tel: 01507 328232
Open: Mar to Nov

Market Deeping

TF1310

▲ **Deepings Caravan & Camping Park,** Outgang Road, Market Deeping, Peterborough, PE6 8LQ
Actual Grid Ref: TF165118
Tel: 01507 472951
Open: Feb to Dec

Market Rasen

TF1089

▲ **Racecourse Caravan Park,** Legsby Road, Market Rasen, Lincolnshire, LN8 3EA
Actual Grid Ref: TF125885
Tel: 01673 842307 / 843434
Fax: 01673 844532
Open: Mar to Oct

▲ **Walesby Woodlands Caravan Park,** Walesby Road, Market Rasen, Lincolnshire, LN8 3UN
Actual Grid Ref: TF117908
Tel: 01673 843285
Open: Mar to Oct

▲ **Manor Farm,** East Firsby, Market Rasen , LN8 2DB
Tel: 0850 679189
Open: All year

Mavis Enderby

TF3666

▲ **Northfield Farm,** Mavis Enderby, Spilsby, Lincs, PE23 4EW
Tel: 01507 588251
Fax: 01507 588251
Open: All year

Metheringham

TF0661

▲ **The White Horse Inn Caravan & Camping Park,** Dunston Fen, Metheringham, Lincoln, LN4 3AP
Tel: 01526 398341
Open: Feb to Dec

▲ **Eclipse Farm,** Martin Moor, Metheringham, Lincoln, LN4 3BQ
Actual Grid Ref: TF107602
Tel: 01526 378491
Open: Mar to Oct

All details shown are as supplied by hostels and campsites in Autumn 2000.

ENGLAND

Stilwell's Hostels & Camping 2002   115

Lincolnshire • MAP PAGE 112

Middle Rasen
TF0888

▲ **The Rother Camp Site,** Gainsborough Road, Middle Rasen, Market Rasen, Lincolnshire, LN8 3JU
Actual Grid Ref: TF083888
Tel: 01673 842433
Open: Mar to Oct

Northgate
TF1926

▲ **The Paddocks,** Northgate, West Pinchbeck, Spalding, Lincolnshire, PE11 3TB
Actual Grid Ref: TF210263
Tel: 01775 640573
Open: Feb to Nov

Old Leake
TF4050

▲ **White Cat Park,** Shaw Lane, Old Leake, Boston, Lincolnshire, PE22 9LQ
Actual Grid Ref: TF410498
AA grade: 3 Pennants
Tel: 01205 870121
Email: mkibby@whitecat.freeserve.co.uk
Tent pitches: 40
Tent rate: £5.75-£6.75
Open: Mar to Nov **Last arr:** 10pm
Dogs allowed • Electric hook-up • Calor Gas/Camping Gaz • Children's play area • Showers • Public phone on site • Shop on site
The White Cat is always quiet and clean. Ideal for Fens.

▲ **White Hart Public House,** Church Road, Old Leake, Boston, Lincs, PE22 9NS
Actual Grid Ref: TF407504
Tel: 01205 870783
Open: All year

Orby
TF4967

▲ **Herons Mead Touring Park,** Marsh Lane, Orby, Skegness, Lincolnshire, PE24 5JA
Actual Grid Ref: TF508673
Tel: 01754 873357
Open: Easter to Oct

Hostels and campsites may vary rates – be sure to check when booking.

Pinchbeck
TF2425

▲ **Lake Ross Caravan Park,** Dozens Bank, West Pinchbeck, Pinchbeck, Spalding, Lincolnshire, PE11 3NA
Actual Grid Ref: TF211222
Tel: 01775 761690
Open: Apr to Oct

Ruckland
TF3378

▲ **Woody's Top Youth Hostel,** Ruckland, Louth, Lincolnshire, LN11 8RQ
Tel: 01507 533323
Fax: 01507 533323
Capacity: 22
Under 18: £5.75
Adults: £8.50
Open: All year, 5.00pm
Self-catering facilities • Showers • Wet weather shelter • Lounge • Drying room • Cycle store • Parking • No smoking • No smoking • WC • Kitchen facilities • Credit cards accepted
Traditional hostel built from converted farm buildings, with comfortable facilities and wood-burning stove, in peaceful countryside.

Salmonby
TF3273

▲ **The Cross Keys Inn,** Salmonby, Horncastle, Lincs, LN9 6PX
Tel: 01507 533206
Open: All year

Saracen's Head
TF3427

▲ **Whaplode Manor Caravan Park,** Saracen's Head, Holbeach, Spalding, Lincs, PE12 8AZ
Actual Grid Ref: TF340278
Tel: 01406 422837
Fax: 01406 426824
Open: Mar to Nov

Scunthorpe
SE8910

▲ **Brookside Camping and Caravan Park,** Stather Road, Burton-Upon-Stather, Scunthorpe, Lincs., DN15 9DH
Actual Grid Ref: SE866186
Tel: 01724 721369
Tent pitches: 35
Tent rate: £5.50-£6.50

Open: All year
Last arr: 9pm
Facilities for disabled people • Dogs allowed • Electric hook-up • Showers • Laundrette on site
A park set in beautiful surroundings with unrivalled facilities.

Skegness
TF5663

▲ **Pine Tree Leisure Park,** Croft Bank, Skegness, Lincs, PE24 4RE
Actual Grid Ref: TF540627
Tel: 01754 762949
Fax: 01754 810866
Tent pitches: 50
Tent rate: £6.00-£8.00
Open: All year
Last arr: 9pm
Facilities for disabled people • Dogs allowed • Electric hook-up • Baths • Calor Gas/Camping Gaz • Picnic/barbecue area on site • Children's play area • Showers • Laundrette on site • Public phone on site • TV room • Indoor swimming pool nearby • Outdoor swimming pool nearby • Golf nearby • Riding nearby • Fishing on site
Well grassed, level pitches near to fishing lake. Historic towns like Boston and Spilsby are within easy reach, only 1.25 miles from beach. Explore the villages in the Lincolnshire Wolds or relax around our lake, and watch the wildlife and marvellous sunsets. Pubs and restaurants all within easy reach.

▲ **Top Yard Farm Caravan Park,** Croft Bank, Croft, Skegness, PE24 4RL
Tel: 01754 880189
Open: Mar to Oct

▲ **Skegness Water Leisure Park,** Walls Lane, Skegness, Lincolnshire, PE25 1JF
Actual Grid Ref: TF565665
Tel: 0500 821963
Open: Mar to Oct

All details shown are as supplied by hostels and campsites in Autumn 2000.

MAP PAGE 112 • **Lincolnshire**

Spalding

TF2422

▲ **Museum of Entertainment Caravan & Camping Site,** Millgate, Whaplode St Catherines, Spalding, Lincs, PE12 6SF
Tel: 01406 540379
Open: Easter to Oct

▲ **The Hamber Caravan and Camping Site,** 5 Vicarage Lane, Spalding, Lincs, PE12 9AF
Actual Grid Ref: TF440215
Tel: 01406 362741
Open: Mar to Nov

▲ **Heron Cottage Camping & Caravanning,** Frostley Gate, Holbeach Fen, Spalding, Lincolnshire, PE12 8SR
Actual Grid Ref: TF363204
Tel: 01406 540435
Open: All year

Stickney

TF3456

▲ **Midville Caravan Park,** Stickney, Boston, Lincolnshire, PE22 8HW
Actual Grid Ref: TF386578
Tel: 01205 270316
Open: Mar to Nov

Sutton on Sea

TF5281

▲ **Cherry Tree Site,** Huttoft Road, Sutton on Sea, Mablethorpe, Lincolnshire, LN12 2RU
Actual Grid Ref: TF525802
Tel: 01507 441626
Open: Mar to Oct

Sutton St Edmund

TF3712

▲ **Orchard View Caravan & Camping Park,** Sutton St Edmund, Spalding, Lincolnshire, PE12 0LT
Actual Grid Ref: TF365108
Tel: 01945 700482 **Open:** Mar to Oct

Sutton St James

TF4018

▲ **Foremans Bridge Caravan Park,** Sutton St James, Spalding, Lincolnshire, PE12 0HU
Actual Grid Ref: TF406195
Tel: 01945 440346
Open: Mar to Nov

Swinderby

SK8763

▲ **Oakhill Farm,** Swinderby, Lincoln, LN6 9QG
Actual Grid Ref: SK879612
Tel: 01522 868771
Fax: 01522 868771
Open: All year

Tallington

TF0908

▲ **Tallington Lakes,** Barholme Road, Tallington, Stamford, Lincolnshire, PE9 4RT
Actual Grid Ref: TF095090
Tel: 01778 347000
Fax: 01778 346213
Open: All year

Tattershall

TF2158

▲ **Willow Holt Caravan & Camping Park,** Lodge Road, Tattershall, Lincoln, LN4 4JS
Actual Grid Ref: TF200595
Tel: 01526 343111
Open: Mar to Oct

▲ **Tattershall Park Country Club,** Sleaford Road, Tattershall, Lincoln, LN4 4LR
Actual Grid Ref: TF205567
Tel: 01526 343193
Open: Mar to Oct

Tattershall Bridge

TF1956

▲ **Holly Farm Caravan Park,** Tattershall Bridge, Lincoln, LN4 4JP
Actual Grid Ref: TF193568
Tel: 01526 342385
Open: Apr to Oct

Thurlby (Bourne)

TF1017

▲ **Thurlby Youth Hostel,** 16 High Street, Thurlby, Bourne, Lincolnshire, PE10 0EE
Actual Grid Ref: TF097168
Tel: 01778 425588
Fax: 01778 425588
Capacity: 24

Under 18: £6.50
Adults: £9.25
Open: All year, 5.00pm
Camping
Self-catering facilities • Showers • Lounge • Dining room • Drying room • Cycle store • No smoking • WC • Kitchen facilities • Credit cards accepted
Originally a C15th forge, with later additions, this traditional hostel has pleasant lawned grounds. There are several walks nearby, s well as cycling, and fishing on Rutland Water. The Wool Churches, built with the profits of the local mediaeval wool trade, are a local attraction.

Trusthorpe

TF5183

▲ **Kirkstead Holiday Park,** North Road, Trusthorpe, Mablethorpe, Lincolnshire, LN12 2QD
Actual Grid Ref: TF509835
Tel: 01507 441483
Open: Mar to Nov

Tydd Gote

TF4518

▲ **Eaudyke Bank Farm Touring Caravan & Camping Site,** Tydd Gote, Wisbech, Lincolnshire, PE13 5NA
Tel: 01945 420630
Open: All year

Wainfleet Bank

TF4659

▲ **Riverside Caravan Park,** Wainfleet Bank, Skegness, Lincolnshire, PE24 4ND
Actual Grid Ref: TF480592
Tel: 01754 880205
Open: Mar to Oct

Walesby

TF1392

▲ **Viking Way Walesby,** Mill House Farm, Walesby, Market Rasen, Lincolnshire, LN8 3UR
Tel: 01673 838333
Open: Mar to Dec

West Ashby

TF2672

▲ **Ashby Park,** West Ashby, Horncastle, Lincs, LN9 5QA
Actual Grid Ref: TF251726
Tel: 01507 527966
Open: Mar to Nov

Lincolnshire • MAP PAGE 112

Woodhall Spa

TF1963

▲ **Jubilee Park,** Stixwould Road, Woodhall Spa, Lincolnshire, LN10 6QH
Actual Grid Ref: TF189637
Tel: 01526 352448
Open: Mar to Nov

▲ **Glen Lodge,** Edlington Moor, Woodhall Spa, LN10 6UL
Tel: 01526 353523
Open: Mar to Nov

▲ **Bainland Country Park,** Horncastle Road, Woodhall Spa, Lincs, LN10 6UY
Actual Grid Ref: TF219642
Tel: 01526 352903
Fax: 01526 353730
Open: All year

Woodthorpe

TF4380

▲ **Woodthorpe Hall Leisure Park,** Woodthorpe, Alford, Lincs, LN13 0DD
Tel: 01507 450294
Open: Mar to Dec

Wrawby

TA0308

▲ **The Jolly Miller,** Brigg Road, Wrawby, Brigg, DN20 8RH
Tel: 01652 655658
Open: All year

You are advised to book in advance for periods of high demand – the Summer months, Half Term holidays and public holidays.

London

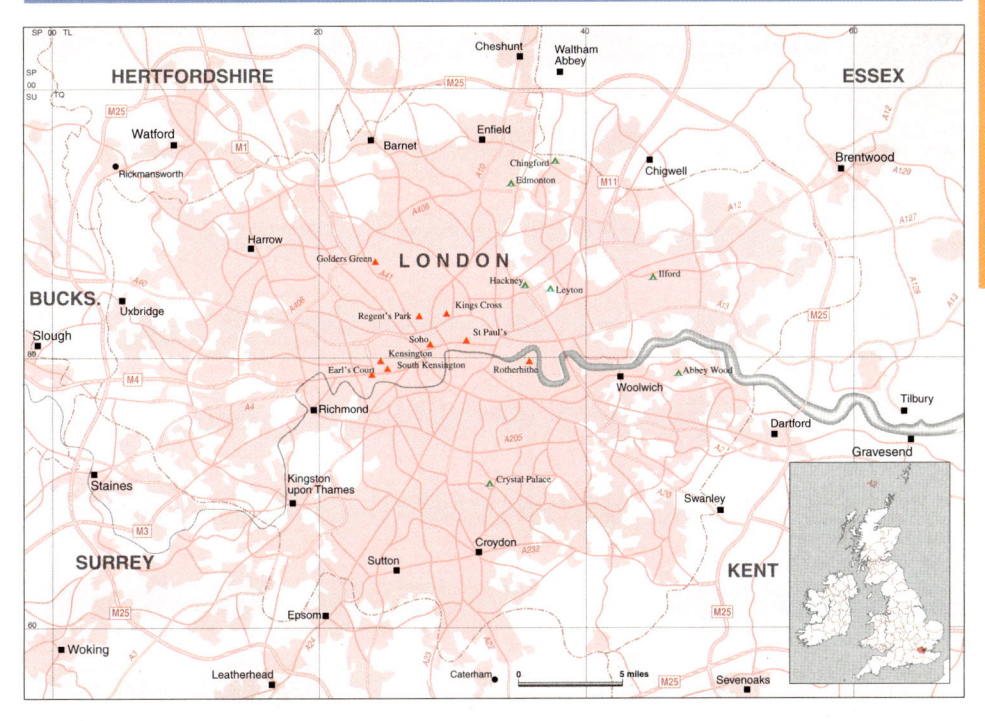

Abbey Wood

TQ4779

▲ **Abbey Wood Caravan & Camping Site,** Federation Road, Abbey Wood, London, SE2 0LS
Tel: 020 8310 2233
Email: cc70@gofornet.co.uk
Open: All year

Chingford

TQ3894

▲ **Lee Valley Campsite,** Sewardstone Road, Chingford, London, E4 7RA
Actual Grid Ref: TQ379968
Tel: 020 8529 5689 **Open:** Apr to Oct

Crystal Palace

TQ3470

▲ **Crystal Palace Caravan Club Site,** Crystal Palace Parade, Crystal Palace, London, SE19 1UF
Tel: 020 8778 7155 **Open:** All year

Earl's Court

TQ2578

▲ **Earl's Court Youth Hostel,** 38 Bolton Gardens, Earl's Court, London, SW5 0AQ
Actual Grid Ref: TQ258783
Tel: 020 7373 7083
Fax: 020 7835 2034
Email: earlscourt@yha.org.uk
Capacity: 159
Under 18: £16.50 **Adults:** £18.50
Open: All year, All day
Television • Television • Showers • Laundry facilities • Lounge • Cycle store • Evening meal available 5.00-8.00pm • Kitchen facilities • Kitchen facilities • Breakfast available • Luggage store • Credit cards accepted
In the heart of a young, international area full of shops, cafes, restaurants and bars as well as being near Earl's Court and Olympia exhibition centres. Small courtyard garden.

All details shown are as supplied by hostels and campsites in Autumn 2000.

Edmonton

TQ3492

▲ **Lee Valley Leisure Centre,** Meridian Way, Edmonton, London, N9 0AS
Actual Grid Ref: TQ363942
Tel: 020 8345 6666 / 020 8803 6900
Fax: 020 8884 4975
Open: All year

Some hostels and campsites impose restrictions on size and type of groups they accept (e.g. not permitting single-sex groups). Always phone to enquire before booking.

London • MAP PAGE 119

ENGLAND

Golders Green
TQ2487

▲ **Hampstead Heath Youth Hostel,** 4 Wellgarth Road, Golders Green, London, NW11 7HR
Actual Grid Ref: TQ258873
Tel: 020 8458 9054
Fax: 020 8209 0546
Email: hampstead@yha.org.uk
Capacity: 199
Under 18: £17.90
Adults: £19.90
Open: All year, All day
Family bunk rooms
Television • Showers • Licensed bar • Laundry facilities • Lounge 2 • Games room • Parking Very limited • Evening meal available 5.00-8.00pm • Breakfast available • Luggage store • Credit cards accepted
Convenient for getting into central London and yet with the feel of a country house, complete with its own lovely garden and access to Hampstead Heath.

Hackney
TQ3584

▲ **Tent City (Hackney),** Millfields Road, Hackney, London, E5 0AR
Actual Grid Ref: TQ366858
Tel: 020 8985 7656
Fax: 020 8749 9074
Email: tentcity@btinternet.com
Open: Jul to Aug

Ilford
TQ4486

▲ **Aldborough Hall Farm,** Aldborough Road North, Ilford, Essex, IG2 7TD
Tel: 020 8590 5882
Open: All year

Kensington
TQ2579

▲ **Holland House Youth Hostel,** Holland House, Holland Walk, Kensington, London, W8 7QU
Actual Grid Ref: TQ249797
Tel: 020 7937 0748
Fax: 020 7376 0667
Email: hollandhouse@yha.org.uk
Capacity: 201
Under 18: £18.50
Adults: £20.50
Open: All year, All day
Self-catering facilities • Television • Showers • Laundry facilities • Lounge • Games room • Security lockers • Evening meal available 5.00-8.00pm • Kitchen facilities • Breakfast available • Luggage store • Credit cards accepted
A former Jacobean mansion built on the edge of the park by the open-air theatre. The windows are onto the park. All the major South Ken museums are within walking distance.

Kings Cross
TQ3083

▲ **St Pancras International Youth Hostel,** 79-81 Euston Road, St Pancras, London, NW1 2QS
Actual Grid Ref: TQ300828
Tel: 020 7388 9998
Fax: 020 7388 6766
Email: stpancras@yha.org.uk
Capacity: 150
Under 18: £19.90
Adults: £23.50
Open: All year, All day
Family bunk rooms
Self-catering facilities • Television • Showers • Licensed bar • Laundry facilities • Lounge • Games room • Security lockers • Cycle store • Evening meal available 6.00-9.00pm • Facilities for disabled people • Luggage store • Credit cards accepted
Modern, comfortable hostel close to St Pancras, King's Cross and Euston stations, the new British Library and Camden Town - live jazz and good Irish pubs. Communications make it ideal for exploring London.

Leyton
TQ3786

▲ **Lee Valley Cycle Circuit Campsite,** Temple Mills Lane, Leyton, London, E15 2EN
Actual Grid Ref: TQ376854
Tel: 020 8534 6085
Open: Mar to Oct

You are advised to book in advance for periods of high demand – the Summer months, Half Term holidays and public holidays.

To stay in a Youth Hostel affiliated to one of the Youth Hostel associations, you need to be a member. You can join at most hostels – phone in advance to check.

Regent's Park
TQ2882

▲ **International Students House,** 229 Great Portland Street, Marylebone, London, W1N 5HD
Tel: 020 7631 8300
Fax: 020 7631 8315
Email: accom@ish.org.uk
Capacity: 550
Adults: £9.99-£31.00
Open: All year, any time
Television • Showers • Licensed bar • Central heating • Laundry facilities • Lounge • Dining room • Games room • Security lockers • Evening meal available 5-7pm • Facilities for disabled people
Central location, close to major tourist attractions and West End.

Rotherhithe
TQ3579

▲ **Rotherhithe Youth Hostel,** Salter Road, Rotherhithe, London, SE16 1PP
Actual Grid Ref: TQ357804
Tel: 020 7232 2114
Fax: 020 7237 2919
Email: rotherhithe@yha.org.uk
Capacity: 320
Under 18: £19.90
Adults: £23.50
Open: All year, All day
Family bunk rooms
Self-catering facilities • Television • Showers • Licensed bar • Laundry facilities • Lounge • Cycle store • Evening meal available 6.00-7.30pm • Facilities for disabled people Category 1 • Credit cards accepted
New purpose-built hostel in a striking modern design on four floors, all bedrooms ensuite. Greenwich is within easy reach, as is the Tower and points west.

Hostels and campsites may vary rates – be sure to check when booking.

MAP PAGE 119 • **London**

Soho
TQ2981

▲ **Oxford Street Youth Hostel,** 14 Noel Street, Soho, London, W1F 8GJ
Tel: 020 7734 1618
Fax: 020 7734 1657
Email: oxfordst@yha.org.uk
Capacity: 75
Under 18: £17.50 **Adults:** £21.50
Open: All year, All day
Self-catering facilities • Television • Showers • Laundry facilities • Lounge • Security lockers • Kitchen facilities • Credit cards accepted
In the middle of lively Soho, you can shop till you drop in Britain's most famous shopping street. Plenty of pubs, clubs & restaurants in the area. You can book tickets to musicals at reception.

All details shown are as supplied by hostels and campsites in Autumn 2000.

South Kensington
TQ2678

▲ **Baden Powell House,** 65-67 Queen's Gate, South Kensington, London, SW7 5JS
Tel: 020 7584 7031
Fax: 020 7590 6902
Email: bph.hostel@scout.org.uk
Capacity: 180
Under 18: £17.00
Adults: £25.00
Open: All year (not Xmas/New Year), any time
Family bunk rooms: £20.00
Television • Central heating • Shop • Laundry facilities • Lounge • Dining room • Games room • Parking • Evening meal available 5-7pm • Facilities for disabled people • No smoking
Modern building opposite Natural History Museum and close to attractions.

Hostels and campsites may vary rates – be sure to check when booking.

St Paul's
TQ3181

▲ **City of London Youth Hostel,** 36 Carter Lane, St Paul's, London, EC4V 5AD
Actual Grid Ref: TQ319811
Tel: 020 7236 4965
Fax: 020 7236 7681
Email: city@yha.org.uk
Capacity: 193
Under 18: £19.90
Adults: £23.50
Open: All year, All day
Family bunk rooms
Television • Showers • Licensed bar • Laundry facilities • Lounge • Evening meal available 5.00-8.00pm • Breakfast available • Luggage store • Credit cards accepted
The one-time Choir School for St Paul's Cathedral has been fully refurbished to modern standards, while the old building retains many of its original features, including the oak panels in the former chapel. It is right in the centre of the City of London.

ENGLAND

Norfolk

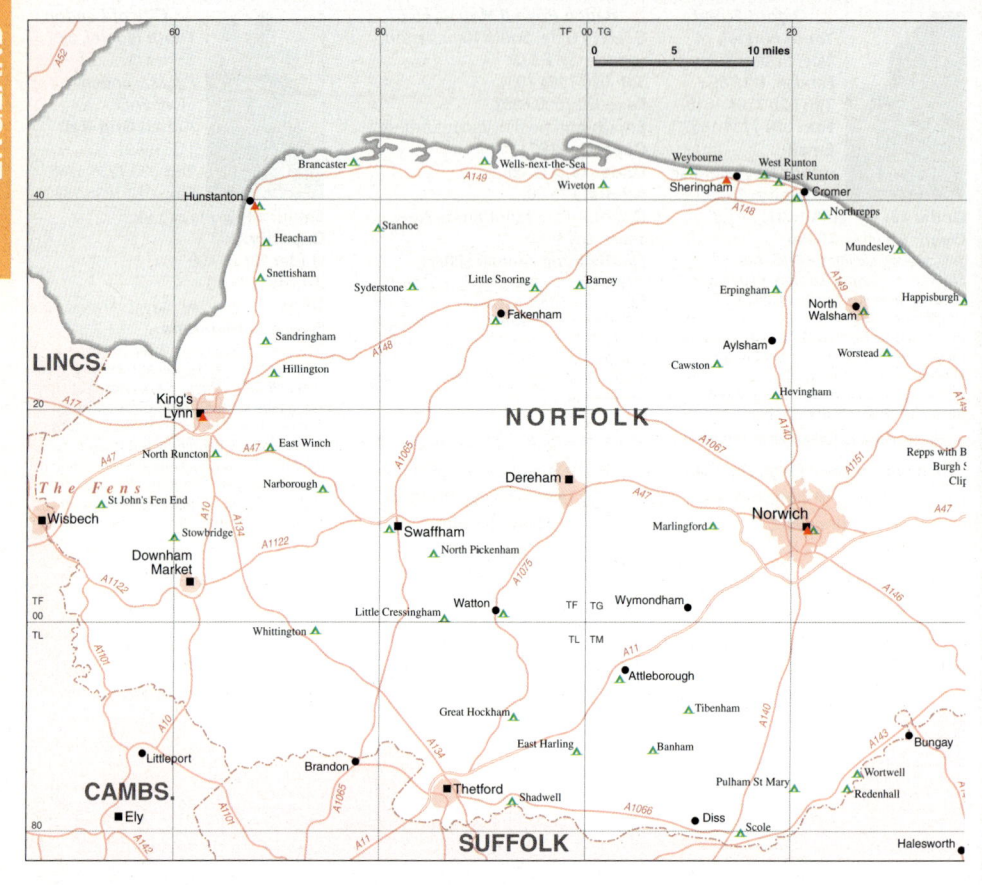

Aldeby
TM4493

▲ **Waveney Lodge Caravan Site,** Elms Road, Aldeby, Beccles, Norfolk, NR34 0EJ
Actual Grid Ref: TM434937
Tel: 01502 677445
Open: All year

Attleborough
TM0495

▲ **Oak Tree Caravan Park,** Norwich Road, Attleborough, Norfolk, NR17 2JX
Actual Grid Ref: TM057960
Tel: 01953 455565
Open: All year

Banham
TM0687

▲ **Farm Meadow Caravan & Camping Park,** The Grove, Banham Zoo, Banham, Norwich, NR16 2HB
Actual Grid Ref: TM056874
Tel: 01953 888370
Fax: 01953 887445
Open: All year

Barney
TF9932

▲ **The Old Brick Kilns Caravan Park,** Barney, Fakenham, Norfolk, NR21 0NL
Actual Grid Ref: TG004332
Tel: 01328 878305
Email: enquire@old-brick-kilns.co.uk
Open: Mar to Dec

Belton
TG4802

▲ **Rose Farm Touring & Camping Park,** Stepshort, Belton, Great Yarmouth, Norfolk, NR31 9JS
Actual Grid Ref: TG488035
Tel: 01493 780896 **Open:** All year

▲ **Wild Duck Holiday Park,** Howards Common, Belton, Great Yarmouth, Norfolk, NR31 9NE
Actual Grid Ref: TG476026
Tel: 01493 780268
Open: Mar to Oct

122   Stilwell's Hostels & Camping 2002

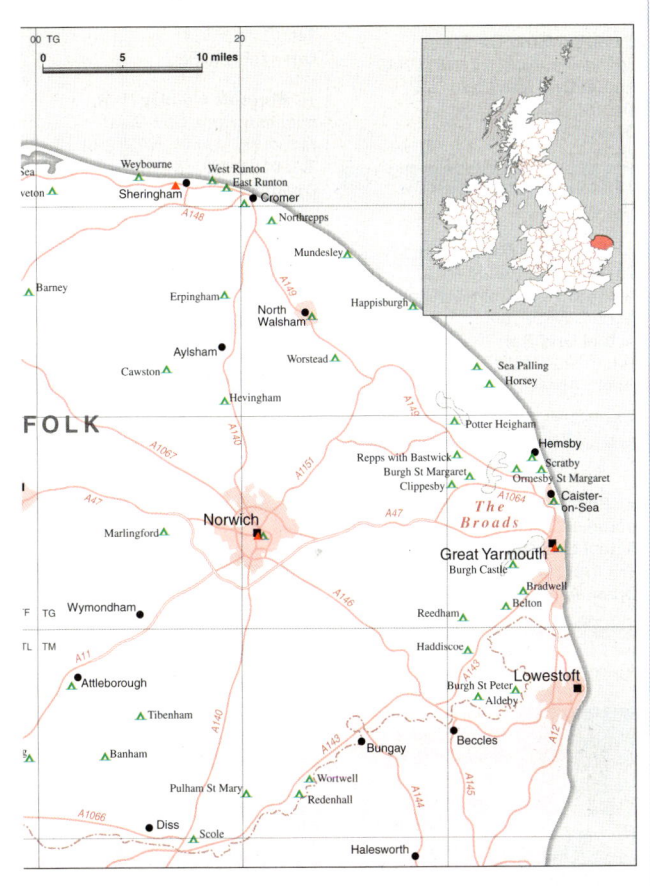

Norfolk

▲ **Cherry Tree Holiday Park,** Mill Road, Burgh Castle, Great Yarmouth, Norfolk, NR31 9QR
Actual Grid Ref: TG490042
Tel: 01493 780024
Open: Mar to Sept

▲ **Burgh Hall Holiday Park,** Lords Lane, Burgh Castle, Great Yarmouth, Norfolk, NR31 9EP
Actual Grid Ref: TG495045
Tel: 01493 780847
Open: Apr to Jan

Burgh St Margaret

TG4414

▲ **Broad Farm Trailer Park,** Fleggburgh, Burgh St Margaret, Great Yarmouth, Norfolk, NR29 3AF
Actual Grid Ref: TG442140
Tel: 01493 369273
Open: Apr to Oct

Burgh St Peter

TM4693

▲ **Waveney River Centre,** Burgh St Peter, Beccles, Suffolk, NR34 0BT
Actual Grid Ref: TM491934
Tel: 01502 677343
Open: Mar to Oct

Caister-on-Sea

TG5112

▲ **Old Hall Leisure Park,** High Street, Caister-on-Sea, Great Yarmouth, Norfolk, NR30 5JL
Actual Grid Ref: TG521122
Tel: 01493 720400
Open: June to Aug

Bradwell

TG5003

▲ **Blue Sky Holiday Park,** Burgh Road, Bradwell, Great Yarmouth, Norfolk, NR31 9ED
Actual Grid Ref: TG502052
Tel: 01493 781234
Open: Apr to Oct

Brancaster

TF7745

▲ **Eastwood Campsite,** Brancaster, King's Lynn, Norfolk, PE31 8AA
Actual Grid Ref: TF776438
Tel: 01485 210491
Open: All year

Burgh Castle

TG4804

▲ **Liffens Holiday Park,** Burgh Castle, Great Yarmouth, Norfolk, NR31 9QB
Actual Grid Ref: TG480042
Tel: 01493 780357
Fax: 01493 782383
Open: Mar to Oct

▲ **Welcome Farm Holiday Park,** Welcome Pit Butt Lane, Burgh Castle, Great Yarmouth, Norfolk, NR29 4EF
Actual Grid Ref: TG483039
Tel: 01493 780481
Open: Apr to Oct

Cawston

TG1323

▲ **Haveringland Hall Caravan Park,** Cawston, Norwich, NR10 4PN
Actual Grid Ref: TG156214
AA grade: 3 Pennants
Tel: 01603 871302
Fax: 01603 879223
Email: haveringland@claranet.com
Tent pitches: 40
Tent rate: £6.50-£8.00
Open: Mar to Oct
Last arr: 8pm
Dogs allowed • Electric hook-up • Calor Gas/Camping Gaz • Picnic/barbecue area on site • Showers • Laundrette on site • Public phone on site • Baby care facilities
Woods and lakes yet minutes from Broads, Norwich and sea.

Norfolk • MAP PAGE 122

You are advised to book in advance for periods of high demand – the Summer months, Half Term holidays and public holidays.

Clippesby
TG4214

▲ **Clippesby Holidays,** Clippesby Hall, Clippesby, Great Yarmouth, Norfolk, NR29 3BL
Actual Grid Ref: TG423145
Tel: 01493 367800
Open: May to Sep

Cromer
TG2142

▲ **Seacroft Camping Park,** Cromer, Norfolk, NR27 9NJ
Actual Grid Ref: TG205424
Tel: 01263 511722
Open: Mar to Oct

East Harling
TL9885

▲ **Dower House Touring Park,** East Harling, Norwich, NR16 2SE
Actual Grid Ref: TL970852
Tel: 01953 717314
Fax: 01953 717843
Open: Mar to Oct

East Runton
TG1942

▲ **Manor Farm Camp Site,** East Runton, Cromer, Norfolk, NR27 9PR
Actual Grid Ref: TG198416
Tel: 01263 512858
Open: Mar to Sept

▲ **Woodhill Park,** Cromer Road, East Runton, Cromer, Norfolk, NR27 9PX
Actual Grid Ref: TG198428
Tel: 01263 512242
Open: Apr to Oct

East Winch
TF6916

▲ **Pentney Lakes Leisure Park,** Common Road, East Winch, Kings Lynn, Norfolk, PE32 1JT
Actual Grid Ref: TF701130
Tel: 01760 338668
Open: All year

Erpingham
TG1932

▲ **Little Haven Caravan & Camping Park,** The Street, Erpingham, Norwich, NR11 7QD
Actual Grid Ref: TG204324
Tel: 01263 768959
Open: Apr to Oct

Fakenham
TF9230

▲ **Fakenham Racecourse Caravan & Camping Park,** Fakenham Racecourse, Fakenham, Norfolk, NR21 7NY
Actual Grid Ref: TF930247
Tel: 01328 862388
Open: All year

Great Hockham
TL9492

▲ **Puddledock Farm,** Great Hockham, Thetford, Norfolk, IP24 1PA
Actual Grid Ref: TL941926
Tel: 01953 498455
Open: All year

Great Yarmouth
TG5207

▲ **Great Yarmouth Youth Hostel,** 2 Sandown Road, Great Yarmouth, Norfolk, NR30 1EY
Actual Grid Ref: TG529083
Tel: 01493 843991
Fax: 01493 856600
Capacity: 40
Under 18: £6.50
Adults: £9.25
Open: All year, 5.00pm
Family bunk rooms
Self-catering facilities • Showers • Wet weather shelter • Lounge • Dining room • Drying room • Cycle store • Evening meal available 7.00pm • No smoking • Kitchen facilities • Luggage store • Credit cards accepted
Victorian house only minutes from the beach and the Broads National Park. Enjoy the kitsch and medieval, coastal and cultural setting of Yarmouth.

All details shown are as supplied by hostels and campsites in Autumn 2000.

▲ **Vauxhall Holiday Park,** 4 Acle New Road, Great Yarmouth, Norfolk, NR30 1TB
Actual Grid Ref: TG519086
Tel: 01493 857231
Open: May to Sep

▲ **Bureside Holiday Park,** Boundary Farm, Oby, Great Yarmouth, Norfolk, NR29 3BW
Tel: 01493 369233
Open: May to Sep

▲ **Burgh Castle Marina,** Great Yarmouth, Norfolk, NR31 9PZ
Actual Grid Ref: TG474042
Tel: 01493 780331
Open: All year

Haddiscoe
TM4497

▲ **Pampas Lodge,** Haddiscoe, Norwich, NR14 6AA
Actual Grid Ref: TM447971
Tel: 01502 677265
Open: Apr to Oct

Happisburgh
TG3731

▲ **Gladhern,** Short Lane, Happisburgh, Norwich, Norfolk, NR12 0RH
Actual Grid Ref: TG375292
Tel: 01692 650402
Open: All year

▲ **Whittletons Farm,** Happisburgh, Norwich, Norfolk, NR12 0RU
Actual Grid Ref: TG371288
Tel: 01692 650485
Open: Apr to Oct

Heacham
TF6737

▲ **Heacham Beach Holiday Park,** South Beach Road, Heacham, Kings Lynn, Norfolk, PE31 7DD
Actual Grid Ref: TF667371
Tel: 01485 570270 **Open:** Apr to Oct

Hemsby
TG4817

▲ **Long Beach Holiday Homes,** Hemsby, Great Yarmouth, Norfolk, NR29 4JD
Actual Grid Ref: TG503178
Tel: 01493 730023
Open: Mar to Oct

MAP PAGE 122 • **Norfolk**

▲ **Newport Caravan Park,** Newport Road, Hemsby, Great Yarmouth, Norfolk, NR29 4NW
Actual Grid Ref: TG502169
Tel: 01493 730405
Open: Mar to Oct

Hevingham

TG1921

▲ **Hevingham Lakes Caravan & Camping,** Hevingham, Norwich, Norfolk, NR10 5QL
Actual Grid Ref: TG182216
Tel: 01603 754368
Open: Apr to Oct

Hillington

TF7125

▲ **Gatton Waters Lakeside Touring Site,** Hillington, King's Lynn, Norfolk, PE31 6BJ
Actual Grid Ref: TF705252
Tel: 01485 600643
Open: Apr to Oct

Horsey

TG4522

▲ **Waxham Sands Holiday Park,** Warren Farm, Horsey, Great Yarmouth, Norfolk, NR29 4EJ
Actual Grid Ref: TG459246
Tel: 01692 598325
Open: May to Sep

Hunstanton

TF6740

▲ **Hunstanton Youth Hostel,** 15 Avenue Road, Hunstanton, Norfolk, PE36 5BW
Actual Grid Ref: TF674406
Tel: 01485 532061
Fax: 01485 532632
Capacity: 45
Under 18: £6.90
Adults: £10.00
Open: All year
Family bunk rooms
Self-catering facilities • Television • Showers • Wet weather shelter • Lounge • Dining room • Drying room • Cycle store • Evening meal available 7.00pm • Kitchen facilities • Luggage store • Credit cards accepted
Large Victorian house in seaside resort with Blue Flag beach, famous for bird and seal watching and ecology studies.

▲ **Searles Holiday Centre,** 3 South Beach Road, Hunstanton, Norfolk, PE36 5BB
Actual Grid Ref: TF672398
Tel: 01485 534211 / 532342 ext 100
Fax: 01485 533815
Open: Apr to Oct

▲ **Inglenook,** Main Road, Holme-next-the-Sea, Hunstanton, Norfolk, PE36 6LA
Actual Grid Ref: TF707429
Tel: 01485 525598
Open: All year

King's Lynn

TF6120

▲ **King's Lynn Youth Hostel,** Thoresby College, College Lane, King's Lynn, Norfolk, PE30 1JB
Actual Grid Ref: TF616199
Tel: 01553 772461
Fax: 01553 764312
Capacity: 35
Under 18: £6.50
Adults: £9.25
Open: All year, 5.00pm
Self-catering facilities • Showers • Lounge • Dining room • Drying room • Cycle store • Evening meal available pre-booked • No smoking • Kitchen facilities • Breakfast available • Credit cards accepted
This is the wing of a 500 year old Chantry college building. It is a ideal base for walking and cycling as well as exploring the many historical and cultural attractions of King's Lynn itself.

Little Cressingham

TF8700

▲ **Sycamore House,** Little Cressingham, Thetford, Norfolk, IP25 6NE
Tel: 01953 881887
Fax: 01953 881887
Open: All year

Little Snoring

TF9532

▲ **Crossways Caravan Site,** Holt Road, Little Snoring, Fakenham, Norfolk, NR21 0AX
Actual Grid Ref: TF961321
Tel: 01328 878335
Fax: 01328 878335
Open: Apr to Oct

Marlingford

TG1309

▲ **Swans Harbour Caravan Park,** Barford Road, Marlingford, Norwich, NR9 4BE
Actual Grid Ref: TG123086
Tel: 01603 759658
Open: All year

Mundesley

TG3136

▲ **Links Caravan Site,** Links Road, Mundesley, Norwich, NR11 8AE
Actual Grid Ref: TG305365
Tel: 01263 720665
Open: Easter to Sep

Narborough

TF7413

▲ **Pentney Park,** Gaynton Road, Narborough, King's Lynn, Norfolk, PE32 1HU
Actual Grid Ref: TF742142
Tel: 01760 337479
Open: All year

North Pickenham

TF8606

▲ **Riverside House,** Meadow Lane, North Pickenham, Swaffham, Norfolk, PE37 8LE
Tel: 01760 440219
Open: All year

North Runcton

TF6415

▲ **King's Lynn Caravan & Camping Park,** New Road, North Runcton, King's Lynn, Norfolk, PE33 0QR
Tel: 01553 840004
Email: klynn.campsite@tesco.net
Tent pitches: 30
Tent rate: £4.50-£8.00
Open: All year
Last arr: 10.30pm
Dogs allowed • Electric hook-up • Picnic/barbecue area on site • Children's play area • Showers
Beautiful 5 acre parkland setting and good food pubs nearby.

Hostels and campsites may vary rates – be sure to check when booking.

Norfolk • MAP PAGE 122

ENGLAND

North Walsham
TG2830

▲ **Two Mills Touring Park,** Scarborough Hill, Old Yarmouth Road, North Walsham, Norfolk, NR28 9NA
Actual Grid Ref: TG291286
Tel: 01692 405829
Open: Mar to Jan

Northrepps
TG2439

▲ **Forest Park Caravan Site,** Northrepps Road, Northrepps, Cromer, Norfolk, NR27 0JR
Actual Grid Ref: TG233405
Tel: 01263 513290
Fax: 01263 513290
Open: Apr to Oct

Norwich
TG2308

▲ **Norwich Youth Hostel,** 112 Turner Road, Norwich, NR2 4HB
Actual Grid Ref: TG213095
Tel: 01603 627647
Fax: 01603 629075
Email: norwich@yha.org.uk
Capacity: 57
Under 18: £6.90
Adults: £10.00
Open: All year, 5.00pm
Family bunk rooms
Self-catering facilities • Television • Showers • Lounge • Drying room • Cycle store • Parking • Evening meal available 7.00pm • Kitchen facilities • Breakfast available • Credit cards accepted
Just a short distance from the city centre, with its medieval cathedral and churches. From Norwich it is easy to reach the seaside and the Broads.

▲ **Camping & Caravanning Club Site,** Martineau Lane, Norwich, NR1 2HX
Actual Grid Ref: TG237063
Tel: 01603 620060
Open: Mar to Aug

You are advised to book in advance for periods of high demand – the Summer months, Half Term holidays and public holidays.

Ormesby St Margaret
TG4915

▲ **The Grange Touring Park,** Ormesby St Margaret, Great Yarmouth, Norfolk, NR29 3QG
Actual Grid Ref: TG512143
Tel: 01493 730306
Fax: 01493 732024
Open: Mar to Oct

Potter Heigham
TG4119

▲ **Causeway Cottage Caravan Park,** Bridge Road, Potter Heigham, Great Yarmouth, Norfolk, NR29 5JB
Actual Grid Ref: TG416187
Tel: 01692 670238
Open: Mar to Oct

Pulham St Mary
TM2085

▲ **Waveney Valley Holiday Park,** Airstation Farm, Pulham St Mary, Diss, Norfolk, IP21 4QF
Actual Grid Ref: TM198832
Tel: 01379 741228
Open: Apr to Oct

Redenhall
TM2684

▲ **Hill Farm,** Redenhall, Harleston, Norfolk, IP20 9QN
Tel: 01379 852289 **Fax:** 01379 852289
Open: Apr to Sep

Reedham
TG4201

▲ **Reedham Ferry Camping & Caravan Park,** Ferry Road, Reedham, Norwich, NR13 3HA
Actual Grid Ref: TG407015
Tel: 01493 700429
Fax: 01493 700999
Open: Mar to Oct

Repps with Bastwick
TG4117

▲ **Willowcroft Camping & Caravan Park,** Staithe Road, Repps with Bastwick, Great Yarmouth, Norfolk, NR29 5JU
Actual Grid Ref: TG414173
Tel: 01962 670380
Fax: 01962 670380
Open: Mar to Oct

▲ **White House Farm,** Main Road, Repps with Bastwick, Great Yarmouth, Norfolk, NR29 5JH
Actual Grid Ref: TG424183
Tel: 01692 670403
Open: Mar to Oct

Sandringham
TF6928

▲ **Camping & Caravanning Club Site,** The Sandringham Estate, Double Lodges, Sandringham, Norfolk, PE35 6EA
Actual Grid Ref: TF683274
Tel: 01485 542555
Open: Mar to Nov

Scole
TM1479

▲ **Willows Camping & Caravan Park,** Diss Road, Scole, Diss, Norfolk, IP21 4DH
Actual Grid Ref: TM147788
Tel: 01379 740271
Open: May to Sep

Scratby
TG5015

▲ **Scratby Hall Caravan Park,** Scratby, Great Yarmouth, Norfolk, NR29 3PH
Actual Grid Ref: TG500156
Tel: 01493 730283
Open: Mar to Oct

▲ **Green Farm Caravan Park,** Beach Road, Scratby, Great Yarmouth, Norfolk, NR29 3NW
Tel: 01263 730440
Open: Apr to Oct

Sea Palling
TG4327

▲ **Golden Beach Holiday Centre,** Beach Road, Sea Palling, Norwich, NR12 0AL
Actual Grid Ref: TG428273
Tel: 01692 598269
Open: Mar to Oct

Shadwell
TL9382

▲ **Thorpe Woodland Caravan & Camping Site,** Shadwell, Thetford, Norfolk, IP24 2RX
Tel: 01842 751042
Open: Easter to Oct

MAP PAGE 122 • **Norfolk**

Sheringham

TG1543

▲ **Sheringham Youth Hostel,** 1 Cremer's Drift, Sheringham, Norfolk, NR26 8BJ
Actual Grid Ref: TG159428
Tel: 01263 823215
Fax: 01263 824679
Email: sheringham@yha.org.uk
Capacity: 100
Under 18: £7.15
Adults: £11.00
Open: Mar to Nov , 1.00pm
Family bunk rooms
Self-catering facilities • Self-catering facilities • Television • Lounge • Dining room • Drying room • Cycle store • Parking • Evening meal available 6.00 to 7.00pm • Facilities for disabled people • Facilities for disabled people • Kitchen facilities • Breakfast available • Credit cards accepted
Victorian building with modern annexe & facilities for disabled. Wide sandy beaches, good birdwatching & a seal colony on this coast.

Snettisham

TF6834

▲ **Diglea Caravan & Camping Park,** Beach Road, Snettisham, King's Lynn, Norfolk, PE31 7RA
Actual Grid Ref: TF654334
Tel: 01485 541367
Open: Apr to Oct

St John's Fen End

TF5411

▲ **Virginia Lake House,** Virginia House, St Johns Fen End, Wisbech, Cambs, PE14 8JF
Actual Grid Ref: TF528113
Tel: 01945 430332
Open: All year

Stanhoe

TF8037

▲ **Rickels Caravan Site,** Bircham Road, Stanhoe, King's Lynn, Norfolk, PE31 8PU
Actual Grid Ref: TF794355
Tel: 01485 518671
Fax: 01485 518671
Open: Mar to Oct

Stowbridge

TF6007

▲ **Woodlakes Leisure Ltd,** Holme Road, Stowbridge, King's Lynn, Norfolk, PE34 3PX
Actual Grid Ref: TF617076
Tel: 01553 810414
Open: Apr to Oct

Swaffham

TF8109

▲ **Breckland Meadows Touring Park,** Lynn Road, Swaffham, Norfolk, PE37 7AY
Actual Grid Ref: TF812093
Tel: 01760 721246
Open: Mar to Oct

Syderstone

TF8232

▲ **The Garden Caravan Site,** Barmer Hall Farm, Barmer, Syderstone, King's Lynn, Norfolk, PE31 8SR
Actual Grid Ref: TF812337
Tel: 01263 579208
Open: Mar to Nov

Tibenham

TM1390

▲ **The Greyhound Public House,** Tibenham, Norfolk, NR16 1PZ
Actual Grid Ref: TM136895
Tel: 01379 677676
Open: Mar to Oct

Watton

TF9100

▲ **Lowe Caravan Park,** Ashdale, Hills Road, Saham Hills, Thetford, Norfolk, IP25 7EW
Tel: 01953 881051
Open: Mar to Oct

Wells-next-the-Sea

TF9143

▲ **Pinewood Holiday Park,** Beach Road, Wells-next-the-Sea, Norfolk, NR23 1DR
Actual Grid Ref: TF913452
Tel: 01328 710439
Fax: 01328 711060
Email: holiday@pinewoods.co.uk
Tent pitches: 200
Tent rate: £7.50-£12.50
Open: Mar to Oct
Facilities for disabled people • Dogs allowed • Electric hook-up • Calor Gas/Camping Gaz • Cafe or Takeaway on site • Picnic/barbecue area on site • Children's play area • Showers • Laundrette on site • Public phone on site • Shop on site • Baby care facilities
Area of Outstanding Natural Beauty. Beautiful sandy beaches. Peaceful, relaxing.

▲ **Stiffkey Campsite,** 6 Green Way, Stiffkey, Wells-next-the-Sea, Norfolk, NR23 1QF
Actual Grid Ref: TF965438
Tel: 01328 830479
Open: Apr to Oct

West Runton

TG1842

▲ **Camping & Caravanning Club Site,** Holygate Lane, West Runton, Cromer, Norfolk, NR27 9NW
Actual Grid Ref: TG189419
Tel: 01263 837544
Open: Mar to Oct

▲ **Beeston Regis Caravan & Camping Park,** Cromer Road, West Runton, Sheringham, Norfolk, NR27 9NG
Actual Grid Ref: TG175432
Tel: 01263 823614
Open: Mar to Oct

▲ **Roman Camp Caravan Park,** West Runton, Cromer, Norfolk, NR27 9ND
Actual Grid Ref: TG184414
Tel: 01263 837256
Open: Apr to Oct

Weybourne

TG1142

▲ **Kelling Heath Holiday Park,** Weybourne, Sheringham, Norfolk, NR25 7HW
Actual Grid Ref: TG118415
Tel: 01263 588181
Open: Mar to Oct

Whittington

TL7198

▲ **Grange Farm,** Whittington, Kings Lynn, Norfolk, PE33 9TE
Actual Grid Ref: TL715994
Tel: 01366 500307
Open: Mar to Oct

Norfolk • MAP PAGE 122

Wiveton
TG0442

▲ **Long Furlong Cottage Caravan Park,** Long Lane, Wiveton, Holt, Norfolk, NR25 7DD
Actual Grid Ref: TG028414
Tel: 01263 740833
Open: Mar to Nov

Worstead
TG3026

▲ **The New Inn,** Worstead, North Walsham, Norfolk, NR28 9RW
Actual Grid Ref: TG302260
Tel: 01692 536296
Open: All year

Wortwell
TM2784

▲ **Little Lakeland Caravan Park,** Wortwell, Harleston, Norfolk, IP20 0EL
Actual Grid Ref: TM279849
Tel: 01986 788646
Open: Mar to Oct

Northamptonshire

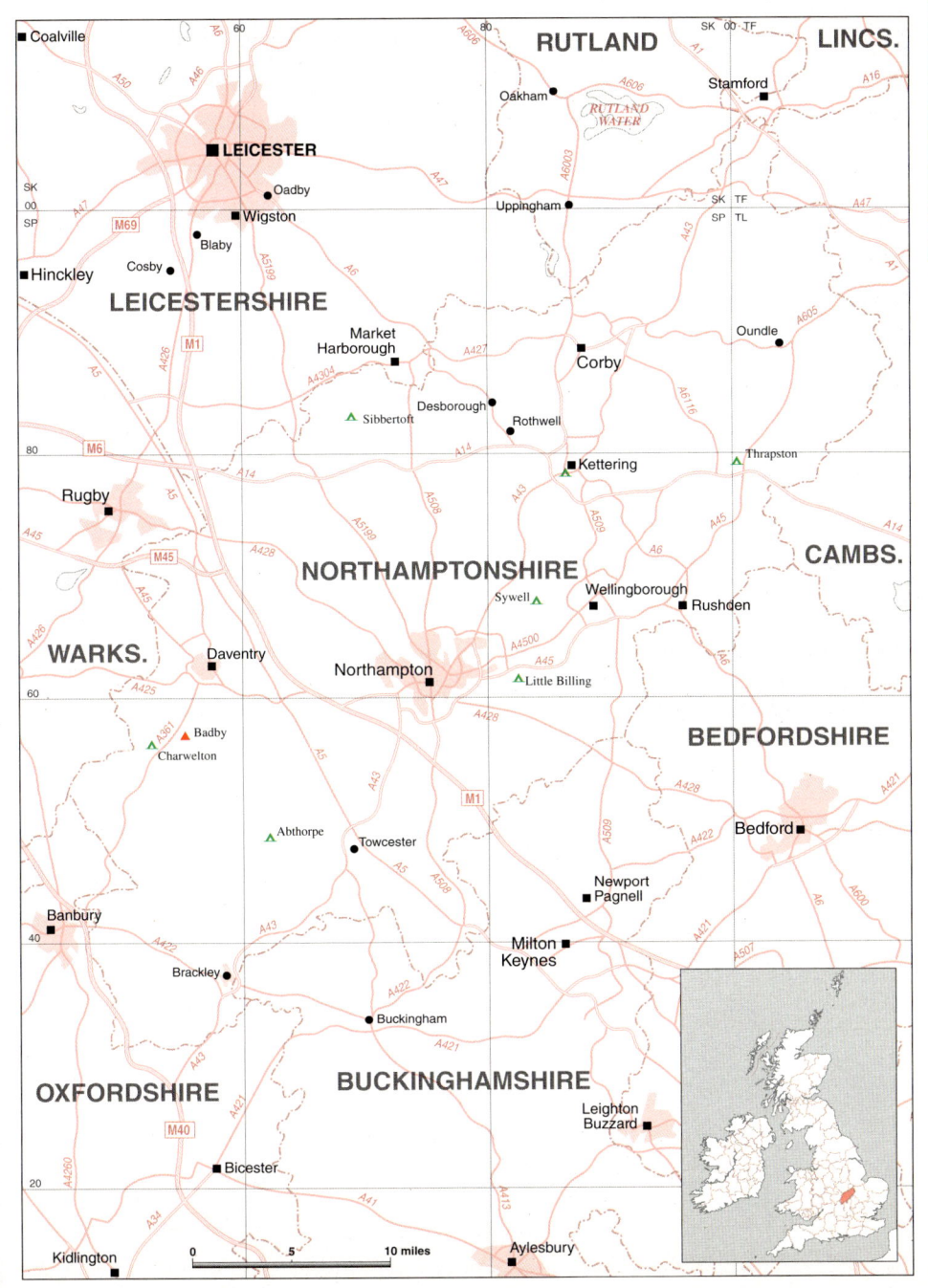

Northamptonshire • MAP PAGE 129

Abthorpe
SP6446

▲ **Stone Cottage,** Main Street, Abthorpe, Towcester, Northants, NN12 8QN
Tel: 01327 857544
Fax: 01327 858654
Open: All year

Badby
SP5558

▲ **Badby Youth Hostel,** Church Green, Badby, Daventry, Northants, NN11 3AS
Actual Grid Ref: SP561588
Tel: 01327 703883
Fax: 01327 703883
Capacity: 30
Under 18: £6.50
Adults: £9.25
Open: All year, 5.00pm
Self-catering facilities • Showers • Shop • Lounge • Dining room • Cycle store • Parking limited • No smoking • WC • Kitchen facilities • Credit cards accepted
C17th cottage on the church green in Badby, retaining its original character.

All details shown are as supplied by hostels and campsites in Autumn 2000.

You are advised to book in advance for periods of high demand – the Summer months, Half Term holidays and public holidays.

Charwelton
SP5356

▲ **Foxhall Farmhouse,** Charwelton, Daventry, Northants, NN11 6YY
Tel: 01327 261817
Fax: 01327 264445
Open: May to Sep

Kettering
SP8778

▲ **Kestrel Caravan Park,** Windy Ridge, Warkton Lane, Kettering, Northamptonshire, NN16 9XG
Actual Grid Ref: SP898791
Tel: 01536 514301
Open: All year

Little Billing
SP8161

▲ **Billing Aquadrome,** Little Billing, Northampton, NN3 4DA
Actual Grid Ref: SP807616
Tel: 01604 408181
Fax: 01604 784412
Open: Mar to Nov

Sibbertoft
SP6882

▲ **Brook Meadow Campsite,** Welford Road, Sibbertoft, Market Harborough, Leics, LE16 9UJ
Actual Grid Ref: SP666830
Tel: 01858 880886
Fax: 01858 880485
Email: brookmeadow@farmline.com
Tent pitches: 12
Tent rate: £5.00
Open: All year
Last arr: 10pm
Facilities for disabled people • Dogs allowed • Electric hook-up • Laundrette on site • Picnic/barbecue area on site
Gently sloping grass site beside Carp fishing lake.

Sywell
SP8266

▲ **Overstone Lakes Caravan Park,** Ecton Lane, Sywell, Northampton, NN6 0BD
Tel: 01604 645255
Open: Mar to Oct

Thrapston
TL0078

▲ **Mill Marina,** Midland Road, Thrapston, Kettering, Northants, NN14 4JR
Actual Grid Ref: SP994781
Tel: 01832 732850
Open: Apr to Nov

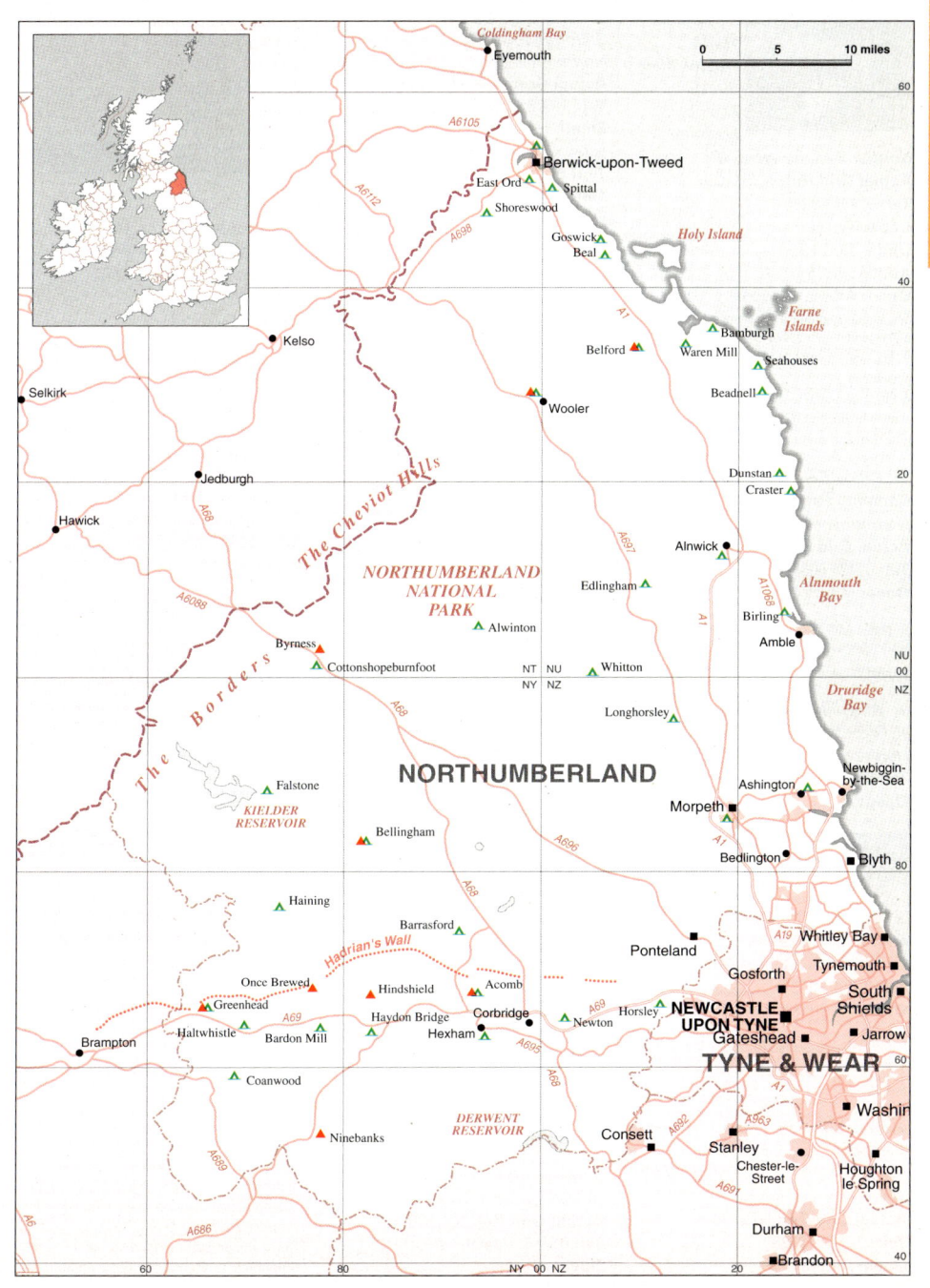

Northumberland

Northumberland • MAP PAGE 131

ENGLAND

Acomb
NY9366

▲ **Acomb Youth Hostel,** Main Street, Acomb, Hexham, Northumberland, NE46 4PL
Actual Grid Ref: NY934666
Tel: 01434 602864
Capacity: 36
Under 18: £4.75
Adults: £6.75
Open: All year, 5oopm
Self-catering facilities • Showers • Lounge • Drying room • Cycle store • No smoking • WC • Kitchen facilities • Credit cards accepted
A simple youth hostel, converted from stable buildings in a small village in the valley of the River Tyne.

▲ **Fallowfield Dene Caravan & Camping Park,** Acomb, Hexham, Northumberland, NE46 4RP
Actual Grid Ref: NY938678
Tel: 01434 603553
Open: Mar to Oct

Alnwick
NU1813

▲ **Alnwick Rugby Club Campsite,** 45 Greenfield Avenue, Alnwick, Northumberland, NE66 1BE
Tel: 01665 602987
Open: Apr to Sep

Alwinton
NT9105

▲ **Clennell Hall,** Clennell, Alwinton, Morpeth, NE65 7BG
Actual Grid Ref: NT928071
Tel: 01669 650341
Open: All year

Ashington
NZ2787

▲ **Wansbeck Riverside Caravan & Camping Park,** Green Lane, Ashington, Northumberland, NE63 8TX
Actual Grid Ref: NZ258864
Tel: 01670 812323
Open: All year

Bamburgh
NU1734

▲ **Glororum Caravan Park,** Glororum Farm, Bamburgh, Northumberland, NE69 7AW
Actual Grid Ref: NU167334
Tel: 01668 214457
Email: info@glororum-caravanpark.co.uk
Tent pitches: 50
Tent rate: £8.00-£12.00
Open: Apr to Oct
Last arr: 10pm
Dogs allowed • Electric hook-up • Calor Gas/Camping Gaz • Children's play area • Showers • Laundrette on site • Public phone on site • Shop on site • Boating/sailing/watersports nearby • Tennis courts nearby • Golf nearby • Riding nearby • Fishing nearby
Beautifully situated 1 mile from Bamburgh on the glorious Northumberland coast. Set in peaceful surroundings within easy reach of Holy Island, Farne Islands, the Cheviots and many historic castles. Please send for our colour brochure and tariff leaflet.

▲ **Waren Caravan Park,** Waren Mill, Bamburgh, Northumberland, NE70 7EE
Actual Grid Ref: NU155342
Tel: 01668 214366
Email: warencp@aol.com
Open: Apr to Oct

▲ **Bradford Kaims Caravan Park,** Bamburgh, Northumberland, NE70 7JT
Tel: 01668 213432
Fax: 01668 213891
Open: Apr to Oct

Bardon Mill
NY7865

▲ **Winshields Campsite,** Once Brewed, Bardon Mill, Hexham, Northd, NE47 7AN
Tel: 01434 344243
Tent pitches: 30
Tent rate: £6.00-£7.00
Open: Apr to Oct
Dogs allowed • Showers • Shop on site
Situated on Hadrian's Wall within walking distance of Roman Forts.

▲ **Ashcroft Farm,** Bardon Mill, Hexham, Northd, NE47 7JA
Actual Grid Ref: NY782645
Tel: 01434 344409
Open: All year

Barrasford
NY9173

▲ **Elwood,** Barrasford, Hexham, Northd, NE48 4AN
Tel: 01434 681421
Fax: 01434 681026
Open: All year

Beadnell
NU2329

▲ **Camping & Caravanning Club Site,** Anstead, Beadnell, Chathill, Northumberland, NE67 5BX
Tel: 01665 720586
Open: Mar to Sep

▲ **Beadnell Links Caravanning,** Beadnell Harbour, Chathill, Northumberland, NE67 5BN
Tel: 01665 720993
Open: Apr to Oct

▲ **The Bunkhouse,** Beadnell, Chathill, Northumberland, NE67 5BT
Tel: 01665 720387
Open: Easter to Oct

Beal
NU0643

▲ **Haggerston Castle Holiday Park,** Beal, Berwick-upon-Tweed, Northumberland, TD15 2PA
Actual Grid Ref: NU041435
Tel: 01289 381333
Open: Mar to Oct

Belford
NU1033

▲ **The Outdoor Trust,** Windy Gyle, Belford, Northumberland, NE70 7QE
Tel: 01668 213289
Fax: 01668 213289
Email: trust@outdoor.demon.co.uk
Capacity: 50
Under 18: £7.50
Adults: £7.50
Open: All year, 9am
Family bunk rooms
Self-catering facilities • Television • Showers • Central heating • Laundry facilities • Wet weather shelter • Lounge • Dining room • Drying room • Facilities for disabled people
Rural village setting, close to all amenities, outdoor activities available.

132 Stilwell's Hostels & Camping 2002

MAP PAGE 131 • **Northumberland**

▲ **Bluebell Farm Caravan Site,**
West Street, Belford,
Northumberland, NE70 7QE
Actual Grid Ref: NU107339
Tel: 01668 213362
Open: Mar to Oct

Bellingham

NY8383

▲ **Bellingham Youth Hostel,**
Woodburn Road, Bellingham,
Hexham, Northumberland, NE48 2ED
Actual Grid Ref: NY843834
Tel: 01434 220313
Fax: 01434 220313
Capacity: 28
Under 18: £5.15
Adults: £8.50
Open: All year, 5.00pm
Self-catering facilities • Showers • Lounge • Cycle store • No smoking • WC • Kitchen facilities
Hostel built of red cedarwood on the Pennine Way, high above the small Borders town of Bellingham. Near Kielder Water (with forest trails and watersports) and Hadrian's Wall.

▲ **Brown Rigg Caravan & Camping Park,** Bellingham,
Hexham, Northumberland, NE48 2JY
Actual Grid Ref: NY834827
AA grade: 4 Pennants
Tel: 01434 220175
Fax: 01434 220175
Email: info@northumberlandcaravanparks.com
Tent pitches: 30
Tent rate: £3.50-£8.50
Open: Apr to Oct
Last arr: 8.30pm
Facilities for disabled people • Dogs allowed • Electric hook-up • Calor Gas/Camping Gaz • Picnic/barbecue area on site • Children's play area • Showers • Laundrette on site • Public phone on site • Shop on site • Games room • Indoor swimming pool nearby • Boating/sailing/watersports nearby • Tennis courts nearby • Golf nearby • Riding nearby • Fishing nearby
A 5 acre level site situated in the beautiful Northumberland National Park half mile south of Bellingham on B6320. The Pennine Way borders the site with the Reivers Cycle Route nearby. Hadrian's Wall and Kielder Water 9 miles.

▲ **Demesne Farm,** Bellingham,
Hexham, Northumberland, NE48 2BS
Actual Grid Ref: NY841833
Tel: 01434 220107
Open: Mar to Oct

Berwick-upon-Tweed

NT9953

▲ **Berwick Holiday Centre,**
Magdalene Fields, Berwick-upon-Tweed, Northumberland, TD15 1NE
Actual Grid Ref: NU000540
Tel: 01289 307113
Open: Mar to Oct

▲ **Marshall Meadows Caravan Site,** Marshall Meadows Farm,
Berwick-upon-Tweed, Northd, TD15 1UT
Actual Grid Ref: NT982567
Tel: 01289 307375
Open: Apr to Oct

▲ **The Friendly Hound,** Ford Common, Berwick-upon-Tweed, Northumberland, TD15 2QD
Actual Grid Ref: NT965389
Tel: 01289 388554
Open: Mar to Jan

Birling

NU2406

▲ **Rose Cottage Campsite,**
Birling, Morpeth, Northumberland, NE65 0XS
Tel: 01665 711459
Open: Apr to Sep

Byrness

NT7602

▲ **Byrness Youth Hostel,** 7 Otterburn Green, Byrness,
Newcastle upon Tyne, NE19 1TS
Actual Grid Ref: NT764027
Tel: 01830 520425
Email: reservations@yha.org.uk
Capacity: 22
Under 18: £4.75
Adults: £6.75
Open: All year, 5.00pm
Self-catering facilities • Showers • Shop • Lounge • Dining room • Games room • Drying room • Cycle store • Parking • No smoking • WC • Kitchen facilities • Credit cards accepted
Formerly two adjoining Forestry Commission houses in peaceful village, in foothills of Cheviot Hills, close to the Scottish border.

You are advised to book in advance for periods of high demand – the Summer months, Half Term holidays and public holidays.

Coanwood

NY6859

▲ **Yont the Cleugh,** Coanwood, Haltwhistle, Northumberland, NE49 0QN
Actual Grid Ref: NY698587
Tourist Board grade: 4 Ticks
Tel: 01434 320274
Tent pitches: 20
Tent rate: £5.00
Open: Mar to Jan
Dogs allowed • Electric hook-up • Calor Gas/Camping Gaz • Children's play area • Showers • Laundrette on site • Public phone on site • Licensed bar on site
A quiet and peaceful spacious park with superb views.

Cottonshopeburnfoot

NT7801

▲ **Border Forest Caravan Park,**
Cottonshopeburnfoot, Otterburn, Newcastle-upon-Tyne, NE19 1TF
Actual Grid Ref: NT779014
Tel: 01830 520259
Open: Mar to Oct

Craster

NU2519

▲ **Proctor's Stead Campsite,**
Craster, Alnwick, Northd, NE66 3TF
Actual Grid Ref: NU248202
Tel: 01665 576613
Open: Mar to Oct

Dunstan

NU2420

▲ **Camping & Caravanning Club Site,** Dunstan Hill, Dunstan,
Alnwick, Northumberland, NE66 3TQ
Tel: 01665 576310
Open: Mar to Nov

East Ord

NT9751

▲ **Ord House Caravan Park,** East Ord, Berwick-upon-Tweed,
Northumberland, TD15 2NS
Actual Grid Ref: NT982515
Tel: 01289 305288
Fax: 01289 330832
Email: enquiries@ordhouse.co.uk
Open: Mar to Jan

ENGLAND

Stilwell's Hostels & Camping 2002

Northumberland • MAP PAGE 131

Edlingham
NU1108

▲ **Cherry Tree Farm,** Edlingham, Alnwick, Northumberland, NE66 2BL
Tel: 01665 574635
Open: Easter to Oct

Falstone
NY7387

▲ **Kielder Water Caravan Club Site,** Leaplish Waterside Park, Falstone, Hexham, Northumberland, NE48 1AX
Tel: 01434 250278
Open: Easter to Sep

Goswick
NU0545

▲ **Beachcomber House Camping Site,** Goswick, Berwick-upon-Tweed, Northd, TD15 2RW
Tel: 01289 381217
Open: Easter to Sep

Greenhead
NY6665

▲ **Greenhead Youth Hostel,** Greenhead, Carlisle, Cumbria, CA6 7HG
Actual Grid Ref: NY659655
Tel: 016977 47401
Fax: 016977 47884
Email: reservations@yha.org.uk
Capacity: 40
Under 18: £6.50
Adults: £9.25
Open: All year, 5.00pm
Self-catering facilities • Showers • Shop • Lounge • Drying room • Cycle store • Evening meal available 7.00pm • No smoking • WC • Kitchen facilities • Breakfast available • Credit cards accepted
This traditional Methodist chapel with its thick stone walls is curiously cosy. Useful for a rest for walkers of the Pennine Way, this is also a popular haunt for cyclists.

▲ **Holmhead Stone Tent,** Holmhead Licensed Guest House, Thirlwall Castle Farm, Hadrian's Wall, Greenhead, Brampton, Cumbria, CA8 7HY
Tel: 016977 47402
Fax: 016977 47402
Email: holmhead@hadrianswall.freeserve.co.uk
Capacity: 4
Under 18: £3.50

Adults: £3.50
Open: Apr to Oct, 4pm
Family bunk rooms: £3.50
Camping for 4 tents: £4.00
Wet weather shelter • Cycle store • No smoking
Stone building. Outside toilet, gas lamp, camping gas, cold water tap. Hadrian's Wall path.

▲ **Roam-n-Rest Caravan Park,** Rayton House, Greenhead, Carlisle, Cumbria, CA6 7HA
Actual Grid Ref: NY656654
Tel: 016977 47213
Open: Mar to Oct

▲ **Holmhead Licensed Guest House,** Thirlwall Castle Farm, Hadrian's Wall, Greenhead, Brampton, Cumbria, CA8 7HY
Tel: 016977 47402
Fax: 016977 47402
Open: All year

Haining
NY7375

▲ **The Haining Farm,** Haining, Wark, Hexham, Northd, NE48 3ED
Tel: 01434 230680
Open: All year

Haltwhistle
NY7064

▲ **Camping & Caravanning Club Site,** Burnfoot, Park Village, Haltwhistle, Northumberland, NE49 0JP
Actual Grid Ref: NY685621
Tel: 01434 320106
Open: Mar to Oct

▲ **Seldom Seen Caravan Park,** Haltwhistle, Northumberland, NE49 0NE
Actual Grid Ref: NY718638
Tel: 01434 320571
Open: Jan to Oct

Haydon Bridge
NY8464

▲ **Poplars Riverside Caravan Park,** Eastlands Ends, Haydon Bridge, Hexham, Northumberland, NE47 6BY
Tel: 01434 684427
Open: Mar to Oct

Hexham
NY9364

▲ **Springhouse Caravan Park,** Staley, Hexham, Northumberland, NE47 0AW
Actual Grid Ref: NY960560
Tel: 01434 673241
Fax: 01434 673034
Email: springhouse.cp@btinternet.com
Tent pitches: 20
Tent rate: £5.00-£8.50
Open: Mar to Oct
Last arr: 9pm
Dogs allowed • Electric hook-up • Calor Gas/Camping Gaz • Picnic/barbecue area on site • Children's play area • Showers • Laundrette on site • Public phone on site
Quiet. Surrounded by forest, with beautiful walks and views. Extensive wildlife.

▲ **Hexham Racecourse Caravan Site,** Hexham Racecourse, Hexham, Northumberland, NE46 3NN
Actual Grid Ref: NY918623
Tel: 01434 606847
Open: May to Sep

▲ **Riverside Leisure,** Tyne Green, Hexham, Northumberland, NE46 3RY
Actual Grid Ref: NY927649
Tel: 01434 604705
Email: riverleis@aol.com
Open: Mar to Jan

▲ **Barrasford Park Caravan Site,** 1 Front Drive, Hexham, Northumberland, NE48 4BE
Actual Grid Ref: NY922769
Tel: 01434 681210
Open: Apr to Oct

▲ **Causey Hill Caravan Park,** Bensonsfell Farm, Causey Hill, Hexham, Northumberland, NE46 2JN
Actual Grid Ref: NY925625
Tel: 01434 602834
Open: Apr to Oct

Some hostels and campsites impose restrictions on size and type of groups they accept (e.g. not permitting single-sex groups). Always phone to enquire before booking.

MAP PAGE 131 • **Northumberland**

Hindshield

NY8367

▲ **Hadrian's Wall Backpackers' Hostel,** Hadrian Lodge Country Hotel, Hindshield Moss, North Road, Haydon Bridge, Hexham, Northumberland, NE47 6NF
Tel: 01434 688688
Fax: 01434 684867
Email: hadrianlodge@hadrianswall.co.uk
Capacity: 50
Under 18: £10.00
Adults: £10.00
Open: Apr to Sep, all day
Family bunk rooms: £10.00
Self-catering facilities • Television • Showers • Licensed bar • Central heating • Laundry facilities • Dining room • Games room • Grounds available for games • Drying room • Parking • Evening meal available • Facilities for disabled people
Near Hadrian's Wall. Beautiful location. Licensed bar/bar meals. Self catering.

Horsley (Newcastle-upon-Tyne)

NZ0965

▲ **Belvedere,** Harlow Hill, Horsley, Newcastle-upon-Tyne, NE15 0QD
Tel: 01661 853689
Open: All year

Kielder

NY6293

▲ **Kielder Campsite,** Kielder, Hexham, Northumberland, NE48 1EJ
Actual Grid Ref: NY626938
Tel: 01434 250291
Open: Apr to Sep

▲ **Leaplish Waterside Park Campsite,** Kielder Water, Hexham, Northumberland, NE48 1BT
Tel: 01434 250312
Open: Easter to Sep

Longhorsley

NZ1494

▲ **Forget-me-Not Caravan Park,** Longhorsley, Morpeth, Northumberland, NE65 8QY
Actual Grid Ref: NZ126946
Tel: 01670 788364
Email: info@forget-me-notcaravanpark.co.uk
Tent pitches: 40
Tent rate: £7.00

All details shown are as supplied by hostels and campsites in Autumn 2000.

Open: Mar to Oct
Last arr: 9pm
Facilities for disabled people • Dogs allowed • Electric hook-up • Calor Gas/Camping Gaz • Cafe or Takeaway on site • Picnic/barbecue area on site • Children's play area • Showers • Laundrette on site • Public phone on site • Licensed bar on site • Shop on site
Picturesque rural location convenient for country and coastal attractions.

Morpeth

NZ2085

▲ **Percy Wood Caravan Park,** Swanlan, Morpeth, Northumberland, NE65 9JW
Actual Grid Ref: NU160042
Tel: 01670 787649
Fax: 01670 787034
Open: Mar to Jan

Newton

NZ0364

▲ **Well House Farm Camping and Caravanning,** Newton, Stocksfield, Northumberland, NE43 7UY
Actual Grid Ref: NZ043666
Tel: 01661 842193
Open: Mar to Jan

Ninebanks

NY7853

▲ **Ninebanks Youth Hostel,** Orchard House, Mohope, Ninebanks, Hexham, Northumberland, NE47 8DQ
Actual Grid Ref: NY771514
Tel: 01434 345288
Fax: 01434 345288
Email: ninebanks@yha.org.uk
Capacity: 26
Under 18: £4.75
Adults: £6.75
Open: All year, 5.00pm
Self-catering facilities • Showers • Shop • Laundry facilities • Lounge • Drying room • Parking • No smoking • WC • Kitchen facilities • Credit cards accepted
Simple accommodation in a 300-year-old lead miner's cottage with a welcoming fire in the peaceful valley of Mohope Burn in North Pennines Area of Outstanding Natural Beauty.

Once Brewed

NY7566

▲ **Once Brewed Youth Hostel,** Military Road, Once Brewed, Bardon Mill, Hexham, Northumberland, NE47 7AN
Actual Grid Ref: NY752668
Tel: 01434 344360
Fax: 01434 344045
Email: oncebrewed@yha.org.uk
Capacity: 90
Under 18: £7.75
Adults: £11.00
Open: Feb to Nov, 1.00pm
Family bunk rooms
Self-catering facilities • Showers • Laundry facilities • Lounge • Dining room • Games room • Drying room • Cycle store • Parking • Evening meal available 6.00-7.00pm • No smoking • WC • Kitchen facilities • Breakfast available
Excellent residential accommodation with small bedrooms and superb range of facilities. Close to Hadrian's Wall and the Roman Forts.

Seahouses

NU2032

▲ **Seafield Caravan Park,** Seahouses, Northumberland, NE68 7SP
Tel: 01665 720088
Email: carolyn@seafieldpark.co.uk
Open: Mar to Dec

Shoreswood

NT9346

▲ **The Salutation,** Shoreswood, Berwick-on-Tweed, Northumberland, TD15 2NL
Actual Grid Ref: NT925467
Tel: 01289 382291
Open: Mar to Nov

Spittal

NU0051

▲ **Seaview Caravan Club Site,** Billendean Road, Spittal, Berwick-upon-Tweed, Northumberland, TD15 1QU
Tel: 01289 305198
Open: Apr to Oct

Hostels and campsites may vary rates – be sure to check when booking.

Northumberland • MAP PAGE 131

Waren Mill

NU1434

▲ **Budle Bay Campsite,** West Street, Belford, Northumberland, NE70 7QE
Actual Grid Ref: NU146341
Tel: 01668 213362
Fax: 01668 213362
Open: Apr to Oct

Whitton

NU0500

▲ **Coquetdale Caravan Park,** Whitton, Morpeth, Northumberland, NE65 7RU
Actual Grid Ref: NU056009
Tel: 01669 620549
Open: Apr to Oct

Wooler

NT9928

▲ **Wooler (Cheviot) Youth Hostel,** 30 Cheviot Street, Wooler, Northumberland, NE71 6LW
Actual Grid Ref: NT991278
Tel: 01668 281365 **Fax:** 01668 282368
Capacity: 52
Under 18: £6.50 **Adults:** £9.25
Open: All year, 5.00pm
Self-catering facilities • Showers • Laundry facilities • Wet weather shelter • Lounge • Drying room • Cycle store • Parking • Evening meal available 7.00pm • Facilities for disabled people Category 2 • No smoking • WC • Kitchen facilities • Breakfast available • Credit cards accepted
On outskirts of the market town of Wooler in the foothills of the Cheviots, close to the Scottish border, the most northerly of the English Youth Hostels is convenient for Holy Island, Lindisfarne and the Farne Islands.

▲ **Highburn House Caravan & Camping Site,** Wooler, Northumberland, NE71 6EE
Actual Grid Ref: NT984282
Tel: 01668 281839
Open: Apr to Oct

▲ **Riverside Holiday Park,** Wooler, Northumberland, NE71 6EE
Actual Grid Ref: NT995279
Tel: 01668 281447
Open: Mar to Nov

If you have to cancel your visit to any hostel or campsite, please let them know – it is always possible to make a bed or a pitch available to someone else.

Nottinghamshire

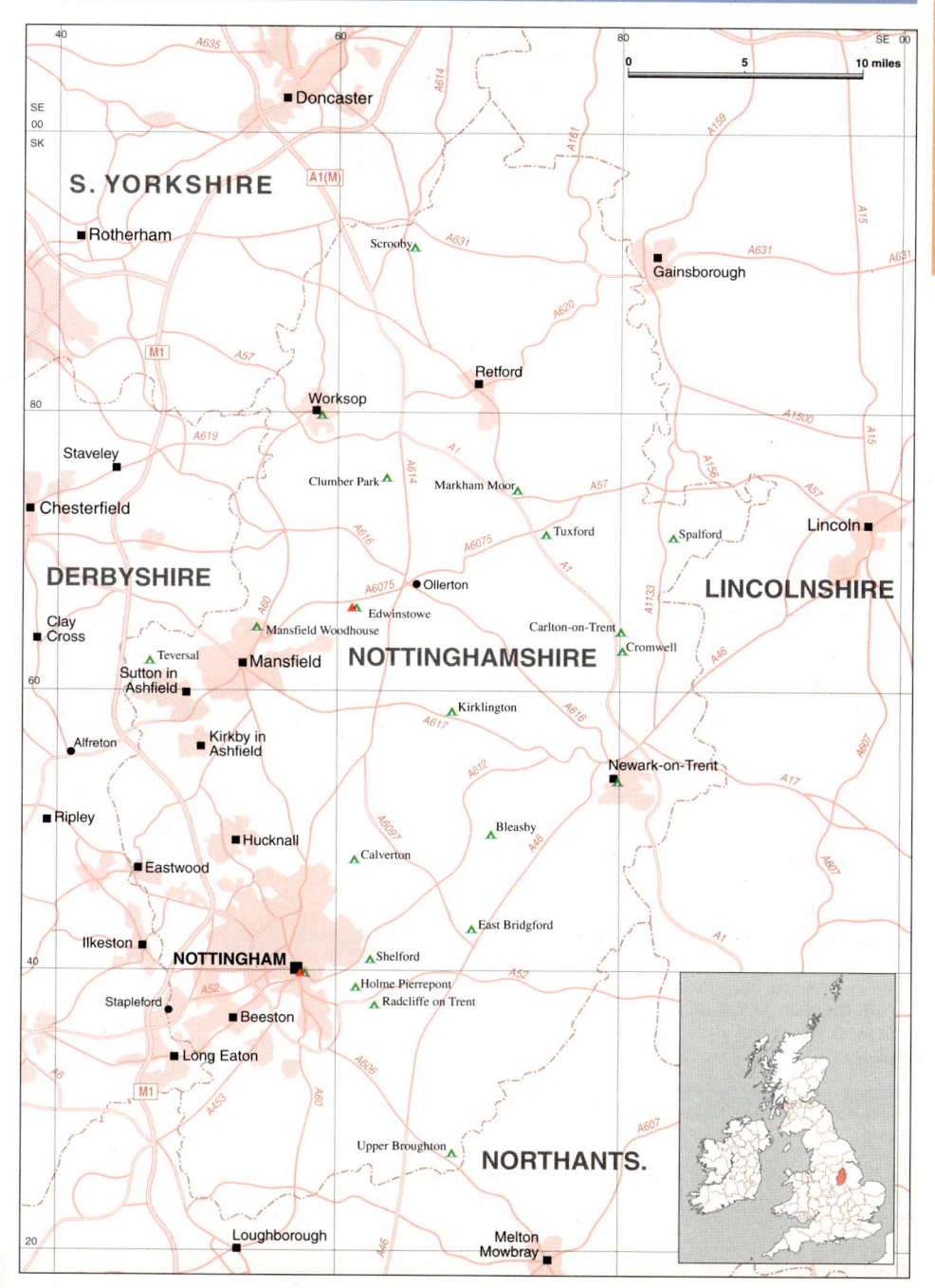

Nottinghamshire • MAP PAGE 137

Bleasby
SK7149

▲ **Boat Lane (Mr Toplis),** Bleasby, Nottingham, NG14 7FT
Actual Grid Ref: SK723492
Tel: 01636 830676
Open: All year

Calverton
SK6149

▲ **Moor Farm Camping,** Calverton, Nottingham, NG14 6ZF
Actual Grid Ref: SK630488
Tel: 0115 965 2426
Open: All year

Carlton-on-Trent
SK8064

▲ **Carlton Manor Caravan Park,** Ossington Road, Carlton-on-Trent, Newark, Notts, NG23 6NU
Actual Grid Ref: SK794640
Tel: 01530 835662
Open: Apr to Oct

Clumber Park
SK6275

▲ **Camping & Caravanning Club Site,** The Walled Garden, Clumber Park, Worksop, Nottinghamshire, S80 3BD
Actual Grid Ref: SK626748
Tel: 01909 482303
Open: Mar to Oct

Cromwell
SK8062

▲ **Milestone Caravan Park,** Milestone House, North Road, Cromwell, Newark, Notts, NG23 6JE
Actual Grid Ref: SK798622
Tel: 01636 821244
Open: All year

East Bridgford
SK6943

▲ **Barn Farm Cottage,** Kneeton Road, East Bridgford, Nottingham, NG13 8PH
Tel: 01949 20196
Open: All year

Edwinstowe
SK6266

▲ **Sherwood Forest (Edwinstowe) Youth Hostel,** Forest Corner, Edwinstowe, Mansfield, Notts, NG21 9RN
Actual Grid Ref: SK625673
Tel: 01623 825794
Fax: 01623 825796
Email: sherwood@yha.org.uk
Capacity: 39
Under 18: £8.50
Adults: £12.50
Open: Feb to Dec (not Xmas) + New Year, 1.00pm
Family bunk rooms
Self-catering facilities • Television • Lounge • Dining room • Drying room • Cycle store • Parking • Evening meal available 7.00pm • Facilities for disabled people • Facilities for disabled people • No smoking • WC • Kitchen facilities • Breakfast available
Purpose-built youth hostel, ideal base for exploring Robin Hood country. Just a short walk to Major Oak and Sherwood Forest Visitor Centre.

▲ **Sherwood Forest Caravan Park,** Cavendish Lodge, Edwinstowe, Mansfield, Notts, NG21 9HW
Actual Grid Ref: SK594650
Tel: 0800 146505
Fax: 01623 823132
Open: Mar to Oct

Holme Pierrepont
SK6339

▲ **National Water Sports Centre & Country Park,** Adbolton Lane, Holme Pierrepont, Nottinghamshire, NG12 2LU
Actual Grid Ref: SK602382
Tel: 0115 982 4721
Open: Apr to Oct

All details shown are as supplied by hostels and campsites in Autumn 2000.

Kirklington
SK6757

▲ **Robin Hood View Caravan Park,** Middle Plantation Farm, Belle Eau Park, Kirklington, Newark, Notts, NG22 8TY
Actual Grid Ref: SK669594
Tel: 01623 870361
Open: All year

Mansfield Woodhouse
SK5463

▲ **Redbrick House Hotel,** Peafield Lane, Mansfield Woodhouse, NG20 0EW
Actual Grid Ref: SK568654
Tel: 01623 846499
Open: All year

Markham Moor
SK7173

▲ **Longbow Caravan Park,** Milton Road, Markham Moor, Retford, Nottinghamshire, NG22 0PP
Actual Grid Ref: SK716736
Tel: 01777 838067
Open: All year

Newark
SK7953

▲ **Smeatons Lakes and Fishing Touring Caravan Park,** Great North Road, Newark, Notts, NG23 6ED
Actual Grid Ref: SK792558
Tel: 01636 605088
Open: Mar to Nov

Nottingham
SK5641

▲ **The Igloo Backpackers Hostel,** 110 Mansfield Road, Nottingham, NG1 3HL
Tel: 0115 947 5250
Email: reception@igloohostel.co.uk
Capacity: 36
Under 18: £10.50
Adults: £10.50
Open: All year (not Xmas/New Year), 9am-3am
Self-catering facilities • Television • Showers • Central heating • Lounge • Dining room • Drying room • Security lockers • Cycle store • Parking • Facilities for disabled people
Award winning hostel in lively city in Robin Hood's world.

MAP PAGE 137 • **Nottinghamshire**

▲ **Holme Pierrepont Caravan & Camping Park,** Nottingham, NG12 2LU
Tel: 0115 982 1212
Open: Apr to Oct

Radcliffe on Trent

SK6538

▲ **Thornton's Holt Camping Park,** Stragglethorpe Road, Radcliffe on Trent, Nottingham, NG12 2JZ
Actual Grid Ref: SK637377
AA grade: 3 Pennants
Tel: 0115 933 2125 / 933 4204
Fax: 0115 933 3318
Tent pitches: 90
Tent rate: £7.50-£8.50
Open: All year
Last arr: 9.30pm
Facilities for disabled people • Dogs allowed • Electric hook-up • Calor Gas/Camping Gaz • Picnic/barbecue area on site • Children's play area • Showers • Laundrette on site • Public phone on site • Shop on site
Comprehensive facilities including an indoor swimming pool and a pub and restaurants within 150m.

Scrooby

SK6590

▲ **Scrooby Caravan Site,** Scrooby, Bawtry, Doncaster, South Yorkshire, DN10 6AS
Actual Grid Ref: SK647910
Tel: 01302 711031
Open: All year

Shelford

SK6642

▲ **Shelford Nurseries Caravan Park,** The Hill, Shelford, Radcliffe-on-Trent, Nottinghamshire, NG12 1ED
Actual Grid Ref: SK663417
Tel: 0115 933 3433
Open: All year

Spalford

SK8369

▲ **Windmill Farm Fisheries,** Spalford, Newark, Nottinghamshire, NG23 7HA
Actual Grid Ref: SK843691
Tel: 01522 778305
Open: Apr to Nov

Teversal

SK4861

▲ **Shardaroba Touring Caravan Park,** Silverhill Lane, Teversal, Sutton in Ashfield, Nottinghamshire, NG17 3JJ
Tel: 01623 551838
Open: All year

You are advised to book in advance for periods of high demand – the Summer months, Half Term holidays and public holidays.

Tuxford

SK7370

▲ **Greenacres Touring Park,** Lincoln Road, Tuxford, Newark, Notts, NG22 0JW
Actual Grid Ref: SK748716
Tel: 01777 870264
Open: Mar to Oct

▲ **Orchard Park Touring Caravan & Camping Park,** Marnham Road, Tuxford, Newark, Notts, NG22 0PY
Actual Grid Ref: SK753708
Tel: 01777 870228 / 0402 433346
Open: Mar to Oct

Upper Broughton

SK6826

▲ **Swan Lodge,** Upper Broughton, Melton Mowbray, Leics, LE14 3BH
Tel: 01664 823686
Open: All year

Worksop

SK5879

▲ **Riverside Caravan Park,** Worksop Cricket Club, Central Avenue, Worksop, Nottinghamshire, S80 1ER
Actual Grid Ref: SK583791
Tel: 01909 474118
Open: All year

Oxfordshire

Oxfordshire

Adderbury
SP4735

▲ **Bo Peep Caravan Park,** Aynho Road, Adderbury, Banbury, Oxfordshire, OX17 3NP
Tel: 01295 810605
Fax: 01295 810605
Open: Apr to Oct

Appleton
SP4401

▲ **West Farm,** Eaton, Appleton, Abingdon, Oxon, OX13 5PR
Tel: 01865 862908
Open: All year

Barford St Michael
SP4332

▲ **The Manor House,** Barford St Michael, Oxford, OX15 0RJ
Actual Grid Ref: SP432326
Tel: 01869 338207
Open: All year

Benson
SU6191

▲ **Benson Cruisers,** Benson, Oxford, OX10 8SJ
Actual Grid Ref: SU613916
Tel: 01491 838304
Open: Mar to Oct

Bicester
SP5822

▲ **Glebe Lakes Caravan Park,** Glebe Farm, Stoke Lyn Road, Fringford, Bicester, Oxon, OX6 9RJ
Tel: 01869 277410
Open: All year

Bletchingdon
SP5018

▲ **Diamond Farm Caravan & Camping Park,** Islip Road, Bletchingdon, Kidlington, Oxfordshire, OX5 3DR
Actual Grid Ref: SP513169
Tourist Board grade: 3 Ticks
AA grade: 3 Pennants
Tel: 01869 350909
Fax: 01869 350909
Email: diamondfarm@supanet.com
Tent pitches: 37
Tent rate: £7.00-£10.00
Open: All year

Last arr: 10pm
Facilities for disabled people • Dogs allowed • Electric hook-up • Baths • Calor Gas/Camping Gaz • Children's play area • Showers • Laundrette on site • Public phone on site • Licensed bar on site • Shop on site
Small family-run site offering excellent facilities.

Cassington
SP4510

▲ **Cassington Mill Caravan Park,** Eynsham Road, Cassington, Witney, Oxfordshire, OX8 1DB
Actual Grid Ref: SP445100
Tel: 01865 881081
Open: Apr to Oct

Chadlington
SP3222

▲ **Camping & Caravanning Club Site,** Chipping Norton Road, Chadlington, Chipping Norton, Oxfordshire, OX7 3PE
Tel: 01608 641993
Open: Mar to Nov

Charlbury
SP3619

▲ **Charlbury Youth Hostel,** The Laurels, The Slade, Charlbury, Chipping Norton, Oxfordshire, OX7 3SJ
Actual Grid Ref: SP361198
Tel: 01608 810202
Fax: 01608 810202
Email: charlbury@yha.org.uk
Capacity: 51
Under 18: £6.90
Adults: £10.00
Open: All year, 5.00pm
Family bunk rooms
Cycle store • Facilities for disabled people • No smoking • WC • Breakfast available
Old glove factory, recently refurbished. 2 bedrooms sleep up to 8.

▲ **Cotswold View Caravan & Camping Site,** Banbury Hill Farm, Enstone Road, Charlbury, Chipping Norton, Oxon, OX7 3JH
Actual Grid Ref: SP363209
Tourist Board grade: 4 Star
AA grade: 4 Pennants
Tel: 01608 810314
Fax: 01608 811891
Email: cotwoldview@cotswoldview.f9.co.uk
Tent pitches: 125
Tent rate: £8.00-£11.00

Open: Mar to Oct
Last arr: 9pm
Dogs allowed • Electric hook-up • Baths • Calor Gas/Camping Gaz • Picnic/barbecue area on site • Children's play area • Showers • Laundrette on site • Public phone on site • Shop on site • Baby care facilities
Beautiful quiet friendly family site, near Blenheim, Burford, Oxford, Stratford.

Clifton
SP4931

▲ **Thames Bridge House Caravan Site,** Clifton, Abingdon, Oxfordshire, OX14 3EH
Tel: 01865 407725
Open: Apr to Oct

Court Hill
SU3885

▲ **Ridgeway Youth Hostel,** Courth Hill Ridgeway Centre, Court Hill, Wantage, Oxfordshire, OX12 9NE
Actual Grid Ref: SU393851
Tel: 01235 760253
Fax: 01235 768865
Capacity: 59
Under 18: £6.90
Adults: £10.00
Open: All year (not Xmas)
Family bunk rooms
Camping
Self-catering facilities • Television • Showers • Showers • Laundry facilities • Lounge • Dining room • Drying room • Cycle store • Parking • Evening meal available 7.00pm • No smoking • WC • Kitchen facilities • Breakfast available • Luggage store • Credit cards accepted
Modern hostel, beautifully reconstructed from five barns, with beechwood grounds, panoramic views and stabling for four horses.

Crowmarsh Gifford
SU6188

▲ **Bridge Villa C & C Site,** Crowmarsh Gifford, Wallingford, Oxfordshire, OX10 8HB
Actual Grid Ref: SU612893
Tel: 01491 836860
Fax: 01491 839103
Tent pitches: 111
Tent rate: £4.00-£8.00
Open: Feb to Dec
Last arr: 8pm
Dogs allowed • Electric hook-up • Calor Gas/Camping Gaz • Showers • Public phone on site • Shop on site
Five minutes' walk from centre of historic market town of Wallingford-on-Thames.

Oxfordshire • MAP PAGE 140

ENGLAND

▲ **Riverside Park,** Crowmarsh Gifford, Wallingford, Oxfordshire, OX10 8EB
Actual Grid Ref: SU612897
Tel: 01491 835232
Fax: 01491 835232
Tent pitches: 28
Tent rate: £5.90-£8.00
Open: May to Sep
Last arr: 7pm
Facilities for disabled people • Picnic/barbecue area on site • Showers • Public phone on site • Shop on site
River Thames location. Picturesque location and very friendly campsite.

▲ **Newnham Manor Touring Caravan Park,** The Street, Crowmarsh Gifford, Wallingford, Oxon, OX10 8EH
Tel: 0118 9412445
Open: Jan to Nov

Cumnor
SP4604

▲ **Spring Farm,** Faringdon Road, Cumnor, Oxford, OX2 9QY
Actual Grid Ref: SP462032
Tel: 01865 863028
Open: Apr to Oct

Deddington
SP4631

▲ **Hill Barn,** Milton Gated Road, Deddington, Banbury, Oxon, OX15 0TS
Tel: 01869 338631
Open: All year

Eynsham
SP4309

▲ **Swinford Farm Camping & Caravan Site,** Swinford, Witney, Oxfordshire, OX8 1BY
Tel: 01865 881368
Open: Apr to Oct

Great Bourton
SP4545

▲ **Barnstones Caravan & Camping Site,** Great Bourton, Banbury, Oxon, OX17 1QU
Actual Grid Ref: SP454454
Tel: 01295 750289
Open: All year

Henley-on-Thames
SU7682

▲ **Swiss Farm International Camping,** Marlow Road, Henley-on-Thames, Oxfordshire, RG9 2HY
Actual Grid Ref: SU761835
Tel: 01491 573419
Open: Mar to Oct

Kidlington
SP4913

▲ **Lince Copse Caravan & Camping Park,** Enslow Wharf, Kidlington, Oxfordshire, OX5 3AY
Actual Grid Ref: SP483182
Tel: 01869 331508
Open: Mar to Oct

Kingham
SP2524

▲ **Churchill Heath Caravan & Camping Site,** Kingham, Chipping Norton, Oxfordshire, OX7 6UJ
Actual Grid Ref: SP263226
Tel: 01608 658317
Open: All year

Mollington
SP4347

▲ **Mollington Touring Caravan Park,** The Yews, Mollington, Banbury, Oxfordshire, OX17 1AZ
Actual Grid Ref: SP443477
Tel: 01295 750731
Open: All year

Moreton
SP6904

▲ **The Dairy,** Moreton, Thame, Oxon, OX9 2HX
Tel: 01844 214075
Open: All year

Nether Westcote
SP2220

▲ **The New Inn,** Nether Westcote, Chipping Norton, Oxfordshire, OX7 6SD
Actual Grid Ref: SP227205
Tel: 01993 830827
Open: Apr to Oct

Oxford
SP5106

▲ **Oxford Backpackers Hostel,** 9a Hythe Bridge Street, Oxford, OX1 2EW
Tel: 01865 721761
Fax: 01865 203293
Email: oxford@hostels.demon.co.uk
Capacity: 92
Adults: £11.00
Open: All year, 8am
Family bunk rooms: £12.00
Self-catering facilities • Television • Showers • Licensed bar • Central heating • Laundry facilities • Wet weather shelter • Lounge • Security lockers • Cycle store
City centre location. Groups welcome. Bar, Internet, kitchen. Great atmosphere.

▲ **New Oxford Youth Hostel,** 2a Botley Road, Oxford, OX2 0AB
Tel: 01865 727275
Fax: 01865 769402
Email: oxford@yha.org.uk
Capacity: 184
Under 18: £13.50
Adults: £18.00
Open: All year, All day
Self-catering facilities • Evening meal available 7.00pm • Facilities for disabled people • Breakfast available
Brand new hostel, opening at Easter 2001, and replacing the former hostel in Jack Straw's Lane.

▲ **Camping & Caravanning Club Site,** 426 Abingdon Road, Oxford, OX1 4XN
Actual Grid Ref: SP518041
Tel: 01865 244088
Open: All year

▲ **Salter Bros Ltd,** Slipway, Meadow Lane, Donnington Bridge, Oxford, OX4 4BL
Actual Grid Ref: SP526044
Tel: 01865 243421
Open: Mar to Oct

Radcot
SU2899

▲ **The Swan Hotel,** Radcot, Bampton, Oxford, OX18 2SX
Actual Grid Ref: SU286995
Tel: 01367 810220
Open: All year

Standlake

SP3903

▲ **Lincoln Farm Park,** High Street, Standlake, Witney, Oxfordshire, OX8 7RH
Actual Grid Ref: SP395028
Tel: 01865 300239
Open: Feb to Nov

▲ **Hardwick Parks,** Downs Road, Standlake, Witney, Oxfordshire, OX8 7PZ
Actual Grid Ref: SP390045
Tel: 01865 300501
Open: Apr to Oct

Steventon

SU4691

▲ **Hill Farm,** Steventon, Abingdon, Oxon, OX13 6SW
Tel: 01235 831910
Open: All year

Upper Heyford

SP4925

▲ **Heyford Leys Farm,** Camp Road, Upper Heyford, Bicester, Oxfordshire, OX6 3LU
Tel: 01869 232048 **Fax:** 01869 232048
Open: Apr to Oct

Rutland

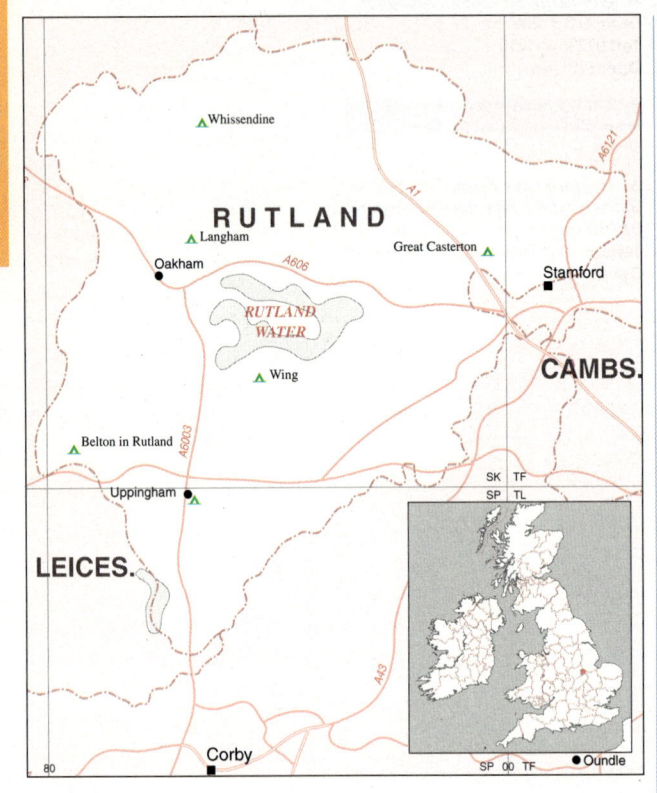

If you have to cancel your visit to any hostel or campsite, please let them know – it is always possible to make a bed or a pitch available to someone else.

Langham

SK8410

⚠ **Ranksborough Hall Camping & Caravan Park,** Langham, Oakham, Rutland, LE15 7EH
Actual Grid Ref: SK835110
Tel: 01572 722984
Open: All year

Uppingham

SP8699

⚠ **Folly Lane Farm,** 56 Newton Road, Uppingham, Oakham, Rutland, LE15 9TS
Tel: 01572 822386
Open: Apr to Oct

Whissendine

SK8214

⚠ **Greendale Farm,** Pickwell Lane, Whissendine, Oakham, Rutland, LE15 7LB
Actual Grid Ref: SK820134
Tel: 01664 474516
Open: All year

Wing

SK8903

⚠ **Wing Caravan & Camping Park,** Wing Hall, Wing, Oakham, Rutland, LE15 8RY
Tel: 01572 737283
Open: All year

Belton in Rutland

SK8101

⚠ **The Old Rectory,** 4 New Road, Belton in Rutland, Oakham, Rutland, LE15 9LE
Tel: 01572 717279 **Fax:** 01572 717343
Open: All year

All details shown are as supplied by hostels and campsites in Autumn 2000.

Great Casterton

TF0009

⚠ **Road End Farm Caravan Site,** Road End Farm, Tollbar, Great Casterton, Stamford, Lincs, PE9 4BB
Actual Grid Ref: TF004086
Tel: 01780 763417 **Fax:** 01780 489212
Tent pitches: 18
Tent rate: £4.00-£5.00
Open: All year **Last arr:** any time
Dogs allowed • Electric hook-up • Calor Gas/Camping Gaz
3 miles from Rutland Water, largest man-made lake in Europe.

Shropshire

Stilwell's Hostels & Camping 2002

Shropshire • MAP PAGE 145

ENGLAND

Battlefield
SJ5115

▲ *Beaconsfield Farm Touring Park,* Battlefield, Shrewsbury, Shropshire, SY4 4AA
Actual Grid Ref: SJ522189
Tel: 01939 210370 / 210399
Fax: 01939 210349
Open: All year

Billingsley
SO7184

▲ *Camp Easy,* Rays Farm Country Matters, Billingsley, Bridgnorth, Shropshire, WV16 6PF
Tel: 01299 841255
Open: May to Sep

Bishop's Castle
SO3288

▲ *Broughton Bunkhouse,* Lower Broughton Farm, Bishop's Castle, Shropshire, SY15 6SZ
Actual Grid Ref: SO313906
Tel: 01588 638393
Capacity: 12
Under 18: £7.50
Adults: £10.00
Open: Mar to Dec, all day
Self-catering facilities • Television • Showers • Central heating • Laundry facilities • Wet weather shelter • Lounge • Dining room • Grounds available for games • Drying room • Cycle store • Parking • No smoking
Comfortable accommodation in C17th barn in Shropshire's walking country.

Bridges
SO3996

▲ *Bridges Long Mynd Youth Hostel,* Bridges, Ratlinghope, Shrewsbury, SY5 0SP
Actual Grid Ref: SO395965
Tel: 01588 650656
Fax: 01588 650531
Capacity: 37
Under 18: £5.75 **Adults:** £8.50
Open: All year, 5.00pm
Camping
Self-catering facilities • Wet weather shelter • Lounge • Drying room • Cycle store • Evening meal available 7.00pm • No smoking • WC • Washing facilities • Kitchen facilities • Breakfast available
Former village school offering basic accommodation in beautiful countryside between Long Mynd and Stiperstones in the Shropshire Hills. Ideal place for walking and birdwatching.

Bridgnorth
SO7193

▲ *Stanmore Hall Touring Park,* Stourbridge Road, Bridgnorth, Shropshire, WV15 6DT
Actual Grid Ref: SO744923
Tel: 01746 761761
Email: stanmore@morris-leisure.co.uk
Open: All year

Broome
SO3980

▲ *Engine & Tender Inn,* Broome, Aston-on-Clun, Craven Arms, Shropshire, SY7 0NT
Actual Grid Ref: SO399812
Tel: 01588 660275
Open: Apr to Sep

Cardington
SO5095

▲ *Ley Hill Caravan Park,* Ley Hill Farm, Cardington, Church Stretton, Shropshire, SY6 7LA
Actual Grid Ref: SO510963
Tel: 01694 771366
Open: Mar to Oct

Chelmarsh
SO7288

▲ *Denn Farm,* Chelmarsh, Bridgnorth, Shropshire, WV16 4RE
Actual Grid Ref: SO719875
Tel: 01746 861192
Open: Easter to Sep

Church Stretton
SO4593

▲ *Botvyle Farm,* All Stretton, Church Stretton, Shropshire, SY6 7JN
Tel: 01694 722869
Open: Easter to Oct

▲ *Spring Bank Farm,* 62 Shrewsbury Road, Church Stretton, Shropshire, SY6 6HB
Actual Grid Ref: SO458945
Tel: 01694 723570
Open: Apr to Sep

To stay in a Youth Hostel affiliated to one of the Youth Hostel associations, you need to be a member. You can join at most hostels – phone in advance to check.

Cleobury Mortimer
SO6775

▲ *Blount Arms Caravan & Camping Site,* Forest Park, Cleobury Mortimer, Kidderminster, Worcestershire, DY14 9BD
Actual Grid Ref: SO703755
Tel: 01299 270423
Open: Mar to Dec

Clun
SO3080

▲ *Clun Mill Youth Hostel,* The Mill, Clun, Craven Arms, Shropshire, SY7 8NY
Actual Grid Ref: SO303812
Tel: 01588 640582
Fax: 01588 640582
Email: reservations@yha.org.uk
Capacity: 24
Under 18: £6.50
Adults: £9.25
Open: All year, 5.00pm
Camping
Self-catering facilities • Showers • Lounge • Cycle store • Parking • No smoking • WC • Kitchen facilities • Credit cards accepted
Former watermill (workings still visible) upgraded yet unspoilt by modern development, set in stone-built town (C16th humpbacked bridge) and Norman castle.

Clunton
SO3381

▲ *Bush Farm,* Clunton, Craven Arms, Shropshire, SY7 0HU
Actual Grid Ref: SO338812
Tel: 01588 660330
Open: Apr to Oct

If you have to cancel your visit to any hostel or campsite, please let them know – it is always possible to make a bed or a pitch available to someone else.

146   Stilwell's Hostels & Camping 2002

MAP PAGE 145 • **Shropshire**

Coalbrookdale
SJ6604

▲ **Ironbridge Gorge Youth Hostel (2),** Paradise, Coalbrookdale, Telford, Shropshire TF8 7HT
Actual Grid Ref: SJ671043
Tel: 01952 588755
Fax: 01952 588722
Email: ironbridge@yha.org.uk
Capacity: 160
Under 18: £7.15
Adults: £11.00
Open: All year, All day
Family bunk rooms
Television • Showers • Lounge • Games room • Drying room • Evening meal available 6.00-7.00pm • WC • Breakfast available
The hostel is sited in C19th Literary and Scientific Institute, a stone's throw from the original Iron Bridge, the birthplace of the Industrial Revolution, now a World Heritage Site. This hostel is paired with the one in Coalbrookdale, 3 miles away.

Coalport
SJ6902

▲ **Ironbridge Gorge Youth Hostel (1),** John Rose Building, High Street, Coalport, Telford, Shropshire, TF8 7HT
Actual Grid Ref: SJ671043
Tel: 01952 588755
Fax: 01952 588722
Capacity: 160
Under 18: £7.15
Adults: £11.00
Open: All year
Family bunk rooms
Self-catering facilities • Television • Showers • Lounge • Drying room • Evening meal available 6.00-7.00pm • Facilities for disabled people • WC • Breakfast available • Credit cards accepted
Fine hostel imaginatively converted in the museum complex of the original Coalport China Works founded by John Rose in 1796. It is paired with the Hostel in Coalbrookdale 3 miles away.

Craven Arms
SO4282

▲ **Kevindale Camping Site,** Kevindale Broome, Craven Arms, Shropshire, SY7 0NT
Tel: 01588 660326
Open: Apr to Sep

Culmington
SO4882

▲ **Sparchford Farm Caravaning & Camping Site,** Culmington, Ludlow, Shropshire, SY8 2DE
Actual Grid Ref: SO496830
Tel: 01584 861222
Open: All year

Dorrington
SJ4703

▲ **The Bridge Inn,** Dorrington, Shrewsbury, SY5 7ED
Actual Grid Ref: SJ475037
Tel: 01743 718209
Open: All year

Edgerley
SJ3518

▲ **Royal Hill Inn,** Edgerley, Kinnerley, Oswestry, SY10 8ES
Actual Grid Ref: SJ352175
Tel: 01743 741242
Open: Apr to Oct

Ellesmere
SJ3934

▲ **Talbot Caravan Park,** Sparbridge, Ellesmere, Shropshire, SY12 0AG
Actual Grid Ref: SJ401350
Tel: 01691 623594
Open: Mar to Oct

Halfway House
SJ3411

▲ **Rowton Grange,** Halfway House, Shrewsbury, Shropshire, SY5 9ET
Actual Grid Ref: SJ372115
Tel: 01743 884258
Open: Apr to Oct

Hampton Loade
SO7486

▲ **Unicorn Inn,** Hampton Loade, Chelmarsh, Bridgnorth, Shropshire, WV16 6BN
Tel: 01746 861515
Open: All year

Hughley
SO5697

▲ **Mill Farm Caravan Park,** Hughley, Shrewsbury, Shropshire, SY5 6NT
Actual Grid Ref: SO564979
Tel: 01746 785208 / 785255
Fax: 01746 785208
Open: Mar to Oct

▲ **Lower Hill Campsite,** Lower Hill Farm, Hughley, Shrewsbury, Shropshire, SY5 6NX
Tel: 01746 785292
Open: Easter to Oct

Kinnerley
SJ3321

▲ **Cranberry Moss Camping & Caravan Park,** Kinnerley, Oswestry, Shropshire, SY10 8DY
Actual Grid Ref: SJ366212
Tel: 01743 741444
Open: Apr to Oct

Little Stretton
SO4491

▲ **Small Batch Site,** Ashe Valley, Little Stretton, Church Stretton, Shropshire, SY6 6PW
Actual Grid Ref: SO440920
Tel: 01694 723358
Open: Mar to Oct

Llanforda
SJ2528

▲ **The Old Mill Inn,** Candy, Llanforda, Oswestry, Shropshire, SY10 9AZ
Tel: 01691 657058
Fax: 01691 657058
Open: All year

Hostels and campsites may vary rates – be sure to check when booking.

Stilwell's Hostels & Camping 2002

Shropshire • MAP PAGE 145

Longville-in-the-Dale
SO5393

▲ **Wilderhope Manor Youth Hostel,** *The John Cadury Memorial Hostel, Longville-in-the-Dale, Easthope, Much Wenlock, Shropshire, TF13 6EG*
Actual Grid Ref: SO544928
Tel: 01694 771363
Fax: 01694 771520
Email: wilderhope@yha.org.uk
Capacity: 70
Under 18: £7.75 **Adults:** £11.00
Open: Feb to Oct + Xmas, 5.00pm
Family bunk rooms
Camping
Self-catering facilities • Showers • Lounge • Games room • Drying room • Parking • Evening meal available 7.00pm • No smoking • WC • Kitchen facilities • Breakfast available • Credit cards accepted
Exquisite Elizabethan manor house owned by the National Trust, with lots of original features, idyllically situated atop Wenlock Edge.

Lyneal
SJ4433

▲ **Fernwood Caravan Park,** *Lyneal, Ellesmere, Shropshire, SY12 0QF*
Actual Grid Ref: SJ445346
Tel: 01948 710221 **Open:** Mar to Nov

Mainstone
SO2787

▲ **New House Farm,** *Mainstone, Clun, Craven Arms, Shropshire, SY7 8NJ*
Tel: 01588 638214
Open: All year

Melverley
SJ3316

▲ **Church House,** *Melverley, Oswestry, Shropshire, SY10 8PJ*
Actual Grid Ref: SJ332165
Tel: 01691 682754
Open: Easter to Oct

Much Wenlock
SO6299

▲ **The Sytche Caravan Site,** *Farley Road, Much Wenlock, Shropshire, TF13 6NA*
Actual Grid Ref: SJ620004
Tel: 01952 727274
Email: derrick.hill@shropshire-cc.uk
Open: Apr to Oct

Nantmawr
SJ2424

▲ **The Engine House,** *Rose Hill, Nantmawr, Oswestry, Shropshire, SY10 9HL*
Actual Grid Ref: SJ253249
Tel: 01691 659358
Fax: 01691 659358
Capacity: 18
Under 18: £12.00 **Adults:** £12.00
Open: All year, until 9pm
Camping for 30 tents: £4.00
Self-catering facilities • Television • Showers • Central heating • Dining room • Parking • Facilities for disabled people
Renovated limestone building. Quality facilities. 250 acre estate. MB centre.

Pant
SJ2722

▲ **Three Firs,** *Pant, Oswestry, Shropshire, SY10 8LB*
Tel: 01691 831375
Open: All year

Ratlinghope
SO4096

▲ **Middle Darnford,** *Ratlinghope, Shrewsbury, SY5 0SR*
Actual Grid Ref: SO422976
Tel: 01694 751320
Open: Mar to Oct

Shelve
SO3398

▲ **The Old School Caravan Park,** *Shelve, Minsterley, Shrewsbury, SY5 0JQ*
Actual Grid Ref: SO322976
Tel: 01588 650410
Open: Mar to Oct

All details shown are as supplied by hostels and campsites in Autumn 2000.

Shrewsbury
SJ4912

▲ **Shrewsbury Youth Hostel,** *The Woodlands, Abbey Foregate, Shrewsbury, Shropshire, SY2 6LZ*
Actual Grid Ref: SJ505120
Tel: 01743 360179
Fax: 01743 357423
Email: shrewsbury@yha.org.uk
Capacity: 60
Under 18: £6.50
Adults: £9.25
Open: Feb to Dec
Self-catering facilities • Television • Laundry facilities • Lounge • Cycle store • Parking • Evening meal available 7.00pm • Kitchen facilities • Breakfast available • Luggage store • Credit cards accepted
Former Victorian ironmaster's house built in red sandstone. The hostel is on the outskirts of the town, but only about a mile from the Abbey and town centre.

▲ **Carref,** *Fords Heath, Shrewsbury, SY5 9GD*
Actual Grid Ref: SJ414915
Tel: 01743 821688
Open: May to Oct

▲ **Oxon Touring Park,** *Welshpool Road, Shrewsbury, SY3 5FB*
Actual Grid Ref: SJ457136
Tel: 01743 340 868
Email: oxon@morris-leisure.co.uk
Open: All year

▲ **Severn House,** *Montford Bridge, Shrewsbury, SY4 1ED*
Actual Grid Ref: SJ433154
Tel: 01743 850229
Open: Apr to Oct

Telford
SJ6909

▲ **Camping & Caravanning Club Site,** *Ebury Hill, Haughton, Telford, Shropshire, TF6 6BU*
Tel: 01743 709334
Open: Mar to Oct

▲ **Severn Gorge Caravan Park,** *Bridgnorth Road, Tweedale, Telford, Shropshire, TF7 4JB*
Actual Grid Ref: SJ704052
Tel: 01952 684789
Fax: 01952 684789
Open: All year

MAP PAGE 145 • **Shropshire**

Wem
SJ5129

▲ **Lower Lacon Caravan Park,** Lerdene, Cabtree Lane, Wemsbrooke Road, Wem, Shrewsbury, Shropshire, SY4 5RP
Actual Grid Ref: SJ529298
Tel: 01939 232376 / 232856
Fax: 01939 233606
Email: info@llcp.co.uk
Open: All year

Wentnor
SO3892

▲ **Cwnd House Farm,** Wentnor, Bishops Castle, Shropshire, SY9 5EQ
Tel: 01588 650237
Open: May to Oct

▲ **The Green Caravan & Camping Park,** Wentnor, Bishops Castle, Shropshire, SY9 5EF
Actual Grid Ref: SO378923
Tel: 01588 650605 / 650231
Open: Mar to Oct

▲ **The Poplars,** Prolley Moor, Wentnor, Bishops Castle, Shropshire, SY9 5EF
Actual Grid Ref: SO396921
Tel: 01588 650383
Open: Mar to Oct

Wheathill
SO6182

▲ **Three Horse Shoes,** Brown Clee View, Wheathill, Burwarton, Bridgnorth, Shropshire, WV16 6QT
Actual Grid Ref: SO600819
Tel: 01584 823206
Open: Mar to Oct

Whitchurch
SJ5441

▲ **Green Lane Farm Camping Site,** Green Lane, Press, Whitchurch, Shropshire, SY13 2AH
Actual Grid Ref: SJ568347
Tel: 01948 840460 **Tent pitches:** 20
Tent rate: £6.00
Open: Mar to Oct **Last arr:** 8.30pm
Dogs allowed • Electric hook-up • Showers
A 'country garden' site, peaceful, quiet with spacious level pitches.

▲ **Brook House Farm,** Grindley Brook, Whitchurch, Shropshire, SY13 4QJ
Actual Grid Ref: SJ526425
Tel: 01948 664557
Open: All year

▲ **Abbey Green Farm Caravan Park,** Whixhall, Whitchurch, Shropshire, SY13 2PT
Tel: 01948 880213
Open: All year

Whixall
SJ5134

▲ **Roden View,** Dobson's Bridge, Whixall, Whitchurch, Shropshire, SY13 2QL
Actual Grid Ref: SJ493343
Tel: 01948 710320
Fax: 01948 710320
Tent pitches: 5 **Tent rate:** £8.50
Open: All year **Last arr:** 10pm
Dogs allowed • Electric hook-up • Cafe or Takeaway on site • Picnic/barbecue area on site • Showers • Laundrette on site • Public phone on site
Small secluded park, close to Shropshire, lakes and canal. Local fishing.

ENGLAND

Somerset

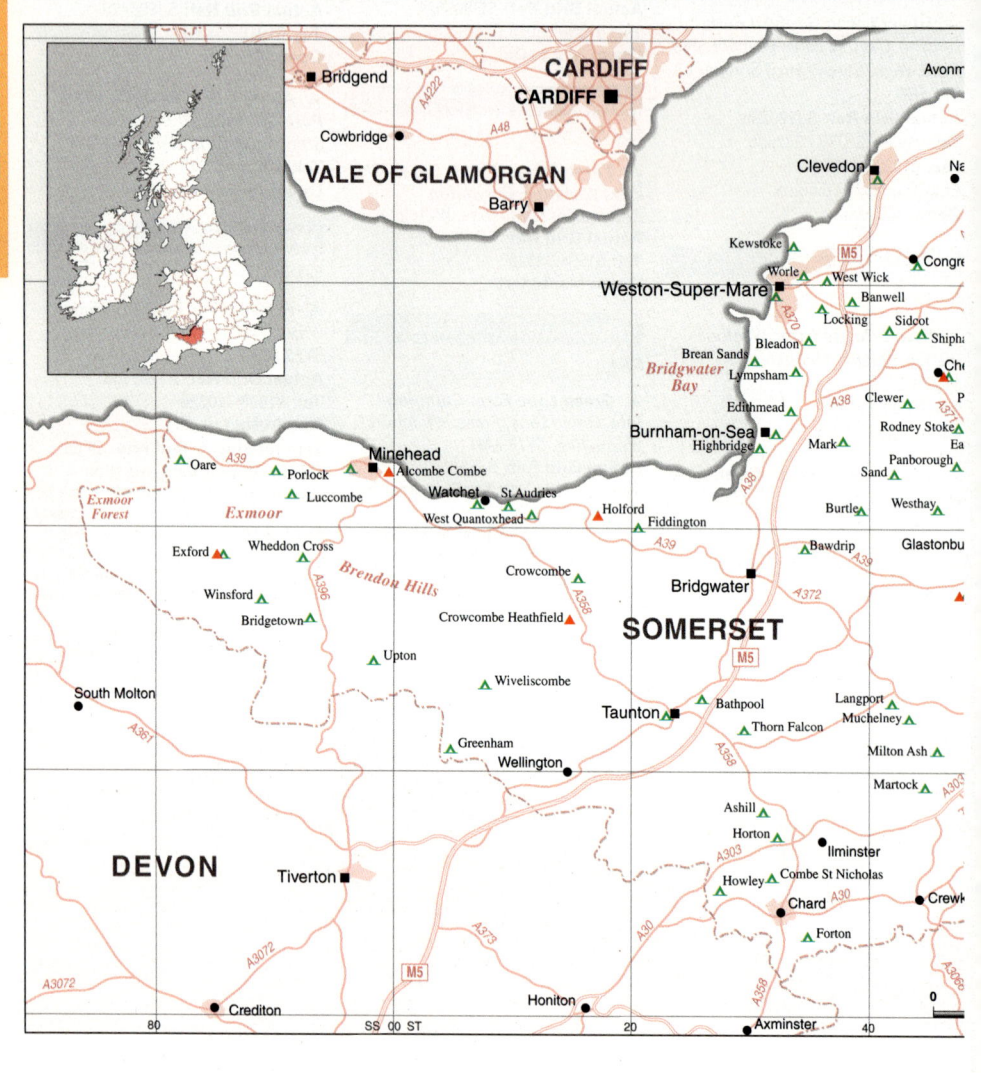

Alcombe Combe

SS9745

▲ **Minehead Youth Hostel,**
Alcombe Combe, Minehead,
Somerset, TA24 6EW
Actual Grid Ref: SS973442
Tel: 01643 702595 **Fax:** 01643 703016
Capacity: 36

Under 18: £6.90 **Adults:** £10.00
Open: All year, 5.00
Family bunk rooms
Self-catering facilities • Showers • Lounge • Dining room • Drying room • Parking Limited • Evening meal available 7.00pm • No smoking • WC • Breakfast available • Credit cards accepted
In a secluded position up a wooded combe on the edge of Exmoor.

Ashill

ST3117

▲ **Stewley Cross Caravan Park,**
Stewley Cross, Ashill, Ilminster,
Somerset, TA19 9NP
Tel: 01823 480314
Open: Apr to Oct

Somerset

Batcombe

ST6837

▲ **Batcombe Vale,** Batcombe, Shepton Mallet, Somerset, BA4 6BW
Actual Grid Ref: ST682379
Tel: 01749 830246
Open: May to Sep

Bath

ST7464

▲ **Bath Youth Hostel,** Bathwick Hill, Bath, Somerset, BA2 6JZ
Actual Grid Ref: ST766644
Tel: 01225 465674
Fax: 01225 482947
Email: bath@yha.org.uk
Capacity: 124
Under 18: £7.75
Adults: £11.00
Open: All year, All day
Self-catering facilities • Television • Showers • Shop • Laundry facilities • Lounge • Drying room • Security lockers • Cycle store • Evening meal available 6.00 to 8.00pm • Kitchen facilities • Breakfast available • Credit cards accepted
Handsome Italianate mansion, set in beautiful, secluded gardens, with views of historic city and surrounding hills.

▲ **Bath Marina & Caravan Park,** Brassmill Lane, Bath, Somerset, BA1 3JT
Actual Grid Ref: ST719655
Tel: 01225 428778 / 424301
Open: All year

Bathpool

ST2425

▲ **Tanpits Cider Farm,** Dyers Lane, Bathpool, Taunton, Somerset, TA2 8BZ
Actual Grid Ref: ST254261
Tel: 01823 270663
Open: Mar to Nov

Bawdrip

ST3339

▲ **Fairways International Touring Caravan & Camp,** Woolavington Corner, Bath Road, Bawdrip, Bridgwater, Somerset, TA7 8PP
Actual Grid Ref: ST348402
Tel: 01278 685569
Open: Mar to Nov

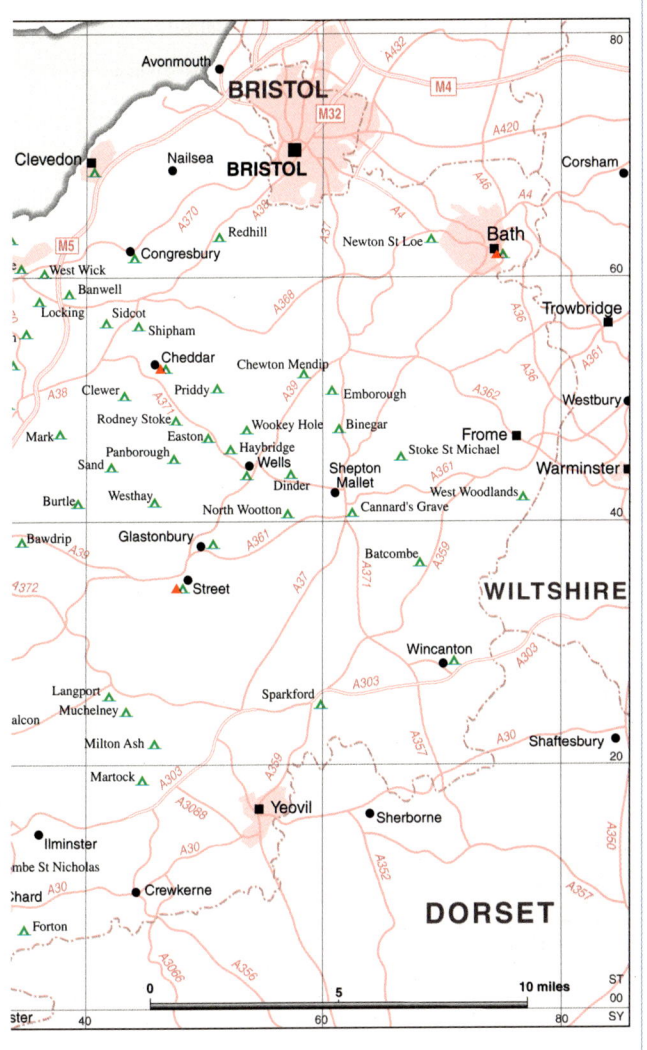

Banwell

ST3959

▲ **Stonebridge Farm,** Wolvershill Road, Banwell, Weston-super-Mare, Somerset, BS24 6DR
Actual Grid Ref: ST392597
Tel: 01934 822115
Open: Apr to Oct

▲ **Myrtle Farm Touring Park,** Summer Lane, Banwell, Weston-super-Mare, Somerset, BS29 6LP
Actual Grid Ref: ST383606
Tel: 01934 823845
Open: Apr to Oct

Somerset • MAP PAGE 150

Binegar
ST6149

▲ **Whitnell Manor,** Binegar, Emborough, Bath, BA3 4UF
Tel: 01749 840277
Fax: 01749 840277
Open: All year

Bleadon
ST3356

▲ **Purn International Holiday Park ,** Bridgewater Road, Bleadon, Weston-super-Mare, North Somerset, BS24 0AN
Actual Grid Ref: ST335567
Tel: 01934 812342
Open: Mar to Nov

Brean Sands
ST2956

▲ **Northam Farm Camping & Caravan Park,** Brean, Burnham-on-Sea, Somerset, TA8 2SE
Actual Grid Ref: ST297535
Tel: 01278 751244 / 751222
Open: Mar to Oct

▲ **Diamond Farm Caravan Park & Touring Park,** Weston Road, Brean, Burnham-on-Sea, Somerset, TA8 2RL
Tel: 01278 751041
Open: Apr to Oct

▲ **Brean Leisure Park,** Coast Road, Brean, Burnham-on-Sea, Somerset, TA8 2RF
Tel: 01278 751595 **Fax:** 01278 751595
Open: May to Oct

▲ **Holiday Resort Unity,** Coast Road, Brean, Burnham-on-Sea, Somerset, TA8 2RB
Tel: 01278 751235
Open: Mar to Nov

▲ **Diamond Farm,** Brean, Burnham-on-Sea, Somerset, TA8 2RS
Tel: 01278 751263
Open: Easter to Oct

Bridgetown
SS9232

▲ **Exe Valley Caravan Site,** Mill House, Bridgetown, Dulverton, Somerset, TA22 9JR
Actual Grid Ref: SS923332
Tel: 01643 851432
Open: Mar to Oct

Burnham-on-Sea
ST3049

▲ **Channel View Caravan & Camping Site,** Brean Down Road, Brean, Burnham-on-Sea, Somerset, TA8 2RR
Actual Grid Ref: ST297577
Tel: 01278 760485
Open: Mar to Oct

Burtle
ST4042

▲ **Ye Olde Burtle Inn,** Catcott Road, Burtle, Bridgwater, Somerset, TA7 8NG
Actual Grid Ref: ST397434
Tel: 01278 722269
Open: All year

▲ **Orchard Camping,** Catcott Road, Burtle, Glastonbury, Somerset
Tel: 01278 722123
Open: All year

Cannard's Grave
ST6241

▲ **Manleaze Caravan Park,** Cannard's Grave, Shepton Mallet, Somerset, BA4 4LY
Actual Grid Ref: ST625420
Tel: 01749 342404
Open: All year

Cheddar
ST4553

▲ **Cheddar Youth Hostel,** Hillfield, Cheddar, Somerset, BS27 3HN
Actual Grid Ref: ST455534
Tel: 01934 742494 **Fax:** 01934 744724
Email: cheddar@yha.org.uk
Capacity: 53
Under 18: £7.75 **Adults:** £11.00
Open: All year (not Xmas/New Year)
Family bunk rooms
Self-catering facilities • Showers • Laundry facilities • Lounge • Lounge • Drying room • Cycle store • Evening meal available 7.00pm • No smoking • WC • Kitchen facilities • Breakfast available
Victorian stone house offering comfortable accommodation in the centre of this world-famous village. Handy for the Gorge and Wookey Hole. Day trips could include Glastonbury, Wells. Walk the Mendips or cycle the Somerset Levels.

▲ **Broadway House Holiday Caravan & Camping Park,** Axbridge Road, Cheddar, Somerset, BS27 3DB
Actual Grid Ref: ST449546
Tel: 01934 742610
Email: broadway.house@btinternet.com
Open: Mar to Nov

▲ **Church Farm Caravan & Camping Park,** Church Street, Cheddar, Somerset, BS27 3RF
Actual Grid Ref: ST459530
Tel: 01934 743048
Open: Mar to Oct

▲ **Froglands Farm Caravan & Camping Park,** Cheddar, Somerset, BS27 3RH
Actual Grid Ref: ST461529
Tel: 01934 742058 / 743304
Open: Mar to Oct

▲ **Woodeaves Camping,** Draycott Road, Cheddar, Somerset, BS27 3RU
Actual Grid Ref: ST472516
Tel: 01934 742556
Open: All year

Chewton Mendip
ST5953

▲ **Chewton Cheese Dairy,** Priory Farm, Chewton Mendip, Bath, N E Somerset, BA3 4NT
Actual Grid Ref: ST591525
Tel: 01761 241666
Open: All year

Clevedon
ST3971

▲ **Colehouse Farm Caravan Park,** Colehouse Farm, Colehouse Lane, Clevedon, North Somerset, BS21 4TQ
Tel: 01275 872680
Open: Mar to Jan

▲ **Warren's Holiday Park,** Lake Farm, Colehouse Lane, Clevedon, North Somerset, BS21 6TQ
Actual Grid Ref: ST406695
Tel: 01275 871666
Open: Mar to Jan

Clewer
ST4350

▲ **Ragwood Farm,** Clewer, Wedmore, Cheddar, Somerset, BS28 4JG
Tel: 01934 742254
Open: June to Aug

Somerset

Combe St Nicholas
ST2911

▲ **Five Acres House,** Beetham, Combe St Nicholas, Chard, Somerset, TA20 3PZ
Actual Grid Ref: ST273125
Tel: 01460 234364
Open: All year

Congresbury
ST4363

▲ **Oak Farm Touring Park,** Weston Road, Congresbury, Weston-super-Mare, North Somerset, BS19 5EB
Actual Grid Ref: ST433640
Tel: 01934 833246
Open: Mar to Oct

Crowcombe
ST1336

▲ **Quantock Orchard Caravan Park,** Crowcombe, Taunton, Somerset, TA4 4AW
Actual Grid Ref: ST142350
Tel: 01984 618618
Fax: 01984 618618
Open: All year

Crowcombe Heathfield
ST1333

▲ **Crowcombe Heathfield Youth Hostel,** Denzel House, Crowcombe Heathfield, Crowcombe, Taunton, Somerset, TA4 4BT
Actual Grid Ref: ST138339
Tel: 01984 667249
Fax: 01984 667249
Capacity: 50
Under 18: £6.50
Adults: £9.25
Open: All year, 5.00pm
Family bunk rooms
Camping
Self-catering facilities • Television • Showers • Shop • Laundry facilities • Laundry rooms • Lounge • Dining room • Grounds available for games • Drying room • Cycle store • WC • Kitchen facilities • Credit cards accepted
In peaceful wooded countryside close to the colourful Quantock Hills, a spacious country house in large grounds. Close to West Somerset Railway steam train.

Dinder
ST5744

▲ **Little Crapnell Farm,** Dinder, Wells, Somerset, BA5 3HQ
Actual Grid Ref: ST599463
Tel: 01749 342692
Open: All year

Easton
ST5047

▲ **Beaconsfield Farm,** Easton, Wells, Somerset, BA5 1DU
Actual Grid Ref: ST515475
Tel: 01749 870308
Open: All year

Edithmead
ST3249

▲ **Home Farm Touring Caravan Camping Park,** Edithmead, Highbridge, Somerset, TA9 4HD
Actual Grid Ref: ST327493
Tel: 01278 788888
Open: All year

Emborough
ST6151

▲ **Old Down Caravan & Camping Park,** Emborough, Bath, Somerset, BA3 4SA
Actual Grid Ref: ST625513
Tel: 01761 232355
Open: Apr to Oct

Exford
SS8538

▲ **Exford (Exmoor) Youth Hostel,** Exe Mead, Exford, Minehead, Somerset, TA24 7PU
Actual Grid Ref: SS853383
Tel: 01643 831288
Fax: 01643 831650
Capacity: 51
Under 18: £7.75
Adults: £11.00
Open: All year, 5.00pm
Family bunk rooms
Self-catering facilities • Showers • Dining room • Drying room • Cycle store • Parking • Evening meal available 7.00pm • WC • Kitchen facilities • Breakfast available • Credit cards accepted
Victorian house and cedarwood annex. Lovely garden with access to riverside.

▲ **Downscombe Farm Camp Site,** Dowsncombe Farm, Exford, Minehead, Somerset, TA24 7NP
Actual Grid Ref: SS844395
Tel: 01643 831239
Open: Apr to Oct

▲ **Westermill Farm,** Exford, Minehead, Somerset, TA24 7NJ
Actual Grid Ref: SS824398
Tel: 01643 831238
Open: All year

Fiddington
ST2140

▲ **Mill Farm Caravan & Camping Park,** Fiddington, Bridgwater, Somerset, TA5 1JQ
Actual Grid Ref: ST219410
Tel: 01278 732286
Open: All year

Forton
ST3306

▲ **Alpine Grove Touring Park,** Forton, Chard, Somerset, TA20 4HD
Actual Grid Ref: ST342070
Tel: 01460 63479
Open: Easter to Sep

Glastonbury
ST5039

▲ **Old Oaks Touring Park,** Wick Farm, Wick, Glastonbury, Somerset, BA6 8JS
Actual Grid Ref: ST521393
Tel: 01458 831437
Open: Mar to Oct

▲ **Isle of Avalon Touring Caravan Park,** Godney Road, Glastonbury, Somerset, BA6 9AF
Actual Grid Ref: ST493397
Tel: 01458 833618
Open: All year

Greenham
ST0720

▲ **Gamlins Farm Caravan Park,** Greenham, Wellington, Somerset, TA21 0LZ
Actual Grid Ref: ST086129
Tel: 01823 672596
Fax: 01823 672324
Open: Mar to Sept

Somerset • MAP PAGE 150

ENGLAND

Haybridge
ST5346

▲ **Haybridge Farm,** Haybridge, Wells, Somerset, BA5 1AJ
Actual Grid Ref: ST532458
Tel: 01749 673681
Open: Apr to Oct

Highbridge
ST3147

▲ **Edithmead Leisure & Park Homes,** Highbridge, Somerset, TA9 4HE
Actual Grid Ref: ST338492
Tel: 01278 783475
Open: Feb to Dec

▲ **New House Farm Caravan & Camping Park,** Walrow, Highbridge, Somerset, TA9 4RA
Actual Grid Ref: ST339469
Tel: 01278 782218 / 783277
Open: Mar to Oct

Holford
ST1541

▲ **Quantock Hills Youth Hostel,** Sevenacres, Holford, Bridgwater, Somerset, TA5 1SQ
Actual Grid Ref: ST146416
Tel: 01278 741224
Fax: 01278 741224
Email: reservations@yha.org.uk
Capacity: 34
Under 18: £6.50
Adults: £9.25
Open: All year
Camping
Self-catering facilities • Shop • Wet weather shelter • Lounge • Dining room • Drying room • Parking Available • No smoking • WC • Kitchen facilities
Overlooking the Bristol Channel, with views across to Wales, this country house is perfect for exploring the Quantocks and its wildlife. Facilities are basic.

Horton
ST3114

▲ **Thornleigh Caravan Park,** Hanning Road, Horton, Ilminster, Somerset, TA19 9QH
Actual Grid Ref: ST324148
Tel: 01460 53450
Open: Mar to Oct

Howley
ST2609

▲ **South Somerset Holiday Park,** Howley, Chard, Somerset, TA20 3EA
Actual Grid Ref: ST275094
Tel: 01460 66036
Open: All year

Kewstoke
ST3363

▲ **Ardnave Holiday Park,** Kewstoke, Weston-super-Mare, North Somerset, BS22 9XJ
Tel: 01934 622319
Open: Mar to Oct

▲ **Rose Tree Caravan Park,** Lower Norton Lane, Kewstoke, Somerset, BS22 9XP
Actual Grid Ref: ST347638
Tel: 01934 620351
Open: Mar to Oct

Langport
ST4126

▲ **Bowdens Crest Caravan & Camping Park,** Bowdens, Langport, Somerset, TA10 0DD
Actual Grid Ref: ST414290
Tel: 01458 250553
Open: Mar to Nov

Locking
ST3559

▲ **Camping & Caravanning Club Site,** West End Farm, Locking, Weston-super-Mare, North Somerset, BS24 8RH
Tel: 01934 822548
Open: Mar to Sept

▲ **West End Farm Caravan & Camping Park,** Locking, Weston-super-Mare, North Somerset, BS24 8RH
Actual Grid Ref: ST353600
Tel: 01934 822529 **Open:** All year

Luccombe
SS9144

▲ **Burrowhayes Farm Caravan & Camping Site,** West Luccombe, Luccombe, Minehead, Somerset, TA24 8HU
Actual Grid Ref: SS899463
Tel: 01643 862463
Open: Mar to Oct

Lympsham
ST3354

▲ **Dulhorn Farm Camping Site,** Weston Road, Lympsham, Weston-super-Mare, Somerset, BS24 0JQ
Actual Grid Ref: ST349534
Tel: 01934 750298
Fax: 01934 750913
Tent pitches: 20
Tent rate: £5.00-£7.00
Open: Mar to Oct
Dogs allowed • Electric hook-up • Calor Gas/Camping Gaz • Showers
Quiet site on working farm in country surroundings. Ideal touring.

Mark
ST3747

▲ **Splott Farm,** Mark, Blackford, Wedmore, Somerset, BS28 4PD
Tel: 01278 641522
Open: Mar to Nov

Martock
ST4619

▲ **Southfork Caravan Park,** Parrett Works, Martock, Somerset, TA12 6AE
Actual Grid Ref: ST446188
Tel: 01935 825661
Open: All year

Milton Ash
ST4621

▲ **Falconers Farm,** Isle Brewers, Taunton, Somerset, TA3 6QN
Tel: 01460 281423
Open: All year

Minehead
SS9646

▲ **Camping & Caravanning Club Site,** Hill Road, North Hill, Minehead, Somerset, TA24 5SF
Actual Grid Ref: SS958471
Tel: 01643 704138
Open: Mar to Sept

▲ **Minehead & Exmoor Caravan Site,** Minehead & Exmoor Caravan Park, Porlock Road, Minehead, Somerset, TA24 8SN
Actual Grid Ref: SS951458
Tel: 01643 703074
Open: Mar to Oct

MAP PAGE 150 • **Somerset**

ENGLAND

▲ **Blue Anchor Bay Caravan Park,** Minehead, Somerset, TA24 6JT
Actual Grid Ref: ST025434
Tel: 01643 821360
Fax: 01643 821572
Open: Mar to Oct

Muchelney

ST4324

▲ **Thorney Lakes Caravan Parks,** Thorney West Farm, Muchelney, Langport, Somerset, TA10 0DW
Actual Grid Ref: ST429232
Tel: 01458 250811
Open: Mar to Nov

Newton St Loe

ST7064

▲ **Newton Mill Touring Centre,** Newton St Loe, Bath, North East Somerset, BA2 9JF
Actual Grid Ref: ST715645
Tel: 01225 333909
Open: All year

North Wootton

ST5641

▲ **Greenacres Camping,** Barrow Lane, North Wootton, Shepton Mallet, Somerset, BA4 4HL
Actual Grid Ref: ST553416
Tel: 01749 890497
Open: Apr to Oct

Oare

SS8047

▲ **Doone Valley Camp Site,** Oare, Brendon, Lynton, Devon, EX35 6NU
Actual Grid Ref: SS795477
Tel: 01598 741267
Open: Mar to Sept

Panborough

ST4745

▲ **Garden End Farm,** Panborough, Wells, Somerset, BA5 1PN
Tel: 01934 712414
Open: Mar to Oct

Porlock

SS8846

▲ **Sparkhayes Farm Camping Site,** Sparkhayes Lane, Porlock, Minehead, Somerset, TA24 8NE
Actual Grid Ref: SS887470
Tel: 01643 862470
Tent pitches: 50 **Tent rate:** £4.00
Open: Apr to Oct **Last arr:** any time
Dogs allowed • Calor Gas/Camping Gaz • Cafe or Takeaway on site nearby • Children's play area nearby • Showers • Laundrette on site • Public phone on site • Licensed bar on site nearby • Shop on site nearby
Level site near village with beautiful hill and sea views.

▲ **Porlock Caravan Park,** Porlock, Minehead, Somerset, TA24 8NS
Actual Grid Ref: SS883468
Tel: 01643 862269
Open: Mar to Oct

▲ **Pool Bridge Campsite,** Porlock, Minehead, Somerset, TA24 8LS
Actual Grid Ref: SS875447
Tel: 01643 862521
Open: May to Oct

Priddy

ST5251

▲ **Mendip Heights Camping & Caravan Park,** Townsend, Priddy, Wells, Somerset, BA5 3BP
Actual Grid Ref: ST523518
Tel: 01749 870241 **Fax:** 01749 870241
Email: mendip@mendipheights.co.uk
Open: Mar to Nov

Redhill

ST4963

▲ **Brook Lodge Camping & Caravan Park,** Cowslip Green, Redhill, Bristol, BS40 5RD
Actual Grid Ref: ST485620
Tel: 01934 862311
Open: Feb to Nov

Rodney Stoke

ST4850

▲ **Bucklegrove Caravan & Camping Park,** Wells Road, Rodney Stoke, Cheddar, Somerset, BS27 3UZ
Actual Grid Ref: ST491495
Tel: 01749 870261
Email: bucklegrove@u.genie.co.uk
Open: Mar to Oct

▲ **Rodney Stoke Camp Site,** Rodney Stoke, Cheddar, Somerset, BS27 3XB
Actual Grid Ref: ST483502
Tel: 01749 870209
Open: All year

Sand

ST4346

▲ **Country View Caravan Park,** Sand Road, Sand Bay, Sand, Weston-super-Mare, North Somerset, BS22 9UJ
Actual Grid Ref: ST335646
Tel: 01934 627595
Open: Mar to Oct

Shipham

ST4457

▲ **Longbottom Farm,** Shipham, Winscombe, Somerset, BS25 1RW
Actual Grid Ref: ST459567
Tel: 01934 743166
Open: All year

Sidcot

ST4257

▲ **Netherdale Caravan & Camping Site,** Bridgwater Road, Sidcot, Winscombe, North Somerset, BS25 1NH
Actual Grid Ref: ST426567
Tel: 01934 843481
Open: Mar to Oct

Sparkford

ST6026

▲ **Long Hazel Camping Caravan Park,** High Street, Sparkford, Yeovil, Somerset, BA22 7JH
Actual Grid Ref: ST604263
Tel: 01963 440002
Open: Mar to Dec

St Audries

ST1042

▲ **Home Farm Holiday Centre,** St Audries Bay, Williton, Taunton, Somerset, TA4 4DP
Actual Grid Ref: ST106432
Tel: 01984 632487
Open: All year

Stoke St Michael

ST6646

▲ **Phippens Farm,** Stoke St Michael, Oakhill, Shepton Mallet, Somerset, BA3 5JH
Actual Grid Ref: ST657470
Tel: 01749 840395
Open: Mar to Sept

Somerset • MAP PAGE 150

Street
ST4836

▲ **Street Youth Hostel,** *The Chalet, Ivythorn Hill, Street, Somerset, BA16 0TZ*
Actual Grid Ref: ST480345
Tel: 01458 442961
Fax: 01458 442738
Capacity: 28
Under 18: £6.50
Adults: £9.25
Open: All year, 5.00pm
Camping
Self-catering facilities • Wet weather shelter • Lounge • Drying room • Cycle store • Parking • No smoking • WC • Kitchen facilities • Credit cards accepted
Former holiday home for workers at Clarks' shoemakers, this traditional hostel is a Swiss-style chalet looking towards Glastonbury Tor.

▲ **Bramble Hill Camping Park,** *Bramble Hill, Walton Street, Street, Somerset, BA16 9RQ*
Actual Grid Ref: ST455362
Tel: 01458 442548
Open: Apr to Sep

▲ **Marshals Elm Farm,** *Street, Somerset, BA16 0TZ*
Actual Grid Ref: ST486345
Tel: 01458 442878
Open: May to Oct

Taunton
ST2324

▲ **Holly Bush Park,** *Culmhead, Taunton, Somerset, TA3 7EA*
Actual Grid Ref: ST222161
Tel: 01823 421515
Email: beaumont@hollybushpark.ndo.co.uk
Open: All year

Thorn Falcon
ST2723

▲ **Ashe Farm Camping & Caravan Site,** *Thorn Falcon, Taunton, Somerset, TA3 5NW*
Actual Grid Ref: ST280224
Tel: 01823 442567
Open: Apr to Oct

Hostels and campsites may vary rates – be sure to check when booking.

Upton
SS9928

▲ **Lowtrow Cross Caravan/Camping Park & Inn,** *Upton, Wiveliscombe, Taunton, Somerset, TA4 2DB*
Actual Grid Ref: ST006292
Tel: 01398 371220 **Open:** Apr to Oct

Watchet
ST0643

▲ **Doniford Bay Holiday Park,** *Watchet, Somerset, TA23 0TJ*
Actual Grid Ref: ST093432
Tel: 01984 632423
Open: Apr to Oct

▲ **Warren Bay Caravan & Camping Park,** *Watchet, Somerset, TA23 0JR*
Actual Grid Ref: ST057430
Tel: 01984 631460
Fax: 01984 633999
Open: Apr to Oct

▲ **Warren Farm,** *Watchet, Somerset, TA23 0JP*
Actual Grid Ref: ST048432
Tel: 01984 631220
Open: Mar to Sept

Wells
ST5445

▲ **Birdwood House,** *Bath Road, Wells, Somerset, BA5 3DH*
Actual Grid Ref: ST572467
Tel: 01749 679250
Open: May to Oct

West Quantoxhead
ST1141

▲ **St Audries Bay Holiday Club,** *West Quantoxhead, Taunton, Somerset, TA4 4DY*
Tel: 01984 632515
Email: mrandle@staudriesbay.demon.co.uk
Open: Easter to Oct

West Wick
ST3661

▲ **Weston Gateway Caravan Site,** *West Wick, Weston-super-Mare, North Somerset, BS24 7TF*
Actual Grid Ref: ST372620
Tel: 01934 510344
Open: All year

Some hostels and campsites impose restrictions on size and type of groups they accept (e.g. not permitting single-sex groups). Always phone to enquire before booking.

West Woodlands
ST7744

▲ **Seven Acres,** *West Woodlands, Frome, Somerset, BA11 5EQ*
Actual Grid Ref: ST777444
Tel: 01373 464222
Open: Mar to Oct

Westhay
ST4342

▲ **Rose Farm,** *Westhay, Glastonbury, Somerset, BA6 9TR*
Tel: 01458 860256
Open: May to Oct

Weston-super-Mare
ST3261

▲ **Rugby Football Club Ground,** *Weston-super-Mare, North Somerset, BS23 3PA*
Tel: 01934 628530
Open: Apr to Oct

Wheddon Cross
SS9238

▲ **Blagdon Farm,** *Wheddon Cross, Minehead, Somerset, TA24 7ED*
Tel: 01643 841280
Open: May to Oct

Wincanton
ST7028

▲ **Wincanton Racecourse Caravan Club Site,** *Wincanton, Somerset, BA9 8BJ*
Actual Grid Ref: ST700300
Tel: 01963 34276
Open: Apr to Sep

All details shown are as supplied by hostels and campsites in Autumn 2000.

Winsford

SS9034

▲ **Halse Farm Caravan & Camping Park,** Winsford, Minehead, Somerset, TA24 7JL
Actual Grid Ref: SS898342
AA grade: 3 Pennants
Tel: 01643 851259 **Fax:** 01643 851592
Email: sm@halsefarm.co.uk
Tent pitches: 22
Tent rate: £6.00-£8.00
Open: Mar to Oct
Last arr: 11pm
Facilities for disabled people • Dogs allowed • Electric hook-up • Calor Gas/Camping Gaz • Children's play area • Showers • Laundrette on site • Public phone on site • Tennis courts nearby • Riding nearby • Fishing nearby
In Exmoor National Park, adjacent to the moor, on working stock farm. Walker's paradise. Quality heated toilet block with free hot showers, baby changing facilities, hand and hair dryers. 1 miles from Winsford with thatched inn, shop and garage. Signposted from A396 and village. More details on website - www.halsefarm.co.uk.

Wiveliscombe

ST0827

▲ **Waterrow Touring Park,** Watterow, Wiveliscombe, Taunton, Somerset, TA4 2AZ
Actual Grid Ref: ST053248
Tel: 01984 623464
Open: Apr to Oct

Wookey Hole

ST5347

▲ **Homestead Caravan & Camping Park,** Wookey Hole, Wells, Somerset, BA5 1BW
Actual Grid Ref: ST532475
AA grade: 3 Pennants
Tel: 01749 673022
Fax: 01749 673022
Email: homestead.park@virgin.net
Tent pitches: 50
Tent rate: £6.00-£9.00
Open: Mar to Oct
Dogs allowed • Electric hook-up • Baths • Calor Gas/Camping Gaz • Showers • Indoor swimming pool nearby • Golf nearby • Riding nearby • Fishing nearby
Nestling at the foot of the Mendip Hills in the historic village of Wookey Hole, this park enjoys a quiet and scenic location close to the heart of rural Somerset. Pleasant & secluded, it offers a peaceful haven for those wanting a quiet holiday in an Area of Outstanding Natural Beauty.

▲ **Ebborlands,** Wookey Hole, Wells, Somerset, BA5 1AY
Actual Grid Ref: ST528478
Tel: 01749 672550
Open: May to Oct

▲ **Lower Milton Farm,** Lower Milton, Wookey Hole, Wells, Somerset, BA5 1DG
Actual Grid Ref: ST538477
Tel: 01749 675326
Open: All year

Worle

ST3562

▲ **Airport View Holiday Park,** Moor Lane, Worle, Weston-super-Mare, North Somerset, BS24 7LA
Actual Grid Ref: ST351611
Tel: 01934 622168
Open: Mar to Oct

Staffordshire

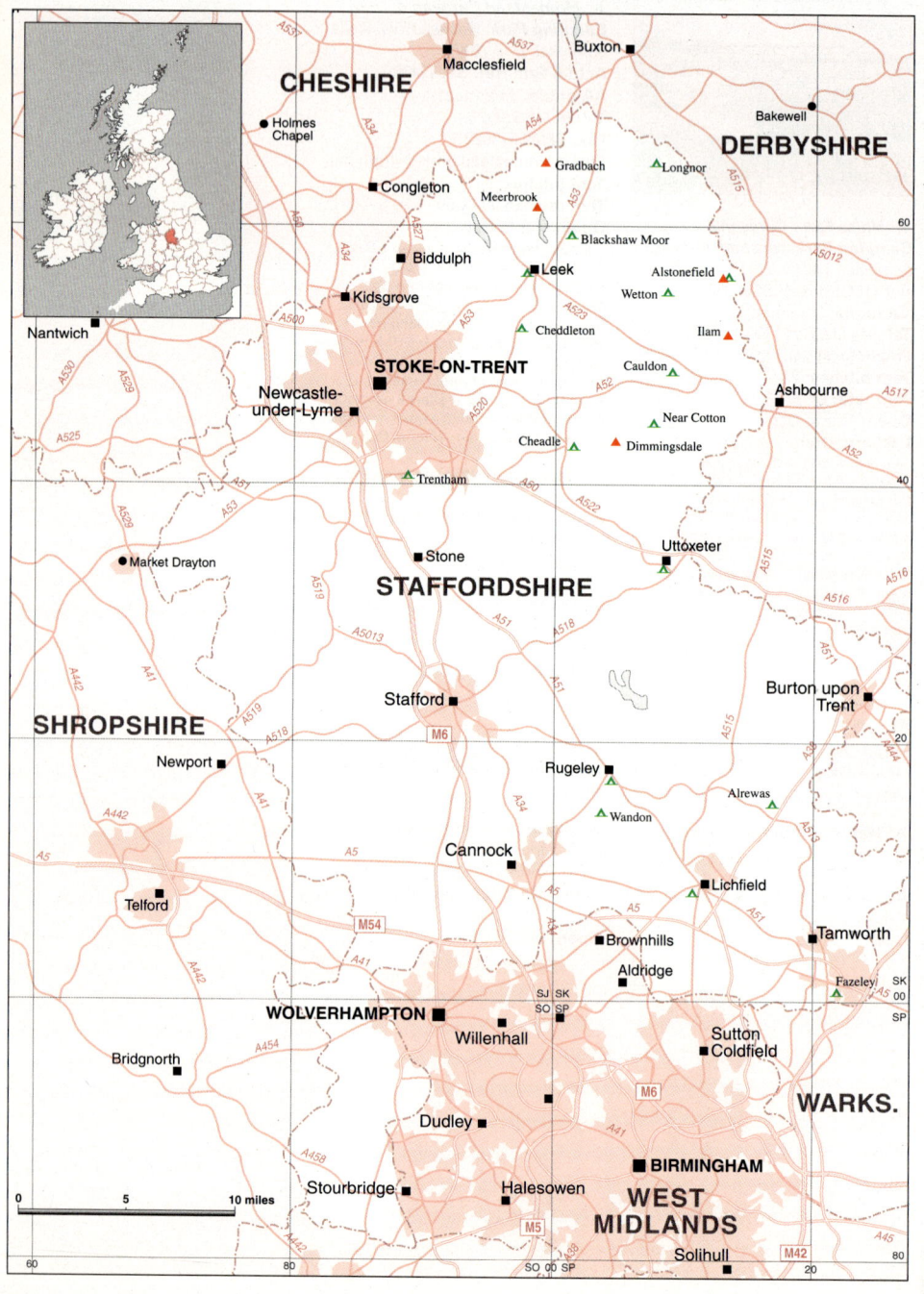

Staffordshire

Alrewas
SK1715

▲ **Woodside Caravan Park,** Fradley Junction, Alrewas, Burton-on-Trent, Staffordshire, DE13 7DN
Actual Grid Ref: SK1398
Tel: 01283 790407
Tent pitches: 10
Tent rate: £7.50-£9.50
Open: Mar to Oct
Last arr: 7pm
Dogs allowed • Electric hook-up • Calor Gas/Camping Gaz • Picnic/barbecue area on site • Children's play area • Showers • Public phone on site
At junction of 2 canals, narrow boats galore and canal-side pub.

▲ **Willowbrook Farm,** Alrewas, Burton-on-Trent, Staffordshire, DE13 7BA
Actual Grid Ref: SK183157
Tel: 01283 790217
Open: All year

Alstonefield
SK1355

▲ **Alstonefield Youth Hostel,** Gypsy Lane, Alstonefield, Derbyshire, DE6 2FZ
Tel: 01335 350212
Fax: 01335 350350
Email: ilam@yha.org.uk
Capacity: 12
Under 18: £7.75
Adults: £11.00
Open: All year, 5.00pm
Family bunk rooms
Self-catering facilities • Lounge • Dining room • Parking • No smoking • Kitchen facilities
Converted from two former barns, the hostel, which overlooks Dovedale, is well-placed for exploring the dales - Dovedale itself, Wolfcote and Beresford Dales and the Manifold Valley.

▲ **The George Hotel,** Alstonefield, Ashbourne, Derbyshire, DE6 2FX
Actual Grid Ref: SK132556
Tel: 01335 310205
Open: All year

Blackshaw Moor
SK0059

▲ **Camping & Caravanning Club Site,** Blackshaw Grange, Blackshaw Moor, Leek, Staffordshire, ST13 8TL
Actual Grid Ref: SK008599
Tel: 01538 300285
Open: All year

Cauldon
SK0749

▲ **The Cross Inn Caravan Park,** The Cross Inn & Restaurant, Cauldon Lowe, Cauldon, Waterhouses, Stoke on Trent, Staffordshire, ST10 3EX
Actual Grid Ref: SK072482
Tel: 01538 308338
Open: Mar to Nov

Cheadle
SK0143

▲ **Quarry Walk Park,** Coppice Lane, Coxden Common, Freehay, Cheadle, Stoke-on-Trent, Staffordshire, ST10 1RQ
Actual Grid Ref: SK045404
Tel: 01538 723495
Open: All year

▲ **Hales Hall Caravan & Camping Park,** Oakamoor Road, Cheadle, Staffordshire, ST10 1BU
Actual Grid Ref: SK020440
Tel: 01538 753305
Fax: 01782 202316
Open: Apr to Nov

Cheddleton
SJ9752

▲ **Glencote Caravan Park,** Station Road, Churnet Valley, Cheddleton, Leek, Staffordshire, ST13 7EE
Actual Grid Ref: SJ982524
Tel: 01538 360745
Fax: 01538 361788
Open: Apr to Oct

Dimmingsdale
SK0443

▲ **Dimmingsdale Youth Hostel,** Little Ranger, Dimmingsdale, Oakmoor, Stoke-on-Trent, Staffordshire, ST10 3AS
Actual Grid Ref: SK052436
Tel: 01538 702304 **Fax:** 01538 702304
Capacity: 20
Under 18: £6.50 **Adults:** £9.25
Open: All year, 5.00pm
Self-catering facilities • Showers • Shop • Lounge • Drying room • Cycle store • Parking • Evening meal available 7.30pm • No smoking • Kitchen facilities • Credit cards accepted
A simple hostel in secluded woods overlooking the Churnet Valley, in a corner of the relatively undiscovered Staffordshire Moorlands.

Fazeley
SK2002

▲ **Drayton Manor Park,** Fazeley, Tamworth, Staffordshire, B78 3TW
Actual Grid Ref: SK195013
Tel: 01827 287979
Fax: 01827 288916
Open: Apr to Oct

Gradbach
SJ9965

▲ **Gradbach Mill Youth Hostel,** Gradbach, Quarnford, Buxton, Derbyshire, SK17 0SU
Actual Grid Ref: SJ993661
Tel: 01260 227625
Fax: 01260 227334
Capacity: 87
Under 18: £6.90
Adults: £10.00
Open: Feb to Nov + New Year, 1.00pm
Family bunk rooms
Self-catering facilities • Television • Showers • Licensed bar • Laundry facilities • Lounge • Drying room • Cycle store • Parking • Evening meal available 7.00pm • No smoking • Kitchen facilities • Breakfast available • Luggage store • Credit cards accepted
An ideal base for climbing the Roaches, or for investigating this lesser known part of the Peaks on foot or on bike. The hostel is in a old mill, on the River Dane, a mere 6 miles from Buxton.

Ilam
SK1350

▲ **Ilam Hall Youth Hostel,** Ilam Hall, Ilam, Ashbourne, Derbyshire, DE6 2AZ
Actual Grid Ref: SK131506
Tel: 01335 350212
Fax: 01335 350350
Email: ilam@yha.org.uk
Capacity: 135
Under 18: £7.75
Adults: £11.00
Open: Feb to Oct, All day
Family bunk rooms
Self-catering facilities • Television • Showers • Licensed bar • Laundry facilities • Lounge • Drying room • Cycle store • Evening meal available 6.00-7.30pm • Facilities for disabled people Category 2 • Kitchen facilities • Breakfast available • Credit cards accepted
A magnificent Victorian Gothic National Trust mansion, beautifully decorated, with formal Italian gardens and open parkland and woodland, on the banks of the River Manifold just 1 mile from Dove Dale.

ENGLAND

Staffordshire • MAP PAGE 158

ENGLAND

Leek
SJ9856

▲ **Birchalls (PF) Ltd,** The Hatcheries, Church Lane, Mount Pleasant, Leek, Staffs, ST13 5ET
Tel: 01538 399552
Open: All year

Lichfield
SK1109

▲ **Cathedral Grange Touring Caravan Park,** Grange Lane, Lichfield, Staffordshire, WS13 8HH
Actual Grid Ref: SK105114
Tel: 01543 251449
Open: Mar to Oct

Longnor
SK0864

▲ **Longnor Wood Over 50s Caravan Park,** Longnor, Buxton, Derbyshire, SK17 0LD
Actual Grid Ref: SK072640
Tel: 01298 83648
Open: Apr to Oct

Meerbrook
SJ9860

▲ **Meerbrook Youth Hostel,** Old School, Meerbrook, Leek, Staffordshire, ST13 8SJ
Actual Grid Ref: SJ989608
Tel: 01538 300148
Email: reservations@yha.org.uk
Capacity: 22
Under 18: £6.50 **Adults:** £9.25
Open: All year, 5.00pm
Self-catering facilities • Showers • Wet weather shelter • Lounge • Drying room • Cycle store • Parking • No smoking • WC • Kitchen facilities
Former school house in the centre of Meerbrook village, within sight of which is the Roaches - a long ridge of millstone grit, popular with climbers.

Near Cotton
SK0646

▲ **The Star Caravan & Camping Park,** Star Road, Near Cotton, Oakamoor, Stoke-on-Trent, ST10 3BN
Actual Grid Ref: SK066456
Tourist Board grade: 3 Star
AA grade: 3 Pennants
Tel: 01538 702256 / 702219
Tent pitches: 60
Tent rate: £6.00-£8.00
Open: Feb to Dec
Last arr: 11.30pm
Dogs allowed • Electric hook-up • Calor Gas/Camping Gaz • Children's play area • Showers • Laundrette on site • Public phone on site • Shop on site • Indoor swimming pool nearby • Golf nearby • Riding nearby • Fishing nearby
Situated off B5417 road, between Leek/Cheadle in Staffordshire. Within 10 miles of the park are market towns of Ashbourne and Uttoxeter (famous for racecourse), with Alton Towers approximately 1 mile away. The nearest public house, Ye Olde Star Inn, offers bar snacks/family room. A variety of eating places within the park.

Rugeley
SK0418

▲ **Silvertrees Caravan Park,** Stafford Brook Road, Penkridge Bank, Rugeley, Staffordshire, WS15 2TX
Tel: 01889 582185
Fax: 01889 582185
Open: Mar to Nov

If you have to cancel your visit to any hostel or campsite, please let them know – it is always possible to make a bed or a pitch available to someone else.

Please respect hostels' policy on smoking. Some hostels do not allow smoking anywhere, some restrict smoking to certain areas.

Trentham
SJ8740

▲ **Trentham Gardens Caravan & Leisure Park,** Trentham Gardens, Stone Road, Trentham, Stoke-on-Trent, ST4 8AX
Actual Grid Ref: SJ863407
Tel: 01782 657519 / 657341
Open: All year

Uttoxeter
SK0933

▲ **Uttoxeter Racecourse Site,** Wood Lane, Uttoxeter, Staffordshire, ST14 8BD
Actual Grid Ref: SK099333
Tel: 01889 564172 / 562561
Open: Mar to Nov

Wandon
SK0314

▲ **Camping & Caravanning Club Site,** Old Youth Hostel, Wandon, Cannock Chase, Rugeley, Staffordshire, WS15 1QW
Actual Grid Ref: SK039145
Tel: 01889 582166
Open: Apr to Oct

Wetton
SK1055

▲ **New House Farm,** Wetton, Ashbourne, Derbyshire, DE6 2AF
Actual Grid Ref: SK108553
Tel: 01335 310204
Open: All year

Stilwell's National Trail Companion

46 Long Distance Footpaths • Where to Stay • Where to Eat

ENGLAND

Other guides may show you where to walk, Stilwell's National Trail Companion shows your where to stay and eat. The perfect companion guide for the British Isles' famous national trails and long distance footpaths, Stilwell's make pre-planning your accommodation easy. It lists B&Bs, hostels, campsites and pubs - in the order they appear along the routes - and includes such vital information as maps, grid references and distance from the path; Tourist Board ratings; the availability of vehicle pick-up, drying facilities and packed lunches. So whether you walk a trail in stages at weekends or in one continuous journey, you'll never be stuck at the end of the day for a hot meal or a great place to sleep.

Enjoy the beauty and adventure of Britain's – and Ireland's – long distance trails with **Stilwell's National Trail Companion**.

Paths in England
Cleveland Way & Tabular Hills Link – Coast to Coast Path – Cotswald Way – Cumbria Way – Dales Way – Essex Way – Greensand Way – Hadrian's Wall – Heart of England Way – Hereward Way – Icknield Way – Macmillan Way – North Downs Way – Oxfordshire Way – Peddars Way and Norfolk Coastal Path – Pennine Way – Ribble Way – The Ridgeway – Shropshire Way – South Downs Way – South West Coast Path – Staffordshire Way – Tarka Trail – Thames Path – Two Moors Way - Vanguard Way – Viking Way – Wayfarer's Walk – Wealdway – Wessex Ridgeway – Wolds Way

Paths in Ireland
Beara Way – Dingle Way – Kerry Way – Ulster Way – Western Way – Wicklow Way

Paths in Scotland
Fife Coastal Walk – Southern Upland Way – Speyside Way – West Highland Way

Paths in Wales
Cambrian Way – Glyndwr's Way – Offa's Dyke Path – Pembrokeshire Coast Path – Wye Valley Walk

£9.95 from all good bookstores (ISBN 1-900861-25-9) or £10.95 (inc p&p) from Stilwell Publishing, 59 Charlotte Road, London EC2A 3QW (020 7739 7179)

Suffolk

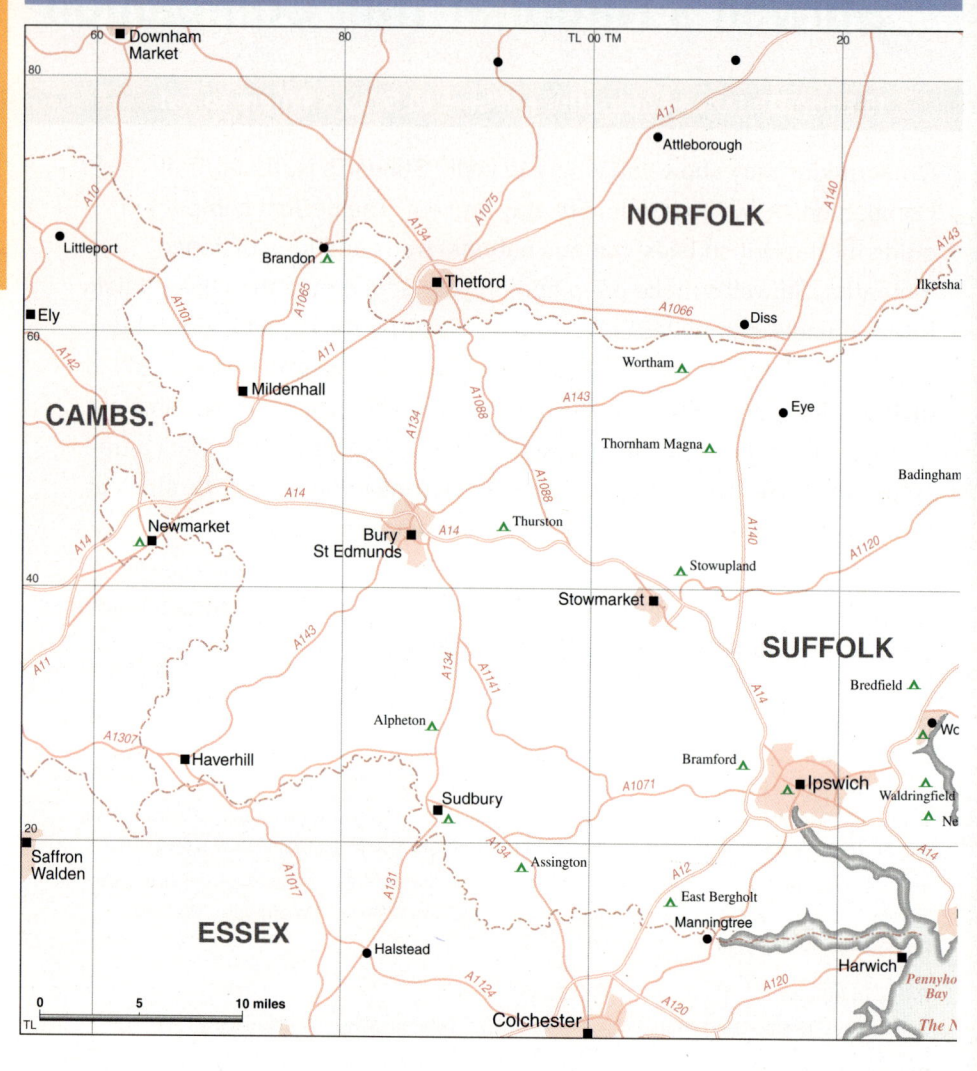

Aldeburgh
TM4656

▲ **Church Farm Caravan Park,** Aldeburgh, Suffolk, IP15 5BH
Actual Grid Ref: TM463569
Tel: 01728 453433
Open: Apr to Oct

Alpheton
TL8850

▲ **Monks Croft,** 8 Bury Road, Alpheton, Sudbury, Suffolk, CO10 9BP
Actual Grid Ref: TL882511
Tel: 01284 828297
Open: Mar to Oct

Assington
TL9338

▲ **Assington Hall,** Assington, Sudbury, Suffolk, CO10 5LQ
Actual Grid Ref: TL936388
Tel: 01787 210314
Open: Mar to Oct

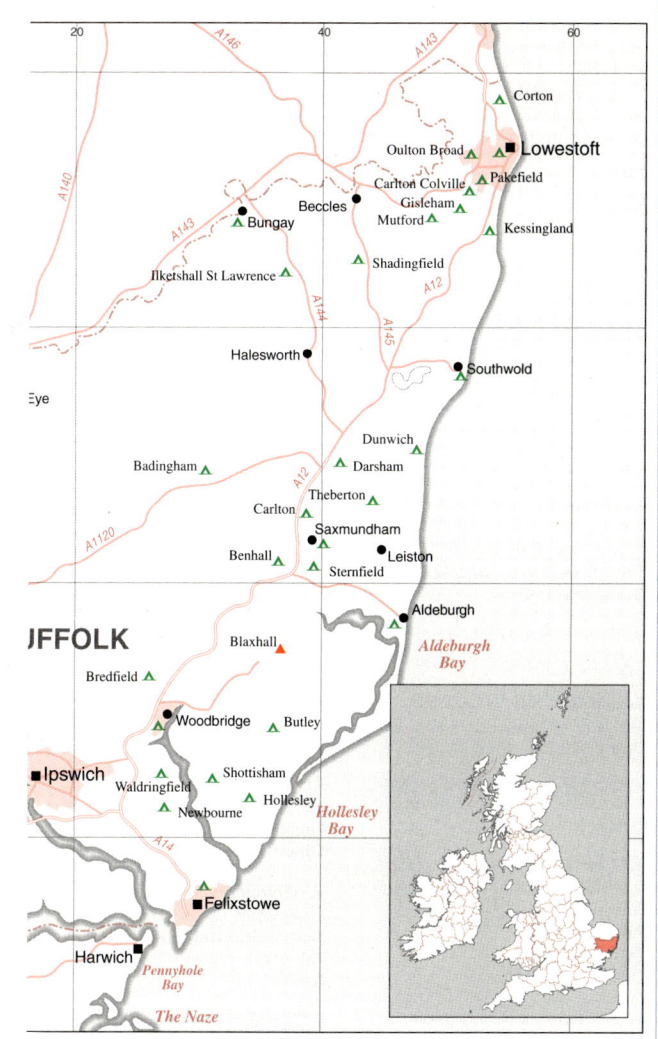

Suffolk

Blaxhall

TM3656

▲ **Blaxhall Youth Hostel,** Heath Walk, Blaxhall, Woodbridge, Suffolk, IP12 2EA
Actual Grid Ref: TM369570
Tel: 01728 688206
Fax: 01728 689191
Capacity: 40
Under 18: £7.75
Adults: £11.00
Open: All year, 5.00pm
Family bunk rooms
Self-catering facilities • Television • Showers • Lounge • Drying room • Security lockers • Cycle store • Parking • Evening meal available 7.00pm • Facilities for disabled people • No smoking • Kitchen facilities • Breakfast available • Credit cards accepted
Traditional hostel, once a village school, offering modest accommodation. RSPB reserves of Minsmere and Havergate nearby. Snape Maltings concert hall 2m.

Bramford

TM1246

▲ **Suffolk Waters Country Park,** Loraine Way, Bramford, Ipswich, Suffolk, IP8 4JS
Actual Grid Ref: TM117485
Tel: 01473 830191
Open: Apr to Oct

Brandon

TL7886

▲ **Riverside Lodge,** 78 High Street, Brandon, Suffolk, IP27 0AU
Tel: 01842 811236
Open: Apr to Oct

Bredfield

TM2652

▲ **Moat Barn Touring Park,** Bredfield, Woodbridge, Suffolk, IP13 6BD
Tel: 01473 737520
Open: Apr to Nov

Bungay

TM3389

▲ **Outney Meadow Caravan Park,** Outney Meadow, Bungay, Suffolk, NR35 1HG
Actual Grid Ref: TM333904
Tel: 01986 892338
Open: All year

Badingham

TM3068

▲ **Colston Hall,** Badingham, Woodbridge, Suffolk, IP13 8LB
Tel: 01728 638175
Fax: 01728 638175
Open: All year

Benhall

TM3760

▲ **Whitearch Touring Caravan Park,** Main Road, Benhall, Saxmundham, Suffolk, IP17 1NA
Actual Grid Ref: TM379610
Tel: 01728 604646 / 603773
Fax: 01728 604646
Open: Apr to Oct

Suffolk • MAP PAGE 162

ENGLAND

Butley
TM3650

▲ **Tangham Campsite,** *Butley, Woodbridge, Suffolk, IP12 3NP*
Actual Grid Ref: TM355485
Tel: 01394 450707
Open: Apr to Jan

Carlton
TM3764

▲ **Lonely Farm Camping & Caravan Site,** *Carlton, Saxmundham, Suffolk, IP17 2QP*
Actual Grid Ref: TM365655
Tel: 01728 663416
Open: Easter to Oct

Carlton Colville
TM5090

▲ **Carlton Manor Caravan Site,** *Chapel Road, Carlton Colville, Lowestoft, Suffolk, NR33 8BL*
Actual Grid Ref: TM506904
Tel: 01502 566511
Fax: 01502 573949
Open: Mar to Oct

Corton
TM5497

▲ **Azure Seas Caravan Park,** *Corton, Lowestoft, Suffolk, NR32 5HN*
Actual Grid Ref: TM544971
Tel: 01502 731403
Open: Mar to Oct

▲ **Church Farm,** *Corton, Lowestoft, NR32 5HX*
Actual Grid Ref: TM538980
Tel: 01502 730359
Open: Mar to Oct

▲ **Taylors Farm,** *Corton, Lowestoft, Suffolk, NR32 5NJ*
Actual Grid Ref: TM529972
Tel: 01502 730241
Open: All year

Darsham
TM4169

▲ **Haw Wood Farm,** *Caravan & Camping Park, Darsham, Saxmundham, Suffolk, IP17 3QT*
Actual Grid Ref: TM424716
Tel: 01986 784248
Open: Apr to Oct

Dunwich
TM4770

▲ **Cliff House,** *Minsmere Road, Dunwich, Saxmundham, Suffolk, IP17 3DQ*
Actual Grid Ref: TM477690
Tel: 01728 648282
Open: Apr to Oct

East Bergholt
TM0735

▲ **The Grange Country Park,** *The Grange, East Bergholt, Colchester, Essex, CO7 6UX*
Actual Grid Ref: TM097352
Tel: 01206 298567 / 298912
Fax: 01206 298770
Open: Feb to Dec

Felixstowe
TM3034

▲ **Peewit Caravan Park,** *Walton Avenue, Felixstowe, Suffolk, IP11 8HB*
Actual Grid Ref: TM288337
Tel: 01394 284511 / 670217
Open: Mar to Oct

▲ **Suffolk Sands Holiday Park,** *Carr Road, Felixstowe, Suffolk, IP11 8TS*
Actual Grid Ref: TM290330
Tel: 01394 273434
Open: Apr to Oct

Gisleham
TM5188

▲ **Chestnut Farm Touring Park,** *Gisleham, Lowestoft, Suffolk, NR33 8EE*
Actual Grid Ref: TM517880
Tel: 01502 740227
Open: Mar to Oct

▲ **Whitehorse Farm Caravans,** *Gisleham, Lowestoft, Suffolk, NR33 8DX*
Tel: 01502 740248
Open: Apr to Oct

Hollesley
TM3444

▲ **The Sandlings Centre (formerly Maple Leaf),** *Lodge Road, Hollesley, Woodbridge, Suffolk, IP12 3NF*
Actual Grid Ref: TM343439
Tel: 01394 411202
Open: Mar to Jan

Ilketshall St Lawrence
TM3783

▲ **The Garage,** *Ilketshall St Lawrence, Beccles, Suffolk, NR34 8WS*
Tel: 01449 612326
Open: Apr to Oct

▲ **The Garage,** *Ilketshall St Lawrence, Beccles, Suffolk, NR34 8LB*
Actual Grid Ref: TM381832
Tel: 01986 781241
Open: Apr to Oct

Ipswich
TM1644

▲ **Low House Touring Caravan Centre,** *Bucklesham Road, Ipswich, IP10 0AU*
Actual Grid Ref: TM225423
Tel: 01473 659437
Fax: 01473 659437
Email: john.e.booth@talk21.com
Tent pitches: 30
Tent rate: £6.50-£8.50
Open: All year
Last arr: 10pm
Dogs allowed • Electric hook-up • Calor Gas/Camping Gaz • Children's play area • Showers • Public phone on site
Camp in beautiful garden with ornamental trees. Abundant wildlife all around.

▲ **Priory Park,** *off Nacton Road, Ipswich, IP10 0JT*
Actual Grid Ref: TM192403
Tel: 01473 727393 / 726373
Fax: 01473 278372
Open: All year

▲ **Orwell Meadows Leisure Park,** *Priory Lane, Ipswich, IP10 0JS*
Actual Grid Ref: TM192402
Tel: 01473 726666
Open: Mar to Jan

Kessingland
TM5286

▲ **Kessingland Beach Holiday Village,** *Beach Road, Kessingland, Lowestoft, Suffolk, NR33 7RN*
Tel: 01502 740636 / 740879
Fax: 01502 740907
Open: Apr to Oct

Hostels and campsites may vary rates – be sure to check when booking.

Suffolk

▲ **Camping & Caravanning Club Site,** Suffolk Wildlife Park, Whites Lane, Kessingland, Lowestoft, Suffolk, NR33 7SL
Actual Grid Ref: TM520860
Tel: 01502 742040
Open: Apr to Oct

▲ **Heathland Beach Caravan Park,** London Road, Kessingland, Lowestoft, Suffolk, NR33 7PJ
Actual Grid Ref: TM535877
Tel: 01502 740337 **Fax:** 01502 742355
Open: Apr to Oct

Lowestoft
TM5493

▲ **North Denes Caravan & Camp Site,** Lowestoft, Suffolk, NR32 1WX
Actual Grid Ref: TM551950
Tel: 01502 573197
Open: Apr to Oct

Mutford
TM4888

▲ **Beulah Hall Caravan Site,** Dairy Lane, Mutford, Beccles, Norfolk, NR34 7QJ
Actual Grid Ref: TM479893
Tel: 01502 476609
Open: Mar to Oct

Newbourne
TM2742

▲ **The Steading,** 10 Ipswich Road, Newbourne, Woodbridge, Suffolk, IP12 4NS
Actual Grid Ref: TM265433
Tel: 01473 736505
Open: Mar to Jan

Newmarket
TL6463

▲ **Camping & Caravanning Club Site,** Rowley Mile Racecourse, Newmarket, Suffolk, CB8 8JL
Actual Grid Ref: TL622625
Tel: 01638 663235 **Open:** May to Sep

Oulton Broad
TM5192

▲ **Broad View Caravans,** Marsh Road, Oulton Broad, Lowestoft, Suffolk, NR33 9JY
Actual Grid Ref: TM516922
Tel: 01502 565587
Open: Apr to Oct

Pakefield
TM5390

▲ **Pakefield Caravan Park,** Arbor Lane, Pakefield, Lowestoft, Suffolk, NR33 7BQ
Tel: 01502 561136
Fax: 01502 539264
Open: Apr to Oct

▲ **Beach Farm Caravan Park,** Arbor Lane, Pakefield, Lowestoft, Suffolk, NR33 7BD
Actual Grid Ref: TM532897
Tel: 01502 572794
Open: Mar to Dec

Saxmundham
TM3863

▲ **Carlton Park Camping Site,** Saxmundham, Suffolk, IP17 1EE
Actual Grid Ref: TM387639
Tel: 01728 604413
Open: Mar to Oct

▲ **Lakeside Leisure Park,** Saxmundham, Suffolk, IP17 2QP
Actual Grid Ref: TM365645
Tel: 01728 603344
Open: Easter to Oct

Shadingfield
TM4384

▲ **Fox County Camping Site,** The Fox Inn, London Road, Shadingfield, Beccles, Suffolk, NR34 8DD
Tel: 01502 575610
Tent pitches: 30
Tent rate: £5.00
Open: All year
Last arr: 10pm
Facilities for disabled people • Dogs allowed • Electric hook-up • Calor Gas/Camping Gaz • Cafe or Takeaway on site • Picnic/barbecue area on site • Children's play area • Showers • Public phone on site • Licensed bar on site Peaceful country site near coast. Good food and beer.

Shottisham
TM3144

▲ **St Margaret's House,** Hollesley Road, Shottisham, Woodbridge, Suffolk, IP12 3HD
Actual Grid Ref: TM322448
Tel: 01394 411247
Open: Apr to Oct

Southwold
TM5076

▲ **The Harbour Camping & Caravan Park,** Ferry Road, Southwold, Suffolk, IP18 6ND
Actual Grid Ref: TM501751
Tel: 01502 722486
Open: Apr to Oct

Sternfield
TM3861

▲ **Marsh Farm Caravan Site,** Sternfield, Saxmundham, Suffolk, IP17 1HW
Actual Grid Ref: TM387608
Tel: 01728 602168
Open: Apr to Oct

Stowupland
TM0659

▲ **Orchard View Caravan Park,** Thorney Green, Stowupland, Stowmarket, Suffolk, IP14 4BJ
Actual Grid Ref: TM067597
Tel: 01449 613249
Open: Apr to Oct

Sudbury
TL8741

▲ **Willowmere Caravan Park,** Bures Road, Little Cornard, Sudbury, Suffolk, CO10 0NN
Actual Grid Ref: TL887389
Tel: 01787 375559
Open: Mar to Oct

Theberton
TM4366

▲ **Cakes & Ale Park,** Abbey Lane, Theberton, Leiston, Suffolk, IP16 4TE
Actual Grid Ref: TM431637
Tel: 01728 831655 / 01473 736650
Fax: 01473 736270
Open: Apr to Oct

Thornham Magna
TM1071

▲ **Red House Farm,** Thornham Magna, Eye, Suffolk, IP23 8EX
Actual Grid Ref: TM097713
Tel: 01379 783262
Open: All year

Suffolk • MAP PAGE 162

Thurston
TL9264

▲ **The Dell Touring Park,** Beyton Road, Thurston, Bury St Edmunds, Suffolk, IP31 3RB
Actual Grid Ref: TL930640
Tel: 01359 270121
Open: All year

Waldringfield
TM2744

▲ **Moon & Sixpence,** Newbourn Road, Waldringfield, Woodbridge, Suffolk, IP12 4PP
Actual Grid Ref: TM262456
Tel: 01473 736650
Open: Apr to Oct

Woodbridge
TM2649

▲ **Staverton Caravan Park,** Wantisden, Woodbridge, Suffolk, IP12 3PJ
Actual Grid Ref: TM354516
Tel: 01394 460783
Open: Feb to Oct

Wortham
TM0776

▲ **Honeypot Camp & Caravan Park,** Wortham, Eye, Suffolk, IP22 1PW
Actual Grid Ref: TM085772
Tel: 01379 783312
Fax: 01379 78233
Open: Apr to Oct

Surrey

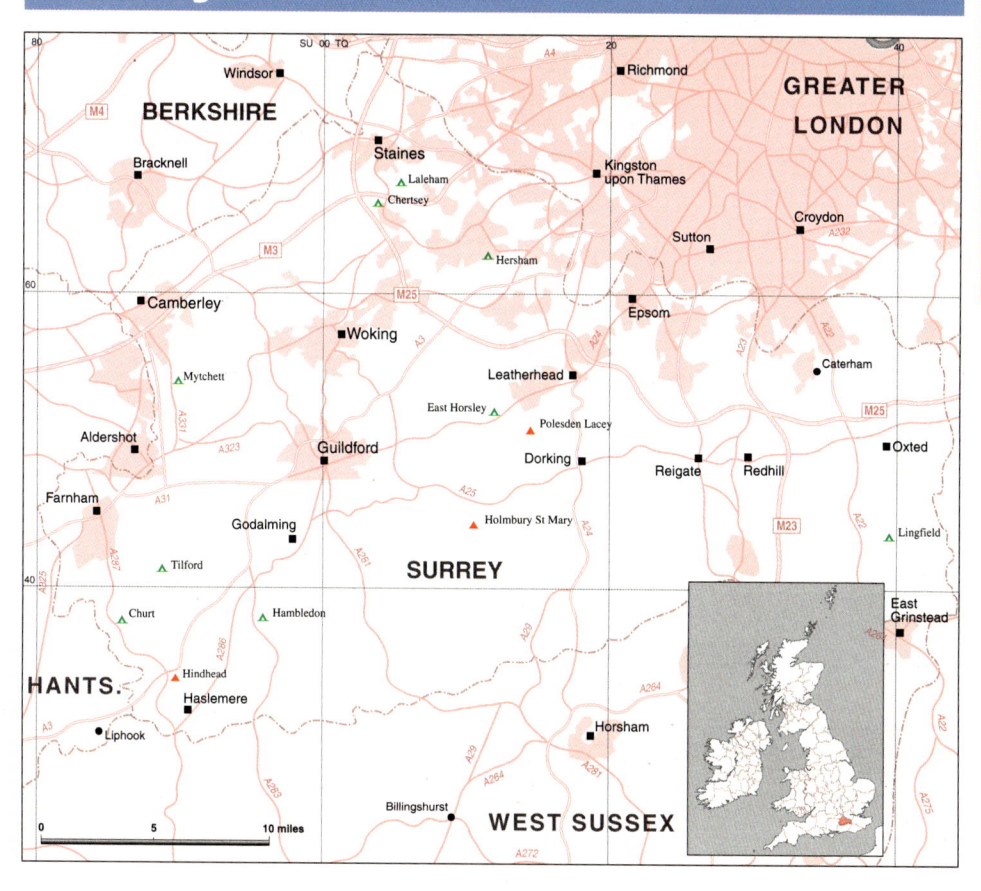

Chertsey

TQ0366

▲ **Camping & Caravanning Club Site,** Bridge Road, Chertsey, Surrey, KT16 8JX
Actual Grid Ref: TQ052667
Tel: 01932 562405
Open: All year

Churt

SU8538

▲ **Symondstone Farm,** Churt, Farnham, Surrey, GU10 2QL
Actual Grid Ref: SU845389
Tel: 01428 712090
Open: Apr to Oct

East Horsley

TQ0952

▲ **Camping & Caravanning Club Site,** Oackham Road North, East Horsley, Leatherhead, Surrey, KT24 6PE
Actual Grid Ref: TQ083552
Tel: 01483 283273
Open: Mar to Oct

Hambledon

SU9638

▲ **The Merry Harriers,** Hambledon, Godalming, Surrey, GU8 4DR
Tel: 01428 682883
Open: All year

Hersham

TQ1164

▲ **Camping & Caravanning Club Site,** Fieldcommon Lane, Hersham, Walton-on-Thames, Surrey, KT12 3QG
Tel: 01932 220392
Open: Mar to Nov

If you have to cancel your visit to any hostel or campsite, please let them know – it is always possible to make a bed or a pitch available to someone else.

Surrey • MAP PAGE 167

If you have to cancel your visit to any hostel or campsite, please let them know – it is always possible to make a bed or a pitch available to someone else.

Hindhead

SU8836

▲ **Hindhead Youth Hostel,** *Highcoombe Bottom, Bowlhead Green, Hindhead, Godalming, Surrey, GU7 6NS*
Actual Grid Ref: SU892368
Tel: 01428 604285
Fax: 01428 604285
Email: reservations@yha.org.uk
Capacity: 16
Under 18: £5.25
Adults: £7.50
Open: All year, 5.00pm
Self-catering facilities • Lounge • No smoking • Kitchen facilities
A superbly simple hostel, set in the peaceful haven of the Devil's Punchbowl, converted from three National Trust cottages and refurbished to a high standard.

Holmbury St Mary

TQ1144

▲ **Holmbury St Mary Youth Hostel,** *Radnor Lane, Holmbury St Mary, Dorking, Surrey, RH5 6NW*
Actual Grid Ref: TQ104450
Tel: 01306 730777
Fax: 01306 730933
Email: holmbury@yha.org.uk
Capacity: 52
Under 18: £6.90
Adults: £10.00
Open: Feb to Nov, 5.00pm
Camping
Self-catering facilities • Showers • Wet weather shelter • Lounge • Drying room • Cycle store • Evening meal available 7.00pm • No smoking • Kitchen facilities • Breakfast available • Credit cards accepted
Set in its own 5,000 acres of woodland grounds, this purpose-built hostel offers tranquil beauty among the Surrey Hills.

Some hostels and campsites impose restrictions on size and type of groups they accept (e.g. not permitting single-sex groups). Always phone to enquire before booking.

Laleham

TQ0468

▲ **Laleham Park Camping Site,** *Thameside, Laleham, Staines, TW18 1SH*
Tel: 01932 564149
Open: Apr to Sep

Lingfield

TQ3843

▲ **Long Acres Caravan & Camping Park,** *Newchapel Road, Lingfield, Surrey, RH7 6LE*
Actual Grid Ref: TQ368424
Tel: 01342 833205 / 884307
Open: All year

Mytchett

SU8854

▲ **Basingstoke Canal Visitor Centre,** *Mytchett Place Road, Mytchett, Camberley, Surrey, GU16 6DD*
Tel: 01252 370073
Open: All year

Polesden Lacey

TQ1352

▲ **Tanners Hatch Youth Hostel,** *Polesden Lacey, Ranmore Road, Dorking, Surrey, RH5 6BE*
Actual Grid Ref: TQ140515
Tel: 01306 877964
Fax: 01306 877964
Email: tanners@yha.org.uk
Capacity: 25
Under 18: £5.75
Adults: £8.50
Open: Jan to Dec + New Year, 5.00pm
Camping
Self-catering facilities • Showers • Lounge • Cycle store • No smoking • WC • Kitchen facilities • Credit cards accepted
A renovated black and white cottage in the Surrey Hills Area of Outstanding Natural Beauty. Facilities are basic, and taking a torch is recommended. The lounge has an open fire.

Tilford

SU8743

▲ **Tilford Touring,** *Tilford, Farnham, Surrey, GU10 2DF*
Actual Grid Ref: SU878424
Tel: 01252 792199
Fax: 01252 781027
Open: All year

Stilwell's Britain Cycleway Companion

ENGLAND

23 Long Distance Cycleways • Where to Stay • Where to Eat

County Cycleways – Sustrans Routes

The first guide of its kind, Stilwell's Britain Cycleway Companion makes planning accommodation for your cycling trip easy. It lists B&Bs, hostels, campsites and pubs– in the order they appear along the selected cycleways – allowing the cyclist to book ahead. No more hunting for a room, a hot meal or a cold drink after a long day in the saddle. Stilwell's gives descriptions of the featured routes and includes such relevant information as maps, grid references and distance from route; Tourist Board ratings; and the availability of drying facilities and packed lunches. No matter which route – or part of a route – you decide to ride, let the Cycleway Companion show you where to sleep and eat.

As essential as your tyre pump – the perfect cycling companion:
Stilwell's Britain Cycleway Companion.

Cycleways – Sustrans
Carlisle to Inverness – Clyde to Forth - Devon Coast to Coast - Hull to Harwich – Kingfisher Cycle Trail - Lon Las Cymru – Sea to Sea (C2C) – Severn and Thames - West Country Way – White Rose Cycle Route

Cycleways – County
Round Berkshire Cycle Route – Cheshire Cycleway – Cumbria Cycleway – Essex Cycle Route – Icknield Way - Lancashire Cycleway – Leicestershire County Cycleway – Oxfordshire Cycleway – Reivers Cycle Route – South Downs Way - Surrey Cycleway – Wiltshire Cycleway – Yorkshire Dales Cycleway

£9.95 from all good bookstores (ISBN 1-900861-26-7) or £10.95 (inc p&p) from Stilwell Publishing, 59 Charlotte Road, London EC2A 3QW (020 7739 7179)

East Sussex

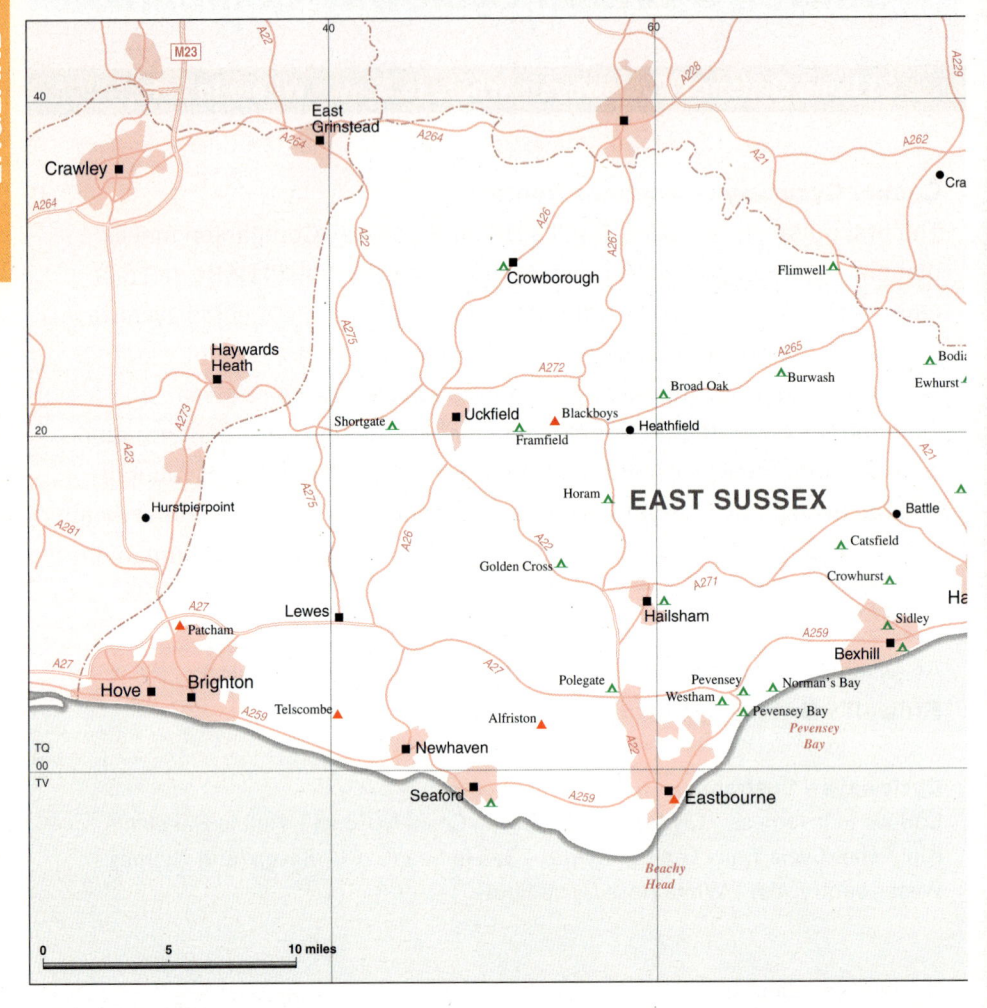

Alfriston

TQ5103

▲ **Alfriston Youth Hostel,** Frog Firle, Alfriston, Polegate, East Sussex, BN26 5TT
Actual Grid Ref: TQ518019
Tel: 01323 870423
Fax: 01323 870615
Email: alfriston@yha.org.uk
Capacity: 68
Under 18: £6.90
Adults: £10.00
Open: Feb to Dec + New Year (x Sun), 5.00pm
Self-catering facilities • Showers • Wet weather shelter • Lounge • Drying room • Parking • Evening meal available 6.30pm • WC • Kitchen facilities • Breakfast available • Credit cards accepted
A comfortable Sussex country house dating from 1530, set in Cuckmere Valley with views over river and Litlington.

Bexhill-on-Sea

TQ7308

▲ **Kloofs Caravan Park,** Sandhurst Lane, Whydown, Bexhill-on-Sea, East Sussex, TN39 4RG
Tel: 01424 842839
Open: Mar to Jan

Stilwell's Hostels & Camping 2002

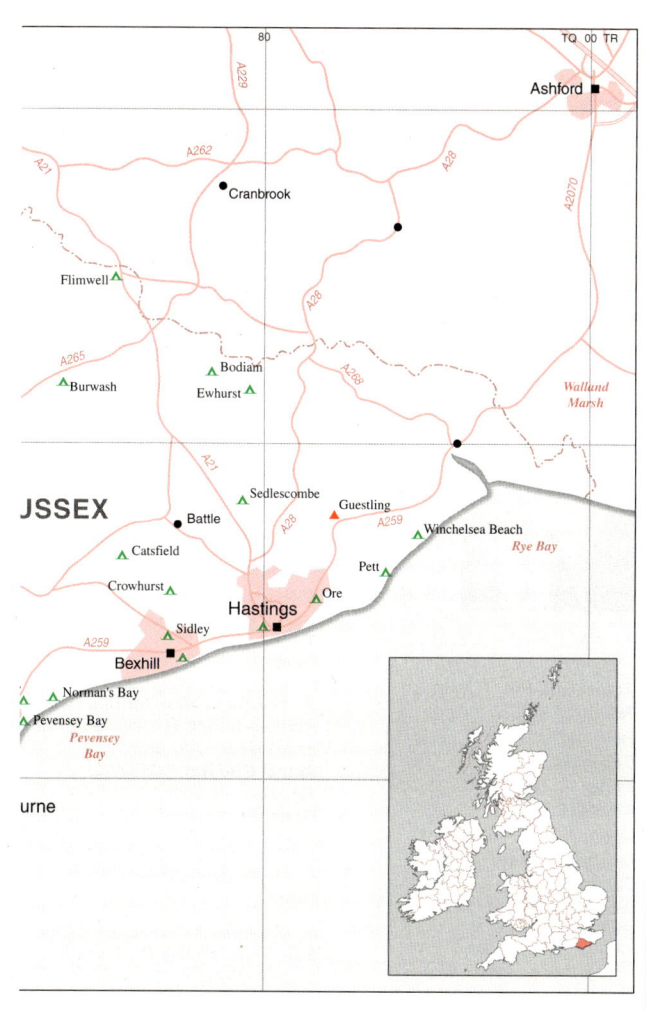

East Sussex

Bodiam
TQ7825

▲ **Park Farm Caravan & Camping Park,** Park Farm, Bodiam, Robertsbridge, East Sussex, TN32 5XA
Actual Grid Ref: TQ767244
Tel: 01580 830514
Fax: 01580 830514
Open: Mar to Sept

Broad Oak (Heathfield)
TQ6022

▲ **Greenview Caravan Park,** Broad Oak, Heathfield, East Sussex, TN21 8RT
Actual Grid Ref: TQ605223
Tel: 01435 863531
Open: Apr to Oct

Burwash
TQ6724

▲ **Park Farm,** Burwash, Etchingham, East Sussex, TN19 7DR
Actual Grid Ref: TQ669233
Tel: 01435 882358
Open: All year

Catsfield
TQ7214

▲ **Senlac Park Caravan & Camping Site,** Main Road, Catsfield, Battle, East Sussex, TN33 9DU
Actual Grid Ref: TQ718152
Tel: 01424 773969 / 752590
Open: Mar to Oct

Crowborough
TQ5230

▲ **Camping & Caravanning Club Site,** Goldsmith Recreation Ground, Crowborough, East Sussex, TN6 2TN
Actual Grid Ref: TQ520315
Tel: 01892 664827
Open: Feb to Dec

Crowhurst
TQ7612

▲ **Brakes Coppice Park,** Forewood Lane, Crowhurst, Battle, East Sussex, TN33 9AB
Actual Grid Ref: TQ764131
Tel: 01424 830322
Open: Mar to Oct

Blackboys
TQ5220

▲ **Blackboys Youth Hostel,** Blackboys, Uckfield, East Sussex, TN22 5HU
Actual Grid Ref: TQ521215
Tel: 01825 890607 **Fax:** 01825 890304
Capacity: 29
Under 18: £6.50
Adults: £9.25
Open: All year, 5.00pm
Camping

Self-catering facilities • Showers • Laundry facilities • Lounge • Drying room • Cycle store • Parking • No smoking • WC • Kitchen facilities • Luggage store • Credit cards accepted

This rustic wooden cabin in a deciduous sylvan setting offers good basic accommodation with a cosy open fire, spacious lounge/dining room & kitchen.

Hostels and campsites may vary rates – be sure to check when booking.

East Sussex • MAP PAGE 170

ENGLAND

Eastbourne
TQ5900

▲ **Eastbourne Youth Hostel**, East Dean Road, Eastbourne, East Sussex, BN20 8ES
Actual Grid Ref: TV588990
Tel: 01323 721081
Fax: 01323 721081
Capacity: 32
Under 18: £6.90
Adults: £10.00
Open: All year, 5.00pm
Family bunk rooms
Self-catering facilities • Showers • Lounge • Dining room • Drying room • Cycle store • Parking Limited • No smoking • WC • Kitchen facilities • Credit cards accepted
Former golf clubhouse on South Downs, 450 ft above sea level with sweeping views across Eastbourne & Pevensey Bay.

Ewhurst
TQ7924

▲ **Lordine Court Caravan Park**, Ewhurst Green, Ewhurst, Staple Cross, Robertsbridge, East Sussex, TN32 5TS
Actual Grid Ref: TQ799225
Tel: 01580 830209
Fax: 01550 830091
Open: Apr to Oct

Flimwell
TQ7131

▲ **Cedar Gables**, Hasting Road, Flimwell, Wadhurst, E. Sussex, TN5 7QA
Actual Grid Ref: TQ695337
Tel: 01892 890566
Fax: 01892 890566
Tent pitches: 15
Tent rate: £5.50
Open: All year
Last arr: 9.30pm
Dogs welcome • Electric hook-up • Picnic/barbecue area on site • Children's play area • Showers
Small farm close to many NT properties and Bewl Water.

You are advised to book in advance for periods of high demand – the Summer months, Half Term holidays and public holidays.

Framfield
TQ4920

▲ **Honeys Green Farm Caravan Park**, Easons Green, Framfield, Uckfield, East Sussex, TN22 5RE
Tel: 01825 840334
Open: Apr to Oct

Golden Cross
TQ5312

▲ **The Old Mill Caravan Park**, Chalvington Road, Golden Cross, Hailsham, East Sussex, BN27 3SS
Actual Grid Ref: TQ537124
Tel: 01825 872532
Open: Apr to Oct

Guestling
TQ8515

▲ **Hastings Youth Hostel**, Guestling Hall, Rye Road, Guestling, Hastings, East Sussex, TN35 4LP
Actual Grid Ref: TQ848133
Tel: 01424 812373
Fax: 01424 812373
Capacity: 52
Under 18: £6.90
Adults: £10.00
Open: Jan to Dec, 5.00pm
Family bunk rooms
Camping
Self-catering facilities • Wet weather shelter • Lounge • Games room • Drying room • Cycle store • Parking 12 cars • Evening meal available 7.00pm • WC • Kitchen facilities • Breakfast available • Credit cards accepted
Victorian house in four acres of grounds with its own small lake and leafy woodland footpaths leading to nearby country park. Hastings town & beach only 4 miles away.

Hailsham
TQ5809

▲ **Chicheley Farm**, Hempstead Lane, Hailsham, East Sussex, BN27 3PR
Tel: 01323 841253
Open: Easter to Nov

Hostels and campsites may vary rates – be sure to check when booking.

Hastings
TQ8110

▲ **Shear Barn Holiday Park**, Barley Lane, Hastings, East Sussex, TN35 5DX
Actual Grid Ref: TQ842107
Tel: 01424 423583 / 716474
Fax: 01424 718740
Open: Mar to Jan

▲ **Stalkhurst Caravan and Camping Site**, Ivyhouse Lane, Hastings, East Sussex, TN35 4NN
Actual Grid Ref: TQ829129
Tel: 01424 439015
Open: Mar to Jan

Horam
TQ5717

▲ **Horam Manor Touring Park**, Horam, Heathfield, East Sussex, TN21 0YD
Actual Grid Ref: TQ576173
Tel: 01435 813662
Open: Mar to Oct

▲ **Woodland View Touring Park**, Horebeech Lane, Horam, Heathfield, East Sussex, TN21 0HR
Actual Grid Ref: TQ580170
Tel: 01435 813597
Open: Apr to Oct

Norman's Bay
TQ6905

▲ **Camping & Caravanning Club Site**, Norman's Bay, Pevensey, East Sussex, BN24 6PP
Actual Grid Ref: TQ682055
Tel: 01323 761190
Open: Mar to Oct

Ore
TQ8311

▲ **Spindlewood Country Holiday Park**, Bricklands Farm, Rock Lane, Ore, Hastings, East Sussex, TN35 4JN
Actual Grid Ref: TQ836119
Tel: 01424 720825
Email: holidays@spindlewood.co.uk
Open: Mar to Oct

Stilwell's Hostels & Camping 2002

MAP PAGE 170 • **East Sussex**

Patcham

TQ3008

▲ **Brighton Youth Hostel,** Patcham Place, London Road, Patcham, Brighton, East Sussex, BN1 8YD
Actual Grid Ref: TQ300088
Tel: 01273 556196
Fax: 01273 509366
Email: brighton@yha.org.uk
Capacity: 84
Under 18: £6.90 **Adults:** £10.00
Open: Feb to Oct and New Year, 1pm to 11pm
Self-catering facilities • Television • Showers • Laundry facilities • Lounge • Games room • Security lockers • Cycle store • Evening meal available 6.30 to 7.30 • Kitchen facilities • Breakfast available • Credit cards accepted
Splendid country house with Queen Anne front, on the edge of Brighton and the South Downs.

Pett

TQ8714

▲ **Carters Farm,** Elm Lane, Pett, Hastings, East Sussex, TN35 4JD
Actual Grid Ref: TQ887144
Tel: 01424 813206 / 812244
Open: Mar to Oct

Pevensey

TQ6404

▲ **Castle View Camping Site,** Eastbourne Road, Pevensey, East Sussex, BN24 6DT
Actual Grid Ref: TQ646032
Tel: 01323 763038
Open: Mar to Oct

Pevensey Bay

TQ6504

▲ **Bayview Caravan & Camping Park,** Old Martello Road, Pevensey Bay, Pevensey, East Sussex, BN24 6DX
Actual Grid Ref: TQ648028
Tourist Board grade: 5 Star
AA grade: 3 Pennants
Tel: 01323 768688 **Fax:** 01323 769263
Email: bayviewcaravanpark@tesco.net
Tent pitches:
Tent rate: £8.50-£13.15

Open: Apr to Oct
Last arr: 10pm
Dogs allowed • Electric hook-up • Calor Gas/Camping Gaz • Children's play area • Showers • Laundrette on site • Public phone on site • Shop on site
Award-winning park next to the beach near Eastbourne's Sunshine Coast.

▲ **Cannon Camping,** Eastbourne Road, Pevensey Bay, East Sussex, BN24 6DT
Actual Grid Ref: TQ647033
Tel: 01323 764634
Open: Mar to Oct

Polegate

TQ5804

▲ **Peel House Farm Caravan Park,** Polegate, East Sussex, BN26 6QX
Actual Grid Ref: TQ589072
Tel: 01323 845629
Open: Apr to Oct

Seaford

TV4898

▲ **Buckle Caravan & Camping Park,** Marine Parade, Seaford, East Sussex, BN25 2QR
Actual Grid Ref: TV467998
Tel: 01323 897801
Open: Mar to Jan

Sedlescombe

TQ7719

▲ **Whydown Farm Caravan Park,** Crazy Lane, Sedlescombe, Battle, East Sussex, TN33 0QT
Actual Grid Ref: TQ782170
Tel: 01424 870147
Fax: 01424 870147
Email: info@crazylane.co.uk
Tent pitches: 36
Tent rate: £8.00-£9.00
Open: Mar to Oct
Last arr: 10pm
Facilities for disabled people • Dogs allowed • Electric hook-up • Calor Gas/Camping Gaz • Showers • Laundrette on site • Public phone on site • Shop on site
Situated in a sun trap valley, heart of 1066 country.

Shortgate

TQ4915

▲ **Bluebell Holiday Park,** The Broyle, Shortgate, Ringmer, Lewes, East Sussex, BN8 6PJ
Tel: 01825 840407
Open: May to Oct

Sidley

TQ7409

▲ **Cobbs Hill Farm Caravan and Camping Park,** Watermill Lane, Sidley, Bexhill-on-Sea, East Sussex, TN39 5JA
Actual Grid Ref: REF1309
Tel: 01424 213460
Fax: 01424 221358
Tent pitches: 45
Tent rate: £4.60-£5.30
Open: Apr to Oct
Last arr: 10pm
Dogs allowed • Electric hook-up • Calor Gas/Camping Gaz • Children's play area • Showers • Laundrette on site • Laundrette on site • Shop on site
Quiet country site, large field for tents. Nearby Hastings, Battle.

Telscombe

TQ4003

▲ **Telscombe Youth Hostel,** Bank Cottages, Telscombe, Lewes, East Sussex, BN7 3HZ
Actual Grid Ref: TQ405033
Tel: 01273 301357
Fax: 01273 301357
Email: reservations@yha.org.uk
Capacity: 22
Under 18: £6.50
Adults: £9.25
Open: All year, 5.00pm
Self-catering facilities • Showers • Lounge • Drying room • Cycle store • Parking By arrangement • No smoking • WC • Kitchen facilities
Three 200-year-old cottages combined into one hostel, next to the Norman church in a small unspoilt village in Sussex Downs Area of Outstanding Natural Beauty.

Westham

TQ6304

▲ **Fairfields Farm,** Westham, Pevensey, East Sussex, BN24 5NG
Actual Grid Ref: TQ638037
Tel: 01323 763165
Open: Apr to Oct

Winchelsea Beach

TQ9116

▲ **Rye Bay Caravan Park,** Pett Level Road, Winchelsea Beach, East Sussex, TN36 4NE
Tel: 01797 226340
Open: Mar to Oct

West Sussex

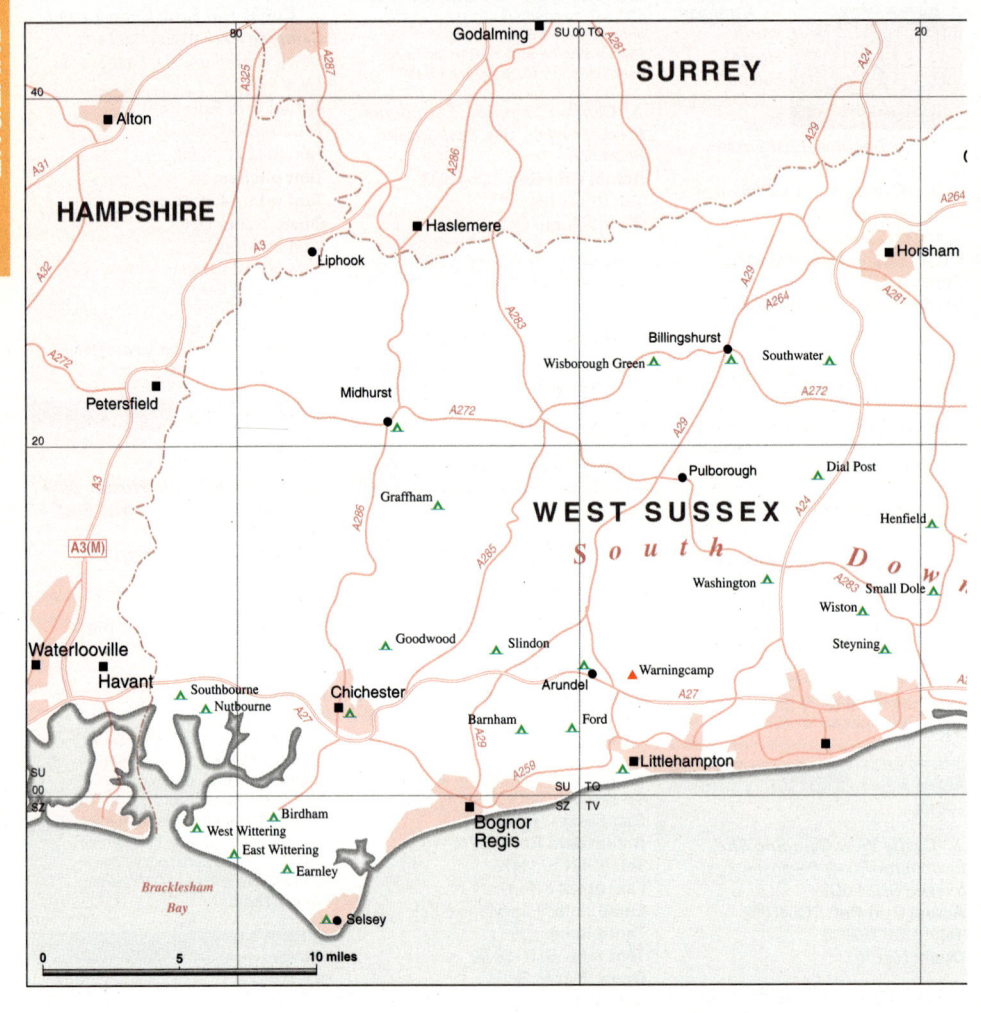

Arundel
TQ0106

▲ **Maynard's Caravan & Camping Park,** Crossbush, Arundel, West Sussex, BN18 9PQ
Actual Grid Ref: TQ029062
Tel: 01903 882075
Open: All year

Barnham
SU9603

▲ **The Lillies Nursery & Caravan Site,** Yapton Road, Barnham, Bognor Regis , West Sussex, PO22 0AY
Actual Grid Ref: SU964050
Tel: 01243 552081
Open: Mar to Oct

Billingshurst
TQ0825

▲ **Limeburner Arms Site,** Newbridge, Billingshurst, West Sussex, RH14 9JA
Actual Grid Ref: TQ073255
Tel: 01403 782311
Open: Apr to Oct

West Sussex

Dial Post

TQ1519

▲ **Honeybridge Park,** *Dial Post, Horsham, West Sussex, RH13 8NX*
Actual Grid Ref: TQ152183
AA grade: 4 Pennants
Tel: 01403 710923
Fax: 01403 710923
Email: enquiries@
honeybridgepark.free-online.co.uk
Tent pitches: 100
Tent rate: £5.00-£9.50
Open: All year
Last arr: 10pm
Facilities for disabled people • Dogs allowed • Electric hook-up • Calor Gas/Camping Gaz • Picnic/barbecue area on site • Children's play area • Showers • Laundrette on site • Public phone on site • Shop on site • Baby care facilities
A delightfully situated spacious 15 acre park. Adjacent to woodland.

Earnley

SZ8196

▲ **Red House Farm Camping Site,** *Bookers Lane, Earnley, Chichester, West Sussex, PO20 7JG*
Actual Grid Ref: SZ815979
Tel: 01243 512959
Fax: 01243 514216
Email:
redhousecamping@talk21.com
Tent pitches: 25
Tent rate: £8.00-£10.00
Open: Apr to Oct
Last arr: 9pm
Dogs allowed • Electric hook-up • Calor Gas/Camping Gaz • Children's play area • Showers • Public phone on site
Quiet country site on working farm 1 mile from beach. Families and couples only.

East Wittering

SZ8096

▲ **The Gees Camp,** *127 Stock Lane, East Wittering, Chichester, West Sussex, PO20 8NY*
Actual Grid Ref: SZ805969
Tel: 01243 670223
Open: Mar to Oct

▲ **Stubcroft Farm Caravanning and Camping,** *Stubcroft Lane, East Wittering, Chichester, West Sussex, PO20 8PJ*
Tel: 01243 671469
Open: All year

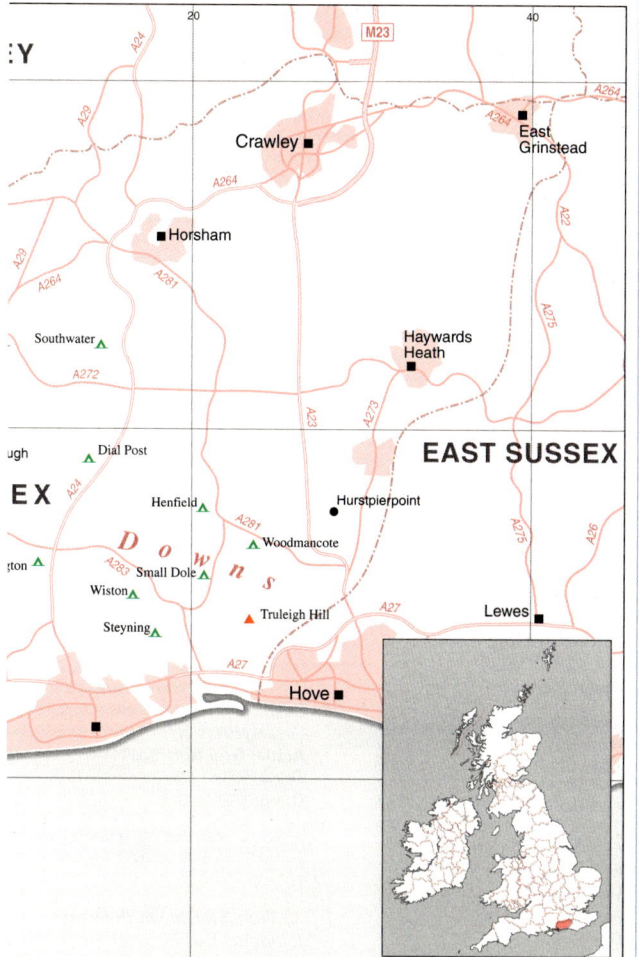

Birdham

SU8200

▲ **Ellscott Park,** *Sidlesham Lane, Birdham, Chichester, West Sussex, PO20 7QL*
Actual Grid Ref: SZ830996
Tel: 01243 512003
Open: Mar to Oct

Chichester

SU8604

▲ **Southern Leisure Lakeside Village,** *Vinnetrow Road, Chichester, West Sussex, PO20 6LB*
Actual Grid Ref: SU878039
Tel: 01243 787715
Open: Apr to Oct

West Sussex • MAP PAGE 174

Ford
SU9903

▲ **Ship & Anchor Marina,** Heywood & Brett Ltd, Ford, Arundel, West Sussex, BN18 0BJ
Actual Grid Ref: TQ002040
Tel: 01243 551262
Fax: 01243 555256
Open: Mar to Oct

Goodwood
SU8808

▲ **Caravan Club Site,** Goodwood Racecourse, Goodwood, Chichester, West Sussex, PO18 0PX
Actual Grid Ref: SU885111
Tel: 01243 774486
Open: Easter to Sep

▲ **Goodwood Racecourse Caravan Park,** Goodwood, Chichester, West Sussex, PO18 0PS
Actual Grid Ref: SU885110
Tel: 01243 755033
Email: racing@goodwood.co.uk
Open: Easter to Sep

Graffham
SU9217

▲ **Camping & Caravanning Club Site,** Great Bury, Graffham, Petworth, West Sussex, GU28 0QJ
Actual Grid Ref: SU941187
Tel: 01798 867476
Open: Mar to Oct

Henfield
TQ2116

▲ **Harwoods Farm,** West End Lane, Henfield, West Sussex, BN5 9RF
Actual Grid Ref: TQ194154
Tel: 01273 492820
Open: Mar to Oct

Littlehampton
TQ0202

▲ **White Rose Touring Park,** Mill Lane, Wick, Littlehampton, West Sussex, BN17 7PH
Actual Grid Ref: TQ027042
Tel: 01903 716176
Fax: 01903 732671
Email: snowdondavid@hotmail.com
Tent pitches: 52
Tent rate: £8.00-£12.00
Open: Mar to Jan
Last arr: 10.30pm
*Facilities for disabled people • Dogs allowed • Electric hook-up • Calor Gas/Camping Gaz • Children's play area • Showers • Laundrette on site • Public phone on site • Shop on site
Friendly family site close to sandy beaches and South Downs.*

▲ **Rutherford's Touring Park,** Cornfield Close, Worthing Road, Littlehampton, West Sussex, BN17 6LD
Actual Grid Ref: TQ035035
Tel: 01903 714240
Open: All year

Midhurst
SU8821

▲ **Oakhurst Cottage,** Carron Lane, Midhurst, W. Sussex, GU29 9LF
Tel: 01730 813523
Open: May to Sep

Nutbourne (Horsham)
SU7805

▲ **Loveders Farm Caravan & Camp Site,** Inlands Road, Nutbourne, Chichester, West Sussex, PO10 8JH
Actual Grid Ref: SU775058
Tel: 01243 372368
Open: Mar to Jan

Selsey
SZ8593

▲ **Warner Farm Touring Park,** Warner Lane, Selsey, Chichester, West Sussex, PO20 9EL
Actual Grid Ref: SZ838937
Tel: 01243 604121 / 604499
Fax: 01243 604499
Open: Mar to Oct

Slindon
SU9608

▲ **Camping & Caravanning Club Site,** Slindon Park, Slindon, Arundel, West Sussex, BN18 0RG
Tel: 01243 814387
Open: Mar to Sep

All details shown are as supplied by hostels and campsites in Autumn 2000.

Small Dole
TQ2112

▲ **Farmhouse Caravan & Camping Site,** Tottington Drive, Small Dole, Henfield, Sussex, BN5 9XZ
Actual Grid Ref: TQ221129
Tel: 01273 493157
Open: Mar to Nov

Southbourne
SU7705

▲ **Camping & Caravanning Club Site,** 343 Main Road, Southbourne, Emsworth, Hants, PO10 8JH
Actual Grid Ref: SU774056
Tel: 01243 373202
Open: All year

Southwater
TQ1525

▲ **Raylands Caravan Park,** Jackrells Lane, Southwater, Horsham, West Sussex, RH13 7DH
Actual Grid Ref: TQ170265
Tel: 01403 730218 / 731822
Open: Mar to Oct

Steyning
TQ1711

▲ **The White House,** Sheep Pen Lane, Newham Lane, Steyning, Sussex, BN44 3LR
Actual Grid Ref: TQ171107
Tel: 01903 813737
Open: Mar to Oct

Truleigh Hill
TQ2210

▲ **Truleigh Hill Youth Hostel,** Tottington Barn, Truleigh Hill, Shoreham-by-Sea, West Sussex, BN43 5FB
Actual Grid Ref: TQ220105
Tel: 01903 813419
Fax: 01903 812016
Capacity: 56
Under 18: £6.90 **Adults:** £10.00
Open: All year, 5.00pm
Family bunk rooms
*Television • Showers • Showers • Lounge • Dining room • Cycle store • Parking • Evening meal available 7.00pm • No smoking • WC • Credit cards accepted
Modern hostel in the Sussex Downs Area of Outstanding Natural Beauty with conservation project and old dew pond in grounds.*

MAP PAGE 174 • **West Sussex**

Warningcamp

TQ0306

▲ **Arundel Youth Hostel,** Warningcamp, Arundel, West Sussex, BN18 9QY
Actual Grid Ref: TQ032076
Tel: 01903 882204
Fax: 01903 882776
Capacity: 60
Under 18: £7.75 **Adults:** £11.00
Open: Jan to Dec (not New Year), 5.00pm
Family bunk rooms
Camping
Self-catering facilities • Television • Showers • Showers • Wet weather shelter • Lounge • Dining room • Games room • Drying room • Cycle store • Parking • Evening meal available 7.00pm • WC • Breakfast available • Breakfast available • Credit cards accepted
Georgian building 1.5 miles from ancient town of Arundel, dominated by its castle & the South Downs.

Washington

TQ1212

▲ **Washington Caravan & Camping Park,** London Road, Washington, Pulborough, West Sussex, RH20 4AJ
Actual Grid Ref: TQ123135
Tel: 01903 892869
Fax: 01903 893252
Open: All year

West Wittering

SZ7798

▲ **Wicks Farm Holiday Park,** Redlands Lane, West Wittering, Chichester, West Sussex, PO20 8QD
Actual Grid Ref: SZ796995
Tourist Board grade: 5 Star
Tel: 01243 513116
Fax: 01243 511296
Email: wicks.farm@virgin.net
Tent pitches: 40
Tent rate: £10.00-£15.00
Open: Mar to Oct
Last arr: 9pm
Dogs allowed • Electric hook-up • Calor Gas/Camping Gaz • Children's play area • Showers • Laundrette on site • Public phone on site • Shop on site • Baby care facilities
Rural park near West Wittering beach and Chichester Harbour at Itchenor.

▲ **Scotts Farm Camping Site,** West Wittering, Chichester, West Sussex, PO20 8ED
Actual Grid Ref: SZ792975
Tel: 01243 671720
Fax: 01243 513669
Open: Mar to Oct

▲ **Nunnington Farm Camping Site,** Rockwood Road, West Wittering, Chichester, West Sussex, PO20 8LZ
Actual Grid Ref: SZ787988
Tel: 01243 514013
Open: Mar to Oct

Wisborough Green

TQ0425

▲ **Bat and Ball Public House,** New Pound, Wisborough Green, Billingshurst, West Sussex, RH14 0EH
Actual Grid Ref: TQ059267
Tel: 01403 700313
Open: All year

Wiston

TQ1414

▲ **Buncton Manor Farm,** Steyning Road, Wiston, Steyning, W. Sussex, BN44 3DD
Tel: 01903 812736
Fax: 01903 814838
Open: All year

Woodmancote (Henfield)

TQ2314

▲ **Downsview Caravan Park,** Bramlands Lane, Woodmancote, Henfield, West Sussex, BN5 9TG
Actual Grid Ref: TQ236138
Tel: 01273 492801
Fax: 01273 495214
Open: Mar to Nov

You are advised to book in advance for periods of high demand – the Summer months, Half Term holidays and public holidays.

Teesside

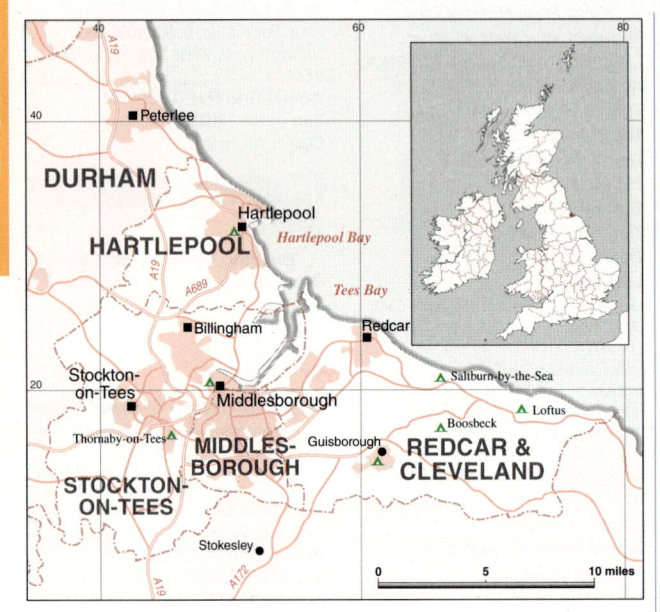

Loftus
NZ7118

▲ **Street House Farm,** Loftus, Saltburn-by-the-Sea, North Yorkshire, TS13 4UX
Tel: 01287 644998
Open: Mar to Oct

Middlesbrough
NZ5118

▲ **Prissick Caravan Park,** Marton Road, Middlesbrough, TS4 3SA
Actual Grid Ref: NZ512172
Tel: 01642 300202
Open: Apr to Oct

Saltburn-by-the-Sea
NZ6722

▲ **Hazelgrove Caravan Park,** Milton Street, Saltburn-by-the-Sea, North Yorkshire, TS12 1DE
Tel: 01287 622014
Open: Mar to Oct

Thornaby-on-Tees
NZ4516

▲ **White Water Caravan Club Site,** Tees Barrage, Stockton-on-Tees, County Durham, TS18 2QW
Tel: 01642 634880
Open: All year

Boosbeck
NZ6517

▲ **Margrove Park Holidays,** Boosbeck, Saltburn-by-the-Sea, North Yorkshire, TS12 3BZ
Actual Grid Ref: NZ653156
Tel: 01287 653616
Open: Apr to Oct

Guisborough
NZ6115

▲ **Tocketts Mill Caravan Park,** Skelton Road, Guisborough, North Yorkshire, TS14 6QA
Actual Grid Ref: NZ626182
Tel: 01287 610182
Open: Mar to Oct

Please respect hostels' policy on smoking. Some hostels do not allow smoking anywhere, some restrict smoking to certain areas.

Hartlepool
NZ5032

▲ **Ash Vale Holiday Park,** Easington Road, Hartlepool, County Durham, TS24 9RF
Actual Grid Ref: NZ481357
Tel: 01429 862111
Email: ashvale@compuserve.com
Open: Apr to Oct

Some hostels and campsites impose restrictions on size and type of groups they accept (e.g. not permitting single-sex groups). Always phone to enquire before booking.

Tyne & Wear

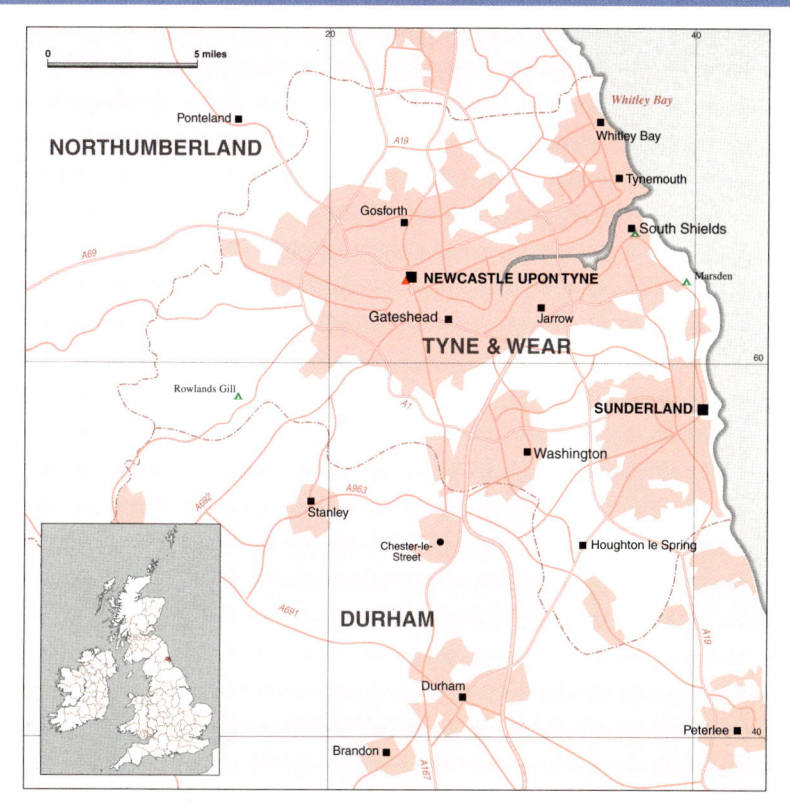

Marsden

NZ4064

⛺ **Lizard Lane Camping & Caravan Park,** The Mill House, Marsden, South Shields, Tyne & Wear, NE34 7AB
Actual Grid Ref: NZ398647
Tel: 0191 454 4982 / 0191 455 7411
Open: Apr to Oct

Newcastle-upon-Tyne

NZ2564

⛺ **Newcastle-upon-Tyne Youth Hostel,** 107 Jesmond Road, Newcastle-upon-Tyne, NE2 1NJ
Actual Grid Ref: NZ257656
Tel: 0191 281 2570
Fax: 0191 281 8779
Email: newcastle@yha.org.uk
Capacity: 60
Under 18: £7.75
Adults: £11.00
Open: All year (not Xmas/New Year)
Self-catering facilities • Television • Showers • Lounge • Dining room • Cycle store • Parking • Evening meal available 7.00pm • Kitchen facilities • Breakfast available • Credit cards accepted
A large town house conveniently located for the centre of this vibrant city, the regional capital of the North East.

Rowlands Gill

NZ1659

⛺ **Derwent Park Caravan Site,** Rowlands Gill, Tyne & Wear, NE39 1LG
Actual Grid Ref: NZ167588
Tel: 01207 543383
Open: Apr to Sep

South Shields

NZ3666

⛺ **Sandhaven Caravan & Camping Park,** Bents Park Road, South Shields, Tyne & Wear, NE33 2NL
Actual Grid Ref: NZ376673
Tel: 0191 454 5594 / 0191 455 7411
Open: Apr to Oct

⛺ **Sandhaven Caravan and Camping Park,** Sea Road, Bents Park Road, South Shields, Tyne & Wear, NE33 2LD
Actual Grid Ref: NZ376672
Tel: 0191 454 4982
Open: Mar to Oct

Hostels and campsites may vary rates – be sure to check when booking.

Warwickshire

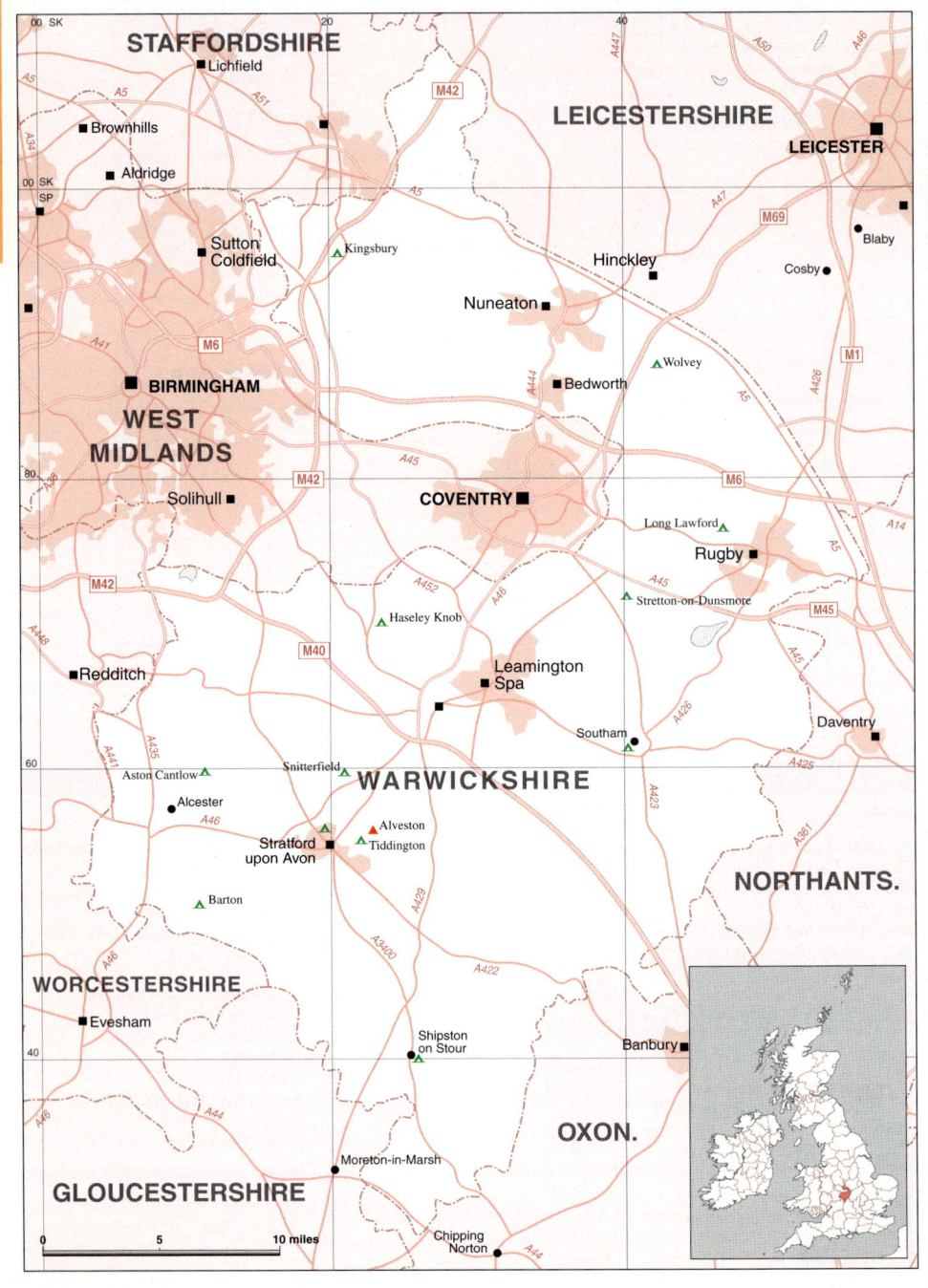

Warwickshire

Alveston
SP2356

▲ **Stratford upon Avon Youth Hostel,** Hemmingford House, Alveston, Stratford-upon-Avon, Warwickshire, CV37 7RG
Actual Grid Ref: SP231562
Tel: 01789 297093 **Fax:** 01789 205513
Email: stratford@yha.org.uk
Capacity: 132
Under 18: £11.50 **Adults:** £15.50
Open: Jan to Dec, All day
Family bunk rooms
Self-catering facilities • Television • Showers • Laundry facilities • Lounge • Games room • Cycle store • Parking • Evening meal available 5.30-7.30pm • Kitchen facilities • Credit cards accepted
Just a mile and a half outside Stratford, and a bare six from Warwick, this Georgian mansion, with its 3 acres of grounds, is an excellent base for exploring Shakespeare's country.

Aston Cantlow
SP1359

▲ **Island Meadow Caravan Park,** The Mill House, Aston Cantlow, Solihull, West Midlands, B95 6JP
Actual Grid Ref: SP135597
Tel: 01789 488273
Open: Mar to Oct

Barton
SP1051

▲ **Cottage of Content,** Welford Road, Barton, Bidford-on-Avon, Alcester, Warwickshire, B50 4NP
Actual Grid Ref: SP107511
Tel: 01789 772279
Open: Mar to Oct

To stay in a Youth Hostel affiliated to one of the Youth Hostel associations, you need to be a member. You can join at most hostels – phone in advance to check.

Haseley Knob
SP2371

▲ **Croft Caravan Site,** The Croft, Haseley Knob, Warwick, CV35 7NL
Tel: 01926 484447 **Fax:** 01926 484447
Email: david@croftguesthouse.co.uk
Tent pitches: 3
Tent rate: £5.00-£10.00
Open: All year **Last arr:** 8pm
Dogs allowed • Electric hook-up • Showers
Certified location convenient for Warwick, Stratford, NEC and Coventry.

Kingsbury
SP2196

▲ **Tame View Caravan Site,** Cliff, Kingsbury, Tamworth, Staffs, B78 2DR
Actual Grid Ref: SP209979
Tel: 01827 873853
Open: All year

Long Lawford
SP4776

▲ **Lodge Farm Caravan and Camping,** Bilton Lane, Long Lawford, Rugby, Warks, CV23 9DU
Actual Grid Ref: SP477549
Tel: 01788 560193
Email: alec@lodgefarm.demon.co.uk
Open: Mar to Oct

Shipston on Stour
SP2540

▲ **Mill Farm,** Long Compton Mill, Shipston on Stour, Warwickshire, CV36 5NZ
Actual Grid Ref: SP278332
Tel: 01608 684663
Open: Mar to Oct

Snitterfield
SP2159

▲ **High Close Farm,** Blackhill, Snitterfield, Stratford-upon-Avon, Warwickshire, CV37 0PH
Actual Grid Ref: SP232597
Tel: 01789 731300
Open: All year

Southam
SP4162

▲ **Holt Farm,** Southam, Leamington Spa, Warwickshire, CV33 0NJ
Actual Grid Ref: SP455593
Tel: 01926 812225
Open: Mar to Oct

Stratford-upon-Avon
SP1955

▲ **Dodwell Park,** Evesham Road, Stratford-upon-Avon, Warwickshire, CV37 9ST
Actual Grid Ref: SP168537
Tel: 01789 204957
Fax: 01926 336476
Open: All year

▲ **Stratford on Avon Racecourse,** Luddington Road, Stratford-upon-Avon, Warwickshire, CV37 9SE
Tel: 01789 267949
Open: Apr to Oct

Stretton-on-Dunsmore
SP4073

▲ **Sherwood Farm,** Stretton-on-Dunsmore, Rugby, Warwickshire, CV23 9JB
Actual Grid Ref: SP444723
Tel: 01788 810325
Open: All year

Tiddington
SP2155

▲ **Riverside Caravan Park,** Tiddington, Stratford-upon-Avon, Warwickshire, CV37 7AB
Actual Grid Ref: SP219559
Tel: 01789 292312
Open: Apr to Oct

Wolvey
SP4388

▲ **Wolvey Villa Farm Caravan & Camping Site,** Wolvey, Hinckley, Leicestershire, LE10 3AF
Actual Grid Ref: SP427869
Tel: 01455 220493 / 220630
Open: All year

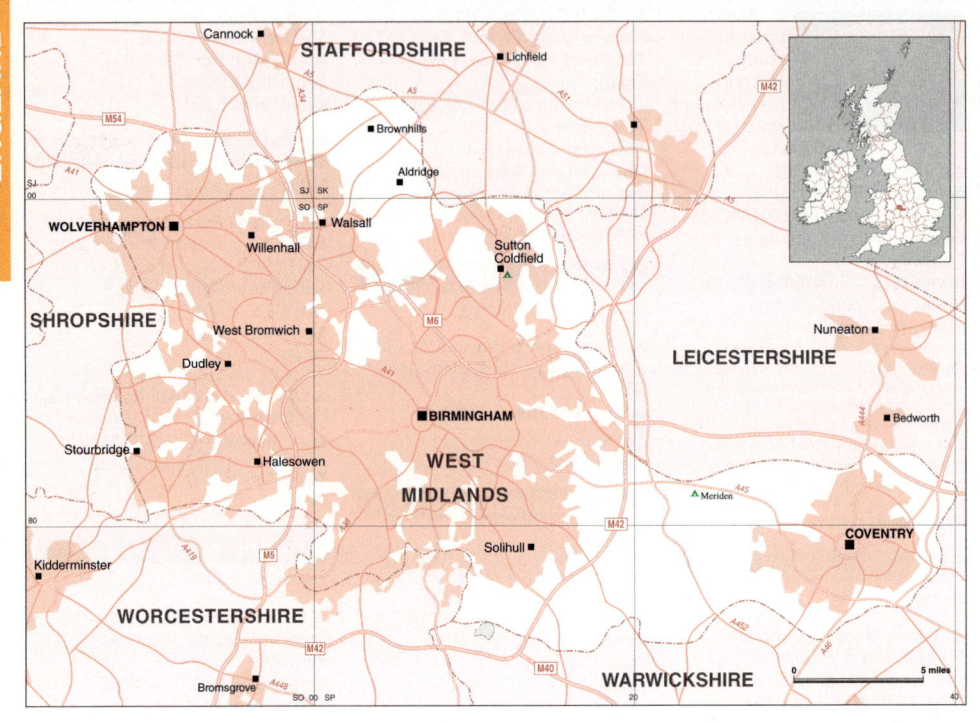

West Midlands

Meriden
SP2482

▲ **Somers Wood Caravan & Camping Park,** Somers Road, Meriden, Coventry, West Midlands, CV7 7PL
Actual Grid Ref: SP228819
Tel: 01676 522978 **Open:** All year

Sutton Coldfield
SP1297

▲ **Camping & Caravanning Club Site,** Kingsbury Water Park, Bodymoor Heath, Sutton Coldfield, West Midlands, B76 0DY
Tel: 01827 874101
Open: Mar to Oct

Some hostels and campsites impose restrictions on size and type of groups they accept (e.g. not permitting single-sex groups). Always phone to enquire before booking.

Wiltshire

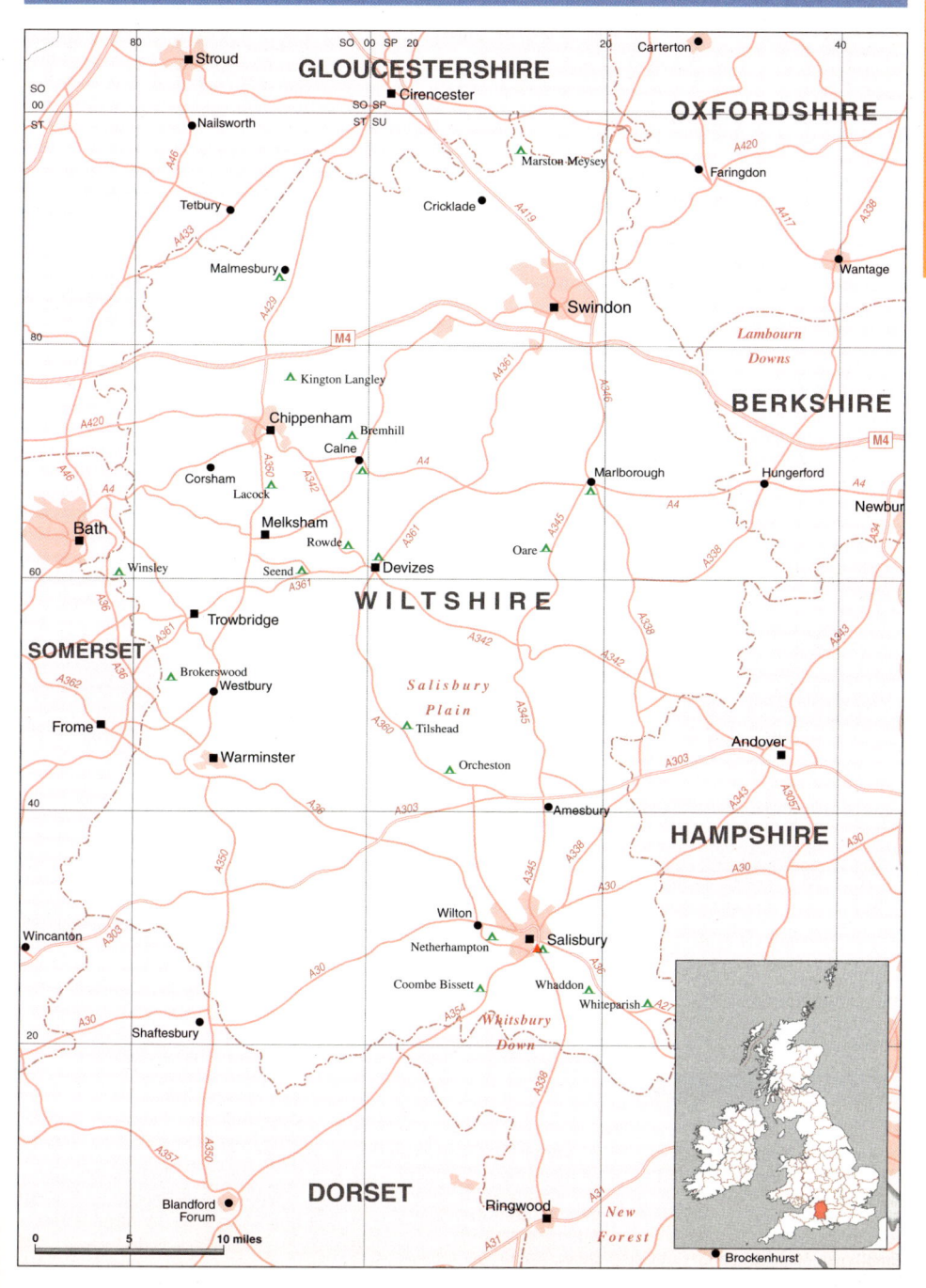

Stilwell's Hostels & Camping 2002

Wiltshire • MAP PAGE 183

ENGLAND

Bremhill
ST9773

▲ **Lowbridge Farm,** Bremhill, Calne, Wilts, SN11 9HE
Tel: 01249 815889
Open: All year

Brokerswood
ST8351

▲ **Brokerswood Country Park,** Brokerswood, Westbury, Wiltshire, BA13 4EH
Actual Grid Ref: ST839524
AA grade: 3 Pennants
Tel: 01373 822238
Fax: 01373 858474
Email: woodland.park@virgin.net
Tent pitches: 16
Tent rate: £8.00-£12.00
Open: All year
Last arr: 9pm
Facilities for disabled people • Dogs allowed • Electric hook-up • Calor Gas/Camping Gaz • Cafe or Takeaway on site • Picnic/barbecue area on site • Children's play area • Showers • Public phone on site • Shop on site • Baby care facilities
Beautiful 5 acre site adjoining 80 acres of woodland.

Calne
ST9971

▲ **Brackland Lakes Holiday & Leisure Centre,** Stockley Lane, Calne, Wiltshire, SN11 0NQ
Actual Grid Ref: SU005689
Tel: 01249 813672
Email: blackland@madasafish.com
Open: All year

Coombe Bissett
SU1026

▲ **Summerlands Caravan Park,** Rockbourne Road, Coombe Bissett, Salisbury, Wiltshire, SP5 4LP
Actual Grid Ref: SU109235
Tel: 01722 718259
Open: Apr to Oct

Devizes
SU0061

▲ **Lower Foxhangers Campsite,** Rowde, Devizes, Wilts, SN10 1SS
Actual Grid Ref: ST968615
Tel: 01380 828254
Fax: 01380 828254
Email: camping@foxhangers.co.uk

Tent pitches: 5
Tent rate: £6.00
Open: Easter to Nov **Last arr:** 9pm
Dogs allowed • Electric hook-up • Calor Gas/Camping Gaz • Showers • Public phone on site
Small, sheltered site beside canal for fishing, walking, cycling.

▲ **Bell Caravan Park,** Andover Road, Lydeway, Devizes, Wiltshire, SN10 3PS
Actual Grid Ref: SU050580
Tel: 01380 840230
Fax: 01380 840137
Tent pitches: 30
Tent rate: £9.00-£11.00
Open: Apr to Sep **Last arr:** 11pm
Dogs allowed • Electric hook-up • Calor Gas/Camping Gaz • Cafe or Takeaway on site • Picnic/barbecue area on site • Children's play area • Showers • Laundrette on site • Public phone on site • Shop on site
Level. Wonderful walking, cycling, canal locks. White horses. Avebury, Stonehenge.

Kington Langley
ST9277

▲ **Plough Lane Caravan Site,** Kington Langley, Chippenham, Wiltshire, SN15 5PS
Actual Grid Ref: ST914764
Tel: 01249 750795
Open: Mar to Oct

Lacock
ST9168

▲ **Picadilly Caravan Site,** Folly Lane West, Lacock, Chippenham, Wiltshire, SN15 2LP
Actual Grid Ref: ST912682
Tel: 01249 730260
Open: Apr to Oct

Malmesbury
ST9387

▲ **Burton Hill Caravan & Camping Park,** Burton Hill, Malmesbury, Wiltshire, SN16 0EH
Tel: 01666 822585
Fax: 01666 822585
Open: Apr to Nov

▲ **Burton Hill Caravan and Camping Park,** Burton Hill, Malmesbury, Wiltshire, SN16 0EJ
Actual Grid Ref: ST935865
Tel: 01666 826880
Open: Apr to Nov

Marlborough
SU1869

▲ **Wernham Farm Camping and Caravanning,** Clench Common, Marlborough, Wilts, SN8 4DR
Tel: 01672 512236
Open: All year

▲ **Postern Hill Caravan & Camping Site,** Savernake Forest, Marlborough, Wiltshire, SN8 4ND
Actual Grid Ref: SU197681
Tel: 01672 515195
Open: Mar to Oct

Marston Meysey
SU1297

▲ **Second Chance Caravan Park,** Marston Meysey, Swindon, Wiltshire, SN6 6SZ
Actual Grid Ref: SU140960
Tel: 01285 810675
Open: Mar to Nov

Netherhampton
SU1030

▲ **Coombe Touring Park,** Race Plain, Netherhampton, Salisbury, Wiltshire, SP2 8PN
Actual Grid Ref: SU098282
Tel: 01722 328451
Open: All year

Oare
SU1563

▲ **Hillview Park,** Oare, Marlborough, Wiltshire, SN8 4JE
Actual Grid Ref: SU156621
Tel: 01672 563151
Open: Apr to Sep

Orcheston
SU0546

▲ **Stonehenge Touring Park,** Orcheston, Salisbury, Wiltshire, SP3 4SH
Actual Grid Ref: SU060455
Tel: 01980 620304
Fax: 01980 621121
Open: All year

Please respect hostels' policy on smoking. Some hostels do not allow smoking anywhere, some restrict smoking to certain areas.

MAP PAGE 183 • **Wiltshire**

Rowde

ST9762

▲ **Lakeside,** Rowde, Devizes, Wiltshire, SN10 2LX
Actual Grid Ref: ST991623
Tel: 01380 722767
Open: Apr to Oct

Salisbury

SU1430

▲ **Salisbury Youth Hostel,** Milford Hill House, Milford Hill, Salisbury, Wiltshire, SP1 2QW
Actual Grid Ref: SU149299
Tel: 01722 327572
Fax: 01722 330446
Email: salisbury@yha.org.uk
Capacity: 70
Under 18: £7.75 **Adults:** £11.00
Open: All year, 1.00pm
Camping
Self-catering facilities • Television • Showers • Laundry facilities • Lounge • Cycle store • Parking • Evening meal available 5.30-7.45pm • Kitchen facilities • Breakfast available • Credit cards accepted
200-year-old Listed building in secluded grounds only a few minutes from the city centre. Enjoy the relaxed atmosphere of the hostel and the well-tended grounds which include a fine old cedar tree.

▲ **Camping & Caravanning Club Site,** Hudson Field, Castle Road, Salisbury, Wiltshire, SP1 3RR
Actual Grid Ref: SU140320
Tel: 01722 320713
Open: Mar to Oct

Seend

ST9461

▲ **Camping & Caravanning Club Site,** Spout Lane, Seend, Melksham, Wiltshire, SN12 6RN
Actual Grid Ref: ST951619
Tel: 01380 828839
Open: All year

Tilshead

SU0348

▲ **Brades Acre,** Tilshead, Salisbury, Wiltshire, SP3 4RX
Actual Grid Ref: SU034477
Tel: 01980 620402
Open: All year

Whaddon

SU1926

▲ **Alderbury Caravan & Camping Park,** Southampton Road, Whaddon, Salisbury, Wiltshire, SP5 3HB
Actual Grid Ref: SU198263
Tel: 01722 710125
Open: All year

Some hostels and campsites impose restrictions on size and type of groups they accept (e.g. not permitting single-sex groups). Always phone to enquire before booking.

Whiteparish

SU2524

▲ **Hillcrest Camp Site,** Southampton Road, Whiteparish, Salisbury, Wiltshire, SP5 2QW
Tel: 01794 884471
Email: hillcrest@dtullis.freeserve.co.uk
Open: All year

Winsley

ST7961

▲ **Church Farm,** Winsley, Bradford on Avon, Wilts, BA15 2JH
Tel: 01225 722246
Fax: 01225 722246
Open: All year

Hostels and campsites may vary rates – be sure to check when booking.

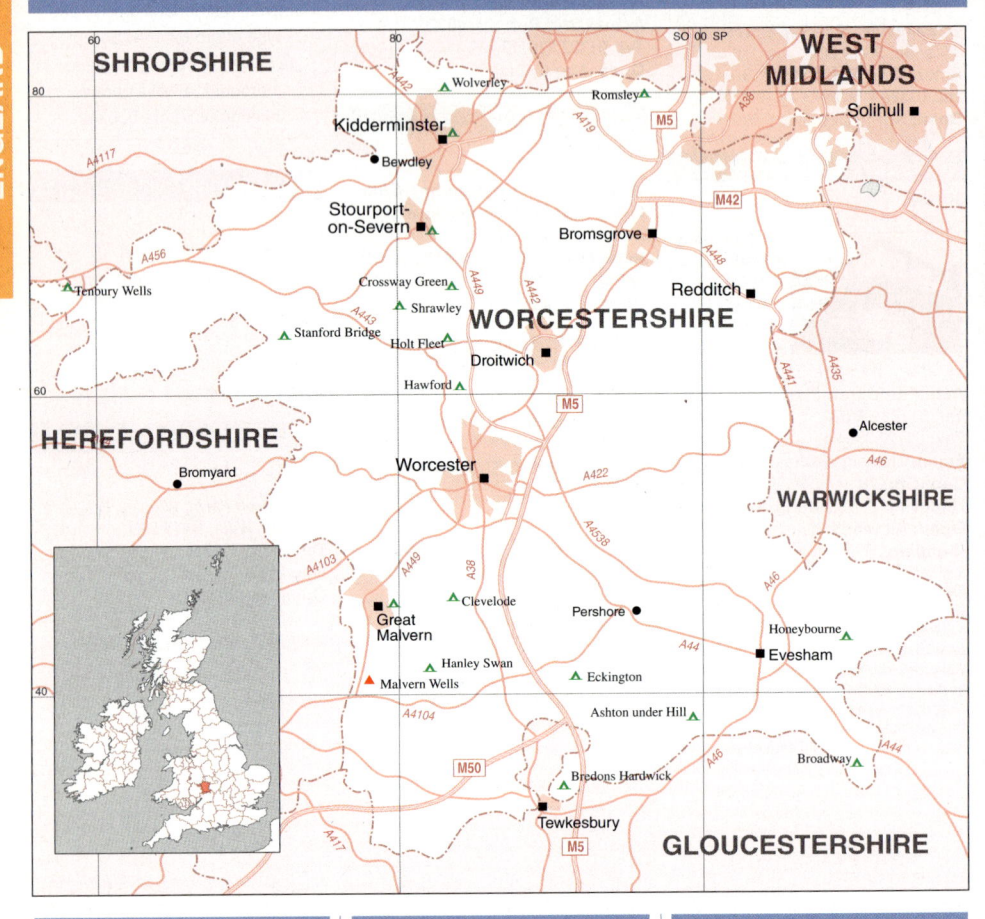

Worcestershire

Ashton under Hill
SO9938

Long Carrant Caravan Park, Cheltenham Road, Ashton-under-Hill, Hereford & Worcester, WR11 6QP
Actual Grid Ref: SP002369
Tel: 01386 881724
Open: All year

To stay in a Youth Hostel affiliated to one of the Youth Hostel associations, you need to be a member. You can join at most hostels – phone in advance to check.

Bredons Hardwick
SO9035

Croft Farm Leisure and Water Park, Croft Farm, Bredons Hardwick, Tewkesbury, Gloucestershire, GL20 7EE
Actual Grid Ref: SO911354
Tel: 01684 772321 **Fax:** 01684 773379
Tent pitches: 76
Tent rate: £6.50-£10.50
Open: Mar to Dec **Last arr:** 9pm
Facilities for disabled people • Electric hook-up • Calor Gas/Camping Gaz • Cafe or Takeaway on site • Picnic/barbecue area on site • Children's play area • Showers • Laundrette on site • Public phone on site • Licensed bar on site • Shop on site Lakeside location with tuition and hire for sailing, windsurfing and canoeing.

Broadway
SP0937

Leedon's Park, Childswickham Road, Broadway, Worcestershire, WR12 7HB
Actual Grid Ref: SP080385
Tel: 01386 852423
Open: All year

Clevelode
SO8745

Riverside Caravan Park, Little Clevelode, Clevelode, Malvern, Worcestershire, WR13 6PE
Actual Grid Ref: SO833463
Tel: 01684 310475
Open: Mar to Dec

186   Stilwell's Hostels & Camping 2002

Worcestershire

Crossway Green
SO8468

▲ **Shorthill Caravan & Camping Centre,** Worcester Road, Crossway Green, Stourport-on-Severn, Worcestershire, DY13 9SH
Actual Grid Ref: SO841689
Tel: 01299 250571
Open: All year

Eckington
SO9241

▲ **Eckington Riverside Caravan Park,** Eckington, Pershore, Worcestershire, WR10 3DD
Tel: 01386 750985
Open: Mar to Oct

Hanley Swan
SO8143

▲ **Camping & Caravanning Club Site,** Hanley Swan, Worcester, WR8 0EE
Actual Grid Ref: SO812440
Tel: 01684 310280
Open: Mar to Nov

Hawford
SO8461

▲ **Mill House Caravan & Camping Site,** Hawford, Worcester, WR3 7SE
Actual Grid Ref: SO848598
Tel: 01905 451283
Fax: 01905 754143
Open: Apr to Oct

Holt Fleet
SO8263

▲ **Holt Fleet Farm,** Holt Heath, Worcester, WR6 6NW
Actual Grid Ref: SO824635
Tel: 01905 620512
Open: Mar to Oct

Honeybourne
SP1044

▲ **The Ranch Caravan Park,** Station Road, Honeybourne, Evesham, Worcs, WR11 5QG
Actual Grid Ref: SP113444
Tel: 01386 830744
Open: Mar to Nov

Kidderminster
SO8276

▲ **Camp Easy,** The Old Vicarage Activity Centre, Stottesdon, Kidderminster, Worcestershire, DY14 8UH
Tel: 01746 718436
Fax: 01746 718420
Open: Mar to Aug

Malvern
SO7846

▲ **Three Counties Park,** Sledge Green, Berrow, Malvern, Worcestershire, WR13 6PE
Actual Grid Ref: SO809347
Tel: 01684 833439
Open: Mar to Sept

▲ **Kingsgreen Caravan Park,** Kingsgreen, Berrow, Malvern, Worcestershire, WR13 6AQ
Actual Grid Ref: SO769337
Tel: 01531 650272
Open: Mar to Nov

▲ **Nether Green Farm,** Ridge Way Cross, Malvern, Worcs, WR13 5JS
Tel: 01886 880387
Open: All year

Malvern Wells
SO7742

▲ **Malvern Hills Youth Hostel,** 18 Peachfield Road, Malvern Wells, Malvern, Worcestershire, WR14 4AP
Actual Grid Ref: SO774440
Tel: 01684 569131
Fax: 01684 565205
Email: malvern@yha.org.uk
Capacity: 59
Under 18: £6.90
Adults: £10.00
Open: Jan to Dec (not Xmas/New Year), 5.00pm
Family bunk rooms
Self-catering facilities • Television • Showers • Shop • Lounge • Dining room • Games room • Drying room • Cycle store • Parking • Evening meal available 7.00pm • No smoking • WC • Kitchen facilities • Breakfast available • Credit cards accepted
On the slopes of the Malverns, with marvellous views over this Area of Outstanding Natural Beauty.

Romsley
SO9680

▲ **Camping & Caravanning Club Site,** Fieldhouse Lane, Romsley, Halesowen, West Midlands, B62 0NH
Actual Grid Ref: SO955795
Tel: 01562 710015
Open: Apr to Oct

Shrawley
SO8065

▲ **Lenchford Caravan Park,** Shrawley, Worcester, WR6 6TB
Tel: 01905 620246
Open: Apr to Oct

Stanford Bridge
SO7165

▲ **The Bridge Caravan & Camping Park,** Stanford Bridge, Worcester, WR6 6RU
Actual Grid Ref: SO715658
Tel: 01886 812771
Open: Mar to Sept

Stourport-on-Severn
SO8171

▲ **Lickhill Manor Caravan Park,** Stourport-on-Severn, Worcestershire, DY13 8RL
Tel: 01299 871041
Open: All year

Tenbury Wells
SO5967

▲ **Palmers Meadow & The Burgage,** Swimming Baths Site, Tenbury Wells, Worcestershire, WR15 8SF
Actual Grid Ref: SO598685
Tel: 01584 810448
Open: Apr to Dec

Wolverley
SO8279

▲ **Camping & Caravanning Club Site,** Brown Westhead Park, Wolverley, Kidderminster, Worcestershire, DY10 3PX
Actual Grid Ref: SO833792
Tel: 01562 850909
Open: Mar to Oct

ENGLAND

East Yorkshire

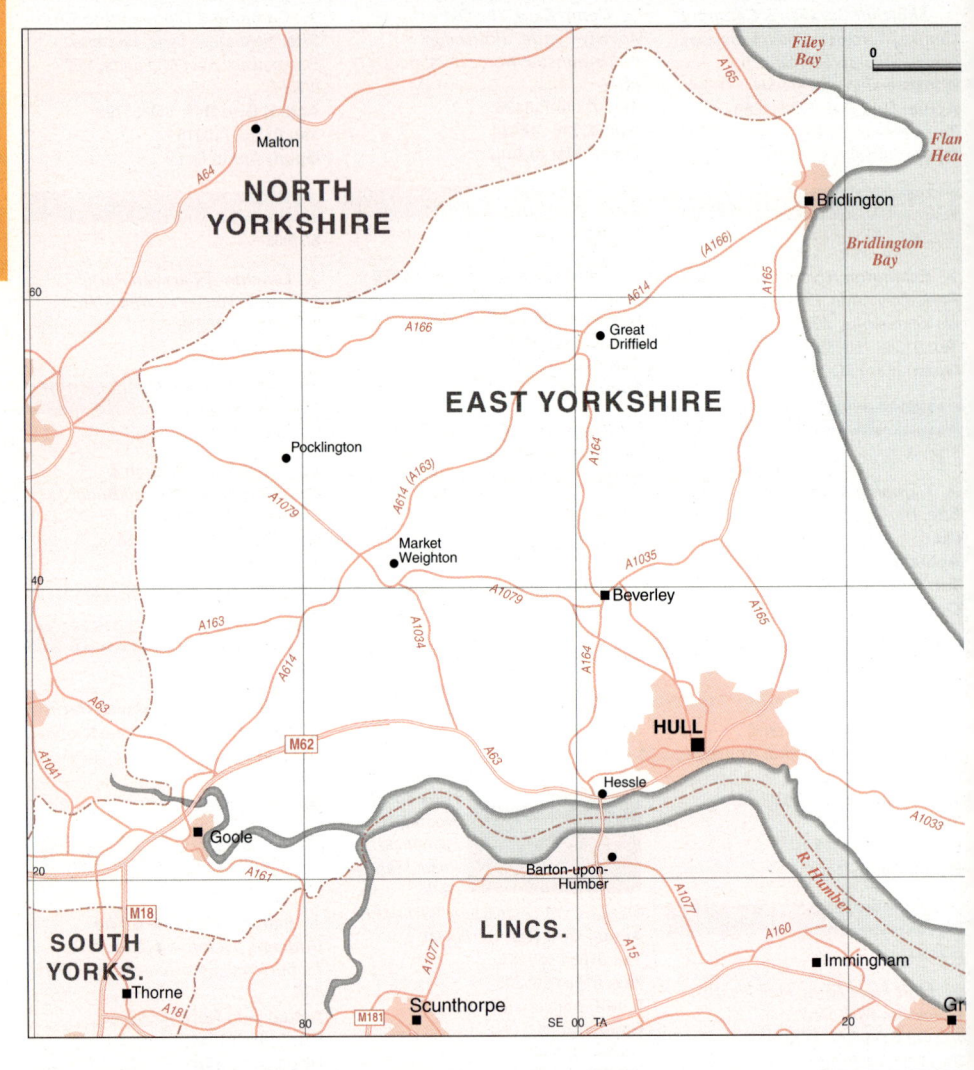

Atwick

TA1950

Four Acres Caravan Park, Atwick, Driffield, East Yorkshire, YO25 8DG
Actual Grid Ref: TA193506
Tel: 01964 536940
Open: Apr to Oct

Barmby Moor

SE7748

The Sycamores Touring Caravan Park, Feoffe Common Lane, Barmby Moor, York, YO4 5HS
Actual Grid Ref: SE764493
Tel: 01759 388838
Open: Mar to Nov

Barmston

TA1658

Barmston Beach Holiday Park, Sands Lane, Barmston, Driffield, East Yorkshire, YO25 8PJ
Tel: 01262 468202
Open: Easter to Oct

East Yorkshire

▲ **Lakeminster Park,** Hull Road, Beverley, East Yorkshire, HU17 0PN
Actual Grid Ref: TA054835
Tel: 01482 882655
Open: All year

Brandesburton

TA1247

▲ **Dacre Lakeside Park,** New Road, Brandesburton, Driffield, East Riding of Yorkshire, YO25 8SA
Actual Grid Ref: TA118469
Tel: 01964 543704 / 542372
Open: Mar to Oct

▲ **Billabong Lakeside Water Sports & Caravan Park,** Hempholme Bridge, Brandesburton, Driffield, East Yorkshire, YO25 8NA
Actual Grid Ref: TA098488
Tel: 01964 543631
Open: Mar to Oct

Bridlington

TA1867

▲ **South Cliff Caravan Park,** Wilstthorpe, Bridlington, East Yorkshire, YO15 3QN
Actual Grid Ref: TA171648
Tel: 01262 671051
Open: Mar to Nov

Fangfoss

SE7653

▲ **Fangfoss Old Station Caravan Park,** Old Station House, Fangfoss, York, YO41 5QB
Actual Grid Ref: SE748527
Tel: 01759 380491
Open: Mar to Oct

Hornsea

TA2047

▲ **Springfield Caravan Park,** Springfield Farm, Atwick Road, Hornsea, East Yorkshire, HU18 1EJ
Tel: 01964 532253
Open: May to Oct

▲ **Springfield Farm,** Atwick Road, Hornsea, East Yorkshire, HU18 1EJ
Actual Grid Ref: TA195487
Tel: 01964 532112
Open: Apr to Oct

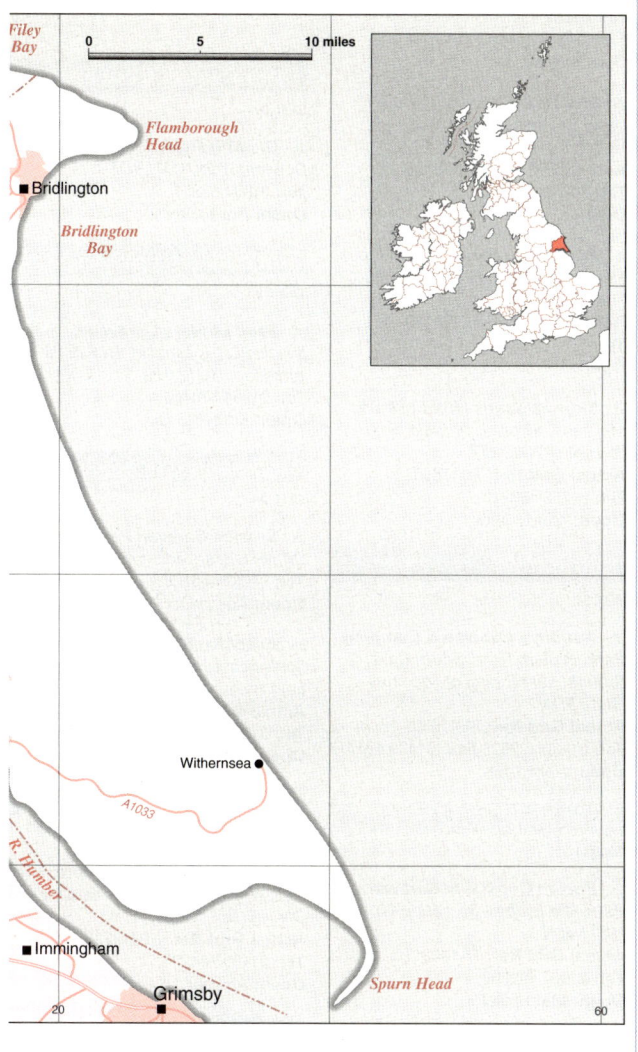

Beverley

TA0440

▲ **Beverley Friary Youth Hostel,** The Friary, Friar's Lane, Beverley, East Yorkshire, HU17 0DF
Actual Grid Ref: TA038393

Tel: 01482 881751
Fax: 01482 880118
Capacity: 34
Under 18: £5.75 **Adults:** £8.50
Open: All year, 5.0pm
Showers • Shop • Lounge • Games room • Drying room • Cycle store • Parking • Evening meal available 7.00pm • Kitchen facilities • Breakfast available • Credit cards accepted
Restored Dominican friary mentioned in the Canterbury Tales and next to Beverley Minster.

East Yorkshire • MAP PAGE 188

Little Weighton
SE9933

▲ **Louvain,** Rowley Road, Little Weighton, Hull, East Yorkshire, HU20 3XJ
Actual Grid Ref: SE983333
Tel: 01482 848249
Open: All year

Newport
SE8530

▲ **Sandholme Lodge Holiday Park,** Sandholme Lodge, Newport, Brough, East Yorkshire, HU15 2QQ
Actual Grid Ref: SE835318
Tel: 01430 440487
Open: Mar to Oct

Rudston
TA0966

▲ **Thorpe Hall Caravan & Camping Site,** Thorpe Hall, Rudston, Driffield, East Riding of Yorkshire, YO25 4JE
Actual Grid Ref: TA108676
Tel: 01262 420393 / 420574
Open: Mar to Oct

Sewerby
TA2068

▲ **The Poplars Motel,** 45 Jewison Lane, Sewerby, Bridlington, East Yorkshire, YO15 1DX
Actual Grid Ref: TA196699
Tel: 01262 677251 **Open:** All year

Skipsea
TA1754

▲ **Far Grange Park,** Windhook, Hornsea Road, Skipsea, Driffield, East Riding of Yorkshire, YO25 8SY
Actual Grid Ref: TA181530
Tel: 01262 468248 / 468293
Fax: 01262 468648
Open: Mar to Oct

All details shown are as supplied by hostels and campsites in Autumn 2000.

▲ **Skirlington Leisure Park,** Low Skirlington, Skipsea, Driffield, East Yorkshire, YO25 8SY
Actual Grid Ref: TA188526
Tel: 01262 468213 / 468466
Fax: 01262 468105
Open: Mar to Oct

▲ **Mill Farm Country Park,** Mill Lane, Skipsea, Driffield, East Yorkshire, YO25 8SS
Actual Grid Ref: TA170555
Tel: 01262 468211
Open: Mar to Oct

▲ **Far Grange Park Ltd,** Windhook, Skipsea, Driffield, East Yorkshire, YO25 8ST
Actual Grid Ref: TA186530
Tel: 01262 468293
Open: Mar to Oct

▲ **Skipsea Sands Holiday Park,** Mill Lane, Skipsea, Driffield, East Yorkshire, YO25 8TZ
Actual Grid Ref: TA176565
Tel: 01262 468210
Open: Mar to Nov

South Cave
SE9231

▲ **Waudby's Caravan & Camping Park,** Brough Road, South Cave, Brough, East Riding of Yorkshire, HU15 2DN
Actual Grid Ref: SE928302
Tel: 01430 422523 **Fax:** 01430 424777
Open: Apr to Jan

Sproatley
TA1934

▲ **Burton Constable Caravan Park,** Old Lodges, Sproatley, Hull, HU11 4LN
Actual Grid Ref: TA186357
Tel: 01964 562508
Open: Mar to Oct

Stamford Bridge
SE7155

▲ **Weir Caravan Park,** Stamford Bridge, York, YO41 1AN
Actual Grid Ref: SE712557
Tel: 01759 371377
Open: Mar to Oct

Hostels and campsites may vary rates – be sure to check when booking.

Sutton upon Derwent
SE7046

▲ **Old Mill Field,** Sutton upon Derwent, York, YO41 4DF
Tel: 01904 85357
Open: Apr to Oct

Tunstall
TA3131

▲ **Sand Le Mere Caravans,** Seaside Lane, Tunstall, Hull, East Yorkshire, HU12 0JQ
Tel: 01964 670403
Open: Easter to Oct

Ulrome
TA1656

▲ **Seaside Caravan Park,** Ulrome, Driffield, East Yorkshire, YO25 8TT
Tel: 01262 468228
Open: Apr to Oct

▲ **Beachbank Caravan Park,** Southfield Lane, Ulrome, Driffield, East Yorkshire, YO25 8BJ
Actual Grid Ref: TA176562
Tel: 01262 468491
Open: Mar to Oct

Whitgift
SE8122

▲ **Whitgift Hall Caravan Site,** The Hall, Whitgift, Goole, Humberside, DN14 8HL
Actual Grid Ref: SE818288
Tel: 01405 704283
Open: All year

Wilberfoss
SE7351

▲ **Steer Inn Caravan Park,** Hull Road, Wilberfoss, York, YO41 5PF
Actual Grid Ref: SE752494
Tel: 01759 380600
Open: Mar to Nov

Britain: Bed & Breakfast

The essential guide to B&Bs in England, Scotland & Wales

The Bed & Breakfast is one of the great British institutions. Like Fish & Chips, it's known by people around the world. But you don't have to be a tourist to enjoy this traditional accommodation. Whether you're travelling, on holiday, away on business or just escaping from it all, the B&B is a great value alternative to expensive hotels and a world away from camping and caravanning.

Stilwell's Britain: Bed & Breakfast 2001 is the most comprehensive guide of its kind, containing over 7,750 entries listed by country, county and location, in England, Scotland and Wales. Each entry includes room rates, facilities, Tourist Board grades and a brief description of the B&B and its location and surroundings.

Stilwell's Britain: Bed & Breakfast 2001: The indispensable guide to great value accommodation:

- Private houses, country halls, farms, cottages, inns, small hotels and guest houses
- Over 7,750 entries
- Average price £19 per person per night
- All official grades shown
- Local maps
- Pubs serving hot evening meals shown
- Tourist Information Centres listed
- Handy size for easy packing

£9.95 from all good bookstores (ISBN 1-900861-22-4) or £11.95 (inc p&p) from Stilwell Publishing, 59 Charlotte Road, London EC2A 3QW (020 7739 7179)

North Yorkshire

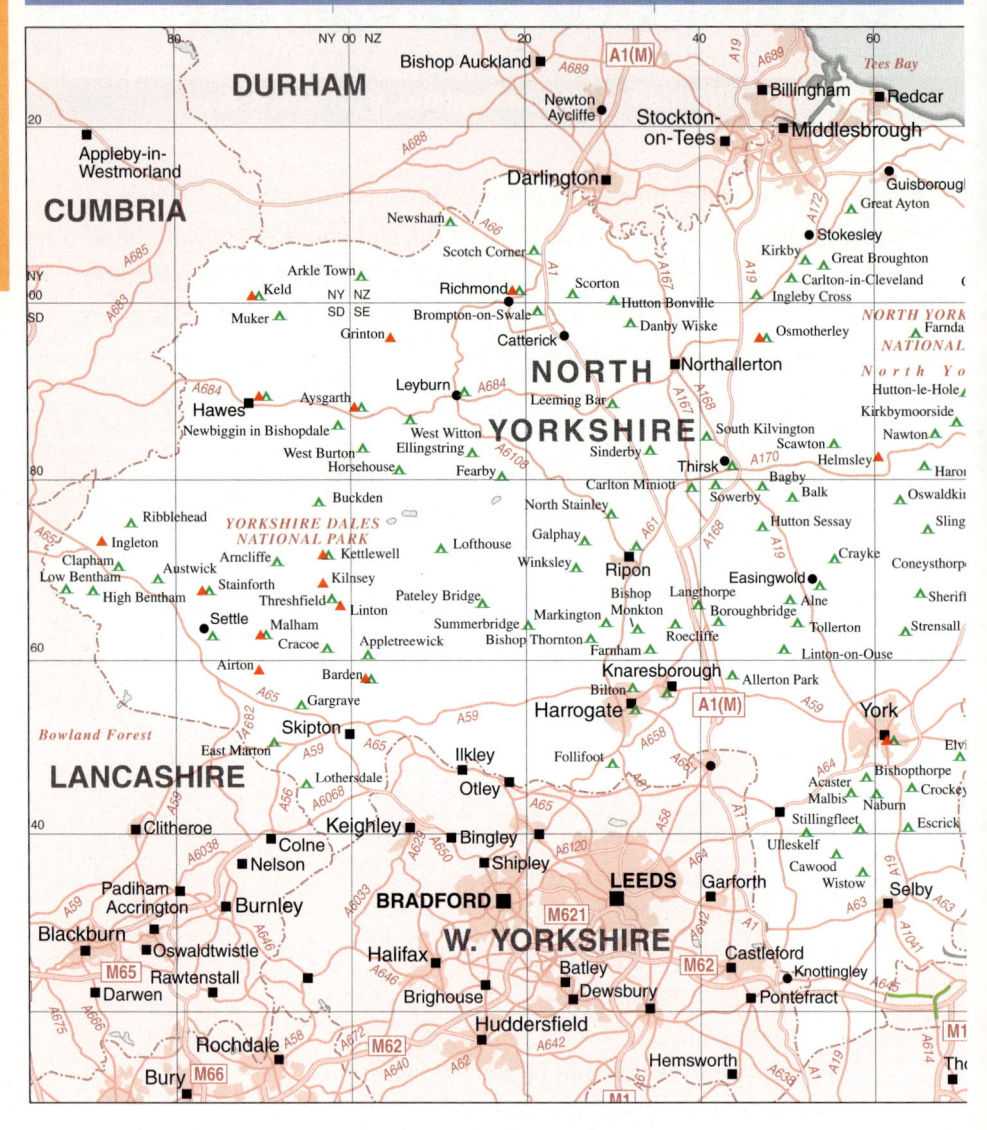

Acaster Malbis

SE5845

▲ **Chestnut Farm Caravan Park,** Acaster Malbis, York, YO23 2UQ
Actual Grid Ref: SE590456
Tel: 01904 704676 **Email:** alison@chestnuthp.freeserve.co.uk
Open: Apr to Sep

▲ **Moor End Farm,** Acaster Malbis, York, YO23 2PY
Actual Grid Ref: SE589458
Tel: 01904 706727 **Open:** Apr to Oct

To stay in a Youth Hostel affiliated to one of the Youth Hostel associations, you need to be a member. You can join at most hostels – phone in advance to check.

Hostels and campsites may vary rates – be sure to check when booking.

192 Stilwell's Hostels & Camping 2002

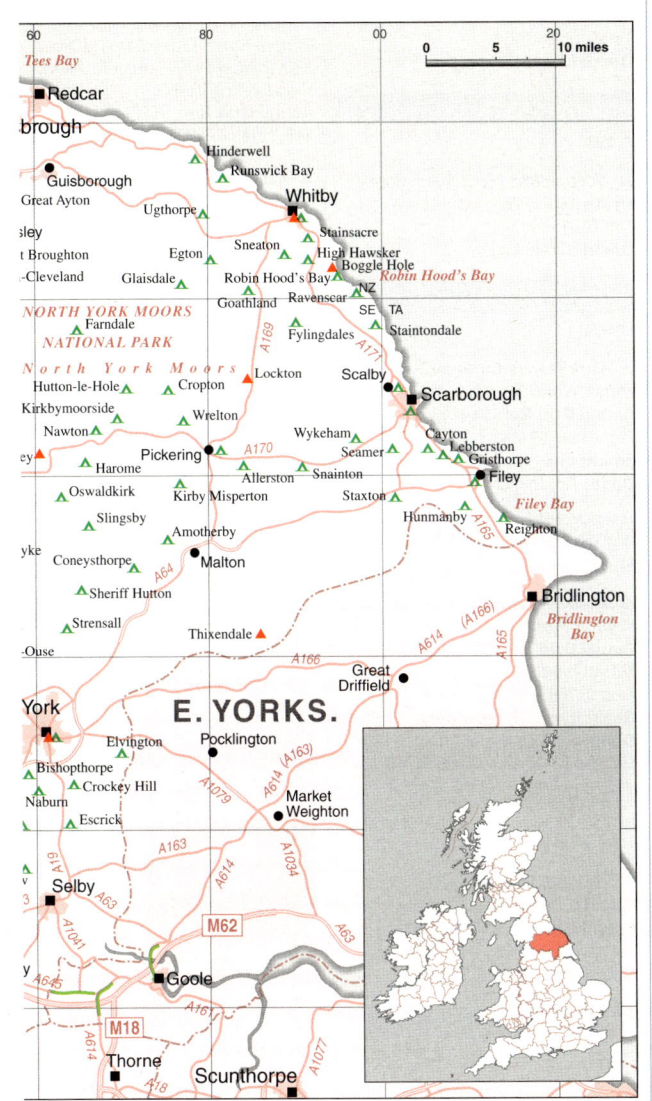

North Yorkshire

Airton

SD9059

▲ **Airton Quaker Hostel,** Airton, Skipton, North Yorkshire, BD23 4AE
Actual Grid Ref: SD904592
Tel: 01729 830263
Capacity: 14
Under 18: £3.00
Adults: £5.00 **Open:** All year
Self-catering facilities • Showers • Dining room • No smoking
Attached to C17th meeting house in quiet Dales village close to Pennine Way.

Allerston

SE8883

▲ **Vale of Pickering Caravan Park,** Carr House Farm, Allerston, Pickering, North Yorkshire, YO18 7PQ
Actual Grid Ref: SE879808
Tel: 01723 859280
Open: Mar to Oct

Allerton Park

SE4158

▲ **Allerton Park Caravan Site,** Allerton Mauleverer, Allerton Park, Knaresborough, North Yorkshire, HG5 0SE
Actual Grid Ref: SE416576
Tel: 01423 330569
Open: All year

Alne

SE4965

▲ **The Alders Caravan Park,** Home Farm, Alne, York, YO61 1TB
Tel: 01347 838722
Open: Mar to Oct

Amotherby

SE7473

▲ **Brickyard Farm,** Amotherby, Malton, N Yorks, YO17 0TL
Actual Grid Ref: SE749744
Tel: 01653 693606
Open: Mar to Oct

Appletreewick

SE0560

▲ **Mill Lane Caravan Park,** Ainhams House, Appletreewick, Skipton, North Yorkshire, BD23 6DD
Actual Grid Ref: SE047603
Tel: 01756 720275
Open: Mar to Oct

▲ **Mount Pleasant Caravan Village,** Acaster Malbis, York, YO23 2UA
Actual Grid Ref: SE583455
Tel: 01904 707078 **Fax:** 01904 707078
Open: Apr to Nov

▲ **Poplar Farm Caravan Park,** Acaster Malbis, York, YO23 2UH
Actual Grid Ref: SE591455
Tel: 01904 706548
Open: Apr to Oct

North Yorkshire • MAP PAGE 192

ENGLAND

Arkle Town

NZ0002

▲ **The Ghyll,** Arkle Town, Arkengarthdale, Richmond, DL11 6EU
Tel: 01748 884353 **Fax:** 01748 884015
Open: All year

Arncliffe

SD9372

▲ **Hawkswick Cote Caravan Park,** Arncliffe, Skipton, North Yorkshire, BD23 5PX
Actual Grid Ref: SD949704
Tel: 01756 770226
Open: Mar to Nov

Austwick

SD7668

▲ **Dalesbridge,** Austwick, Lancaster, LA2 8AZ
Actual Grid Ref: SD762676
Tel: 015242 51021
Fax: 015242 51021
Email: info@dalesbridge.co.uk
Tent pitches: 60
Tent rate: £3.25-£10.00
Open: All year **Last arr:** 11pm
Facilities for disabled people • Dogs allowed • Electric hook-up • Cafe or Takeaway on site • Picnic/barbecue area on site • Showers • Public phone on site • Licensed bar on site • Shop on site •
Eight self-catering bunkhouses for groups/individuals, with outstanding views.

Aysgarth

SE0088

▲ **Aysgarth Falls Youth Hostel,** Aysgarth, Leyburn, North Yorkshire, DL8 3SR
Actual Grid Ref: SE012884
Tel: 01969 663260
Fax: 01969 663110
Email: aysgarth@yha.org.uk
Capacity: 67
Under 18: £6.25
Adults: £9.25
Open: Feb to Nov, 5.00pm
Family bunk rooms
Self-catering facilities • Television • Showers • Shop • Lounge • Dining room • Games room • Drying room • Cycle store • Parking • Evening meal available 7.00pm • Kitchen facilities • Credit cards accepted
Just outside the village, and minutes' walk from Aysgarth Falls and woodland trail, a good base for exploring Wensleydale.

▲ **Westholme Caravan Park,** Aysgarth, Leyburn, North Yorkshire, DL8 3SP
Actual Grid Ref: SE017882
Tel: 01969 663268
Open: Mar to Oct

Bagby

SE4580

▲ **Scenecliffe,** Moor Road, Bagby, Thirsk, YO7 2PN
Tel: 01845 597368
Open: Mar to Oct

Balk

SE4779

▲ **York House Caravan Park,** Balk, Thirsk, North Yorkshire, YO7 2AQ
Actual Grid Ref: SE474809
Tel: 01845 597495
Email: phil.brierley@which.net
Open: Apr to Oct

Barden (Skipton)

SE0557

▲ **Barden Bunk Barn,** Barden, Skipton, North Yorkshire, BD23 6AS
Actual Grid Ref: SD051572
Tel: 01756 720330
Fax: 01756 720330
Capacity: 25 **Groups only**
Open: All year (not Jan)
Self-catering facilities • Showers • Central heating • Lounge • Dining room • Drying room • Cycle store • Parking
200 year old barn. Unique historic location in Wharfedale.

▲ **Howgill Lodge,** Barden, Skipton, N. Yorks, BD23 6DJ
Actual Grid Ref: SE064592
Tel: 01756 720655
Open: Apr to Oct

Bilton (Harrogate)

SE3056

▲ **Bilton Park Village Farm,** Bilton Lane, Harrogate, North Yorkshire, HG1 4DH
Actual Grid Ref: SE319578
Tel: 01423 863121
Open: Apr to Oct

Hostels and campsites may vary rates – be sure to check when booking.

Bishop Monkton

SE3266

▲ **Church Farm Caravan Park,** Church Farm, Knaresborough Road, Bishop Monkton, Harrogate, North Yorkshire, HG3 3QQ
Actual Grid Ref: SE286658
Tel: 01765 677405 **Open:** Apr to Oct

▲ **Church Farm,** Knaresborough Road, Bishop Monkton, Ripon, North Yorkshire, HG3 3QQ
Actual Grid Ref: SE328658
Tel: 01765 677668
Open: Apr to Oct

Bishop Thornton

SE2663

▲ **Chequers Inn,** Bishop Thornton, Harrogate, North Yorkshire, HG3 3JN
Actual Grid Ref: SE268639
Tel: 01423 771544
Open: Apr to Oct

Bishopthorpe

SE5947

▲ **Riverside Caravan & Camping Park,** Ferry Lane, Bishopthorpe, York, YO23 2SB
Tel: 01904 704442
Open: Easter to Oct

Boggle Hole

NZ9504

▲ **Boggle Hole Youth Hostel,** Mill Beck, Boggle Hole, Robin Hood's Bay, Whitby, North Yorkshire, YO22 4UQ
Actual Grid Ref: NZ954040
Tel: 01947 880352 **Fax:** 01947 880987
Email: bogglehole@yha.org.uk
Capacity: 80
Under 18: £6.75 **Adults:** £10.00
Open: Feb to Nov + New Year, 1.00pm
Family bunk rooms
Self-catering facilities • Television • Showers • Licensed bar • Lounge • Dining room • Cycle store • Parking • Evening meal available 6.00 to 7.00pm • WC • Drying facilities • Kitchen facilities • Breakfast available • Credit cards accepted
A former mill in a wooded ravine, Boggle Hole has the North Sea tide coming up to the doorstep and the North York Moors behind.

---

194   Stilwell's Hostels & Camping 2002

MAP PAGE 192 • **North Yorkshire**

ENGLAND

Boroughbridge

SE3966

▲ **Blue Bell Hotel Caravan Site,** Kirby Hill, Boroughbridge, York, YO51 9DN
Tel: 01423 322380
Open: Apr to Oct

Brompton-on-Swale

SE2199

▲ **Brompton Caravan & Camping Park,** Brompton-on-Swale, Richmond, N Yorks, DL10 7EZ
Actual Grid Ref: NZ197004
Tel: 01748 824629
Open: Apr to Oct

Buckden

SD9477

▲ **West Deepdale,** Buckden, Skipton, N Yorks, BD23 5JJ
Tel: 01756 760204
Open: All year

Carlton Miniott

SE3981

▲ **Carlton Miniott Park,** Carlton Miniott, Thirsk, North Yorkshire, YO7 4NH
Actual Grid Ref: SE400816
Tel: 01845 523106
Open: Apr to Oct

Carlton-in-Cleveland

NZ5004

▲ **Carlton Caravan Park,** Carlton-in-Cleveland, Middlesbrough, TS9 7DJ
Tel: 01642 712550
Open: Mar to Dec

Cawood

SE5737

▲ **Cawood Holiday Park,** Ryther Road, Cawood, Selby, North Yorkshire, YO8 3TT
Actual Grid Ref: SE567384
Tel: 01757 268450
Open: All year

All details shown are as supplied by hostels and campsites in Autumn 2000.

Cayton

TA0583

▲ **Cayton Village Caravan Park,** Mill Lane, Cayton, Scarborough, North Yorkshire, YO11 3NN
Actual Grid Ref: TA057837
Tel: 01723 583171
Open: Apr to Oct

Clapham

SD7469

▲ **Flying Horseshoe Hotel,** Clapham, Lancaster, LA2 8ES
Actual Grid Ref: SD733678
Tel: 015242 51229
Fax: 015242 51229
Open: Mar to Oct

Coneysthorpe

SE7171

▲ **Castle Howard Caravan & Camp Site,** Coneysthorpe, York, YO60 7DD
Actual Grid Ref: SE712712
Tel: 01653 648366 / 648316
Email: admin@castlehoward.demon.co.uk
Open: Mar to Oct

Cracoe

SD9860

▲ **Threaplands House Farm,** Cracoe, Skipton, North Yorkshire, BD23 6LD
Actual Grid Ref: SD985606
Tel: 01756 730248
Tent pitches: 30
Tent rate: £7.00
Open: Mar to Oct
Last arr: 9pm
Facilities for disabled people • Dogs allowed • Electric hook-up • Calor Gas/Camping Gaz • Picnic/barbecue area on site • Children's play area • Showers nearby
Yorkshire Dales National Park, walking from site, grass field with roads.

Crayke

SE5670

▲ **The Hermitage,** Crayke, York, YO61 4TB
Tel: 01347 821635
Open: All year

Crockey Hill

SE6246

▲ **Wigman Hall,** Wheldrake Lane, Crockey Hill, York, YO19 4SQ
Tel: 01904 448221
Open: Mar to Oct

▲ **Swallow Hall Caravan Park,** Crockey Hill, York, YO19 4SG
Actual Grid Ref: SE657462
Tel: 01904 448219
Open: Mar to Oct

Cropton

SE7589

▲ **Spiers House Campsite,** Cropton, Pickering, North Yorkshire, YO18 8ES
Actual Grid Ref: SE756918
Tel: 01751 417591
Open: Apr to Sep

Danby Wiske

SE3398

▲ **The White Swan Inn,** Danby Wiske, Northallerton, N. Yorks, DL7 0NQ
Tel: 01609 770122
Open: All year

Easingwold

SE5369

▲ **Easingwold Caravan & Camping Park,** White Horse Farm, Thirsk Road, Easingwold, York, YO61 3NF
Actual Grid Ref: SE510708
Tel: 01347 821479
Open: Mar to Oct

▲ **Holly Brook Caravan Park,** Penny Carr Lane, Easingwold, York, YO61 3EU
Actual Grid Ref: SE534684
Tel: 01347 821906
Email: hollybrookcaravan@hotmail.com
Open: Mar to Dec

▲ **Low Shires Farm,** Forest Lane, Easingwold, York, YO61 3PF
Tel: 01347 838823
Open: Easter to Nov

▲ **Far Shires Farm,** York Road, Easingwold, York, YO61 3EJ
Tel: 01347 838256
Open: Apr to Sep

Stilwell's Hostels & Camping 2002   195

North Yorkshire • MAP PAGE 192

East Marton
SD9050

▲ **Sawley House,** East Marton, Skipton, N. Yorks, BD23 3LP
Tel: 01282 843207
Open: All year

Egton
NZ8006

▲ **Ladycross Plantation Caravan Park,** Egton, Whitby, North Yorkshire, YO21 1UA
Actual Grid Ref: NZ821080
Tel: 01947 895502
Open: Easter to Oct

Ellingstring
SE1684

▲ **Ellingstring Youth Hostel,** Holybreen, Ellingstring, Masham, Ripon, HG4 4PW
Tel: 01677 460132
Fax: 01677 460132
Capacity: 18
Under 18: £4.75 **Adults:** £6.25
Open: All year, 5.00pm
Showers • Shop • Lounge • Drying room • Cycle store • Parking • No smoking
A basic hostel in a stone cottage on the eastern edge of the Yorkshire Dales National Park. Cyclists and walkers can explore the byways, and historians can visit Fountains, Jervaulx and Ripon.

Elvington
SE7047

▲ **The Old Gate House,** Wheldrake Lane, Elvington, York, YO41 4AZ
Tel: 01904 608225
Open: Mar to Oct

Escrick
SE6342

▲ **Approach Farm Caravan Site,** Escrick, York, YO19 6EE
Tel: 01757 248250
Open: All year

Farndale
SE6697

▲ **Oak House,** Farndale, Kirkbymoorside, North Yorkshire, YO6 6LH
Actual Grid Ref: SE659986
Tel: 01751 433053
Open: Apr to Oct

Farnham
SE3460

▲ **Kingfisher Caravan Park,** Low Moor Lane, Farnham, Knaresborough, North Yorkshire, HG5 9DQ
Actual Grid Ref: SE335600
Tel: 01423 869411
Open: Mar to Oct

Fearby
SE1981

▲ **Black Swan Caravan and Campsite,** Fearby, Masham, Ripon, North Yorkshire, HG4 4NF
Actual Grid Ref: SE194809
Tel: 01765 689477
Open: Mar to Oct

Filey
TA1180

▲ **Filey Brigg Touring Caravan & Country Park,** North Cliff, Filey, North Yorkshire, YO14 0SS
Actual Grid Ref: TA118815
Tel: 01723 513852
Open: Mar to Sept

▲ **Primrose Valley Holiday Centre,** Primrose Valley, Filey, North Yorkshire, YO14 9RF
Tel: 01723 513771
Open: Easter to Oct

Follifoot
SE3352

▲ **Rudding Holiday Park,** Follifoot, Harrogate, N Yorks, HG3 1JH
Actual Grid Ref: SE333530
Tel: 01423 870439
Email: hpreception@rudding-park.co.uk
Open: Mar to Oct

Fylingdales
SE9199

▲ **Grouse Hill Caravan Park,** Flask Bungalow Farm, Fylingdales, Whitby, North Yorkshire, YO22 4QH
Actual Grid Ref: NZ930005
Tel: 01947 880543
Open: Apr to Oct

Hostels and campsites may vary rates – be sure to check when booking.

Galphay
SE2572

▲ **Gold Coin Farm,** Galphay, Ripon, North Yorkshire, HG4 3NJ
Actual Grid Ref: SE254726
Tel: 01765 658508
Open: Apr to Oct

Gargrave
SD9354

▲ **Eshton Road Caravan Site,** Gargrave, Skipton, North Yorkshire, BD23 3PN
Actual Grid Ref: SD935547
Tel: 01756 749229
Open: All year

Glaisdale
NZ7603

▲ **Hollins Farm,** Glaisdale, Whitby, N. Yorks, YO21 2PZ
Actual Grid Ref: NZ753042
Tel: 01947 897516
Tent pitches: 10
Tent rate: £2.00
Open: All year
Last arr: 10pm
Dogs allowed • Showers • Calor Gas/Camping Gaz • Picnic/barbecue area on site • Children's play area
Campsite charging £2 per person. Breakfast available by arrangement.

Goathland
NZ8301

▲ **Abbot's House Farm,** Goathland, Whitby, North Yorkshire, YO22 5NH
Actual Grid Ref: NZ838005
Tel: 01947 896270 or 896026
Email: ivegill@enterprise.net
Tent pitches: 90
Tent rate: £4.50-£7.50
Open: Mar to Oct
Last arr: any time
Dogs allowed • Calor Gas/Camping Gaz • Showers • Public phone on site • Shop on site
Backpacker's discount. Steam railway. Heartbeat country. Holiday apartment. Caravan hire.

▲ **Jackson's Camp Site,** Goathland, Whitby, North Yorkshire, YO22 5NP
Tel: 01947 896274
Open: Mar to Nov

MAP PAGE 192 • **North Yorkshire**

Great Ayton

NZ5611

▲ **Whinstone View Farm,** Great Ayton, Middlesbrough, Cleveland, TS9 6QG
Actual Grid Ref: NZ554123
Tel: 01642 723285
Open: Mar to Oct

Great Broughton

NZ5406

▲ **White House Farm Caravan Park,** Ingleby Road, Great Broughton, Middlesbrough, North Yorkshire, TS9 5JE
Actual Grid Ref: NZ555071
Tel: 01642 712148
Tent pitches: 30
Tent rate: £2.00-£3.00
Open: Mar to Oct
Last arr: 10pm
Dogs allowed • Electric hook-up • Picnic/barbecue area on site • Children's play area • Showers • Laundrette on site 1.5 acre fishing lake - carp to 16 lb.

Grinton

SE0498

▲ **Grinton Lodge Youth Hostel,** Grinton Lodge, Grinton, Richmond, N. Yorks, DL11 6HS
Tel: 01748 884206
Fax: 01748 884876
Email: grinton@yha.org.uk
Capacity: 69
Under 18: £6.90
Adults: £10.00
Open: Feb to Nov + New Year, 5.00pm
Family bunk rooms
Self-catering facilities • Television • Showers • Laundry facilities • Lounge • Games room • Drying room • Cycle store • Evening meal available 7pm • WC • Breakfast available • Credit cards accepted
A useful stopover for the Coast to Coast path and the Yorkshire Dales Cycleway. Harkerside Moor has traditional drystone walling and field barns. The hostel itself was once a shooting lodge and retains its log fires among other original features.

Gristhorpe

TA0981

▲ **Crow's Nest Caravan Park,** Gristhorpe Bay, Filey, North Yorkshire, YO14 9PS
Actual Grid Ref: TA086834
Tel: 01723 582206
Open: Mar to Oct

▲ **Blue Dolphin Holiday Centre,** Gristhorpe Bay, Gristhorpe, Filey, North Yorkshire, YO14 9PU
Actual Grid Ref: TA093830
Tel: 01723 515155
Open: Mar to Oct

Harome

SE6482

▲ **Foxholme Caravan Park,** Harome, York, YO62 5JG
Actual Grid Ref: SE661831
Tel: 01439 770416
Fax: 01439 771744
Open: Apr to Oct

Harrogate

SE3055

▲ **High Moor Farm Park,** Skipton Road, Harrogate, North Yorkshire, HG3 2LT
Actual Grid Ref: SE244559
Tel: 01423 563637
Open: Apr to Oct

▲ **Ripley Caravan Park,** Knaresborough Road, Harrogate, North Yorkshire, HG3 3AU
Actual Grid Ref: SE288602
Tel: 01423 770050
Open: Apr to Oct

▲ **Shaw's Trailer Park,** Knaresborough Road, Harrogate, North Yorkshire, HG2 7NE
Actual Grid Ref: SE324558
Tel: 01423 884432
Open: All year

Hawes

SD8789

▲ **Hawes Youth Hostel,** Lancaster Terrace, Hawes, N Yorks, DL8 3LQ
Actual Grid Ref: SD867897
Tel: 01969 667368
Fax: 01969 667723
Capacity: 58
Under 18: £6.90
Adults: £10.00
Open: Feb to Dec + Xmas
Self-catering facilities • Television • Laundry facilities • Lounge • Games room • Drying room • Cycle store • Evening meal available 7.00pm • No smoking • Kitchen facilities • Breakfast available • Credit cards accepted
Friendly and attractively refurbished purpose-built hostel overlooking Hawes and Wensleydale.

▲ **Bainbridge Ings Caravan & Camping Site,** Hawes, North Yorkshire, DL8 3NU
Actual Grid Ref: SD875894
Tel: 01969 667354
Tent pitches: 40
Tent rate: £3.00-£7.00
Open: Apr to Oct
Last arr: 9.30pm
Dogs allowed • Electric hook-up • Calor Gas/Camping Gaz • Showers
Quiet, clean, well organised family-run site. Marvellous views.

▲ **Brown Moor,** Hawes, North Yorkshire, DL8 3PS
Tel: 01969 667338
Open: Easter to Jan

▲ **Shaw Ghyll Farm Caravan & Camping Site,** Simonstone, Hawes, N Yorks, DL8 3LY
Actual Grid Ref: SD868919
Tel: 01969 667359
Open: Mar to Oct

Helmsley

SE6184

▲ **Helmsley Youth Hostel,** Carlton Lane, Helmsley, York, North Yorkshire, YO62 5HB
Tel: 01439 770433
Fax: 01439 770433
Capacity: 36
Under 18: £6.50 **Adults:** £9.25
Open: All year, 5.00pm
Self-catering facilities • Showers • Laundry facilities • Lounge • Dining room • Drying room • Cycle store • Evening meal available 7.00pm • No smoking • Kitchen facilities • Breakfast available • Credit cards accepted
The hostel is in the centre of the market town of Helmsley, a short distance from both the market square and the castle. It is a great base for walkers, starting the Cleveland Way.

High Bentham

SD6669

▲ **Riverside Caravan Park,** Wenning Avenue, High Bentham, Lancaster, LA2 7HS
Actual Grid Ref: SD668688
Tel: 01524 261272
Open: Mar to Oct

▲ **Curlew Camping,** Tennant House, High Bentham, Lancaster, LA2 7AH
Actual Grid Ref: SD684693
Tel: 015242 62176
Open: Apr to Oct

Stilwell's Hostels & Camping 2002

North Yorkshire • MAP PAGE 192

ENGLAND

High Hawsker
NZ9207

▲ **York House Caravan Park,** High Hawsker, Whitby, North Yorkshire, YO22 4LW
Actual Grid Ref: NZ927074
Tel: 01947 880354
Open: Mar to Oct

Hinderwell
NZ7916

▲ **'Serenity' Touring Caravan & Camping Park,** High Street, Hinderwell, Saltburn-by-the-Sea, North Yorkshire, TS13 5JH
Actual Grid Ref: NZ792168
Tel: 01947 841122
Open: Mar to Oct

Horsehouse
SE0481

▲ **The Thwaite Arms,** Horsehouse, Leyburn, N. Yorks, DL8 4TS
Tel: 01969 640206
Open: All year

Hunmanby
TA0977

▲ **Orchard Farm Holiday Village,** 143 Stonegate, Hunmanby, Filey, North Yorks, YO14 0PU
Actual Grid Ref: TA105779
Tel: 01723 891582
Open: All year

Hutton Bonville
NZ3400

▲ **Hutton Bonville Caravan Park & Camping Site,** Church Lane, Hutton Bonville, Northallerton, North Yorkshire, DL7 0NR
Tel: 01609 881416
Open: Mar to Oct

Hutton Sessay
SE4776

▲ **White Rose Caravan Park Ltd,** Hutton Sessay, Thirsk, North Yorkshire, YO7 3BA
Tel: 01845 501215
Open: Mar to Oct

To stay in a Youth Hostel affiliated to one of the Youth Hostel associations, you need to be a member. You can join at most hostels – phone in advance to check.

Hutton-le-Hole
SE7089

▲ **The Crown,** Hutton-le-Hole, York, YO62 6UA
Tel: 01751 417343
Open: All year

Ingleby Cross
NZ4500

▲ **Blue Bell Inn,** Ingleby Cross, Northallerton, N. Yorks, DL6 3NF
Tel: 01609 882272
Open: All year

Ingleton
SD6973

▲ **Ingleton Youth Hostel,** Greta Tower, Sammy Lane, Ingleton, Carnforth, LA6 3EG
Actual Grid Ref: SD695733
Tel: 015242 41444
Fax: 015242 41854
Capacity: 58
Under 18: £7.75
Adults: £11.00
Open: All year, 5.00pm
Family bunk rooms
Self-catering facilities • Showers • Lounge • Dining room • Drying room • Cycle store • Parking • Evening meal available 7.00pm • No smoking • WC • Kitchen facilities • Breakfast available • Credit cards accepted
The hostel has been refurbished recently, and is ideally placed for family holidays, being on the edge of the Yorkshire Dales National Park. It is also a good base for climbers, pot-holers and walkers of all levels.

Some hostels and campsites impose restrictions on size and type of groups they accept (e.g. not permitting single-sex groups). Always phone to enquire before booking.

Keld
NY8901

▲ **Keld Youth Hostel,** Keld Lodge, Keld, Upper Swaledale, Richmond, N. Yorks, DL11 6LL
Tel: 01748 886259
Fax: 01748 886013
Capacity: 38
Under 18: £6.50
Adults: £9.25
Open: All year, 5.00pm
Family bunk rooms
Self-catering facilities • Television • Showers • Lounge • Dining room • Drying room • Cycle store • Evening meal available 7.00pm • No smoking • Kitchen facilities • Breakfast available • Credit cards accepted
Close to both the Pennine and the Coast-to-Coast long distance paths, this onetime shooting lodge is ideal for walkers. Swaledale has moorland, waterfalls, and abundant wildlife.

▲ **Park Lodge Farm,** Keld, Richmond, N Yorks, DL11 6LJ
Actual Grid Ref: NY892013
Tel: 01748 886274
Open: Apr to Sep

▲ **Park House Camping & Caravans,** Keld, Swaledale, North Yorkshire, DL11 6DZ
Actual Grid Ref: NY887015
Tel: 01748 886549
Open: Apr to Sep

Kettlewell
SD9772

▲ **Kettlewell Youth Hostel,** Whernside House, Kettlewell, Skipton, North Yorkshire, BD23 5QU
Actual Grid Ref: SD970724
Tel: 01756 760232
Fax: 01756 760402
Capacity: 43
Under 18: £6.90
Adults: £10.00
Open: All year, 5.00pm
Self-catering facilities • Television • Showers • Lounge • Drying room • Cycle store • Parking Lomoted • Evening meal available 7.00pm • No smoking • Kitchen facilities • Breakfast available • Luggage store • Credit cards accepted
Large house right in the middle of pretty Wharfedale village of Kettlewell, ideal for families and small groups.

▲ **Fold Farm,** Kettlewell, Skipton, N. Yorks, BD23 5RH
Tel: 01756 760886
Open: All year

---

198   Stilwell's Hostels & Camping 2002

MAP PAGE 192 • **North Yorkshire**

Kilnsey

SD9767

▲ **Skirfare Bridge Dales Barn,** Kilnsey, Skipton, N. Yorks, BD23 5PT
Tel: 01756 752465
Fax: 01756 752465
Email: skirfarebridgebarn@farmersweekly.net
Capacity: 25
Under 18: £8.00 **Adults:** £8.00
Open: All year, 4pm-10.30am
Self-catering facilities • Showers • Central heating • Wet weather shelter • Lounge • Dining room • Grounds available for games • Drying room • Cycle store • Parking • Evening meal available by arrangement
Converted stone barn in beautiful limestone countryside of upper Wharfedale, ideally situated for outdoor activities. All inclusive, warm and well-equipped. Own recreation area. Adjacent to B6160, north of Kilnsey Crag. Pub (700m), trout fishing, pony trekking, leisure centre, picturesque villages nearby. Catering by arrangement. Groups, students and individuals welcomed.

Kirby Misperton

SE7779

▲ **Flamingoland Theme Park & Holiday Village,** Kirby Misperton, Malton, North Yorkshire, YO17 0UX
Actual Grid Ref: SE778800
Tel: 01653 668585
Open: Apr to Oct

▲ **Ashfield Caravan & Camping Park,** Kirby Misperton, Malton, N Yorks, YO17 6UU
Actual Grid Ref: SE778794
Tel: 01653 668555
Open: Mar to Oct

Kirkby

NZ5306

▲ **Toft Hill Caravan Park,** Kirkby, Great Broughton, Middlesbrough, TS9 7HJ
Actual Grid Ref: NZ537043
Tel: 01642 712469
Open: Apr to Oct

Kirkbymoorside

SE6987

▲ **Wombleton Caravan Park,** The Airfield, Wombleton, York, YO62 7RY
Actual Grid Ref: SE669834
Tel: 01751 431634
Open: Mar to Oct

Hostels and campsites may vary rates – be sure to check when booking.

Knaresborough

SE3557

▲ **The Lido Caravan Park,** Wetherby Road, Knaresborough, North Yorkshire, HG5 8LR
Actual Grid Ref: SE362560
Tel: 01423 865169
Open: Feb to Nov

Langthorpe

SE3867

▲ **Old Hall Caravan Park,** Langthorpe, Boroughbridge, North Yorkshire, YO5 9BZ
Actual Grid Ref: SE392672
Tel: 01423 322130
Open: Apr to Oct

Lebberston

TA0782

▲ **Lebberston Touring Caravan Park,** Beckfield Green, Lebberston, Scarborough, North Yorkshire, YO11 3PF
Actual Grid Ref: TA077824
Tel: 01723 585723 / 582254
Open: Mar to Oct

▲ **Flower of May Caravan Park,** Lebberston Cliff, Lebberston, Scarborough, North Yorkshire, YO11 3NU
Tel: 01723 582324
Open: Easter to Oct

Leeming Bar

SE2890

▲ **Pembroke Park,** Leases Road, Leeming Bar, Northallerton, North Yorkshire, DL7 9SW
Actual Grid Ref: SE285905
Tel: 01677 422652
Open: Apr to Sep

Leyburn

SE1190

▲ **Akebar Park,** Leyburn, North Yorkshire, DL8 5LY
Actual Grid Ref: SE192906
Tel: 01677 450201
Open: Mar to Jan

Linton

SD9962

▲ **Linton Youth Hostel,** The Old Rectory, Linton, Skipton, North Yorkshire, BD23 5HH
Actual Grid Ref: SD998627
Tel: 01756 752400
Fax: 01756 752400
Capacity: 36
Under 18: £6.90
Adults: £10.00
Open: All year, 5.00pm
Self-catering facilities • Wet weather shelter • Dining room • Drying room • Cycle store • Parking • Evening meal available 7.00pm • No smoking • WC • Kitchen facilities
C17th former rectory in own grounds, across the stream from the village green, in one of Wharfedale's most picturesque and unspoilt villages.

Linton-on-Ouse

SE4960

▲ **Linton Lock Leisureways,** Linton-on-Ouse, York, YO30 2AZ
Tel: 01347 848486
Open: Mar to Oct

Lockton

SE8489

▲ **Lockton Youth Hostel,** The Old School, Lockton, Pickering, North Yorkshire, YO18 7PY
Actual Grid Ref: SE844900
Tel: 01751 460376
Capacity: 22
Under 18: £5.20
Adults: £7.50
Open: All year, 5.00pm
Self-catering facilities • Showers • Cycle store • Parking • No smoking • WC • Kitchen facilities • Credit cards accepted
Former village school in rural hamlet just off main Pickering-Whitby road. Enjoy walks in Cropton and Dalby Forests.

Lofthouse

SE0973

▲ **Studdfold Farm,** Lofthouse, Harrogate, North Yorkshire, HG3 5SG
Actual Grid Ref: SE099733
Tel: 01423 755210
Open: Apr to Oct

All details shown are as supplied by hostels and campsites in Autumn 2000.

ENGLAND

North Yorkshire • MAP PAGE 192

ENGLAND

Lothersdale
SD9645

▲ **Lynmouth,** Dale End, Lothersdale, Skipton, N Yorks, BD20 8EH
Tel: 01535 632744
Fax: 01535 632744
Open: All year (not Xmas)

Low Bentham
SD6469

▲ **Goodenbergh Caravan Park,** Low Bentham, Lancaster, LA2 7EW
Tel: 01524 262022
Open: Mar to Oct

Malham
SD9062

▲ **Malham Youth Hostel,** John Dower Memorial Hostel, Malham, Skipton, North Yorkshire, BD23 4DE
Actual Grid Ref: SD901629
Tel: 01729 830321
Fax: 01729 830551
Email: malham@yha.org.uk
Capacity: 82
Under 18: £7.75 **Adults:** £11.00
Open: All year, 5.00pm
Family bunk rooms
Self-catering facilities • Television • Showers • Shop • Laundry facilities • Drying room • Security lockers • Cycle store • Parking • Evening meal available 7.00pm • WC • Kitchen facilities • Breakfast available • Credit cards accepted
Superbly located purpose-built hostel close to centre of picturesque Malham village, in the middle of caving, walking and cycling district.

▲ **Gordale Scar Camping Site,** Malham, Skipton, North Yorkshire, BD23 4DL
Tel: 01729 830333
Open: Mar to Oct

Markington
SE2865

▲ **Yorkshire Hussar Inn Holiday Caravan Park,** Markington, Harrogate, North Yorkshire, HG3 3NR
Actual Grid Ref: SE288650
Tel: 01765 677137
Open: Mar to Nov

Muker
SD9098

▲ **Usha Gap,** Muker, Richmond, N Yorks, DL11 4DW
Tel: 01748 886214
Open: All year

Naburn
SE5945

▲ **Naburn Lock Caravan Site,** Naburn, York, YO19 4RU
Actual Grid Ref: SE595445
Tel: 01904 728697
Fax: 01904 728697
Email: nablock@easynet.co.uk
Open: Mar to Oct

Nawton
SE6584

▲ **Wrens of Ryedale Caravan Site,** Gale Lane, Nawton, York, YO62 7SD
Actual Grid Ref: SE656841
Tel: 01439 771260
Open: Apr to Oct

Newbiggin in Bishopdale
SD9985

▲ **Street Head Caravan Park,** Newbiggin in Bishopdale, Leyburn, North Yorkshire, DL8 3TE
Actual Grid Ref: SD998862
Tel: 01969 663472
Open: Mar to Oct

Newsham
NZ1010

▲ **Tavern House Caravan Park,** Newsham, Richmond, N. Yorks, DL11 7RA
Actual Grid Ref: NZ106101
Tel: 01833 621223
Open: Mar to Oct

North Stainley
SE2876

▲ **Sleningford Water Mill Caravan & Camping Park,** North Stainley, Ripon, North Yorkshire, HG4 3HQ
Actual Grid Ref: SE288775
Tel: 01765 635201
Open: Apr to Oct

Osmotherley
SE4597

▲ **Osmotherley Youth Hostel,** Cote Ghyll, Osmotherley, Northallerton, North Yorkshire, DL6 3AH
Actual Grid Ref: SE461981
Tel: 01609 883575
Fax: 01609 883715
Email: Osmotherley@yha.org.uk
Capacity: 72
Under 18: £6.90
Adults: £10.00
Open: All year (not Xmas/New Year), 1.00pm
Family bunk rooms
Self-catering facilities • Television • Showers • Laundry facilities • Wet weather shelter • Lounge • Games room • Drying room • Cycle store • Parking • Evening meal available 7.00pm • No smoking • WC • Kitchen facilities • Breakfast available • Credit cards accepted
Surrounded by woodland, the youth hostel is fully modernised with excellent facilities, right on the edge of the North York Moors National Park.

▲ **Cote Ghyll Caravan Park,** Osmotherley, Northallerton, North Yorkshire, DL6 3AH
Actual Grid Ref: SE460983
Tel: 01609 883425
Open: Apr to Oct

Oswaldkirk
SE6279

▲ **Golden Square Caravan & Camping Park,** Country Cottages, Golden Square Farm, Oswaldkirk, York, YO62 5YQ
Actual Grid Ref: SE603798
Tel: 01439 788269
Open: Mar to Oct

Pateley Bridge
SE1565

▲ **Riverside Caravan Park,** Low Wath Road, Pateley Bridge, Harrogate, North Yorkshire, HG3 5HL
Actual Grid Ref: SE154658
Tel: 01423 711383
Open: Apr to Oct

MAP PAGE 192 • **North Yorkshire**

▲ **Westfield Caravan Site,**
Heathfield, Pateley Bridge,
Harrogate, North Yorkshire, HG3 5PU
Actual Grid Ref: SE133666
Tel: 01423 711410
Open: Apr to Oct

▲ **Low Wood Caravan Site,** Spring House, Heathfield, Pateley Bridge, Harrogate, North Yorkshire, HG3 5PZ
Actual Grid Ref: SE135664
Tel: 01423 711433 **Open:** Apr to Oct

Pickering

SE7984

▲ **Rosedale Caravan & Camping Parks,** Rosedale Abbey, Pickering, North Yorkshire, YO18 8SA
Actual Grid Ref: SE724957
AA grade: 3 Pennants
Tel: 01751 417272
Email: rosedale@flowerofmay.com
Tent pitches: 80
Tent rate: £3.00-£11.00
Open: Mar to Oct **Last arr:** 9pm
Dogs allowed • Electric hook-up • Calor Gas/Camping Gaz • Picnic/barbecue area on site • Children's play area • Showers • Laundrette on site • Public phone on site • Shop on site • Baby care facilities • Games room • Indoor swimming pool nearby • Outdoor swimming pool nearby • Golf nearby • Riding nearby • Fishing nearby
Gloriously situated in the North Yorkshire Moors 7 miles from Pickering with all its attractions. York and Helmsley close by with country houses, museums and history right on your doorstep. The park meanders through majestic countryside following the river, magical & restful. All mains facilities, some super pitches for tents and touring caravans.

▲ **Upper Carr Touring Park,**
Upper Carr Lane, Malton Road, Pickering, North Yorkshire, YO18 7JP
Actual Grid Ref: SE803815
Tel: 01751 473115
Email: green@uppercarr.demon.co.uk
Open: Mar to Oct

▲ **The Black Bull Camp & Caravan Park,** Malton Road, Pickering, North Yorkshire, YO18 8EA
Actual Grid Ref: SE802815
Tel: 01751 472528
Open: Apr to Oct

▲ **Overbrook Caravan Site,**
Maltongate, Thornton-le-Dale, Pickering, North Yorkshire, YO18 7XS
Tel: 01751 474417
Open: Mar to Oct

Ravenscar

NZ9801

▲ **Bent Rigg Farm,** Ravenscar, Scarborough, N. Yorks, YO13 0NG
Actual Grid Ref: NZ985008
Tel: 01723 870475
Open: May to Oct

Reighton

TA1374

▲ **Reighton Sands Holiday Park,** Reighton Gap, Reighton, Filey, North Yorkshire, YO14 9SJ
Actual Grid Ref: TA135152
Tel: 01723 890476
Open: Easter to Oct

Ribblehead

SD7778

▲ **The Station Inn,** Ribblehead, Ingleton, Carnforth, LA6 3AS
Tel: 015242 41274
Open: All year

Richmond

NZ1701

▲ **The Bunkhouse,** Richmond Equestrian Centre, Brough Park, Richmond, N. Yorks, DL10 7PL
Tel: 01748 811629
Fax: 01748 818019
Email: info@richmondec.co.uk
Capacity: 18
Under 18: £12.50 **Adults:** £12.50
Open: All year, 8am
Family bunk rooms: £40.00
Self-catering facilities • Television • Showers • Licensed bar • Laundry facilities • Lounge • Dining room • Drying room • Parking • Facilities for disabled people • No smoking
Riding school, overlooking the Dales and North York Moors.

▲ **Swale View Caravan Site,** Reeth Road, Richmond, N Yorks, DL10 4SF
Actual Grid Ref: NZ135012
Tel: 01748 823106
Open: Apr to Oct

Ripon

SE3171

▲ **Riverside Meadows Country Caravan Park,** Ure Bank Top, Ripon, North Yorkshire, HG4 1JD
Actual Grid Ref: SE317727
Tel: 01765 602964 / 607764
Open: Mar to Oct

Robin Hood's Bay

NZ9504

▲ **Hooks House Farm Camp Site,** Whitby Road, Robin Hood's Bay, Whitby, North Yorkshire, YO22 4PE
Actual Grid Ref: NZ946058
Tel: 01947 880283
Tent pitches: 50
Tent rate: £3.00
Open: All year
Last arr: 10pm
Dogs allowed • Electric hook-up • Showers • Indoor swimming pool nearby • Outdoor swimming pool nearby • Boating/sailing/watersports nearby • Tennis courts nearby • Golf nearby • Riding nearby • Fishing nearby
Small, friendly family-run caravan and camping site situated on the B1447 (Whitby Road), half mile from Robin Hood's Bay. Every pitch has magnificent panoramic sea views. All amenities are included in the site fee. The prices quoted are per person. Open all year. Also available self-catering cottage and caravan.

▲ **Middlewood Farm Holiday Park,** Middlewood Lane, Robin Hood's Bay, Fylingthorpe, Whitby, North Yorkshire, YO22 4UF
Actual Grid Ref: NZ945045
AA grade: 3 Pennants
Tel: 01947 880414
Fax: 01947 880414
Email: info@middlewoodfarm.fsnet.co.uk
Tent pitches: 100
Tent rate: £5.00
Open: Mar to Nov
Last arr: 10pm
Dogs allowed • Electric hook-up • Calor Gas/Camping Gaz • Children's play area • Showers • Laundrette on site • Public phone on site • Baby care facilities
Quiet, peaceful, magnificent views. Superb facilities. 10 minutes' walk - beach/pub/shops.

▲ **Flask Holiday Home Park,** Robin Hood's Bay, Fylingdales, Whitby, YO22 4QH
Tel: 01947 880305
Open: Mar to Oct

Stilwell's Hostels & Camping 2002   **201**

North Yorkshire • MAP PAGE 192

Roecliffe

SE3765

▲ **Camping & Caravanning Club Site,** Bar Lane, Roecliffe, Boroughbridge, York, YO51 9LS
Tel: 01423 322683
Open: All year

Runswick Bay

NZ8016

▲ **Runswick Bay Caravan & Camping Park,** Hinderwell Lane, Runswick Bay, Saltburn-by-the-Sea, North Yorkshire, TS13 5HR
Actual Grid Ref: NZ805162
Tel: 01947 840997
Open: Easter to Oct

Scalby

TA0190

▲ **Scarborough Youth Hostel,** The White House, Burniston Road, Scalby, Scarborough, North Yorkshire, YO13 0DA
Actual Grid Ref: TA026907
Tel: 01723 361176
Fax: 01723 500054
Email: scarborough@yha.org.uk
Capacity: 50
Under 18: £6.90
Adults: £10.00
Open: All year, 5.00pm
Family bunk rooms
Self-catering facilities • Showers • Laundry facilities • Lounge • Drying room • Cycle store • Parking • Evening meal available 7.00pm • No smoking • WC • Kitchen facilities • Breakfast available • Credit cards accepted
A converted water mill by a bridge on the Sea Cut, just outside Scarborough, 10 minutes' walk from the Cleveland Way.

Scarborough

TA0388

▲ **Jacobs Mount Caravan Park,** Jacobs Mount, Stepney Road, Scarborough, North Yorkshire, YO12 5NL
Actual Grid Ref: TA021876
Tel: 01723 361178
Open: Mar to Oct

▲ **Scalby Manor Caravan & Camping Park,** Field Lane, Burniston Road, Scarborough, North Yorkshire, YO11 2EP
Actual Grid Ref: TA025911
Tel: 01723 366212
Open: Mar to Oct

▲ **Scalby Close Park,** Burniston Road, Scarborough, N Yorks, YO13 0DA
Actual Grid Ref: TA021918
Tel: 01723 365908
Open: Mar to Oct

▲ **Flower of May Caravan Park,** Lebberston Cliff, Scarborough, North Yorkshire, YO11 3NU
Actual Grid Ref: TA080838
Tel: 01723 584311
Open: Apr to Oct

Scawton

SE5484

▲ **Bungdale Head Farm,** Scawton, Thirsk, North Yorkshire, YO7 2HH
Tel: 01439 770589
Open: Easter to Oct

Scorton

NZ2500

▲ **Ellerton Park,** Ellerton North Farm, Scorton, Richmond, North Yorkshire, DL10 6AP
Actual Grid Ref: SE251981
Tel: 01748 811373
Open: Mar to Nov

Scotch Corner

NZ2105

▲ **Scotch Corner Caravan Park,** Scotch Corner, Richmond, N Yorks, DL10 6NS
Actual Grid Ref: NZ213052
Tel: 01748 822530
Open: Apr to Oct

Seamer (Scarborough)

TA0282

▲ **Arosa Caravan & Camping Park,** Seamer, Scarborough, North Yorkshire, YO12 4QB
Actual Grid Ref: TA012830
Tel: 01723 862166
Open: Mar to Jan

Settle

SD8163

▲ **Langcliffe Caravan Park,** Settle, North Yorkshire, BD24 9LX
Tel: 01729 822387
Open: Mar to Oct

Sheriff Hutton

SE6466

▲ **Camping & Caravanning Club Site,** Bracken Hill, Sheriff Hutton, York, YO60 6QG
Actual Grid Ref: SE638652
Tel: 01347 878660
Open: Mar to Oct

Sinderby

SE3482

▲ **Quernhow Cafe and Caravan Site,** Great North Road, Sinderby, Thirsk, North Yorkshire, YO7 4LG
Actual Grid Ref: SE335813
Tel: 01845 567221
Open: All year

Slingsby

SE6975

▲ **Robin Hood Caravan & Camping Park,** Green Dyke Lane, Slingsby, York, YO62 4AP
Actual Grid Ref: SE700748
Tel: 01653 628391 Open: Mar to Oct

▲ **Camping & Caravanning Club Site,** Railway Street, Slingsby, York, YO62 4AA
Tel: 01653 628335
Open: Mar to Oct

Snainton

SE9282

▲ **Jasmine Caravan Park,** Cross Lane, Snainton, Scarborough, North Yorkshire, YO13 9BE
Actual Grid Ref: SE928813
Tel: 01723 859240 Open: Mar to Dec

Sneaton

NZ8907

▲ **Lound House Farm,** Littlebeck Lane, Sneaton, Whitby, North Yorkshire, YO22 5HY
Actual Grid Ref: NZ890065
Tel: 01947 810383
Open: All year

MAP PAGE 192 • **North Yorkshire**

South Kilvington

SE4284

▲ **Beechwood Caravan Park,**
South Kilvington, Thirsk, YO7 2LZ
Actual Grid Ref: SE426837
Tel: 01845 522348
Open: Mar to Oct

Sowerby

SE4281

▲ **Sowerby Caravan Park,**
Sowerby, Thirsk, North Yorkshire,
YO7 3AG
Actual Grid Ref: SE437801
Tel: 01845 522753
Open: Mar to Oct

Stainforth

SD8267

▲ **Stainforth Youth Hostel,**
Taitlands, Stainforth, Settle, North
Yorkshire, BD24 9PA
Actual Grid Ref: SD821668
Tel: 01729 823577
Fax: 01729 825404
Email: stainforth@yha.org.uk
Capacity: 48
Under 18: £7.75 **Adults:** £11.00
Open: Feb to Nov, 1.00pm
Family bunk rooms
Self-catering facilities • Showers • Lounge • Dining room • Drying room • Cycle store • Parking • Evening meal available 7.00pm • Facilities for disabled people • No smoking • Kitchen facilities • Breakfast available • Credit cards accepted
Georgian listed building with fine interior, set in extensive grounds with grazing paddock, a short walk from the village. Central for many walks, including the Pennine and Ribble Ways, and the Yorkshire Dales Cycleway.

▲ **Knight Stainforth Hall Caravan
& Campsite,** Cross Lane, Stainforth,
Settle, North Yorkshire, BD24 0DP
Actual Grid Ref: SD815645
Tel: 01729 822200
Fax: 01729 823387
Open: Mar to Oct

Stainsacre

NZ9108

▲ **Rigg Farm Caravan Park,**
Stainsacre, Whitby, North Yorkshire,
YO22 4LP
Actual Grid Ref: NZ915061
Tel: 01947 880430
Open: Mar to Oct

Staintondale

SE9998

▲ **Lowfield Camping Site,**
Downdale Road, Staintondale,
Scarborough, North Yorkshire, YO13 0EZ
Actual Grid Ref: TA001977
Tel: 01723 870574
Open: All year

Staxton

TA0278

▲ **Spring Willows Touring
Caravan Park,** Main Road, Staxton
Roundabout, Staxton, Scarborough,
North Yorkshire, YO12 4SB
Actual Grid Ref: TA024794
Tel: 01723 891505
Open: Mar to Dec

Stillingfleet

SE5841

▲ **Home Farm Caravan &
Camping,** Moreby, Stillingfleet, York,
YO19 6HN
Actual Grid Ref: SE595428
Tel: 01904 728263
Open: Feb to Dec

Strensall

SE6361

▲ **Moorside Caravan Park,** Flaxton
Road, Strensall, York, YO32 5XJ
Tel: 01904 491208
Open: Mar to Oct

Summerbridge

SE2062

▲ **Manor House Farm Caravan
Park,** Manor House Farm,
Summerbridge, Harrogate, North
Yorkshire, HG3 3JS
Tel: 01423 780322
Open: Mar to Oct

Thirsk

SE4282

▲ **Trax Caravan Club Site,** Station
Road, Thirsk, North Yorkshire, YO7 1QL
Actual Grid Ref: SE420820
Tel: 01845 525266
Open: Apr to Oct

Thixendale

SE8461

▲ **Thixendale Youth Hostel,** The
Village Hall, Thixendale, Malton,
North Yorkshire, YO17 8TG
Actual Grid Ref: SE843610
Tel: 01377 288238
Capacity: 18
Under 18: £4.65
Adults: £6.80
Open: Apr to Sep
No smoking
The old school in a quiet village, near the foot of a remarkable chalk dry valley.

Threshfield

SD9863

▲ **Wood Nook Caravan Park,**
Skirethorns, Threshfield, Skipton,
North Yorkshire, BD23 5NU
Actual Grid Ref: SD974641
Tel: 01756 752412
Open: Mar to Oct

Tollerton

SE5164

▲ **Tollerton Park,** Station Road,
Tollerton, York, YO61 1RD
Actual Grid Ref: SE515645
Tel: 01347 838313
Open: Mar to Oct

Ugthorpe

NZ7911

▲ **Burnt House Holiday Park,**
Ugthorpe, Whitby, North Yorkshire,
YO21 2BG
Actual Grid Ref: NZ785114
Tel: 01947 840448
Open: Mar to Oct

▲ **Ugthorpe Lodge ,** Guisborough
Road, Ugthorpe, Whitby, North
Yorkshire, YO21 2BE
Actual Grid Ref: NZ784112
Tel: 01947 840518
Open: Apr to Oct

Ulleskelf

SE5140

▲ **Whitecote Caravan Park,** Ryther
Road, Ulleskelf, Tadcaster, North
Yorkshire, LS24 9DY
Actual Grid Ref: SE526397
Tel: 01937 835231
Open: All year

North Yorkshire • MAP PAGE 192

ENGLAND

West Burton
SE0186

▲ **Little Cote Farm,** West Burton, Leyburn, North Yorkshire, DL8 4JY
Tel: 01969 666450
Open: Mar to Oct

West Witton
SE0688

▲ **Chantry Caravan Park,** West Witton, Leyburn, N Yorks, DL8 4NA
Tel: 01969 622372
Open: Mar to Jan

Whitby
NZ8910

▲ **Whitby Youth Hostel,** East Cliff, Whitby, North Yorkshire, YO22 4JT
Actual Grid Ref: NZ902111
Tel: 01947 602878
Fax: 01947 602878
Capacity: 58
Under 18: £6.90
Adults: £10.00
Open: Feb to Dec + New Year, 5.00pm
Family bunk rooms
Self-catering facilities • Showers • Lounge • Dining room • Drying room • Security lockers • Cycle store • Evening meal available 7.00pm • No smoking • Kitchen facilities • Breakfast available • Credit cards accepted
Converted stable range near abbey, at top of 199 steps above the harbour of this ancient fishing town.

▲ **Northcliffe Holiday Park,** High Hawsker, Whitby, North Yorkshire, YO22 4LL
Actual Grid Ref: NZ942079
Tel: 01947 880477
Email: enquiries@northcliffe.com
Open: Apr to Oct

▲ **Haven Holiday Village,** Saltwick Bay, Whitby, North Yorkshire, YO22 4JX
Actual Grid Ref: NZ915015
Tel: 01947 602664
Open: Mar to Sept

▲ **Sandfield House Farm Caravan Park,** Sandsend Road, Whitby, North Yorkshire, YO21 3SR
Actual Grid Ref: NZ875115
Tel: 01947 602660
Email: sandfieldw@aol.com
Open: Mar to Oct

▲ **Manor House Farm,** Hawsker, Whitby, North Yorkshire, YO22 4JZ
Actual Grid Ref: NZ920096
Tel: 01947 603107
Open: Apr to Sep

Winksley
SE2471

▲ **Woodhouse Farm Caravan & Camping Park,** Winksley, Ripon, North Yorkshire, HG4 3PG
Actual Grid Ref: SE241715
Tel: 01765 658309
Fax: 01765 658882
Email: woodhouse.farm@talk21.com
Tent pitches: 50
Tent rate: £7.00-£9.00
Open: Mar to Oct **Last arr:** 9pm
Dogs allowed • Electric hook-up • Calor Gas/Camping Gaz • Picnic/barbecue area on site • Children's play area • Showers • Laundrette on site • Public phone on site • Shop on site
Glorious countryside to discover, close to Fountains Abbey, Brimham Rocks.

Wistow
SE5935

▲ **Scalm Park Farm,** Wistow, Selby, YO8 3RD
Tel: 01757 704873
Email: scalmpark@aol.com
Open: All year

Wrelton
SE7686

▲ **Wayside Caravan Park,** Wrelton, Pickering, North Yorkshire, YO18 8PG
Actual Grid Ref: SE766860
Tel: 01751 472608
Open: Apr to Oct

Wykeham (Scarborough)
SE9683

▲ **St Helens Caravan Park,** St Helens in the Park, Wykeham, Scarborough, North Yorkshire, YO13 9QD
Actual Grid Ref: SE967534
Tel: 01723 862771
Open: All year

York
SE5951

▲ **The Racecourse Centre,** Tadcaster Road, York, YO24
Tel: 01904 636553
Fax: 01904 612815
Email: info@racecoursecentre.co.uk
Capacity: 134
Under 18: £17.50 **Adults:** £18.50
Open: All year, 10am
Television • Showers • Central heating • Lounge • Dining room • Games room • Grounds available for games • Security lockers • Cycle store • Parking • Evening meal available 6pm • Facilities for disabled people
Easily accessible by road and rail, the centre provides excellent value budget accommodation for groups of all ages throughout the year. 134 beds in single, twin and family rooms. Cafeteria style dining room and a large recreation room suitable for receptions, meetings and leisure. Excellent coach/car parking.
GROUPS ONLY.

▲ **York International Youth Hostel,** Water End, Clifton, York, YO30 6LP
Actual Grid Ref: SE589528
Tel: 01904 653147
Fax: 01904 651230
Email: york@yha.org.uk
Capacity: 150
Under 18: £11.50
Adults: £15.50
Open: All year, All day
Family bunk rooms
Self-catering facilities • Television • Licensed bar • Laundry facilities • Lounge • Games room • Cycle store • Parking • Evening meal available 5.30-7.30pm • Kitchen facilities • Breakfast available • Luggage store • Credit cards accepted
Comfortable Victorian house with spacious grounds in a peaceful location just a walk along the river from the city. The hostel has its own restaurant.

MAP PAGE 192 • **North Yorkshire**

▲ ***York Youth Hotel,*** *11/17*
Bishophill Senior, York, YO1 6EF
Actual Grid Ref: SE601515
Tel: 01904 625904
Fax: 01904 612494
Email: info@yorkyouthhotel.com
Capacity: 120
Under 18: £11.00 **Adults:** £12.00
Open: All year, any time
Family bunk rooms: £36.00
Self-catering facilities • Television • Showers • Licensed bar • Central heating • Shop • Laundry facilities • Lounge • Dining room • Games room • Drying room • Cycle store • Parking • Evening meal available for groups only • No smoking
Large Georgian house in city centre location.

▲ ***Micklegate House Youth Hotel,***
88-90 Micklegate, York, YO1 6JX
Tel: 01904 627720
Fax: 01904 339350
Email: mail@micklegatehouse.com
Capacity: 135
Under 18: £9.00 **Adults:** £9.00
Open: All year
Family bunk rooms: £30.00
Self-catering facilities • Television • Showers • Licensed bar • Central heating • Shop • Laundry facilities • Lounge • Dining room • Games room • Drying room • Security lockers • Cycle store • Evening meal available
1752 Georgian mansion, located in the heart of medieval York.

▲ ***Rawcliffe Manor Caravan Site,***
Manor Lane, Shipton Road, Rawcliffe, York, YO30 5TZ
Actual Grid Ref: SE583552
Tel: 01904 624422
Open: All year

▲ ***Goosewood Caravan Park,***
Sutton On The Forest, York, YO61 1ET
Actual Grid Ref: SE595636
Tel: 01347 810829
Open: Mar to Oct

Hostels and campsites may vary rates – be sure to check when booking.

South Yorkshire

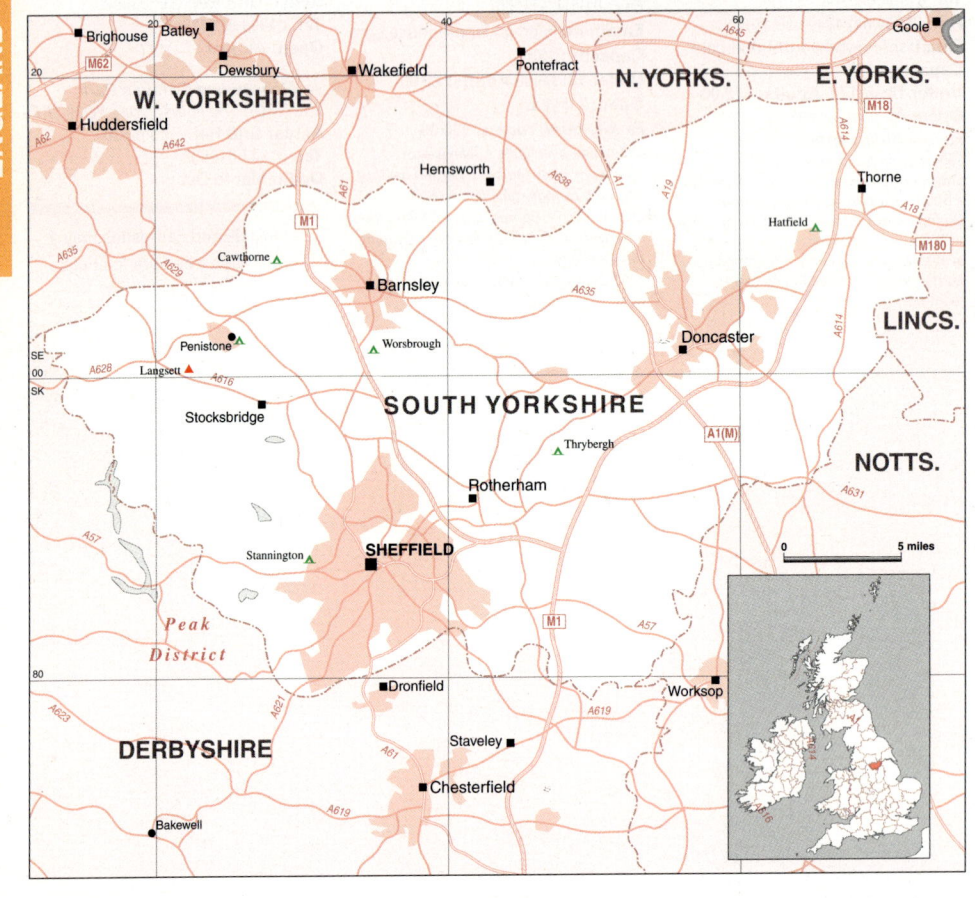

Cawthorne

SE2807

▲ **Cinderhills Farm,** Cawthorne, Barnsley, S. Yorks, S75 4JA
Tel: 01226 790318
Open: All year

Hatfield

SE6609

▲ **Hatfield Water Park,** Hatfield, Doncaster, South Yorkshire, DN7 6EQ
Actual Grid Ref: SE670110
Tel: 01302 841572 / 737263
Open: Apr to Oct

Langsett

SE2100

▲ **Langsett Youth Hostel,** Langsett, Stocksbridge, Sheffield, S36 4GY
Tel: 01226 761548
Fax: 01226 761548
Email: reservations@yha.org.uk
Capacity: 27
Under 18: £5.75 **Adults:** £8.50
Open: All year, 5.00pm
Self-catering facilities • Showers • Lounge • Drying room • Cycle store • No smoking • WC • Kitchen facilities
Open fires in this moorland hostel, close to 'Last of the Summer Wine' country. It has easy access to the Derwent Valley.

Penistone

SE2403

▲ **Woodland View Caravan Site,** 322 Barnsley Road, Hoylandswaine, Sheffield, S36 7HA
Actual Grid Ref: SE268048
Tel: 01226 761906
Open: Apr to Nov

Sheffield - Stannington

SK3088

▲ **Fox Hagg Farm Caravan Site,** Lodge Lane, Rivelin, Sheffield, S6 5SN
Tel: 0114 230 5589
Open: Apr to Oct

South Yorkshire

Thrybergh

SK4695

▲ **Thrybergh Country Park Touring & Camping Site,**
Doncaster Road, Thrybergh,
Rotherham, S65 4NU
Actual Grid Ref: SK474963
Tel: 01709 850353 **Fax:** 01709 851532
Tent pitches: 25
Tent rate: £3.00-£5.40
Open: All year **Last arr:** 6pm
Facilities for disabled people • Dogs allowed • Electric hook-up • Cafe or Takeaway on site • Picnic/barbecue area on site • Children's play area • Showers • Public phone on site • Shop on site • Fishing on site

Set in a country park adjacent to a fly fishing lake. Between villages of Thrybergh and Hooton Roberts on the A630. Showers, shop and cafe on site. Excellent place from which to explore the South Yorkshire countryside. Conisbrough Castle and Earth Centre a short distance away. Dogs welcome.

Worsbrough

SE3503

▲ **Greensprings Touring Park,**
Rockley Abbey Farm, Rockley Lane,
Worsbrough, Barnsley, South Yorkshire, S75 3DS
Actual Grid Ref: SE330019
Tel: 01226 288298
Open: Apr to Oct

West Yorkshire

ENGLAND

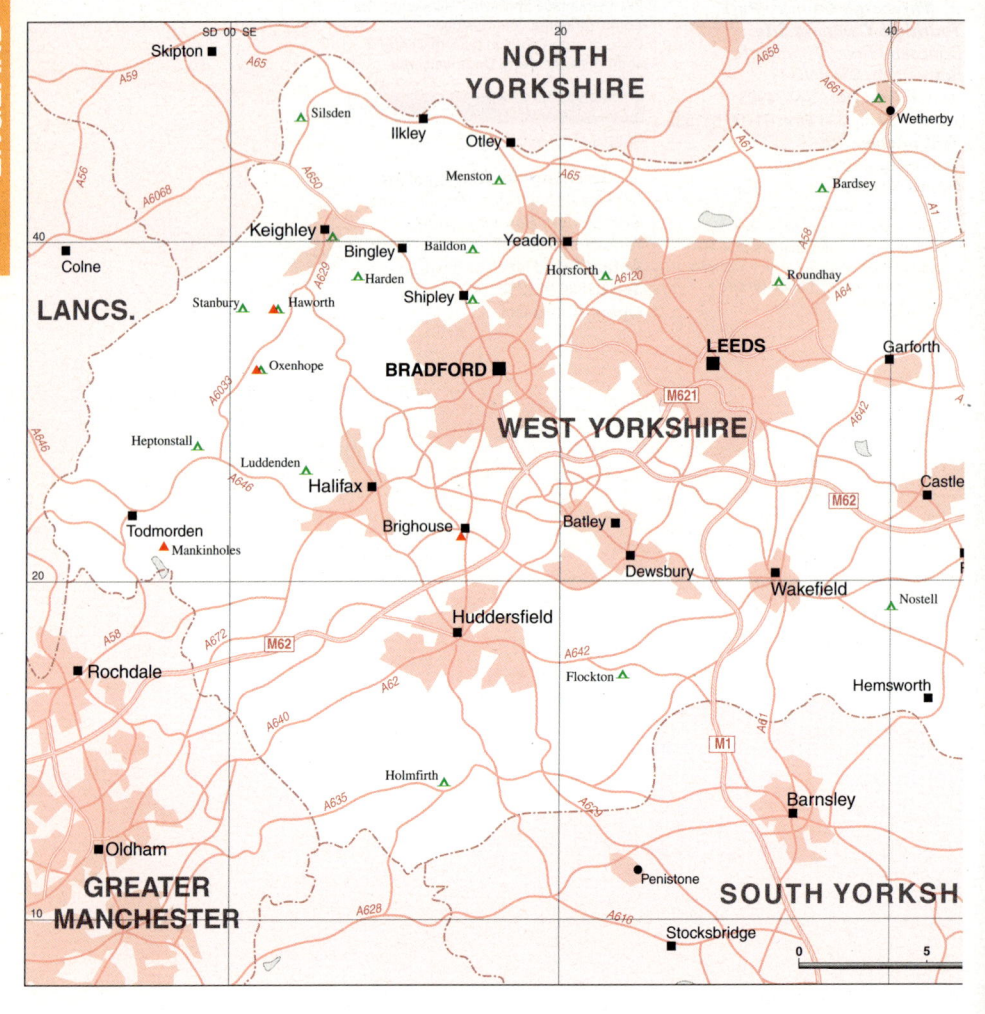

To stay in a Youth Hostel affiliated to one of the Youth Hostel associations, you need to be a member. You can join at most hostels – phone in advance to check.

Some hostels and campsites impose restrictions on size and type of groups they accept (e.g. not permitting single-sex groups). Always phone to enquire before booking.

Baildon

SE1539

▲ **Dobrudden Caravan Park,**
Baildon Moors, Baildon, Shipley,
West Yorkshire, BD17 5EE
Tel: 01274 581016
Open: Mar to Dec

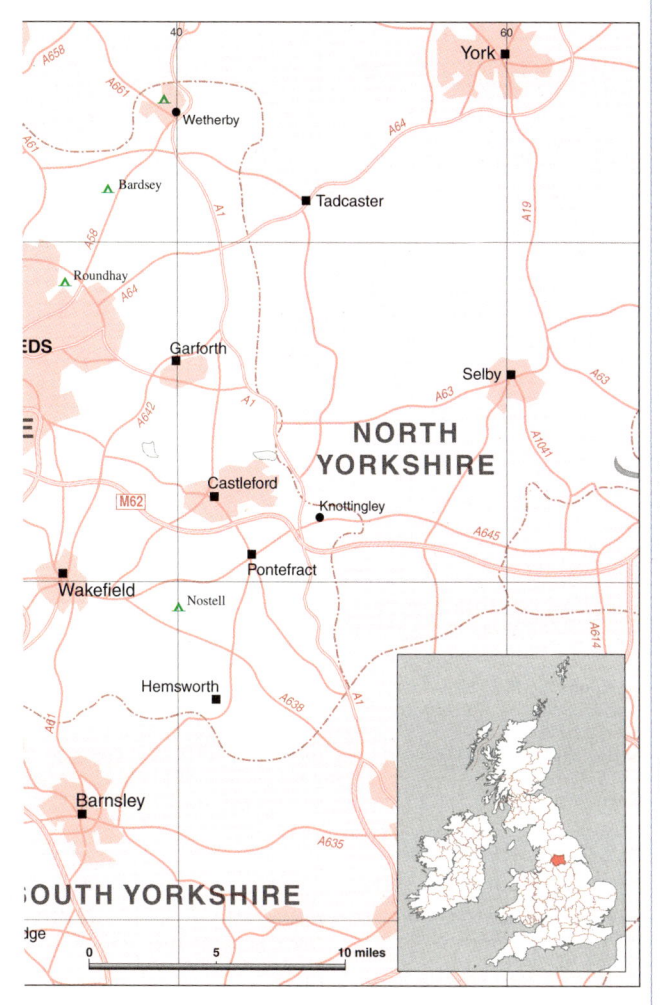

West Yorkshire

Brighouse
SE1423

▲ **Naturefriends House,** Ebor Mount, 67 Lightcliffe Road, Brighouse, HD6 2EX
Actual Grid Ref: SE141236
Tel: 01484 710113
Fax: 01484 710113
Email: b.k.s@btinternet.com
Capacity: 12
Under 18: £5.00 **Adults:** £10.00
Open: All year, all day
Self-catering facilities • Television • Showers • Central heating • Laundry facilities • Lounge • Dining room • Grounds available for games • Parking • Facilities for disabled people • No smoking
Beautiful Victorian house in a secluded garden 0.75 mile from town centre, making excellent base for South Pennine exploration. Open fire & barbecue. Available for members of 'Naturefriends' (international green tourism organisation). Guests welcome. Yearly subscription: over 18 (£8) under 18 (£5) plus £1 joining fee. Membership forms available at the house.

Flockton
SE2314

▲ **Highfield House Caravan Park,** Highfield House, Clough Road, Flockton, Wakefield, WF4 4DQ
Actual Grid Ref: SE246145
Tel: 01924 840124
Open: All year

Harden
SE0838

▲ **Harden & Bingley Caravan Park,** Goit Stock Private Estate, Goit Stock Lane, Harden, Bingley, West Yorkshire, BD16 1DF
Tel: 01535 273810
Open: Apr to Oct

Bardsey
SE3643

▲ **Moor Lodge Caravan Park,** Blackmore Lane, Bardsey, Leeds, LS17 9DZ
Actual Grid Ref: SE352423
Tel: 01937 572424
Open: All year

▲ **Glenfield Caravan Park,** Fernleigh Bungalow, Blackmoor Lane, Bardsey, Leeds, LS17 9DZ
Actual Grid Ref: SE351421
Tel: 01937 574657
Open: All year

All details shown are as supplied by hostels and campsites in Autumn 2000.

Hostels and campsites may vary rates – be sure to check when booking.

West Yorkshire • MAP PAGE 208

Haworth
SE0337

▲ **Haworth Youth Hostel,** Longlands Hall, Longlands Drive, Lees Lane, Haworth, Keighly, West Yorkshire, BD22 8RT
Actual Grid Ref: SE038378
Tel: 01535 642234
Fax: 01535 643023
Email: haworth@yha.org.uk
Capacity: 100
Under 18: £6.90 **Adults:** £10.00
Open: Feb to Dec + New Year (not Xmas), All day
Self-catering facilities • Showers • Laundry facilities • Lounge • Games room • Drying room • Cycle store • Parking • Evening meal available 6.30pm • No smoking • WC • Kitchen facilities • Breakfast available • Credit cards accepted
Victorian mill owner's mansion with interesting architectural features, set in extensive grounds just outside the Bronte village. Good home-cooked meals.

▲ **Upwood Holiday Park,** Blackmoor Road, Haworth, Keighley, W. Yorks, BD22 9SS
Tel: 01535 644242
Open: Mar to Oct

▲ **Westfield Farm,** Tim Lane, Haworth, Keighley, W. Yorks, BD22 7SA
Tel: 01535 644568 **Fax:** 01535 644568
Open: All year

Heptonstall
SD9728

▲ **Pennine Camp & Caravan Site,** High Greenwood House, Heptonstall, Hebden Bridge, West Yorkshire, HX7 7AZ
Actual Grid Ref: SD969308
Tel: 01422 842287
Open: Apr to Oct

Holmfirth
SE1408

▲ **Holme Valley Camping & Caravan Park,** Thongsbridge, Holmfirth, Huddersfield, West Yorkshire, HD7 2TD
Actual Grid Ref: SE152105
Tel: 01484 665819 **Fax:** 01484 663870
Open: Easter to Dec

All details shown are as supplied by hostels and campsites in Autumn 2000.

Horsforth
SE2338

▲ **St Helenas Caravan Site,** None-Go-Bye Farm, Otley Old Road, Horsforth, Leeds, LS18 5HZ
Actual Grid Ref: SE240420
Tel: 0113 284 1142
Open: Apr to Oct

Keighley
SE0541

▲ **Brown Bank Caravan Park,** Brown Bank Lane, Slisden, Keighley, West Yorkshire, BD20 0NN
Tel: 01535 653241
Open: Apr to Oct

▲ **Bronte Caravan Park,** Halifax Road, Keighley, W.Yorks, BD21 5QF
Tel: 01535 691746
Open: Apr to Oct

Leeds - Roundhay
SE3337

▲ **Roundhay Park Site,** Roundhay Park, Elmete Lane, Wetherby Road, Leeds, LS8 2LG
Actual Grid Ref: SE339376
Tel: 0113 265 2354
Open: Mar to Oct

Luddenden
SE0426

▲ **Jerusalem Farm Camp Site,** Jerusalem Lane, Booth, Luddenden, Halifax, HX2 6XB
Actual Grid Ref: SE036279
Tel: 01422 883246
Open: Apr to Sep

Mankinholes
SD9623

▲ **Mankinholes Youth Hostel,** Mankinholes, Todmorden, West Yorkshire, OL14 6HR
Actual Grid Ref: SD960235
Tel: 01706 812340
Fax: 01706 812340
Capacity: 32
Under 18: £6.90 **Adults:** £10.00
Open: All year, 5.00pm

Family bunk rooms
Self-catering facilities • Showers • Laundry facilities • Dining room • Parking • Evening meal available 7.00pm • Facilities for disabled people • No smoking • WC • Kitchen facilities • Luggage store • Credit cards accepted
Listed ancient manor house in a conservation village with typical South Pennine architecture, surrounded by moorland.

Menston
SE1743

▲ **Yorkshire Clarion Clubhouse Ltd,** Chevin Road, Menston, Ikley, West Yorkshire, LS29 6BL
Tel: 01924 382952
Open: Apr to Oct

Nostell
SE4017

▲ **Nostell Priory Holiday Park,** Nostell, Wakefield, West Yorkshire, WF4 1QD
Actual Grid Ref: SE404184
Tel: 01924 863938
Fax: 01924 862226
Open: Apr to Sep

Oxenhope
SE0335

▲ **Westfield Lodge Moorside Bunkhouses,** Westfield Lodge, New Westfield Farm, Upper Marsh, Oxenhope, Keighley, W.Yorks, BD22 9RH
Tel: 01535 646900
Capacity: 87
Under 18: £7.00
Adults: £7.00
Open: All year, 10am
Showers • Licensed bar
Close to Pennine Way, Yorkshire Moors and Dales. Superb views.

▲ **Marsh Top Farm,** Marsh Lane, Oxenhope, Keighley, W.Yorks, BD22 9RN
Tel: 01535 642184
Open: Easter to Oct

▲ **Westfield Lodge,** Moorside Bunkhouse, New Westfield Farm, Upper Marsh, Oxenhope, Keighley, W.Yorks, BD22 9RH
Tel: 01535 646900
Fax: 01535 646900
Open: All year

MAP PAGE 208 • **West Yorkshire**

Shipley

SE1437

▲ **Crook Farm Caravan Park,** Glen Road, Shipley, Bradford, West Yorkshire, BD17 5ED
Tel: 01274 584339 **Open:** Mar to Jan

Silsden

SE0446

▲ **Dales Bank Holiday Park,** Low Lane, Silsden, Keighley, West Yorkshire, BD20 9JH
Actual Grid Ref: SE035484
Tel: 01535 653321 / 656523
Open: Apr to Oct

▲ **Lower Heights Farm,** Bradley Road, Silsden, Keighley, W. Yorks, BD20 9HW
Tel: 01535 653035
Open: Easter to Nov

Stanbury

SE0137

▲ **Upper Heights Farm,** Stanbury, Keighley, W. Yorks, BD22 0HH
Actual Grid Ref: SD994362
Tel: 01535 644592
Open: Apr to Oct

Wetherby

SE4048

▲ **Maustin Caravan Park,** Kearby with Netherby, Wetherby, West Yorkshire, LS22 4DA
Tel: 0113 288 6234
Open: Mar to Oct

You are advised to book in advance for periods of high demand – the Summer months, Half Term holidays and public holidays.

ENGLAND

Isle of Man

Douglas
SC3875

⛺ **Glenlough Farm Campsite,** Union Mills, Douglas, Isle of Man, IM4 4AT
Actual Grid Ref: SC343782
Tel: 01624 851326 **Open:** Apr to Sep

⛺ **Nobles Park Campsite,** Douglas, Isle of Man, IM2 4BD
Actual Grid Ref: SC384774
Tel: 01624 621132
Open: Jun to Sep

Glenroy
SC4083

⛺ **Laxey Commissioners Campsite,** Quarry Road, Laxey, Isle of Man, IM4 7DU
Actual Grid Ref: SC438841
Tel: 01624 861241 / 861816
Open: Apr to Oct

Hillberry
SC3880

⛺ **Glen Dhoo Farm Camp Site,** Hillberry, Onchan, Douglas, Isle of Man, IM4 5BJ
Actual Grid Ref: SC383796
Tel: 01624 621254
Open: Apr to Oct

Kirk Michael
SC3190

⛺ **Glen Wyllin Campsite,** Kirk Michael, Isle of Man, IM6 1AL
Actual Grid Ref: SC314903
Tel: 01624 878231 / 878836
Open: May to Sep

Hostels and campsites may vary rates – be sure to check when booking.

Peel
SC2484

⛺ **Peel Camping Park,** Derby Road, Peel, Isle of Man, IM5 1RG
Actual Grid Ref: SC252840
Tel: 01624 842341 / 843667
Open: May to Sep

St John's
SC2782

⛺ **Ballaspit Farm,** Patrick Road, St John's, Douglas, Isle of Man, IM4 3BP
Tel: 01624 842574
Open: All year

All details shown are as supplied by hostels and campsites in Autumn 2000.

County Antrim

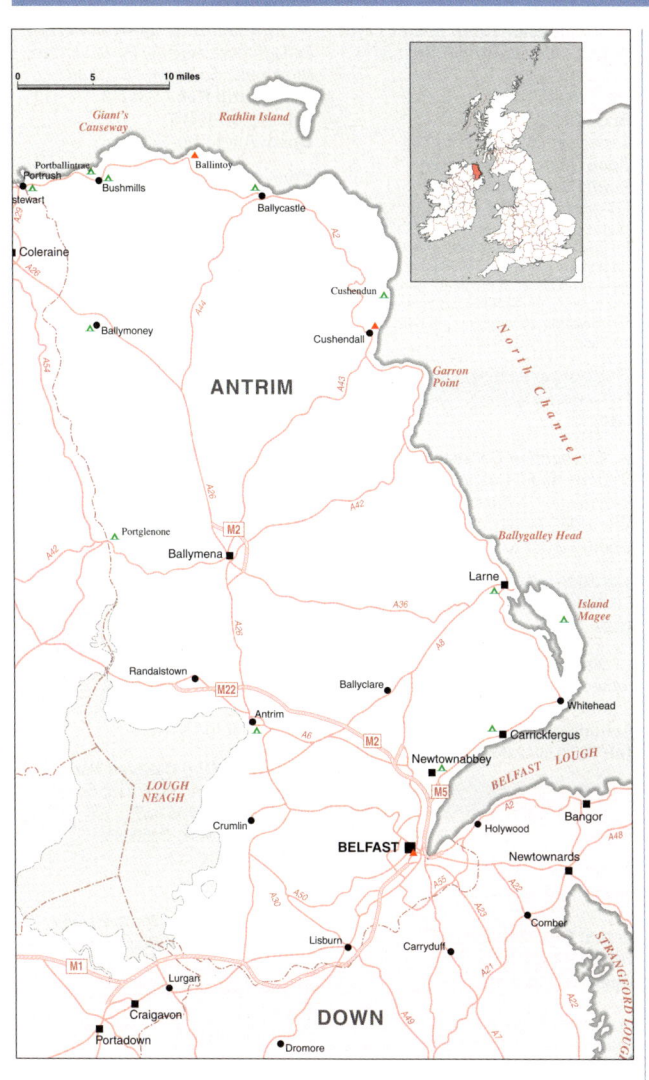

Ballintoy
D0444

▲ **Whitepark Bay International Youth Hostel,** 157 Whitepark Road, Ballintoy, Ballycastle, Co Antrim BT54 6NH
Tel: 028 2073 1745
Fax: 028 2073 2034
Capacity: 62 **Adults:** £10.50
Open: All year, all day Apr to Sep; from 5pm Oct to Mar
Family bunk rooms
Television • Laundry facilities • Evening meal available • Facilities for disabled people
With magnificent views over the sea, this is a new, purpose-built hostel, in its own secluded grounds.

Ballycastle
D1241

▲ **Silvercliffs Holiday Village,** 21 Clare Road, Ballycastle, Co Antrim, BT54 5DB
Actual Grid Ref: D111418
Tel: 01265 762550
Open: Mar to Oct

Ballymoney
C9425

▲ **Drumaheglis Marina & Caravan Park,** 36 Glenstall Road, Ballymoney, Co Antrim, BT53 7QN
Actual Grid Ref: C899261
Tourist Board grade: 5 Ticks
Tel: 028 2766 6466/2766 2280 x 227
Fax: 028 2766 7659
Email: info@ballymoney.gov.uk
Tent pitches: 20
Tent rate: £9.00-£11.00
Open: Apr to Oct **Last arr:** 9pm
Facilities for disabled people • Dogs allowed • Electric hook-up • Calor Gas/Camping Gaz • Picnic/barbecue area on site • Children's play area • Showers • Laundrette on site • Public phone on site
Perfect riverside location, ideal for exploring Causeway Coast and Glens.

Antrim
J1587

▲ **Sixmilewater Caravan Park,** Lough Road, Antrim, Co Antrim, BT28 2PQ
Actual Grid Ref: J140870
Tel: 01849 464131
Open: Apr to Sep

Some hostels and campsites impose restrictions on size and type of groups they accept (e.g. not permitting single-sex groups). Always phone to enquire before booking.

County Antrim • MAP PAGE 213

Belfast
J3374

▲ Belfast International Youth Hostel, 22 Donegal Road, Belfast BT12 5JN
Tel: 028 9032 4733
Fax: 028 9043 9699
Capacity: 124
Adults: £9.00
Open: All year, All day
Family bunk rooms
Television • Central heating • Shop • Laundry facilities • Cycle store • Parking • Evening meal available • Facilities for disabled people
Modern and cosmopolitan, this purpose-built hostel is ideally sited in the Belfast University area. It is highly popular with visitors of all descriptions.

Bushmills
C9440

▲ Bush Caravan Park, 95 Priestland Road, Bushmills, Co Antrim, BT57 8UJ
Actual Grid Ref: C902308
Tel: 028 2073 1678
Open: Apr to Oct

Carrickfergus
J4187

▲ Beechgrove, 412 Upper Road, Trooperslane, Carrickfergus, Co Antrim, BT38 8PW
Tel: 028 9336 3204
Open: All year

If you have to cancel your visit to any hostel or campsite, please let them know – it is always possible to make a bed or a pitch available to someone else.

Cushendall
D2427

▲ Cushendall Youth hostel, Layde Road, Cushendall, Co Antrim BT44 0NQ
Tel: 028 2177 1344
Fax: 028 2177 2042
Capacity: 56 **Adults:** £10.50
Open: March to Dec, 5pm
Family bunk rooms
Self-catering facilities • Television • Dining room • Cycle store
The hostel, an historic house, is on the outskirts of Cushendell village, itself on the Antrim coast. It has large gardens, and courses on Nature studies and conservation are encouraged here and in the Field Study Centre.

Cushendun
D2533

▲ Cushenden Caravan Park, 14 Glendun Road, Cushendun, Ballymena, Co Antrim, BT44 0PX
Tel: 01266 74254
Open: Easter to Sep

Islandmagee
J4699

▲ Brown's Bay Caravan Park, Brown's Bay, Islandmagee, Larne, Co Antrim
Actual Grid Ref: J437028
Tel: 028 9338 2497 **Open:** Apr to Sep

Larne
D4002

▲ Carnfunnock Country Park, Coast Road, Drains Bay, Larne, Co Antrim, BT40 2QZ
Actual Grid Ref: D383067
Tel: 01574 260088
Open: Easter to Sep

▲ Curran Caravan Park, 131 Curran Road, Larne, Co Antrim, BT40 1DD
Actual Grid Ref: D410030
Tel: 01574 260088
Open: Easter to Sep

Newtownabbey
J3580

▲ Jordanstown Loughshore Park, Shore Road, Newtownabbey, Co Antrim, BT39 9BA
Actual Grid Ref: J366835
Tel: 028 9086 8751
Open: All year

Portballintrae
C9241

▲ Portballintrae Caravan Park, Ballaghmore Avenue, Portballintrae, Bushmills, Co Antrim, BT57 8RX
Actual Grid Ref: C936418
Tel: 01265 731478
Open: Apr to Oct

Portglenone
C9703

▲ Kingfisher Angling Centre, 24A Hiltonstown Road, Portglenone, Ballymena, Co Antrim, BT44 8EG
Tel: 01266 821630
Open: Mar to Oct

Portrush
C8540

▲ The Skerries Holiday Park, 126 Dunluce Road, Portrush, Co Antrim, BT56 8NB
Actual Grid Ref: C875398
Tel: 01265 822531
Open: Mar to Oct

▲ Hilltop Holiday Park, 60 Loguestown Road, Portrush, Co Antrim, BT56 8PD
Actual Grid Ref: C806308
Tel: 01265 823537
Open: Mar to Oct

▲ Carrick-Dhu Caravan Park, 12 Ballyreagh Road, Portrush, Co Londonderry, BT56 8LS
Actual Grid Ref: C850395
Tel: 028 7082 3712
Open: Apr to Oct

▲ Blairs Caravan Park, 29 Dhu Varren, Portstewart Road, Portrush, Co Antrim, BT56 8EW
Actual Grid Ref: C805309
Tel: 028 7082 2760
Open: Apr to Oct

▲ Ballymacrea Touring Caravan Park, 220 Ballybogy Road, Portrush, Co Antrim, BT56 8NE
Actual Grid Ref: C809401
Tel: 028 7082 4357
Open: All year

You are advised to book in advance for periods of high demand – the Summer months, Half Term holidays and public holidays.

County Armagh

Armagh
H8745

▲ **Armagh Youth Hostel,** 39 Abbey Street, Armagh BT61 7EB
Tel: 028 9032 4733
Fax: 028 9051 1801
Capacity: 62
Adults: £10.50
Open: All year (not Xmas/New Year), 5pm
Family bunk rooms
Self-catering facilities • Television • Central heating • Shop • Laundry facilities • Dining room • Cycle store • Parking • Evening meal available • Facilities for disabled people
This is a brand new hostel, with a variety of types of accommodation. Armagh was St Patrick's headquarters, and is the seat of both the Roman Catholic and Anglican archbishops.

Lurgan
J0758

▲ **Kinnego Caravan Site,** Kinnego Marina, Oxford Island, Lurgan, Craigavon, Co Armagh, BT66 6NJ
Actual Grid Ref: J081630
Tel: 01762 327573
Open: Mar to Oct

Markethill
H9638

▲ **Gosford Forest Park,** 54 Gosford Road, Markethill, Armagh, BT60 1UG
Actual Grid Ref: H968405
Tel: 01861 551277
Open: Apr to Sep

County Down

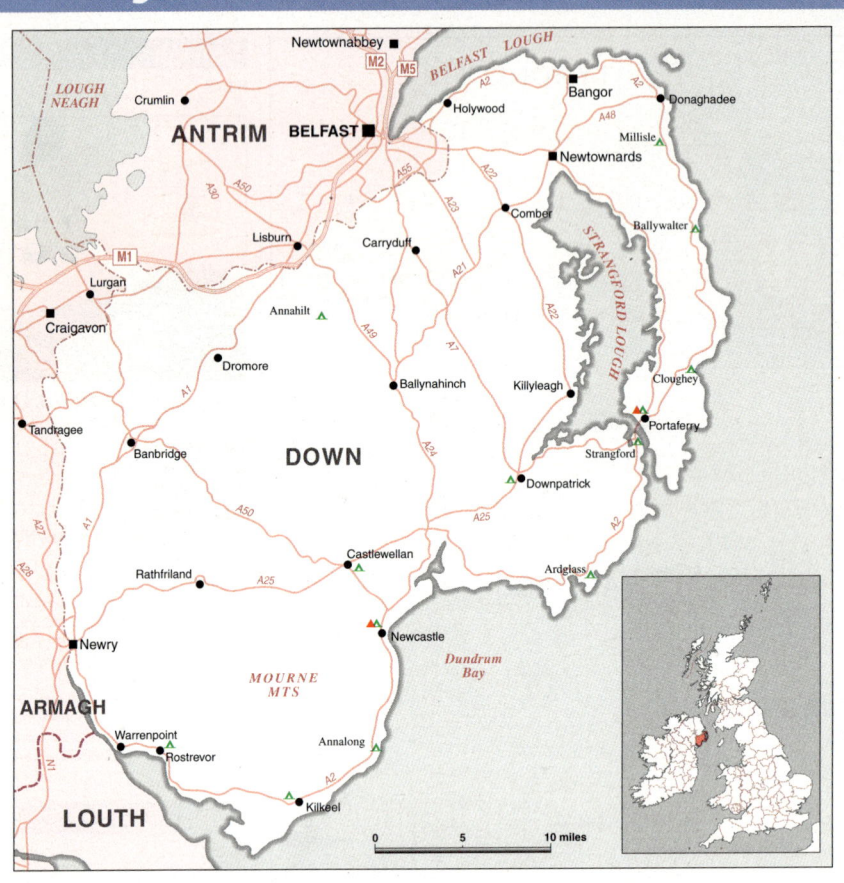

Annahilt

J2956

▲ **Lakeside View Caravan Park,** 71 Magheraconluce Road, Annahilt, Hillsborough, Co Down, BT26 6PR
Actual Grid Ref: J330356
Tel: 028 9268 2098
Open: Easter to Oct

Annalong

J3618

▲ **Annalong Caravan Park,** 38 Kilkeel Road, Annalong, Co Down, BT34 4TZ
Actual Grid Ref: J373193
Tel: 013967 68248
Open: Apr to Oct

Ardglass

J5637

▲ **Coney Island Caravan Park,** 74 Killough Road, Ardglass, Downpatrick, Co Down, BT30 7UH
Tel: 01396 841448
Open: Easter to Nov

Ballywalter

J6268

▲ **Rosebank Caravan Park,** 199 Whitechurch Road, Ballywalter, Newtownards, Co Down, BT22 2JZ
Actual Grid Ref: J610730
Tel: 028 4275 8211
Open: Apr to Oct

▲ **Rockmore Caravan Park,** 69 Whitechurch Road, Ballywalter, Newtownards, Co Down, BT22 2JZ
Actual Grid Ref: J635674
Tel: 028 4276 1428
Open: Apr to Oct

▲ **Sandycove Caravan Park,** 191 Whitechurch Road, Ballywalter, Newtownards, Co Down, BT22 2JZ
Actual Grid Ref: J630705
Tel: 028 4275 8062
Open: Mar to Nov

Please respect hostels' policy on smoking. Some hostels do not allow smoking anywhere, some restrict smoking to certain areas.

County Down

Castlewellan
J3435

▲ **Castlewellan Forest Park,** The Grange, Castlewellan, Co Down, BT31 9BU
Actual Grid Ref: J348382
Tel: 013967 78664
Open: All year

Cloughey
J6356

▲ **Kirkistown Caravan Park,** 55 Main Road, Cloughey, Newtownards, Co Down, BT22 1JB
Actual Grid Ref: J648572
Tel: 012477 71183
Open: Mar to Oct

Downpatrick
J4844

▲ **Minerstown Caravan Park,** Downpatrick, Co Down, BT30 8LS
Tel: 01396 851527
Open: Apr to Nov

Kilkeel
J3014

▲ **Chestnutt Caravan Park,** 3 Grange Road, Cranfield West, Kilkeel, Newry, Co Down, BT34 4LW
Actual Grid Ref: J271110
Tel: 016937 62653
Open: Apr to Oct

▲ **Leestone Caravan Park,** Leestone Road, Kilkeel, Newry, Co Down, BT34 4NW
Actual Grid Ref: J332151
Tel: 028 4176 2567
Open: Apr to Oct

Millisle
J6076

▲ **Rathlin Touring & Holiday Home Park,** 41-45 Moss Road, Millisle, Newtownards, Co Down, BT22 2DS
Tel: 01247 861386
Open: Mar to Sept

▲ **Ballywhiskin Caravan & Camping Park,** 216 Ballywalter Road, Millisle, Newtownards, Co Down, BT21 2LY
Actual Grid Ref: J618723
Tel: 01247 862162
Open: Mar to Nov

▲ **Seaview Caravan Park,** 1 Donaghadee Road, Millisle, Newtownards, Co Down, BT22 2BY
Actual Grid Ref: J590760
Tel: 028 9186 1248
Open: Apr to Oct

Newcastle
J3731

▲ **Newcastle Youth Hostel,** 30 Downs Road, Newcastle, Co Down BT33 0AG
Tel: 028 4372 2133
Capacity: 44
Adults: £10.50
Open: March to Dec, 5pm
Family bunk rooms
Self-catering facilities • Television • Central heating • Laundry facilities • Dining room • Cycle store • Evening meal available
This townhouse hostel is convenient for exploring the Mountains of Mourne.

▲ **Tollymore Forest Park,** 176 Tullybrannigan Road, Newcastle, Co Down, BT33 0PW
Actual Grid Ref: J357318
Tel: 013967 22428
Open: All year

▲ **Windsor Caravan Park ,** 138 Dundrum Road, Newcastle, Co Down, BT33 0LN
Actual Grid Ref: J385330
Tel: 028 4372 3367
Open: Mar to Nov

▲ **Mourneview Caravan Park,** 195 Dundrum Road, Newcastle, Co Down, BT33 0LW
Actual Grid Ref: J409346
Tel: 028 4372 3327
Open: Apr to Oct

Some hostels and campsites impose restrictions on size and type of groups they accept (e.g. not permitting single-sex groups). Always phone to enquire before booking.

Portaferry
J5950

▲ **Portaferry Youth Hostel,** Barholm, 11 The Strand, Portaferry, Co Down BT22 1PF
Tel: 028 4272 9598
Fax: 028 4272 9784
Capacity: 42
Adults: £10.50
Open: All year (not Xmas/New Year), all day
Family bunk rooms
Self-catering facilities • Television • Central heating • Shop • Laundry facilities • Dining room • Cycle store • Evening meal available
Not only an Area of Outstanding Natural Beauty, this is also a Area of Special Scientific Study. The hostel itself in in an Edwardian house, which overlooks Strangford Lough.

▲ **Silver Bay Caravan Park,** 15 Ard Minnan Road, Portaferry, Newtownards, Co Down, BT22 1QJ
Actual Grid Ref: J636560
Tel: 012477 71321
Open: Apr to Oct

▲ **Tara Caravan Park,** 4 Ballyquintin Road, Portaferry, Newtownards, Co Down, BT22 1RE
Actual Grid Ref: J632476
Tel: 028 4272 8459
Open: Apr to Oct

▲ **The NI Aquarium,** The Ropewalk, Castle Street, Portaferry, Co Down, BT22 1NZ
Actual Grid Ref: J600510
Tel: 028 4272 8610
Open: Apr to Sep

Rostrevor
J1718

▲ **Kilbroney Park,** Shore Road, Rostrevor, Newry, Co Down, BT34 3DQ
Actual Grid Ref: J191178
Tel: 016937 38134
Open: Apr to Oct

Strangford
J5948

▲ **The National Trust,** Castleward, Strangford, Downpatrick, Co Down, BT30 7LS
Actual Grid Ref: J580495
Tel: 028 4488 1680
Open: Mar to Sept

County Fermanagh

Blaney
H1553

▲ **Blaney Caravan Park,** Blaney, Enniskillen, Co Fermanagh, BT93 7ER
Actual Grid Ref: H154540
Tel: 01365 641634
Open: All year

Church Hill
H1155

▲ **Loughshore Road Campsite,** 383 Loughshore Road, Tully, Church Hill, Enniskillen, Co Fermanagh, BT93 6HP
Tel: 028 6864 1656
Open: All year

Enniskillen
H2344

▲ **Lakeland Canoe Centre Campsite,** Castle Island, Enniskillen, Co Fermanagh, BT74 5HH
Tel: 01365 324250
Open: Easter to Oct

Irvinestown
H2358

▲ **Castle Archdale Youth Hostel,** Castle Archdale Country Park, Irvinestown, Co Fermanagh BT94 1PP
Tel: 028 6862 8118
Capacity: 44 **Adults:** £10.50
Open: March to Oct, 5pm
Family bunk rooms
Self-catering facilities • Television • Central heating • Shop • Laundry facilities • Dining room • Cycle store • Evening meal available
On the shores of Lower Lough Erne. The hostel is located in an C18th house within the Castle Archdale country park. It is suitable for visitors of all description, wanting to explore Co Fermanagh.

Hostels and campsites may vary rates – be sure to check when booking.

County Fermanagh

Kesh

H1863

▲ **Lakeland Caravan Park,** Boa Island Road, Kesh, Co Fermanagh, BT93 1AE
Actual Grid Ref: H170650
Tel: 028 6863 1578
Open: Feb to Nov

Lisnarrick

H1958

▲ **Castle Archdale Caravan Park & Camp Site Ltd,** Castle Archdale, Lisnarrick, Irvinestown, Enniskillen, Co Fermanagh, BT94 1PP
Actual Grid Ref: H180590
Tel: 01365 621333
Open: Apr to Sep

Some hostels and campsites impose restrictions on size and type of groups they accept (e.g. not permitting single-sex groups). Always phone to enquire before booking.

Lisnaskea

H3633

▲ **Share Centre,** Smiths Strand, Shanaghy, Lisnaskea, Enniskillen, Co Fermanagh, BT92 0EQ
Actual Grid Ref: H340290
Tel: 028 6772 2122
Fax: 028677 21893
Email: share@d.net.co.uk
Capacity: 198
Under 18: £10.00
Adults: £12.00
Open: All year, 8am-12pm
Family bunk rooms: £10.00
Camping: £7.00
Self-catering facilities • Television • Showers • Licensed bar • Central heating • Shop • Laundry facilities • Wet weather shelter • Lounge • Dining room • Games room • Grounds available for games • Drying room • Parking • Evening meal available 5.30pm • Facilities for disabled people
Beautiful 23 acre lake shore site. Learns to sail, windsurf or canoe on site. TV room, play areas, arts/drama activities. enjoy membership of leisure club for duration of stay. Indoor swimming pool children's pool, sauna/steam rooms. Coffee shop on site during summer months.

▲ **Share Holiday Village ,** Share Centre, Smiths Strand, Shanaghy, Lisnaskea, Enniskillen, Co Fermanagh, BT92 0EQ
Actual Grid Ref: H330280
Tel: 028 6772 2122
Fax: 028 6772 1893
Email: share@dnet.co.uk
Tent pitches: 13
Tent rate: £7.00-£10.00
Open: All year **Last arr:** 10pm
Facilities for disabled people • Dogs allowed • Electric hook-up • Cafe or Takeaway on site • Picnic/barbecue area on site • Children's play area • Showers • Laundrette on site • Public phone on site • Licensed bar on site • Shop on site • TV room • Games room • Indoor swimming pool on site • Boating/sailing/watersports on site • Golf nearby • Fishing nearby
Beautiful 23 acre lake shore site. Learn to sail, windsurf or canoe on site. TV room, play areas, arts/drama activities. Enjoy membership of leisure club for duration of stay - indoor swimming pool, children's pool, sauna/steam rooms. Coffee shop on site during summer months.

▲ **Lisnaskea Caravan Park,** Mullynascarty, Lisnaskea, Enniskillen, Co Fermanagh, BT92 0NZ
Actual Grid Ref: H330350
Tel: 028 6672 1040
Open: Easter to Oct

IRELAND

County Londonderry

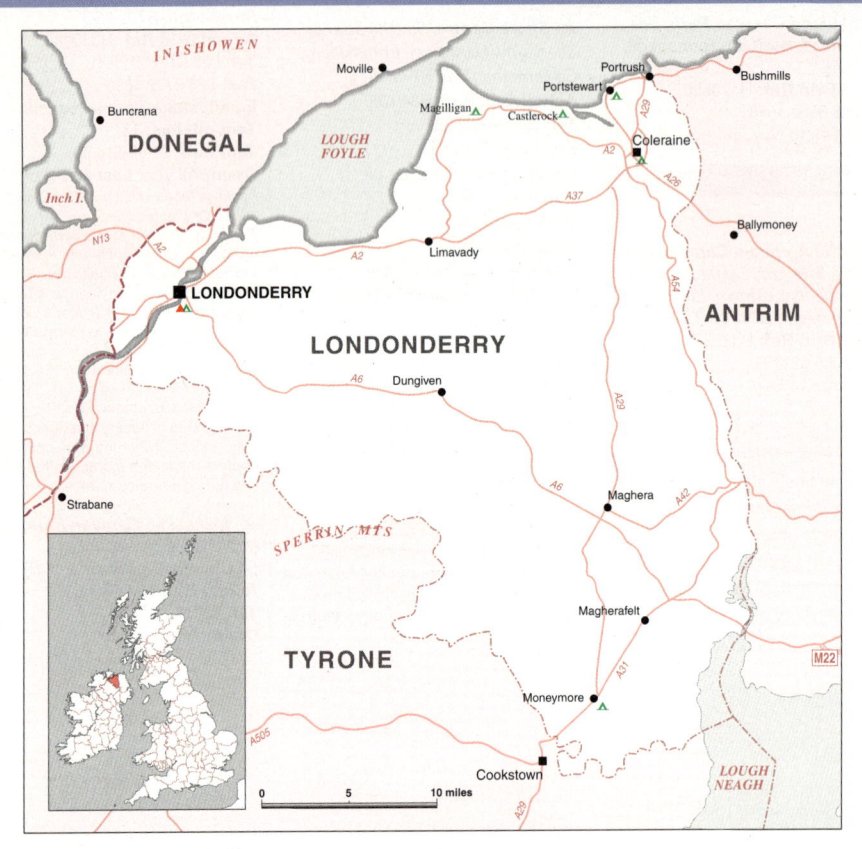

Castlerock

C7736

▲ **Castlerock Holiday Park,** 24 Sea Road, Castlerock, Coleraine, Co Londonderry, BT51 4TN
Actual Grid Ref: C768360
Tel: 01265 843381
Open: Apr to Oct

Coleraine

C8532

▲ **Tullans Farm Caravan Park,** 46 Newmills Road, Coleraine, Co Londonderry, BT52 2JB
Actual Grid Ref: C872314
Tel: 028 7034 2309
Open: Mar to Oct

Londonderry

C4316

▲ **Derry City Youth Hostel,** 4-6 Magazine Street, Londonderry BT48 6HJ
Tel: 028 7137 2273
Fax: 028 7137 2409
Capacity: 120 **Adults:** £10.50
Open: All year, all day
Family bunk rooms
Self-catering facilities • Television • Central heating • Shop • Laundry facilities • Dining room • Games room • Cycle store • Evening meal available • Facilities for disabled people
Derry is the last intact walled city in both Britain and Ireland. The hostel, which is purpose-built is inside the walls.

▲ **Banks of the Faughan Motel,** 69 Clooney Road, Londonderry, BT47 3PA
Tel: 028 7186 0242
Fax: 028 7186 0242
Email: bf.motel@talk21.com
Tent pitches: 6
Tent rate: £7.50-£11.50
Open: All year
Last arr: 10pm
Dogs allowed • Electric hook-up • Picnic/barbecue area on site • Showers • Laundrette on site • Public phone on site
Attractions, city tours, walls, museums, visitors' centre, sports facilities, walking.

Hostels and campsites may vary rates – be sure to check when booking.

Stilwell's Hostels & Camping 2002

County Londonderry

Magilligan
C7034

▲ **Benone Tourist Complex,** 53 Benone Avenue, Magilligan, Limavady, Co Londonderry, BT49 0LQ
Actual Grid Ref: C720360
Tel: 015047 50555 **Open:** All year

▲ **Golden Sands Caravan Parks,** Benone Strand Caravans Ltd, 26 Benone Avenue, Magilligan, Limavady, Co Londonderry, BT49 0LQ
Actual Grid Ref: C708357
Tel: 015047 50324
Open: Apr to Oct

Moneymore
H8683

▲ **The National Trust,** c/o H P Law, Springhill, Moneymore, Magherafelt, Co Londonderry, BT45 7NQ
Actual Grid Ref: H869828
Tel: 028 8674 8210
Open: All year

All details shown are as supplied by hostels and campsites in Autumn 2000.

Portstewart
C8137

▲ **Portstewart Holiday Park,** 80 Mill Road, Portstewart, Co Londonderry, BT55 7SW
Tel: 01265 833308
Open: Easter to Oct

▲ **Juniper Hill Caravan Park,** 70 Ballyreagh Road, Portstewart, Co Londonderry, BT55 7PT
Actual Grid Ref: C839390
Tel: 028 7083 2023
Open: Apr to Oct

IRELAND

County Tyrone

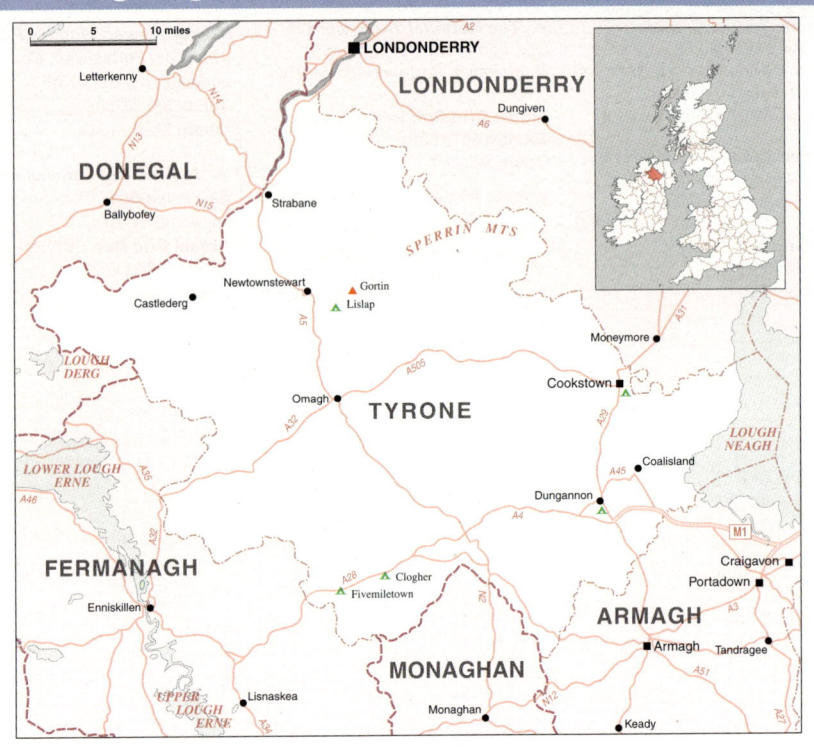

IRELAND

Clogher
H5351

▲ **Clogher Valley Country Caravan Park,** 9 Fardross Road, Clogher, Co Tyrone, BT76 0HG
Actual Grid Ref: H520494
Tel: 016625 48932
Open: Mar to Nov

Cookstown
H8177

▲ **Drum Manor Forest Park,** Oaklands, Cookstown, Co Tyrone, BT70 3DS
Actual Grid Ref: H760780
Tel: 028 8676 2774
Open: All year

You are advised to book in advance for periods of high demand – the Summer months, Half Term holidays and public holidays.

Dungannon
H7962

▲ **Killymaddy Tourist Amenity Centre,** Killymaddy Evans, Ballygawley Road, Dungannon, Co Tyrone, BT70 1TF
Actual Grid Ref: H720603
Tel: 01868 767259
Fax: 01868 767911
Open: All year

Fivemiletown
H4448

▲ **Round Lake Caravan Park,** Dungannon & South Tyrone BC, Circular Road, Dungannon, Co Tyrone, BT71 6DT
Tel: 01868 725311 **Open:** All year

Hostels and campsites may vary rates – be sure to check when booking.

Gortin
H5085

▲ **Gortin Outdoor Centre Hostel,** Glenpark Road, Gortin, Omagh, Co Tyrone, BT79 8PJ
Tel: 028 8164 8207 **Fax:** 028 816 48599
Email: lucinda@bhestate.co.uk
Capacity: 18
Under 18: £6.00 **Adults:** £6.00
Open: All year, 9am-10.30pm
Self-catering facilities • Television • Showers • Laundry facilities • Wet weather shelter • Lounge • Dining room • Grounds available for games • Drying room • Parking
Old schoolhouse close to all local amenities and Sperrin Mountains.

Lislap
H4782

▲ **Gortin Glen Forest Park,** 163 Glenpark Road, Lislap, Omagh, Co Tyrone, BT79 7AU
Actual Grid Ref: H492820
Tel: 028 8164 8217
Open: All year

County Cavan

Ballyconnell

H2718

▲ **Sandville House Hostel,** Ballyconnell, Co Cavan
Actual Grid Ref: H291152
Tel: 049 9526297
Email: sandville@eircom.net
Capacity: 30
Under 18: IR£2.00-IR£7.50
Adults: IR£7.50
Open: All year, until 10pm
Camping for 4 tents: IR£6.00

Self-catering facilities • Television • Showers • Central heating • Laundry facilities • Wet weather shelter • Lounge • Dining room • Games room • Grounds available for games • Parking • Facilities for disabled people

Restored barn hostel in quiet setting. Beautiful, well equipped, totally informal. Large family rooms. gardens, play space. 4 km Ballyconnell, signed from Belturbet Road. Express bus Dublin 2.5 hrs. Explore rich landscape of Cavan and Leitrim. Lakes, hill walks, archaeology. Unmissable Marble Arch Caves 25 km. Good touring base. Occasionally private for retreats.

County Clare

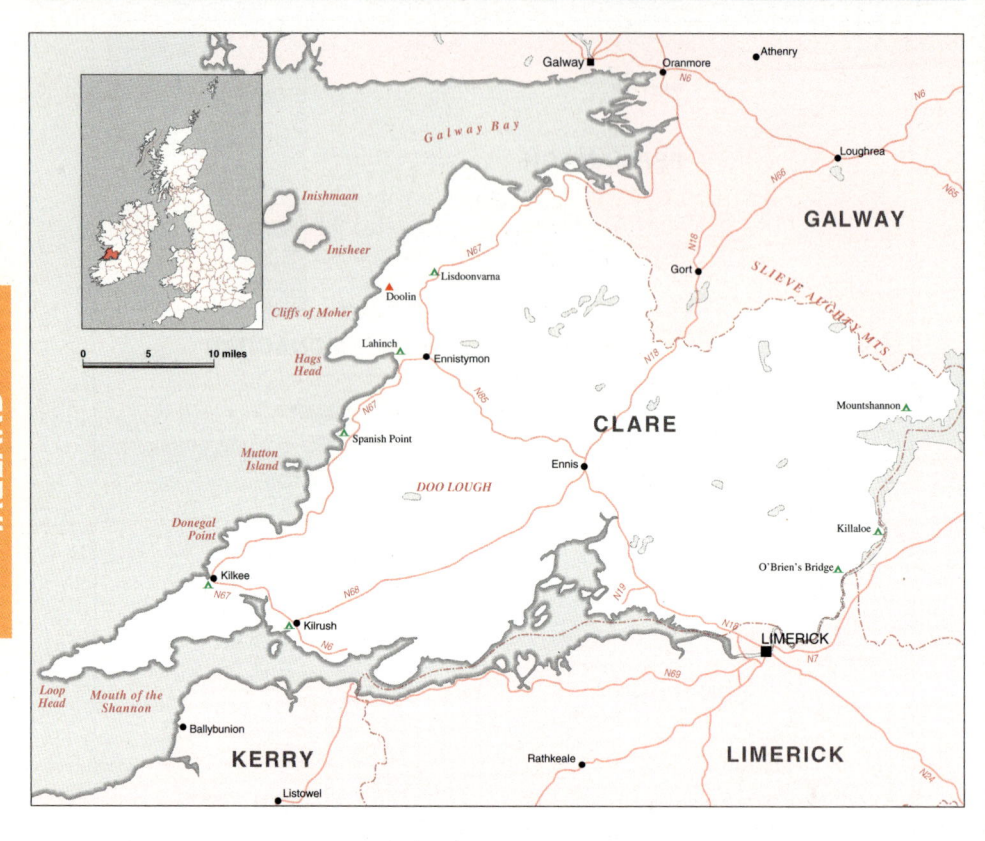

IRELAND

Doolin
R0897

▲ **Aille River Tourist Hostel,** *Doolin, Ennis, County Clare*
Actual Grid Ref: R072966
Tel: 065 7074260
Email: ailleriver@esatclear.ie
Capacity: 32
Under 18: IR£7.50 **Adults:** IR£7.50
Open: All year, all day
Family bunk rooms: IR£8.00
Camping for 15 tents: IR£4.00
Self-catering facilities • Showers • Central heating • Laundry facilities • Wet weather shelter • Lounge • Dining room • Grounds available for games • Drying room •

Security lockers • Cycle store • Parking Aille River Hostel is situated on a quiet road by the banks of the Aille River, halfway between Doolins two famous Irish music villages. You will experience a warm and friendly atmosphere in our old world surroundings. Camping provided adjacent to cliffs of Moher Arran Islands, the Burren. Come and stay!

Kilkee
Q8860

▲ **Cunningham Caravan & Camping Park,** *Kilkee, Kilrush, Co Clare*
Tel: 061 451009
Open: May to Sep

Killaloe
R7073

▲ **Lough Derg Holiday Park,** *Killaloe, Limerick*
Tel: 061 376329
Open: May to Sep

Kilrush
Q9955

▲ **Aylevarroo Caravan Park,** *Kilrush, Co Clare*
Tel: 065 51102
Open: May to Sep

County Clare

Lahinch
R0988

▲ **Lahinch Camping & Caravan Park,** Lahinch, Ennis, Co Clare
Tel: 065 81424
Fax: 065 81194
Open: May to Sep

Lisdoonvarna
R1398

▲ **Gleannbui,** Ballyconnoe, Lisdoonvarna, Ennis, Co Clare
Tel: 065 7074352
Open: Apr to Oct

Mountshannon
R7186

▲ **Lakeside Caravan & Camping Park,** Mountshannon, Limerick
Tel: 061 927225
Open: Apr to Nov

O'Brien's Bridge
R6667

▲ **The Shannon Cottage Caravan Park,** O'Brien's Bridge, Killaloe, Limerick
Tel: 061 377118
Open: All year

Spanish Point
R0377

▲ **Lahiffs Caravan & Camping Park,** Spanish Point, Milltown Malbay, Co Clare
Tel: 065 84006
Open: Apr to Sep

Phoning from outside the Republic? Dial 00353 and omit the initial '0' of the area code.

County Cork

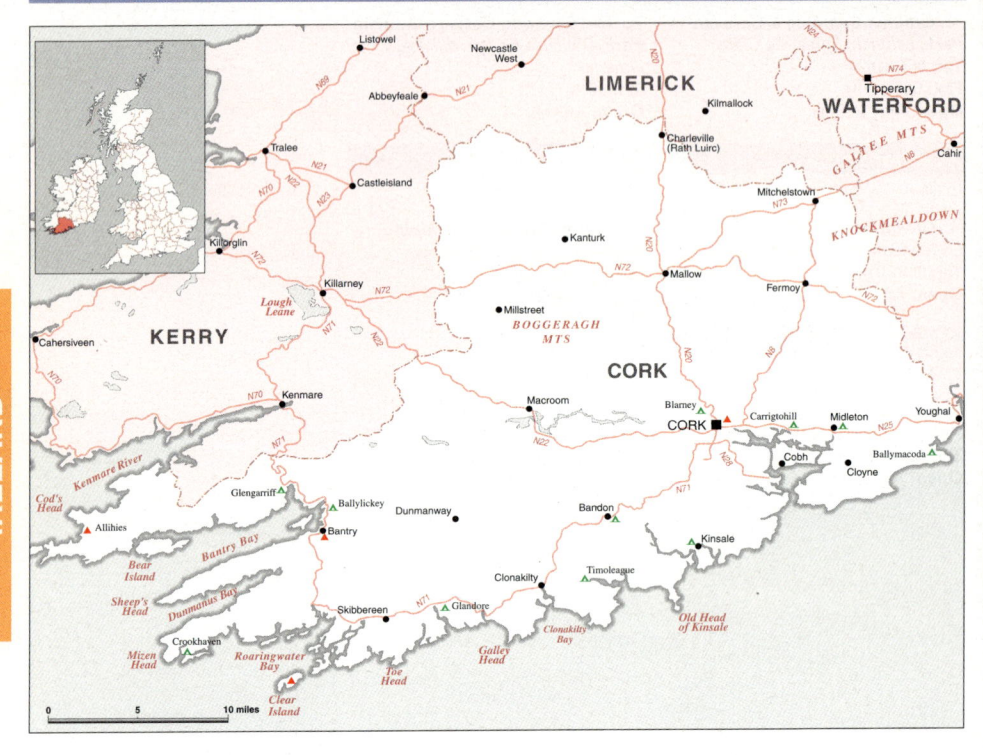

Allihies
V5845

▲ **Allihies Youth Hostel**, Allihies, Bantry, County Cork
Tel: 027 73014
Email: mailbox@anoige.ie
Capacity: 34 **Under 18:** IR£5.50
Adults: IR£7.00 **Open:** June to Sep
Self-catering facilities • Shop 2 km away • Laundry facilities • Parking
Set on the remote Beara Peninsula, the hostel is surrounded by mountains and overlooks the Atlantic. Explore sandy beaches, old copper mines, stone circles.

▲ **Allihies Village Hostel**, Allihies, Bantry, County Cork
Tel: 027 73107
Capacity: 50
Under 18: IR£5.50 **Adults:** IR£8.00
Open: All year, 7am-midnight
Self-catering facilities • Television • Showers • Central heating • Laundry facilities • Wet weather shelter • Lounge • Dining room • Cycle store • Parking • Facilities for disabled people • No smoking
Award-winning hostel nestled in the beautiful village of Allihies, surrounded by mountains and the wild Atlantic Ocean, Allihies is renowned for its friendliness, traditional music and spectacular scenery.

Ballylickey
W0053

▲ **Eagle Point Camping**, Ballylickey, Bantry, Co Cork
Tel: 027 50630
Open: May to Sep

Ballymacoda
X0471

▲ **Sonas Caravan & Camping Park**, Glenawilling, Ballymacoda, Cork
Tel: 024 98132
Open: June to Sept

Bandon
W4955

▲ **Murray's Caravan & Camping**, Kilbrogan Farm, Bandon, Co Cork
Tel: 023 41332
Open: Apr to Sep

You are advised to book in advance for periods of high demand – the Summer months, Half Term holidays and public holidays.

County Cork

Bantry
W0048

▲ **Bantry Independent Hostel,**
Bishop Lucey Place, Bantry, County Cork
Tel: 027 51050
Email: bantryhostel@eircom.net
Capacity: 30 **Adults:** IR£8.00
Open: All year, 11am
Family bunk rooms: IR£35.00
Self-catering facilities • Television • Showers • Central heating • Laundry facilities • Dining room • Parking • No smoking
Near shops, bike hire, sea 300 metres, Internet access, BBQ, wooded setting.

Blarney
W6175

▲ **Blarney Caravan & Camping Park,** Stone View, Blarney, Cork
Tel: 021 385167
Open: All year

Cape Clear Island
V9521

▲ **Cape Clear Island Youth Hostel,** South Harbour, Cape Clear Island, Skibbereen, County Cork
Tel: 028 39198 **Fax:** 028 39144
Email: lasmuigh@tinet.ie
Capacity: 40
Under 18: IR£5.50-IR£6.00
Adults: IR£7.00-IR£8.00
Open: March to Nov
Family bunk rooms
Self-catering facilities • Shop nearby • Laundry facilities • Meals available breakfast for groups 10+
Excellent walking and whale, dolphin and bird watching. New adventure centre at the hostel. Superb scenery.

Carrigtohill
W8172

▲ **Jasmine Villa Caravan & Camping Park,** Carrigtohill, Co Cork
Tel: 021 883234
Open: All year

Cork
W6571

▲ **Cork International Youth Hostel,**
1 Redclyffe, Western Road, Cork
Tel: 021 543289 **Fax:** 021 343715
Email: mailbox@anoige.ie
Capacity: 100
Under 18: IR£7.50-IR£9.00
Adults: IR£8.00-IR£9.50
Open: All year
Family bunk rooms
Self-catering facilities • Shop nearby • Parking • Meals available on request
Ideal for exploring the magnificent city of Cork, with its Cathedral, Blarney Castle and Shandon Steeple. Gateway to the county.

Crookhaven
V8024

▲ **Barleycove Caravan & Camping Park,** Crookhaven, Skibbereen, Co Cork
Tel: 028 35302
Open: June to Aug

If you have to cancel your visit to any hostel or campsite, please let them know – it is always possible to make a bed or a pitch available to someone else.

Glandore
W2235

▲ **The Meadow Camping Park,** Glandore, Skibbereen, Co Cork
Tel: 028 33280
Open: Mar to Oct

Glengarriff
V9256

▲ **Dowling's Caravan & Camping Park,** Glengarriff, Bantry, Co Cork
Tel: 027 63154
Open: Mar to Oct

▲ **O'Shea's Caravan & Camping Park,** Glengarriff, Bantry, Co Cork
Tel: 027 63140
Open: Mar to Oct

Kinsale
W6450

▲ **Garrettstown House Caravan & Camping Park,** Kinsale, Co Cork
Tel: 021 778156
Open: May to Sep

Midleton
W8873

▲ **Trabolgan Holiday Village,** Midleton, Co Cork
Tel: 021 661551
Open: Apr to Nov

Timoleague
W4743

▲ **Sexton's Caravan & Camping Park,** Timoleague, Bandon, Co Cork
Tel: 023 46347
Open: All year

You are advised to book in advance for periods of high demand – the Summer months, Half Term holidays and public holidays.

IRELAND

County Donegal

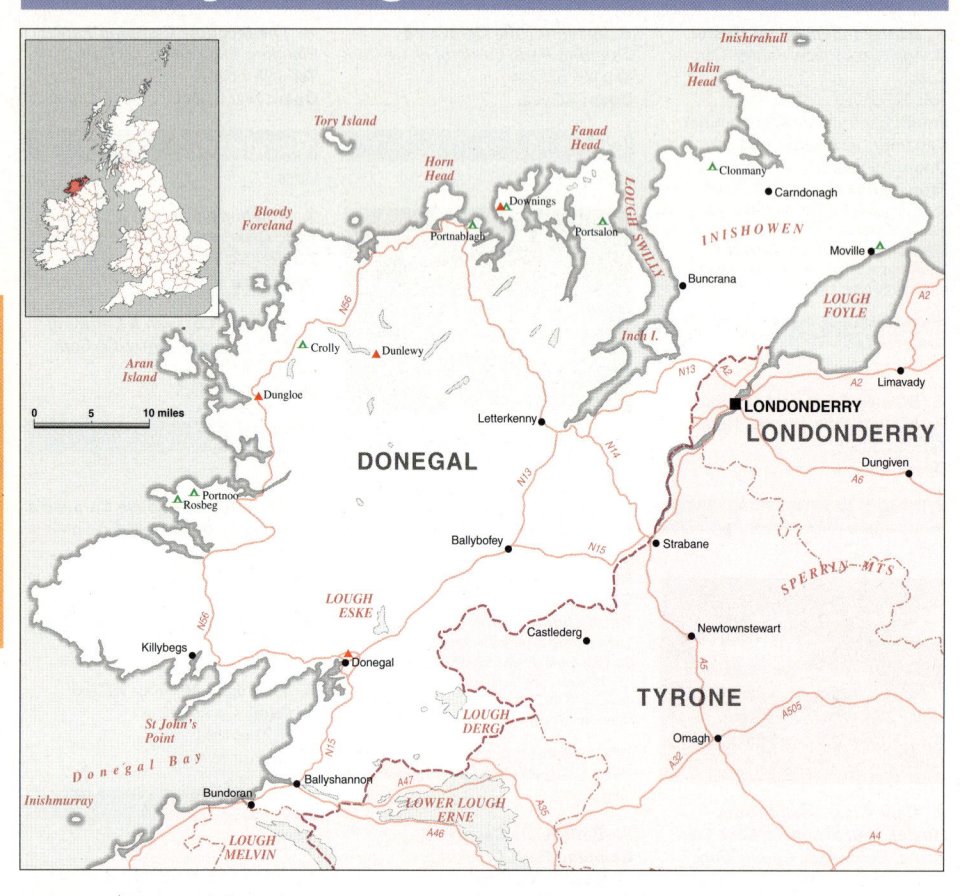

Clonmany

C3746

⛺ **Tullagh Bay Caravan & Camping Park,** Clonmany, Lifford, Co Donegal
Tel: 077 76189 **Open:** May to Sep

Crolly

B8220

⛺ **Coillin Darach Caravan Park,** Crolly, Letterkenny, Co Donegal
Tel: 075 31306
Open: All year

Donegal

G9076

▲ **Ball Hill Youth Hostel,** Ball Hill, Donegal Town, Co Donegal

Tel: 073 21174
Fax: 023 21174
Email: mailbox@anoige.ie
Capacity: 66
Under 18: IR£5.50-IR£6.00
Adults: IR£6.50-IR£7.50
Open: Easter to Sep
Family bunk rooms
• Self-catering facilities • Shop 2 km away
Former coastguard station with stunning views over Donegal Bay. Good walking on the shores of Lough Eske and the Blue Stack Mountains. Open at weekends out of season.

228   Stilwell's Hostels & Camping 2002

County Donegal

Downings
C1242

▲ **Tra na Rosann Youth Hostel,** Downings, Letterkenny, County Donegal
Tel: 074 55374
Email: mailbox@anoige.ie
Capacity: 34
Under 18: IR£5.50-IR£6.00
Adults: IR£6.50-IR£7.50
Open: Easter to Sep
Self-catering facilities • Shop 6 km away • Parking
This former hunting lodge is Ireland's most northerly hostel, situated on the Rosguill Peninsula. Ideal for exploring northern Donegal. Doe Castle nearby.

▲ **Casey's Caravan & Camping Park,** Downings, Letterkenny, Co Donegal
Tourist Board grade: 2 Ticks
Tel: 074 55376
Tent pitches: 15
Tent rate: IR£8.00-IR£12.00
Open: Apr to Sep
Last arr: 10pm
Dogs allowed • Electric hook-up • Showers • Golf • Riding
25 miles North of Letterkenny, situated on a lovely beach in the fishing village of Downings 200 yds from shops, bar, hotel, laundrette, restaurants. Takeaway.

To stay in a Youth Hostel affiliated to one of the Youth Hostel associations, you need to be a member. You can join at most hostels – phone in advance to check.

Dungloe
B7108

▲ **Crohy Head Youth Hostel,** Crohy Head, Dungloe, County Donegal
Tel: 075 21950
Email: mailbox@anoige.ie
Capacity: 38
Under 18: IR£5.00-IR£5.50
Adults: IR£6.50-IR£7.50
Open: Easter to Sep
Family bunk rooms
Self-catering facilities • Shop 2 km away • Parking
Overlooking Boylagh Bay and the Atlantic. Fine sea cliffs, caves and beaches. Great fishing.

Dunlewy
B9120

▲ **Errigal Youth Hostel,** Errigal, Dunlewy, Gweedore, Co Donegal
Tel: 075 31180
Fax: 075 31292
Email: mailbox@anoige.ie
Capacity: 46
Under 18: IR£5.50-IR£6.00
Adults: IR£7.00-IR£8.00
Open: All year
Family bunk rooms
Self-catering facilities • Shop nearby • Parking
This hostel is on the Ulster Way and at the foot of Donegal's highest mountain, Errigal. Glenveagh Castle and National Park are close by.

Moville
C6138

▲ **Gulladuff House,** Malin Road, Moville, Lifford, Co Donegal
Tel: 077 82378
Fax: 028 7137 2187
Open: All year

Portnablagh
C0436

▲ **Johnston's Caravans & Camping,** Marble Hill, Portnablagh, Letterkenny, Co Donegal
Tel: 074 36155
Open: Easter to Sep

Portnoo
G6999

▲ **Dunmore Caravans,** Strand Road, Portnoo, Donegal
Tel: 075 45121
Open: Mar to Oct

Portsalon
C2339

▲ **Knockalla Caravan & Camping Park,** Portsalon, Letterkenny, Co Donegal
Tel: 074 59108 / 53213
Open: Apr to Sep

Rosbeg
G6697

▲ **Tramore Beach Caravan & Camping Park,** Campbell's Holiday Hostel, Glenties, Donegal
Tel: 075 51491
Open: Easter to Sep

IRELAND

County Dublin

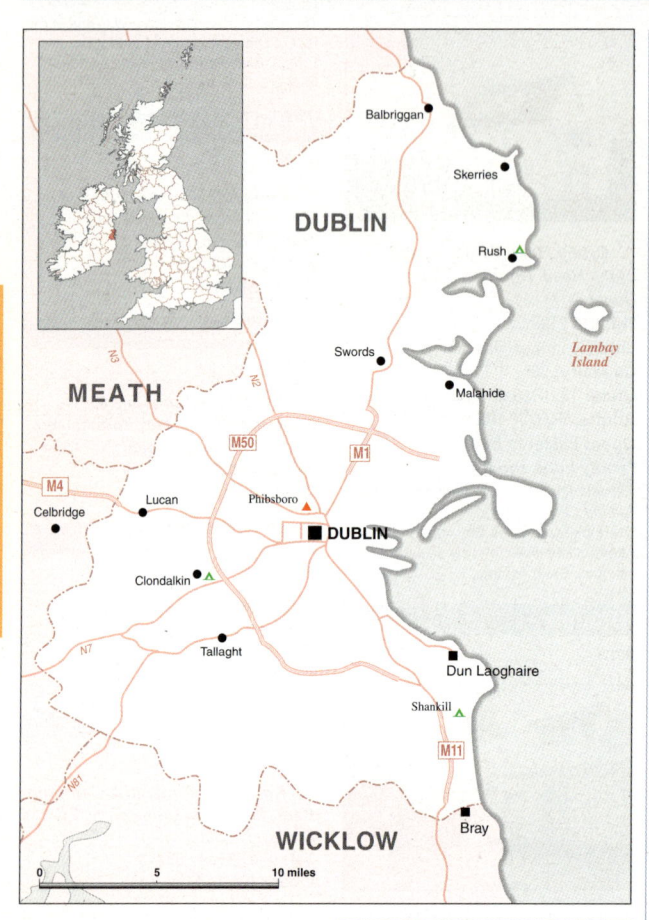

Dublin - Phibsboro
O1436

▲ **Dublin International Youth Hostel,** 61 Mountjoy Street, Dublin 7
Tel: 01 8301766
Fax: 01 8301600
Email: dublin-international@anoige.ie
Capacity: 369
Under 18: IR£10.00-IR£13.50
Adults: IR£10.00-IR£13.50
Open: All year
Family bunk rooms
Self-catering facilities • Laundry facilities • Parking • Meals available
This hostel is at the heart of Dublin, with easy access to museums, galleries, parks and pubs. Newly refurbished, it includes conference facilities and a games room.

Rush
O2553

▲ **North Beach Caravan & Camping Park,** Rush, Co Dublin
Tel: 01 8437131
Open: Mar to Oct

Dublin - Clondalkin
O0730

▲ **Camac Valley Tourist Caravan & Camping Park,** Corkagh Park, Nass Road, Clondalkin, Dublin 22
Tel: 01 4640644 **Fax:** 01 4640643
Open: All year

Shankill
O2421

▲ **Shankill Caravan & Camping Park (Rent a Sprite Ltd),** Shankill, Co Dublin
Tel: 011 2820011
Open: All year

Ireland: Bed & Breakfast 2001

The essential guide to B&Bs in the Republic of Ireland and Northen Ireland

Think of Ireland and you think of that famous Irish hospitality. The warmth of the welcome is as much a part of this great island as the wild and beautiful landscapes, the traditional folk music and the Guiness. Wherever you go, town or country, North or South, you can't escape it.

There are few better ways of experiencing this renowned hospitality, when travelling through Ireland, than by staying at one of the country's many Bed & Breakfasts. They offer a great value alternative to expensive hotels, each has its own individual charm and you get a home cooked breakfast to help you start your day.

Stilwell's Ireland: Bed & Breakfast 2001 is the most comprehensive guide of its kind, with over 1,400 entries listed by county and location, in both Northern Ireland and the Republic of Ireland. Each entry includes room rates, facilities, Tourist Board grades, local maps and a brief description of the B&B, its location and surroundings.

Treat yourself to some Irish hospitality with Stilwell's Ireland: Bed & Breakfast 2001.

- Private houses, country halls, farms, cottages, inns, small hotels and guest houses
- Over 1,400 entries
- Average price £18 per person per night (US$32 per person per night)
- All official grades shown
- Local maps
- Pubs serving hot evening meals shown
- Tourist Information Centres listed
- Handy size for easy packing

£6.95 from all good bookstores (ISBN 1-900861-24-0) or £7.95 (inc p&p) from Stilwell Publishing, 59 Charlotte Road, London EC2A 3QW (020 7739 7179)

IRELAND

County Galway

Aran Islands - Inisheer
L9702

▲ **Bru Radharc na Mara Hostel,** *Inisheer, Galway*
Tel: 099 75024 **Fax:** 099 75024
Email: maire.searraigh@oceanfree.net
Capacity: 40
Under 18: IR£8.00
Adults: IR£8.00
Open: All year, all day
Self-catering facilities • Television • Showers • Central heating • Laundry facilities • Wet weather shelter • Lounge • Dining room • Grounds available for games • Cycle hire • Evening meal available
Situated on beautiful Inisheer. Sandy beach, historical ruins, tranquil surroundings.

Aran Islands - Inishmor
L8408

▲ **Kilronan Hostel,** *Inishmor, Aran Islands, Co Galway*
Actual Grid Ref: L885089
Tel: 099 61255
Capacity: 44
Under 18: IR£10.00
Adults: IR£10.00
Open: All year, 8am-8pm
Family bunk rooms: IR£50.00
Self-catering facilities • Television • Showers • Central heating • Laundry facilities • Wet weather shelter • Lounge • Dining room • No smoking
Ideally located, spectacular views, 2 minutes' walk from pier.

Barna
M2222

▲ **Barna House Caravan & Camping Park,** *Barna, Galway*
Tel: 091 92469 **Open:** May to Sep

Ben Lettery
L7748

232 Stilwell's Hostels & Camping 2002

County Galway

Claddaghduff

L5856

▲ **Actons,** Leegawn, Claddaghduff, Galway
Tel: 095 44339
Open: Apr to Oct

Galway

M2925

▲ **Galway International Youth Hostel,** St Mary's College, St Mary's Road, Galway
Tel: 091 527411 **Fax:** 091 528710
Email: mailbox@anoige.ie
Capacity: 120 **Under 18:** IR£10.00
Adults: IR£10.00
Open: June to Aug
Family bunk rooms
Self-catering facilities • Shop nearby • Laundry facilities • Parking • Meals available groups only, by prior arrangement
This hostel is set between the city centre and the beach at Salthill. Galway City is a cultural and historical centre and is the gateway to the stunning Connemara landscape.

▲ **Barna House Caravan Park,** Barna Road, Galway
Tel: 091 592469
Open: May to Sep

▲ **Ballyloughane Caravan & Camping Park,** Galway
Tel: 091 755338
Open: Apr to Sep

Inishbofin Island

L5365

▲ **Inishbofin Island Hostel,** Inishbofin Island, Galway
Tel: 095 45855
Fax: 095 45803
Capacity: 38
Under 18: IR£7.00-IR£8.00
Adults: IR£7.00-IR£8.00
Open: Apr to Oct, 8am-11pm
Family bunk rooms
Camping for 6 tents: IR£8.00

Self-catering facilities • Showers • Central heating • Laundry facilities • Wet weather shelter • Lounge • Dining room • Drying room • Cycle store • Parking • No smoking
Converted farmhouse, sandy beaches, spectacular views, excellent walking, traditional music.

Kinvara

M3512

▲ **Doorus House (Burren) Youth Hostel,** Doorus House, Kinvara, Co Galway
Tel: 091 637512
Fax: 091 637512
Email: mailbox@anoige.ie
Capacity: 56
Under 18: IR£5.50-IR£6.00
Adults: IR£7.00-IR£8.00
Open: All year
Self-catering facilities • Shop 2 km away • Parking
Spectacular landscape including the Burren limestone plateau, Lisdoonvara Hot Springs, Dunguire Castle, Ailwee Caves and the Cliffs of Moher.

▲ **Johnston's Independent Hostel,** Main Street, Kinvara, Galway
Actual Grid Ref: M373104
Tel: 091 637164
Capacity: 36
Under 18: IR£8.00 **Adults:** IR£8.00
Open: July to Aug, 9am
Camping for 25 tents: IR£9.00
Self-catering facilities • Showers • Central heating • Laundry facilities • Wet weather shelter • Lounge • Dining room • Drying room
In centre of rural, seaside, fishing village. Gateway to Burren National Park. Archaeology/Botany Burren tours available. Short bus ride to Galway city. Blue flag beach nearby. Large, spacious, C19th building. Huge dining hall/lounge. Well equipped kitchen. Comfortable. Private. Picturesque, sheltered campsite. C16th castle in village - medieval banquets.

Letterfrack

L7157

▲ **Connemara Caravan & Camping Park,** Letterfrack, Galway
Tel: 095 43406
Open: May to Sep

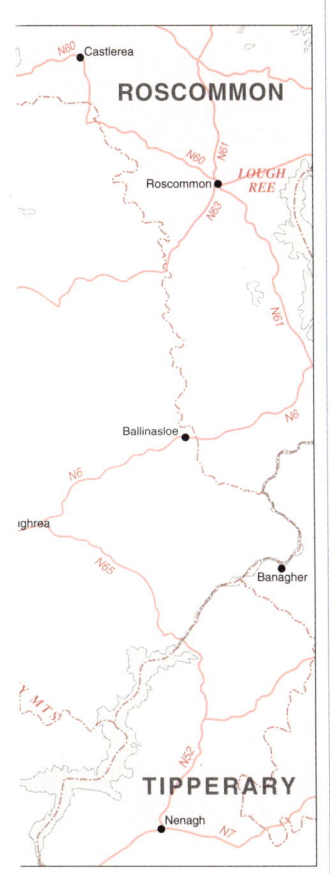

▲ **Ben Lettery Youth Hostel,** Ben Lettery, Ballinafad, Co Galway
Actual Grid Ref: L777483
Tel: 095 51136 **Fax:** 095 51136
Email: mailbox@anoige.ie
Capacity: 50
Under 18: IR£5.50-IR£6.00
Adults: IR£7.00-IR£8.00
Open: Easter to Sep
Self-catering facilities • Shop • Parking
Ferry to Inishboffin, island of legend. Wonderful walking and fishing area. Visit nearby villages of Recess and Roundstone.

You are advised to book in advance for periods of high demand – the Summer months, Half Term holidays and public holidays.

Phoning from outside the Republic? Dial 00353 and omit the initial '0' of the area code.

County Galway • MAP PAGE 232

Renvyle

L7664

▲ *Killary Harbour Youth Hostel,*
Rosroe, Renvyle, Co Galway
Tel: 095 43417
Email: mailbox@anoige.ie
Capacity: 44
Under 18: IR£5.50-IR£6.00
Adults: IR£7.00-IR£8.00
Open: Mar to Sep
Self-catering facilities • Shop 5 km away • Parking
The fishing hamlet of Rosroe is set on the mouth of Killary Harbour, one of Ireland's largest fjords. Spectacular scenery. Adventure centre next door. Hostel is open for groups out of season, by request.

▲ *Renvyle Beach Caravan & Camping Site,* *Tullybeg, Renvyle, Co Galway*
Tel: 095 43462
Open: Easter to Sep

County Kerry

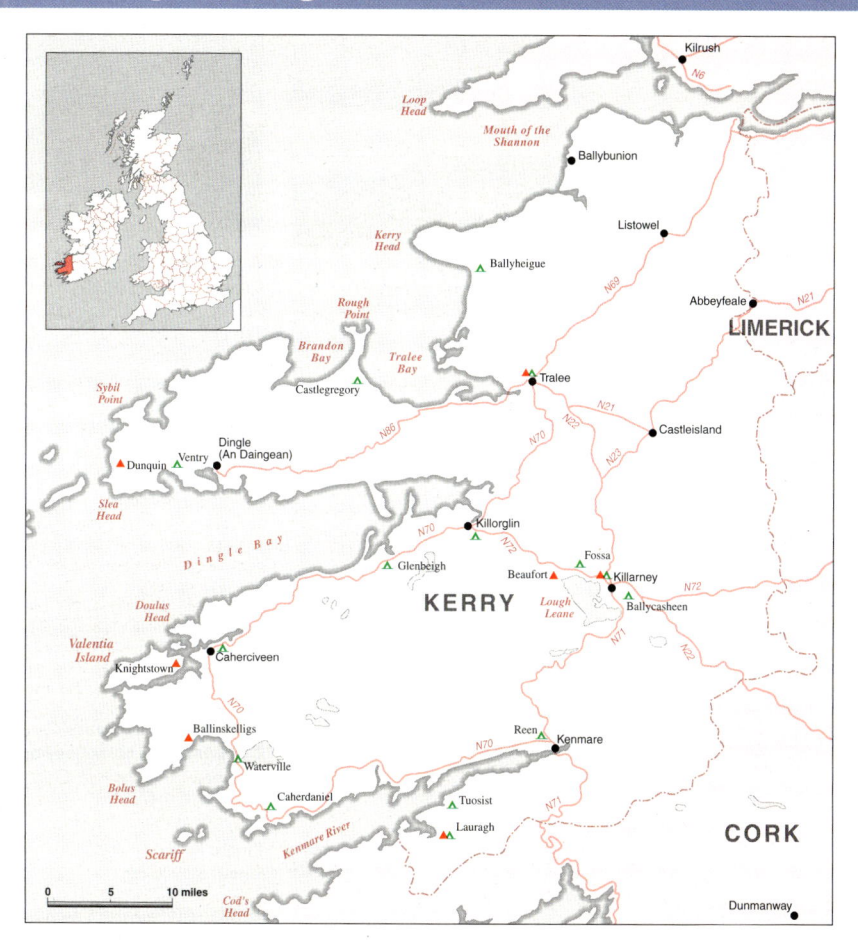

Ballinskeligs
V4366

▲ **Ballinskelligs Youth Hostel,**
Prior House, Ballinskelligs, County Kerry
Tel: 066 947 9229
Email: mailbox@anoige.ie
Capacity: 22
Under 18: IR£5.00-IR£5.50
Adults: IR£6.00-IR£7.50
Open: Apr to Sep
Family bunk rooms
Self-catering facilities • Shop • Parking • Meals available
Skellig Heritage Centre, gentle hillwalking, fishing and excellent beaches all nearby. Boat trips to Skellig Michael, with its lighthouse and ruined monastic settlement.

Ballycasheen
V9790

▲ **Fleming's Whitebridge Caravan Park,** Ballycasheen, Killarney, Co Kerry
Tel: 064 31590
Fax: 064 37474
Open: Mar to Oct

All details shown are as supplied by hostels and campsites in Autumn 2000.

County Kerry • MAP PAGE 235

Ballyheigue
Q7528

▲ **Cassey's Caravan & Camping Park,** Ballyheigue, Tralee, Co Kerry
Tel: 066 33195
Open: May to Sep

Beaufort
V8682

▲ **Black Valley Youth Hostel,** Black Valley, Beaufort, Killarney, County Kerry
Tel: 064 34712
Email: mailbox@anoige.ie
Capacity: 50
Under 18: IR£5.50-IR£6.00
Adults: IR£7.00-IR£8.00
Open: March to Nov
Family bunk rooms
Self-catering facilities • Shop • Drying room • Parking • Meals available groups only, by prior arrangement
Ireland's highest mountains, the Macgillycuddy's Reeks, are nearby; also the Ring of Kerry and Beara Peninsula. Open for groups out of season, by request only.

Caherciveen
V4779

▲ **Mannix Point Camping & Caravan Park,** Caherciveen, Co Kerry
Tel: 066 72806
Open: Mar to Sept

Caherdaniel
V5459

▲ **Wave Crest Caravan Park,** Caherdaniel, Killarney, Co Kerry
Tel: 066 75188
Open: Mar to Oct

Castlegregory
Q6113

▲ **Anchor Caravan Park,** Castlegregory, Tralee, Co Kerry
Tel: 066 39157
Open: Easter to Sep

▲ **Green Acres Caravan & Camping Park,** Castlegregory, Tralee, Co Kerry
Tel: 066 39158
Open: Apr to Sep

Dunquin
Q3101

▲ **Dunquin Youth Hostel,** Dunquin, Tralee, County Kerry
Tel: 066 915 6121
Fax: 066 915 6355
Email: mailbox@anoige.ie
Capacity: 52
Under 18: IR£5.50-IR£6.00
Adults: IR£6.50-IR£7.00
Open: All year **Family bunk rooms**
Self-catering facilities • Shop 8 km, or limited supplies at hostel • Drying room • Parking • Meals available groups by prior arrangement
Situated on the Dingle Way, this is the most westerly hostel in Europe. Good hillwalking and cycling plus many archaeological sites.

Fossa
V9191

▲ **Fossa Caravan & Camping Park,** Fossa, Killarney, County Kerry
Tel: 064 31497
Open: Easter to Sep

Glenbeigh
V6891

▲ **Glenross Caravan & Camping Park ,** Glenbeigh, Killarney, Co Kerry
Tel: 066 68451 Open: May to Sep

▲ **Falvey's Camping Site,** Caherciveen Road, Glenbeigh, Killarney, Co Kerry
Tel: 066 9768238
Open: Easter to Oct

▲ **Falvey's Caravan & Camping Park,** Glenbeigh, Killarney, Co Kerry
Tel: 066 68238
Open: Easter to Oct

Phoning from outside the Republic? Dial 00353 and omit the initial '0' of the area code.

Killarney
V1992

▲ **Killarney International Youth Hostel,** Aghadoe House, Killarney, County Kerry
Tel: 064 31240
Fax: 064 34300
Email: anoige@killarney.iol.ie
Capacity: 200
Under 18: IR£7.50-IR£9.00
Adults: IR£8.00-IR£9.50
Open: All year
Family bunk rooms
Self-catering facilities • Shop • Laundry facilities • Parking • Facilities for disabled people • Meals available groups only, by prior arrangement
This recently renovated C18th mansion is set in 75 acres of lawns and forests, overlooking Killarney's National Park. Ideal base for touring the Ring of Kerry, Gap of Dunloe and Dingle Peninsula.

▲ **The Flesk Muckross Caravan & Camping Park,** Muckross Road, Killarney, Co Kerry
Tel: 064 31704
Fax: 064 35439
Email: killarneylakes@tinet.ie
Open: May to Sep

▲ **White Villa Farm Camping & Caravan Park, Cork Road,** Woodford, Cork Road, Killarney, Co Kerry
Tel: 064 32456
Open: Apr to Oct

▲ **Beech Grove Caravan Park,** Killarney, Co Kerry
Tel: 064 31727
Open: Mar to Oct

Killorglin
V7796

▲ **West's Caravan & Camping Park,** Killorglin, Co Kerry
Tel: 066 61240
Open: Apr to Oct

MAP PAGE 235 • **County Kerry**

Knightstown
V4277

▲ **Valentia Island Youth Hostel,**
Knightstown, Valentia Island,
County Kerry
Tel: 066 947 6154
Email: mailbox@anoige.ie
Capacity: 40
Under 18: IR£5.00
Adults: IR£7.50
Open: June to Sep
Family bunk rooms
Self-catering facilities • Shop nearby • Parking
This former coastguard station overlooks Beginish Island with lovely sandy beaches. Check out the petrified dinosaur tracks or go whale spotting (in season). Magnificent scenery.

Lauragh
V7754

▲ **Glanmore Lake Youth Hostel,**
Glenmore Lake, Lauragh, Killarney,
Co Kerry
Tel: 064 83181
Email: mailbox@anoige.ie
Capacity: 36
Under 18: IR£5.00-IR£5.50
Adults: IR£6.50-IR£7.50
Open: Apr to Sep
Self-catering facilities • Shop 6 km away • Parking
This old school house is set at the foot of the Tim Healy pass and near the Beara Way. Magnificent views of the sea, mountains, forests and lakes.

▲ **Creveen Lodge Caravan & Camping Park,** Healy Pass Road, Lauragh, Killarney, Co Kerry
Tel: 064 83131
Open: Easter to Oct

Reen
V8870

▲ **Ring of Kerry Caravan & Camping Park,** Reen, Kenmare, Co. Kerry
Tel: 064 41648
Open: Apr to Oct

Tralee
Q8413

▲ **Collis-Sandes House Hostel,**
Oakpark, Tralee, County Kerry
Tel: 066 7128 658
Fax: 066 7128 658
Email: colsands@indigo.ie
Capacity: 100
Under 18: IR£7.00 **Adults:** IR£7.50
Open: All year, 8am-11pm
Family bunk rooms: IR£30.00
Camping for 50 tents: IR£8.00
Self-catering facilities • Television • Showers • Licensed bar • Central heating • Laundry facilities • Wet weather shelter • Lounge • Dining room • Grounds available for games • Drying room • Security lockers • Cycle store • Parking • Evening meal available by arrangement • Facilities for disabled people • No smoking
Listed as 'one of the very best hostels' by the world's best-selling budget travellers' guide (Let's Go 2000). 20,000 sq ft Venetian Gothic mansion set in 20 acres of mature woodland approximately 1.5 miles from Tralee town centre. Adjoins 18-hole pitch and putt course and tennis club. Beginning of Dingle Way/Peninsula.

▲ **Tralee Bayview Caravan & Camping Park,** Bayview Caravan Park, Tralee, Co Kerry
Tel: 066 71 26140
Fax: Bayviewtralee@ericom.net
Tent pitches: 53

Tent rate: IR£5.00-IR£8.00
Open: All year **Last arr:** 10pm
Facilities for disabled people • Dogs allowed • Electric hook-up • Calor Gas/Camping Gaz • Children's play area • Showers • Laundrette on site • Public phone on site • Shop on site • Baby care facilities • TV room • Games room • Indoor swimming pool nearby • Outdoor swimming pool nearby • Boating/sailing/watersports nearby • Tennis courts nearby • Golf nearby • Riding nearby • Fishing nearby
Established over 20 years and registered with the Irish Tourist Board. Rural tree-lined park with all modern facilities. Ideal base for holidays in Kerry and South West. SPECIAL PROMOTION: 1 night in 3 FREE in Tralee. Stay for 3 nights, pay for 2.

▲ **Seaside Caravan & Camping Park,** Tralee, Co Kerry
Tel: 066 7130161
Fax: 066 7130331
Tent pitches: 30
Tent rate: IR£6.80-IR£8.80
Open: All year
Last arr: 9pm
Dogs allowed • Electric hook-up • Calor Gas/Camping Gaz • Children's play area • Showers • Laundrette on site • Public phone on site • Shop on site
Beautiful seaside location. Beach, sand, sea.

Tuosist
V7962

▲ **Camping 'The Peacock',**
Coormagillagh, Tuosist, Killarney, Co Kerry
Tel: 064 84287
Open: All year

Ventry
Q3800

▲ **Brosnans Camping Site,**
Ballymore, Ventry, Tralee, Co Kerry
Tel: 066 59087
Open: Mar to Nov

Waterville
V5066

▲ **Waterville Caravan & Camping Park,** Waterville, Killarney, Co Kerry
Tel: 066 74191
Fax: 066 74538
Open: Easter to Sep

County Kildare

Rathangan

N6719

▲ **Carasali Caravan & Camping Park,** Tobarban, Rathangan, Kildare
Tel: 045 524331
Open: Apr to Oct

County Kilkenny

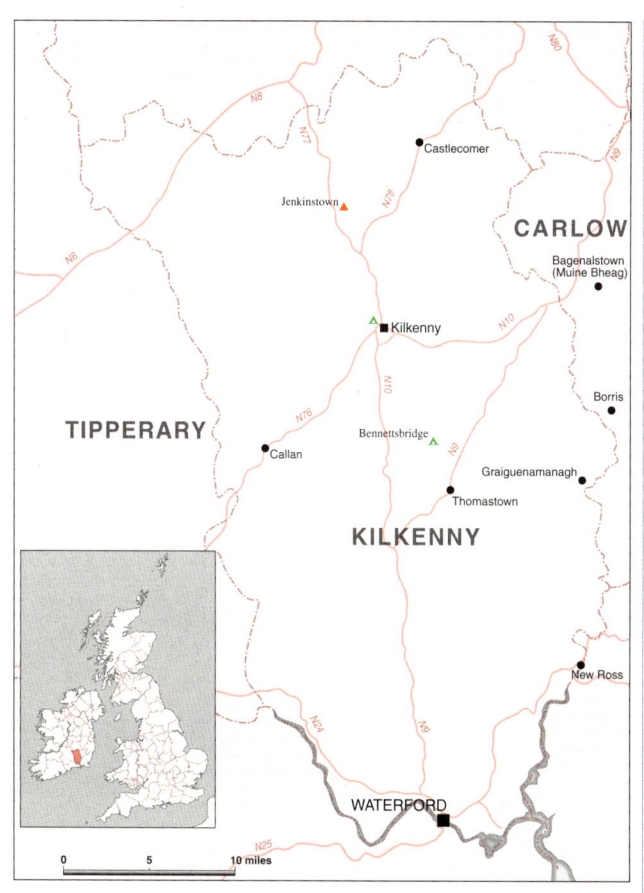

Email: norevalleypark@eircom.net
Tent pitches: 35
Tent rate: IR£5.50-IR£8.00
Open: Mar to Oct
Last arr: 10.30pm
Facilities for disabled people • Dogs allowed • Electric hook-up • Calor Gas/Camping Gaz • Cafe or Takeaway on site • Picnic/barbecue area on site • Children's play area • Showers • Laundrette on site • Public phone on site • Shop on site • Baby care facilities
Peaceful farm setting. Home baking a speciality. Breakfasts June-August.

Jenkinstown

S4666

▲ **Foulksrath Castle Youth Hostel,** *Foulksrath Castle, Jenkinstown, Co Kilkenny*
Tel: 056 67674
Fax: 056 67744
Email: mailbox@anoige.ie
Capacity: 52
Under 18: IR£5.00-IR£5.50
Adults: IR£6.50-IR£7.50
Open: All year
Self-catering facilities • Shop nearby • Parking
This C16th Norman Tower House, built by the Purcell family, is set in a picturesque garden. Ideal base for exploring the area's many heritage sites.

Bennettsbridge

S5549

▲ **Nore Valley Park,** *Annamult, Bennettsbridge, Kilkenny*
Actual Grid Ref: S547459
Tourist Board grade: 3 Ticks
Tel: 056 27229
Fax: 056 27748

Kilkenny

S5156

▲ **Tree Grove Caravan & Camping Park,** *Danville House, Kilkenny*
Tel: 056 70302
Fax: 056 21512
Open: Apr to Oct

County Laois

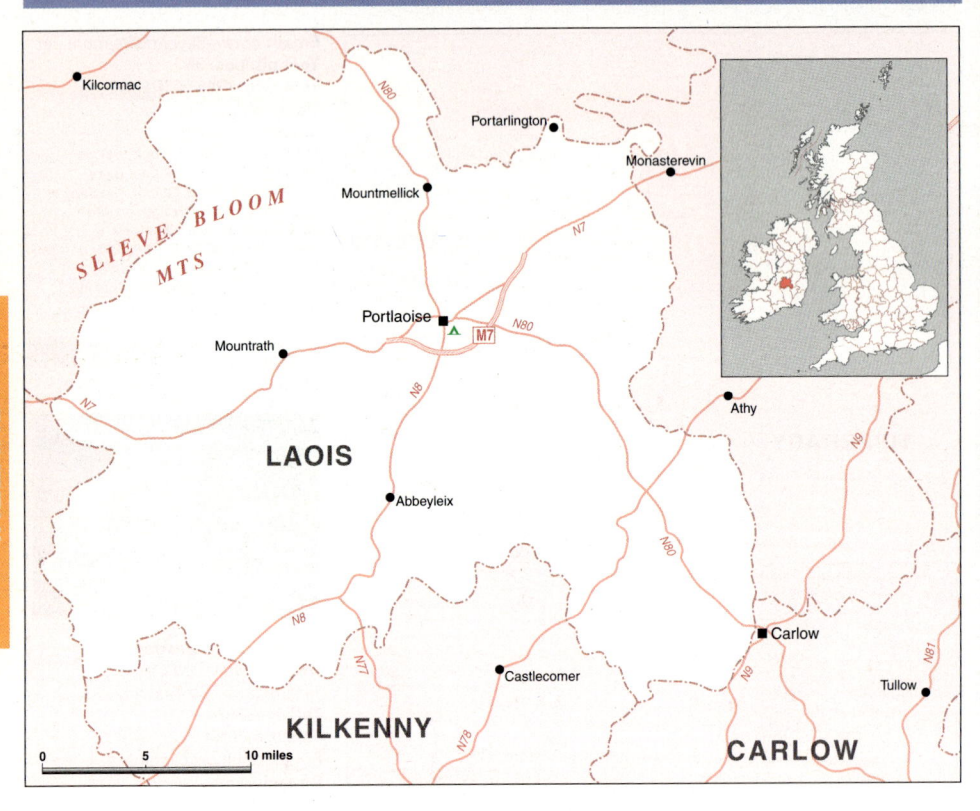

Portlaoise

S4698

▲ **Kirwans Caravan & Camping Park,** N7 Limerick Road, Portlaoise, Co Laois
Tel: 0502 21688
Open: Apr to Oct

County Limerick

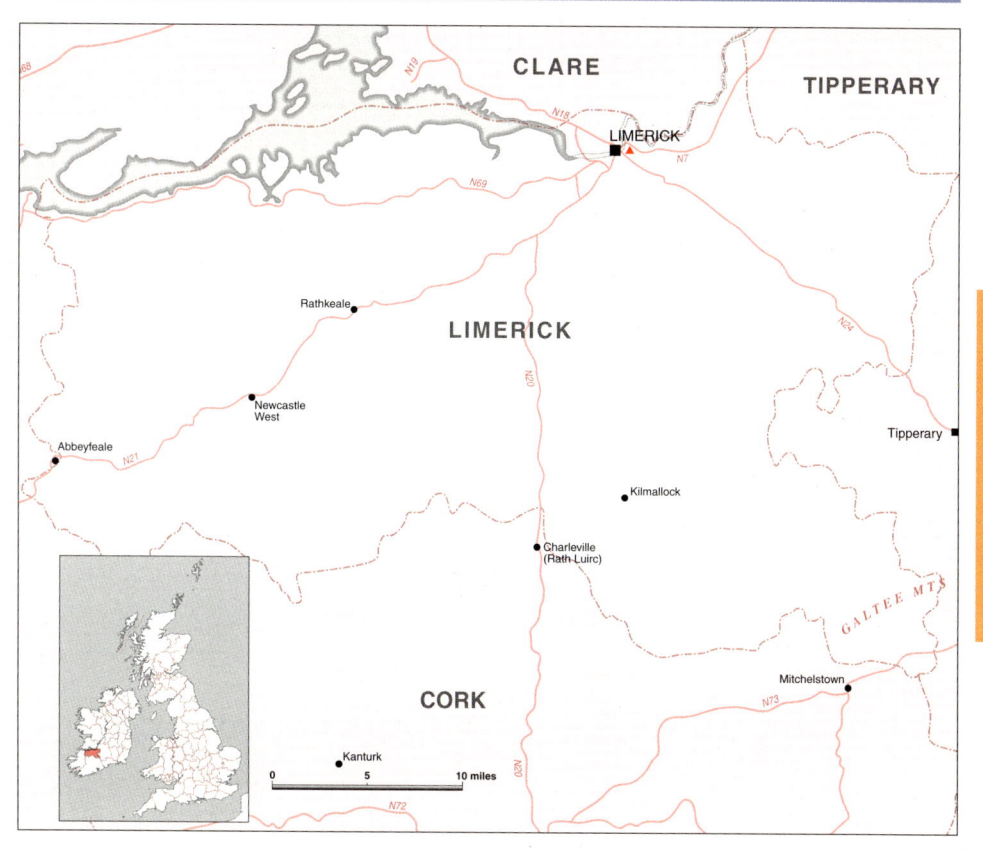

Limerick

R7185

▲ **Limerick City Youth Hostel,** 1 Pery Square, Limerick
Tel: 061 314672
Fax: 061 314672
Email: mailbox@anoige.ie
Capacity: 66
Under 18: IR£6.50-IR£7.50
Adults: IR£7.50-IR£8.50
Open: All year
Self-catering facilities • Shop nearby • Parking • Meals available
Located on a quiet square of this historical city. Limerick is the gateway to Clare and the Shannon area. Bunratty Castle 13 km away.

County Louth

Omeath
J1316

▲ **Tain Holiday Village,**
Carlingford Lough, Ballynoonan,
Omeath, Dundalk, Co Louth
Tel: 042 9375385
Fax: 042 9375417
Tent pitches: 10
Tent rate: IR£17.00-IR£19.00
Open: Mar to Oct **Last arr:** 9pm
Facilities for disabled people • Electric hook-up • Calor Gas/Camping Gaz • Cafe or Takeaway on site • Picnic/barbecue area on site • Children's play area • Showers • Laundrette on site • Public phone on site • Licensed bar on site • Shop on site • Baby care facilities • TV room • Games room • Indoor swimming pool on site • Boating/sailing/watersports on site • Tennis courts on site • Golf nearby • Riding nearby
Torin Holiday village & Torin Outdoor Adventure Centre is situated along shore of Carlingford Lough at foot of Cooley Mountains. New for 2000. Pirate lagoon, windsurfing and sailing. Leisure facilities include steam room, jacuzzi and indoor heated swimming pool. Torin offers a unique holiday experience to be enjoyed by all.

County Mayo

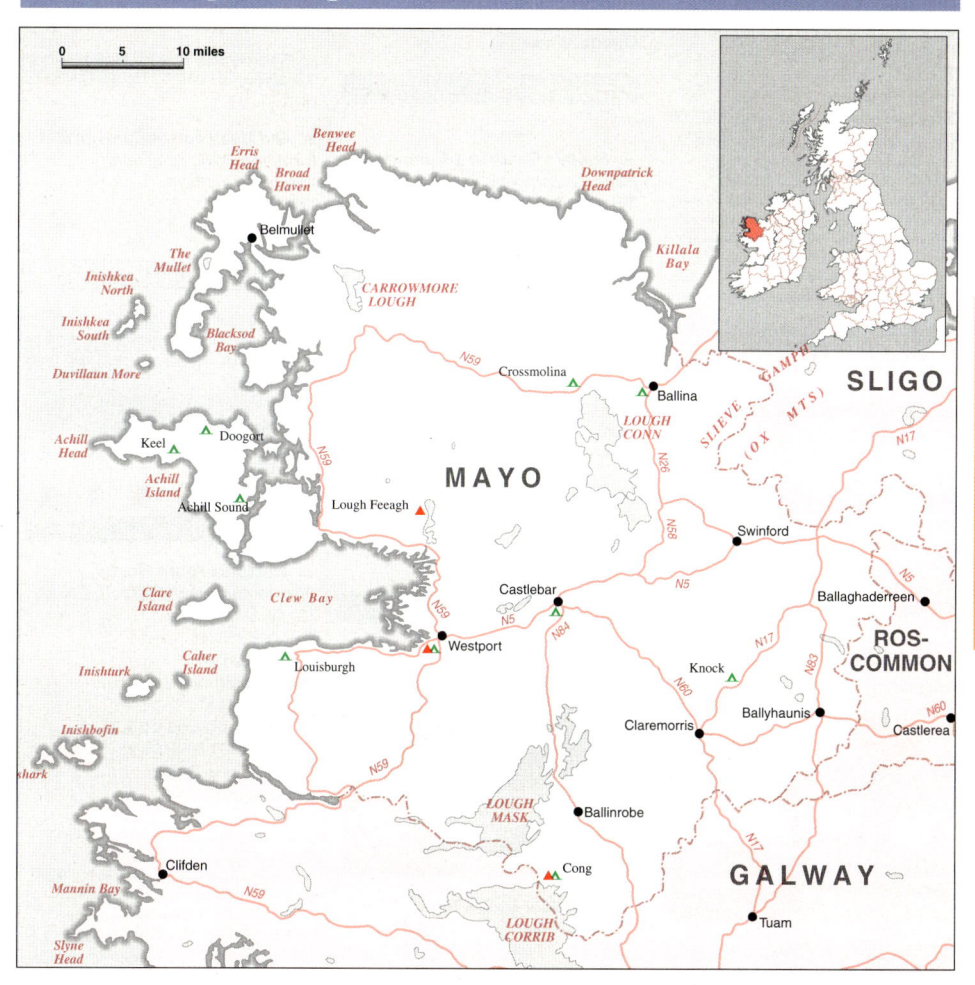

Achill Island - Achill Sound
L7399

▲ **Lavelle's Caravan & Camping Park,** Achill Sound, Westport, Co Mayo

Tel: 098 47232
Tent pitches: 10
Tent rate: IR£6.00-IR£8.50
Open: Easter to Oct
Last arr: 11pm
Facilities for disabled people • Electric hook-up • Calor Gas/Camping Gaz • Children's play area • Showers • Laundrette on site • Public phone on site • Shop on site
Lavelle's Golden Strand Caravan Camping Park is situated on one of Mayo's finest EU Blue Flag beaches, direct access from park onto the beach. Scenic walks in the surrounding area. Also sea. Rock fishing available.

Achill Island - Doogort
F6608

▲ **Seal Caves Caravan Park,** Strand, Doogort, Achill Island, Westport, Co Mayo
Tel: 098 43262 **Open:** Apr to Sep

Achill Island - Keel
F6305

▲ **Keel Sandybanks Caravan & Camping Park,** Keel Holiday Cottages, Belcarra, Castlebar, Co Mayo
Tel: 094 32054 **Open:** May to Sep

County Mayo • MAP PAGE 243

Ballina
G2418

⛺ Belleek Caravan & Camping Park, Ballina, Co Mayo
Tel: 096 71533
Email: lenahan@indigo.ie
Tent pitches: 58 **Tent rate:** IR£7.00
Open: Mar to Oct **Last arr:** 9pm
Facilities for disabled people • Dogs allowed • Electric hook-up • Calor Gas/Camping Gaz • Picnic/barbecue area on site • Children's play area • Showers • Laundrette on site • Public phone on site • Shop on site • Baby care facilities
Excellent facilities. Family run. Sheltered, ideal for touring, fishing or relaxing.

Castlebar
M1490

⛺ Carra Caravan & Camping Park, Keel Holiday Cottages, Belcarra, Castlebar, Co Mayo
Tel: 094 32054
Open: June to Sept

⛺ Camp Carrowkeel Caravan & Camping Park, Castlebar, Co Mayo
Tel: 094 31264
Open: Apr to Sep

Cong
M1554

▲ Cong Youth Hostel, Lisloughrey, Quay Road, Cong, Claremorris, County Mayo
Tel: 092 46089 **Fax:** 092 46448
Email: quiet.man.cong@iol.ie
Capacity: 104
Under 18: IR£6.50-IR£7.50
Adults: IR£7.00-IR£7.50
Open: All year
Family bunk rooms
Camping
Self-catering facilities • Parking • Meals available groups only, by prior arrangement
Modern hostel near Loughs Mask, Cara and Corrib. Rich archaeological interest with Cong Abbey, Ashford Castle and stone circles nearby.

⛺ Cong Caravan & Camping Park, Lisloughrey, Quay Road, Cong, Claremorris, County Mayo
Tel: 092 46089
Open: All year

Crossmolina
G1317

⛺ Hiney's Caravan & Camping Park, Crossmolina, Ballina, Co Mayo
Tel: 096 31262
Open: Mar to Oct

Knock
M3983

⛺ Knock Caravan & Camping Park, Claremorris Road, Knock, Claremorris, Co Mayo
Tel: 094 88100 / 88223
Fax: 094 88295
Open: Mar to Nov

⛺ Knock Caravan & Camping Park, Knock, Claremorris, Co Mayo
Tel: 094 88223
Open: Mar to Nov

Lough Feeagh
L9401

▲ Traenlaur Lodge Youth Hostel, Traenlaur Lodge, Lough Feeagh, Newport, County Mayo
Tel: 098 41358
Email: mailbox@anoige.ie
Capacity: 32
Under 18: IR£5.50-IR£6.00
Adults: IR£7.00-IR£8.00
Open: Easter to Sep
Self-catering facilities • Shop • Parking • Meals available groups only, by prior arrangement

You are advised to book in advance for periods of high demand – the Summer months, Half Term holidays and public holidays.

The hostel, an old fishing lodge with its own harbour, overlooks Lough Feeagh from the crossroads of the Western Way and the Bangor Trail. Great walking, cycling, fishing and swimming.

Louisburgh
L8080

⛺ Old Head Forest Caravan & Camping Park, Louisburgh, Westport, Co Mayo
Tel: 098 66021
Open: May to Sep

Westport
M0084

▲ Westport Youth Hostel, Altamount Street, Westport, County Mayo
Tel: 098 26644
Fax: 098 26241
Email: mailbox@anoige.ie
Capacity: 140
Under 18: IR£6.50-IR£7.00
Adults: IR£7.50-IR£8.00
Open: Mar to Oct
Family bunk rooms
Camping
Shop • Laundry facilities • Facilities for disabled people • Meals available
Purpose-built modern hostel in heritage town of Westport. Visit Ireland's Holy Mountain and Achill Island. Leisure complex nearby; blue flag beaches; hillwalking.

⛺ Parkland Caravan & Camping Park, Westport, Co Mayo
Tel: 098 27766
Open: May to Sep

⛺ Emania, Castlebar Road, Sheeaune, Westport, Co Mayo
Tel: 098 26459
Open: May to Sep

Hostels and campsites may vary rates – be sure to check when booking.

County Roscommon

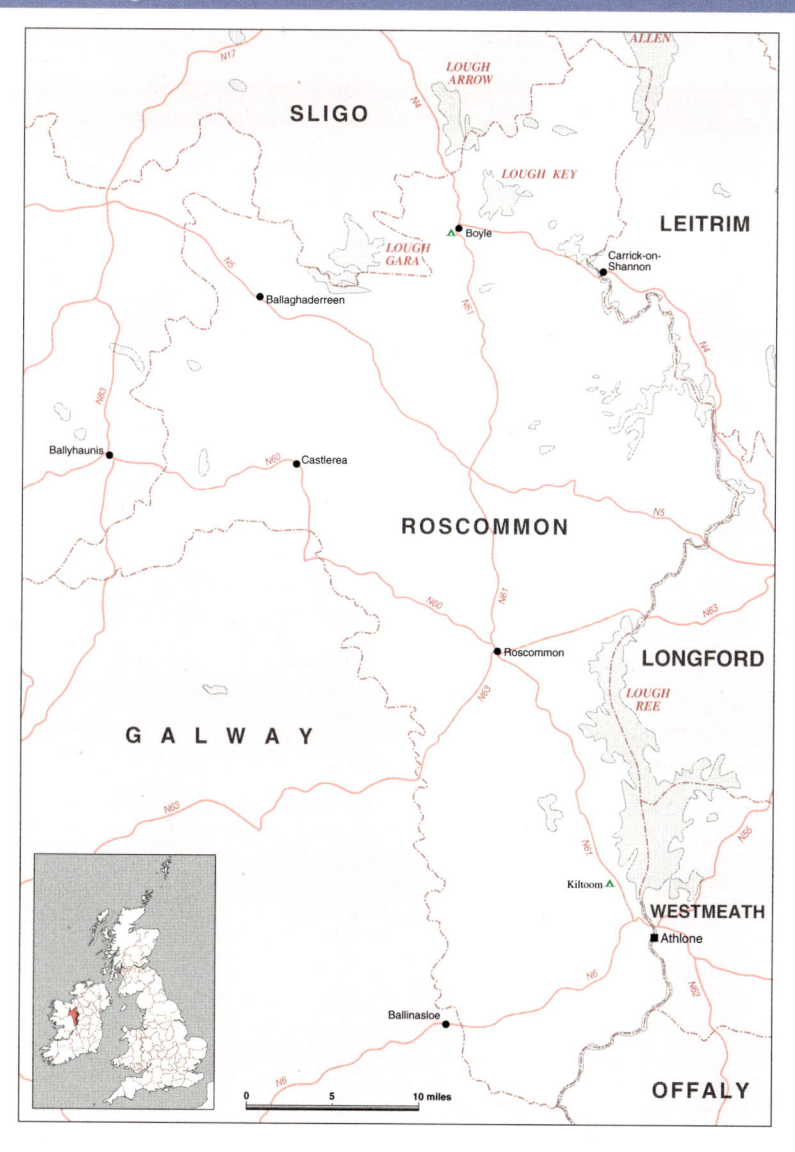

Boyle
G8002

▲ **Lough Key Caravan & Camping Park,** Lough Key Caravan & Camping Park, Boyle, Co Roscommon
Tel: 079 62212 **Open:** May to Aug

Kiltoom
M9847

▲ **Hodson Bay Caravan & Camping Park,** Kiltoom, Athlone, Co Westmeath
Tel: 0902 92448
Open: June to Aug

Ireland: Bed & Breakfast 2001

The essential guide to B&Bs in the Republic of Ireland and Northen Ireland

Think of Ireland and you think of that famous Irish hospitality. The warmth of the welcome is as much a part of this great island as the wild and beautiful landscapes, the traditional folk music and the Guiness. Wherever you go, town or country, North or South, you can't escape it.

There are few better ways of experiencing this renowned hospitality, when travelling through Ireland, than by staying at one of the country's many Bed & Breakfasts. They offer a great value alternative to expensive hotels, each has its own individual charm and you get a home cooked breakfast to help you start your day.

Stilwell's Ireland: Bed & Breakfast 2001 is the most comprehensive guide of its kind, with over 1,400 entries listed by county and location, in both Northern Ireland and the Republic of Ireland. Each entry includes room rates, facilities, Tourist Board grades, local maps and a brief description of the B&B, its location and surroundings.

Treat yourself to some Irish hospitality with Stilwell's Ireland: Bed & Breakfast 2001.

- Private houses, country halls, farms, cottages, inns, small hotels and guest houses
- Over 1,400 entries
- Average price £18 per person per night (US$32 per person per night)
- All official grades shown
- Local maps
- Pubs serving hot evening meals shown
- Tourist Information Centres listed
- Handy size for easy packing

£6.95 from all good bookstores (ISBN 1-900861-24-0) or £7.95 (inc p&p) from Stilwell Publishing, 59 Charlotte Road, London EC2A 3QW (020 7739 7179)

IRELAND

County Sligo

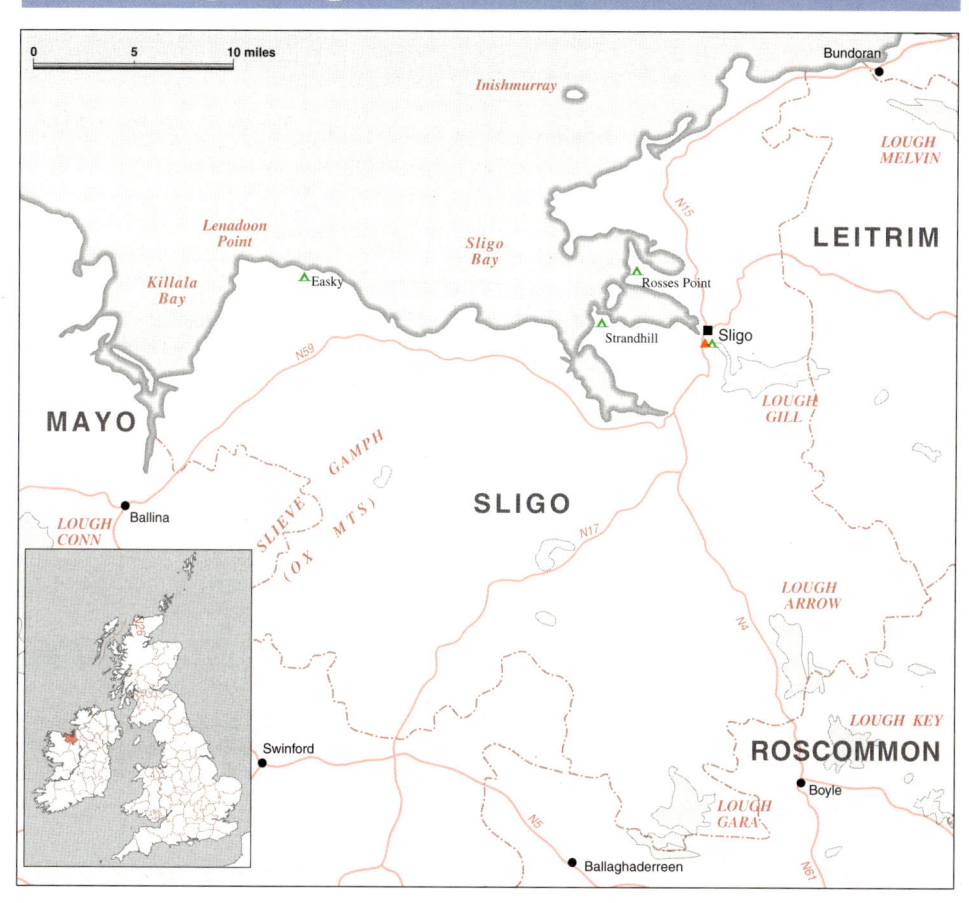

Easky
G3738

▲ **Atlantic n Riverside,** Easky, Ballina, Co Mayo
Tel: 096 49001
Open: Apr to Sep

Rosses Point
G6341

▲ **Greenlands Caravan & Camping Park,** Rosses Point, Sligo
Tel: 071 77113 / 45618
Fax: 071 45618
Open: Easter to Sep

Sligo
G6936

▲ **Eden Hill Holiday Hostel,** Marymount, Pearse Road, Sligo
Tel: 071 43204 / 071 44113
Fax: 00353 7143204
Email: edenhill@iol.ie
Capacity: 32 **Adults:** IR£7.50
Open: All year (not Xmas), 8am-12pm
Family bunk rooms: IR£19.00
Camping for 7 tents: IR£4.00
Self-catering facilities • Television • Showers • Central heating • Laundry facilities • Lounge • Dining room • Drying room • Cycle store • Parking • No smoking Late Victorian period house. Ten minutes city centre/tourist office.

▲ **Gateway Caravan & Camping Centre,** Ballinode, Sligo
Tel: 071 45618
Open: All year

▲ **Gateway Caravan & Camping Park,** Ballinode, Sligo
Tel: 071 45618
Open: All year

Strandhill
G6136

▲ **Strandhill Caravan & Camping Park,** Strandhill, Sligo
Tel: 071 68120
Open: Easter to Sep

County Tipperary

Burncourt

S9220

▲ **Mountain Lodge Youth Hostel,** Mountain Lodge, Burnacourt, County Tipperary
Tel: 052 67277
Email: mailbox@anoige.ie
Capacity: 30
Under 18: IR£5.00-IR£5.50
Adults: IR£6.50-IR£7.50
Open: Mar to Sep
Family bunk rooms
Self-catering facilities • Shop 5 km away • Drying room • Parking
This gaslit hostel is an old shooting lodge set in the forests of the Galtee Mountains. The Rock of Cashel, Swiss Cottage, Mitchelstown Caves and the Tipperary Way are all nearby.

▲ **The Apple Camping & Caravan Park,** Moorstown, Cahir, Co Tipperary
Tel: 052 41459
Fax: 052 42774
Open: May to Sep

Carrick-on-Suir

S4021

▲ **Carrick-on-Suir Caravan & Camping Park,** Kilkenny Road, Ballirichard, Carrick-on-Suir, Co Tipperary
Tel: 051 640461
Open: All year

Clogheen

S0013

▲ **Parsons Green Caravan & Camping Park,** Clogheen, Cahir, Co Tipperary
Tel: 052 65290
Open: All year

Ballinderry

R8597

▲ **Tavern Caravan & Camping Park,** Ballinderry, Nenagh, Co Tipperary
Tel: 067 22026
Open: Easter to Oct

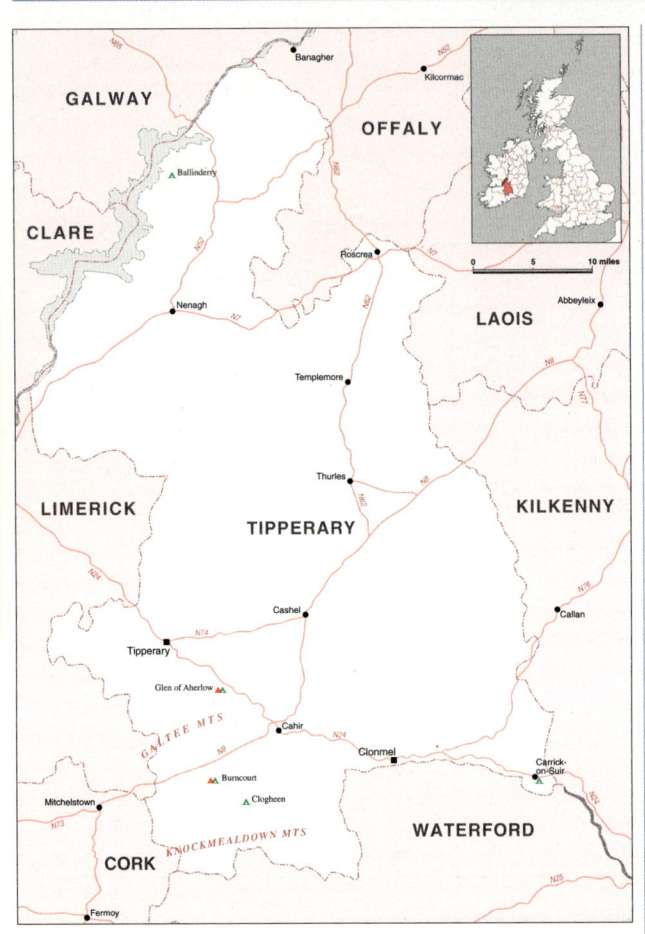

To stay in a Youth Hostel affiliated to one of the Youth Hostel associations, you need to be a member. You can join at most hostels – phone in advance to check.

Phoning from outside the Republic? Dial 00353 and omit the initial '0' of the area code.

County Tipperary

Glen of Aherlow

R9728

▲ **Ballydavid Wood Youth Hostel,** Ballydavid Wood House, Glen of Aherlow, Bansha, Co Tipperary
Tel: 062 54148

Capacity: 40
Under 18: IR£6.00
Adults: IR£8.00
Open: Mar to Nov + weekends
Family bunk rooms
Self-catering facilities • Shop 5 km away • Parking • Meals available groups only, by prior arrangement
An old shooting lodge close to the Tipperary Way. Many historical and archaeological sites of interest including the Rock of Cashel, Mitchelstown Caves and Cappauniacke Castle ruins. Open weekends out of season.

▲ **Ballinacourt House Caravan Park,** Glen of Aherlow, Tipperary
Tel: 062 56230
Open: Easter to Sep

County Waterford

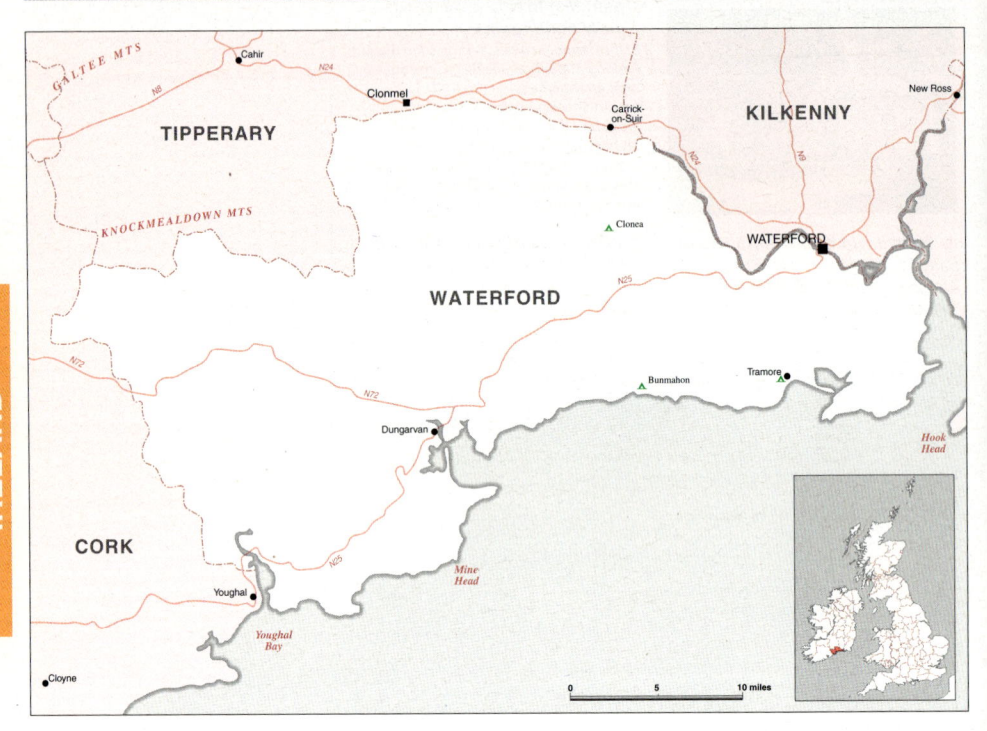

Bunmahon
X4298

▲ **Bonmahon Caravan & Camping Park,** Bunmahon, Kilmacthomas, Co Waterford
Tel: 051 92239 **Open:** May to Sep

Clonea
S3714

▲ **Casey's Caravan Park,** Clonea, Dungarvan, Co Waterford
Tel: 058 41919
Open: May to Aug

Tramore
S5801

▲ **Newtown Cove Camping & Caravan Park,** Tramore, Waterford
Tel: 051 381979 / 381121
Open: May to Sep

County Westmeath

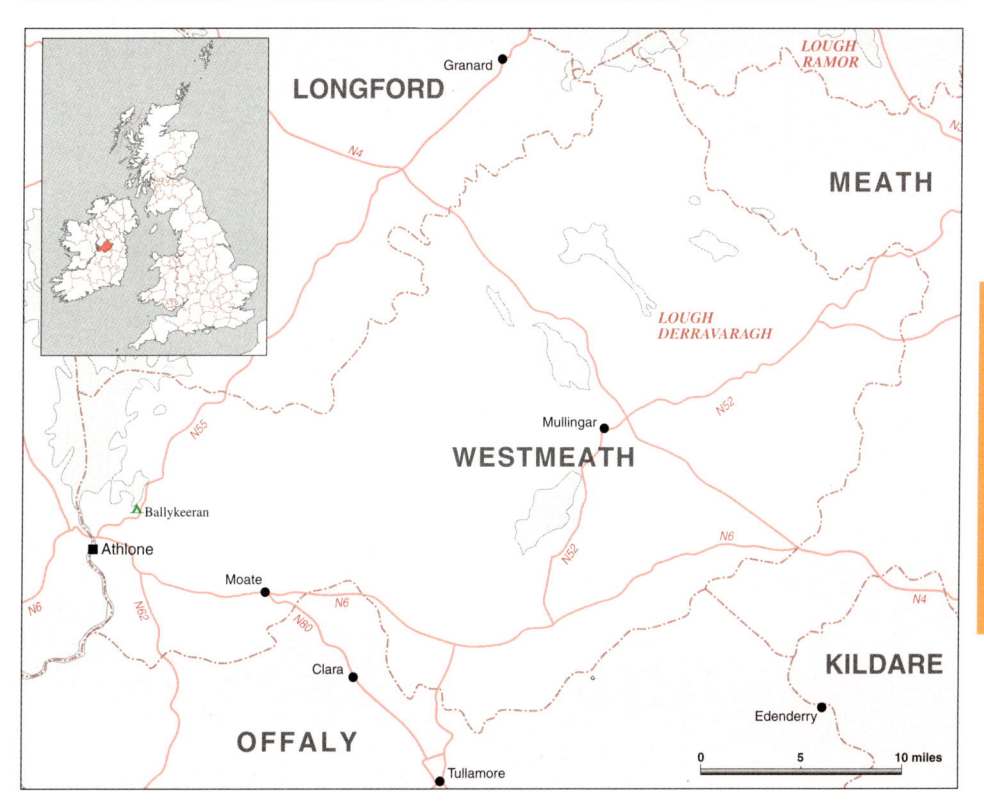

Ballykeeran

N0743

▲ *Lough Ree (East) Caravan & Camping Park,* Ballykeeran, Athlone, Co Westmeath
Tel: 0902 78561 / 74414
Open: Apr to Sep

County Wexford

Arthurstown
S7110

▲ **Arthurstown Youth Hostel,**
Arthurstown, New Ross, County Wexford
Tel: 051 389411
Email: mailbox@anoige.ie
Capacity: 30 **Under 18:** IR£6.00
Adults: IR£7.50
Open: June to Sep
Family bunk rooms
• Self-catering facilities • Shop nearby
This old coastguard station lies at the head of Waterford Harbour. Visit Tintern and Dunbrody Abbeys, the fishing village of Dunmore East and the resort of Tramore.

Ferns
T0149

▲ **Clone House,** Ferns, Enniscorthy, Co Wexford
Tel: 054 66113 **Fax:** 054 66225
Open: Apr to Oct

All details shown are as supplied by hostels and campsites in Autumn 2000.

County Wexford

Kilmuckridge

T1641

▲ **Morriscastle Strand Caravan & Camping Park,** Kilmuckridge, Gorey, Co Wexford
Tel: 053 30124 / 30212
Fax: 053 30365
Open: July to Aug

Lady's Island

T1007

▲ **St Margaret's Caravan & Camping Park,** Lady's Island, Wexford
Tel: 053 31169
Open: Mar to Oct

New Ross

S7227

▲ **MacMurrough Farm Hostel,** MacMurrough, New Ross, County Wexford
Tel: 051 421383
Email: machostel@eircom.net
Capacity: 18
Under 18: IR£8.00
Adults: IR£8.00
Open: All year, 8am
Family bunk rooms: IR£8.00
Camping for 1 tents: IR£5.00
Self-catering facilities • Showers • Wet weather shelter • Lounge • Dining room • Grounds available for games • Cycle store • Parking • No smoking
Quiet country cottage hostel. A real change from city rush.

Newbawn

S8222

▲ **Cypress House,** Newbawn, Wexford
Tel: 051 428335 **Fax:** 051 428148
Open: Apr to Nov

Rosslare

T1015

▲ **Burrow Holiday Caravan & Camping Park,** Rosslare, Wexford
Tel: 053 32190
Open: Mar to Nov

Rosslare Harbour

T1312

▲ **Rosslare Youth Hostel,** Goulding Street, Rosslare Harbour, Co Wexford
Tel: 053 33399
Fax: 053 33624
Email: rosslareyh@oceanfree.net
Capacity: 68
Under 18: IR£7.00-IR£8.00
Adults: IR£8.00-IR£9.50
Open: All year
Family bunk rooms
Self-catering facilities • Shop nearby • Parking
Relax on the sandy beaches, go horse riding, walk the Wexford Coastal Path and visit Lady's Island or the Viking town of Wexford.

Wexford

T0421

▲ **Ferrybank Caravan & Camping Park,** Wexford
Tel: 053 42611
Open: Apr to Sep

County Wicklow

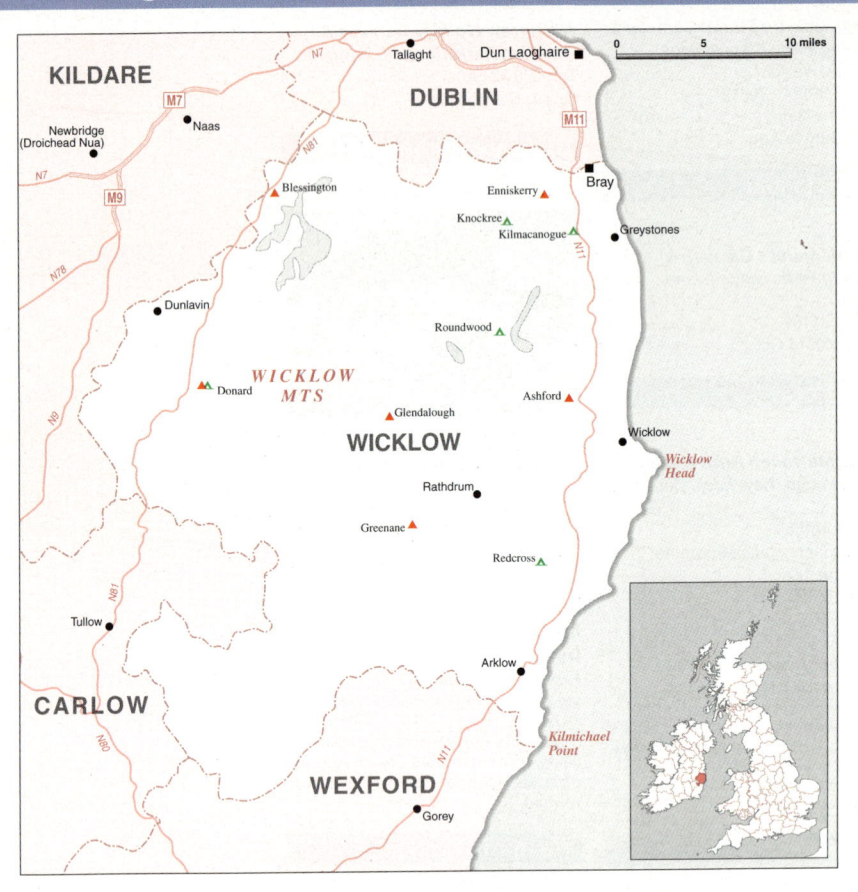

Ashford
T2398

▲ **Tiglin (Devil's Glen) Youth Hostel,** Tiglin Youth Hostel, Devil's Glen, Ashford, Wicklow
Tel: 0404 49049 **Fax:** 0404 49049
Email: mailbox@anoige.ie
Capacity: 52
Under 18: IR£5.00-IR£5.50
Adults: IR£6.50-IR£7.50
Open: All year **Family bunk rooms**
Self-catering facilities • Shop • Parking
A C19th farmhouse set in the forest, where wild deer roam close to the hostel. A local outdoor sculpture exhibition is worth a visit.

254 Stilwell's Hostels & Camping 2002

County Wicklow

Blessington
N9814

▲ **Baltyboys Youth Hostel,** Blessington, County Wicklow
Tel: 045 867266
Fax: 045 867032
Email: mailbox@anoige.ie
Capacity: 36
Under 18: IR£5.00-IR£5.50
Adults: IR£6.50-IR£7.50
Open: Mar to Nov
Self-catering facilities • Shop 5 km away • Parking
Old schoolhouse in secluded woodland area overlooking Blessington Lakes. Great walking, cycling, fishing, boating and watersports. Open weekends out of season.

Donard
S9396

▲ **Ballinclea Youth Hostel,** Ballinclea, Donard, County Wicklow
Tel: 045 404657
Fax: 045 404657
Email: mailbox@anoige.ie
Capacity: 40
Under 18: IR£5.00-IR£5.50
Adults: IR£6.50-IR£7.50
Open: Mar to Nov
Family bunk rooms
Self-catering facilities • Shop 2 km away • Parking
This charming old farmhouse is a great base for hillwalking, including Lugnaquilla, Wicklow's highest mountain. Horse riding and orienteering also available.

▲ **Moat Farm Caravan & Camping Park,** Donard, Dunlavin, Co Wicklow
Tel: 045 404727
Open: All year

Enniskerry
O2217

▲ **Glencree Youth Hostel,** Stone House, Glencree, Enniskerry, County Wicklow
Tel: 01 2864037
Email: mailbox@anoige.ie
Capacity: 40
Under 18: IR£5.00-IR£5.50
Adults: IR£6.50-IR£7.50
Open: All year
Family bunk rooms
Self-catering facilities • Shop nearby, limited
Charming old stone house, next to a stream. The area is well-known for its excellent hillwalking. Visit the German War Cemetery in the village.

Glendalough
T1296

▲ **Glendalough Youth Hostel,** The Lodge, Glendalough, Bray, County Wicklow
Actual Grid Ref: T122968
Tel: 0404 45342
Fax: 0404 45690
Email: mailbox@anoige.ie
Capacity: 120
Under 18: IR£8.50-IR£10.50
Adults: IR£10.50-IR£12.50
Open: All year
Family bunk rooms

If you have to cancel your visit to any hostel or campsite, please let them know – it is always possible to make a bed or a pitch available to someone else.

Self-catering facilities • Shop 2 km or limited supplies at hostel • Laundry facilities • Parking • Facilities for disabled people • Meals available
Situated in a wooded glacial valley in a National Park area. Ideal for historians, geographers and naturalists; great for fishing, cycling and walking the Wicklow Way.

Greenane
T0694

▲ **Glenmalure Youth Hostel,** Glenmalure, Greenane, Co Wicklow
Tel: 01 8304555 **Fax:** 01 8305808
Email: mailbox@anoige.ie
Capacity: 19
Under 18: IR£5.00-IR£5.50
Adults: IR£6.50-IR£7.50
Open: Jun to Aug
Family bunk rooms
Self-catering facilities • Shop 10 km away
Simple mountain hut set in the valley where the Battle of Glenmalure was fought in 1798. Please call head office for reservations: 01 830 4555. Open Sat nights throughout year.

Kilmacanogue
O2614

▲ **Valleyview,** Killough, Kilmacanogue, Bray, Co Wicklow
Tel: 01 2829565
Open: Apr to Oct

To stay in a Youth Hostel affiliated to one of the Youth Hostel associations, you need to be a member. You can join at most hostels – phone in advance to check.

IRELAND

Stilwell's Hostels & Camping 2002 255

County Wicklow • MAP PAGE 254

Knockree

O1915

▲ **Knockree Youth Hostel,** Lacken House, Knockree, Enniskerry, County Wicklow
Actual Grid Ref: O192151
Tel: 01 2864036
Email: mailbox@anoige.ie
Capacity: 58
Under 18: IR£5.00-IR£5.50
Adults: IR£6.50-IR£7.50
Open: All year

Self-catering facilities • Shop 7 km away • Parking
Converted farmhouse, set at the bottom of Knockree, overlooking Glencree Mountains. The Wicklow Way passes through the hostel grounds. Call head office for reservations: 01 830 4555

Redcross

T2584

▲ **Johnson's Caravan & Camping Park,** Redcross, Wicklow
Tel: 0404 48133
Open: Apr to Sep

Roundwood

O1802

▲ **Roundwood Caravan & Camping Park,** Roundwood, Bray, Co Wicklow
Tel: 01 2818163
Open: Apr to Sep

Aberdeenshire & Moray

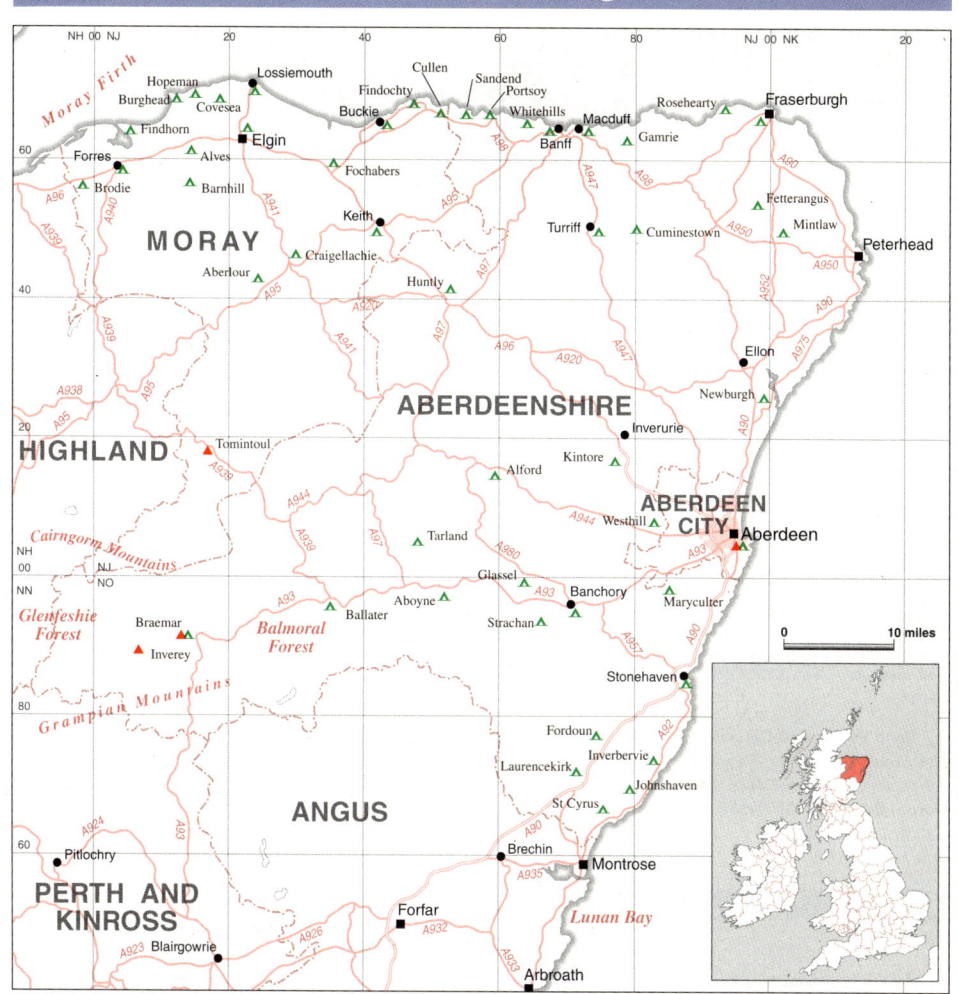

Aberdeen
NJ9306

▲ **Aberdeen Youth Hostel**, 8 Queen's Road, Aberdeen, AB15 4ZT
Actual Grid Ref: NJ922058
Tel: 01224 646988
Email: aberdeenshire@syha.org.uk
Capacity: 116 **Under 18:** £6.00-£11.35
Adults: £9.00-£13.25
Open: All year **Family bunk rooms**
Self-catering facilities • Shop nearby • Laundry facilities
Ideal for enjoying the city and countryside. Sail to Orkney & Shetland.

▲ **Hazlehead Caravan & Camping Site**, Groats Road, Aberdeen, AB15 8BE
Actual Grid Ref: NJ894057
Tel: 01224 647647 / 321268
Open: Mar to Oct

Aberlour
NJ2642

▲ **Aberlour Gardens Caravan Park**, Aberlour, Banffshire, AB38 9LD
Actual Grid Ref: NJ282437
Tel: 01340 871586
Email: Abergard@compuserve.com
Open: Mar to Oct

Aboyne
NO5298

▲ **Aboyne Loch Caravan Park**, Aboyne, Aberdeenshire, AB34 5BR
Actual Grid Ref: NO538998
Tel: 013398 86244 / 01330 811351
Open: Apr to Oct

▲ **Aboyne Loch Holdiay Park**, Aboyne, Aberdeenshire, AB34 5BR
Actual Grid Ref: NO538998
Tel: 01339 886244
Open: Apr to Oct

Aberdeenshire & Moray • MAP PAGE 257

Alford
NJ5716

▲ **Haughton House Caravan Park,** Montgarrie Road, Alford, Aberdeenshire, AB33 8NA
Actual Grid Ref: NJ583169
Tel: 01975 562107
Open: Apr to Sep

Alves
NJ1362

▲ **North Alves Caravan Park,** Alves, Elgin, Moray, IV30 3XD
Actual Grid Ref: NJ122633
Tel: 01343 850223
Open: Apr to Oct

Ballater
NO3695

▲ **Ballater Caravan Park,** Anderson Road, Ballater, Aberdeenshire, AB35 5QW
Actual Grid Ref: NO371954
Tel: 013397 55727
Open: Apr to Oct

Banchory
NO7095

▲ **Banchory Lodge Caravan Site,** Dee Street, Banchory, Kincardineshire, AB31 4DN
Actual Grid Ref: NO698954
Tel: 01330 822246
Open: Apr to Oct

Banff
NJ6864

▲ **Banff Links Caravan Park,** Banff, Aberdeenshire, AB45 2JJ
Actual Grid Ref: NJ673645
Tel: 01261 812228
Open: Apr to Oct

Barnhill
NJ1457

▲ **Windsor Holiday Park,** Barrhill, Girvan, Ayrshire, KA26 0PZ
Actual Grid Ref: NJ215836
Tel: 01465 821355
Email: bookings@windsor-park.freeserve.co.uk
Open: Mar to Oct

Braemar
NO1491

▲ **Braemar Youth Hostel,** Corrie Feragie, 21 Glenshee Road, Braemar, Ballater, AB35 5YQ
Actual Grid Ref: NO155909
Tel: 01339 741659
Email: braemar@syha.org.uk
Capacity: 59
Under 18: £5.00-£8.00
Adults: £8.00-£9.25 **Open:** Dec to Oct
Self-catering facilities • Shop • Laundry facilities
Braemar is the setting for the Royal Highland Games in September. Royal Deeside provides unsurpassed beauty in its majestic mountains and pine-clad glens.

▲ **Rucksacks Bunkhouse,** 15 Mar Road, Braemar, Aberdeenshire, AB35 5YL
Tel: 013397 41517
Open: All year

Brodie
NH9757

▲ **Old Mill Holiday Park,** Brodie, Forres, Moray, IV36 0TD
Actual Grid Ref: NH980570
Tel: 01309 641244
Open: Apr to Oct

Buckie (Spey Bay)
NJ4165

▲ **Strathlene Caravan Site,** Great Eastern Road, Buckie, Banffshire, AB56 1SR
Tel: 01542 834851
Open: Apr to Oct

Burghead
NJ1169

▲ **Red Craig Hotel Caravan & Camping Park,** Burghead, Elgin, Moray, IV30 2XX
Actual Grid Ref: NJ122687
Tel: 01343 835663
Open: Apr to Oct

▲ **Burghead Caravan Site,** Burghead, Elgin, Morayshire, IV30 2UN
Actual Grid Ref: NJ114686
Tel: 01343 830084
Open: Apr to Oct

Covesea
NJ1870

▲ **Silver Sands Leisure Park,** Covesea, West Beach, Lossiemouth, Moray, IV31 6SP
Actual Grid Ref: NJ205710
Tel: 01343 813262
Fax: 01343 815203
Email: holidays@silversands.freeserve.co.uk
Open: Apr to Oct

Craigellachie
NJ2845

▲ **Camping & Caravanning Club Site,** Elchies, Craigellachie, Aberlour, Banffshire, AB38 9SD
Actual Grid Ref: NJ257449
Tel: 01340 810414
Open: All year

Cullen
NJ5167

▲ **Cullen Caravan Site,** Logie Drive, Cullen, Banffshire, AB56 2TW
Actual Grid Ref: NJ516676
Tel: 01542 840766
Open: Apr to Sep

Cuminestown
NJ8050

▲ **East Balthangie Caravan Park,** Cuminestown, Turriff, Aberdeenshire, AB53 7XY
Actual Grid Ref: NJ841516
Tel: 01888 544261
Open: Mar to Oct

▲ **East Balthangie Caravan Park,** Cuminestown, Turriff, Grampian, AB53 5XY
Actual Grid Ref: NJ842517
Tel: 01888 544921
Fax: 01888 544261
Open: Mar to Oct

All details shown are as supplied by hostels and campsites in Autumn 2000.

Aberdeenshire & Moray

Elgin
NJ2162

▲ **Riverside Caravan Park,** Elgin, Moray, IV30 3UN
Actual Grid Ref: NJ197627
Tel: 01343 542813
Open: Apr to Oct

Fetterangus
NJ9951

▲ **Greens of Gaval,** Fetterangus, Peterhead, Aberdeenshire, AB42 4HB
Actual Grid Ref: NJ982507
Tel: 01771 623696
Open: All year

Findhorn
NJ0464

▲ **Findhorn Sands Caravan Park,** Findhorn, Forres, Moray, IV36 0YZ
Actual Grid Ref: NJ036646
Tel: 01309 690324
Open: Apr to Oct

▲ **Findhorn Bay Caravan Park,** Findhorn, Forres, IV36 0TY
Actual Grid Ref: NJ051635
Tel: 01309 690203
Open: Apr to Oct

Findochty
NJ4668

▲ **Moray Council Caravan Site,** Findochty, Buckie, Banffshire, AB56 4QA
Actual Grid Ref: NJ459679
Tel: 01542 835303
Open: Apr to Sep

Fochabers
NJ3458

▲ **Burnside Caravan Site,** The Nurseries, Keith Road, Fochabers, Moray, IV32 7PF
Actual Grid Ref: NJ350580
Tel: 01343 820511 **Open:** Apr to Oct

Fordoun
NO7575

▲ **Brownmuir Caravan Park,** Fordoun, Laurencekirk, Kincardineshire, AB30 1SJ
Actual Grid Ref: NO740772
Tel: 01561 320786
Open: Apr to Oct

All details shown are as supplied by hostels and campsites in Autumn 2000.

Forres
NJ0358

▲ **River View Caravan Park,** Mundole Court, Forres, Morayshire, IV36 0SZ
Actual Grid Ref: NJ013572
Tel: 01309 673932
Fax: 01309 675822
Open: Mar to Nov

Fraserburgh
NJ9967

▲ **Kessock Caravan Park,** Kessock Road, Fraserburgh, Aberdeenshire, AB43 8UE
Actual Grid Ref: NJ999661
Tel: 01346 510041
Open: Apr to Sep

▲ **Esplanade Caravan Park,** Kessock Road, Fraserburgh, Aberdeenshire, AB43 8UE
Actual Grid Ref: NK000662
Tel: 01346 510041
Open: Apr to Oct

Gamrie
NJ7965

▲ **Wester Bonnyton Farm Site,** Gamrie, Banff, Banffshire, AB45 3EP
Actual Grid Ref: NJ740636
Tel: 01261 832470
Open: Apr to Oct

Glassel
NO6599

▲ **Campfield Caravan Site,** Glassel, Banchory, Aberdeenshire, AB31 4DN
Actual Grid Ref: NJ652004
Tel: 013398 82250
Open: Apr to Sep

Some hostels and campsites impose restrictions on size and type of groups they accept (e.g. not permitting single-sex groups). Always phone to enquire before booking.

Hopeman
NJ1469

▲ **Station Caravan Park,** West Beach, Hopeman, Elgin, Moray, IV30 2RU
Actual Grid Ref: NJ28/142696
Tourist Board grade: 2 Ticks
Tel: 01343 830880
Fax: 01343 830880
Email: stationcaravanpark@talk21.com
Tent pitches: 35
Tent rate: £3.50-£10.00
Open: Mar to Nov **Last arr:** 8pm
Dogs allowed • Electric hook-up • Calor Gas/Camping Gaz • Showers • Laundrette on site • Public phone on site • Boating/sailing/watersports nearby • Tennis courts nearby • Golf nearby • Riding nearby • Fishing nearby
Family-run park on Hopeman's West Beach which is sandy and safe, adjacent to harbour, which is ideal for boating enthusiasts. Dolphins can often be seen in the bay. Ideal centre for exploring Moray, Whisky and Castle Trails. Shops, pubs, takeaways in Hopeman. Caravans to rent, many with sea views.

▲ **Hopeman Sands Caravan Park,** Hopeman, Elgin, IV30 2RU
Actual Grid Ref: NJ142696
Tel: 01343 830880
Fax: 01343 830880
Open: Apr to Oct

Huntly
NJ5240

▲ **Huntly Castle Caravan Park,** The Meadow, Huntly, AB54 4UJ
Actual Grid Ref: NJ528405
Tel: 01466 794999
Open: Mar to Oct

Inverbervie
NO8372

▲ **Burgh Haugh Caravan Park,** Inverbervie, Montrose, DD10 0SP
Actual Grid Ref: NO834724
Tel: 01561 361182
Open: Apr to Oct

SCOTLAND

Stilwell's Hostels & Camping 2002

Aberdeenshire & Moray • MAP PAGE 257

Inverey

NO0889

▲ **Inverey Youth Hostel,** Inverey, Braemar, Ballater, Aberdeenshire, AB35 5YB
Actual Grid Ref: NO077896
Tel: 08701 553255 (SYHA Central Booking Service)
Capacity: 17
Under 18: £5.75
Adults: £7.00
Open: May to Oct
Self-catering facilities • Shop 5 miles away Ideal base for climbers. Lairig Ghru and the Cairngorms are close. Corrour Bothy is 10 miles away. Mountain bikes can be hired locally.

Johnshaven

NO7966

▲ **Wairds Park Caravan Site,** Johnshaven, Montrose, Angus, DD10 0HD
Actual Grid Ref: NO800672
Tel: 01561 362395
Open: Apr to Oct

Keith

NJ4250

▲ **Keith Caravan Site,** Dunnyduff Road, Keith, Banffshire, AB55 3JG
Actual Grid Ref: NJ434498
Tel: 01542 882078
Open: Apr to Sep

Kintore

NJ7915

▲ **Hillhead Caravan Park,** Kintore, Inverurie, Aberdeenshire, AB51 0YX
Actual Grid Ref: NJ762161
Tel: 01467 632809
Fax: 01467 633173
Email: deacon@not4zero.com
Tent pitches: 29
Tent rate: £5.90-£8.20
Open: Easter to Oct
Last arr: 10pm

Facilities for disabled people • Dogs allowed • Electric hook-up • Calor Gas/Camping Gaz • Picnic/barbecue area on site • Children's play area • Showers • Laundrette on site • Public phone on site • Shop on site • Golf nearby • Riding nearby • Fishing nearby
Family-run park set on wooded hilltop. Quiet and secluded, sheltered flat grass. Picturesque area. Static caravans, disabled facilities. Forest walks, 13 miles from Aberdeen, famed Castle and Whisky Trails, 9 golf courses nearby. Park signposted off A96 Aberdeen-Inverness.

Laurencekirk

NO7171

▲ **Dovecot Caravan Park,** Northwaterbridge, Laurencekirk, Kincardineshire, AB30 1QL
Actual Grid Ref: NO648663
Tel: 01674 840630
Fax: 01674 840630
Open: Apr to Oct

Lossiemouth

NJ2370

▲ **Lossiemouth Caravan Site,** Lossiemouth, Moray, IV31 6JJ
Actual Grid Ref: NJ237702
Tel: 01343 813980
Open: Apr to Sep

Macduff

NJ7064

▲ **Myrus Caravan Site,** Macduff, Aberdeenshire, AB44 1QP
Actual Grid Ref: NJ710633
Tel: 01261 812845
Open: Apr to Oct

Maryculter

NO8499

▲ **Lower Deeside Holiday Park,** Maryculter, Aberdeen, AB12 5FX
Actual Grid Ref: NO845998
Tel: 01224 733860
Fax: 01224 732490
Open: All year

Mintlaw

NK0048

▲ **Aden Country Park Caravan Park,** Mintlaw, Peterhead, Aberdeenshire, AB42 8FQ
Actual Grid Ref: NJ985483
Tel: 01771 623460
Open: Mar to Oct

Newburgh (Ellon)

NJ9925

▲ **Ythan Hotel Caravan Site,** Newburgh, Aberdeenshire, AB41 6BE
Actual Grid Ref: NJ998248
Tel: 01358 789272
Open: May to Sep

Portsoy

NJ5866

▲ **Portsoy Caravan Park,** Maclean Terrace, Portsoy, Banff, AB45 2RQ
Actual Grid Ref: NJ592662
Tel: 01261 842695
Open: Apr to Oct

Rosehearty

NJ9367

▲ **Rosehearty Caravan Park,** Rosehearty, Fraserburgh, AB43 7JQ
Actual Grid Ref: NJ934676
Tel: 01346 571658
Open: Apr to Sep

Sandend

NJ5566

▲ **Sandend Caravan Park,** Sandend, Portsoy, Banff, AB45 2UA
Actual Grid Ref: NJ555663
Tel: 01261 842660
Open: Apr to Oct

St Cyrus

NO7464

▲ **East Bowstrips Caravan Park,** St Cyrus, Montrose, Angus, DD10 0DE
Actual Grid Ref: NO746655
Tel: 01674 850328
Fax: 01674 850328
Open: Apr to Oct

▲ **Lauriston Caravan Park,** St Cyrus, Montrose, Angus, DD10 0DJ
Actual Grid Ref: NO764657
Tel: 01674 850316
Open: All year

▲ **Miltonhaven Seaside Caravan Park,** St Cyrus, Montrose, Angus, DD10 0DL
Actual Grid Ref: NO775655
Tel: 01674 850413
Open: Apr to Oct

MAP PAGE 257 • **Aberdeenshire & Moray**

Stonehaven

NO8786

▲ *Queen Elizabeth Caravan Park,*
Queen Elizabeth Park, Stonehaven, Aberdeenshire, AB39 2RD
Actual Grid Ref: NO879867
Tel: 01569 764014
Open: Apr to Oct

Strachan

NO6792

▲ *Feughside Caravan Park,*
Strachan, Banchory, Aberdeenshire, AB31 6NT
Actual Grid Ref: NO642925
Tel: 01330 850669
Open: Apr to Oct

▲ *Silver Ladies Leisure Park,*
Strachan, Banchory, Aberdeenshire, AB31 6NL
Actual Grid Ref: NO692936
Tel: 01330 822800
Open: Apr to Oct

Tarland

NJ4704

▲ *Camping & Caravanning Club Site,* Tarland, Aboyne, Aberdeenshire, AB34 4UP
Actual Grid Ref: NJ477044
Tel: 01339 881388
Open: Mar to Nov

Tomintoul

NJ1618

▲ *Tomintoul Youth Hostel,* Main Street, Tomintoul, Ballindalloch, Banffshire, AB37 9HA
Actual Grid Ref: NJ165190
Tel: 01807 580282
Email: reservations@syha.org.uk
Capacity: 38
Under 18: £6.00
Adults: £6.75
Open: May to Oct
Self-catering facilities • Shop nearby
Go for the 47-mile Speyside Way walk, explore the Cairngorms, try rock climbing or abseiling and savour the Whisky Trail.

Turriff

NJ7250

▲ *Turriff Caravan Park,* Station Road, Turriff, Aberdeenshire, AB53 7ER
Actual Grid Ref: NJ725494
Tel: 01888 562205
Open: Apr to Oct

Westhill

NJ8306

▲ *Skene Caravan Park,* Mains of Keir, Skene, Westhill, Aberdeenshire, AB32 6YA
Actual Grid Ref: NJ810082
Tel: 01224 743282
Open: Apr to Oct

Whitehills

NJ6565

▲ *Blackpotts Cottages,* Whitehills, Banff, Grampian, AB45 2JN
Actual Grid Ref: NJ662658
Tel: 01261 861396
Open: Apr to Oct

Angus

Acharn
NO2876

Glendoll Youth Hostel, Acharn, Clova, Kirriemuir, Angus, DD8 4RD
Actual Grid Ref: NO278763
Tel: 01575 550236
Capacity: 45
Under 18: £7.00
Adults: £8.25
Open: March to Oct
Family bunk rooms
Self-catering facilities • Shop
Unspoilt mountain region, with many fine circular walks. Nature reserve and lochs nearby, many Munros within reach. Good winter climbing and skiing.

Airlie
NO3150

The Brae Of Airlie Farmhouse, The Kirkton of Airlie, Airlie, Kirriemuir, Angus, DD8 5NJ
Tel: 01575 530293 **Fax:** 01575 530293
Open: All year

Hostels and campsites may vary rates – be sure to check when booking.

262   Stilwell's Hostels & Camping 2002

Angus

Arbroath
NO6441

▲ **Seaton Estate Caravan Site,** Seaton House, Arbroath, Angus, DD11 5SE
Tel: 01241 874762
Open: Easter to Oct

Brechin
NO6059

▲ **Eastmill Road Caravan Site,** Eastmill Road, Brechin, Angus, DD9 7EL
Actual Grid Ref: NO606595
Tel: 01356 622810
Open: Apr to Sep

Carnoustie
NO5634

▲ **Woodlands Caravan Park,** Newton Road, Carnoustie, Angus, DD7 6HR
Actual Grid Ref: NO558350
Tel: 01241 853246
Fax: 01307 461889
Open: Apr to Oct

Edzell
NO6068

▲ **Glenesk Caravan Park,** Edzell, Brechin, Angus, DD9 7YP
Actual Grid Ref: NO602721
Tel: 01356 648565
Open: Apr to Oct

Forfar
NO4550

▲ **Lochside Caravan/Camping Site,** Forfar Country Park, Forfar, Angus, DD8 1BT
Actual Grid Ref: NO450506
Tel: 01307 468917
Open: Apr to Oct

Memus
NO4259

▲ **The Glens Caravan Site,** Memus, Forfar, Angus, DD8 3TY
Actual Grid Ref: NO426591
Tel: 01307 860258
Open: Apr to Oct

Monifieth
NO4932

▲ **Tayview Holiday Park,** Monifieth, Dundee, Tayside, DD5 4NH
Actual Grid Ref: NO502322
Tel: 01382 532837
Open: Apr to Oct

Montrose
NO7157

▲ **South Links Caravan Park,** Traill Drive, Montrose, Angus, DD10 8NN
Actual Grid Ref: NO725575
Tel: 01674 672105
Open: Apr to Sep

Roundyhill
NO3750

▲ **Drumshademuir Caravan Park,** Roundyhill, Forfar, Angus, DD8 1QT
Actual Grid Ref: NO380505
Tel: 01575 573284
Open: Mar to Oct

Argyll & Bute

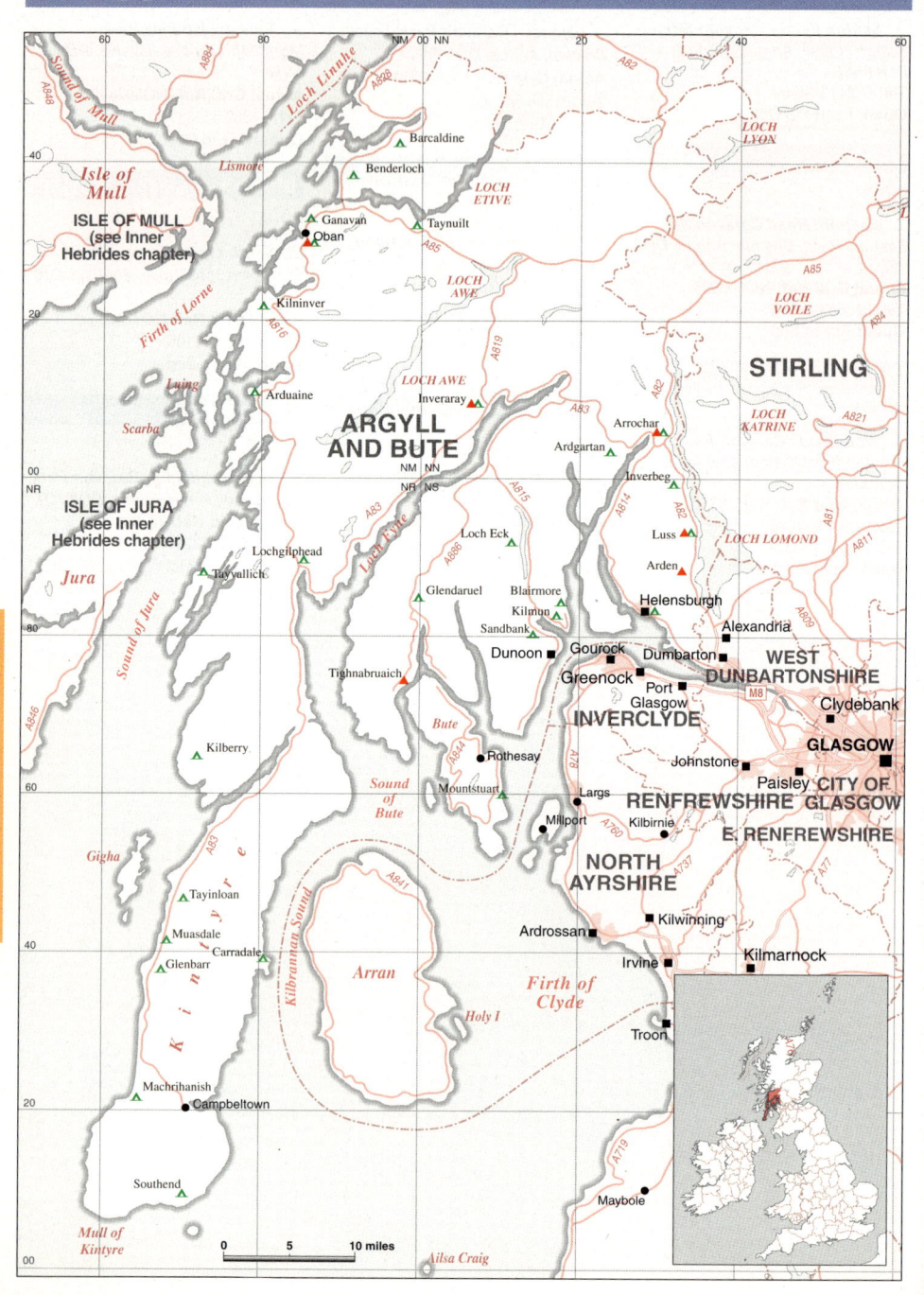

Argyll & Bute

Arden
NS3684

▲ Loch Lomond Youth Hostel,
Arden, Alexandria, G83 8RB
Actual Grid Ref: NS368834
Tel: 01389 850226
Email: loch.lomond@syha.org.uk
Capacity: 160
Under 18: £10.50-£11.75
Adults: £11.75-£13.25
Open: All year
Family bunk rooms
Self-catering facilities • Shop • Laundry facilities • Evening meal available groups only
Set in beautiful grounds, a fine centre for walking and climbing. Watersports and boat trips available on the loch.

Ardgartan
NN2703

▲ Camping & Caravanning Club Site, Collesan Road, Ardgartan, Arrochar, Argyll, G83 7AR
Tel: 01301 702253
Open: Apr to Sep

Arduaine
NM8010

▲ Arduaine Caravan & Camping Park, Arduaine, Kilmelford, Oban, Argyll, PA34 4XA
Actual Grid Ref: NM802102
Tel: 01852 200331
Open: Apr to Oct

Arrochar
NN2904

▲ Ardgartan Youth Hostel, Arrochar, Dunbartonshire G83 7AR
Actual Grid Ref: NN272028
Tel: 01301 702362
Email: ardgartan@syha.org.uk
Capacity: 60
Under 18: £6.25-£8.00
Adults: £7.50-£9.25
Open: March to Nov
Family bunk rooms
Self-catering facilities • Shop • Laundry facilities • Group evening meal available
Superb hostel set on the banks of Loch Long. Ideal base for all grades of walking, mountain biking and rock climbing. Loch Lomond cruises from nearby Tarbert.

▲ Ardgartan Caravan & Campsite, Arrochar, Argyll, G83 7AL
Actual Grid Ref: NN275030
Tel: 01301 702293
Open: Easter to Oct

Barcaldine
NM9641

▲ Camping & Caravanning Club Site, Barcaldine, Oban, Argyll, PA37 1SG
Actual Grid Ref: NM966420
Tel: 01631 720348 **Open:** Apr to Oct

Benderloch
NM9038

▲ Highfield, 3 Kiel Croft, Benderloch, Oban, Argyll, PA37 1QS
Actual Grid Ref: NM904392
Tel: 01631 720262 **Open:** May to Nov

Blairmore
NS1982

▲ Gairletter Caravan Park, Blairmore, Dunoon, Argyll, PA23 8TP
Tel: 01369 810208 **Open:** Mar to Oct

Bute - Mountstuart
NS1059

▲ New Farm, Mountstuart, Rothesay, Isle of Bute, PA20 9NA
Tel: 01700 831646 **Fax:** 01700 831646
Open: All year

Carradale
NR8138

▲ Carradale Bay Caravan Site, Kintyre, Carradale, Campbeltown, Argyll, PA28 6QG
Actual Grid Ref: NR805374
Tel: 01583 431665 **Open:** Apr to Sep

Ganavan
NM8532

▲ Ganavan Sands Touring Caravan Park, Ganavan, Oban, Argyll, PA34 5TU
Actual Grid Ref: NM862325
Tel: 01631 562179 **Open:** Apr to Oct

Glenbarr
NR6736

▲ Killegruer Caravan Site, Glenbarr, Tarbert, Argyll, PA29 6XB
Actual Grid Ref: NR663357
Tel: 01583 421241
Open: Apr to Sep

Glendaruel
NR9985

▲ Glendaruel Caravan Park, Glendaruel, Colintraive, Argyll, PA22 3AB
Actual Grid Ref: NS002868
Tel: 01369 820267
Open: Apr to Oct

Helensburgh
NS2982

▲ Roseneath Castle Caravan Park, Helensburgh, Argyll, G84 0QS
Actual Grid Ref: NS268822
Tel: 01436 831208
Open: Mar to Jan

Inveraray
NN0908

▲ Inveraray Youth Hostel, Dalmally Road, Inveraray, Argyll, PA32 8XD
Actual Grid Ref: NN093087
Tel: 01499 302454
Capacity: 38 **Under 18:** £7.00-£7.25
Adults: £8.25-£8.50
Open: March to Oct
Family bunk rooms
Self-catering facilities • Shop nearby
The scenic town of Inveraray is always worth a visit, with its lovely castle and the 'Arctic Penguin' ship with maritime museum. Sea bathing and fishing in Loch Fyne.

▲ Argyll Caravan & Camping Park, Inveraray, Argyll, PA32 8XT
Actual Grid Ref: NN075055
Tel: 01499 302285
Fax: 01499 302421
Open: Apr to Oct

Argyll & Bute • MAP PAGE 264

Hostels and campsites may vary rates – be sure to check when booking.

All details shown are as supplied by hostels and campsites in Autumn 2000.

Inverbeg
NS3497

▲ **Inverbeg Holiday Park,** Inverbeg, Luss, Alexandria, Dunbartonshire, G83 8PD
Tel: 01436 860267
Open: Mar to Oct

Kilberry
NR7163

▲ **Port Ban,** Kilberry, Tarbert, Argyll, PA29 6YD
Actual Grid Ref: NR705655
Tel: 01880 770224
Open: Apr to Oct

Kilmun
NS1781

▲ **Cot House Caravan Park,** Cot House, Kilmun, Dunoon, PA23 8QS
Actual Grid Ref: NS154831
Tel: 01369 840351
Open: Apr to Oct

Kilninver
NM8221

▲ **Glen Gallain Caravan Park,** Kilninver, Oban, Argyll, PA34 4UU
Tel: 01852 316200
Open: Apr to Oct

Loch Eck
NS1391

▲ **Stratheck Caravan Park,** Loch Eck, Dunoon, Argyll, PA23 8SG
Actual Grid Ref: NS143865
Tel: 01369 840472
Fax: 01369 840472
Open: Mar to Dec

Lochgilphead
NR8687

▲ **Lochgilphead Caravan Park,** Bank Park, Lochgilphead, Argyll, PA31 8NX
Actual Grid Ref: NR859881
Tel: 01546 602003
Fax: 01546 603699
Open: Apr to Oct

Luss
NS3592

▲ **Edentaggart Bothy,** Edentaggart, Glen Luss, Luss, Alexandria, Dunbartonshire, G83 8PB
Actual Grid Ref: NS325940
Tel: 01436 860226
Capacity: 2
Under 18: £8.00
Adults: £12.00
Open: All year, 8am-8pm
Self-catering facilities • Television • Showers • Parking • No smoking
Wonderful walking area with beautiful views. Bunks, shower, cooking facilities, open fire.

▲ **Camping & Caravanning Club Site,** Luss Road, Loch Lomond, Glasgow, G51 3YD
Actual Grid Ref: NS360936
Tel: 01436 860658
Open: Mar to Oct

Machrihanish
NR6320

▲ **Camping & Caravanning Club Site,** East Trodigal Farm Camping & Caravan Site, Machrihanish, Campbeltown, Argyll, PA28 6PT
Actual Grid Ref: NR647208
Tel: 01586 810366
Open: Mar to Sept

Muasdale
NR6840

▲ **Muasdale Holiday Park,** Muasdale, Tarbert, Argyll, PA29 6XD
Actual Grid Ref: NR680402
Tel: 01546 602003
Fax: 01546 603699
Open: Apr to Sep

You are advised to book in advance for periods of high demand – the Summer months, Half Term holidays and public holidays.

Oban
NM8630

▲ **Oban Youth Hostel,** Esplanade, Oban, Argyll, PA34 5AF
Actual Grid Ref: NM854307
Tel: 01631 562025
Capacity: 94
Under 18: £6.00-£11.75
Adults: £9.00-£13.25
Open: All year
Family bunk rooms
Self-catering facilities • Shop nearby • Laundry facilities
Castles: Dunollie, Gylen and Dunstaffnage; swimming, sub-aqua, fishing, sailing; Sea Life Centre; walking; steamer to Mull, Colonsay, Iona and Lismore.

▲ **Oban Waterfront Lodge,** Victoria Crescent, Esplanade, Oban, PA34 5PN
Tel: 01631 566040
Fax: 01631 566940
Capacity: 67
Under 18: £10.00
Adults: £10.00-£20.00
Open: All year, any time
Self-catering facilities • Showers • Showers • Central heating • Laundry facilities • Lounge • Dining room
On the water front - great views. Twin, double, family rooms available.

▲ **Oban Lodge Youth Hostel,** Esplanade, Oban, Argyll, PA34 5AF
Actual Grid Ref: NM854307
Tel: 01631 562025
Capacity: 42
Under 18: £6.00-£11.75
Adults: £9.00-£13.25
Open: All year
Family bunk rooms
Self-catering facilities • Shop nearby • Laundry facilities
Brand new seafront hostel with ensuite facilities. Go island-hopping to Mull, Colonsay, Lismore and Iona.

▲ **Oban Caravan & Camping Park,** Gallachmore Farm, Oban, Argyll, PA34 4QH
Actual Grid Ref: NM830275
Tel: 01631 562425
Fax: 01631 566624
Open: Apr to Sep

MAP PAGE 264 • **Argyll & Bute**

▲ **Oban Divers Caravan Park,**
Gleshellach Road, Oban, Argyll, PA34 4QJ
Actual Grid Ref: NM841277
Tel: 01631 562755
Open: Mar to Nov

Sandbank

NS1680

▲ **Invereck Caravan Park,**
Sandbank, Dunoon, Argyll, PA23 8QS
Actual Grid Ref: NS148830
Tel: 01369 705544
Open: Apr to Oct

Southend

NR6907

▲ **Machribeg Caravan Site,**
Southend, Campbeltown, Argyll, PA28 6RW
Tel: 01586 820249
Open: Easter to Sep

▲ **Machribeg Caravan Site,**
Machribeg, Southend, Campbeltown, Argyll, PA28 6RW
Actual Grid Ref: NR686080
Tel: 01586 830249
Open: Apr to Sep

Tayinloan

NR6945

▲ **Point Sands Caravan Park,**
Tayinloan, Tarbert, Argyll, PA29 6XG
Actual Grid Ref: NR698484
Tel: 01583 441263
Fax: 01583 441216
Open: Apr to Oct

Taynuilt

NN0031

▲ **Crunachy Caravan & Camping Site,** Bridge of Awe, Taynuilt, Argyll, PA35 1HT
Actual Grid Ref: NN032297
Tel: 01866 822612
Open: Mar to Oct

Tayvallich

NR7487

▲ **Tayvallich Camping Site,**
Leachive Farm, Tayvallich, Lochgilphead, Strathclyde, PA31 8PL
Actual Grid Ref: NR745875
Tel: 01546 870226
Open: Easter to Oct

Tighnabruaich

NR9773

▲ **Tighnabruaich Youth Hostel,**
High Road, Tighnabruaich, Argyll, PA21 2BD
Actual Grid Ref: NR975728
Tel: 01700 811622
Capacity: 40
Under 18: £6.25
Adults: £7.50
Open: Mar to Oct
Seated high on a hillside overlooking the Kyles of Bute, with views of unsurpassed beauty. Popular with artists and photographers. Sailing School nearby.

Ayrshire & Arran

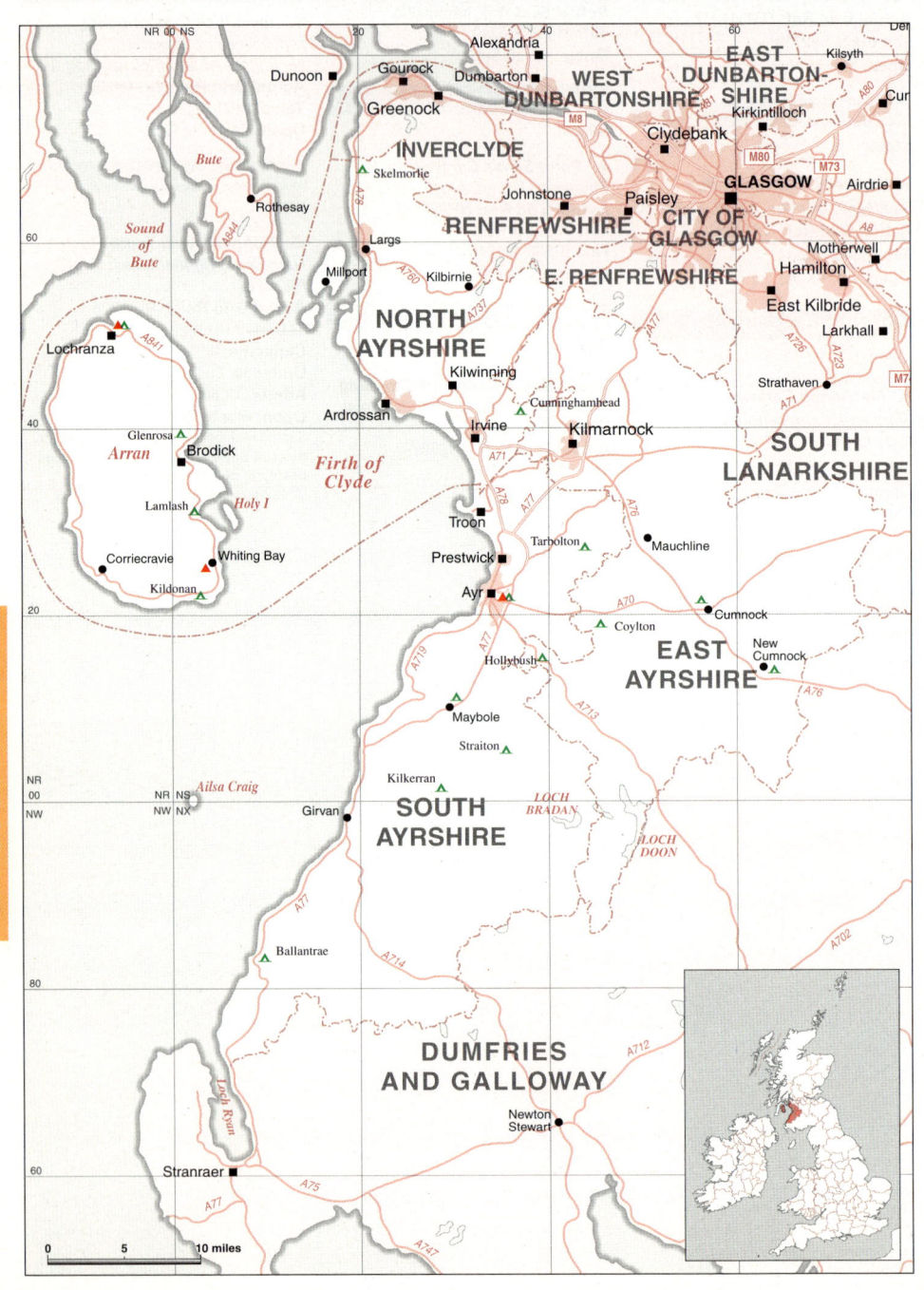

Ayrshire & Arran

Arran - Glenrosa
NS0037

▲ **Glen Rosa Farm,** Glenrosa, Brodick, Isle of Arran, KA27 8DF
Tel: 01770 302380
Email: campbellseaton@hotmail.com
Open: All year

Arran - Kildonan
NS0320

▲ **Breadalbane Caravan & Camping Site,** Breadalbane Lodge Park, Kildonan, Brodick, Isle of Arran, KA27 8SE
Actual Grid Ref: NS020210
Tel: 01770 820210
Open: Apr to Oct

▲ **Kildonan Hotel Camping & Touring Site,** Kildonan, Brodrick, Isle of Arran, KA27 8SE
Actual Grid Ref: NS020210
Tel: 01770 820320
Open: Apr to Oct

Arran - Lamlash
NS0230

▲ **Middleton Caravan & Camping Park,** Lamlash, Brodick, Isle of Arran, KA27 8NN
Actual Grid Ref: NS026302
Tel: 01770 600251
Open: Apr to Oct

Arran - Lochranza
NR9349

▲ **Lochranza Youth Hostel,** Lochranza, Brodick, Isle of Arran, KA27 8HL
Actual Grid Ref: NR935204
Tel: 01770 830631 **Capacity:** 68
Under 18: £5.00-£8.00
Adults: £8.50-£9.25
Open: March to Oct
Family bunk rooms
Self-catering facilities • Shop • Laundry facilities

The Isle of Arran has everything - safe sea bathing, excellent hill and ridge walking, climbing. C14th castle; classic geological location. Great cycling, fishing and watersports.

▲ **Lochranza Caravan & Camp Site,** Lochranza, Brodick, Isle of Arran, KA27 8HL
Actual Grid Ref: NR942499
Tel: 01770 830273
Email: office@lochgolf.demon.co.uk
Open: Apr to Oct

Arran - Whiting Bay
NS0425

▲ **Whiting Bay Youth Hostel,** Shore Road, Whiting Bay, Brodick, Isle of Arran, KA27 8QW
Actual Grid Ref: NS046251
Tel: 01770 700339
Capacity: 48
Under 18: £7.00-£7.50
Adults: £8.25-£9.00
Open: March to Oct
Family bunk rooms
Self-catering facilities • Shop nearby
Whiting Bay has a good beach and is within easy reach of other island attractions. Glenashdale Falls and Brodick Castle nearby. Try walking Goatfell, hire bikes locally or go sea fishing.

Ayr
NS3422

▲ **Ayr Youth Hostel,** 5 Craigwell Road, Ayr, KA7 2XJ
Actual Grid Ref: NS331211
Tel: 01292 262322
Capacity: 60
Under 18: £8.00 **Adults:** £9.25
Open: March to Oct
Family bunk rooms
Self-catering facilities • Shop nearby • Laundry facilities
An excellent family base, with a barbecue, a 3-mile sandy beach and plenty to see nearby, including Burns Cottage, Culzean Castle and a Gold Cup racecourse.

▲ **Crofthead Caravan Park,** Ayr, KA6 6EN
Actual Grid Ref: NS365200
Tel: 01292 263516
Open: Mar to Oct

Ballantrae
NX0982

▲ **Laggan House Leisure Park,** Ballantrae, Girvan, Ayrshire, KA26 0LL
Tel: 01465 831229
Open: Mar to Oct

Coylton
NS4219

▲ **Sundrum Castle Holiday Park,** Coylton, Ayr, KA6 6HX
Actual Grid Ref: NS404206
Tel: 01292 570057
Open: Mar to Oct

Cumnock
NS5719

▲ **Woodroad Park Caravan Site,** Wood Road, Cumnock, Ayrshire, KA18 1RP
Actual Grid Ref: NS572205
Tel: 01290 422318
Open: Apr to Sep

Cunninghamhead
NS3741

▲ **Cunninghamhead Estate Caravan Park,** Irvine, Ayrshire, KA3 2PE
Actual Grid Ref: NS368416
Tel: 01294 850238
Open: Apr to Sep

Hollybush
NS3914

▲ **Skeldon Caravan Park,** Hollybush, Ayr, Strathclyde, KA6 7EB
Actual Grid Ref: NS389144
Tel: 01292 560502
Open: Apr to Oct

To stay in a Youth Hostel affiliated to one of the Youth Hostel associations, you need to be a member. You can join at most hostels – phone in advance to check.

SCOTLAND

Stilwell's Hostels & Camping 2002   269

Ayrshire & Arran • MAP PAGE 268

Kilkerran
NS3002

▲ **The Walled Garden Caravan & Camping Park,** Kilkerran, Maybole, Ayrshire, KA19 7SL
Actual Grid Ref: NS309034
Tel: 01655 740323
Email: walledgardencp@clara.co.uk
Open: Apr to Oct

Maybole
NS2909

▲ **Camping & Caravanning Club Site,** Culzean Castle, Maybole, Ayrshire, KA19 8JX
Actual Grid Ref: NS247103
Tel: 01655 760627
Open: Apr to Oct

New Cumnock
NS6113

▲ **Glenafton Park,** Afton Road, New Cumnock, Cumnock, Ayrshire, KA18 4PR
Tel: 01290 338847
Open: All year

Skelmorlie
NS1967

▲ **Mains Camping & Caravan Park,** Skelmorlie, Ayrshire, PA17 5EU
Actual Grid Ref: NS198664
Tel: 01475 520794
Fax: 01745 520794
Open: Apr to Oct

Straiton
NS3804

▲ **Three Thorns Farm,** Straiton, Maybole, Ayrshire, KA19 7QR
Tel: 01655 770221
Fax: 01655 770221
Open: All year

Tarbolton
NS4327

▲ **Middlemuir Holiday Park,** Tarbolton, Mauchline, Ayr, KA5 5NR
Actual Grid Ref: NS440263
Tel: 01292 541647
Fax: 01292 541649
Open: Apr to Oct

Borders

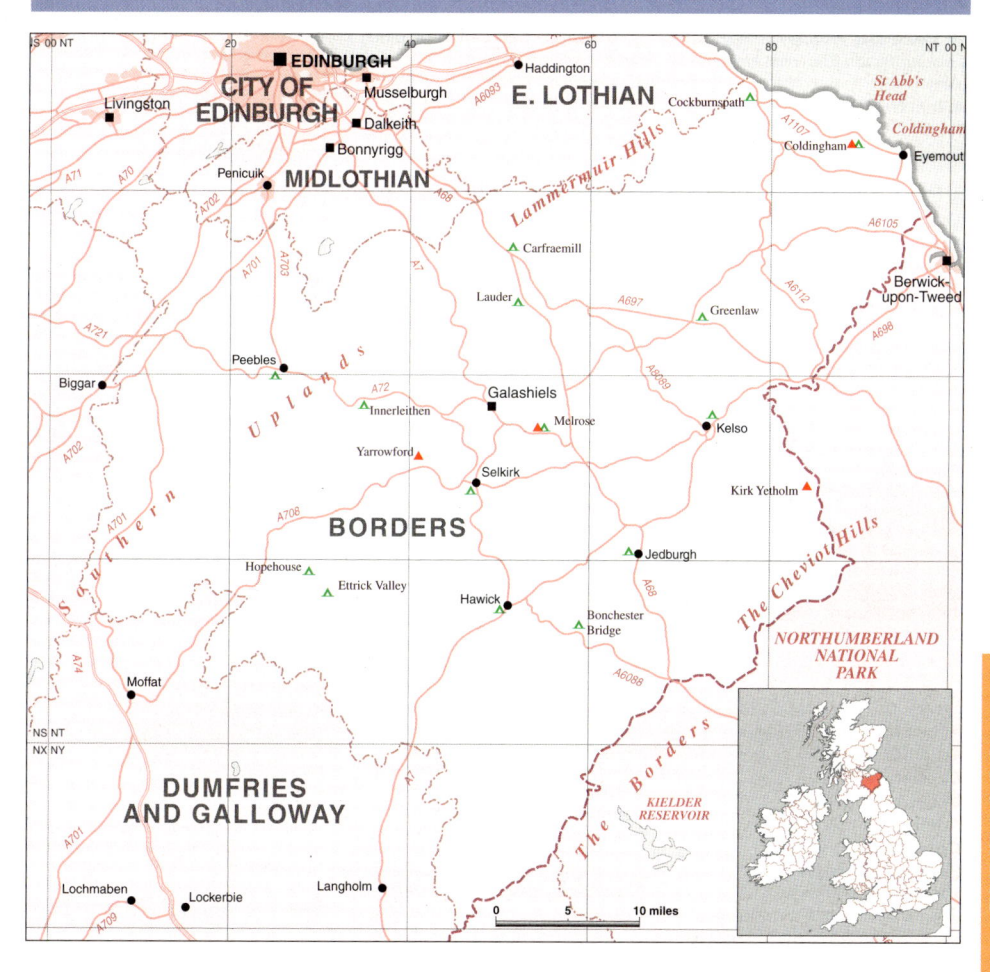

Bonchester Bridge

NT5811

▲ **Bonchester Bridge Caravan Park,** Bonchester Bridge, Hawick, Roxburghshire, TD9 8JN
Actual Grid Ref: NT587121
Tel: 01450 860676
Open: Apr to Oct.

Carfraemill

NT5153

▲ **Camping & Caravanning Club Site,** Carfraemill, Lauder, Berwickshire, TD2 6RA
Tel: 01578 750697
Open: Mar to Oct

▲ *The Carfraemill Campsite,* Carfraemill, Oxton, Lauder, Borders, TD2 6RA
Actual Grid Ref: NT509535
Tel: 01578 750215
Open: Mar to Oct

Borders • MAP PAGE 271

Cockburnspath
NT7770

▲ **Pease Bay Holiday**, Pease Bay, Cockburnspath, Berwickshire, TD13 5YP
Actual Grid Ref: NT794708
Tel: 01368 830206
Open: Mar to Dec

▲ **Chesterfield Caravan Park,** The Neuk, Cockburnspath, Berwickshire, TD13 5YH
Actual Grid Ref: NT770693
Tel: 01368 830459
Open: Apr to Oct

Coldingham
NT9066

▲ **Coldingham Youth Hostel,** Coldingham Sands, Coldingham, Eyemouth, Berwickshire, TD14 5PA
Actual Grid Ref: NT915664
Tel: 01890 771298
Capacity: 46
Under 18: £7.00-£8.25
Adults: £7.00-£8.25
Open: March to Oct
Family bunk rooms
Self-catering facilities • Shop
Situated by grand cliff scenery and famous Coldingham Sands. Popular centre for scuba diving, sea bathing and coastal walks.

▲ **Scoutscroft Holiday Centre,** St Abb's Road, Coldingham, St Abb's, Borders, TD14 5NB
Actual Grid Ref: NT908661
Tel: 01890 771338
Open: Mar to Oct

Ettrick Valley
NT3018

▲ **Angecroft Caravan Park,** Ettrick Valley, Selkirk, TD7 5HY
Actual Grid Ref: NT277135
Tel: 01750 62251
Open: All year

Greenlaw
NT7146

▲ **Greenlaw Caravan Park,** Bank Street, Greenlaw, Duns, Berwickshire, TD10 6XX
Actual Grid Ref: NT711464
Tel: 01361 810341
Open: Mar to Nov

Hawick
NT5015

▲ **Hawick Riverside Caravan Park Ltd,** Hornshole Bridge, Hawick, Roxburghshire, TD9 8SY
Actual Grid Ref: NT537169
Tel: 01450 373785
Open: Mar to Oct

Hopehouse
NT2916

▲ **Honey Cottage Caravan Park,** Hopehouse, Ettrick Valley, Selkirk, TD7 5HU
Actual Grid Ref: NT295165
Tel: 01750 62246
Open: All year

Innerleithen
NT3336

▲ **Tweedale Caravan Park,** Montgomery Street, Innerleithen, Peebleshire, EH44 6JP
Tel: 01896 831271
Open: Apr to Oct

Jedburgh
NT6520

▲ **Camping & Caravanning Club Site,** Elliot Park, Jedburgh, Roxburghshire, TD8 6EF
Actual Grid Ref: NT658219
Tel: 01835 863393
Open: Apr to Oct

▲ **Jedwater Caravan Park,** Jedburgh, Roxburghshire, TD8 6PJ
Actual Grid Ref: NT665160
Tel: 01835 840219
Open: Easter to Oct

▲ **Lilliardsedge Park,** Jedburgh, Roxburghshire, TD8 6TZ
Actual Grid Ref: NT620267
Tel: 01835 830271
Open: Apr to Sep

Kelso
NT7234

▲ **Springwood Caravan Park,** Springwood Estate, Kelso, Roxburghshire, TD5 8LS
Actual Grid Ref: NT720333
Tel: 01573 224596
Fax: 01573 224033
Open: Mar to Oct

Kirk Yetholm
NT8228

▲ **Kirk Yetholm Youth Hostel,** Kirk Yetholm, Kelso, Roxburghshire, TD5 8PG
Actual Grid Ref: NT826282
Tel: 01573 420631
Capacity: 27
Under 18: £7.00
Adults: £8.25
Open: March to Oct
Family bunk rooms
Self-catering facilities • Shop nearby • Lounge • Parking limited • No smoking • WC • Kitchen facilities
Kirk Yetholm is at the north end of the Pennine Way and mid-point on St Cuthbert's Way. Many abbeys and castles to visit. Good cycling, including the Tweed Cycle Way.

Lauder
NT5247

▲ **Thirlestane Castle Caravan & Camping,** Lauder, Berwickshire, TD2 6RU
Actual Grid Ref: NT536473
Tourist Board grade: 4 Star
AA grade: 3 Pennants
Tel: 01578 722254 or 0976231032
Fax: 01578 718749
Tent pitches: 50
Tent rate: £8.00
Open: Apr to Sep
Last arr: any time
Dogs allowed • Electric hook-up • Picnic/barbecue area on site • Showers • Laundrette on site • Public phone on site
Set in rolling parkland with glorious views across wooded countryside to the Lammermuir Hills.

MAP PAGE 271 • **Borders**

Melrose

NT5433

▲ *Melrose Youth Hostel,*
Priorwood, Melrose, Roxburghshire, TD6 9EF
Actual Grid Ref: NT549339
Tel: 01896 822521
Capacity: 86
Under 18: £8.00-£10.00
Adults: £11.25
Open: All year
Family bunk rooms
Self-catering facilities • Shop nearby • Laundry facilities • Meals available groups only
Imposing stone-built Georgian mansion surrounded by own grounds, overlooking Melrose Abbey. Set on the Southern Upland and St Cuthbert's Ways.

▲ *Gibson Park Caravan Club Site,* Melrose, Roxburghshire, TD6 9RY
Actual Grid Ref: NT544341
Tel: 01896 822969
Open: Mar to Nov

Peebles

NT2540

▲ *Rosetta Caravan & Camping Park,* Rosetta Road, Peebles, EH45 8PG
Actual Grid Ref: NT244414
Tel: 01721 720770
Open: Apr to Oct

▲ *Crossburn Caravans,* Skerryvore, 93 Edinburgh Road, Peebles, EH45 8ED
Actual Grid Ref: NT249417
Tel: 01721 720501
Email: enquiries@crossburncaravans.co.uk
Open: Apr to Oct

Selkirk

NT4728

▲ *Victoria Park Caravan Site,* Victoria Park, Buccleugh Road, Selkirk, TD7 5DN
Actual Grid Ref: NT465288
Tel: 01750 20897
Fax: 01896 757003
Open: Apr to Oct

Yarrowford

NT4029

▲ *Broadmeadows Youth Hostel,* Old Broadmeadows, Yarrowford, Selkirk, TD7 5LZ
Actual Grid Ref: NT417303
Tel: 01750 76262
Capacity: 28
Under 18: £6.25
Adults: £7.50
Open: Mar to Oct
Self-catering facilities • Shop 5 miles away • Facilities for disabled people
The first SYHA hostel, opened in 1931. Visit Newark Castle ruins. Fishing, pony trekking, scenic cycle routes.

SCOTLAND

Dumfries & Galloway

Annan
NY1966

▲ **Galabank Camping Site,**
Annan, Dumfriesshire, DG12 5BQ
Actual Grid Ref: NY192676
Tel: 01461 23311
Open: May to Sep

▲ **Galabank Caravan & Camping Site,** North Street, Annan, DG12 5DQ
Tel: 01556 503806
Open: May to Sep

Auchenmalg
NX2352

▲ **Cock Inn Caravan Park,**
Auchenmalg, Glenluce, Newton Stewart, Wigtownshire, DG8 0JH
Actual Grid Ref: NX236518
Tel: 01581 500227
Open: Mar to Oct

Balminnoch
NX2665

▲ **Three Lochs Caravan Park,**
Balminnoch, Kirkcowan, Newton Stewart, DG8 0EP
Actual Grid Ref: NX272654
Tel: 01671 830304 **Fax:** 01671 830335
Open: Apr to Oct

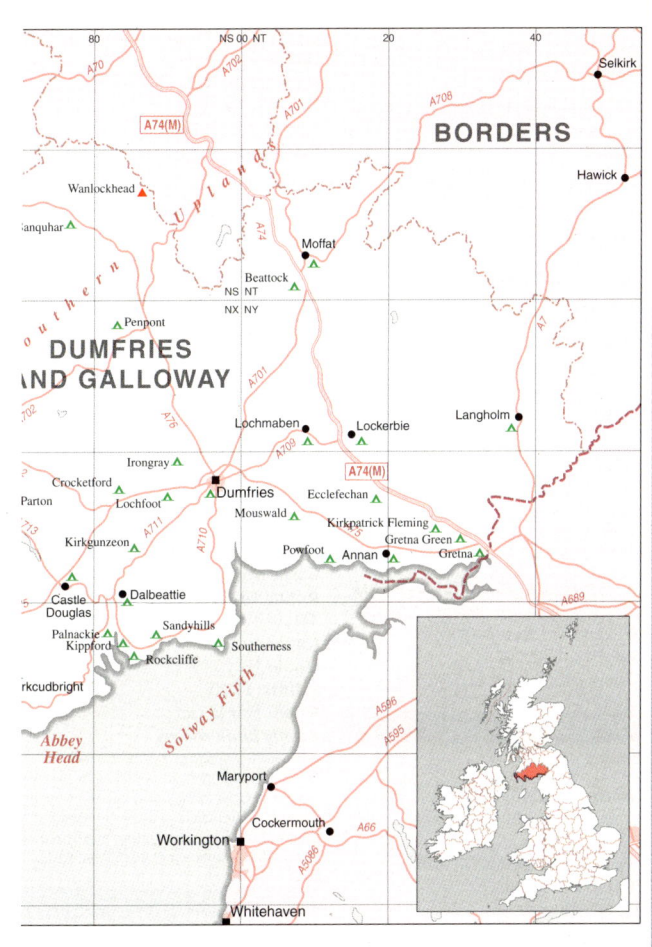

Dumfries & Galloway

▲ **Craigielands Country Park,**
Beattock, Moffat, Dumfries & Galloway, DG10 9RB
Actual Grid Ref: NT078019
Tel: 01683 300591
Open: All year

Castle Douglas

NX7662

▲ **Lochside Caravan Park,** Castle Douglas, Kirkcudbrightshire, DG7 1EZ
Actual Grid Ref: NX765619
Tel: 01556 502949
Fax: 01556 502521
Open: Apr to Oct

Creetown

NX4758

▲ **Castle Cary Holiday Park,** Creetown, Newton Stewart, DG8 7DQ
Actual Grid Ref: NX477576
Tel: 01671 820264
Open: All year

▲ **Ferry Croft Holiday Caravan Park,** Creetown, Wigtownshire, DG8 7JS
Actual Grid Ref: NX480590
Tel: 01671 820502
Open: Easter to Sep

▲ **Creetown Caravan Park,** Silver Street, Creetown, Newton Stewart, DG8 7HU
Actual Grid Ref: NX474586
Tel: 01671 820377
Open: Mar to Oct

Crocketford

NX8372

▲ **Galloway Arms Hotel,** Crocketford or Ninemile Bar, Dumfries, DG2 8RA
Tel: 01556 690248
Open: Apr to Oct

▲ **Park of Brandedleys,** Crocketford, Dumfries, Dumfries & Galloway, DG2 8RG
Actual Grid Ref: NX830725
Tel: 01556 690250
Open: Mar to Oct

Bargrennan

NX3576

▲ **Caldons Campsite,** Bargrennan, Newton Stewart, Wigtownshire, DG8 6SU
Actual Grid Ref: NX400790
Tel: 01671 840218
Open: Easter to Sep

▲ **Glen Trool Holiday Park,** GlenTrool Holiday Park, Bargrennan, Newton Stewart, DG8 6RN
Actual Grid Ref: NX354735
Tel: 01671 840280
Open: Mar to Oct

Beattock

NT0802

▲ **Beattock House Hotel Caravan Park,** Beattock House Hotel, Beattock, Moffat, Dumfriesshire, DG10 9QB
Actual Grid Ref: NT080025
Tel: 01683 300403
Open: Apr to Oct

▲ **Middlegill,** Beattock, Moffat, Dumfriesshire, DG10 9SW
Tel: 01683 300612
Open: All year

All details shown are as supplied by hostels and campsites in Autumn 2000.

Dumfries & Galloway • MAP PAGE 274

Dalbeattie
NX8361

▲ Islecroft Caravan & Camping Site, Dalbeattie, Kirkcudbrightshire, DG5 4HE
Actual Grid Ref: NX835615
Tel: 01556 610012
Fax: 01556 502521
Open: Apr to Oct

▲ Glenearly Caravan Park, Park Farm, Dalbeattie, Kirkcudbrightshire, DG5 4NE
Actual Grid Ref: NX838628
Tel: 01556 611393
Open: All year

Drummore
NX1337

▲ Clashwhannon Caravan Site & Public House, Drummore, Stranraer, Wigtownshire, DG9 9QE
Tel: 01776 840374
Open: Mar to Oct

Dumfries
NX9776

▲ Mossband Caravan Park, Dumfries, DG2 8JP
Actual Grid Ref: NX872665
Tel: 01387 760208
Open: Mar to Oct

▲ Parkend Touring Park, Glasgow Road, Newbridge, Dumfries & Galloway, DG2 0LF
Actual Grid Ref: NX950790
Tel: 01387 720927
Open: Apr to Oct

Ecclefechan
NY1974

▲ Cressfield Caravan Park, Ecclefechan, Lockerbie, Dumfriesshire, DG11 3DR
Actual Grid Ref: NY196744
Tel: 01576 300702
Open: All year

Gatehouse of Fleet
NX6056

▲ Auchenlarie Holiday Park, Gatehouse of Fleet, Castle Douglas, DG7 2EX
Actual Grid Ref: NX536522
Tel: 01557 840251
Open: Mar to Oct

▲ Mossyard Caravan Site, Gatehouse of Fleet, Castle Douglas, Kirkcudbrightshire, DG7 4QL
Actual Grid Ref: NX546518
Tel: 01557 840226
Open: Apr to Nov

Glenluce
NX1957

▲ Glenluce Caravan & Camping, Glenluce, Newton Stewart, DG8 0QR
Actual Grid Ref: NX200575
AA grade: 3 Pennants
Tel: 01581 300412
Fax: 0807 137 1489
Email: peter@glenlucecaravan.co.uk
Tent pitches: 18
Tent rate: £5.50-£8.20
Open: Apr to Oct **Last arr:** 9pm
Facilities for disabled people • Dogs allowed • Electric hook-up • Calor Gas/Camping Gaz • Picnic/barbecue area on site • Children's play area • Showers • Laundrette on site • Public phone on site
Peaceful, secluded, sun trap. Park close to village amenities, indoor pool.

▲ Whitecairn Farm Caravan Park, Glenluce, Newton Stewart, DG8 0NZ
Actual Grid Ref: NX208598
Tel: 01581 300267
Open: Mar to Oct

Gretna
NY3167

▲ Braids Caravan Park, Annan Road, Gretna, Dumfriesshire, DG16 5DQ
Actual Grid Ref: NY314675
Tel: 01461 337409
Open: All year

Gretna Green
NY3168

▲ Old Toll Bar, Sark Bridge Road, Gretna Green, Dumfries & Galloway, DG16 5JD
Actual Grid Ref: NY325670
Tel: 01461 337439
Open: Apr to Oct

Innermessan
NX0963

▲ Ryanbay Caravan Park, Innermessan, Stranraer, Wigtownshire, DG9 8QP
Tel: 01776 703346
Open: Mar to Oct

Irongray
NX9179

▲ Barnsoul Farm, Irongray, Dumfries, DG2 9SQ
Actual Grid Ref: NX876777
Tel: 01387 730249
Fax: 01387 730249
Open: Apr to Oct

Isle of Whithorn
NX4737

▲ Burrow Head Holiday Village, Tonderghie Road, Isle of Whithorn, Newton Stewart, DG8 8OA
Actual Grid Ref: NX450345
Tel: 01988 500252
Fax: 01988 500855
Open: Mar to Oct

Kendoon
NX6087

▲ Kendoon Youth Hostel, Kendoon, St John's Town of Dalry, Castle Douglas, DG7 3UD
Actual Grid Ref: NX616883
Tel: 01644 460680
Capacity: 36
Under 18: £6.25
Adults: £7.50
Open: Mar to Oct
Family bunk rooms
Self-catering facilities • Shop 5 miles
Good hillwalking countryside, with the Southern Upland Way only 1.5 miles away. Fishing available close by on the Black Water and River Ken. Picturesque Threave Castle and Gardens just 20 miles away.

Kippford
NX8354

▲ Kippford Caravan Park, Kippford, Dalbeattie, DG5 4LF
Actual Grid Ref: NX843563
Tel: 01556 620636
Fax: 01556 620636
Open: Mar to Oct

Kirkcudbright
NX6850

▲ Silvercraigs Caravan & Camping Site, Kirkcudbright, DG6 4BT
Actual Grid Ref: NX685510
Tel: 01557 330123
Fax: 01556 502521
Open: Apr to Oct

MAP PAGE 274 • **Dumfries & Galloway**

▲ *Brighouse Bay Holiday Park,*
Borgue, Kirkcudbright, Dumfries &
Galloway, DG6 4TS
Actual Grid Ref: NX626451
Tel: 01557 870267
Open: All year

▲ *Seaward Caravan Park,*
Kirkcudbright, Dumfries & Galloway,
DG6 4TS
Actual Grid Ref: NX664494
Tel: 01557 331079
Open: Mar to Oct

Kirkgunzeon
NX8666

▲ *Beeswing Caravan Park,*
Drumjohn Moor, Kirkgunzeon,
Dumfries, DG2 8JL
Actual Grid Ref: NX885685
Tel: 01387 760242
Open: Mar to Oct

Kirkpatrick Fleming
NY2770

▲ *King Robert the Bruce's Cave
Caravan & Camping Site,*
Kirkpatrick Fleming, Lockerbie,
Dumfries & Galloway, DG11 3AT
Actual Grid Ref: NY267705
Tel: 01461 800285
Open: All year

Langholm
NY3684

▲ *Ewes Water Caravan &
Camping Park,* Milntown,
Langholm, Dumfriesshire, DG13
Actual Grid Ref: NY365855
Tel: 01387 380386
Open: Apr to Sep

Lochfoot
NX9073

▲ *Auchenfranco Caravan & Camp
Site,* Lochfoot, Dumfries, DG2 8NZ
Actual Grid Ref: NX890725
Tel: 01387 730473
Fax: 01387 730473
Email:
cpe@auchenfranco.freeserve.co.uk
Tent pitches: 10
Tent rate: £4.00
Open: All year
Last arr: dusk
*Dogs allowed • Electric hook-up • Indoor
swimming pool nearby • Watersports nearby • Golf
Boating/sailing/watersports nearby • Golf
nearby • Riding nearby • Fishing on site*
Auchenfranco is a very quiet site set in 63
acres of meadows, woodland, reedbeds,
where you are welcome to walk, coarse
fish in loch, or birdwatch. A place to
unwind and take life easy. Sorry no
children. Fresh vegetables, free range
eggs. Portaloo for hire. National cycle
route nearby.

Lochmaben
NY0882

▲ *Halleaths Touring Camping &
Caravan Park,* Lochmaben,
Lockerbie, Dumfriesshire, DG11 1NA
Actual Grid Ref: NY098818
Tel: 01387 810630
Fax: 01387 810630
Open: Mar to Nov

▲ *Kirkloch Caravan & Camping
Site,* Kirkloch Brae, Lochmaben,
Lockerbie, Dumfries & Galloway,
DG11 1PZ
Actual Grid Ref: NY081826
Tel: 01387 810265
Open: Apr to Oct

Lockerbie
NY1381

▲ *Hoddom Castle Caravan Park,*
Hoddom, Lockerbie, Dumfriesshire,
DG11 1AS
Actual Grid Ref: NY155730
Tel: 01576 300251
Fax: 01576 300757
Open: Apr to Oct

▲ *Dinwoodie Lodge,* Country
House Hotel, Johnstone Bridge,
Lockerbie, Dumfries & Galloway, DG11 2SL
Actual Grid Ref: NY106902
Tel: 01576 470289
Open: All year

Minnigaff
NX4166

▲ *Minnigaff Youth Hostel,*
Minnigaff, Newton Stewart,
Wigtownshire, DG8 6PL
Actual Grid Ref: NX411663
Tel: 01671 402211 Capacity: 36
Under 18: £7.00-£7.25
Adults: £8.25-£8.50
Open: March to Oct
*Self-catering facilities • Shop nearby •
Facilities for disabled people*
Galloway Forest Park and RSPB reserve
are nearby. Good area for hillwalking,
cycling and pony trekking. Fishing in the
River Cree; day trips to wild goat park and
nature trails.

Moffat
NT0805

▲ *Camping & Caravanning Club
Site,* Hammerlands Farm, Moffat,
Dumfriesshire, DG10 9QL
Actual Grid Ref: NT085050
Tel: 01683 220436
Open: Mar to Oct

Monreith
NX3641

▲ *Knock School Caravan Park,*
Monreith, Newton Stewart,
Wigtownshire, DG8 8NJ
Actual Grid Ref: NX368405
Tel: 01988 700414
Open: Apr to Sep

Mouswald
NY0672

▲ *Mouswald Caravan Park,*
Mouswald Place, Mouswald,
Dumfries, DG1 4JS
Actual Grid Ref: NY060740
Tel: 01387 830226
Open: Mar to Oct

Newton Stewart
NX4065

▲ *Creebridge Caravan Park,*
Newton Stewart, DG8 6AJ
Actual Grid Ref: NX416656
Tel: 01671 402324
Open: Mar to Oct

▲ *Talnotry Campsite,* Galloway
Forest Park, Newton Stewart,
Wigtownshire, DG8 7BL
Actual Grid Ref: NX488715
Tel: 01671 402170
Open: Apr to Sep

Palnackie
NX8566

▲ *Barlochan Caravan Park,*
Palnackie, Castle Douglas,
Kirkcudbrightshire, DG7 1PF
Actual Grid Ref: NX819572
Tel: 01556 600256
Open: Apr to Oct

Hostels and campsites may
vary rates – be sure to check
when booking.

SCOTLAND

Dumfries & Galloway • MAP PAGE 274

Parton
NX6970

▲ **Loch Ken Holiday Park,** Boreland Of Parton, Parton, Castle Douglas, Dumfries & Galloway, DG7 3NE
Actual Grid Ref: NX685705
Tel: 01644 470282
Open: Apr to Oct

Penpont
NX8494

▲ **Penpont (Floors) Caravan Park,** Penpont, Thornhill, Dumfriesshire, DG3 4BH
Actual Grid Ref: NX850949
Tel: 01848 330470
Open: Apr to Oct

Port William
NX3343

▲ **West Barr Farm Caravan Park,** Port William, Newton Stewart, DG8 9QS
Actual Grid Ref: NX316462
Tel: 01988 700367
Open: All year

Portpatrick
NW9954

▲ **Galloway Point Holiday Park,** Portpatrick, Stranraer, Wigtownshire, DG9 9AA
Actual Grid Ref: NX008538
AA grade: 3 Pennants
Tel: 01776 810561
Fax: 01776 810561
Tent pitches: 40
Tent rate: £7.00-£10.00
Open: Mar to Oct
Last arr: midnight
Dogs allowed • Electric hook-up • Calor Gas/Camping Gaz • Cafe or Takeaway on site • Children's play area • Showers • Laundrette on site • Public phone on site • Licensed bar on site
Coastal panoramic views, fishing, golf, walking, gardens all nearby.

▲ **Castle Bay Caravan Park,** Portpatrick, Stranraer, DG9 9AA
Actual Grid Ref: NX008536
Tel: 01776 810462
Open: Mar to Oct

▲ **Sunnymeade Caravan Park,** Portpatrick, Stranraer, DG9 8LN
Actual Grid Ref: NX005540
Tel: 01776 810293
Open: Apr to Oct

Powfoot
NY1465

▲ **Queensberry Bay Caravan Park,** Powfoot, Annan, Dumfriesshire, DG12 5PU
Actual Grid Ref: NY138653
Tel: 01461 700205
Open: Apr to Oct

Rockcliffe
NX8453

▲ **Castle Point Caravan Park,** Rockcliffe, Dalbeattie, Kirkcudbrightshire, DG5 4QL
Actual Grid Ref: NX855532
Tel: 01556 630248
Open: Apr to Oct

Sandhead
NX0950

▲ **Sandhead Caravan Park,** Sandhead, Stranraer, Wigtownshire, DG9 9JN
Actual Grid Ref: NX102508
Tel: 01776 830296
Open: Apr to Oct

Sandyhills
NX8855

▲ **Sandyhills Bay Leisure Park,** Sandyhills, Dalbeattie, Kirkcudbrightshire, DG5 4PT
Actual Grid Ref: NX890549
Tel: 01387 780257
Open: Apr to Oct

Sanquhar
NS7809

▲ **Castleview Caravan Park,** Sanquhar, Dumfries & Galloway, DG4 6AX
Actual Grid Ref: NS787095
Tel: 01659 50291
Open: Apr to Sep

Southerness
NX9754

▲ **Southerness Holiday Village,** Southerness, Dumfries, DG2 8AZ
Actual Grid Ref: NX976546
Tel: 01387 880256
Fax: 01387 880429
Open: Mar to Oct

To stay in a Youth Hostel affiliated to one of the Youth Hostel associations, you need to be a member. You can join at most hostels – phone in advance to check.

▲ **Lighthouse Leisure,** Southerness, Dumfries, DG2 8AZ
Tel: 01387 880277
Open: Mar to Oct

Stranraer
NX0560

▲ **Cairnryan Caravan & Chalet Park,** Cairnryan, Stranraer, Wigtownshire, DG9 8QX
Actual Grid Ref: NX075674
Tel: 01581 200231
Fax: 01581 200207
Tent pitches: 15
Tent rate: £5.00
Open: Apr to Oct
Last arr: 11pm
Dogs allowed • Electric hook-up • Children's play area • Showers • Laundrette on site • Public phone on site • Licensed bar on site
Superbly situated overlooking Loch Ryan. Handy P&O Scottish-Irish ferry port.

▲ **Sands of Luce Caravan Park,** Stanhead, Stranraer, DG9 9JR
Actual Grid Ref: NX100511
Tel: 01776 830456
Fax: 01776 830456
Open: Apr to Oct

▲ **Aird Donald Caravan Park,** Stranraer, Wigtownshire, DG9 8RN
Actual Grid Ref: NX075605
Tel: 01776 702025
Open: All year

▲ **Wig Bay Holiday Park,** Loch Ryan, Stranraer, DG9 0PS
Actual Grid Ref: NX034655
Tel: 01776 853233
Open: Mar to Oct

Some hostels and campsites impose restrictions on size and type of groups they accept (e.g. not permitting single-sex groups). Always phone to enquire before booking.

Dumfries & Galloway

Wanlockhead
NS8712

▲ **Wanlockhead Youth Hostel,**
Lotus Lodge, Wanlockhead, Biggar, Lanarkshire, ML12 6UT
Actual Grid Ref: NS874131
Tel: 01659 74252
Capacity: 28
Under 18: £7.00
Adults: £8.25
Open: March to Oct
Self-catering facilities • Shop nearby
Lovely old white house in Scotland's highest village, famous for gold-panning and silver and lead mining. Great base for exploring the Lowther Hills.

Whithorn
NX4440

▲ **Castlewigg Caravan Park,**
Whithorn, Newton Stewart, Wigtownshire, DG8 8DL
Actual Grid Ref: NX432431
Tel: 01988 500616
Tent pitches: 20
Tent rate: £5.00-£8.00
Open: Mar to Oct
Last arr: 11pm
Dogs allowed • Electric hook-up • Calor Gas/Camping Gaz • Picnic/barbecue area on site • Children's play area • Showers • Laundrette on site • Public phone on site • Licensed bar on site
Family site set in a beautiful walled garden, lovely countryside, close to sea.

You are advised to book in advance for periods of high demand – the Summer months, Half Term holidays and public holidays.

SCOTLAND

Fife

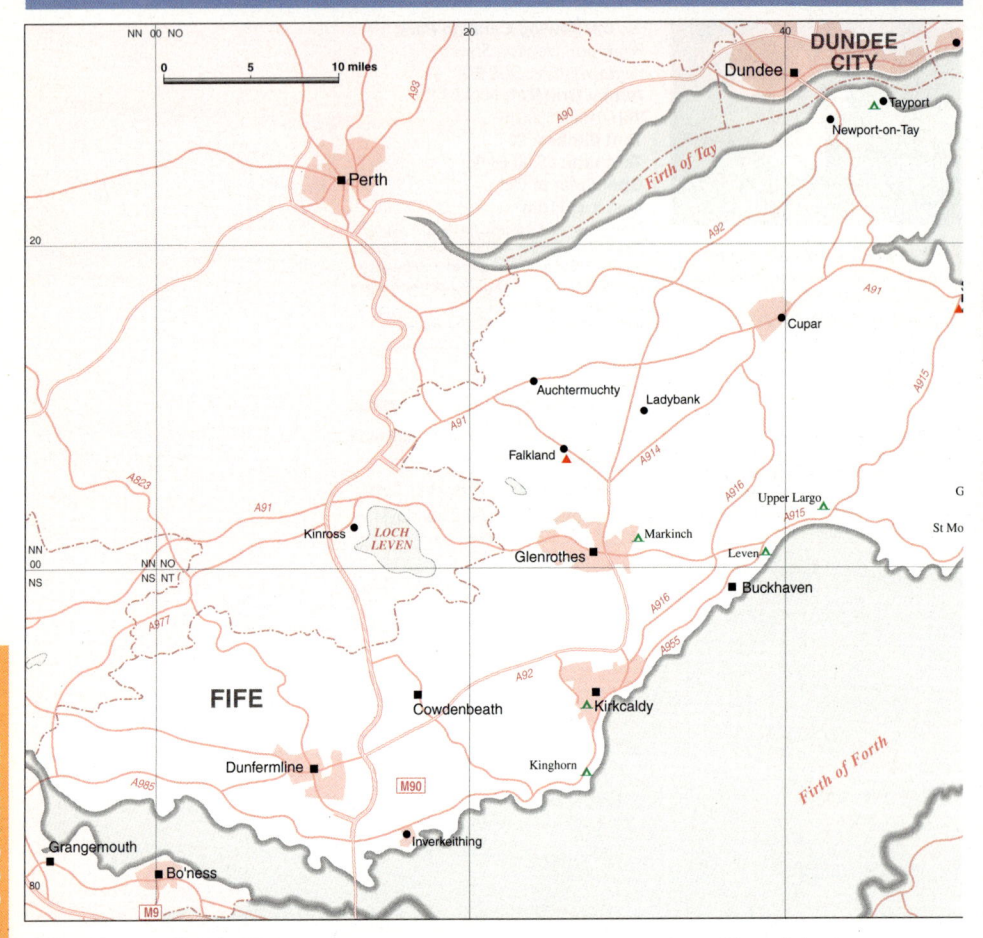

Anstruther
NO5603

▲ **3 Thirdpart Holidays,** West Pitcorthie, Anstruther, Fife, KY10 3LE
Actual Grid Ref: NO571071
Tel: 01333 310271 **Open:** May to Oct

Crail
NO6107

▲ **Ashburn House Caravan Site,** St Andrews Road, Crail, Anstruther, Fife, KY10 3UL
Actual Grid Ref: NO613080
Tel: 01333 450314
Open: Apr to Oct

▲ **Sauchope Links Caravan Park,** Crail, Anstruther, Fife, KY10 3XJ
Actual Grid Ref: NO624080
Tel: 01333 450460
Open: Mar to Oct

Falkland
NO2507

▲ **Falkland Youth Hostel,** Back Wynd, Falkland, Fife, KY15 7BX
Actual Grid Ref: NO253074
Tel: 01337 857710
Email: falkland@backpackers.connectfree.co.uk
Capacity: 38
Under 18: £6.25 **Adults:** £7.50
Open: Mar to Oct
Situated in one of the auld toons of the Kingdom of Fife, near Falkland Palace. The Lomond Hills are excellent for walking. Nearby are St Andrews, and Loch Leven with its island castle where Mary, Queen of Scots was imprisoned.

Grangemuir
NO5303

▲ **Grangemuir Woodland Park,** Grangemuir, Pittenween, Fife, KY10 2RB
Actual Grid Ref: NO540040
Tel: 01333 311213
Fax: 01333 312796
Open: Apr to Oct

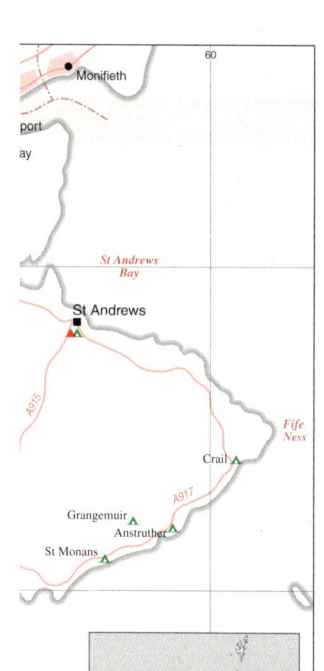

Fife

Hostels and campsites may vary rates – be sure to check when booking.

Kirkcaldy
NT2791

▲ **Dunnikier Caravan Park,** Dunnikier Way, Kirkcaldy, Fife, KY1 3DN
Actual Grid Ref: NT282940
Tel: 01592 267563
Open: Mar to Jan

Leven
NO3800

▲ **Woodland Gardens Caravan & Camping Site,** Blindwell Road, Lunden Links, Leven, Fife, KY8 5QG
Actual Grid Ref: NO417036
Tel: 01333 360319
Email: woodlandgardens@lineone.net
Open: Mar to Oct

▲ **Letham Feus Caravan Park,** Cupar Road, Leven, KY8 5NT
Tel: 01333 351900
Open: Mar to Oct

Markinch
NO2901

▲ **Balbirnie Park Caravan Club Site,** Markinch, Glenrothes, Fife, KY7 6NR
Tel: 01592 759130
Open: Apr to Oct

St Andrews
NO5116

▼ **St Andrews Tourist Hostel,** Inchape House
St Marys Place
St Andrews
KY16 9QP
Tel: 01334 479911
Fax: 01334 479988
Email: lee@eastgatehostel.com
Capacity: 44
Under 18: £10.00 **Adults:** £10.00
Open: All year
Family bunk rooms: £10.00
Self-catering facilities • Television • Showers • Central heating • Laundry facilities • Lounge • Dining room • Cycle store • Parking
Located in heart of the historic old town, this newly opened hostel is 5 mins from bus station. Lively hostel with cosy atmosphere and friendly staff. Self catering kitchen, free tea/coffee, no curfew. 5 mins from pubs/clubs. Attractions - St Andrews cathedral, castle, St Rules Tower, Royal Golf Club, St Mary's House.

▲ **Clayton Caravan Park,** St Andrews, Fife, KY16 9YA
Tel: 01334 870242
Fax: 01334 870057
Email: claytoncpk@aol.com
Open: Mar to Oct

▲ **Craigtoun Meadows Holiday Park,** Mount Melville, St Andrews, Fife, KY16 8PQ
Actual Grid Ref: NO483151
Tel: 01334 475959
Fax: 01334 476424
Open: Mar to Oct

▲ **Cairnsmill Caravan Park,** Largo Road, St Andrews, Fife, KY16 8NN
Actual Grid Ref: NO498147
Tel: 01333 311213
Open: Apr to Oct

▲ **Kinkell Braes Caravan Park,** Kinkell Braes, St Andrews, Fife, KY16 8PX
Actual Grid Ref: NO522156
Tel: 01334 474250
Open: Mar to Oct

St Monans
NO5201

▲ **St Monans Caravan Site,** The Common, St Monans, Anstruther, Fife, KY10 2DN
Actual Grid Ref: NO531019
Tel: 01333 730778
Open: Mar to Oct

Tayport
NO4528

▲ **Tayport Caravan Park,** Tayport, Fife, DD6 9ES
Actual Grid Ref: NO465285
Tel: 01382 552334
Email: largo_leisure@bigfoot.com
Open: Apr to Oct

Upper Largo
NO4203

▲ **Forth House Camping & Caravan Club,** Newburn, Upper Largo, Leven, KY8 6JG
Tel: 01333 360231
Open: All year

Kinghorn
NT2687

▲ **Pettycur Bay Caravan Park,** Kinghorn Road, Kinghorn, Burntisland, Fife, KY3 9YE
Actual Grid Ref: NT260864
Tel: 01592 890913
Fax: 01592 891420
Open: Mar to Oct

You are advised to book in advance for periods of high demand – the Summer months, Half Term holidays and public holidays.

Britain: Bed & Breakfast

The essential guide to B&Bs in England, Scotland & Wales

The Bed & Breakfast is one of the great British institutions. Like Fish & Chips, it's known by people around the world. But you don't have to be a tourist to enjoy this traditional accommodation. Whether you're travelling, on holiday, away on business or just escaping from it all, the B&B is a great value alternative to expensive hotels and a world away from camping and caravanning.

Stilwell's Britain: Bed & Breakfast 2001 is the most comprehensive guide of its kind, containing over 7,750 entries listed by country, county and location, in England, Scotland and Wales. Each entry includes room rates, facilities, Tourist Board grades and a brief description of the B&B and its location and surroundings.

Stilwell's Britain: Bed & Breakfast 2001: The indispensable guide to great value accommodation:

- Private houses, country halls, farms, cottages, inns, small hotels and guest houses
- Over 7,750 entries
- Average price £19 per person per night
- All official grades shown
- Local maps
- Pubs serving hot evening meals shown
- Tourist Information Centres listed
- Handy size for easy packing

£9.95 from all good bookstores (ISBN 1-900861-22-4) or £11.95 (inc p&p) from **Stilwell Publishing, 59 Charlotte Road, London EC2A 3QW (020 7739 7179)**

Glasgow & District

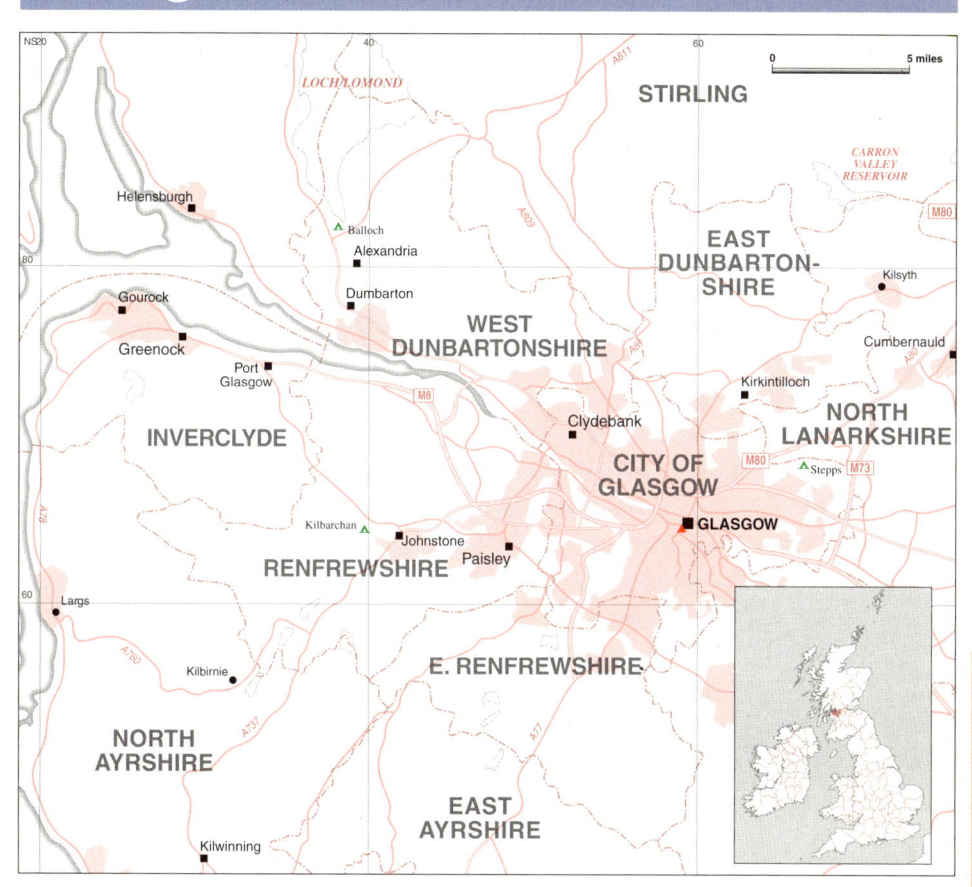

Balloch
NS3982

▲ **Tullichewan Holiday Park,** Old Luss Road, Balloch, Alexandria, Dunbartonshire, G83 8QP
Actual Grid Ref: NS382816
Tel: 01389 759475
Fax: 01389 755563
Open: Jan to Nov

All details shown are as supplied by hostels and campsites in Autumn 2000.

Glasgow - Central
NS5865

▲ **Euro Hostel Glasgow,** 318 Clyde Street, Glasgow G1 4NR
Actual Grid Ref: NS593645
Tel: 0141 222 2828 **Fax:** 0141 222 2829
Email: info@euro-hostels.com
Capacity: 360
Adults: £13.75-£25.00
Open: All year, any time
Laundry facilities • Games room • Security lockers • Cycle store • Facilities for disabled people • No smoking
Centrally located, overlooking River Clyde. All rooms ensuite: 3 single, 70 twin, 3 triple, 32 x 4 person/family, 3 x 8 person, 4 x 14 person - most combinations of requirements can be catered for. Close Central/Queen Street rail stations/Buchanan Street Bus Station; overnight parking available at nearby St Enoch Square.

Glasgow & District • MAP PAGE 283

▲ **Glasgow Youth Hostel,** 7/8 Park Terrace, Glasgow, G3 6BY
Actual Grid Ref: NS575662
Tel: 0141 332 3004
Email: glasgow@syha.org.uk
Capacity: 150
Under 18: £8.50-£10.00
Adults: £10.00-£11.50
Open: All year
Family bunk rooms
Self-catering facilities • Shop nearby • Laundry facilities • Evening meal available groups only
Glasgow has something for everyone, from city parks to free museums and galleries, and great nightlife. Good base for touring the Trossachs, the Clyde Coast and Loch Lomond.

Kilbarchan
NS4063

▲ **Barnbrock Camping Site,** Barnbrock Farm, Kilbarchan, Johnstone, Renfrewshire, PA10 2PZ
Tel: 01505 614791
Open: Mar to Oct

Stepps
NS6668

▲ **Craigendmuir Park,** 3 Campsie View, Stepps, Glasgow, G33 6AF
Tel: 0141 779 4159
Fax: 0141 779 4057
Open: June to Sept

▲ **Craigendmuir Caravan Park,** Craigendmuir Park, Craigendmuir, Stepps, Strathclyde, G33 6AE
Actual Grid Ref: NS659678
Tel: 01417 794159
Open: All year

Some hostels and campsites impose restrictions on size and type of groups they accept (e.g. not permitting single-sex groups). Always phone to enquire before booking.

Highland

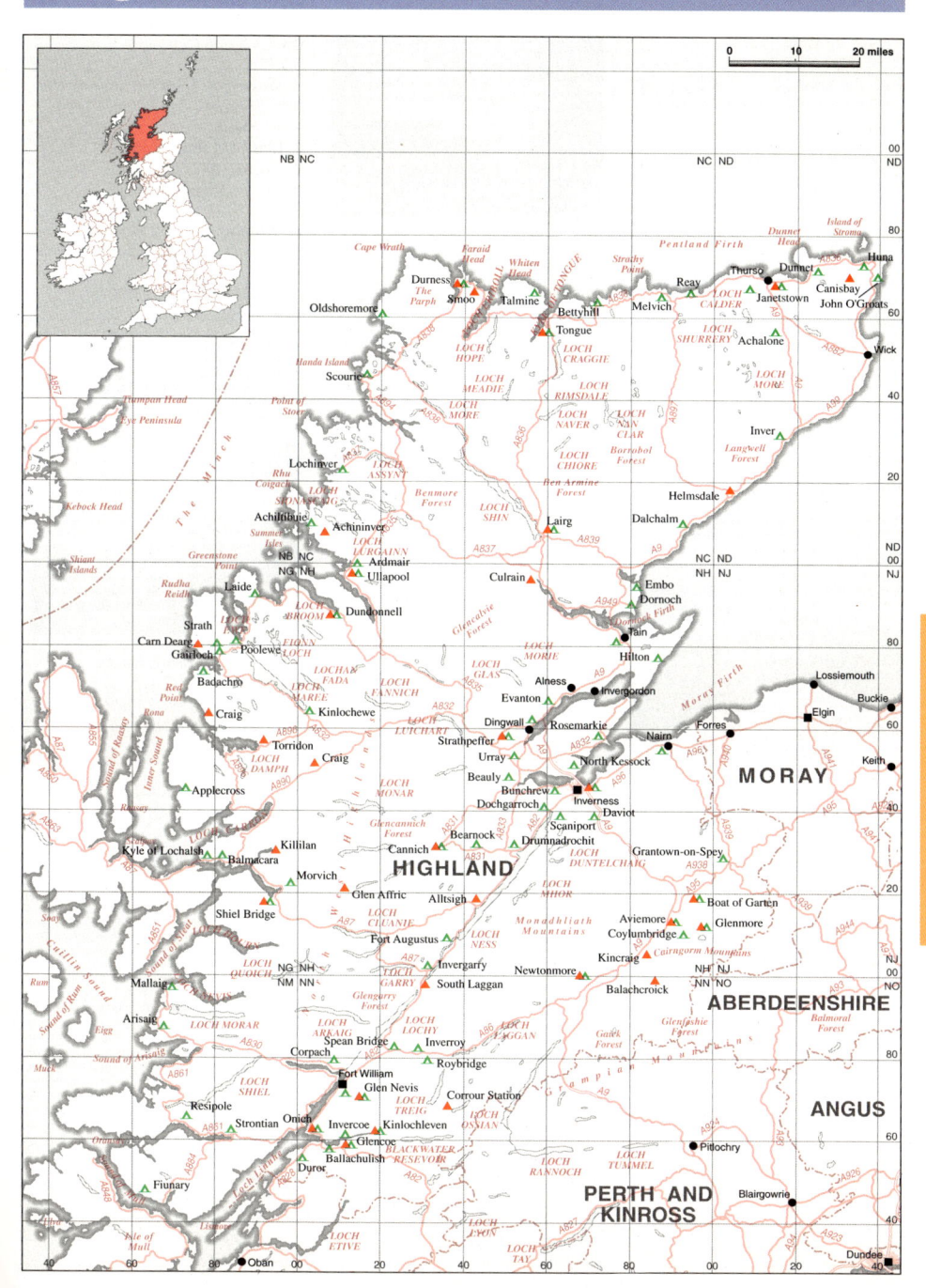

Highland • MAP PAGE 285

All details shown are as supplied by hostels and campsites in Autumn 2000.

Achalone
ND1556

▲ **Achalone Activities,** North Achalone, Halkirk, Caithness, KW12 6XA
Tel: 01847 831326
Open: All year

Achiltibuie
NC0209

▲ **Achnahaird Caravan and Camping Site,** Achiltibuie, Ullapool, Ross-shire, IV26 2YT
Actual Grid Ref: NC015136
Tel: 01854 622348
Fax: 01854 622348
Open: May to Sep

Achininver
NC0405

▲ **Achininver Youth Hostel,** Achininver, Achiltibuie, Ullapool, Ross-shire, IV26 2YL
Actual Grid Ref: NC042056
Tel: 01854 622254
Capacity: 20
Under 18: £6.25
Adults: £7.50
Open: May to Oct
Self-catering facilities • Shop 3 miles away
Small hostel in picturesque setting ideal for coastal and hill walks, and climbing the wild rugged peaks surrounding the hostel. Beach for swimmers, high season sails to the Summer Isles.

If you have to cancel your visit to any hostel or campsite, please let them know – it is always possible to make a bed or a pitch available to someone else.

Alltsigh
NH4518

▲ **Loch Ness Youth Hostel,** Alltsigh, Invermoriston, Glenmoriston, Inverness, IV63 7YD
Actual Grid Ref: NH457191
Tel: 01320 351274
Capacity: 54
Under 18: £7.00-£7.25
Adults: £8.25-£8.50
Open: March to Oct
Family bunk rooms
Self-catering facilities • Shop
Cruise the loch from Drumnadrochit or hire a boat at Fort Augustus. Fort Augustus Abbey and Urquhart Castle nearby. Drumnadrochit Highland Games in August. Great Glen Cycle Track for mountain biking.

Applecross
NG7144

▲ **Applecross Campsite,** via Loch Carron, Applecross, Strathcarron, Wester Ross, IV54 8ND
Actual Grid Ref: NG711442
Tel: 01520 744268 / 744284
Fax: 01520 744268
Open: Apr to Oct

Ardmair
NH1098

▲ **Ardmair Point Caravan Park,** Ardmair, Ullapool, Ross-shire, IV26 2TN
Actual Grid Ref: NH109983
Tel: 01854 612054
Fax: 01854 612757
Open: May to Sep

Arisaig
NM6586

▲ **Gorten Sands Caravan Site,** Gorten Farm, Arisaig, Inverness-shire, PH39 4NS
Actual Grid Ref: NM643878
Tel: 01687 450283
Open: Apr to Sep

▲ **Portnadoran Caravan Site,** Arisaig, Inverness-shire, PH39 4NT
Actual Grid Ref: NM650891
Tel: 01687 450267
Open: Apr to Oct

▲ **Skyeview Caravan & Camping Site,** Skyeview, Arisaig, Inverness-shire, PH39
Actual Grid Ref: NM655881
Tel: 01687 450209
Open: Apr to Oct

▲ **Kilmartin Guest House,** Kinloid Farm, Arisaig, Inverness-shire, PH39 4NS
Actual Grid Ref: NM662878
Tel: 01687 450366
Open: Apr to Oct

Aviemore
NH8912

▲ **Aviemore Youth Hostel,** 25 Grampian Road, Aviemore, Inverness-shire, PH22 1PR
Actual Grid Ref: NH893119
Tel: 01479 810345
Capacity: 114
Under 18: £6.00-£10.75
Adults: £9.00-£12.25
Open: All year
Family bunk rooms
Self-catering facilities • Shop • Laundry facilities • Facilities for disabled people
Set in birch woodlands next to a nature reserve, ideal base to explore Strathspey. Gliding, ski-ing, snowboarding, canoeing, golf available locally.

▲ **Dalraddy Holiday Park,** Alvie Estate, Aviemore, Inverness-shire, PH22 1QB
Actual Grid Ref: NH857083
Tel: 01479 810330
Open: All year

▲ **Aviemore Mountain Resort Caravan Park,** Aviemore, Inverness-shire, PH22 1PF
Actual Grid Ref: NH894120
Tel: 01479 810751
Open: Dec to Oct

MAP PAGE 285 • **Highland**

▲ **High Range Caravan Park,** High Range Holiday Chalets, Grampian Road, Aviemore, Inverness-shire, PH22 1PT
Actual Grid Ref: NH892118
Tel: 01479 810636
Open: Dec to Oct

Badachro

NG7773

▲ **Primrose Cottage,** Badachro, Gairloch, Ross-shire, IV21 2AB
Tel: 01445 741317
Fax: 01445 741377
Open: All year

Balachcroick

NH8400

▲ **Glenfeshie Hostel,** Balachcroick House, Glenfeshie, Kincraig, Kingussie, Inverness-shire, PH21 1NH
Actual Grid Ref: NH849009
Tel: 01540 651323
Email: glenfeshiehostel@totalise.co.uk
Capacity: 14
Under 18: £8.00
Adults: £8.00
Open: All year
Family bunk rooms: £28.00
Self-catering facilities • Showers • Shop • Wet weather shelter • Lounge • Dining room • Drying room • Cycle store • Parking • Evening meal available • No smoking
Warm, friendly accommodation, set beside the Cairngorm National Nature Reserve.

Ballachulish

NN0858

▲ **Glencoe Campsite,** Ballachulish, Argyll, PA39 4LA
Actual Grid Ref: NN112576
Tel: 01855 811397
Open: Easter to Oct

Balmacara

NG8026

▲ **Balmacara Caravan and Campsite,** Balmacara, Kyle of Lochalsh, Ross-shire, IV40 8DN
Actual Grid Ref: NG803279
Tel: 01599 566317
Open: Apr to Sep

Bearnock

NH4130

▲ **Glen Urquhart Campsite,** Bearnock, Glen Urquhart, Inverness, Highlands, IV3 6TN
Actual Grid Ref: NH413303
Tel: 01456 476353
Open: All year

Beauly

NH5246

▲ **Lovat Bridge Camping Site,** Lovat Bridge, Beauly, Inverness-shire, IV4 7AY
Tel: 01463 782374
Open: Mar to Oct

Bettyhill

NC7061

▲ **Cragdhu Caravan & Camping Site,** Bettyhill, Thurso, Caithness, KW14 7SP
Actual Grid Ref: NC709620
Tel: 01641 521273
Open: Apr to Oct

Boat of Garten

NH9418

▲ **Fraoch Lodge,** Mountain Innovations, Deshar Road, Boat of Garten, Invernesshire, PH24 3BN
Actual Grid Ref: NH938190
Tel: 01479 831331
Fax: 01479 831331
Email: info@scotmountain.co.uk
Capacity: 18
Under 18: £7.50-£10.00
Adults: £7.50-£12.00
Open: All year, any time
Family bunk rooms: £40.00
Self-catering facilities • Showers • Central heating • Laundry facilities • Lounge • Dining room • Grounds available for games • Cycle store • Parking • Evening meal available • No smoking
Cairngorms route/weather info, local pub, breakfast available, friendly atmosphere.

▲ **Loch Garten Lodges & Caravan Park,** Croft Na-Carn, Loch Garten Road, Boat of Garten, Inverness-shire, PH24 3BY
Tel: 01479 831769
Fax: 01479 831708
Tent pitches: 20
Tent rate: £7.00-£9.00
Open: All year
Last arr: 10pm

Dogs allowed • Electric hook-up • Cafe or Takeaway on site • Picnic/barbecue area on site • Showers • Laundrette on site • Public phone on site
Wilderness - Tranquillity - Luxury. The camping site comprises just 20 pitches in 3 acres. If you are looking for a natural uncrowded location then this is for you. The pitches are level and grassy and set in clearings amongst the trees. The site has facilities for motor caravans, touring caravans and tents.

▲ **Boat of Garten Caravan & Camping Park,** Boat of Garten, Inverness-shire, PH24 3BN
Actual Grid Ref: NH938191
Tel: 01479 831652
Fax: 01479 831652
Open: All year

▲ **Croft na Carn Caravan Park,** Hopeman, Elgin, IV30 2RU
Actual Grid Ref: NH965195
Tel: 01343 830880
Fax: 01343 830880
Open: All year

Bunchrew

NH6245

▲ **Bunchrew Caravan Park,** Bunchrew, Inverness, IV3 8TD
Actual Grid Ref: NH616459
Tel: 01463 237802
Fax: 01463 225803
Open: Mar to Dec

Canisbay

ND3472

▲ **John O'Groats Youth Hostel,** Canisbay, Wick, Caithness, KW1 4YH
Actual Grid Ref: ND348721
Tel: 01955 611424
Capacity: 40
Under 18: £7.00-£7.25
Adults: £8.25-£8.50
Open: March to Oct
Self-catering facilities • Shop 3 miles away
Fantastic cliffs with puffin colonies. Ferries to Orkney. Many ancient cairns and brochs. See the Fossil Visitor Centre and the Last House in Scotland.

If you have to cancel your visit to any hostel or campsite, please let them know – it is always possible to make a bed or a pitch available to someone else.

SCOTLAND

Highland • MAP PAGE 285

Cannich
NH3331

▲ **Cannich Youth Hostel,**
Cannich, Beauly, Inverness-shire, IV4 7LT
Actual Grid Ref: NH339315
Tel: 01456 415244
Capacity: 54
Under 18: £7.00-£7.25
Adults: £8.25-£8.50
Open: March to Oct
Family bunk rooms
Self-catering facilities • Shop nearby • Facilities for disabled people
Interesting walks around Strathglass, Glen Urquhart, Glen Affric and Glen Cannich. Visit Beauly Priory, Cluanie Deer Park and the Loch Ness Monster Centre.

▲ **Cannich Caravan & Camping Park,** Cannich, Beauly, Inverness-shire, IV4 7LN
Actual Grid Ref: NH341314
Tel: 01456 415364
Fax: 01456 415263
Open: Mar to Oct

Carn Dearg
NG7678

▲ **Carn Dearg Youth Hostel,** Carn Dearg, Gairloch, Ross-shire, IV21 2DJ
Actual Grid Ref: NG763776
Tel: 01445 712219
Capacity: 44
Under 18: £7.50
Adults: £8.75
Open: May to Oct
Self-catering facilities • Shop
Ideally situated by Loch Gairloch, just nine miles from famous Inverewe Garden. Paragliding, abseiling, canoeing, water-skiing, windsurfing.

Corpach
NN0976

▲ **Linnhe Caravan & Chalet Park,** Corpach, Fort William, Inverness-shire, PH33 7NL
Actual Grid Ref: NN073776
Tourist Board grade: 5 Star

AA grade: 5 Pennants
Tel: 01397 772376
Fax: 01397 772007
Email: holidays@linnhe.demon.co.uk
Tent pitches: 20
Tent rate: £8.50-£10.50
Open: Dec to Oct
Last arr: 7pm
Dogs allowed • Electric hook-up • Baths • Calor Gas/Camping Gaz • Picnic/barbecue area on site • Children's play area • Showers • Laundrette on site • Public phone on site • Shop on site • Baby care facilities • Indoor swimming pool nearby • Boating/sailing/watersports on site • Golf nearby • Riding nearby • Fishing on site
STB/Calor 'Best Park in Scotland' 1999 award. Almost a botanical garden and probably the most beautiful lochside park in Scotland. Near Ben Nevis and Fort William, Scotland's adventure capital. Explore or relax and soak up the scenery in lovely surroundings. Private beach and free fishing. Luxury chalets and holiday caravans for hire.

Corrour Station
NN3566

▲ **Loch Ossian Youth Hostel,** Corrour, Fort Wiliam, Inverness-shire, PH30 4AA
Actual Grid Ref: NN370671
Tel: 01397 732207
Capacity: 20
Under 18: £5.75 **Adults:** £7.00
Open: March to Oct
Self-catering facilities
High moorland, ideal for walkers and anglers - free fishing. Densely-populated red deer country, excellent birdwatching. No shop for 20 miles, no car access, no laundry. Bring own sleeping bag.

Coylumbridge
NH9110

▲ **Rothiemurchus Forest Camping & Caravan Park,** Coylumbridge, Aviemore, Inverness-shire, PH22 1QU
Actual Grid Ref: NH916108
Tel: 01479 810120
Open: All year

▲ **Rothiemurchus Caravan Park,** Coylumbridge, Aviemore, Inverness-shire, PH22 1QU
Actual Grid Ref: NH915106
Tel: 01479 812800
Open: All year

Craig (Glen Carron)
NH0349

▲ **Gerry's Achnashellach Hostel,** Craig, Achnashellach, Strathcarron, Wester Ross, IV54 8YU
Actual Grid Ref: NH037493
Tel: 01520 766232
Email: gerryshostel@freedomland.co.uk
Capacity: 20
Under 18: £9.00
Adults: £9.00-£10.00
Open: All year, 5-8.30pm
Family bunk rooms
Self-catering facilities • Showers • Central heating • Shop • Laundry facilities • Wet weather shelter • Lounge • Dining room • Grounds available for games • Drying room • Parking • No smoking
Terrace 3 cottages/Kyle-Inverness railway/A890. Central hills. Wildlife.

Craig (Loch Torridon)
NG7763

▲ **Craig Youth Hostel,** Craig, Diabaig, Achnasheen, Ross-shire, IV22 2HE
Actual Grid Ref: NT774638
Tel: 08701 553255 (SYHA Central Booking Service)
Capacity: 16
Under 18: £5.75
Adults: £7.00
Open: May to Oct
Self-catering facilities
A real 'get-away-from-it-all' hostel - small cottage on the north shore of Loch Torridon with views to Skye and the Outer Isles. No shop for 12 miles. Bring own sleeping bag.

MAP PAGE 285 • **Highland**

Culrain

NH5794

▲ **Carbisdale Castle Youth Hostel,** Culrain, Ardgay, Sutherland, IV24 3DP
Actual Grid Ref: NH574954
Tel: 01549 421232
Email: carbisdale@syha.org.uk
Capacity: 197
Under 18: £9.00-£12.50
Adults: £13.50-£14.00
Open: March to Oct
Family bunk rooms
Self-catering facilities • Shop • Laundry facilities • Evening meal available • Facilities for disabled people
Unique, statue-filled castle hostel in a commanding position overlooking the Kyle of Sutherland. See salmon jumping at the Falls of Shin.

Dalchalm

NC9105

▲ **Greenpark Caravan Site,** Dalchalm, Brora, Sutherland, KW9 6LP
Actual Grid Ref: NC913059
Tel: 01408 621513
Open: Apr to Oct

Daviot

NH7239

▲ **Auchnahillin Caravan Park,** Daviot, Inverness, IV1 2XQ
Actual Grid Ref: NH741387
Tel: 01463 772286
Fax: 01463 772286
Open: Apr to Oct

▲ **Loch Ness Caravan & Camping Centre,** Invermoriston, Inverness, IV63 7YE
Actual Grid Ref: NH425210
Tel: 01320 351207
Open: Mar to Oct

Dingwall

NH5458

▲ **Camping & Caravanning Club Site,** Jubilee Park Road, Dingwall, Ross-shire, IV15 9QZ
Actual Grid Ref: NH555588
Tel: 01349 862236
Open: Apr to Oct

▲ **Torridon Camp Site,** High Street, Dingwall, Ross-shire, IV15 9QN
Tel: 01349 868486
Open: All year

Dochgarroch

NH6040

▲ **Culloden Moor Caravan Site,** Dochgarroch, Inverness, IV1 2EF
Tel: 01463 790625
Email: cc115@gofornet.co.uk
Open: Apr to Oct

▲ **Dochgarroch Caravan Park,** Dochgarroch, Inverness, Highlands, IV3 6SY
Actual Grid Ref: NH620407
Tel: 01463 861333
Open: Apr to Sep

Dornoch

NH8089

▲ **Dornoch Caravan & Camping Site,** The Links, Dornoch, Sutherland, IV25 3LX
Actual Grid Ref: NH804887
Tel: 01862 810423
Open: Apr to Oct

▲ **Pitgrudy Caravan Park,** Poles Road, Dornoch, Sutherland, IV25 3HY
Actual Grid Ref: NH795911
Tel: 01862 821253
Fax: 01862 821382
Open: May to Sep

Drumnadrochit

NH5030

▲ **Borlum Farm Caravan Park,** Drumnadrochit, Inverness, IV63 6XN
Actual Grid Ref: NH518291
Tel: 01456 450220
Open: Apr to Oct

Dundonnell

NH0887

▲ **Sail Mhor Croft Hostel,** Camusnagaul, Dundonnell, Garve, Ross-shire, IV23 2QT
Tel: 01854 633224
Email: sailmhor@btinternet.com
Capacity: 16
Under 18: £9.00
Adults: £9.00
Open: All year (not Xmas/New Year), 10am-11pm
Self-catering facilities • Showers • Central heating • Lounge • Dining room • Drying room • Parking • Evening meal available 6.30-8pm • No smoking
Friendly, rural setting amongst some of Scotland's finest mountains.

▲ **Badrallach Bothy and Campsite,** Croft 9, Badrallach, Dundonnell, Garve, Ross-shire, IV23 2QP
Actual Grid Ref: NH065915
Tel: 01854 633281
Open: All year

Dunnet

ND2271

▲ **Dunnet Bay Caravan Club Site,** Dunnet, Thurso, Caithness, KW14 8XD
Actual Grid Ref: ND219705
Tel: 01847 821319 / 01955 607772
Open: May to Sep

Durness

NC4067

▲ **Lazy Crofter Bunkhouse,** Parkhill Hotel, Durness, Lairg, Sutherland, IV27 4PN
Actual Grid Ref: NC406679
Tel: 01971 511209
Fax: 01971 511321
Email: mackay@bosinternet.com
Capacity: 25
Under 18: £9.00
Adults: £9.00
Open: All year
Self-catering facilities • Television • Showers • Central heating • Laundry facilities • Wet weather shelter • Lounge • Dining room • Drying room • Security lockers • Cycle store • Parking • No smoking
Small highland hostel, big highland hospitality. All facilities - quality accommodation.

SCOTLAND

Highland • MAP PAGE 285

Sango Sands Camping & Caravan Site, Sangomore, Durness, Lairg, Sutherland, IV27 4PP
Actual Grid Ref: NC405678
Tel: 01971 511262
Fax: 01971 511205
Open: Apr to Oct

Duror
NM9955

Auchindarroch Farm Caravan Park, Duror, Appin, Argyll, PA38 4BS
Actual Grid Ref: NM998555
Tel: 01631 740177
Open: Mar to Oct

Embo
NH8193

Grannies Heilan Hame Holiday Park, Embo, Dornoch, Sutherland, IV25 3QD
Actual Grid Ref: NH818926
Tel: 01862 810383 / 810753
Open: Mar to Oct

Evanton
NH6066

Black Rock Caravan Park, Evanton, Dingwall, Ross-shire, IV16 9UN
Actual Grid Ref: NH605665
Tel: 01349 830917
Fax: 01349 830321
Open: Apr to Oct

Fiunary
NM6146

Fiunary Caravan and Camping Park, Fiunary, Morvern, Oban, Argyll, PA34 5XX
Actual Grid Ref: NM614467
Tel: 01967 421225
Open: Apr to Oct

Fort Augustus
NH3709

Fort Augustus Caravan & Camping Site, Fort Augustus, Inverness-shire, PH32 4DS
Actual Grid Ref: NH373084
Tel: 01320 366360
Open: Apr to Sep

Fort William
NN1073

Lochy Caravan Park Ltd, Fort William, Inverness-shire, PH33 7NF
Actual Grid Ref: NN126764
Tel: 01397 703446
Open: All year

Gairloch
NG8076

Sands Holiday Centre, Gairloch, Ross-shire, IV21 2DL
Actual Grid Ref: NG760785
Tel: 01445 712152
Fax: 01445 712518
Open: Apr to Oct

Glen Affric
NH088230

Glen Affric Youth Hostel, Allt Beithe, Glen Affric, Cannich, Beauly, Inverness-shire, IV4 7ND
Actual Grid Ref: NH079202
Tel: 08701 553255 (SYHA Central Booking Service) **Capacity:** 26
Under 18: £7.50 **Adults:** £8.75
Open: March to Oct
Self-catering facilities
Nestling in beautiful scenery, this remote hostel is surrounded by fine mountains. The Falls of Glomach are 7 miles away. No shop for 21 miles. Bring own sleeping bag.

Glen Nevis
NN1272

Glen Nevis Youth Hostel, Glen Nevis, Fort William, Inverness-shire, PH33 6ST
Actual Grid Ref: NN127716
Tel: 01397 702336
Capacity: 109
Under 18: £6.00-£11.75
Adults: £9.00-£13.25
Open: All year
Family bunk rooms
Self-catering facilities • Shop • Laundry facilities • Facilities for disabled people
Large weather-boarded hostel right at the foot of Ben Nevis. Summer boat trips from Fort William. Highland games in August.

Glen Nevis Caravan & Camping Park, Glen Nevis Holiday Cottages, Glen Nevis, Fort William, Inverness-shire, PH33 6SX
Actual Grid Ref: NN125723
Tel: 01397 702191
Open: Mar to Oct

Glencoe
NN1058

Glencoe Youth Hostel, Glencoe, Ballachulish, Argyll, PA39 4HX
Actual Grid Ref: NN118577
Tel: 01855 811219
Capacity: 62
Under 18: £5.00-£8.00
Adults: £8.50-£9.50
Open: All year
Family bunk rooms
Self-catering facilities • Shop • Laundry facilities • Facilities for disabled people
All grades of rock climbing are on hand, winter skiing is available. Live music and good food at the local inn. Aonach Eagach, the finest mainland ridge, is within reach of the hostel.

Red Squirrel Camping Site, Leacantuim Farm, Glencoe, Ballachulish, Argyll, PA39 4HX
Actual Grid Ref: NN120574
Tel: 01855 811256
Open: All year

Glenmore
NH9809

Loch Morlich Youth Hostel, Glenmore, Aviemore, Inverness-shire, PH22 1QY
Actual Grid Ref: NH976099
Tel: 01479 861238
Capacity: 82
Under 18: £6.00-£8.00
Adults: £9.25
Open: All year
Family bunk rooms
Self-catering facilities • Shop • Laundry facilities • Evening meal available
All grades of rock climbing/hillwalking in summer; skiing/snowboarding in winter. There are orienteering trails in the forest and mountain bikes can be hired. Special diets catered for on request.

Glenmore Forest Camping & Caravan Park, Glenmore, Aviemore, Inverness-shire, PH22 1QU
Actual Grid Ref: NH976097
Tel: 01479 861271
Open: Dec to Oct

MAP PAGE 285 • **Highland**

Grantown-on-Spey

NJ0327

▲ **Grantown-on-Spey Caravan Park,** Seafield Avenue, Grantown-on-Spey, Moray, PH26 3JQ
Actual Grid Ref: NJ028283
Tel: 01479 872474
Fax: 01479 873696
Open: Apr to Sep

Helmsdale

ND0215

▲ **Helmsdale Youth Hostel,** Helmsdale, Sutherland, KW8 6JR
Actual Grid Ref: ND028155
Tel: 01431 821577
Capacity: 38
Under 18: £6.25
Adults: £7.50
Open: May to Oct
Self-catering facilities • Shop nearby
Scenic area abounding in red deer and bird life. Hill and seashore walks and good summer swimming from sandy beaches. Boat trips for birdwatching, sea angling and sight-seeing.

Hilton

NH9285

▲ **Seaview Farm Caravan Park,** Seaview, Hilton, Dornoch, Sutherland, IV25 3PW
Actual Grid Ref: NH807916
Tel: 01862 810294
Open: Apr to Oct

Huna

ND3673

▲ **Stroma View,** Huna, John O'Groats, Wick, Caithness, KW1 4YL
Actual Grid Ref: ND362732
Tel: 01955 611313
Open: Apr to Oct

Hostels and campsites may vary rates – be sure to check when booking.

Inver (Dunbeath)

ND1630

▲ **Inver Guest House,** Inver, Dunbeath, Caithness, KW6 6EH
Actual Grid Ref: ND166300
Tel: 01593 731252
Open: Apr to Oct

Invercoe

NN1059

▲ **Invercoe Caravan & Camping Park,** Invercoe, Ballachulish, Argyll, PA39 4HP
Actual Grid Ref: NN098594
Tel: 01855 811210
Fax: 01855 811210
Open: Apr to Oct

Invergarry

NH3001

▲ **Faichem Park,** Tigh a Fiadh Madadah, Ardgarry Farm, Faichem, Invergarry, Inverness-shire, PH35 4HG
Actual Grid Ref: NH287015
AA grade: 3 Pennants
Tel: 01809 501226
Fax: 01809 501 307
Email: ardgarry.farm@lineone.net
Tent pitches: 15
Tent rate: £7.00-£7.50
Open: Mar to Oct
Last arr: 10pm
Dogs allowed • Electric hook-up • Calor Gas/Camping Gaz • Picnic/barbecue area on site • Showers • Public phone on site
Set amidst mountains and pines with panoramic views. Brochure available.

▲ **Faichemard Farm Camping & Caravan Site,** Invergarry, Inverness-shire, PH35 4HG
Actual Grid Ref: NH285018
Tel: 01809 501314
Open: Apr to Oct

Inverness

NH6645

▲ **Inverness Milburn Youth Hostel,** Victoria Drive, Inverness, IV2 3BQ
Actual Grid Ref: NH667449
Tel: 01463 231771
Capacity: 166
Under 18: £6.00-£12.25
Adults: £9.00-£13.75
Open: All year
Family bunk rooms

Self-catering facilities • Shop nearby • Laundry facilities • Evening meal available groups only • Facilities for disabled people
Modern hostel close to town centre and all its amenities, the shops, cafes and the lively Eden Court Theatre. The gateway to the Highlands.

▲ **Eastgate Hostel,** 38 Eastgate, Inverness, Inverness-shire, IV2 3NA
Tel: 01463 718756
Fax: 01463 718756
Email: lee@eastgatehostel.com
Capacity: 48
Under 18: £9.00-£11.00
Adults: £9.00-£11.00
Open: All year
Family bunk rooms: £9.00
Self-catering facilities • Television • Showers • Licensed bar • Central heating • Wet weather shelter • Lounge • Dining room • Drying room • Cycle store • Parking
Eastgate Hostel is located in the city centre - 5 mins from train/bus station. Relaxed atmosphere, friendly staff, newly opened pub/restaurant with live music. Free tea/coffee, no curfew, 5 mins from pubs and clubs, supermarket. Visit Loch Ness, Inverness Castle, Culloden Battlefield and our lovely dolphins.

▲ **Bught Caravan & Camping Site,** Inverness, IV3 5JR
Tel: 01463 239111
Open: Easter to Oct

▲ **Campbells Cullen View Caravan Site,** 3 Upper Breakish, Upper Breakish, Isle of Skye, IV42 8PY
Tel: 01471 822248
Open: All year

▲ **Bught Caravan & Camping Site,** Bught, Inverness, IV3 5SR
Actual Grid Ref: NH657435
Tel: 01463 236920
Open: Apr to Sep

▲ **Torvean Caravan Park,** Glenurquhart Road, Inverness, Highlands, IV3 6JL
Actual Grid Ref: NH654438
Tel: 01463 220582
Open: Apr to Oct

Inverroy

NN2681

▲ **Hillcrest,** Inverroy, Roybridge, Inverness-shire, PH31 4AQ
Tel: 01397 81205
Open: May to Oct

Highland • MAP PAGE 285

Janetstown
ND0866

▲ **Riverside Caravan Club Site,** Janetstown, Wick, Caithness, KW1 5SR
Actual Grid Ref: ND361509
Tel: 01955 605420
Open: Apr to Sep

John O' Groats
ND3773

▲ **John o' Groats Caravan Site,** John O'Groats, Wick, Caithness, KW1 4YS
Actual Grid Ref: ND381734
Tel: 01955 611329
Open: Apr to Oct

Killilan
NG9430

▲ **Tigh Iseabail Bunkhouse,** 1 Camusluinie, Killilan, Kyle of Lochalsh, Ross-shire, IV40 8EA
Actual Grid Ref: NG947284
Tel: 01599 588205
Fax: 01599 588205
Email: wfholidays@aol.com
Capacity: 10
Under 18: £7.50 **Adults:** £7.50
Open: All year, any time
Family bunk rooms: £20.00
Self-catering facilities • Showers • Central heating • Laundry facilities • Wet weather shelter • Games room • Drying room • Cycle store • Parking • No smoking
Original croft house converted to warm comfortable bunkhouse. Fairly isolated being 7 miles from nearest shop or pub. Set in the most beautiful glen in Scotland. Surrounded by Munros and Corbets and close to the dramatic falls of Glomach and Eilean Donan Castle. Fresh free range eggs included in price.

Kincraig
NH8305

▲ **Badenoch Christian Centre,** Kincraig, Kingussie, Inverness-shire, PH21 1QD
Tel: 01540 651373
Fax: 01540 651 373
Email: badenoch@dial.pipex.com
Capacity: 36
Under 18: £8.00 **Adults:** £9.50
Open: All year, 9am-11pm
Self-catering facilities • Television • Showers • Central heating • Lounge • Dining room • Games room • Grounds available for games • Drying room • Cycle store • Parking • Facilities for disabled people

Comfortable purpose built centre with 2 or 4 people in well fitted bunk rooms. Great area for water sports and mountain activities including skiing. Many visitor attractions close by. suitable for groups or individuals, also families rooms and self contained family suite. Occasional programmed activities and quiet retreat days.

▲ **Kirkbeag Hostel,** Kirkbeag, Milehead, Kincraig, Kingussie, Inverness-shire, PH21 1ND
Actual Grid Ref: NH840068
Tel: 01540 651298
Fax: 01540 651298
Email: kirkbeag@kincraig.com
Capacity: 6
Under 18: £8.50 **Adults:** £9.00
Open: All year, 9am-10pm
Family bunk rooms: £25.50
Self-catering facilities • Television • Showers • Lounge • Dining room • Grounds available for games • Drying room • Parking
Sleeps max. 6. Quiet country location, ideal for walking/climbing.

Kinlochewe
NH0261

▲ **Kinlochewe Caravan Club Site,** Kinlochewe, Achnasheen, Ross-shire, IV22 2PA
Actual Grid Ref: NH025620
Tel: 01445 760239
Open: Apr to Sep

Kinlochleven
NN1861

▲ **Blackwater Hostel and Campsite,** Lab Road, Kinlochleven, Argyll, PA40
Tel: 01855 831253
Fax: 01631740549
Email: black.water@virgin.net
Capacity: 39
Under 18: £10.00 **Adults:** £10.00
Open: All year, any time
Family bunk rooms: £10.00
Camping for 30 tents: £4.00
Self-catering facilities • Television • Showers • Central heating • Laundry facilities • Wet weather shelter • Lounge • Dining room • Grounds available for games • Cycle store • Parking • Facilities for disabled people
Rooms of 2, 3, 4, 8 beds all room en suite, with TVs. Breakfast and packed lunches available on request. In the centre of scenic village, amenities: supermarket, post office, shops and pubs. Regular bus service to Fort William. Activities: walking, climbing, skiing, fishing, pony trekking, most water sports available nearby.

▲ **Caolasnacon Caravan & Camping Park,** Kinlochleven, Argyll, PA40 4RJ
Actual Grid Ref: NN138608
Tel: 01855 831279
Open: Apr to Oct

Kyle of Lochalsh
NG7627

▲ **Reraig Caravan Site,** Kyle of Lochalsh, Ross-shire, IV40 8DH
Actual Grid Ref: NG816272
Tel: 01599 566215
Open: May to Sep

Laide
NG8992

▲ **Gruinard Bay Caravan Park,** Laide, Gairloch, Achnasheen, Ross-shire, IV22 2ND
Actual Grid Ref: NG906918
Tel: 01445 731225
Fax: 01445 731225
Open: Apr to Oct

Lairg
NC5806

▲ **Achmelvich Youth Hostel,** Recharn, Lairg, Sutherland, IV27 4JB
Actual Grid Ref: NC059248
Tel: 01571 844480
Capacity: 36
Under 18: £6.35
Adults: £7.50
Open: Mar to Oct
Family bunk rooms
Self-catering facilities • Shop 4 miles away
Beautiful coastal scenery surrounds hostel. Area of geological interest. Caving; climbing; sea fishing. NB no showers.

You are advised to book in advance for periods of high demand – the Summer months, Half Term holidays and public holidays.

MAP PAGE 285 • **Highland**

▲ **Dunroamin Caravan Park,** Main Street, Lairg, Sutherland, IV27 4AR
Actual Grid Ref: NC585062
Tel: 01549 402447
Fax: 01549 402447
Open: Mar to Oct

▲ **Woodend Caravan & Camping Park,** Archnairn, Lairg, Sutherland, IV27 4DN
Actual Grid Ref: NC558127
Tel: 01549 402248
Open: Apr to Sep

Lochinver

NC0922

▲ **Shore Caravan Site,** 106 Achmelvich, Lochinver, Lairg, Sutherland, IV27 4JB
Actual Grid Ref: NC055248
Tel: 01571 844393
Open: Apr to Oct

▲ **102 Achmelvich,** Lochinver, Lairg, Sutherland, IV27 4JB
Actual Grid Ref: NC059240
Tel: 01571 844262
Open: Apr to Sep

Mallaig

NM6796

▲ **Glenancross,** Morar, Mallaig, Inverness-shire, PH40 4PD
Tel: 01687 450362
Fax: 01687 450325
Open: All year

Melvich

NC8865

▲ **Halladale Inn Caravan Park,** Melvich, Thurso, Sutherland, KW14 7YJ
Actual Grid Ref: NC887640
Tel: 01641 541182
Open: Apr to Sep

Morvich (Shiel Bridge)

NG9620

▲ **Morvich Caravan Club Site,** Morvich, Inverinate, Kyle of Lochalsh, IV40 4HQ
Actual Grid Ref: NG964210
Tel: 01599 511354
Open: Apr to Sep

Nairn

NH8856

▲ **Spindrift Caravan Park,** Little Kildrummie, Nairn, IV12 5QU
Actual Grid Ref: NH873537
Tel: 01667 453992
Open: Apr to Oct

▲ **Nairn Lochloy Holiday Park,** East Beach, Nairn, IV12 4PH
Actual Grid Ref: NH890572
Tel: 01667 453764
Open: Mar to Nov

▲ **Delnies Wood Caravan Park,** Delnies Wood, Nairn, Inverness, Highlands, IV12 5NX
Actual Grid Ref: NH847551
Tel: 01667 455281
Open: Mar to Oct

Newtonmore

NN7199

▲ **Strathspey Mountain Hostel,** Main Street, Newtonmore, Inverness-shire, PH20 1DR
Actual Grid Ref: NN716993
Tel: 01540 673694
Email: strathspey@newtonmore.com
Capacity: 24
Adults: £7.50-£9.00
Open: All year, all day
Self-catering facilities • Television • Showers • Central heating • Laundry facilities • Wet weather shelter • Lounge • Dining room • Drying room • Security lockers • Cycle store • Parking • Facilities for disabled people
Brilliant, central location for walkers, cyclists, golfers, skiers, birdwatchers, fishermen, families, groups and individuals. Fully modernised highland villa. C/W, full CH, excellent showers and comprehensive self-catering facilities. STB 2 Star Hostel Award and Eco Tourism Award. Coal fire, cosy TV lounge. Excellent local information from outdoor activist owners. 6-bed cottage also available.

▲ **Croft Holidays Hostel,** Croft Holidays, Newtonmore, Inverness-shire, PH20 1BA
Actual Grid Ref: NH721001
Tel: 01540 673504
Fax: 01540 673504
Email: crofthols@newtonmore.com
Capacity: 12
Under 18: £9.00-£10.00
Adults: £9.00-£10.00
Open: All year, 4pm
Self-catering facilities • Television • Showers • Central heating • Laundry facilities • Lounge • Dining room • Grounds available for games • Drying room • Cycle store • Parking • Facilities for disabled people • No smoking
Flexible accommodation, half mile from Newtonmore in foothills of Monadhliaths.

▲ **Invernahavon Holiday Park,** Glentruim, Newtonmore, Inverness-shire, PH20 1BE
Actual Grid Ref: NN688920
Tel: 01540 673504
Open: Apr to Oct

▲ **Spey Bridge Caravan Site,** Newtonmore, Inverness, Highlands, PH20 1BB
Actual Grid Ref: NN709982
Tel: 01540 673275
Open: Apr to Oct

North Kessock

NH6548

▲ **Coulmore Bay Camping Site,** North Kessock, Inverness, IV1 3XB
Actual Grid Ref: NH619482
Tel: 01463 731322
Open: Apr to Oct

Oldshoremore

NC2058

▲ **Oldshoremore Caravan Site,** Kinlochbervie, Lairg, Sutherland, IV27 4RS
Actual Grid Ref: NC211586
Tel: 01971 521281
Open: Apr to Sep

To stay in a Youth Hostel affiliated to one of the Youth Hostel associations, you need to be a member. You can join at most hostels – phone in advance to check.

SCOTLAND

Highland • MAP PAGE 285

All details shown are as supplied by hostels and campsites in Autumn 2000.

Onich

NN0261

▲ **The Inchree Centre,** Onich, Fort William, Inverness-shire, PH33 6SD
Actual Grid Ref: NN025632
Tel: 01855 821287
Fax: 01855 821287
Email: enquiry@hostel-scotland.com
Capacity: 51
Under 18: £7.00-£12.00
Adults: £7.00-£12.00
Open: All year
Family bunk rooms: £30.00
Self-catering facilities • Television • Showers • Licensed bar • Central heating • Laundry facilities • Lounge • Dining room • Grounds available for games • Drying room • Cycle store • Parking • Evening meal available 6pm-9.30pm • Facilities for disabled people
Situated midway between the Ben Nevis & Glencoe mountains in a spectacular rural setting. Ideal location for all mountain sports. Deluxe hostel with ensuite rooms. Bunkhouse available for exclusive group use. Bar/bistro on site. Canyoning, funyakking & archery activities available. Outdoor climbing wall, Internet/email access.

▲ **Corran Caravans,** Moss Cottage, Onich, Fort William, Inverness-shire, PH33 6SE
Actual Grid Ref: NN020625
Tel: 01855 821208
Fax: 01397 700133
Open: All year

Poolewe

NG8580

▲ **Camping & Caravanning Club Site,** Inverewe Gardens, Poolewe, Achnasheen, Ross-shire, IV22 2LG
Actual Grid Ref: NG862812
Tel: 01445 781249
Open: Apr to Oct

Reay

NC9665

▲ **Dunvegan Caravan Site,** Reay, Caithness, KW14 7RQ
Actual Grid Ref: NC957646
Tel: 01847 811405
Open: May to Sep

Resipole

NM7263

▲ **Resipole Caravan Park,** Loch Sunart, Salen, Acharacle, Argyll, PH36 4HX
Actual Grid Ref: NM723638
Tel: 01967 431235
Open: Apr to Oct

Rosemarkie

NH7357

▲ **Camping & Caravanning Club Site,** Well Road, Rosemarkie, Fortrose, Ross-shire, IV10 8UW
Actual Grid Ref: NH739569
Tel: 01381 621117
Open: Apr to Oct

Roybridge

NN2781

▲ **Bunroy Holiday Park,** Roybridge, Inverness-shire, PH31 4AG
Actual Grid Ref: NN275807
Tel: 01397 712332
Open: Mar to Oct

▲ **Inveroy Caravan Park,** Roybridge, Inverness-shire, PH31 4AQ
Actual Grid Ref: NN257813
Tel: 01397 712275
Open: All year

Scaniport

NH6239

▲ **Scaniport Camping & Caravanning Park,** Scaniport, Inverness, IV1 2DL
Actual Grid Ref: NH630399
Tel: 01463 751351
Open: Apr to Sep

Scourie

NC1544

▲ **Scourie Caravan & Camping Park,** Harbour Road, Scourie, Lairg, Sutherland, IV27 4TG
Actual Grid Ref: NC154446
Tel: 01971 502060
Open: Apr to Sep

Hostels and campsites may vary rates – be sure to check when booking.

If you have to cancel your visit to any hostel or campsite, please let them know – it is always possible to make a bed or a pitch available to someone else.

Shiel Bridge

NG9318

▲ **Ratagan Youth Hostel,** Glenshiel, Kyle of Lochalsh, Ross-shire, IV40 8HP
Actual Grid Ref: NG918199
Tel: 01599 511243
Capacity: 44
Under 18: £6.00-£8.00
Adults: £9.25
Open: March to Oct
Self-catering facilities • Shop • Laundry facilities • Facilities for disabled people
Stunning location with several Munros nearby. Visit Donan Castle, Falls of Glomach and Kylerhea otter haven; take the ferry to Skye.

▲ **Shiel Bridge,** Shielbridge, Glenshiel, Kyle of Lochalsh, Ross-shire, IV40 8HW
Actual Grid Ref: NG940185
Tel: 01599 511221
Fax: 01599 511432
Email: lynnefivesisters@aol.com
Tent pitches: 50
Tent rate: £4.00
Open: Mar to Oct
Last arr: 10pm
Dogs allowed • Calor Gas/Camping Gaz • Cafe or Takeaway on site • Showers • Laundrette on site • Public phone on site • Licensed bar on site • Shop on site • Indoor swimming pool nearby • Boating/sailing/watersports nearby • Golf nearby • Riding nearby
Situated in an Area of Outstanding Natural Beauty with wonderful views over to the Five Sisters of Kintail. This rural campsite, with stream running parallel to it, is situated 13 miles from Cluanie and 18 miles from the Skye Bridge. Hill walker's and birdwatcher's paradise with Sea/Loch fishing available locally.

MAP PAGE 285 • **Highland**

Smoo

NC4166

▲ **Durness Youth Hostel,** Smoo, Lairg, Sutherland, IV27 4QA
Actual Grid Ref: NC417672
Tel: 01971 511244
Capacity: 40
Under 18: £6.25
Adults: £7.50
Open: Mar to Oct
Self-catering facilities • Shop 1 mile away
Magnificent northern setting, with mysterious Smoo Cave and clean sandy beaches nearby. Great hillwalking, Ranger-led guided walks.

South Laggan

NN2996

▲ **Loch Lochy Youth Hostel,** South Laggan, Spean Bridge, Inverness-shire, PH34 4EA
Actual Grid Ref: NN293972
Tel: 01809 501239
Capacity: 60
Under 18: £7.00-£7.25
Adults: £8.25-£8.50
Open: March to Oct
Self-catering facilities • Shop
Good walking on the north side of the loch. Windsurfing equipment, boats, fishing tackle and mountain bikes can all be hired at the Great Glen Water Park.

Spean Bridge

NN2281

▲ **Stronaba Caravan Site,** Spean Bridge, Inverness-shire, PH34 4DX
Actual Grid Ref: NN204843
Tel: 01397 712259
Open: Apr to Oct

▲ **Gairlochy Holiday Park,** Old Station, Gairlochy Road, Spean Bridge, Inverness-shire, PH34 4EQ
Actual Grid Ref: NN190835
Tel: 01397 712711
Open: Apr to Oct

Strath (Gairloch)

NG7977

▲ **Gairloch Caravan & Camping Park,** Strath, Gairloch, Ross-shire, IV21 2BT
Actual Grid Ref: NG798773
Tel: 01505 614343 / 01445 712373
Open: Apr to Oct

▲ **Gairloch Caravan and Camping Park,** Mihol Road, Strath, Gairloch, Highlands, IV21 2BX
Actual Grid Ref: NG797774
Tel: 01445 712373
Open: Apr to Oct

Strathpeffer

NH4858

▲ **Strathpeffer Youth Hostel,** Strathpeffer, Ross-shire, IV14 9BT
Actual Grid Ref: NH478574
Tel: 01997 421532
Capacity: 54
Under 18: £7.00-£7.75
Adults: £8.25-£9.00
Open: May to Oct
Self-catering facilities • Shop nearby
Excellent centre for walking and cycling; ospreys at Kinelloch Loch and Loch Ord; a Pictish stone surrounded by mystery and legend.

▲ **Riverside Chalets & Caravan Park,** Strathpeffer, Ross-shire, IV14 9ES
Actual Grid Ref: NH456562
Tel: 01997 421351
Open: All year

Strontian

NM8161

▲ **Glenview Caravan Park,** Strontian, Loch Sunart, Acharacle, Argyll, PH36 4JD
Actual Grid Ref: NM817617
Tel: 01967 402123
Open: Mar to Jan

Tain (Dornoch Firth)

NH7881

▲ **Meikle Ferry Caravan Park,** Meikle Ferry, Tain, Ross-shire, IV19 1JX
Actual Grid Ref: NH748843
Tel: 01862 892292
Open: All year

Talmine

NC5863

▲ **Bayview Caravan Site,** Talmine, Lairg, Sutherland, IV27 4YS
Actual Grid Ref: NC585627
Tel: 01847 601225
Open: Apr to Sep

Thurso

ND1168

▲ **Thurso Youth Club Hostel,** Old Mill, Millbank, Thurso, Caithness, KW14 8PS
Actual Grid Ref: ND116678
Tel: 01847 892964
Email: t.y.c.hostel@btinternet.com
Capacity: 22
Under 18: £7.00
Adults: £8.00
Open: July to Aug, any time
Self-catering facilities • Television • Showers • Central heating • Laundry facilities • Wet weather shelter • Lounge • Dining room • Games room • Grounds available for games • Drying room • Cycle store • Parking
Our hostel occupies part of a converted 200 year old water mill which has a riverside location overlooking the town's main park. An excellent base for exploring the north of Scotland and a convenient stopover for ferry, coaches and train connections. Price includes all bed linen, showers and continental breakfast.

▲ **Dunvegan,** Rea, Thurso, Caithness, KW14 7RQ
Tel: 01847 81405
Open: May to Oct

▲ **Thurso Camping & Caravan Site,** Smith Terrace, Scrabster Road, Thurso, Caithness, KW14 7JY
Tel: 01847 894545
Open: May to Sep

▲ **Thurso Caravan and Camping Park,** Scrabster Road, Thurso, Highlands, KW14 7JY
Actual Grid Ref: ND112688
Tel: 01847 894631
Open: Apr to Sep

Some hostels and campsites impose restrictions on size and type of groups they accept (e.g. not permitting single-sex groups). Always phone to enquire before booking.

Highland • MAP PAGE 285

Tongue
NC5956

▲ **Tongue Youth Hostel,** Tongue, Lairg, Sutherland, IV27 4XH
Actual Grid Ref: NC586584
Tel: 01847 611301
Capacity: 40
Under 18: £7.00
Adults: £8.25
Open: March to Oct
Self-catering facilities • Shop 1 mile away
A remote land of huge beaches, vast moorlands with river valleys, and great mountains. Ideal for pony trekking or climbing; you can view wading birds, seals and otters.

▲ **Kincraig Caravan and Camping Site,** Tongue, Sutherland, IV27 4XE
Actual Grid Ref: NC592564
Tel: 01847 611218
Open: Mar to Oct

Some hostels and campsites impose restrictions on size and type of groups they accept (e.g. not permitting single-sex groups). Always phone to enquire before booking.

All details shown are as supplied by hostels and campsites in Autumn 2000.

Torridon
NG9056

▲ **Torridon Youth Hostel,** Torridon, Ross-shire, IV22 2EZ
Actual Grid Ref: NG904559
Tel: 01445 791284
Capacity: 60 **Under 18:** £6.00-£8.00
Adults: £8.75-£9.25
Open: March to Oct
Family bunk rooms
Self-catering facilities • Shop • Laundry facilities
Set in some of Britain's most spectacular mountain scenery, this is a great area for hillwalking and climbing. Loch Torridon is within easy reach, with good fishing.

If you have to cancel your visit to any hostel or campsite, please let them know – it is always possible to make a bed or a pitch available to someone else.

Ullapool
NH1294

▲ **Ullapool Youth Hostel,** Shore Street, Ullapool, Ross-shire, IV26 2UJ
Actual Grid Ref: NH129940
Tel: 01854 612254
Capacity: 62
Under 18: £7.25-£8.75
Adults: £8.50-£10.00 **Open:** All year
Self-catering facilities • Shop nearby • Laundry facilities
The hostel overlooks the harbour, surrounded by mountains. Try hillwalking, cycling, seafood restaurants and cruises to the Summer Isles to see seabirds, dolphins and seals.

▲ **Broomfield Holiday Park,** Rhodos, Garve Road, Ullapool, Ross-shire, IV26 2SX
Actual Grid Ref: NH125938
Tel: 01854 612020
Open: Apr to Sep

Urray
NH5053

▲ **Druimorrin Caravan & Camping Park,** Orrin Bridge, Urray, Muir of Ord, Ross-shire, IV6 7UL
Actual Grid Ref: NH506534
Tel: 01997 433252
Open: May to Sep

Inner Hebrides

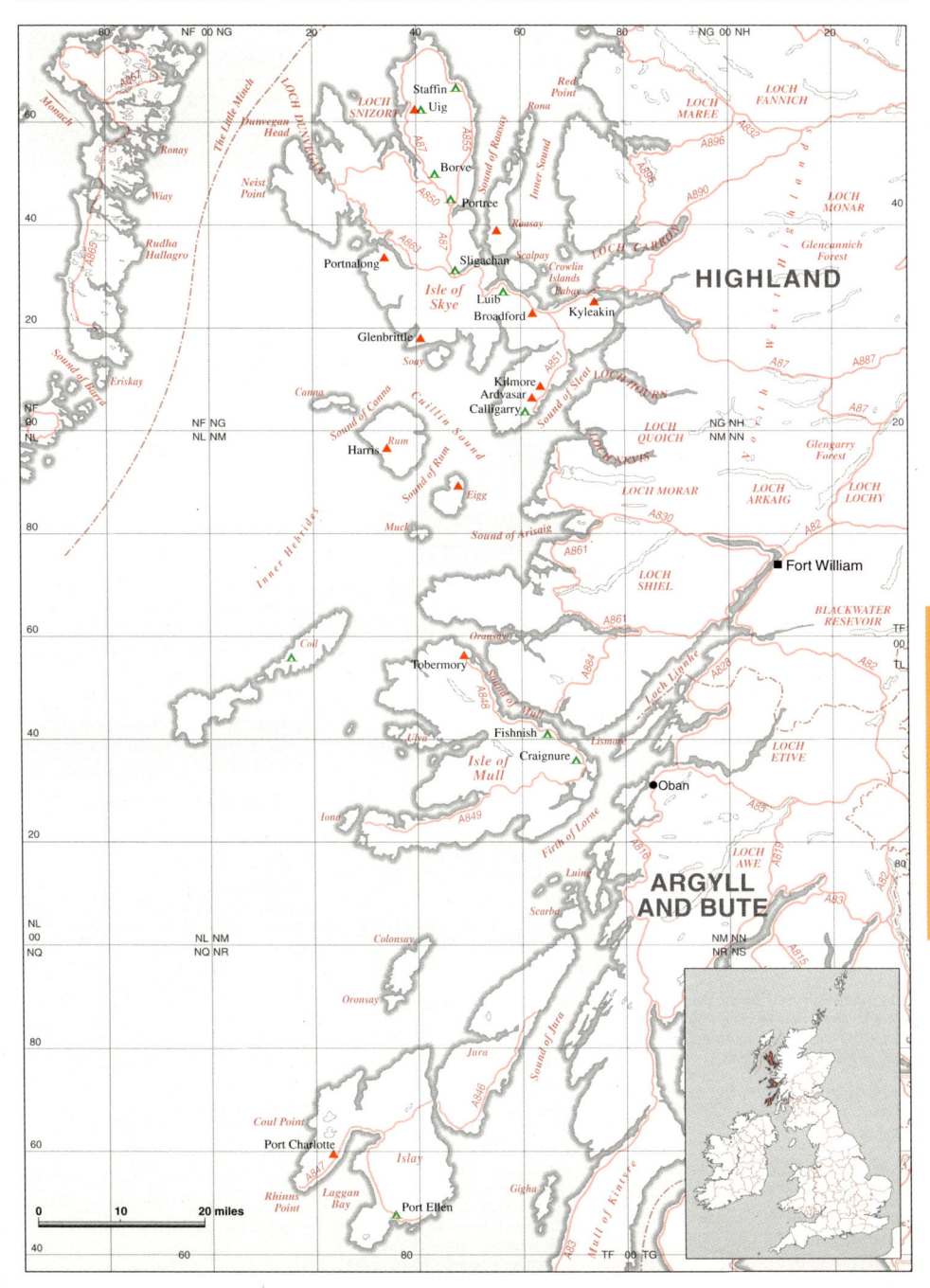

Inner Hebrides • MAP PAGE 297

Coll

NM1955

▲ **Garden House,** Isle of Coll, PA78 6TB
Actual Grid Ref: NM166542
Tel: 01879 230374
Fax: 01879 230374
Open: Apr to Sep

Eigg

NM4884

▲ **The Glebe Barn,** Field Study Centre & Hostel, Isle of Eigg, PH42 4RL
Actual Grid Ref: NM483852
Tel: 01687 482417
Fax: 01687 482417
Email: glebebarneigg@compuserve.com
Capacity: 24
Under 18: £9.50
Adults: £9.50
Open: Mar to Oct
Family bunk rooms: £8.50
Self-catering facilities • Showers • Central heating • Laundry facilities • Lounge • Dining room • Drying room • No smoking
Incredible views, location and facilities. Daily ferries Mallaig/Arisaig. Individuals or exclusive let.

Islay - Port Charlotte

NR2557

▲ **Islay Youth Hostel,** Port Charlotte, Isle of Islay, PA48 7TX
Actual Grid Ref: NR259584
Tel: 01496 850385
Capacity: 42
Under 18: £7.75
Adults: £9.00
Open: March to Oct
Family bunk rooms
Self-catering facilities • Shop • Laundry facilities
Islay is famous for its towering cliffs, beautiful sandy beaches and distilleries. Try hillwalking, cycling, birdwatching, pony trekking, golf and diving.

Islay - Port Ellen

NR3645

▲ **Kintra Farm,** Kintra Beach, Port Ellen, Isle of Islay, PA42 7AT
Actual Grid Ref: NR320483
Tel: 01496 302051
Open: Apr to Sep

Mull - Craignure

NM7136

▲ **Shieling Holidays,** Craignure, Isle of Mull, PA65 6AY
Actual Grid Ref: NM724369
Tel: 01680 812496
Open: Apr to Oct

Mull - Fishnish

NM6641

▲ **Balmeanach Park,** Balmeanach Holiday Park, Isle of Mull, PA65 6BA
Actual Grid Ref: NM657415
Tel: 01680 300342
Open: Mar to Oct

Mull - Tobermory

NM5055

▲ **Tobermory Youth Hostel,** Main Street, Tobermory, Isle of Mull, PA75 6NU
Actual Grid Ref: NM507554
Tel: 01688 302481
Capacity: 40
Under 18: £7.50
Adults: £8.75
Open: March to Oct
Self-catering facilities • Shop nearby
Excellent coastal and woodland walking; boat trips to Iona and Staffa, home of Fingal's Cave; the UK's smallest theatre at Dervaig.

Raasay

NG5537

▲ **Raasay Youth Hostel,** Creachan Cottage, Raasay, Kyle of Lochalsh, IV40 8NT
Actual Grid Ref: NG553378
Tel: 01478 660240
Capacity: 30
Under 18: £5.75 **Adults:** £7.00
Open: May to Oct
Self-catering facilities • Shop 2 miles away
Charming island with unique views of the mainland and Skye. Conservation area of special interest to ornithologists, botanists, geologists and archaeologists. Unrestricted walking and cycling routes.

Skye - Ardvasar

NG6203

▲ **Armadale Youth Hostel,** Ardvasar, Sleat, Isle of Skye, IV45 8RS
Actual Grid Ref: NG638039
Tel: 01471 844260
Capacity: 42
Under 18: £7.00-£7.25
Adults: £8.25-£8.50
Open: March to Oct
Self-catering facilities • Shop 1 mile
Sleat, known as the Garden of Skye, has abundant wildlife - otters, dear, eagles. Views across Armadale Bay. Delicious local seafood.

Skye - Borve

NG4448

▲ **Loch Greshonish Caravan & Camping Site,** Borve, Edinbane, Portree, Isle of Skye, IV51 9PS
Actual Grid Ref: NG345527
Tel: 01470 582230
Open: Apr to Oct

Skye - Broadford

NG6423

▲ **Broadford Youth Hostel,** Broadford, Isle of Skye, IV49 9AA
Actual Grid Ref: NG642241
Tel: 01471 822442
Capacity: 66
Under 18: £7.25-£8.25
Adults: £8.50-£9.50
Open: March to Oct
Family bunk rooms
Self-catering facilities • Shop • Laundry facilities
Ideal centre for exploring Skye. Climb the challenging Cuillin range or walk the scenic Ord -Tarskavaig road. Boat trips to Loch Coruisk.

If you have to cancel your visit to any hostel or campsite, please let them know – it is always possible to make a bed or a pitch available to someone else.

Inner Hebrides

Skye - Calligarry
NG6203

▲ **1/2 10 Calligarry,** Calligarry, Ardvasar, Isle of Skye, IV45 8RY
Tel: 01471 844312
Open: All year

Skye - Glenbrittle
NG4121

▲ **Glenbrittle Youth Hostel,** Glenbrittle, Carbost, Isle of Skye, IV47 8TA
Actual Grid Ref: NG408224
Tel: 01478 640278
Capacity: 39
Under 18: £7.00-£7.50
Adults: £8.25-£8.75
Open: March to Oct
Self-catering facilities • Shop
Ideal base for the magnificent rock climbing and hillwalking in the Cuillin. Popular base for field studies.

Skye - Kilmore
NG6507

▲ **Flora Macdonald Hostel,** Kilmore, Sleat, Isle of Skye, IV44 8RG
Actual Grid Ref: NG657070
Tel: 01471 844440
Capacity: 24
Under 18: £8.00
Adults: £8.00
Open: All year, 9am-11pm
Family bunk rooms: £40.00
Camping for 40 tents: £6.00
Self-catering facilities • Television • Showers • Laundry facilities • Wet weather shelter • Lounge • Dining room • Drying room • Cycle store • Parking
2.5 miles north of Armadale Pier at the foot of hills 5 minutes from sea. Land tours and sea trips available. Free trout fishing, good walks and mountain climbing. Discount for groups = 20% and for individuals staying a week or more. Geologists paradise, best wildlife in UK, Highland cattle and ponies on croftland.

Skye - Kyleakin
NG7526

▲ **Kyleakin Youth Hostel,** Kyleakin, Isle of Skye, IV41 8PL
Actual Grid Ref: NG752264
Tel: 01599 534585
Capacity: 125
Under 18: £6.00-£9.50
Adults: £9.00-£11.00
Open: All year
Family bunk rooms
Self-catering facilities • Shop • Laundry facilities • Evening meal available groups only • Facilities for disabled people
Ideal centre for exploring Skye. Viking Castle Moil sits high above the harbour. Seal cruises from the local pier, summer cruises to Mallaig.

Skye - Luib
NG5627

▲ **Glen Dochart Caravan Park,** Luib, Crianlarich, Stirlingshire, FK20 8QT
Actual Grid Ref: NG477279
Tel: 01567 820637
Open: Mar to Oct

Skye - Portnalong
NG348353

▲ **Skyewalker Independent Hostel,** Old School, Fiscavaig Road, Portnalong, Carbost, Isle of Skye, IV47 8SL
Tel: 01478 640250
Fax: 01478 640420
Email: skyewalker.hostel@virgin.net
Capacity: 36
Under 18: £7.50
Adults: £7.50
Open: All year
Camping for 6 tents: £2.50
Self-catering facilities • Television • Showers • Central heating • Shop • Laundry facilities • Wet weather shelter • Lounge • Dining room • Grounds available for games • Cycle store • Parking • Facilities for disabled people
Situated close to the Cuillin Hills in an area of outstanding natural beauty the hostel provides the perfect base for outdoor activities and is within easy reach of the popular tourist areas. The accommodation comprises a variety of dormitory, family and 2 bedded rooms. A warm welcome awaits you.

▲ **Croft Bunkhouses & Bothies,** 7 Portnalong, Portnalong, Carbost, Isle of Skye, IV47 8SL
Tel: 01478 640254
Fax: 01478 640254
Capacity: 30
Under 18: £7.00-£8.50
Adults: £7.00-£8.50
Open: All year, all day
Family bunk rooms: £78.50
Camping for 12 tents: £3.50
Self-catering facilities • Showers • Laundry facilities • Wet weather shelter • Lounge • Dining room • Games room • Grounds available for games • Drying room • Cycle store • Parking
Five adjacent hostels on 12 acre croft overlooking sea and mountains.

Skye - Portree
NG4843

▲ **Torvaig Caravan & Camping Site,** Portree, Isle of Skye, IV51 9HU
Actual Grid Ref: NG490450
Tel: 01478 612209
Open: Apr to Oct

▲ **4-5 Peinaha,** Glenhinisdale, Portree, Isle of Sky, Highlands, IV51 9UZ
Actual Grid Ref: NG405578
Tel: 01470 542476
Open: Apr to Sep

Skye - Sligachan
NG4829

▲ **Glen Brittle Camping Site,** Glen Brittle, Sligachan, Isle of Sky, IV47 8TA
Actual Grid Ref: NG412205
Tel: 01478 640404
Open: Apr to Oct

▲ **Sligachan Camp and Caravan Site,** Sligachan, Carbost, Isle of Skye, IV47 8SW
Actual Grid Ref: NG486300
Tel: 01478 650303
Open: Apr to Oct

Skye - Staffin
NG4867

▲ **Staffin Caravan & Camping Site,** Lag-Uaine, Staffin, Portree, Isle of Skye, IV51 9JX
Actual Grid Ref: NG496668
Tel: 01470 562213
Open: Apr to Oct

Inner Hebrides • MAP PAGE 297

Skye - Uig (Uig Bay)

NG3963

▲ **Uig Youth Hostel,** Uig, Portree, Isle of Skye, IV51 9YD
Actual Grid Ref: NG396630

Tel: 01470 542211
Capacity: 62
Under 18: £7.00-£7.75
Adults: £8.25-£9.00
Open: March to Oct
Family bunk rooms
Self-cateriµng facilities • Shop
Breathtaking views; a standing stone close to the hostel; cycling, canoeing, pony trekking. Music festival in July, water gala in September. Boats to Tarbert and Lochmaddy.

▲ **Uig Bay Camping & Caravan Site,** 10 Idrigill, Uig, Portree, Isle of Skye, IV51 9XU
Tel: 01470 542360
Open: Mar to Oct

Lanarkshire

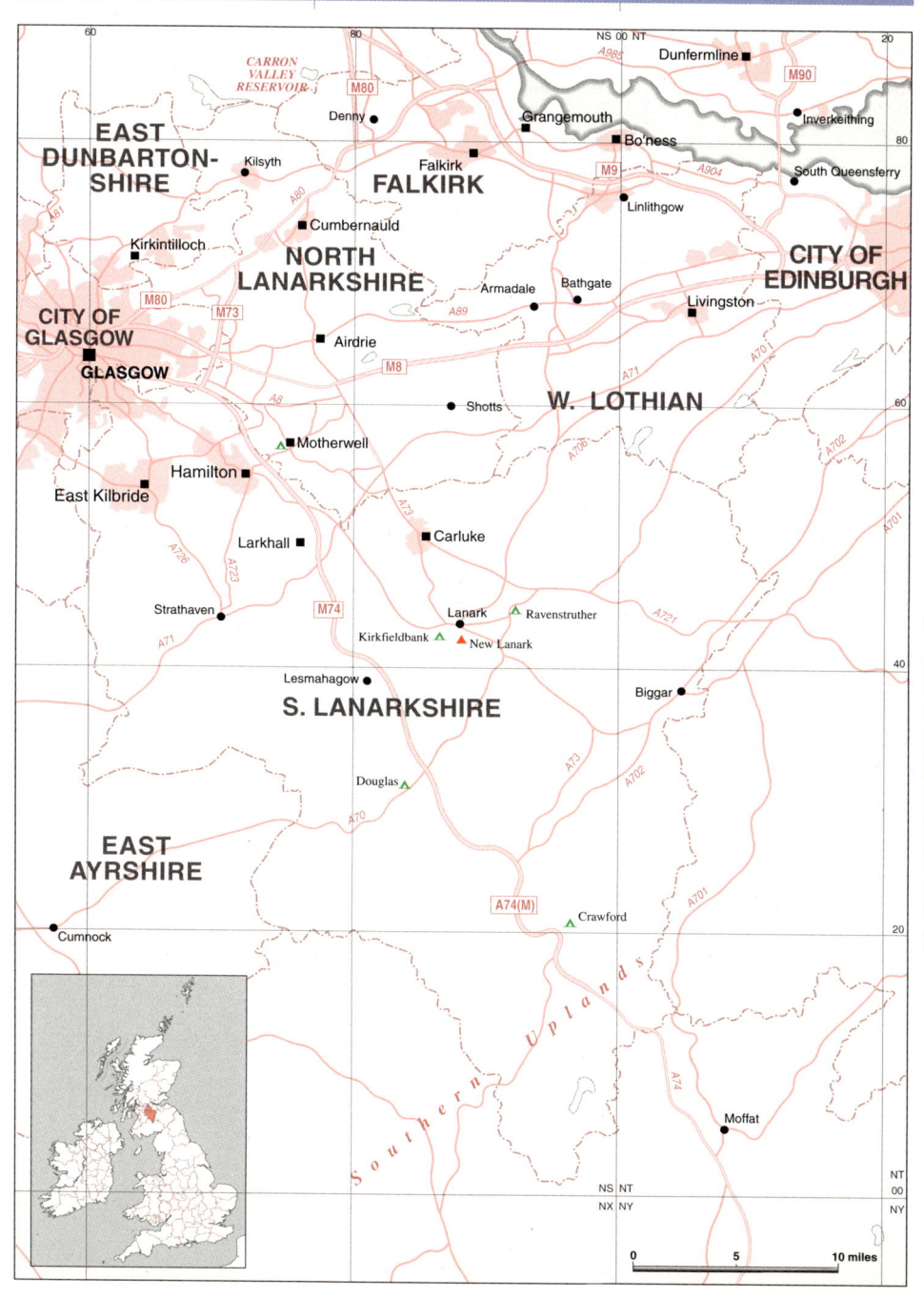

Lanarkshire • MAP PAGE 301

Crawford

NS9520

▲ **Crawford Caravan & Camping Site,** Carlisle Road, Crawford, South Lanarkshire, ML21 6TW
Actual Grid Ref: NS957204
Tel: 01864 502258
Open: Apr to Oct

Douglas

NS8330

▲ **Crossburn Caravan Park,** Douglas, Lanark, ML11 0QA
Actual Grid Ref: NS837308
Tel: 01555 851029
Open: All year

Kirkfieldbank

NS8643

▲ **Clyde Valley Caravan Park,** Kirkfieldbank, Lanark, ML11 9JW
Actual Grid Ref: NS868440
Tel: 01555 663951
Open: Apr to Oct

Motherwell

NS7556

▲ **Strathclyde Country Park,** 366 Hamilton Road, Motherwell, ML1 3ED
Actual Grid Ref: NS719587
Tel: 01698 266155
Fax: 01698 252925
Open: Apr to Oct

New Lanark

NS8742

▲ **New Lanark Youth Hostel,** Wee Row, Rosedale Street, Lanark, ML11 9DJ
Actual Grid Ref: NS878429
Tel: 01555 666710
Email: new.lanark@syha.org.uk
Capacity: 64
Under 18: £7.25-£8.00
Adults: £8.50-£9.25
Open: March to Oct
Family bunk rooms
Self-catering facilities • Shop nearby • Laundry facilities • Evening meal available
New Lanark is a 200-year-old beautifully restored riverside conservation village surrounded by woodland. Waterfalls of Corra Linn; Scottish Wildlife Visitor Centre.

Ravenstruther

NS9245

▲ **Newhouse Caravan & Camping Park,** Ravenstruther, Lanark, ML11 8NP
Actual Grid Ref: NS927457
Tel: 01555 870228
Email: newhousepark@btinternet.com
Open: Mar to Oct

Hostels and campsites may vary rates – be sure to check when booking.

SCOTLAND

Stilwell's National Trail Companion

46 Long Distance Footpaths • Where to Stay • Where to Eat

Other guides may show you where to walk, Stilwell's National Trail Companion shows your where to stay and eat. The perfect companion guide for the British Isles' famous national trails and long distance footpaths, Stilwell's make pre-planning your accommodation easy. It lists B&Bs, hostels, campsites and pubs - in the order they appear along the routes - and includes such vital information as maps, grid references and distance from the path; Tourist Board ratings; the availability of vehicle pick-up, drying facilities and packed lunches. So whether you walk a trail in stages at weekends or in one continuous journey, you'll never be stuck at the end of the day for a hot meal or a great place to sleep.

Enjoy the beauty and adventure of Britain's – and Ireland's – long distance trails with **Stilwell's National Trail Companion**.

Paths in England
Cleveland Way & Tabular Hills Link – Coast to Coast Path – Cotswald Way – Cumbria Way – Dales Way – Essex Way – Greensand Way – Hadrian's Wall – Heart of England Way – Hereward Way – Icknield Way – Macmillan Way – North Downs Way – Oxfordshire Way – Peddars Way and Norfolk Coastal Path – Pennine Way – Ribble Way – The Ridgeway – Shropshire Way – South Downs Way – South West Coast Path – Staffordshire Way – Tarka Trail – Thames Path – Two Moors Way - Vanguard Way - Viking Way – Wayfarer's Walk – Wealdway – Wessex Ridgeway – Wolds Way

Paths in Ireland
Beara Way – Dingle Way – Kerry Way – Ulster Way – Western Way – Wicklow Way

Paths in Scotland
Fife Coastal Walk – Southern Upland Way – Speyside Way – West Highland Way

Paths in Wales
Cambrian Way – Glyndwr's Way – Offa's Dyke Path – Pembrokeshire Coast Path – Wye Valley Walk

£9.95 from all good bookstores (ISBN 1-900861-25-9) or £10.95 (inc p&p) from Stilwell Publishing, 59 Charlotte Road, London EC2A 3QW (020 7739 7179)

Lothian & Falkirk

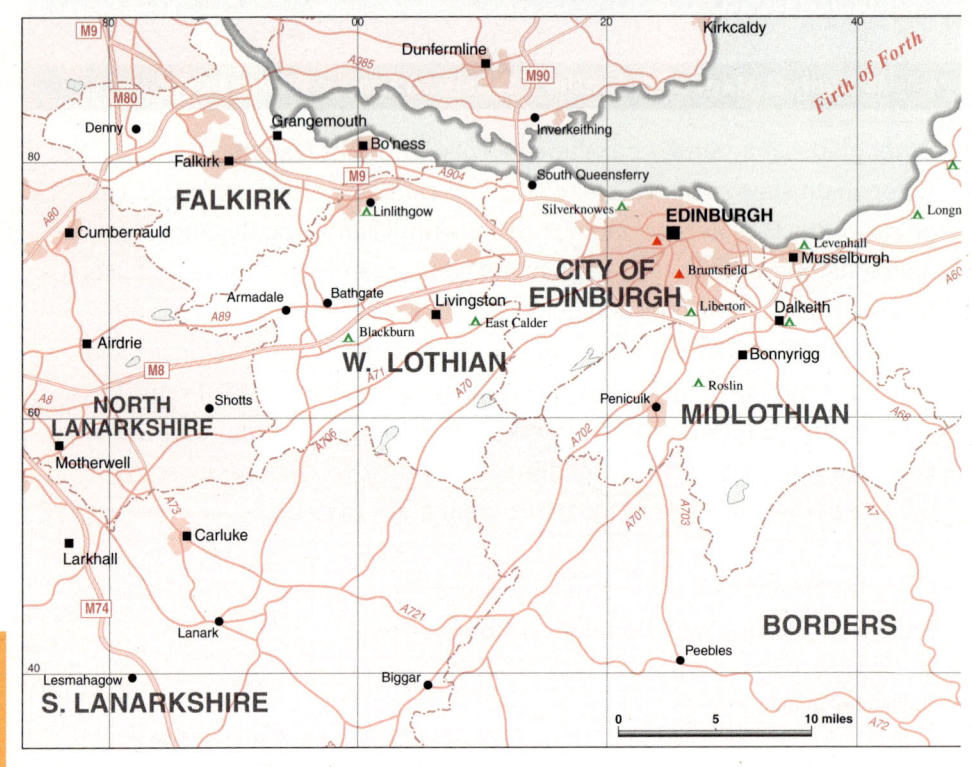

Aberlady

NT4680

Aberlady Station, Haddington Road, Aberlady, Longniddry, E. Lothian, EH32 0PZ
Tel: 01875 870666
Open: Mar to Oct

Blackburn

NS9865

Blackburn Mosshall Farm Caravan Park, Mosshall Farm, Blackburn, Bathgate, West Lothian, EH47 7DB
Actual Grid Ref: NS974647
Tel: 01501 762318
Open: All year

Dalkeith

NT3467

Fordel Caravan & Camping Park, Lauder Road, Dalkeith, Midlothian, EH22 2PH
Actual Grid Ref: NT359668
Tel: 0131 660 3921
Fax: 0131 663 8891
Open: Apr to Sep

Dunbar

NT6779

Camping & Caravanning Club Site, Barns Ness, Dunbar, East Lothian, EH42 1QP
Actual Grid Ref: NT723773
Tel: 01368 863536
Fax: 01620 895623
Open: Mar to Oct

Belhaven Bay Camping & Caravan Park, Dunbar Road, North Berwick, EH39 5NJ

Actual Grid Ref: NT662785
Tel: 01620 893348
Open: Mar to Oct

East Calder

NT0867

East Calder Linwater Caravan Park, West Clifton, East Calder, Livingston, EH53 0HT
Actual Grid Ref: NT104696
Tel: 0131 333 3326
Open: Apr to Oct

All details shown are as supplied by hostels and campsites in Autumn 2000.

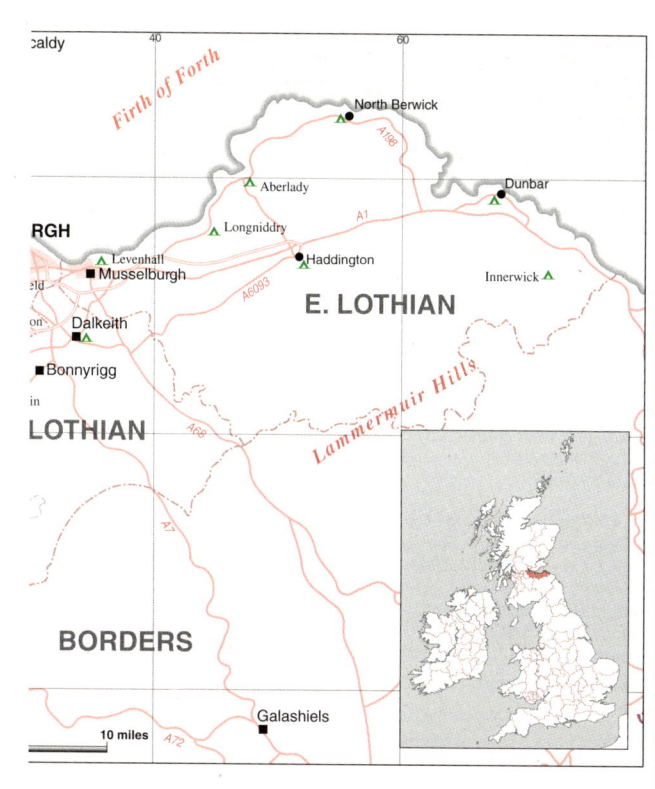

Lothian & Falkirk

▲ **Edinburgh Central Youth Hostel,** Robertson Close/College Wynd, Cowgate, Edinburgh, EH1 1LY
Tel: 08701 553255
Capacity: 121
Under 18: £14.00-£16.75
Adults: £14.00-£16.75
Open: July to Aug
Family bunk rooms
Self-catering facilities • Shop nearby • Laundry facilities
Edinburgh's cobbled streets provide a wealth of history, superb restaurants and spectacular views. The Arts festival runs every summer.

▲ **Edinburgh Pleasance Youth Hostel,** New Arthur Place, Edinburgh, EH8 9TH
Tel: 08701 553255
Capacity: 115
Under 18: £14.00-£16.75
Adults: £14.00-£16.75
Open: July to Aug
Family bunk rooms
Self-catering facilities • Shop nearby • Laundry facilities
Edinburgh's cobbled streets provide a wealth of history, superb restaurants and spectacular views. The Arts festival runs every summer.

▲ **Brodies Backpackers Hostel,** 12 High Street, Edinburgh, EH1 1TB
Actual Grid Ref: NT262737
Tel: 0131 556 6770 **Fax:** 0131 556 6770
Email: reception@brodieshostels.co.uk
Capacity: 56
Adults: £10.20-£14.90
Open: All year, 7am-midnight
Showers • Central heating • Laundry facilities • Lounge • Security lockers • No smoking
Edinburgh's friendliest wee hostel. Superb location, quality facilities, great atmosphere.

Edinburgh - Bruntsfield

NT2572

▲ **Edinburgh Bruntsfield Youth Hostel,** 7 Bruntsfield Crescent, Edinburgh, EH10 4EZ
Actual Grid Ref: NT249720
Tel: 0131 447 2994
Capacity: 130
Under 18: £8.50-£9.75
Adults: £9.75-£11.00
Open: All year
Self-catering facilities • Shop nearby • Laundry facilities
Edinburgh's cobbled streets provide a wealth of history, superb restaurants and spectacular views. The Arts festival runs every summer.

Edinburgh - Central

NT2573

▲ **Edinburgh Eglinton Youth Hostel,** 18 Eglinton Crescent, Edinburgh, EH12 5DD
Actual Grid Ref: NT238735
Tel: 0131 337 1120
Email: eglinton@syha.org.uk
Capacity: 150
Under 18: £10.50-£12.50
Adults: £12.00-£14.00
Open: All year
Self-catering facilities • Shop • Laundry facilities • Evening meal available groups only
Edinburgh's cobbled streets provide a wealth of history, superb restaurants and spectacular views. The Arts festival runs every summer.

▲ **Cowgate Tourist Hostel,** 112 Cowgate , Edinburgh, EH1 1JN
Tel: 0131 226 2153 **Fax:** 0131 226 7355
Email: lee@eastgatehostel.com
Capacity: 50120
Under 18: £11.00-£16.00
Adults: £11.00-£16.00 **Open:** All year
Family bunk rooms: £11.00
Self-catering facilities • Television • Showers • Central heating • Laundry facilities • Wet weather shelter • Lounge • Dining room • Drying room • Security lockers • Cycle store • Parking
Located in the heart of the historic old town, close to attractions. This hostel is made up of large apartments with own bathrooms and kitchen, with TV. 10 mins from train/bus station. 5 mins from pubs/clubs. This hostel has a relaxed atmosphere with friendly staff.

Lothian & Falkirk • MAP PAGE 304

Edinburgh - Liberton
NT2769

▲ **Mortonhall Caravan Park,** 36 Mortonhall Gate, Frogston Road East, Edinburgh, EH16 6TJ
Actual Grid Ref: NT262683
Tel: 0131 664 1533 **Fax:** 0131 664 5387
Open: Apr to Oct

Edinburgh - Silverknowes
NT2075

▲ **Edinburgh Caravan Club Site,** Marine Drive, Edinburgh, EH4 5EN
Actual Grid Ref: NT213769
Tel: 0131 312 6874 **Open:** All year

Haddington
NT5173

▲ **The Monks' Muir,** Haddington, East Lothian, EH41 3SB
Actual Grid Ref: NT559760
Tel: 01620 860340
Fax: 01620 860340
Open: All year

Innerwick
NT7174

▲ **Thurston Manor Holiday Home Park,** Innerwick, Dunbar, East Lothian, EH42 1SA
Actual Grid Ref: NT719745
Tel: 01368 840643
Open: Mar to Oct

Levenhall
NT3673

▲ **Drum Mohr Caravan Park,** Levenhall, Musselburgh, Midlothian, EH21 8JS
Tel: 0131 665 6867 **Fax:** 0131 653 6859
Open: Mar to Oct

▲ **Drum Mohr Caravan Park,** Levenhall, Musselburgh, Lothian, EH21 8JS
Actual Grid Ref: NT371735
Tel: 01316 656867
Fax: 01316 536859
Open: Mar to Oct

Linlithgow
NS9977

▲ **Loch House Farm Site,** Linlithgow, West Lothian, EH49 7RG
Tel: 01506 842144
Open: All year

▲ **Linlithgow Beecraigs Caravan & Camping Site,** Beescraig Country Park, Linlithgow, West Lothian, EH49 6PL
Actual Grid Ref: NT008749
Tel: 01506 844516
Open: All year

Hostels and campsites may vary rates – be sure to check when booking.

Longniddry
NT4476

▲ **Seton Sands Holiday Park,** Longniddry, East Lothian, EH32 0QF
Actual Grid Ref: NT420759
Tel: 01875 813333
Open: Mar to Oct

North Berwick
NT5585

▲ **Gilsland Caravan Park,** Newhouse Road, North Berwick, EH39 5JA
Tel: 01620 892205
Open: Mar to Oct

▲ **North Berwick Tantallon Caravan Park,** Dunbar Road, North Berwick, EH39 5NJ
Actual Grid Ref: NT570850
Tel: 01620 893348
Open: Mar to Oct

Roslin
NT2763

▲ **Roslin Slatebarns Caravan Park,** Slatebarns Farm, Roslin, Midlothian, EH25 9PU
Actual Grid Ref: NT277632
Tel: 0131 440 1608
Email: ian.g.hogg@btinternet.com
Open: Easter to Oct

Orkney

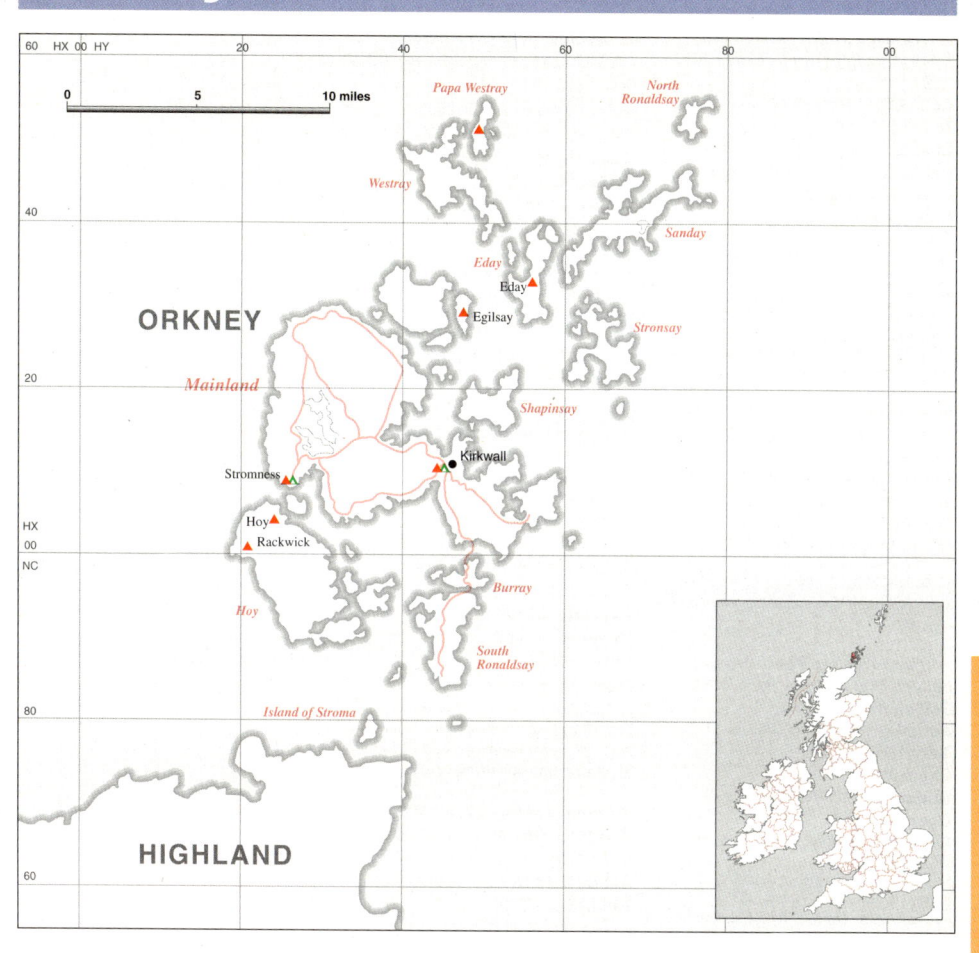

Eday
HY5531

▲ **Eday Youth Hostel,** London Bay, Eday, Orkney, KW17 2AB
Actual Grid Ref: HY562333
Tel: 01857 622206
Capacity: 24
Under 18: £6.25
Adults: £7.50
Open: March to Sep
Self-catering facilities • Shop 1 1/2 miles away
Eday, one of the Orkney Isles, offers numerous archaeological sites, standing stones and Iron Age houses as well as excellent birdwatching.

Egilsay
HY4730

▲ **The Egilsay Science Club,** Netherskaill, Egilsay, Orkney, KW17 2QD
Actual Grid Ref: HY462302
Tel: 01856 821357
Capacity: 5
Under 18: £2.50 **Adults:** £2.50
Open: All year, until last ferry
Camping for 10 tents: £1.50
Self-catering facilities • Laundry facilities • Wet weather shelter • Grounds available for games • Parking • Facilities for disabled people
Island's harbour frontage. Bring all food. Egilsay has no shop!

Hoy
HY2303

▲ **Hoy Youth Hostel,** Hoy, Stromness, Orkney, KW16 3NJ
Actual Grid Ref: HY233037
Tel: 01856 873535
Capacity: 26
Under 18: £6.25
Adults: £7.50
Open: May to Sep
Self-catering facilities • Facilities for disabled people
Hoy, with its magnificent cliff scenery, is the second largest island in the Orkneys. The Old Man of Hoy is a particular challenge to experienced climbers. No shop for 10 miles. Bed linen not provided.

Orkney • MAP PAGE 307

Kirkwall

HY4510

▲ **Kirkwall Youth Hostel,** Old Scarpa Road, Kirkwall, Orkney, KW15 1BB
Actual Grid Ref: HY444101
Tel: 01856 872243
Capacity: 90
Under 18: £7.75 **Adults:** £9.00
Open: March to Oct
Family bunk rooms
Self-catering facilities • Shop nearby • Laundry facilities • Facilities for disabled people
The capital of the Orkney Isles, Kirkwall is dominated by C12th St Magnus' Cathedral. Quiet sandy beach nearby. Guided historical and nature tours, daily ferries to islands.

▲ **Pickaquoy Caravan & Camp Site,** Pickaquoy Road, Kirkwall, Orkney, KW15 1RR
Actual Grid Ref: HY440115
Tel: 01856 873535
Fax: 01856 876227
Open: May to Sep

Papa Westray

HY4851

▲ **Papa Westray Youth Hostel,** Beltane House Hotel, Papa Westray, Orkney, KW17 2BU
Actual Grid Ref: HY493515
Tel: 01857 644267
Capacity: 16
Under 18: £6.25 **Adults:** £7.50
Open: All year
Self-catering facilities • Shop • Facilities for disabled people
For historians, the oldest dwelling in Europe is at Knap of Howar; for naturalists the North Hill bird sanctuary has Europe's largest colony of Arctic Terns, and seals are regular visitors too.

Rackwick (Hoy)

ND2099

▲ **Rackwick Youth Hostel,** Rackwick, Stromness, Orkney, KW16 3NJ
Actual Grid Ref: ND199998
Tel: 01856 873535 ext 2404
Capacity: 8
Under 18: £6.25
Adults: £7.50
Open: Mar to Sep
Self-catering facilities
Hostel in scenic Rackwick Valley area of Hoy, the second largest island in the Orkneys. The Old Man of Hoy is a particular challenge to experienced climbers. No shop for 15 miles. No bed linen provided.

Stromness

HY2509

▲ **Stromness Youth Hostel,** Hellihole Road, Stromness, Orkney, KW16 3DE
Actual Grid Ref: HY251088
Tel: 01856 850589
Capacity: 38
Under 18: £7.00
Adults: £8.25
Open: May to Oct
Self-catering facilities • Shop nearby
Fantastic coastal walks; huge variety of flora and fauna (seabirds, puffins, seals, Scottish primrose); diving and fishing.

▲ **Point of Ness Caravan & Camping Site,** Well Park, Ness Road, Stromness, Orkney, KW16 3DN
Actual Grid Ref: HY256079
Tel: 01856 873535
Fax: 01856 876227
Open: May to Sep

Perthshire & Kinross

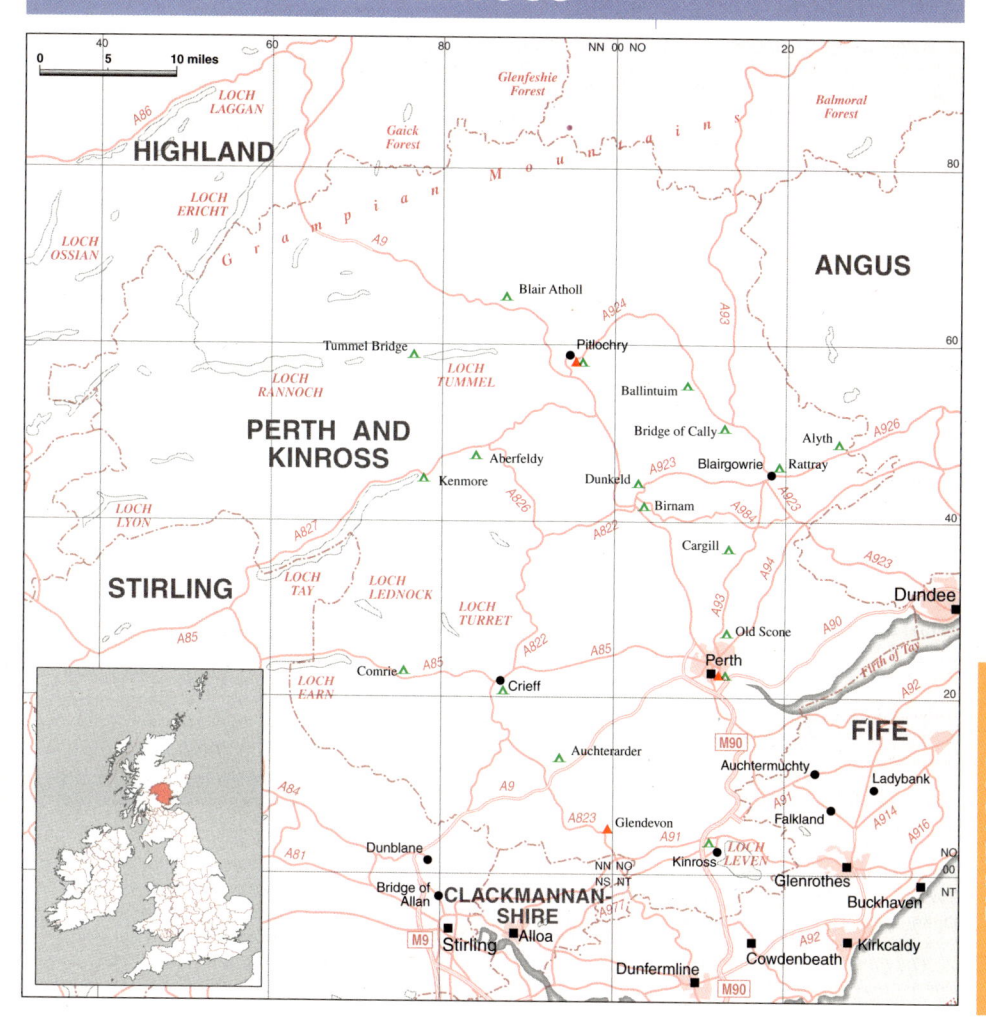

Aberfeldy

NN8549

▲ **Aberfeldy Caravan Park,**
Dunkeld Road, Aberfeldy, Perthshire,
PH15 2AQ
Actual Grid Ref: NN859494
Tel: 01887 820662
Open: Apr to Oct

Alyth

NO2448

▲ **Nether Craig Caravan Park,**
Alyth, Blairgowrie, Perthshire,
PH11 8HN
Actual Grid Ref: NO268528
Tel: 01575 560204 **Fax:** 01575 560315
Email: nethercraig@lineone.net
Open: Mar to Oct

Auchterarder

NN9412

▲ **Auchterarder Caravan Park,**
Auchterarder, Perthshire,
PH3 1ET
Actual Grid Ref: NN964137
Tel: 01764 663119
Open: All year

Perthshire & Kinross • MAP PAGE 309

Ballintuim
NO1054

▲ **Ballintuim Caravan Park,** Ballintuim, Bridge of Cally, Blairgowrie, Perthshire, PH10 7NH
Actual Grid Ref: NO103549
Tel: 01250 886276
Open: All year

Balloch
NO2828

▲ **Inchmartine Caravan Park & Nurseries,** Inchture, Perth, PH14 9QQ
Actual Grid Ref: NO263277
Tel: 01821 670212
Fax: 01821 670266
Open: Mar to Oct

Birnam
NO0341

▲ **Erigmore House Holiday Park,** Birnam, Dunkeld, Perthshire, PH8 9XX
Actual Grid Ref: NO036416
Tel: 01350 727236
Open: Mar to Oct

Blair Atholl
NN8764

▲ **Blair Castle Caravan Park,** Blair Atholl, Pitlochry, Perthshire, PH18 5SR
Actual Grid Ref: NN875652
Tel: 01796 481263
Open: Apr to Oct

▲ **The River Tilt Caravan Park,** Vale of Atholl Country Cottages, Bridge of Tilt, Blair Atholl, PH18 5TE
Actual Grid Ref: NN872656
Tel: 01796 481467
Open: Mar to Nov

Bridge of Cally
NO1351

▲ **Corriefodly Holiday Park,** Bridge of Cally, Blairgowrie, Perthshire, PH10 7JG
Actual Grid Ref: NO135514
Tel: 01250 886236
Open: Dec to Oct

Cargill
NO1537

▲ **Beech Hedge Caravan Park,** Cargill, Perth, PH2 6DU
Actual Grid Ref: NO165374
Tel: 01250 883249
Open: Apr to Oct

Comrie
NN7722

▲ **West Lodge Caravan Park,** Comrie, Crieff, Perthshire, PH6 2LS
Actual Grid Ref: NN784225
Tel: 01764 670354
Open: Apr to Jan

▲ **Twenty Shilling Wood Caravan Park,** Comrie, Crieff, PH6 2JY
Actual Grid Ref: NN762222
Tel: 01764 670411
Open: Mar to Oct

▲ **Riverside Caravan Park,** Comrie, Perthshire, PH6 2EA
Actual Grid Ref: NN780223
Tel: 01764 670555
Open: Apr to Oct

Crieff
NN8621

▲ **Thornhill Lodge Tenting Park,** Monzievaird, Crieff, Perthshire, PH7 4JU
Actual Grid Ref: NN822219
Tel: 01764 655382
Open: Apr to Oct

▲ **Crieff Holiday Village,** Somerton House, Turret Bank, Crieff, Perthshire, PH7 4JN
Actual Grid Ref: NN858226
Tel: 01764 653513
Open: All year

Dunkeld
NO0243

▲ **Kilvrecht Camping & Caravan Site,** Tay District Forestry Commission, Inver Park, Dunkeld, Perthshire, PH8 0JR
Actual Grid Ref: NO617566
Tel: 01350 727284
Fax: 01350 728635
Open: Apr to Sep

▲ **Inver Mill Farm Caravan Park,** Inver Mill, Dunkeld, Perthshire & Kinross, PH8 0JR
Actual Grid Ref: NO016420
Tel: 01350 727477
Open: Apr to Oct

Glendevon
NN9904

▲ **Glendevon Youth Hostel,** Glendevon, Dollar, Clackmannanshire, FK14 7JY
Actual Grid Ref: NN989046
Tel: 01259 781206
Capacity: 36
Under 18: £6.25
Adults: £7.50
Open: Mar to Oct
Family bunk rooms
Self-catering facilities • Shop 3 miles
The Ochil Hills offer beautiful scenery and ideal country for walking or cycling. Pony trekking in July and August.

Kenmore
NN7745

▲ **Kenmore Caravan & Camping Park,** Taymouth Farm, Mains of Taymouth, Kenmore, Aberfeldy, Perthshire, PH15 2HN
Actual Grid Ref: NN773458
Tel: 01887 830226
Open: Mar to Oct

Kinross
NO1102

▲ **Gairney Bridge Caravan Site,** Kinross, KY13 7JZ
Actual Grid Ref: NT129985
Tel: 01577 862336
Open: May to Oct

▲ **Gallowhill Farm Caravan Park,** Gallowhill Road, Kinross, KY13 7RD
Tel: 01577 862364
Open: Mar to Oct

MAP PAGE 309 • **Perthshire & Kinross**

Old Scone

NO1127

▲ **Camping & Caravanning Club Site,** Scone Palace Caravan Park, Old Scone, Perth, PH2 6BB
Tel: 01738 552323
Open: Mar to Oct

Perth

NO1123

▲ **Perth Youth Hostel,** Glasgow Road, Perth, PH2 0NS
Actual Grid Ref: NO103232
Tel: 01738 623658
Capacity: 62
Under 18: £7.50-£8.00
Adults: £8.75-£9.25
Open: March to Oct
Family bunk rooms
Self-catering facilities • Shop nearby • Laundry facilities
Ideal touring base in central location. Visit the art gallery, museum, theatre, sports centre, ice rink and harbour.

▲ **Cleeve Caravan Park,** Glasgow Road, Perth, PH2 0PH
Actual Grid Ref: NO096226
Tel: 01738 639521
Open: Apr to Oct

Pitlochry

NN9458

▲ **Pitlochry Youth Hostel,** Knockard Road, Pitlochry, PH16 5HJ
Actual Grid Ref: NN943584
Tel: 01796 472308
Capacity: 75
Under 18: £6.00-£8.25
Adults: £8.00-£9.50 **Open:** All year
Family bunk rooms
Self-catering facilities • Shop nearby • Laundry facilities • Evening meal available groups only
Pitlochry is a bustling small town at the very centre of Scotland. Scenic countryside ideal for climbing. The Festival Theatre is open May-October - outdoor shows all summer. The Highland Games are in September.

▲ **Milton of Fonab Caravan Site,** Pitlochry, PH16 5NA
Actual Grid Ref: NN945572
Tourist Board grade: 4 Star
Tel: 01796 472882 **Fax:** 01796 474363
Email: fonab@dial.pipex.com
Tent pitches: 30
Tent rate: £10.00-£10.50
Open: Mar to Oct **Last arr:** 9pm
Facilities for disabled people • Dogs allowed • Electric hook-up • Baths • Calor Gas/Camping Gaz • Showers • Laundrette on site • Public phone on site • Shop on site
Quiet family-run site; couples and families only.

▲ **Faskally Home Farm Caravan Site,** Pitlochry, PH16 5LA
Actual Grid Ref: NN922598
Tel: 01796 472007 **Fax:** 01796 474363
Email: ehay@easynet.co.uk
Open: Mar to Oct

▲ **Glengoulandie Farm Site,** Pitlochry, Perthshire, PH15 6NL
Tel: 01887 830261
Open: Apr to Oct

Rattray

NO1845

▲ **Blairgowrie Holiday Park,** Rattray, Blairgowrie, Perthshire, PH10 7AL
Actual Grid Ref: NO182460
Tel: 01250 872941
Email: blairgowrie@holiday-parks.co.uk
Open: All year

Tummel Bridge

NN7659

▲ **Tummel Valley Holiday Park,** Tummel Bridge, Pitlochry, Perthshire, PH16 5SA
Tel: 01862 634221 **Open:** Mar to Jan

▲ **Tummel Valley Holiday Park,** Tummel Bridge, Pitlochry, Perthshire, PH16 5SA
Actual Grid Ref: NN764592
Tel: 01882 634221
Fax: 01882 634302
Open: Mar to Oct

SCOTLAND

Shetland

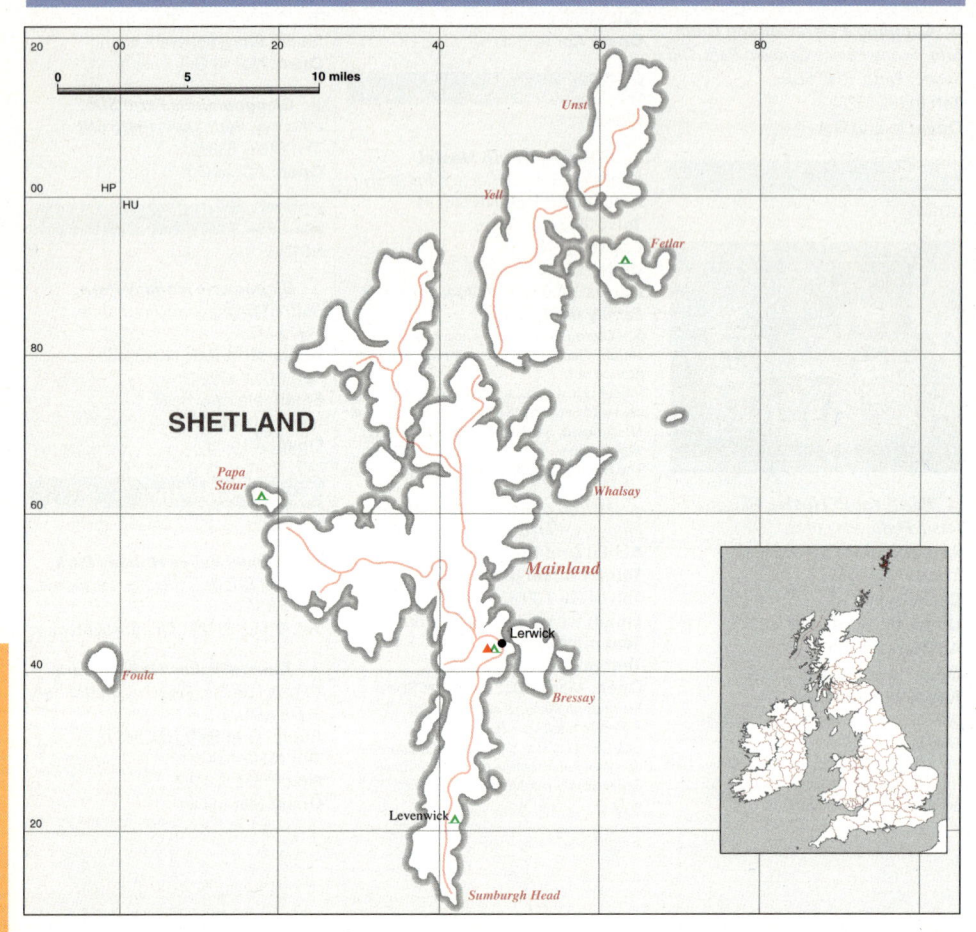

Fetlar
HU6291

▲ **The Garths Campsite,** Fetlar, Shetland, ZE2 9DJ
Actual Grid Ref: HU604916
Tel: 01957 733227
Fax: 01957 733227
Open: May to Sep

Lerwick
HU4741

▲ **Lerwick Youth Hostel,** Isleburgh House, King Harald Street, Lerwick, Shetland, ZE1 0EQ
Actual Grid Ref: HU473413
Tel: 01595 692114
Capacity: 64
Under 18: £6.50
Adults: £7.75
Open: Apr to Oct
Family bunk rooms
Self-catering facilities • Shop • Laundry facilities • Evening meal available • Facilities for disabled people
Beautifully refurbished hostel. Ideal centre to explore Shetland's historical sites. Wildlife in abundance. Warm welcome guaranteed.

▲ **Clickimin Camp Site,** Lochside, Lerwick, Shetland, ZE1 0PJ
Actual Grid Ref: HU466416
Tel: 01595 741000
Open: Apr to Oct

Levenwick
HU4021

▲ **Levenwick Campsite,** South Mainland, Shetland Islands, ZE1 0PJ
Actual Grid Ref: HU408215
Tel: 01950 422207
Open: Apr to Sep

Papa Stour
HU1660

▲ **Northouse,** Papa Stour, Shetland, ZE2 9PW
Tel: 01595 873238
Open: All year

Stirling & the Trossachs

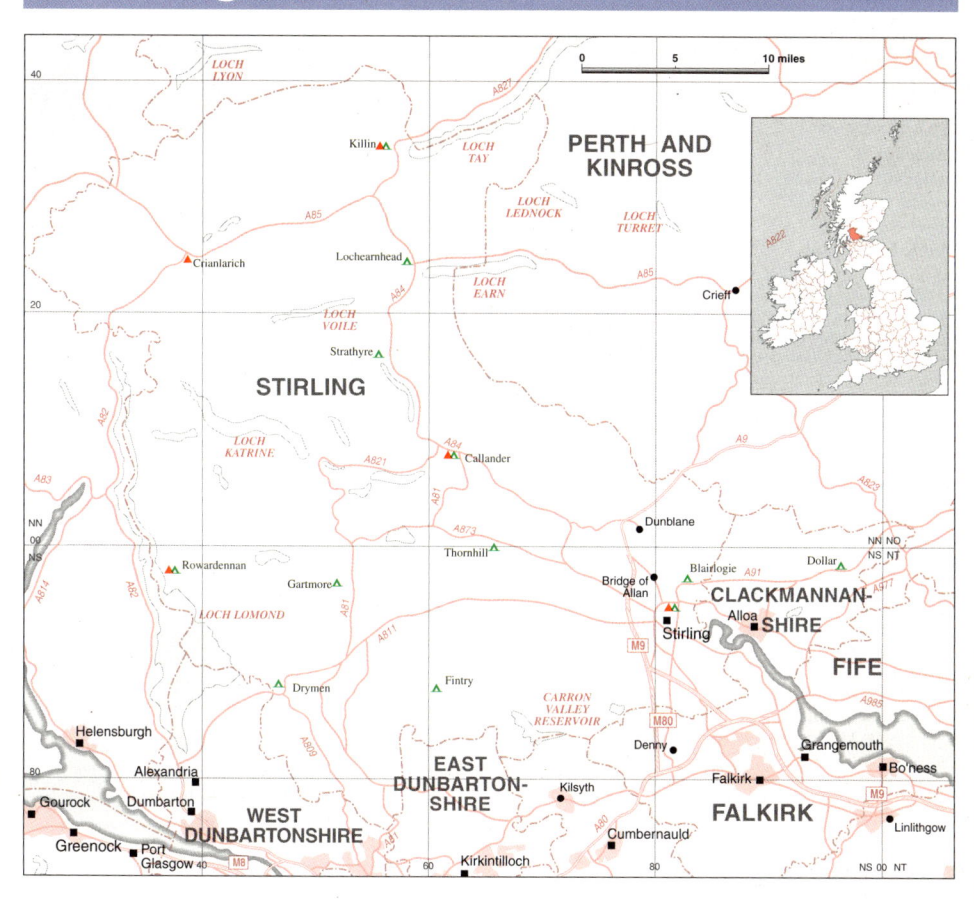

Blairlogie

NS8296

▲ **Witches Craig Caravan Park,**
Blairlogie, Stirling, FK9 5PX
Actual Grid Ref: NS822968
Tel: 01786 474947
Open: Apr to Oct

Callander

NN6307

▲ **Trossachs Backpackers,**
Invertrossachs Road, Callander, Perthshire, FK17 8HW
Actual Grid Ref: NN606072
Tel: 01877 331200
Fax: 01877 331200

Email: trosstel@aol.com
Capacity: 30
Under 18: £10.00-£15.00
Adults: £12.50-£15.00
Open: All year
Self-catering facilities • Television • Showers • Central heating • Shop • Laundry facilities • Wet weather shelter • Lounge • Dining room • Games room • Grounds available for games • Drying room • Cycle store • Parking • Facilities for disabled people • No smoking
Luxurious hostel in idyllic national park setting. Many local attractions.

Hostels and campsites may vary rates – be sure to check when booking.

▲ **Keltie Bridge Caravan Park,**
Keltie Bridge, Callander, FK17 8LQ
Tel: 01877 330811
Fax: 01877 330075
Open: Apr to Oct

▲ **Gart Caravan Park,** *Callander, FK17 8HW*
Actual Grid Ref: NN643070
Tel: 01877 330002
Open: Apr to Oct

You are advised to book in advance for periods of high demand – the Summer months, Half Term holidays and public holidays.

Stilwell's Hostels & Camping 2002

Stirling & the Trossachs • MAP PAGE 313

Crianlarich
NN3825

▲ **Crianlarich Youth Hostel,** Station Road, Crianlarich, Perthshire, FK20 8QN
Actual Grid Ref: NN386250
Tel: 01838 300260
Capacity: 76
Under 18: £6.00-£8.00
Adults: £9.25
Open: Feb to Dec
Family bunk rooms
Self-catering facilities • Shop • Laundry facilities • Facilities for disabled people
Crianlarich marks the halfway point of the West Highland Way; ideal stop for walkers and climbers. Trout fishing nearby. (No family rooms Jun-Aug.)

Dollar
NS9597

▲ **Riverside Caravan Park,** Dollar, Clackmannanshire, FK14 7LX
Actual Grid Ref: NS962970
Tel: 01259 742896
Open: Apr to Sep

Drymen
NS4788

▲ **Easter Drumquhassle Farm,** Gartness Road, Drymen, Glasgow, G63 0DN
Tel: 01360 660893
Fax: 01360 660282
Open: All year

Fintry
NS6186

▲ **Balgair Castle Caravan Park,** Overglinns, Fintry, Glasgow, G63 0LP
Actual Grid Ref: NS614885
Tel: 01360 860283
Fax: 01360 860200
Open: Mar to Oct

Gartmore
NS5297

▲ **Trossachs Holiday Park,** Gartmore, Aberfoyle, Stirling, FK8 3SA
Actual Grid Ref: NS537966
Tel: 01877 382614
Fax: 01877 382732
Open: Mar to Oct

▲ **Cobeland Caravan & Camping Site,** Gartmore, Aberfoyle, Stirling, FK8
Actual Grid Ref: NS532987
Tel: 01877 382392
Open: Easter to Oct

Killin
NN5732

▲ **Killin Youth Hostel,** Killin, Perthshire, FK21 8TN
Actual Grid Ref: NN569338
Tel: 01567 820546
Capacity: 42
Under 18: £6.00-£7.50
Adults: £8.75
Open: March to Oct
Self-catering facilities • Shop nearby • Facilities for disabled people
Picturesque Killin has the impressive Falls of Dochart and standing stones from the Bronze Age. Good walks with views of Ben Lawers and Loch Tay and a wide range of wildlife.

▲ **High Creagan Caravan Site,** High Creagan, Killin, Perthshire, FK21 8TX
Actual Grid Ref: NN594352
Tel: 01567 820449
Open: Apr to Oct

▲ **Cruachan Caravan & Camping Site,** Killin, Perthshire, FK21 8TY
Actual Grid Ref: NN613558
Tel: 01567 820302
Open: Apr to Oct

Lochearnhead
NN5823

▲ **Balquhidder Braes Caravan & Camping Park,** Balquidder Station, Lochearnhead, Perthshire, FK19 8NX
Actual Grid Ref: NN581218
Tel: 01567 830293
Open: Mar to Oct

Rowardennan
NS3598

▲ **Rowardennan Youth Hostel,** Rowardennan, Loch Lomond, Glasgow, G63 0AR
Actual Grid Ref: NS359992
Tel: 01360 870259
Capacity: 80
Under 18: £6.00-£7.00
Adults: £9.00-£9.50
Open: March to Oct
Family bunk rooms
Self-catering facilities • Shop • Evening meal available • Facilities for disabled people
Beautiful setting, right on the banks of Loch Lomond. Relax on the beach, go fishing, walk the West Highland Way or take a boat trip round the islands. National Nature Reserve and Queen Elizabeth Forest Park nearby.

▲ **Cashel Caravan & Campsite,** Rowardennan, Glasgow, G63 0AW
Actual Grid Ref: NS395941
Tel: 01360 870234
Open: Easter to Sep

Stirling
NS7993

▲ **Stirling Youth Hostel,** St John Street, Stirling, FK8 1EA
Tel: 01786 473442
Capacity: 126
Under 18: £8.00-£12.25
Adults: £10.00-£13.75
Open: All year
Family bunk rooms
Self-catering facilities • Shop nearby • Laundry facilities • Evening meal available groups only • Facilities for disabled people
Enjoy Stirling's dramatic skyline and history from this hostel in the heart of the town - the Castle, Guildhall and Tolbooth are all nearby. Excellent shopping and leisure facilities.

MAP PAGE 313 • **Stirling & the Trossachs**

▲ *Stirling Youth Hostel Annexe,*
Union Street, Stirling,
FK8 1NZ
Tel: 01786 473442
Capacity: 96
Under 18: £8.50
Adults: £10.00
Open: July to Aug
Family bunk rooms
Self-catering facilities • Shop nearby
Enjoy Stirling's dramatic skyline and history from this hostel in the heart of the town - the Castle, Guildhall and Tolbooth are all nearby. Excellent shopping and leisure facilities. The annexe is particularly suitable for families.

▲ *Auchenbowie Caravan Site,*
Auchenbowie, Stirling, FK7 8HE
Actual Grid Ref: NS795879
Tel: 01324 822141
Open: Apr to Oct

Strathyre
NN5617

▲ *Immervoulin Caravan & Camping Park,* Strathyre, Callander, Perthshire, FK18 8NJ
Actual Grid Ref: NN560164
Tel: 01877 384285
Open: Apr to Sep

Thornhill
NS6699

▲ *Mains Farm Camping,*
Thornhill, Stirling, FK8 3QR
Actual Grid Ref: NS663997
Tel: 01786 850605 **Fax:** 01786 850605
Tent pitches: 34
Tent rate: £5.00
Open: Apr to Oct **Last arr:** 10.30pm
Facilities for disabled people • Dogs allowed • Electric hook-up • Calor Gas/Camping Gaz • Cafe or Takeaway on site • Picnic/barbecue area on site • Children's play area • Showers • Public phone on site • Shop on site
Panoramic views. Near Loch Lomond/Trossachs National Park. Historic Stirling.

SCOTLAND

Stilwell's Hostels & Camping 2002 315

Western Isles

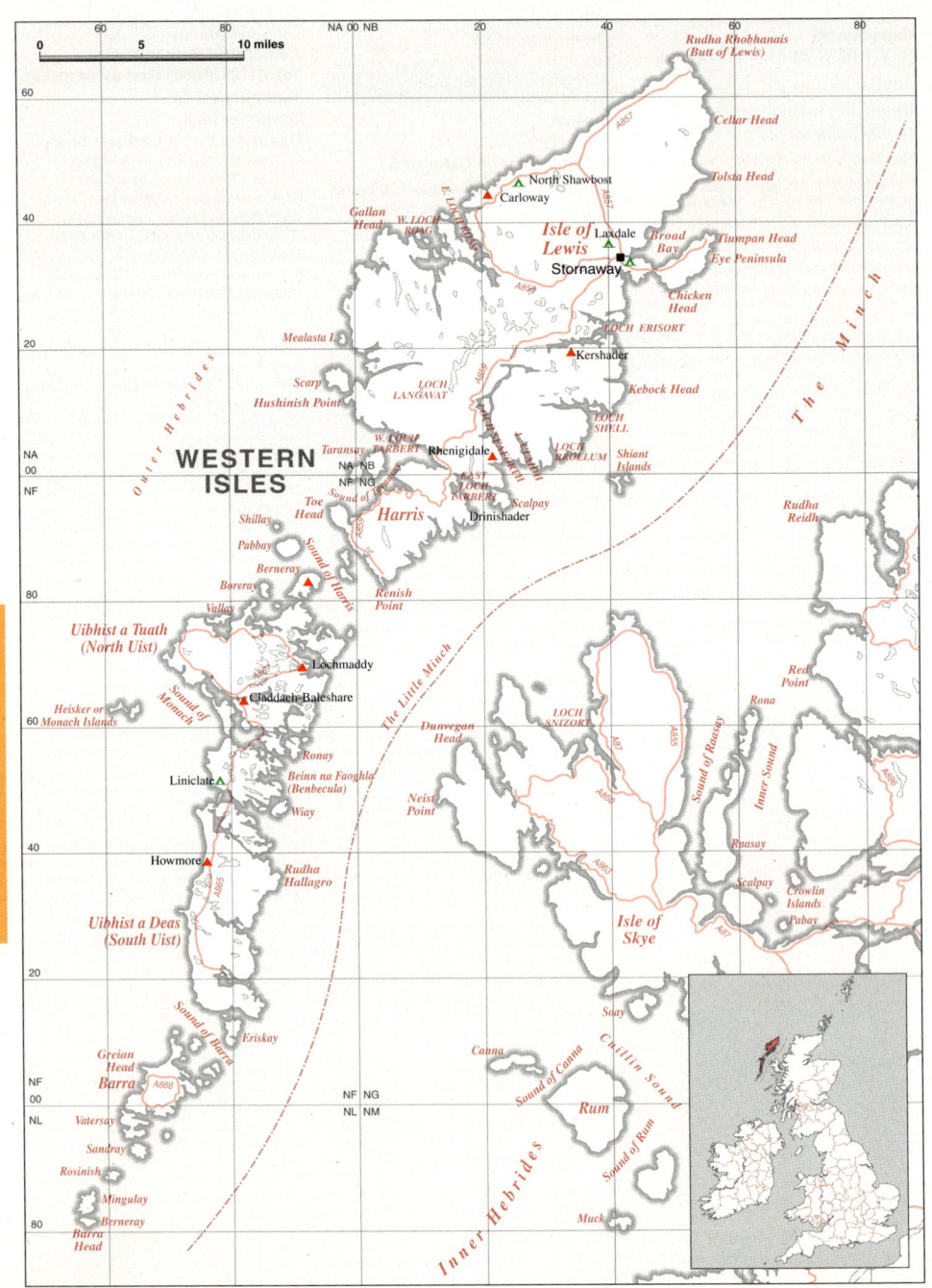

Western Isles

Benbecula - Liniclate
NF7849

▲ **Shell Bay Holiday Park**, Liniclate, Isle of Benbecula, HS7 5PJ
Actual Grid Ref: NF779500
Tel: 01870 602447 **Open:** Mar to Sept

Harris - Drinishader
NG1794

▲ **Minch View Caravan Site**, 10 Drinishader, Drinishader, Harris, Western Isles, HS3 3DX
Actual Grid Ref: NG173947
Tel: 01859 511207
Open: Apr to Sep

Harris - Kyles Stockinish
NG1391

▲ **Stockinish Youth Hostel**, Kyles Stockinish, Isle of Harris, HS3 3EN
Actual Grid Ref: NG136910
Tel: 01859 530373
Capacity: 32
Under 18: £6.25 **Adults:** £7.50
Open: Mar to Oct
Hostel on the East Coast of Harris with rocky hills and lochs, peace and quiet, bathing and fishing.

Harris - Rhenigidale
NB2201

▲ **Rhenigidale Youth Hostel**, Rhenigidale, Isle of Harris, HS3 3BD
Actual Grid Ref: NB229018
Tel: 08701 553255 (SYHA Central Booking Service)
Capacity: 11 **Under 18:** £6.25
Adults: £7.50 **Open:** All year
Self-catering facilities
Traditional croft house in a remote village overlooking the Minch. Clisham, the highest Hebridean peak, is 8 miles away. Excellent birdwatching, including golden eagles.

Lewis - Carloway
NB2042

▲ **Garenin Youth Hostel**, Carloway, Isle of Lewis, HS2 9AL

Actual Grid Ref: NB193442
Tel: 08701 553255 (SYHA Central Booking Service) **Capacity:** 14
Under 18: £6.25 **Adults:** £7.50
Open: All year
Self-catering facilities • Shop 1 mile away • Facilities for disabled people
Old black house restored by the Garenin Trust, in a village set in a peaceful bay on the rugged west coast of Lewis. No advance bookings accepted. No bed linen provided.

Lewis - Kershader
NB3320

▲ **Kershader Youth Hostel**, Ravenspoint, Kershader, Isle of Lewis, HS2 9QA
Actual Grid Ref: NB342203
Tel: 01851 880236 **Capacity:** 14
Under 18: £6.50 **Adults:** £7.75
Open: All year
Self-catering facilities • Shop • Laundry facilities
Peace and tranquillity on the Isle of Lewis. Hillwalking, watersports, and bird, otter and whale watching. Next door to cafe and craft shop.

Lewis - Laxdale
NB4234

▲ **Laxdale Holiday Park**, 6 Laxdale Lane, Laxdale, Isle of Lewis, HS2 0DR
Actual Grid Ref: NB423349
Tel: 01851 703234 **Email:** gordon@laxdaleholidaypark.force9.co.uk
Open: Mar to Oct

Lewis - North Shawbost
NB2647

▲ **Eilean Fraoich Camp Site**, North Shawbost, Isle of Lewis, HS2 9BQ
Actual Grid Ref: NB254464
Tel: 01851 710504 **Open:** May to Sep

Lewis - Stornoway
NB4232

▲ **Broadbay Caravans**, Broadbay, Stornoway, Isle of Lewis, HS2 0LT
Actual Grid Ref: NB462583
Tel: 01851 703561
Open: Apr to Sep

North Uist - Berneray
NF9282

▲ **Berneray Youth Hostel**, Isle of Berneray, Lochmaddy, North Uist, HS6 5BQ
Actual Grid Ref: NF932814

Tel: 08701 553255 (SYHA Central Booking Service) **Capacity:** 16
Under 18: £6.25 **Adults:** £7.50
Open: All year
Self-catering facilities
On beach overlooking the Sound of Harris. A walk around the island is only 8 miles. No advance bookings accepted. No bed linen provided.

North Uist - Claddach-Baleshare
NF8162

▲ **Taigh mo Sheanair Hostel**, Carnach, Claddach-Baleshare, Lochmaddy, Isle of North Uist, HS6 5ET
Actual Grid Ref: NF804637
Tel: 01876 580246 **Fax:** 01876 580246
Email: sheanair@hotmail.com
Capacity: 10
Under 18: £9.00 **Adults:** £9.00
Open: All year, all day
Camping for 6 tents: £8.00
Self-catering facilities • Showers • Central heating • Laundry facilities • Lounge • Grounds available for games • Parking • No smoking
Renovated traditional croft house on working croft. Extensive knowledge of local culture, traditions, genealogy.

North Uist - Lochmaddy
NF9168

▲ **Lochmaddy Youth Hostel**, Ostram House, Lochmaddy, North Uist, HS6 5AE
Actual Grid Ref: NF918687
Tel: 01876 500368
Capacity: 36
Under 18: £6.25 **Adults:** £7.50
Open: May to Oct
Sea bathing, archaeological excavations, Highland Games, local history and birdwatching are among the attractions of North Uist.

South Uist - Howmore
NF7536

▲ **Howmore Youth Hostel**, Howmore, Lochboisdale, South Uist, HS8 5SH
Actual Grid Ref: NF757265
Tel: 08701 553255 (SYHA Central Booking Service) **Capacity:** 17
Under 18: £6.25 **Adults:** £7.50
Open: All year
Self-catering facilities basic • Shop nearby
Small crofthouse, handy for the magnificent, peaceful island beaches. Good hillwalking. Loch Druidibeg nature reserve is nearby. No advance bookings accepted. Bring own quilted sleeping bag.

SCOTLAND

Stilwell's Hostels & Camping 2002

Anglesey

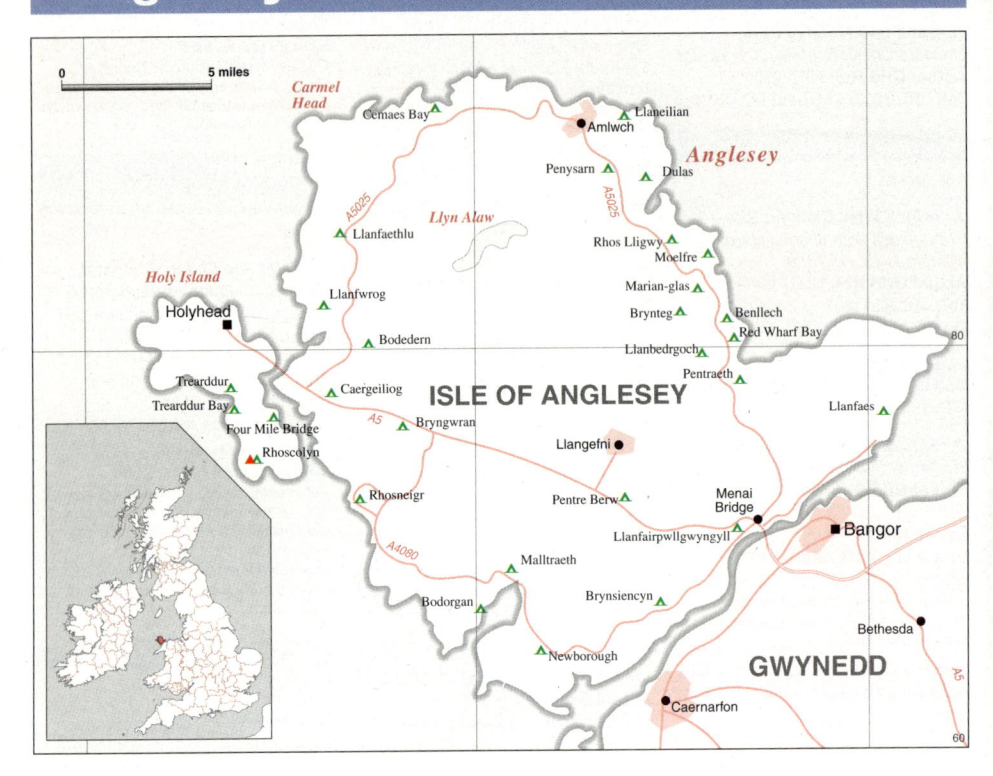

Benllech
SH5182

▲ **Bodafon Caravan & Camping Park,** Benllech, Tynygongl, Anglesey, LL74 8RU
Actual Grid Ref: SH516836
Tel: 01248 852417
Fax: 01248 852417
Tent pitches: 25
Tent rate: £5.00-£8.00
Open: Mar to Oct
Last arr: 9pm
Facilities for disabled people • Dogs allowed • Electric hook-up • Calor Gas/Camping Gaz • Showers • Public phone on site
Half mile from village. Close to sandy beach. Nice views.

▲ **Plas Uchaf Caravan & Camping Park,** Benllech Bay, Benllech, Tynygongl, Anglesey, LL74 8NU
Actual Grid Ref: SH509835
Tel: 01407 763012
Open: Mar to Oct

▲ **Bwlch Holiday Park,** Benllech, Tynygongl, Anglesey, LL74 8RF
Tel: 01248 852914
Open: Mar to Dec

▲ **Golden Sunset Holidays,** Benllech, Tynygongl, Anglesey, LL74 8SW
Tel: 01248 852345
Open: Easter to Oct

Bodedern
SH3380

▲ **Bodowyr Caravan and Camping Park,** Bodowyr, Bodedern, Holyhead, Anglesey, LL65 3SS
Actual Grid Ref: SH322792
Tel: 01407 741171
Email: bodowyr@yahoo.com
Tent pitches: 30
Tent rate: £5.00-£6.00
Open: Mar to Oct
Dogs allowed • Electric hook-up • Showers • Laundrette on site • Public phone on site • Children's play area • TV room • Indoor swimming pool nearby • Outdoor swimming pool nearby • Boating/sailing/watersports nearby • Tennis courts nearby • Golf nearby • Riding nearby • Fishing nearby
Bodowyr Farm is set in a lovely rural location about 6 miles from Holyhead, convenient for ferries/port. The site is level and grassy and the pitch fee includes free hot showers. Breakfast and evening meals available July/August. Ideal base for visiting Anglesey. Beaches within 2-3 miles.

Bodorgan
SH3867

▲ **Tregof Caravan Park,** Bodorgan, Anglesey, LL62 5EH
Tel: 01407 720315
Open: Mar to Oct

Hostels and campsites may vary rates – be sure to check when booking.

WALES

318   Stilwell's Hostels & Camping 2002

Anglesey

Bryngwran
SH3577

▲ **Tyn Llidiart Camping Site,** Towan Trewan, Bryngwran, Holyhead, Anglesey, LL65 3SW
Tel: 01407 810678
Open: All year

Brynsiencyn
SH4867

▲ **Fron Caravan & Camping Site,** Brynsiencyn, Llanfairpwllgwyngyll, Anglesey, LL61 6TX
Actual Grid Ref: SH472668
Tel: 01248 430310
Open: Apr to Sep

Brynteg
SH4983

▲ **Ad Astra Caravan Park,** Brynteg, Anglesey, LL78 7JH
Actual Grid Ref: SH489820
Tel: 01248 853283
Open: Mar to Oct

▲ **Glan Gors (Tyddyn Llwyd),** Brynteg, Anglesey, LL78 8QA
Actual Grid Ref: SH499819
Tel: 01248 852334
Open: Mar to Aug

▲ **Min-y-Ffrwd Caravan Park,** Brynteg, Anglesey, LL78 7JQ
Tel: 01248 852607
Open: Mar to Oct

▲ **Nant Newydd Park,** Brynteg, Anglesey, LL78 7JH
Actual Grid Ref: SH486816
Tel: 01248 852266 **Open:** Mar to Oct

▲ **Garnedd Touring & Camping Site,** Long Bryn Mair, Brynteg, Anglesey, LL78 8QA
Actual Grid Ref: SH495818
Tel: 01248 853240
Open: Mar to Oct

▲ **Ysgubor Fadog Caravan & Camping Site,** Brynteg, Isle of Anglesey, LL78 8QA
Actual Grid Ref: SH497819
Tel: 01248 852681
Open: Apr to Sep

▲ **Pen Parc Caravan Park,** Brynteg, Benllech, Isle of Anglesey, LL78 8JG
Actual Grid Ref: SH495833
Tel: 01248 852500 **Open:** All year

Caergeiliog
SH3178

▲ **Alltwen Goch,** Caergeiliog, Isle of Anglesey, LL65 3DX
Actual Grid Ref: SH332778
Tel: 01407 741289
Open: All year

Cemaes Bay
SH3694

▲ **Park Lodge,** Cemaes Bay, Anglesey, LL67 0HF
Actual Grid Ref: SH365935
Tel: 01407 710103
Open: Mar to Oct

Dulas
SH4789

▲ **Tyddyn Isaf Camping & Caravan Site,** Dulas, Anglesey, LL70 9PQ
Actual Grid Ref: SH486874
Tel: 01248 410203
Fax: 01248 410667
Open: Mar to Oct

▲ **Green Acres,** Dulas, Anglesey, LL70 9DZ
Tel: 01248 410471
Open: Mar to Sept

▲ **Melin Rhos Farm Caravan & Camping Site,** Lligwy Bay, Dulas, Anglesey, LL70 9HQ
Actual Grid Ref: SH493864
Tel: 01248 410213
Open: Apr to Oct

▲ **Capel Elen Caravan Park,** Lligwy Beach, Dulas, Isle of Anglesey, LL70 9PQ
Actual Grid Ref: SH484874
Tel: 01248 410670 **Open:** Mar to Oct

▲ **Tan-y-Banc Camping Park,** Dulas, Isle of Anglesey, LL70 9PQ
Actual Grid Ref: SH488884
Tel: 01248 410504
Open: All year

Four Mile Bridge
SH2778

▲ **Pen-y-Bont Farm,** Four Mile Bridge, Valley, Holyhead, Anglesey, LL65 3EY
Actual Grid Ref: SH282787
Tel: 01407 740481
Open: May to Oct

Llanbedrgoch
SH5080

▲ **Ty Newydd Caravan & Country Club,** Llanbedrgoch, Anglesey, LL76 8TZ
Actual Grid Ref: SH509812
Tel: 01248 450677
Fax: 01248 450711
Open: Mar to Oct

Llaneilian
SH4693

▲ **Plas Ellian,** Llaneilian, Amlwch, Anglesey, LL68 9LS
Actual Grid Ref: SH469929
Tel: 01407 830323
Open: May to Oct

▲ **Point Lynas Caravan Park,** Llaneilian, Amlwch, Anglesey, LL68 9LT
Actual Grid Ref: SH474930
Tel: 01407 831130
Open: Mar to Oct

Llanfaes
SH6078

▲ **Kingsbridge Caravan Park,** Llanfaes, Beaumaris, Anglesey, LL58 8LR
Actual Grid Ref: SH606785
Tel: 01248 490636
Open: Mar to Oct

Llanfaethlu
SH3187

▲ **Graenfa,** Llanfaethlu, Holyhead, Anglesey, LL65 4NL
Actual Grid Ref: SH320855
Tel: 01407 730274
Open: Apr to Oct

Llanfairpwllgwyngyll
SH5372

▲ **Plas Coch Caravan & Leisure Park,** Llanedwen, Llanfairpwllgwyngyll, Anglesey, LL61 6EZ
Tel: 01248 714346
Tent pitches: 100
Tent rate: £8.00
Open: Mar to Oct
Dogs allowed • Electric hook-up • Children's play area • Showers • Public phone on site • Licensed bar on site
Half hour drive from Irish ferry terminal. 2 miles mainline rail station.

WALES

Stilwell's Hostels & Camping 2002 319

Anglesey • MAP PAGE 318

Llanfwrog

SH3084

▲ **Penrhyn Bay Caravan & Camping Site,** Llanfwrog, Holyhead, Anglesey, LL65 4YG
Actual Grid Ref: SH287840
Tel: 01407 730496
Open: Apr to Oct

▲ **Sandy Beach Camping Site,** Porth Tywyn Mawr, Llanfwrog, Holyhead, Anglesey, LL65 4YH
Actual Grid Ref: SH286848
Tel: 01407 730302
Open: Apr to Oct

Malltraeth

SH4068

▲ **Pen-y-Bont Touring Site,** Malltraeth, Bodorgan, Anglesey, LL62 5BA
Actual Grid Ref: SH417686
Tel: 01407 840209
Open: Apr to Sep

Marian-glas

SH5084

▲ **Home Farm Caravan Park,** Marianglas, Anglesey, LL73 8PH
Actual Grid Ref: SH495850
Tel: 01248 410614
Open: Apr to Oct

Moelfre

SH5186

▲ **Tyn Rhos,** Lligwy, Moelfre, Isle of Anglesey, LL72 8NL
Actual Grid Ref: SH499865
Tel: 01248 410808
Open: All year

▲ **Nant Bychan Farm,** Moelfre, Isle of Anglesey, LL72 8HE
Actual Grid Ref: SH507854
Tel: 01248 410269
Open: May to Sep

Newborough

SH4265

▲ **Awelfryn Caravan Park,** Newborough, Llanfairpwllgwyngyll, Anglesey, LL61 6SG
Actual Grid Ref: SH419653
Tel: 01248 440210
Open: Apr to Sep

Pentraeth

SH5278

▲ **Rhos Caravan Park,** Pentraeth, Anglesey, LL75 8DZ
Actual Grid Ref: SH518794
Tel: 01248 450214
Fax: 01248 450214
Open: Mar to Oct

Pentre Berw

SH4772

▲ **Mornest Caravan Park,** Pentre Berw, Ynys Mon, Gaerwen, Anglesey, LL60 6HU
Actual Grid Ref: SH473722
Tel: 01248 421249
Open: Apr to Oct

Penysarn

SH4590

▲ **Tyn Rhos Farm,** Penysarn, Amlwch, Anglesey, LL69 9YR
Actual Grid Ref: SH462902
Tel: 01407 830574
Open: May to Sep

Red Wharf Bay

SH5281

▲ **St David's Estate Caravan Park,** Red Wharf Bay, Isle of Anglesey, LL75 8RJ
Actual Grid Ref: SH531818
Tel: 01248 852341
Fax: 01248 852777
Open: Mar to Oct

Rhos Lligwy

SH4886

▲ **Bronllwyn,** Rhos Lligwy, Dulas, Anglesey, LL70 9HX
Tel: 01248 410758
Open: Mar to Oct

You are advised to book in advance for periods of high demand – the Summer months, Half Term holidays and public holidays.

Rhoscolyn

SH2675

▲ **Outdoor Alternative Hostel,** Cerrig-yr-Adar, Rhoscolyn, Holyhead, Anglesey, LL65 2NQ
Actual Grid Ref: SH278752
Tel: 01407 860469
Fax: 01407 860469
Email: centre@outdooralternative.org
Capacity: 36
Adults: £10.95
Open: All year, any time
Family bunk rooms: £32.00
Camping for 20 tents: £6.00
Self-catering facilities • Showers • Central heating • Wet weather shelter • Lounge • Dining room • Grounds available for games • Drying room • Cycle store • Parking • Evening meal available by arrangement • Facilities for disabled people • No smoking
Comfortable accommodation facility for groups using outdoors, 300m from sea.

▲ **Silver Bay Caravan Park,** Pentre Gwyddel, Rhoscolyn, Holyhead, Anglesey, LL65 2RZ
Actual Grid Ref: SH287753
Tel: 01407 860374
Open: Apr to Oct

▲ **Penrhosedd,** Bryngoleu Farm, Rhoscolyn, Isle of Anglesey, LL65 2SJ
Actual Grid Ref: SH762272
Tel: 01407 860413
Open: Apr to Oct

Rhosneigr

SH3273

▲ **Plas Caravan Park,** Llanfaelog, Rhosneigr, Anglesey, LL63 5TU
Actual Grid Ref: SH331738
Tel: 01407 810234
Fax: 01407 811052
Email: gail@plascaravanpark.co.uk
Tent pitches: 17
Tent rate: £9.25-£12.75
Open: Mar to Oct
Last arr: 10pm
Dogs allowed • Electric hook-up • Showers • Laundrette on site • Public phone on site
Family-run park, rural surroundings, Rhosneigr and Llanfaelog beaches close by.

▲ **Bodfan Farm,** Rhosneigr, Anglesey, LL64 5XA
Tel: 01407 810563
Open: Apr to Sep

Anglesey

▲ **Shoreside Camp & Caravan Site,** Crigyll View, Station Road, Rhosneigr, Anglesey, LL64 5QX
Actual Grid Ref: SH324737
Tel: 01407 810279
Open: Apr to Sep

▲ **Ty Hen Touring & Holiday Park,** Rhosneigr, Anglesey, LL64 5QZ
Actual Grid Ref: SH323737
Tel: 01407 810331
Open: Mar to Oct

Trearddur
SH2579

▲ **Tyn Rhos Camping Site,** Ravenspoint Road, Trearddur Bay, Holyhead, LL65 2AZ
Actual Grid Ref: SH258778
Tel: 01407 860369
Open: Mar to Oct

All details shown are as supplied by hostels and campsites in Autumn 2000.

Trearddur Bay
SH2578

▲ **Bagnol Caravan Park,** Ravens Point Road, Trearddur Bay, Holyhead, Anglesey, LL65 2AZ
Actual Grid Ref: SH260780
Tel: 01407 860223 **Open:** Mar to Oct

▲ **Valley of the Rocks Camping & Caravan Park,** Porthdafarch Road, Trearddur Bay, Holyhead, Anglesey, LL65 2LL
Tel: 01407 765787
Open: Mar to Oct

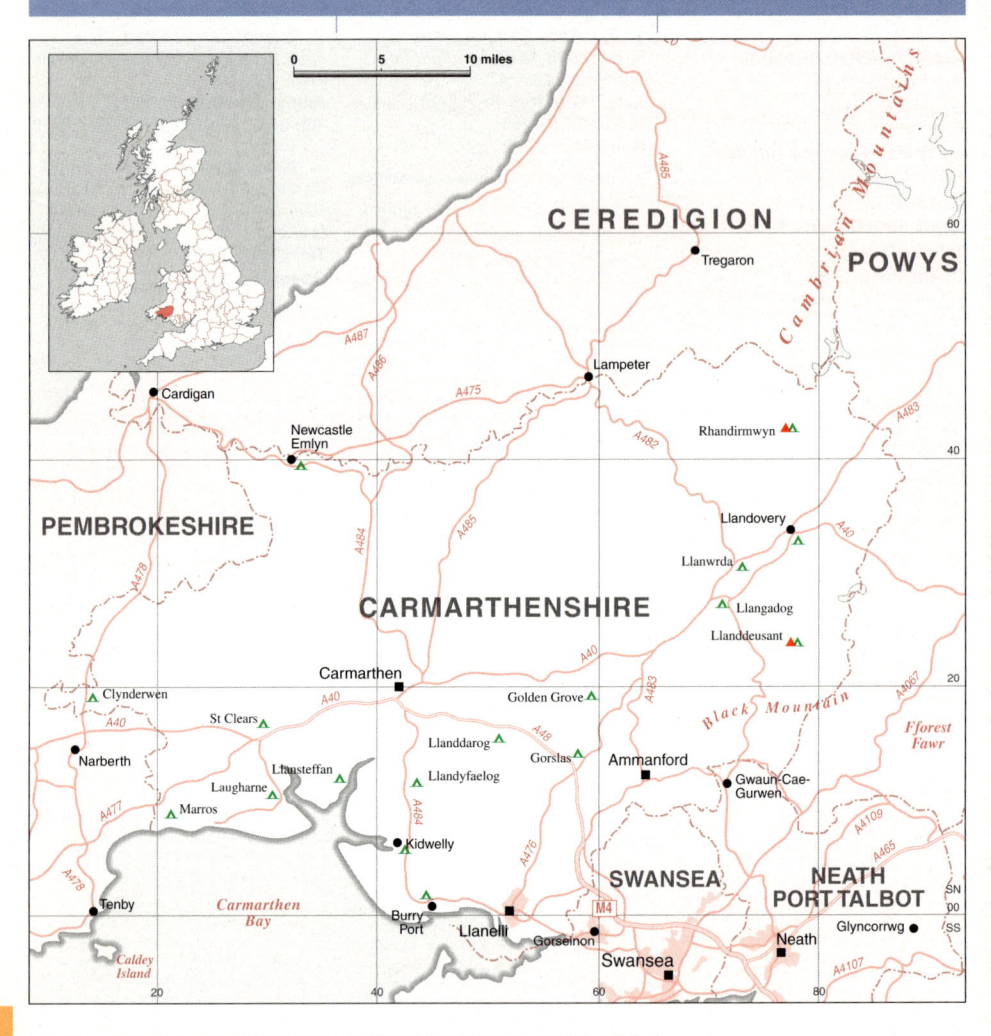

Carmarthenshire

Burry Port
SN4401

▲ **Shoreline Caravan & Chalet Park,** Burry Port, Llanelli, Carmarthenshire, SA16 0HD
Tel: 01554 832657
Open: Mar to Nov

Clynderwen
SN1219

▲ **Derwenlas Caravan Park,** Clynderwen, Narberth, Carmarthenshire, SA66 7SU
Actual Grid Ref: SN122205
Tel: 01437 563504 **Open:** Mar to Oct

▲ **Llandissilio Caravan Park,** Clynderwen, Pembrokeshire, SA66 7TT
Actual Grid Ref: SN122222
Tel: 01437 563408
Open: Mar to Oct

Golden Grove
SN5919

▲ **Grove Hill B&B,** Golden Grove, Carmarthen, SA32 8NW
Tel: 01558 823576
Open: All year

Hostels and campsites may vary rates – be sure to check when booking.

All details shown are as supplied by hostels and campsites in Autumn 2000.

Carmarthenshire

Gorslas
SN5713

▲ **Black Lion Caravan Park,** 78 Black Lion Road, Gorslas, Cross Hands, Llanelli, Carmarthenshire, SA14 6RU
Actual Grid Ref: SN519161
Tel: 01269 845365
Open: Mar to Jan

Kidwelly
SN4006

▲ **Carmarthen Bay Touring & Camping Site,** Tanylan Farm, Kidwelly, Carmarthenshire, SA17 5HJ
Tel: 01267 267306
Open: Easter to Sep

Laugharne
SN3010

▲ **Ants Hill Caravan & Camping Park,** Laugharne, Carmarthen, SA33 4QN
Actual Grid Ref: SN300118
Tourist Board grade: 3 Ticks
Tel: 01994 427293
Fax: 01994 427293
Email: antshill@tinyworld.co.uk
Tent pitches: 20
Tent rate: £6.00-£10.00
Open: Mar to Oct **Last arr:** 11pm
Dogs allowed • Electric hook-up • Calor Gas/Camping Gaz • Cafe or Takeaway on site • Children's play area • Showers • Laundrette on site • Public phone on site • Licensed bar on site • Shop on site • TV room • Games room • Outdoor swimming pool on site • Boating/sailing/watersports nearby • Golf nearby • Riding nearby • Fishing nearby
Beautifully landscaped park in Dylan Thomas's countryside and near the famous golden sands of Pendine. Well-maintained park with all amenities, ideal for both inland and coastal touring.

▲ **Broadway Caravan & Camping Park,** Laugharne, Carmarthen, SA33 4NU
Tel: 01994 427272
Open: Mar to Oct

Llanddarog
SN5016

▲ **Coedhirion Farm,** Llanddarog, Carmarthen, Carmarthenshire, SA32 8BH
Actual Grid Ref: SN516163
Tel: 01267 275666
Open: Mar to Dec

Llanddeusant
SN7724

▲ **Llanddeusant Youth Hostel,** The Old Red Lion, Llanddeusant, Llangadog, Carmarthenshire, SA19 6UL
Actual Grid Ref: SN776245
Tel: 01550 740218
Capacity: 28
Under 18: £5.75
Adults: £8.50
Open: Apr to Oct, 5.00pm
Camping
Self-catering facilities • Showers • Lounge • Drying room • Cycle store • Parking • No smoking • Kitchen facilities
A simple traditional hostel converted from an inn, overlooking Sawdde Valley. The area has Roman and Iron Age remains. There is an open fire in the hostel lounge.

▲ **Cross Inn & Black Mountain Caravan Park,** Llanddeusant, Llangadog, Carmarthenshire, SA19 9YG
Actual Grid Ref: SN773258
Tel: 01550 740621
Open: All year

▲ **Blaenau Farm,** Llanddeusant, Llangadog, Carmarthenshire, SA19 9UN
Tel: 01550 740277
Open: Easter to Oct

▲ **The Pont Aber Inn,** Gwynfe, Llanddeusant, Llangadog, Carmarthenshire, SA19 9TA
Tel: 01550 740202
Open: Easter to Oct

Llandovery
SN7634

▲ **Erwlon Caravan & Camping Park,** Llandovery, Carmarthenshire, SA20 0RD
Actual Grid Ref: SN779543
Tel: 01550 720332
Open: All year

Llandyfaelog
SN4111

▲ **Creative Journeys Enterprises Ltd,** Ystrad Fach Farm, Llandyfaelog, Kidwelly, Carmarthenshire, SA17 5NY
Actual Grid Ref: SN4111
Tel: 01269 861170
Fax: 01269 861170
Tent pitches: 3

Tent rate: £4.00-£5.00
Open: Mar to Oct
Last arr: 9pm
Facilities for disabled people • Dogs allowed • Running water • WC • Camper vans accepted • Cars accepted • Motorcycles accepted • Adjacent parking • Electric hook-up • Children's play area • Public phone on site • Shop on site
Tranquil farm surroundings between Carmarthen and Kidwelly. Superb views. Walks.

Llangadog
SN7028

▲ **Abermarlais Caravan Park,** Llangadog, Carmarthenshire, SA19 9NG
Actual Grid Ref: SN695298
Tel: 01550 777868
Open: Feb to Dec

Llansteffan
SN3510

▲ **Sunrise Bay Holiday Park,** Llansteffan, Carmarthen, SA33 5LP
Tel: 01267 241394
Open: Apr to Oct

Llanwrda
SN7131

▲ **Maesbach Caravan Park,** Farmers, Llanwrda, Carmarthenshire, SA19 8EX
Actual Grid Ref: SN661452
Tel: 01558 650413
Email: hugh.t.thomas@talk21.com
Tent pitches: 20
Tent rate: £6.00
Open: Apr to Oct
Last arr: 10pm
Dogs allowed • Electric hook-up • Calor Gas/Camping Gaz • Showers
Open rural views in red kite country. Peace lover's paradise.

▲ **Penlanwen,** Llanwrda, Carmarthenshire, SA19 8RR
Tel: 01558 650667
Open: All year

▲ **Llandovery Rugby Club,** Dan-y-Coed, Llanwrda, Llandovery, Carmarthenshire, SA20 0EE
Actual Grid Ref: SN760340
Tel: 01550 721110
Open: All year

Carmarthenshire • MAP PAGE 322

Marros

SN2008

▲ **Springfield Site,** Marros, Pendine, Pembrokeshire, SA33 4PW
Actual Grid Ref: SN195088
Tel: 01994 453208
Open: Apr to Oct

Newcastle Emlyn

SN3040

▲ **Afon Teifi Caravan & Camping Park,** Pentre Cagal, Newcastle Emlyn, Carmarthenshire, SA38 9HT
Actual Grid Ref: SN335405
Tel: 01559 370532
Open: Mar to Nov

▲ **Dolbryn Farm Camp Site,** Capel Iwan Road, Newcastle Emlyn, Carmarthenshire, SA38 9LP
Actual Grid Ref: SN296384
Tel: 01239 710683
Open: Apr to Oct

▲ **Moelfryn Caravan and Camping Park,** Pant-y-Bwlch, Newcastle Emlyn, Carmarthenshire, SA38 9JE
Tel: 01559 371231
Email: moelfryn@tinyonline.co.uk
Open: Mar to Jan

Rhandirmwyn

SN7843

▲ **Bryn Poeth Uchaf Youth Hostel,** Hafod-y-Pant, Rhandirmwyn, Cynghordy, Llandovery, Carmarthenshire, SA20 0NB
Actual Grid Ref: SN796439
Tel: 01550 750235
Capacity: 22
Under 18: £4.65
Adults: £6.80
Open: Apr to Sep
No smoking
Formerly an old farmhouse, this hostel is quite simple and isolated, but provides great views back to the Brecon Beacons.

▲ **Camping & Caravanning Club Site,** Rhandirmwyn, Llandovery, Carmarthenshire, SA20 0NT
Actual Grid Ref: SN779435
Tel: 01550 760257
Open: Mar to Oct

▲ **Clynmawr,** Rhandirmwyn, Llandovery, Carmarthenshire, SA20 0NG
Tel: 01550 20462 **Open:** Apr to Oct

▲ **Galltyberau,** Rhandirmwyn, Llandovery, Carmarthenshire, SA20 0PH
Actual Grid Ref: SN772458
Tel: 01550 760218
Open: Mar to Oct

St Clears

SN2716

▲ **Parciau Bach Caravan & Camping Park,** St Clears, Carmarthen, SA33 4LG
Actual Grid Ref: SN275198
Tel: 01994 230647
Open: Mar to Jan

Ceredigion

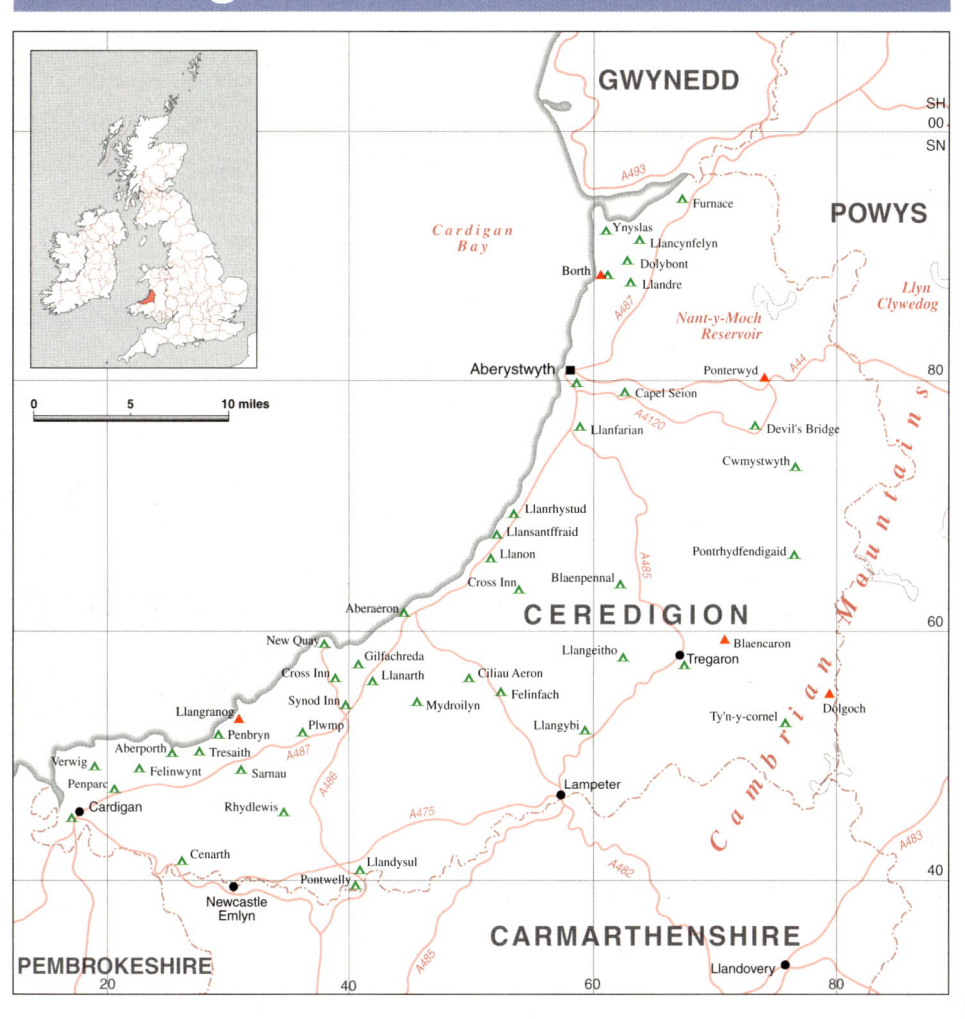

Aberaeron
SN4562

▲ **Aeron Coast Caravan Park,** North Road, Aberaeron, Ceredigion, SA46 0JF
Actual Grid Ref: SN460632
Tel: 01545 570349
Open: Apr to Oct

Aberporth
SN2651

▲ **Dolgelynen,** Aberporth, Cardigan, SA43 2HS
Actual Grid Ref: SN271508
Tel: 01239 811095
Open: Apr to Oct

Aberystwyth
SN5881

▲ **Aberystwyth Holiday Village,** Penparcau Road, Aberystwyth, Ceredigion, SY23 1BP
Actual Grid Ref: SN585811
Tel: 01970 624211
Open: Mar to Oct

Ceredigion • MAP PAGE 325

▲ **Bryncarnedd Caravan Park,**
Clarach Road, Aberystwyth,
Ceredigion, SY23 3DG
Actual Grid Ref: SN602830
Tel: 01970 615271 **Open:** All year

▲ **Glan-y-Mor Leisure Park,**
Clarach Bay, Aberystwyth,
Ceredigion, SY23 3DT
Actual Grid Ref: SN587841
Tel: 01970 828900
Email: holidays-in-wales@sunbourne.co.uk
Open: Mar to Oct

▲ **Midfield Caravan Park,**
Southgate, Aberystwyth, Ceredigion,
SY23 4DX
Actual Grid Ref: SN594798
Tel: 01970 612542
Open: Mar to Oct

▲ **Ocean View Caravan Park,**
North Beach, Clarach Bay,
Aberystwyth, Ceredigion, SY23 3DL
Actual Grid Ref: SN591842
Tel: 01970 828425
Email: alan@grover10.freeserve.co.uk
Open: Apr to Oct

Blaencaron

SN7160

▲ **Blaencaron Youth Hostel,**
Blaencaron, Tregaron,
Cardiganshire, SY25 6HL
Actual Grid Ref: SN713608
Tel: 01974 298441 **Capacity:** 16
Under 18: £4.75 **Adults:** £6.75
Open: Apr to Sep, 5.00pm
Camping
Self-catering facilities • Showers • Drying room • Cycle store • Parking • No smoking • WC • Kitchen facilities
Old village school set in the unspoilt Afon Groes Valley, west of the Cambrian Mountains.

Blaenpennal

SN6364

▲ **Aeron View Caravan Park,**
Blaenpennal, Aberystwyth,
Ceredigion, SY23 4TW
Actual Grid Ref: SN633643
Tel: 01974 251488
Open: Mar to Oct

Borth

SN6089

▲ **Borth Youth Hostel,** Morlais,
Borth, Ceredigion, SY24 5JS
Actual Grid Ref: SN608907
Tel: 01970 871498
Fax: 01970 871827
Email: borth@yha.org.uk
Capacity: 60
Under 18: £6.90
Adults: £10.00
Open: All year, 5.00pm
Family bunk rooms
Self-catering facilities • Television • Showers • Shop • Lounge • Dining room • Games room • Drying room • Cycle store • Parking • Evening meal available 5.30-7.30pm • WC • Kitchen facilities • Breakfast available • Credit cards accepted
Edwardian house overlooking the sea and just across the road from the beach and within 10 miles of Aberystwyth and not far from the Centre for Alternative Technology. From the hostel, you can walk to The Animalarium, Fast Trax and Ynyslas Nature Reserve.

▲ **Glanlerry Caravan Park,**
Glanywern, Borth, Ceredigion, SY254 5LU
Actual Grid Ref: SN617886
Tel: 01970 871413
Open: Mar to Oct

▲ **Brynrodyn Caravan & Leisure Park,** Borth, Ceredigion, SY24 5NR
Actual Grid Ref: SN608908
Tel: 01970 871472
Open: Mar to Oct

▲ **Brynowen Holiday Village,**
Borth, Aberystwyth, Ceredigion,
SY24 5IS
Actual Grid Ref: SN612887
Tel: 01970 871366
Open: Apr to Oct

Capel Seion

SN6379

▲ **Pantmawr Camping Site,**
Pisgah, Capel Seion, Aberystwyth,
Ceredigion, SY23 4ED
Tel: 01970 84449
Open: Easter to Oct

▲ **Pantmawr,** Pisgah, Capel Seion,
Aberystwyth, Ceredigion, SY23 4NE
Actual Grid Ref: SN688783
Tel: 01970 880449
Open: Mar to Oct

Cardigan

SN1746

▲ **Camping Blaenwaun,** Mwnt,
Cardigan, SA43 1QF
Actual Grid Ref: SN204513
Tel: 01239 612165
Open: Mar to Sept

▲ **Plas Y Wern,** Tanygroes,
Cardigan, SA43 2JP
Tel: 01239 811506
Fax: 01239 811506
Open: Easter to Oct

Cenarth

SN2641

▲ **Cenarth Falls Holiday Park,**
Cenarth, Newcastle Emlyn,
Carmarthenshire, SA38 9JS
Actual Grid Ref: SN267421
Tel: 01239 710345
Fax: 01239 710345
Email: cenarth.falls@sagnet.co.uk
Open: Mar to Jan

Ciliau Aeron

SN5058

▲ **Tan-yr-allt Farm,** Ciliau-Aeron,
Lampeter, Ceredigion, SA48 8BU
Actual Grid Ref: SN513586
Tel: 01570 470211
Open: All year

Cross Inn (Nebo)

SN5464

▲ **Brynarian Caravan Park,** Cross
Inn, Llanon, Carmarthenshire, SY23 5NA
Actual Grid Ref: SN540646
Tel: 01974 272231
Open: Mar to Oct

Cross Inn (New Quay)

SN3856

▲ **Pencnwc Holiday Park,** Cross
Inn, Llandysul, Ceredigion, SA44 6NL
Actual Grid Ref: SN386563
Tel: 01545 560479
Open: Mar to Jan

▲ **Penion Caravan Park,** Cross
Inn, Llandysul, Ceredigion, SA44 6JY
Tel: 01545 560620
Open: Mar to Oct

MAP PAGE 325 • **Ceredigion**

Cwmystwyth

SN7874

▲ **Tyllwyd,** Cwmystwyth, Aberystwyth, Cardiganshire, SY23 4AG
Actual Grid Ref: SN822752
Tel: 01974 282216
Open: May to Sep

Devil's Bridge

SN7376

▲ **Erwbarfe Farm,** Devil's Bridge, Ponterwyd, Aberystwyth, Ceredigion, SY23 3JR
Actual Grid Ref: SN749735
Tel: 01970 890665
Open: Mar to Oct

▲ **The Woodlands Caravan Park,** Devil's Bridge, Aberystwyth, Ceredigion, SY23 3JW
Actual Grid Ref: SN744773
Tel: 01970 890233
Open: Mar to Oct

Dolgoch

SN8056

▲ **Dolgoch Youth Hostel,** Dolgoch, Tregaron, Cardiganshire, SY25 6NR
Actual Grid Ref: SH806561
Tel: 01974 298680
Email: reservations@yha.org.uk
Capacity: 22
Under 18: £4.75
Adults: £6.75 **Open:** Apr to Sep
Self-catering facilities • Showers • Shop • Wet weather shelter Limited • Parking • No smoking • WC • Kitchen facilities Mountain hostel in large farmhouse with gas lighting open fires and no electricity. The Tywi Valley is beautiful, remote, and ideal for birdwatching, trekking by foot or by pony.

Dolybont

SN6287

▲ **Mill House Caravan & Camping Park,** Dolybont, Borth, Ceredigion, SY24 5LX
Actual Grid Ref: SN626881
Tel: 01970 871481
Open: Mar to Oct

Felinfach

SN5255

▲ **Hafod Brynog Park,** Yastra Aeron, Felinfach, Lampeter, Ceredigion, SA48 8AE
Actual Grid Ref: SN525563
Tel: 01570 470084
Open: Apr to Oct

Felinwynt

SN2250

▲ **Pen-y-Graig,** Felinwynt, Verwig, Ceredigion, SA43 1QQ
Actual Grid Ref: SN219518
Tel: 01239 810664
Open: Jun to Oct

Furnace

SN6894

▲ **Furnace Farm,** Furnace, Machynlleth, Powys, SY20 8ND
Actual Grid Ref: SN683951
Tel: 01654 781264
Open: All year

Gilfachreda

SN4058

▲ **Wern Mill Campsite,** Gilfachreda, New Quay, Ceredigion, SA45 9SP
Actual Grid Ref: SN409589
Tel: 01545 580699
Open: Mar to Oct

Llanarth

SN4257

▲ **Llain Activity Centre,** Llain Farm, Llanarth, Ceredigion, SA47 0PZ
Tel: 01545 580127
Open: Mar to Oct

▲ **Llanina Touring Caravan Site,** Llanarth, Ceredigion, SA47 0NP
Actual Grid Ref: SN421575
Tel: 01545 580000
Open: Mar to Oct

Llandre

SN6286

▲ **Riverside Park,** Lon Glanfed, Llandre, Bow Street, Ceredigion, SY24 5BY
Actual Grid Ref: SN633879
Tel: 01970 820070
Open: Mar to Oct

Llandysul

SN4140

▲ **Camping & Caravanning Club Site,** Llwynhelyg, Llandysul, Ceredigion, SA44 6LW
Tel: 01545 560029
Open: Mar to Sept

▲ **Pantgwyn Farm,** Synod Inn, Llandysul, Ceredigion, SA44 6JN
Tel: 01545 580320
Open: Easter to Sep

Llanfarian

SN5877

▲ **Morfa Bychan Holiday Park,** Llanfarian, Aberystwyth, Ceredigion, SY23 4QQ
Actual Grid Ref: SN566772
Tel: 01970 617254
Open: Mar to Oct

Llangeitho

SN6259

▲ **Hendrewen Caravan Park,** Pencarn, Llangeitho, Tregaron, Ceredigion, SY25 6QU
Actual Grid Ref: SN642590
Tel: 01974 298410
Open: Apr to Oct

Llangranog

SN3153

▲ **Y Beudy,** Maes y Morfa, Llangranog, Llandysul, Ceredigion, SA44 6RU
Actual Grid Ref: SN310533
Tel: 01239 654561
Email: beudy@maesymorfa.fsnet.co.uk
Capacity: 20
Under 18: £3.50
Adults: £3.50
Open: All year
Family bunk rooms: £3.50
Camping for 2 tents: £3.50
*Self-catering facilities • Showers • Wet weather shelter • Lounge • Dining room • Grounds available for camping • Drying room • Parking
Your group rents the barn. Organic smallholding by sea, beach, village, cliff walks.*

WALES

Ceredigion • MAP PAGE 325

Llangybi
SN6053

▲ **Moorlands Caravan Park,** Llangybi, Lampeter, Ceredigion, SA48 8NN
Actual Grid Ref: SN598543
Tel: 01570 493543
Open: Mar to Oct

Llanon
SN5166

▲ **Woodlands Caravan Park,** Llanon, Ceredigion, SY23 5LX
Actual Grid Ref: SN510668
Tel: 01974 202342
Open: Mar to Oct

Llanrhystud
SN5369

▲ **Pengarreg Caravan Park,** Llanrhystud, Ceredigion, SY23 5JD
Actual Grid Ref: SN531698
Tel: 01974 202247
Open: Mar to Jan

▲ **Morfa Caravan Park,** Llanrhystud, Ceredigion, SY23 5BU
Actual Grid Ref: SN526696
Tel: 01974 202253
Open: Apr to Sep

Llansantffraid
SN5167

▲ **Vyrnwy Caravan Park,** Llansantffraid, Powys, SY22 6SY
Actual Grid Ref: SN246195
Tel: 01691 828217
Open: Apr to Oct

Mydroilyn
SN4655

▲ **Bardsey View Holiday Park,** Mydroilyn, New Quay, Lampeter, Ceredigion, SA48 8NN
Tel: 01545 580270
Open: Easter to Oct

New Quay
SN3859

▲ **Cei Bach Country Club,** New Quay, Ceredigion, SA45 9SL
Actual Grid Ref: SN426590
Tel: 01545 580237
Fax: 01545 580237
Open: Apr to Sep

Penbryn
SN2951

▲ **Maes Glas Caravan Park,** Penbryn, Sarnau, Llandysul, Ceredigion, SA44 6QE
Actual Grid Ref: SN300520
Tel: 01239 654268
Open: Apr to Oct

▲ **Talywerydd Touring Caravan Park,** Penbryn Sands, Penbryn, Sarnau, Llandysul, Ceredigion, SA44 6QY
Actual Grid Ref: SN298507
Tel: 01239 810322
Open: Mar to Oct

Penparc
SN2147

▲ **Brongwyn Mawr Farm,** Penparc, Cardigan, Ceredigion, SA43 1SA
Tel: 01239 613644
Open: Mar to Oct

Plwmp
SN3652

▲ **Greenfields Caravan & Camping Park,** Plwmp, Llandysul, Pentregat, Ceredigion, SA44 6HE
Actual Grid Ref: SN355524
Tel: 01239 654333
Open: Mar to Oct

Ponterwyd
SN7480

▲ **Maesnant,** Ponterwyd, Aberystwyth, Dyfed, SY23 3AG
Tel: 020 8421 4648
Capacity: 16
Under 18: £5.00
Adults: £5.00
Open: Mar to Oct
Camping for 10 tents: £5.00
Self-catering facilities • Showers • Lounge • Dining room • Grounds available for games
Bungalow and outbuildings set in wild open country about 5 miles from village. Located on the slopes of Plynlimon mountain, overlooking Nant-y-Moch Reservoir. Ideal base for youth groups undertaking Duke of Edinburgh's and similar expedition training. Local attractions include Llywernog Mine Museum, Devil's Bridge and Vale of Rheidol Railway.

Pontrhydfendigaid
SN7366

▲ **Red Lion Hotel,** Pontrhydfendigaid, Ystrad Meurig, Ceredigion, SY25 6BH
Tel: 01974 831232
Open: Mar to Nov

Pontwelly
SN4139

▲ **Rhydygalfe Caravan Park,** Pontwelly, Llandysul, Ceredigion, SA44 5AP
Actual Grid Ref: SN407403
Tel: 01559 362738
Open: All year

Rhydlewis
SN3447

▲ **Pilbach Caravan Park,** Betws Ifan, Rhydlewis, Llandysul, Ceredigion, SA44 5RT
Actual Grid Ref: SN308477
Tel: 01239 851434
Open: Mar to Oct

Sarnau
SN3150

▲ **Brynawelon Touring Caravan Park,** Sarnau, Llangranog, Llandysul, Ceredigion, SA44 6RE
Actual Grid Ref: SN322508
Tel: 01239 654584
Email: bryncwelontouring-camping@distantshore.com
Tent pitches: 10
Tent rate: £7.50
Open: Mar to Oct **Last arr:** 9pm
Facilities for disabled people • Dogs allowed • Electric hook-up • Calor Gas/Camping Gaz • Picnic/barbecue area on site • Children's play area • Showers
Quiet family-run level site with sea and mountain views.

▲ **Treddafydd Caravan Site,** Sarnau, Llandysul, Ceredigion, SA44 6PZ
Actual Grid Ref: SN305514
Tel: 01239 654551
Open: Mar to Oct

Hostels and campsites may vary rates – be sure to check when booking.

Ceredigion

▲ **Manorafon,** *Sarnau, Llandysul, Ceredigion, SA44 5RT*
Actual Grid Ref: SN299521
Tel: 01239 810564
Open: Mar to Oct

Synod Inn
SN4054

▲ **Brownhill Caravan Park,** *Pentre r Bryn, Synod Inn, Llandysul, Ceredigion, SA44 6JZ*
Tel: 01545 560 288
Open: Mar to Oct

Tregaron
SN6759

▲ **Neuadd Brenig,** *Abergwesyn Road, Tregaron, Ceredigion, SY25 6NG*
Actual Grid Ref: SN684598
Tel: 01974 298543
Open: Apr to Oct

Tresaith
SN2751

▲ **Llety Caravan Park,** *Tresaith, Aberporth, Cardigan, SA43 2ED*
Tel: 01239 810354
Fax: 01239 810354
Open: Mar to Oct

Verwig
SN1849

▲ **Ty-Gwyn Farm,** *Mwnt, Verwig, Cardigan, SA43 1PL*
Tel: 01239 612164
Open: Apr to Oct

All details shown are as supplied by hostels and campsites in Autumn 2000.

Ynyslas
SN6092

▲ **Cambrian Coast Holiday Park,** *Aberferi Farm, Ynyslas, Borth, Ceredigion, SY24 5JU*
Actual Grid Ref: SN841588
Tel: 01970 871233
Email: holidays-in-wales@sunbourne.co.uk
Open: Mar to Oct

▲ **Ty Mawr Caravan Park,** *Ynyslas, Borth, Ceredigion, SY24 5LB*
Actual Grid Ref: SN630927
Tel: 01970 871327
Open: Mar to Oct

▲ **Ty Gwyn Camping Site,** *Ty Gwyn Farm, Ynyslas, Borth, Ceredigion, SY24 5LA*
Actual Grid Ref: SN611925
Tel: 01970 871323
Open: May to Sep

Denbigh & Flint

Bangor-is-y-coed

SJ3845

▲ **Camping & Caravanning Club Site,** The Racecourse, Bangor-Is-Y-Coed, Wrexham, Clwyd, LL13 0DA
Tel: 01978 781009
Open: Apr to Oct

Bwlchgwyn

SJ2653

▲ **Cae Adar Farm,** Bwlchgwyn, Wrexham, Denbighshire, LL11 5UE
Actual Grid Ref: SJ267529
Tel: 01978 757385
Open: Apr to Oct

Caerwys

SJ1272

▲ **Barlow Caravan Park,** Caerwys, Mold, Denbighshire, CH7 5BY
Actual Grid Ref: SJ119737
Tel: 01352 720625
Open: Mar to Oct

Denbigh & Flint

Corwen
SJ0743

▲ **Llawr Betws Farm,** Glan-yr-afon, Corwen, LL21 0HD
Actual Grid Ref: SJ016424
Tel: 01490 460224
Open: Mar to Oct

Cynwyd
SJ0541

▲ **Cynwyd Youth Hostel,** The Old Mill, Cynwyd, Corwen, Denbighshire, LL21 0LW
Actual Grid Ref: SJ057409
Tel: 01490 412814
Fax: 01490 412814
Capacity: 30
Under 18: £5.25
Adults: £7.50
Open: Apr to Sep, 5.00pm
Camping
Self-catering facilities • Showers • Shop • Lounge 6056 • Drying room • Cycle store • Parking • No smoking • No smoking • WC • Credit cards accepted
Former woollen mill offering basic accommodation in tranquil setting on river bank in good cycling country.

Denbigh
SJ0566

▲ **Tyn-Yr-Eithin,** Mold Road, Denbigh, LL16 4BH
Actual Grid Ref: SJ061673
Tel: 01745 813211
Open: Apr to Oct

▲ **Station House Caravan Park,** Bodfari, Mold Road, Denbigh, Denbighshire, LL16 4DA
Actual Grid Ref: SJ094700
Tel: 01745 710372
Open: Apr to Oct

Eyton
SJ3444

▲ **Plassey Touring Caravan & Leisure Park,** Eyton, Wrexham, Denbighshire, LL13 0SP
Actual Grid Ref: SJ349454
Tel: 01978 780277
Fax: 01978 780019
Email: jbrookshaw@aol.com
Open: Mar to Oct

Froncysyllte
SJ2740

▲ **Argoed Farm,** Froncysyllte, Llangollen, Clwyd, LL20 7RH
Tel: 01691 772367
Open: All year

Glyn Ceiriog
SJ2038

▲ **Pont Bell,** Glan Llyn, Glyn Ceiriog, Llangollen, Denbighshire, LL20 7AB
Tel: 01691 718320
Open: Easter to Oct

▲ **Ddol Hir Caravan Park,** Pandy Road, Glyn Ceiriog, Llangollen, Denbighshire, LL20 7PD
Actual Grid Ref: SJ200370
Tel: 01691 718681 **Open:** All year

Gronant
SJ0983

▲ **St Marys Holiday Touring & Camping Park,** Mostyn Road, Gronant, Prestatyn, Denbighshire, LL19 9TB
Actual Grid Ref: SJ100835
Tel: 01745 853951
Open: Apr to Oct

Hawarden
SJ3165

▲ **Greenacres Farm Park,** Mancot, Deeside, Flintshire, CH5 2AZ
Actual Grid Ref: SJ317671
Tel: 01244 531147
Open: Apr to Sep

Hendre
SJ1867

▲ **Fron Farm,** Hendre, Mold, Flintshire, CH7 5QW
Actual Grid Ref: SJ188688
Tel: 01352 741217
Open: Apr to Oct

Llandrillo
SJ0337

▲ **Hendwr Caravan Park,** Llandrillo, Corwen, Denbighshire, LL21 0SN
Actual Grid Ref: SJ036387
Tel: 01490 440210
Open: All year

▲ **Y Felin Caravan Park,** Llandrillo, Corwen, Denbighshire, LL21 0TD
Tel: 01490 440333
Open: Easter to Oct

▲ **Cilan Caravan Park,** Llandrillo, Corwen, Denbighshire, LL21 0SY
Actual Grid Ref: SJ029378
Tel: 01490 440440
Open: Mar to Oct

Llangollen
SJ2141

▲ **Wern Isaf Farm,** Llangollen, Denbighshire, LL20 8DU
Actual Grid Ref: SJ225426
Tel: 01978 860632
Open: Apr to Oct

▲ **Tower Camping & Caravanning Site,** Tower Farm, Llangollen, Denbighshire, LL20 8TE
Actual Grid Ref: SJ213428
Tel: 01978 860798
Open: All year

▲ **'Eirianfa' Riverside Holiday Park,** Berwyn Road, Llangollen, Denbighshire, LL20 8AD
Actual Grid Ref: SJ208432
Tel: 01978 860919
Open: All year

Lloc
SJ1376

▲ **Misty Waters Country Lodge Hotel,** Lloc, Holywell, CH8 8RG
Actual Grid Ref: SJ135771
Tel: 01352 720497
Fax: 01352 720497
Open: Apr to Nov

Maeshafn
SJ2061

▲ **Maeshafn Youth Hostel,** Holt Hostel, Maeshafn, Mold, CH7 5LR
Actual Grid Ref: SJ208606
Tel: 01352 810320
Capacity: 31
Under 18: £5.75
Adults: £8.50
Open: All year, 5.00pm
Self-catering facilities • Showers • Shop • Lounge • Drying room • Cycle store • Parking • No smoking • Kitchen facilities
Swiss chalet-style building designed by Clough Williams-Ellis. Set in peaceful woodland setting, on edge of Clwydian Hills only 3 miles from Offa's Dyke footpath.

WALES

Denbigh & Flint • MAP PAGE 330

Overton-on-Dee
SJ3742

▲ **The Trotting Mare Caravan Park,** Overton-on-Dee, Wrexham, LL13 0LE
Actual Grid Ref: SJ379387
Tel: 01978 710743
Open: All year

Pentre Saron
SJ0260

▲ **Caer-Mynydd Caravan Park,** Pentre Saron, Denbigh, LL16 4TL
Tel: 01745 550302
Open: Mar to Oct

Pentredwr
SJ1946

▲ **Pentredwr Farm,** Pentredwr, Llangollen, Denbighshire, LL20 8DG
Actual Grid Ref: SJ199466
Tel: 01978 860021
Open: Apr to Dec

All details shown are as supplied by hostels and campsites in Autumn 2000.

Prestatyn
SJ0682

▲ **Nant Mill Touring Caravan & Tent Park,** Gronant Road, Prestatyn, Denbighshire, LL19 9LY
Actual Grid Ref: SJ074831
Tel: 01745 852360
Open: Apr to Oct

▲ **Tan-y-Don Caravan Park,** 263 Victoria Road, Prestatyn, Denbighshire, LL19 7UT
Tel: 01745 853749
Open: Mar to Oct

Rhuallt
SJ0775

▲ **The White House Hotel,** Rhuallt, St Asaph, Denbighshire, LL17 0AW
Actual Grid Ref: SJ069750
Tel: 01745 582155
Open: Mar to Jan

Ruthin
SJ1258

▲ **Minffordd,** Llanber, Ruthin, Clwyd, Denbighshire, LL15 1TS
Actual Grid Ref: SJ123606
Tel: 01824 707169
Open: Jun to Aug

Tyndwr
SJ2341

▲ **Llangollen Youth Hostel,** Tyndwr Hall, Tyndwr Road, Tyndwr, Llangollen, Denbighshire, LL20 8AR
Actual Grid Ref: SK232413
Tel: 01978 860330
Fax: 01978 861709
Email: llangollen@yha.org.uk
Capacity: 134
Under 18: £6.90 **Adults:** £10.00
Open: All year, 1.00pm
Family bunk rooms
Self-catering facilities • Self-catering facilities • Television • Showers • Licensed bar • Lounge • Drying room • Parking • Evening meal available 6.00-7.30pm • Kitchen facilities • Breakfast available • Credit cards accepted
Victorian half-timbered manor house & coach house, extensively refurbished, set in 5 acres of wooded grounds in the Vale of Llangollen.

Hostels and campsites may vary rates – be sure to check when booking.

The Glamorgans

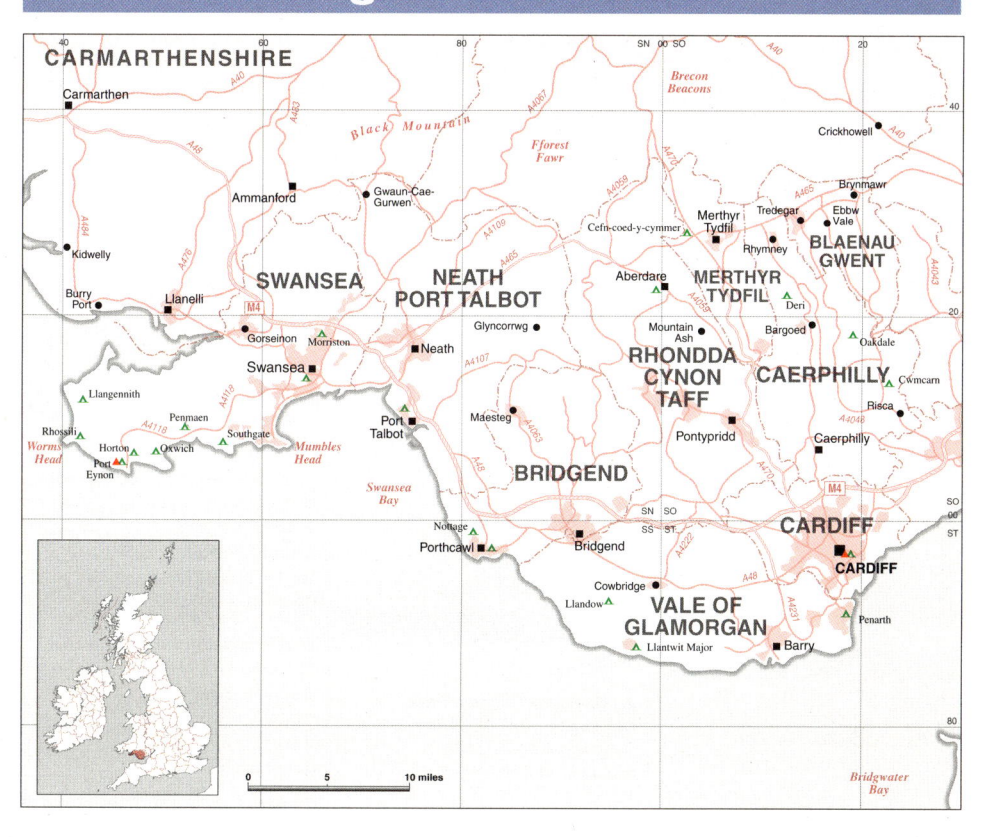

Aberdare

SN9902

Dare Valley Country Park,
Aberdare, Mid Glam, CF44 7RG
Actual Grid Ref: SN985027
Tel: 01685 874672
Open: All year

Cardiff

ST1677

Cardiff Backpacker Caerdydd,
98 Neville Street, Riverside, Cardiff, CF11 6LS
Actual Grid Ref: ST176763
Tel: 029 2034 5577
Fax: 029 2034 5577
Capacity: 80
Adults: £13.50
Open: All year, 7.30am
Self-catering facilities • Television • Showers • Licensed bar • Central heating • Shop • Laundry facilities • Lounge • Dining room • Games room • Security lockers • Cycle store • Parking • No smoking

Cardiff's only central tourist hostel, located within five minutes walk from train/bus stations and all civic amenities. Relax and socialise in a lively Welsh atmosphere with travellers from all over the world or explore the nearby Brecon Beacons National Park and breathtaking castles, museums and coastline. WTB 4 Star Hostel.

Cardiff Youth Hostel,
Ty Croeso, 2 Wedal Road, Roath Park, Cardiff, CF2 5PG
Actual Grid Ref: ST185788
Tel: 029 2046 2303
Fax: 029 2046 4571
Email: cardiff@yha.org.uk
Capacity: 64
Under 18: £10.20
Adults: £13.50
Open: All year, All day
Self-catering facilities • Television • Showers • Shop • Laundry facilities • Lounge 2 • Cycle store • Parking • Kitchen facilities • Breakfast available • Luggage store • Credit cards accepted

Conveniently located hostel near the city centre and Roath Park Lake, with cycling & sailing facilities.

Stilwell's Hostels & Camping 2002

The Glamorgans • MAP PAGE 333

▲ **Pontcanna Caravan Site,** Pontcanna Fields, Sophia Close, Riverside, Cardiff, CF1 9JJ
Tel: 01222 398362 / 471612
Open: All year

Cefn-coed-y-cymmer

SO0308

▲ **Grawen Farm Camping & Caravan Site,** Cwyn Taff, Cefn-coed-y-cymmer, Merthyr Tydfil, Mid Glam, CF48 2HS
Actual Grid Ref: SO016112
Tel: 01685 723740
Open: Apr to Oct

Cwmcarn

ST2193

▲ **Cwmcarn Forest Drive Campsite,** Nant Carn Valley, Cwmcarn, Crosskeys, Newport, Monmouthshire, NP1 7FA
Actual Grid Ref: ST230935
Tel: 01495 272001
Open: All year

Deri

SO1201

▲ **Parc Cwm Darran,** Deri, Bargoed, Caerphilly, CF8 9AB
Actual Grid Ref: SO113057
Tel: 01443 875557
Open: Mar to Dec

Horton

SS4785

▲ **Bank Farm Holiday Park,** Horton, Gower, Swansea, W Glam, SA3 1LL
Actual Grid Ref: SS465863
Tel: 01792 390228
Open: Apr to Oct

Llandow

SS9472

▲ **Llandow Touring Caravan Park,** Llandow, Cowbridge, S Glam, CF71 7PB
Actual Grid Ref: SS954773
Tel: 01446 794527
Open: Feb to Nov

Llangennith

SS4391

▲ **Kennexstone Farm,** Llangennith, Swansea, W Glam, SA3 1HS
Actual Grid Ref: SS450916
Tel: 01792 386225
Open: Mar to Oct

▲ **Hillend Holiday Cottages,** Llangennith, Gower, Swansea, W. Glam, SA3 1JD
Actual Grid Ref: SS413909
Tel: 01792 386204
Open: Apr to Oct

Llantwit Major

SS9768

▲ **Acorn Camping & Caravanning,** Rosedew Farm, Hamlane South, Llantwit Major, S Glam, CF61 1RP
Actual Grid Ref: SS974678
Tel: 01446 794024
Open: Apr to Oct

Morriston

SS6797

▲ **Riverside Caravan Park,** Ynysforgan Farm, Morriston, Swansea, W Glam, SA6 6QL
Actual Grid Ref: SS680995
Tel: 01792 775587
Open: All year

Nottage

SS8177

▲ **Brodawel Camping Park,** Moor Lane, Nottage, Porthcawl, Mid Glam, CF36 3EJ
Actual Grid Ref: SS816790
Tel: 01656 783231
Open: Mar to Oct

Oakdale

ST1898

▲ **Pen-y-fan Caravan & Leisure Park,** Manmoel Road, Oakdale, Blackwood, Monmouthshire, NP2 0HY
Actual Grid Ref: SO190011
Tel: 01493 226636
Fax: 01493 227778
Open: All year

Oxwich

SS4986

▲ **Oxwich Camping Park,** Oxwich, Swansea, Glamorgan, SA3 1LS
Actual Grid Ref: SS497870
Tel: 01792 390777
Open: Easter to Sep

Penarth

ST1871

▲ **Lavernock Point Holiday Estate,** Fort Road, Penarth, S Glam, CF64 5XQ
Tel: 029 2070 7310
Open: May to Sep

Penmaen

SS5388

▲ **Three Cliffs Bay Holiday Park,** North Hill Farm, Penmaen, Swansea, W Glam, SA3 2HB
Actual Grid Ref: SS535887
Tel: 01792 371218
Open: Mar to Oct

▲ **Nicholaston Farm Caravan & Camping Site,** Nicholaston Farm, Penmaen, Swansea, W. Glam, SA3 2HL
Tel: 01792 371209
Open: Easter to Sep

Port Eynon

SS4685

▲ **Port Eynon Youth Hostel,** The Old Lifeboat House, Port Eynon, Swansea, West Glamorgan, SA3 1NN
Actual Grid Ref: SS468848
Tel: 01792 390706
Fax: 01792 390706
Capacity: 30
Under 18: £6.50
Adults: £9.25
Open: All year, 5.00pm
Family bunk rooms
Self-catering facilities • Showers • Lounge • Drying room • Cycle store • No smoking • WC • Kitchen facilities • Credit cards accepted
A former lifeboat station near Port Eynon village providing a friendly atmosphere and marvellous views - seals can often be seen. The Gower peninsula has 34 miles of heritage coast with many good beaches and walks.

MAP PAGE 333 • **The Glamorgans**

▲ **Carreglwyd Camping & Caravan Park,** Port Eynon, Swansea, Glamorgan, SA3 1NN
Actual Grid Ref: SS469848
Tel: 01792 390795
Fax: 01792 390796
Email: rwgrove@compuserve.com
Open: Mar to Dec

▲ **Newpark Holiday Park,** Port Eynon, Swansea, W. Glam, SA3 1NL
Actual Grid Ref: SS465858
Tel: 01792 390292
Fax: 01792 391245
Email: llechwedd@aol.com
Open: Mar to Oct

Port Talbot
SS7489

▲ **Afan Forest Park,** Cynonville, Port Talbot, SA13 3HG
Actual Grid Ref: SS812952
Tel: 01639 850564
Open: Apr to Oct

Porthcawl
SS8277

▲ **Happy Valley Caravan Park,** Wigfach, Porthcawl, Mid Glam, CF32 0NG
Actual Grid Ref: SS849784
Tel: 01656 782144
Open: Apr to Sep

Rhossili
SS4188

▲ **Pitton Cross Caravan Park,** Rhossili, Swansea, W Glam, SA3 1PH
Actual Grid Ref: SS434878
Tourist Board grade: 3 Ticks
AA grade: 3 Pennants
Tel: 01792 390593 **Fax:** 01792 391010
Email: rogerbuttonmm@tesco.net
Tent pitches: 100
Tent rate: £8.00-£11.25
Open: Mar to Oct **Last arr:** 9pm
Dogs allowed • Electric hook-up • Calor Gas/Camping Gaz • Children's play area • Showers • Laundrette on site • Public phone on site • Shop on site • Baby care facilities • Indoor swimming pool nearby • Boating/sailing/watersports nearby • Tennis courts nearby • Golf nearby • Riding nearby • Fishing nearby
We pride ourselves in providing excellent camping facilities over many years. In a superb location close to beautiful coves and sandy beaches and some of the finest countryside in Wales. Clean, modern facilities, no dog field, level pitches, over 50s £40 p/w when pre-booked, low/mid season.

All details shown are as supplied by hostels and campsites in Autumn 2000.

Southgate
SS5588

▲ **Llanmadoc Camping Site,** Llanmadoc, Gower, Swansea, W Glam, SA3 1DE
Actual Grid Ref: SS427930
Tel: 01792 386202
Open: Apr to Oct

Swansea
SS6592

▲ **Blackhills Caravan & Camping Park,** Fairwood Common, Swansea, W Glam, SA2 7JN
Actual Grid Ref: SS583913
Tel: 01792 207065
Open: Apr to Oct

If you have to cancel your visit to any hostel or campsite, please let them know – it is always possible to make a bed or a pitch available to someone else.

WALES

Stilwell's Hostels & Camping 2002   335

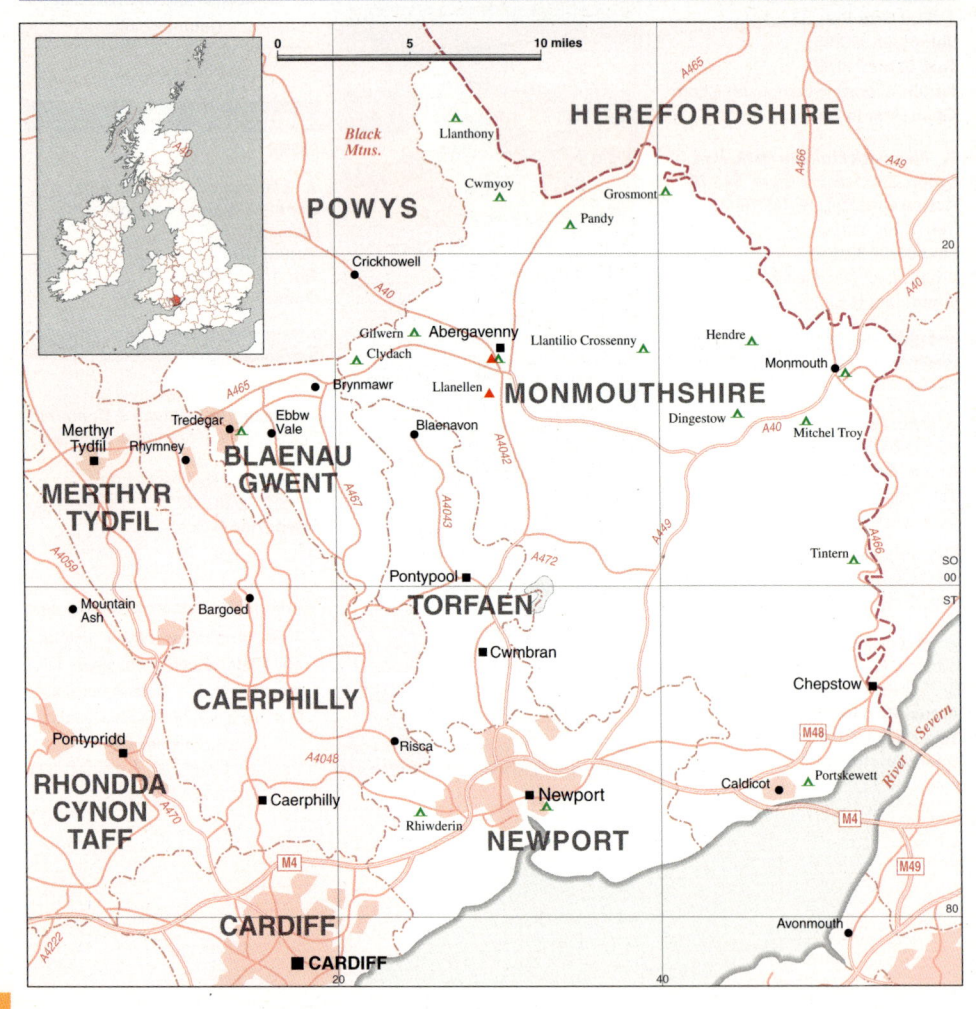

Monmouthshire

Abergavenny
SO2914

▲ **Ty'r Morwydd House,** Pen-y-Pound, Abergavenny, Monmouthshire, NP7 5UD
Actual Grid Ref: SO297147
Tel: 01873 855959
Fax: 01873 855443
Email: tyrmorwydd@aol.com
Capacity: 72
Under 18: £16.50
Adults: £16.50
Open: All year

Showers • Central heating • Lounge • Dining room • Games room • Drying room • Parking • Evening meal available 6pm • No smoking
Quality group accommodation, conferences, training etc. Advance bookings only.

▲ **Pysgodlyn Farm Caravan and Camping Site,** Llanwenarth Citra, Abergavenny, Monmouthshire, NP7 7ER
Actual Grid Ref: SO266156
Tel: 01873 853271
Open: Mar to Oct

▲ **Wernddu Farm,** Old Ross Road, Abergavenny, Gwent, NP7 8NG
Tel: 01873 855289
Open: Feb to Nov

Clydach
SO2213

▲ **Clydach Gorge Caravan & Camping,** Station Road, Clydach, Gilwern, Monmouthshire, NP7 0HD
Actual Grid Ref: SO233137
Tel: 01633 644856
Open: Apr to Sep

Monmouthshire

Cwmyoy
SO2923

▲ **Neuadd Farm,** Cwmyoy, Abergavenny, Monmouthshire, NP7 7NS
Actual Grid Ref: SO295233
Tel: 01873 890276
Open: Mar to Nov

Dingestow
SO4510

▲ **Bridge Caravan Park Camping Site,** Dingestow, Monmouth, NP25 4DY
Actual Grid Ref: SO459103
Tel: 01600 740241
Open: Mar to Oct

Gilwern
SO2414

▲ **Aberbalden Caravan & Camping Park,** Gilwern, Abergavenny, Monmouthshire, NP7 0EF
Tel: 01873 830157
Open: Apr to Oct

Grosmont
SO4024

▲ **Lower Tresenny Farm Camp Site,** Grosmont, Abergavenny, Monmouthshire, NP7 8LN
Actual Grid Ref: SO409241
Tel: 01981 240438
Open: Mar to Sept

Hendre
SO4614

▲ **The Hendre Farmhouse,** Hendre, Monmouth, NP25 4DJ
Tel: 01600 740484
Fax: 01600 740484
Open: All year

Llanellen
SO3010

▲ **Middle Ninfa Farm Bunkhouse,** Middle Ninfa Farm, Llanellen, Abergavenny, Monmouthshire, NP7 9LE
Tel: 01873 854662
Email: middleninfa.farm@ntlworld.com
Capacity: 6
Under 18: £9.00

Adults: £9.00
Open: All year, 4pm
Self-catering facilities • Television • Showers • Grounds available for games • Cycle store • Parking
Recently converted stone barn on small holding. Wonderful views over Usk Valley. Double divan downstairs, 4 single beds on mezzanine. Tennis, croquet. Ideal families. Abergavenny shops, castle, theatre, vineyard, train station 3 miles. Scenic canal and National Cycle Network 1 mile. Industrial heritage, walking, caving, hang gliding, pony trekking locally. Leaflet available.

Llanthony
SO2827

▲ **Court Farm,** Llanthony, Abergavenny, Monmouthshire, NP7 7NN
Tel: 01873 890359
Open: All year

Llantilio Crossenny
SO3914

▲ **Treloyvan Farm,** Llantilio Crossenny, Abergavenny, Monmouthshire, NP7 8UE
Tel: 01600 780478
Open: Mar to Oct

Mitchel Troy
SO4910

▲ **Glen Trothy Caravan & Camping Park,** Mitchel Troy, Monmouth, Monmouthshire, NP25 4BD
Actual Grid Ref: SO496106
Tourist Board grade: 3 Star
Tel: 01600 712295
Tent pitches: 50
Tent rate: £7.00-£11.00
Open: Mar to Oct
Last arr: 9pm
Facilities for disabled people • Dogs allowed • Electric hook-up • Showers • Laundrette on site • Public phone on site • Calor Gas/Camping Gaz • Children's play area • Indoor swimming pool nearby • Boating/sailing/watersports nearby • Tennis courts nearby • Golf nearby • Riding nearby • Fishing on site
Beautiful countryside setting on edge of Wye Valley and Forest of Dean. Level 6.5 acre park. Disabled facilities. Children's play area. Booking advisable peak season and bank holidays. Pub/restaurant adjacent. 1.5 miles SW of Monmouth off A40. Good motorway access. Telephone or send for free colour brochure.

Monmouth
SO5012

▲ **Monmouth Caravan Park,** Rockfield Road, Monmouth, Monmouthshire, NP25 3BA
Actual Grid Ref: SO498135
Tel: 01600 716690
Open: Mar to Oct

▲ **Monmouth Caravan Park,** Rockfield Road, Monmouth, NP25 5BA
Actual Grid Ref: SO504129
Tel: 01600 714745
Open: Mar to Oct

▲ **Great Hall,** Welsh Newton Common, Monmouth, NP5 3RR
Actual Grid Ref: SO515182
Tel: 01989 770473
Open: Apr to Oct

Newport
ST3188

▲ **Tredegar House & Park,** Newport, Monmouthshire, NP1 9YW
Actual Grid Ref: ST2844854
Tel: 01633 816650
Fax: 01633 815895
Open: Apr to Oct

Pandy
SO3322

▲ **The Offa's Tavern,** Pandy, Abergavenny, Monmouthshire, NP7 8DL
Tel: 01873 890254
Open: All year

▲ **Ty Newydd Farm,** Pandy, Abergavenny, Monmouthshire, NP7 8DW
Tel: 01873 890235
Open: All year

Portskewett
ST4988

▲ **St Pierre Caravan Park,** Portskewett, Chepstow, Monmouthshire, NP6 4TT
Actual Grid Ref: ST510895
Tel: 01291 425114
Open: All year

WALES

Stilwell's Hostels & Camping 2002 337

Monmouthshire • MAP PAGE 336

Rhiwderin
ST2687

▲ **Pentre Tai Farm,** *Rhiwderin, Newport, Monmouthshire, NP10 9RQ*
Tel: 01633 893284
Fax: 01633 893284
Open: Easter to Oct

Tintern
SO5300

▲ **Craigo Farm,** *Tintern, Chepstow, Monmouthshire, NP16 6SN*
Tel: 01291 689757
Fax: 01291 689365
Open: All year

Tredegar
SO1408

▲ **Bryn Bach Park,** *Merthyr Road, Tredegar, Monmouthshire, NP22 3AY*
Actual Grid Ref: SO126102
Tel: 01495 711816
Fax: 01495 726630
Open: All year

North West Wales

Aberdaron

SH1726

Caerau Camping & Caravan Site, Aberdaron, Pwllheli, Gwynedd, LL53 8BG
Actual Grid Ref: SH176270

Tel: 01758 760237 or 01758 760481
Tent pitches: 30
Tent rate: £5.00-£6.00
Open: Mar to Oct **Last arr:** 10pm
Facilities for disabled people • Dogs allowed • Electric hook-up • Calor Gas/Camping Gaz • Showers • Laundrette on site • Indoor swimming pool nearby • Boating/sailing/watersports nearby • Golf nearby • Riding nearby • Fishing nearby
Family-run business, working farm only 5 minutes from sea and shops. Excellent views of sea and mountains. Local activities include pony trekking - book direct from the camp site as the owners' son runs the pony trekking business - beautiful cliff walks (up to 8 miles), safe sandy beach within few minutes' walk.

Mur Melyn, Aberdaron, Pwllheli, Gwynedd, LL53 8LW
Actual Grid Ref: SH177289
Tel: 01758 760522
Open: Apr to Aug

Tir Glyn Farm, Aberdaron, Pwllheli, Gwynedd, LL53 8DA
Actual Grid Ref: SH158256
Tel: 01758 760248
Fax: 01758 760248
Open: Apr to Oct

North West Wales • MAP PAGE 339

▲ **Dwyros Campsite,** Aberdaron, Pwllheli, Gwynedd, LL53 8BS
Actual Grid Ref: SH167267
Tel: 01758 760295
Open: Mar to Oct

Abergele
SH9477

▲ **Henllys Farm,** Towyn Road, Towyn, Abergele, LL22 9HF
Actual Grid Ref: SH972792
Tel: 01745 351208
Fax: 01745 351208
Open: Apr to Sep

▲ **Gwrch Towers Camp,** Llandulas Road, Abergele, LL22 8ET
Actual Grid Ref: SH939775
Tel: 01745 832109
Open: Jun to Sep

▲ **Manorafon Farm,** Gwrych Park, Abergele, Clwyd, Conwy, LL22 8ET
Actual Grid Ref: SH936774
Tel: 01745 833207
Open: Apr to Sep

Abergynolwyn
SH6706

▲ **Riverside House,** Abergynolwyn, Tywyn, LL36 9YR
Tel: 01654 782235
Fax: 01654 782235
Open: July to Oct

Abersoch
SH3128

▲ **Seaside Camping Site,** Lon Golff, Abersoch, Pwllheli, Gwynedd
Tel: 01758 712271
Open: May to Oct

▲ **The Warren Touring Park,** Abersoch, Pwllheli, Gwynedd, LL53 7AY
Tel: 01758 712043 **Open:** Mar to Oct

▲ **Tyn-y-Mur Camping & Touring Park,** Lon Garmon, Abersoch, Pwllheli, Gwynedd, LL53 7UL
Actual Grid Ref: SH300290
Tel: 01758 712328
Open: Mar to Oct

▲ **Deucoch Camp Site & Touring Caravans,** Sam Bach, Abersoch, Pwllheli, Gwynedd, LL53 7LD
Actual Grid Ref: SH303269
Tel: 01758 713293
Open: Mar to Oct

Arthog
SH6414

▲ **Garthyfog Camp Site,** Arthog, Gwynedd, LL39 1AX
Actual Grid Ref: SH636139
Tel: 01341 250338
Open: All year

▲ **Pant-y-Cae,** Arthog, Gwynedd, LL39 1LJ
Actual Grid Ref: SH652148
Tel: 01341 250892
Open: All year

▲ **Graig Wen Guest House,** Arthog, LL39 1BQ
Actual Grid Ref: SH656158
Tel: 01341 250900
Fax: 01341 250482
Open: Mar to Oct

Bala
SH9235

▲ **Pen-y-Bont Touring & Camping Park,** Llangynog Road, Bala, Gwynedd, LL23 7PH
Actual Grid Ref: SH931350
Tel: 01678 520549
Fax: 01678 520006
Open: Apr to Oct

▲ **Ty-Isaf Farm,** Llangywog Road, Bala, Gwynedd, LL23 7PP
Actual Grid Ref: SH956355
Tel: 01678 520574
Open: Apr to Oct

▲ **Tylandderwen Caravan Park,** Bala, Gwynedd, LL23 7EP
Actual Grid Ref: SH952363
Tel: 01678 520273
Open: Apr to Oct

Bangor
SH5771

▲ **Bangor Youth Hostel,** Tan-y-Bryn, Bangor, Gwynedd, LL57 1PZ
Actual Grid Ref: SH590722
Tel: 01248 353516
Fax: 01248 371176
Email: bangor@yha.org.uk
Capacity: 84
Under 18: £7.75 **Adults:** £11.00
Open: All year (not Xmas/New Year), All day

Family bunk rooms
Self-catering facilities • Showers • Shop • Laundry facilities • Lounge • Dining room • Games room • Drying room • Parking • Evening meal available 6.00 to 7.00pm • Kitchen facilities • Credit cards accepted
Set against the backdrop of the Snowdonia Mountains with good road and rail links, large Victorian house in city with Victorian pier, cathedral and maritime centre.

▲ **Treborth Hall Farm Camping & Caravan,** Treborth Road, Bangor, Gwynedd, LL57 2RX
Actual Grid Ref: SH553708
Tel: 01248 364399 or 364104
Fax: 01248 364333
Email: treborth@freenetname.co.uk
Tent pitches: 32
Tent rate: £4.00-£7.00
Open: Mar to Oct
Last arr: any time
Facilities for disabled people • Dogs allowed • Electric hook-up • Picnic/barbecue area on site • Children's play area • Showers • Public phone on site • Indoor swimming pool nearby • Outdoor swimming pool nearby • Boating/sailing/watersports nearby • Tennis courts nearby • Golf on site • Fishing on site
Set in a beautiful area of North Wales between the Britannia and the Menai Suspension Bridge. Close to Menai Straits. Sheltered level touring site contained in old walled orchard with hard standing for caravans. Close to the mountains of Snowdonia and beaches of Anglesey. Trout fishing available by arrangement.

Barmouth
SH6115

▲ **Hendre Mynach Touring Caravan & Camping,** Llanaber Road, Barmouth, Gwynedd, LL42 1YR
Actual Grid Ref: SH608168
Tel: 01341 280262
Fax: 01341 280586
Open: Mar to Nov

Beddgelert
SH5948

▲ **Beddgelert Forest Camping Site,** Forest Enterprise, Beddgelert, Caernarfon, Gwynedd, LL55 4UU
Actual Grid Ref: SH579492
Tel: 01768 890288
Open: All year

Stilwell's Hostels & Camping 2002

MAP PAGE 339 • **North West Wales**

Bethania (Nantgwynant)

SH6250

▲ **Bryn Dinas Hostel,** Bethania, Nant Gwynant, Beddgelert, Caernarfon, LL55 4NH
Actual Grid Ref: SH625503
Tel: 01766 890234 **Fax:** 01766 890234
Email: vince@bryndinasbunkhouse.co.uk
Capacity: 52
Under 18: £6.50 **Adults:** £6.50
Open: All year, any time
Family bunk rooms
Self-catering facilities • Showers • Lounge • Dining room • Grounds available for games • Drying room • Cycle store • Parking • Evening meal available by arrangement
In the heart of Snowdonia close to the Watkin Path.

Betws Garmon

SH5357

▲ **Bryn Loch Caravan & Camping Park,** Betws Garmon, Caernarfon, Gwynedd, LL54 7YY
Actual Grid Ref: SH535575
Tel: 01286 650216
Fax: 01286 650216
Open: All year

▲ **Amos Jones Camping,** Bryn Afon, Betws Garmon, Caernarfon, Gwynedd, LL54 7YU
Actual Grid Ref: SH536572
Tel: 01286 650537
Open: All year

Betws-y-Coed

SH7956

▲ **Camp Snowdonia,** Pont-y-Pant, Dolwyddelan, LL25 0LZ
Actual Grid Ref: SH772538
Tel: 01690 750225
Fax: 01690 750457
Email: info@campsnowdonia.fsnet.co.uk
Tent pitches: 25
Tent rate: £3.00-£12.00
Open: All year
Last arr: 9.30pm
Dogs allowed • Showers
A stunning and tranquil riverside setting. Campfires permitted. Wonderfully uncommercialised.

▲ **Hendre Farm,** Betws-y-Coed, LL24 0BN
Actual Grid Ref: SH784566
Tel: 01690 710612
Open: Mar to Oct

▲ **Riverside Caravan & Camping Park,** Old Church Road, Betws-y-Coed, LL24 0BA
Actual Grid Ref: SH797569
Tel: 01690 710310
Open: Mar to Oct

▲ **Rynys Farm Camping Site,** Betws-y-Coed, LL26 0RU
Actual Grid Ref: SH814536
Tel: 01690 710218
Open: All year

▲ **Cwmllanerch Farm,** Betws-y-Coed, Gwynedd, LL24 0BG
Tel: 01690 710363
Open: Mar to Oct

Betws-yn-Rhos

SH9073

▲ **Hunters Hamlet Touring Park,** Sirior Goch Farm, Betws-yn-Rhos, Abergele, LL22 8PL
Actual Grid Ref: SH928736
Tel: 01745 832237
Open: Mar to Oct

Brithdir

SH7618

▲ **Llwyn-yr-Helm Farm,** Brithdir, Dolgellau, Gwynedd, LL40 2SA
Actual Grid Ref: SH778191
Tel: 01341 450254
Open: Apr to Oct

Bryncroes

SH2231

▲ **Ty Mawr Caravan Park,** Bryncroes, Sarn, Pwllheli, Gwynedd, LL53 8EH
Actual Grid Ref: SH218316
Tel: 01248 351537 **Open:** Apr to Oct

Bryncrug

SH6003

▲ **Woodlands Holiday Park,** Bryncrug, Tywyn, Gwynedd, LL36 9UH
Actual Grid Ref: SH618035
Tel: 01654 710471
Fax: 01654 710100
Open: Apr to Oct

▲ **Tynllwyn Caravan & Camping Park,** Bryncrug, Tywyn, Gwynedd, LL36 9RD
Actual Grid Ref: SH615023
Tel: 01654 710370
Open: Mar to Dec

Brynrefail

SH5662

▲ **Snowdon View Caravan Park,** Brynrefail, Caernarfon, Gwynedd, LL55 3PD
Actual Grid Ref: SH563634
Tel: 01286 870349
Open: Mar to Jan

Bwlchtocyn

SH3125

▲ **Sarnlys,** Bwlchtocyn, Pwllheli, Gwynedd, LL53 7BS
Actual Grid Ref: SH309268
Tel: 01758 712956
Open: Apr to Oct

Caeathro

SH5061

▲ **Glan Gwna Holiday Park,** Caeathro, Caernarfon, Gwynedd, LL55 2SG
Actual Grid Ref: SH502622
Tel: 01286 673456
Fax: 01286 673456
Open: Apr to Sep

Caernarfon

SH477627

▲ **Totters,** Plas Porth Yr Aur, 2 High Street, Caernarfon, Gwynedd, LL55 1RN
Tel: 01286 672963
Email: bob@totters.free-online.co.uk
Capacity: 30
Under 18: £10.00
Adults: £10.00
Open: All year, all day
Family bunk rooms: £35.00
Self-catering facilities • Television • Showers • Central heating • Wet weather shelter • Lounge • Dining room • Games room • Drying room • Security lockers • Cycle store • Parking • No smoking
Totters is situated within historic walled town of Caernarfon, only 100m from the castle and 20m from the sea. Caernarfon has plenty of pubs and restaurant and acts as a perfect base for exploring Snowdonia and Anglesey. Why not visit our web page or simply phone for a chat.

Hostels and campsites may vary rates – be sure to check when booking.

WALES

North West Wales • MAP PAGE 339

▲ **Cadnant Valley Caravan & Camping Park,** Llanberis Road Carenarfon, Gwynedd, LL55 2DF
Actual Grid Ref: SH627488
AA grade: 3 Pennants
Tel: 01286 673196
Tent pitches: 35
Tent rate: £5.00-£9.00
Open: Mar to Oct
Last arr: 8pm
*Dogs allowed • Electric hook-up • Calor Gas/Camping Gaz • Children's play area • Showers • Laundrette on site • Public phone on site
Walking distance of town. Snowdonia National Park in easy reach.*

▲ **Plas Gwyn Caravan Park,** Llanberis Road, Caernarfon, Gwynedd, LL55 2AQ
Tel: 01286 672619
Open: Mar to Oct

▲ **Rhyd-y-Galen,** Bethel Road, Caernarfon, Gwynedd, LL55 3PS
Actual Grid Ref: SH508644
Tel: 01248 670110
Open: Apr to Oct

▲ **Parsal Farm,** Clynnog Fawr, Caernarfon, Gwynedd, LL54 5PS
Actual Grid Ref: SH389474
Tel: 01286 660222
Open: Mar to Oct

Capel Curig
SH7258

▲ **Capel Curig Youth Hostel,** Plas Curig, Capel Curig, Betws-y-Coed, LL24 0EL
Actual Grid Ref: SH726579
Tel: 01690 720225
Fax: 01690 720270
Capacity: 52
Under 18: £6.90
Adults: £10.00
Open: Feb to Dec + New Year, 5.00pm
Family bunk rooms
*Self-catering facilities • Showers • Shop • Lounge 2 • Dining room • Drying room • Cycle store • Parking Limited • Evening meal available 7.00pm • WC • Kitchen facilities • Breakfast available • Credit cards accepted
Overlooking a river and forest with views of Moel Siabod. Ideal for mountain sports, riverside walks and forest tracks.*

▲ **Bryn Glo Cafe,** Capel Curig, Betws-y-Coed, LL24 0DT
Tel: 01690 720215
Open: All year

▲ **Bryn Gefeiliau,** Capel Curig, Betws-y-Coed, Conwy, LL24 0EB
Actual Grid Ref: SH745571
Tel: 01690 720284
Open: All year

▲ **Garth,** Capel Curig, Betws-y-Coed, Conwy, LL24 0ES
Actual Grid Ref: SH701570
Tel: 01690 720212
Open: Mar to Oct

▲ **Gwern Gof Isaf Farm,** Capel Curig, Betws-y-Coed, Conwy, LL24 0EU
Actual Grid Ref: SH685602
Tel: 01690 720276
Open: All year

Cefn-ddwysarn
SH9638

▲ **Camping & Caravanning Club Site,** Crynierth Caravan Park, Cefn-Ddwysarn, Bala, Gwynedd, LL23 7LN
Tel: 01678 530324
Open: Mar to Oct

Cerrigydrudion
SH9549

▲ **White Lion,** Cerrigydrudion, Corwen, LL21 9SW
Tel: 01490 420202
Open: All year

Chwilog
SH4338

▲ **Tyddyn Heilyn Farm,** Chwilog, Pwllheli, Gwynedd, LL53 6SW
Actual Grid Ref: SH455394
Tel: 01766 810441
Open: Apr to Nov

Cilan
SH2923

▲ **Bryn Celyn Isaf Camping Site,** Bryn Celyn Isaf, Cilan, Aberdaron, Pwllheli, Gwynedd, LL53 7DB
Actual Grid Ref: SH302258
Tel: 01758 713583
Open: Apr to Oct

▲ **Tai'r Lon,** Cilan, Abersoch, Pwllheli, Gwynedd, LL53 7DB
Actual Grid Ref: SH304257
Tel: 01758 712600
Open: All year

To stay in a Youth Hostel affiliated to one of the Youth Hostel associations, you need to be a member. You can join at most hostels – phone in advance to check.

Clynnog-Fawr
SH4149

▲ **Aberafon Gyrn Goch,** Clynnog-Fawr, Caernarfon, Gwynedd, LL54 5PN
Actual Grid Ref: SH400485
Tel: 01286 660295
Fax: 01286 660582
Open: Mar to Sept

Conwy
SH7777

▲ **Conwy Youth Hostel,** Larkhill, Schymant Pass Road, Conwy, LL32 8AJ
Actual Grid Ref: SH775773
Tel: 01492 593571
Fax: 01492 593580
Email: conwy@yha.org.uk
Capacity: 80
Under 18: £8.50
Adults: £12.50
Open: All year (not Xmas), All day
Family bunk rooms
*Self-catering facilities • Television • Showers • Shop • Laundry facilities • Lounge • Dining room • Games room • Drying room • Security lockers • Cycle store • Parking • Evening meal available 6.00 to 7.30pm • Facilities for disabled people Category 3 • Kitchen facilities • Breakfast available • Credit cards accepted
Former hotel, very modern; overlooking the castle and the bay.*

▲ **Conwy Touring Park,** Trefriw Road, Conwy, North West Wales, LL32 8UX
Actual Grid Ref: SH775758
Tel: 01492 592856
Fax: 01492 580024
Open: Apr to Oct

All details shown are as supplied by hostels and campsites in Autumn 2000.

MAP PAGE 339 • **North West Wales**

Corris

SH7507

▲ **Corris Youth Hostel,** Old School, Old Road, Corris, Machynlleth, Powys, SY20 9QT
Actual Grid Ref: SH753080
Tel: 01654 761686
Fax: 01654 761686
Capacity: 48
Under 18: £6.50
Adults: £9.25
Open: All year (not Xmas), 5.00pm
Self-catering facilities • Showers • Laundry facilities • Wet weather shelter • Lounge • Drying room • Security lockers • Cycle store • Parking • Evening meal available 7.00pm • No smoking • Kitchen facilities • Breakfast available
Picturesque former village school, recently renovated, with panoramic views of Corris.

Criccieth

SH4938

▲ **Llwyn Bugeilydd Farm,** Criccieth, Gwynedd, LL52 0PN
Actual Grid Ref: SH498398
Tel: 01766 522235
Open: Apr to Oct

▲ **Mynydd Du Farm,** Criccieth, Gwynedd, LL52 0PS
Actual Grid Ref: SH515395
Tel: 01766 522533
Open: Apr to Oct

▲ **Tyddyn Cethin,** Criccieth, Gwynedd, LL52 0NF
Actual Grid Ref: SH491403
Tel: 01766 522149
Open: Mar to Oct

▲ **Cae-Canol,** Rhoslan, Criccieth, Gwynedd, LL52 0NB
Actual Grid Ref: SH484402
Tel: 01766 522351
Open: Mar to Oct

▲ **Bontfechan Farm,** Criccieth, Llanystumdwy, Gwynedd, LL52 0LS
Actual Grid Ref: SH463380
Tel: 01766 522604
Open: Mar to Sept

▲ **Llwyn Mafon Isaf,** Criccieth, Gwynedd, LL52 0RE
Actual Grid Ref: SH520413
Tel: 01766 530618
Open: Apr to Oct

▲ **Glan Byl Farm Caravan & Camp Site,** Criccieth, Gwynedd, LL52 0RD
Actual Grid Ref: SH528410
Tel: 01766 530644
Open: Apr to Oct

Dinas Dinlle

SH4356

▲ **Dinlle Caravan Park,** Dinas Dinlle, Caernarfon, Gwynedd, LL54 7TW
Actual Grid Ref: SH438568
Tel: 01286 830324
Fax: 01286 831526
Open: Mar to Oct

▲ **Morfa Lodge Caravan Park,** Dinas Dinlle, Caernarfon, Gwynedd, LL54 5TP
Actual Grid Ref: SH442585
Tel: 01286 830205
Open: Mar to Oct

Dinas-Mawddwy

SH8514

▲ **Tyn-y-Pwll Camping Site,** Dinas Mawddwy, Machynlleth, Powys, SY20 9JF
Actual Grid Ref: SH862152
Tel: 01650 531326
Open: All year
Dogs allowed • Electric hook-up • Children's play area • Showers • Licensed bar on site
Take A470 for 1 mile from Mallwyd to Dinas Mawddwy. Level grass, scenic views.

▲ **Celyn Brithion,** Dinas-Mawddwy, Machynlleth, Powys, SY20 9LP
Actual Grid Ref: SH860139
Tel: 01650 531344
Open: Apr to Oct

Dolgellau

SH7217

▲ **Dolgamedd Caravan & Camping Site,** Gwanas Farm, Bontnewydd/Brithdir, Dolgellau, LL40 2SH
Actual Grid Ref: SH773202
Tel: 01341 422624 or 450221
Fax: 01341 450221 or 422624
Tent pitches: 50 **Tent rate:** £4.00
Open: Apr to Oct **Last arr:** 12pm
Dogs allowed • Electric hook-up • Picnic/barbecue area on site • Showers
6 acres, level, sheltered, beside river, swimming, fishing. Near sea and mountains.

▲ **Tanyfron Caravan & Camping Park,** Arran Road, Dolgellau, North West Wales, LL40 2AA
Actual Grid Ref: SH735176
Tel: 01341 422638
Open: All year

▲ **Vanner Abbey Farm Site,** Lanelltyd, Dolgellau, Gwynedd, LL40 2HE
Actual Grid Ref: SH725194
Tel: 01341 422854
Open: Mar to Oct

▲ **Bryn-y-Gwin Farm,** Cader Road, Dolgellau, Gwynedd, LL40 1TE
Actual Grid Ref: SH718177
Tel: 01341 422733
Open: All year

▲ **Dolserau Uchaf,** Dolgellau, Gwynedd, LL40 2DE
Actual Grid Ref: SH762198
Tel: 01341 422639
Open: Apr to Oct

Dolwyddelan

SH7352

▲ **Bryn Tirion Farm,** Dolwyddelan, LL25 0JD
Actual Grid Ref: SH723525
Tel: 01690 750366
Open: Mar to Oct

Dyffryn Ardudwy

SH5822

▲ **Murmur-yr-Afon Touring,** Dyffryn Ardudwy, Gwynedd, LL44 2BE
Actual Grid Ref: SH586236
Tourist Board grade: 4 Star
AA grade: 2 Pennants
Tel: 01341 247353
Fax: 01341 247353
Email: mills@murmuryrafon25.freeserve.co.uk
Tent pitches: 17
Tent rate: £5.00-£9.25
Open: Mar to Oct
Last arr: 10.30pm
Facilities for disabled people • Dogs allowed • Electric hook-up • Children's play area • Showers • Laundrette on site • Public phone on site
Set in Snowdonia National Park. Sheltered site, close to beaches.

▲ **Dyffryn Seaside Estate Co Ltd,** Dyffryn Ardudwy, Gwynedd, LL44 2HD
Actual Grid Ref: SH573232
Tel: 01341 247220
Open: Apr to Sep

Stilwell's Hostels & Camping 2002 — 343

North West Wales • MAP PAGE 339

▲ **Parc Isaf Farm,** Dyffryn Ardudwy, Gwynedd, LL44 2RJ
Actual Grid Ref: SH595226
Tel: 01341 247447
Open: Mar to Oct

▲ **Parc yr Onnen,** Dyffryn Ardudwy, Gwynedd, LL44 2DU
Tel: 01341 247033
Open: All year

▲ **Tynywern,** Dyffryn Ardudwy, Gwynedd, LL44 2BP
Tel: 01341 247381
Open: May to Oct

▲ **Tyn-y-Pant,** Dyffryn Ardudwy, Gwynedd, LL44 2HX
Actual Grid Ref: SH586243
Tel: 01341 247288
Open: Apr to Oct

▲ **Tanforhesgan Caravan & Camping Site,** Ynys, Talsarnau, Gwynedd, LL47 6RL
Actual Grid Ref: SH584344
Tel: 01766 780465
Open: Apr to Oct

Frongoch
SH9039

▲ **Tyn Cornel Camping & Caravanning Park,** Frongoch, Bala, Gwynedd, LL23 7NU
Actual Grid Ref: SH895400
Tel: 01678 520759
Open: Mar to Oct

Halfway Bridge
SH6068

▲ **Dinas Farm Camping & Touring Site,** Halfway Bridge, Bangor, Gwynedd, LL57 4NB
Actual Grid Ref: SH608685
Tel: 01248 364227
Open: Apr to Oct

Harlech
SH5831

▲ **Min-y-Don Caravan Park,** Beach Road, Harlech, Gwynedd, LL46 2UD
Actual Grid Ref: SH575317
Tel: 01766 780286 **Open:** Apr to Oct

▲ **Merthyr Farm,** Harlech, Gwynedd, LL46 2TP
Actual Grid Ref: SH602318
Tel: 01766 780344
Open: Mar to Oct

Islaw'r Dref
SH6815

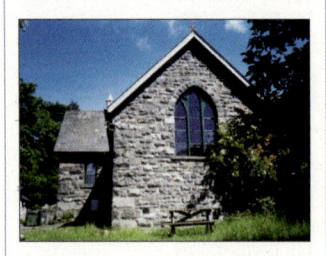

▲ **Caban Cader Idris,** Islaw'r Dref, Dolgellau, LL40 1TS
Actual Grid Ref: SH682169
Tel: 01766 762588 / 07887 954301
Fax: 01766 762588
Email: dafydd@cabancaderidris.com
Capacity: 19
Under 18: £4.50
Adults: £4.50
Open: All year
Camping for 3 tents: £4.00
Self-catering facilities • Showers • Central heating • Lounge • Drying room • Parking • No smoking
Ideal group accommodation, sleeps 19, kitchen/dining room, heating, shower, drying room, parking, picnic/BBQ area. Listed former school in secluded wooded valley 3 miles from Dolgellau in Snowdonia National Park. Within walking distance of Cader Idris Range, Cregennen Lake and Mawddach Estuary. Other local activities include: mountain biking, pony trekking, skiing, fishing, beaches.

▲ **Kings (Dolgellau) Youth Hostel,** Islaw'r Dref, Penmaenpool, Dolgellau, Gwynedd, LL40 1TB
Actual Grid Ref: SH683161
Tel: 01341 422392
Fax: 01341 422477
Capacity: 42
Under 18: £6.50
Adults: £9.25
Open: All year, 5.00pm
Family bunk rooms
Camping
Self-catering facilities • Showers • Shop • Lounge • Dining room • Drying room • Cycle store • Parking • No smoking • WC • Kitchen facilities • Credit cards accepted
Traditional hostel set in idyllic wooded valley, with magnificent views up to Cader Idris and Rhinog mountain ranges.

All details shown are as supplied by hostels and campsites in Autumn 2000.

Llanaber
SH6017

▲ **Trawsdir Farm,** Llanaber, Barmouth, Gwynedd, LL42 1RR
Actual Grid Ref: SH596198
Tel: 01341 280611
Open: Mar to Oct

▲ **Trawsdir Touring Caravan and Camping Site,** Llanaber, Barmouth, North West Wales, LL42 1RR
Actual Grid Ref: SH596198
Tel: 01341 280999
Email: rhian@caerddaniel.freeserve.co.uk
Open: Mar to Oct

Llanbedr
SH5826

▲ **Llanbedr Youth Hostel,** Plas Newydd, Llanbedr, Gwynedd, LL45 2LE
Tel: 01341 241287
Fax: 01341 241389
Capacity: 42
Under 18: £6.50
Adults: £9.25
Open: All year, 5.00pm
Family bunk rooms
Self-catering facilities • Showers • Shop • Lounge • Dining room • Games room • Drying room • Cycle store • Parking • Evening meal available 7.00pm • No smoking • Kitchen facilities • Breakfast available • Credit cards accepted
Set in the southern part of the Snowdonian National Park, and close to the seashore as well as the mountains. Ideal for families and singles alike.

▲ **Dinas Farm,** Llanbedr, Gwynedd, LL45 2PH
Actual Grid Ref: SH610291
Tel: 01341 241585
Open: All year

▲ **Shell Island,** Llanbedr, Gwynedd, LL45 2PJ
Actual Grid Ref: SH557267
Tel: 01341 241453
Fax: 01341 241501
Open: Mar to Nov

▲ **Hendy Farm House,** Llanbedr, Gwynedd, LL45 2LT
Actual Grid Ref: SH586257
Tel: 01341 241263
Open: Mar to Oct

MAP PAGE 339 • **North West Wales**

Llanbedrog

SH3331

▲ **Bodwrog Farm,** Llanbedrog, Pwllheli, Gwynedd, LL53 7RE
Actual Grid Ref: SH318315
Tel: 01758 740341
Tent pitches: 20
Tent rate: £5.00-£6.00
Open: Apr to Oct
Last arr: 10pm
Facilities for disabled people • Dogs allowed • Electric hook-up • Calor Gas/Camping Gaz • Showers • Boating/sailing/watersports nearby • Golf nearby • Riding nearby • Fishing nearby
2 acre mostly level camping and caravan site with superb views over Cardigan Bay to Snowdonia mountains. New block with showers, toilets, washbasins. Vast sandy beaches and small coves, water sports, art gallery, sporting clays, pubs and restaurants locally. Safe off-road environment for children. Ideal walking area. Rallies welcome.

▲ **Refail Caravan & Camping Site,** Refail, Llanbedrog, Pwllheli, Gwynedd, LL53 7NP
Tel: 01258 740511
Open: Easter to Sep

▲ **Bol Mynydd Caravan & Camping Site,** Bolmynydd, Llanbedrog, Pwllheli, Gwynedd, LL53 7UP
Actual Grid Ref: SH325314
Tel: 01758 740511
Open: Easter to Oct

▲ **Refail Caravan and Camping Site,** Bolmynydd, Llanbedrog, Pwllheli, Gwynedd, LL53 7UP
Actual Grid Ref: SH328319
Tel: 01758 740511
Open: Apr to Sep

Llanberis

SH5760

▲ **Llanberis Youth Hostel,** Llwyn Celyn, Llanberis, Carnarfon, Gwynedd, LL55 4SR
Actual Grid Ref: SH574596
Tel: 01286 870280
Fax: 01286 870936
Email: llanberis@yha.org.uk
Capacity: 60
Under 18: £6.90
Adults: £10.00
Open: All year (not Xmas/New Year), 5.00pm
Self-catering facilities • Television • Showers • Shop • Lounge • Dining room • Drying room • Cycle store • Parking

Evening meal available 7.00pm • No smoking • Kitchen facilities • Breakfast available • Credit cards accepted
Overlooking lakes, with views towards summit of Snowdon. The starting point of the walks of all levels, or just 0.5 mile from the Mountain Railway Station.

Llandanwg

SH5628

▲ **Glan-Y-Gors,** Llandanwg, Harlech, LL46 2SD
Tel: 01341 241410
Open: Mar to Oct

Llandderfel

SH9837

▲ **Bryn-Melyn Country Holiday Park,** Llandderfel, Bala, Gwynedd, LL23 7RA
Actual Grid Ref: SH995365
Tel: 01678 530212
Open: Mar to Oct

Llanddulas

SH9078

▲ **Bron-Y-Wendon Caravan Park,** Wern Road, Llanddulas, Colwyn Bay, North Wst Wales, LL22 8HG
Actual Grid Ref: SH904786
Tel: 01492 512903
Open: Mar to Oct

Llandwrog

SH4456

▲ **White Tower Caravan Park,** Llandwrog, Caernarfon, Gwynedd, LL54 5UH
Actual Grid Ref: SH453582
Tel: 01286 830649
Open: Mar to Oct

Llanegryn

SH6005

▲ **Waenfach Caravan Site,** Llanegryn, Tywyn, Gwynedd, LL36 9SB
Actual Grid Ref: SH591050
Tel: 01654 710375
Open: Apr to Oct

▲ **Glanywern,** Llanegryn, Gwynedd, LL36 9TH
Actual Grid Ref: SH631068
Tel: 01654 782247
Open: Apr to Oct

Llanfair

SH5729

▲ **Cae Cethin Farm Camp Site,** Llanfair, Harlech, Gwynedd, LL46 2SA
Actual Grid Ref: SH578287
Tel: 01766 780247
Open: Apr to Nov

▲ **Hengaeau,** Llanfair, Harlech, Gwynedd, LL46 2TE
Actual Grid Ref: SH586293
Tel: 01766 780347
Open: All year

▲ **Uwchglan Farm,** Llanfair, Harlech, Gwynedd, LL46 2RW
Actual Grid Ref: SH577295
Tel: 01766 780656
Open: All year

Llanfihangel-y-pennant

SH6608

▲ **Tynybryn,** Llanfihangel-y-Pennant, Tywyn, Gwynedd, LL36 9TN
Actual Grid Ref: SH660080
Tel: 01654 782277
Open: All year

Llangwnnadl

SH2033

▲ **Pen-y-Bont Bach,** Llangwnnadl, Pwllheli, Gwynedd, LL53 8NS
Actual Grid Ref: SH210326
Tel: 01758 770252
Open: Apr to Oct

▲ **Llecyn,** Llangwnnadl, Pwllheli, Gwynedd, LL53 8NT
Actual Grid Ref: SH196336
Tel: 01758 770347
Open: Apr to Oct

Llanrug

SH5462

▲ **Brynteg CaravanPark,** Llanrug, Caernarfon, Gwynedd, LL55 4RF
Actual Grid Ref: SH543624
Tel: 01286 871374
Open: Mar to Jan

▲ **Challoner Camp Site,** Erw Hywel, Llanrug, Caernarfon, Gwynedd, LL55 2AJ
Actual Grid Ref: SH582635
Tel: 01286 672985
Open: Apr to Oct

North West Wales • MAP PAGE 339

Tyn-y-Coed Farm, Llanrug, Caernarfon, Gwynedd, LL55 2AQ
Tel: 01286 673565
Open: Apr to Sep

Twll Clawdd Caravan Site, Llanrug, Caernarfon, Gwynedd, LL55 2AZ
Actual Grid Ref: SH528635
Tel: 01286 672838
Open: Mar to Oct

Llanrwst
SH7961

Bodnant Caravan Park, Nebo Road, Llanrwst, Gwynedd, LL26 0SD
Actual Grid Ref: SH803613
AA grade: 3 Pennants
Tel: 01492 640248
Tent pitches: 16 **Tent rate:** £7.00-£9.00
Open: Mar to Oct **Last arr:** 10pm
Dogs allowed • Electric hook-up • Calor Gas/Camping Gaz • Picnic/barbecue area on site • Children's play area • Showers • Public phone on site
Small select site. Wales in Bloom winner 26 years.

Llanuwchllyn
SH8730

Glanllyn Caravan & Camping Park, Glanllyn Farm, Llanuwchllyn, Bala, Gwynedd, LL23 7ST
Actual Grid Ref: SH894324
Tel: 01678 540227 **Open:** Mar to Oct

Bryn Gwyn Farm Caravan Park, Godre'r Aran, Llanuwchllyn, Bala, Gwynedd, LL23 7UB
Actual Grid Ref: SH865308
Tel: 01678 540687
Open: Apr to Oct

Llanycil
SH9134

Brynmoel, Llanycil, Bala, Gwynedd, LL23 7YG
Actual Grid Ref: SH909347
Tel: 01678 520143
Open: Mar to Oct

Llanystumdwy
SH4738

Camping & Caravanning Club Site, Tyddyn Sianel, Llanystumdwy, Criccieth, Gwynedd, LL52 0LS
Actual Grid Ref: SH469384
Tel: 01766 522855
Open: Apr to Oct

Llwyngwril
SH5909

Borthwen Farm, Llwyngwril, Gwynedd, LL37 2JJ
Actual Grid Ref: SH588099
Tel: 01341 250322
Open: Jun to Oct

Llysfaen
SH8977

Ty-Ucha Farm Camping Site, Tan-y-Craig Road, Llysfaen, Colwyn Bay, LL29 8UD
Tel: 01492 517051
Open: Easter to Oct

Maentwrog
SH6640

Llechrwd Farm, Maentwrog, Blaenau Ffestiniog, Gwynedd, LL41 4HF
Actual Grid Ref: SH678413
Tel: 01766 590240
Tent pitches: 22
Tent rate: £5.00-£8.00
Open: Easter to Oct **Last arr:** 10pm
Dogs allowed • Electric hook-up • Calor Gas/Camping Gaz • Showers
Riverside site located in heart of Snowdonia National Park.

Morfa Bychan
SH5436

Black Rock Touring & Camping Park, Morfa Bychan, Porthmadog, Gwynedd, LL49 9LD
Actual Grid Ref: SH527376
Tel: 01766 513919 **Open:** Mar to Oct

Garreg Goch Caravan Park, Black Rock Sands, Morfa Bychan, Porthmadog, Gwynedd, LL49 9YD
Actual Grid Ref: SH542372
Tel: 01766 512210
Open: Mar to Oct

Gwyndy Caravan Park, Black Rock Sands, Morfa Bychan, Porthmadog, Gwynedd, LL49 9YB
Actual Grid Ref: SH543371
Tel: 01766 512047
Open: Mar to Oct

Glan Morfa Mawr, Morfa Bychan, Porthmadog, Gwynedd, LL49 9YH
Actual Grid Ref: SH537376
Tel: 01766 513333
Open: Apr to Oct

Mynytho
SH3030

Brynitirion Caravan Site, Mynytho, Pwllheli, Gwynedd, LL53 7RW
Actual Grid Ref: SH306316
Tel: 01758 740850
Open: Mar to Oct

Nant Peris
SH6058

Snowdon House, 3 Gwastadnant, Nant Peris, Caernarfon, LL55 4UL
Tel: 01286 870356
Open: All year

Nantgwynant
SH6250

Bryn Gwynant Youth Hostel, Nantgwynant, Caernarfon, Gwynedd, LL55 4NP
Actual Grid Ref: SH641513
Tel: 01766 890251
Fax: 01766 890479
Email: bryngwynant@yha.org.uk
Capacity: 77
Under 18: £6.90 **Adults:** £10.00
Open: Jan to Oct + Xmas, 5.00pm
*Family bunk rooms Camping
Self-catering facilities • Showers • Shop • Lounge • Games room • Drying room • Cycle store • Parking • Evening meal available 7.00pm • WC • Kitchen facilities • Breakfast available • Credit cards accepted*
Recently refurbished impressive stone mansion with 40 acres of grounds, overlooking Llyn Gwynant lake and close to Snowdon.

Nantlle
SH5153

Talymignedd Isaf, Nantlle, Penygroes, Caernarfon, Gwynedd, LL54 6BT
Actual Grid Ref: SH531531
Tel: 01286 880374
Open: Apr to Oct

Nefyn
SH3140

Wern Farm, Nefyn, Pwllheli, Gwynedd, LL53 6LW
Actual Grid Ref: SH316416
Tel: 01758 720432
Open: Mar to Oct

MAP PAGE 339 • **North West Wales**

Pen-y-Pass

SH6455

▲ **Pen-y-Pass Youth Hostel,** Pen-y-Pass, Nantgwynant, Caernarfon, Gwynedd, LL55 4NY
Actual Grid Ref: SH647556
Tel: 01286 870428
Fax: 01286 872434
Email: panypass@yha.org.uk
Capacity: 84
Under 18: £7.75 **Adults:** £11.00
Open: All year, All day
Self-catering facilities • Television • Showers • Shop • Lounge 2 • Dining room • Games room • Drying room • Security lockers • Cycle store • Evening meal available 7.00pm • Facilities for disabled people Category 2 • Kitchen facilities • Breakfast available
A converted pub that has become the largest hostel in Snowdonia, situated right at the head of the Llanberis Pass.

Penmaenmawr

SH7176

▲ **Woodlands Camping Park,** Pendyffrin Hall, Penmaenmawr, LL34 6UF
Actual Grid Ref: SH740778
Tel: 01492 623219
Open: Easter to Oct

▲ **Trwyn-yr-Wylfa Farm,** Conway Old Road, Penmaenmawr, LL34 6SF
Tel: 01492 622357
Open: May to Sep

▲ **Tyddyn Du Touring Park,** Conwy Old Road, Penmaenmawr, North West Wales, LL34 6RE
Actual Grid Ref: SH730770
Tel: 01492 622300
Open: Mar to Oct

Penrhyndeudraeth

SH6139

▲ **Blaen Cefn Farm,** Penrhyndeudraeth, Gwynedd, LL48 6NA
Actual Grid Ref: SH620398
Tel: 01766 770981
Open: Apr to Oct

Pentrefelin (Porthmadog)

SH5239

▲ **Eisteddfa Caravan & Camping Park,** Pentrefelin, Criccieth, Gwynedd, LL52 0PT
Tel: 01766 522104
Open: Mar to Oct

Pistyll

SH3241

▲ **Tir Bach,** Pistyll, Pwllheli, Gwynedd, LL53 6LW
Actual Grid Ref: SH319419
Tel: 01758 720074
Open: May to Sep

Pont Pen-y-benglog

SH6560

▲ **Idwal Cottage Youth Hostel,** Pont Pen-y-benglog, Bethesda, Bangor, Gwynedd, LL57 3LZ
Actual Grid Ref: SH648603
Tel: 01248 600225
Fax: 01248 602952
Capacity: 44
Under 18: £5.75
Adults: £8.50
Open: Jan to Sept
Camping
Self-catering facilities • Showers • Lounge • Dining room • Drying room • Cycle store • Parking • Evening meal available 5.00pm • No smoking • WC • Kitchen facilities • Credit cards accepted
Originally a quarry manager's cottage, by Ogwen Lake below the Glyder Mountains and overlooking the Nant Ffrancon Pass. This is a good walking area. It may be closed for refurbishment from September 2001.

Pont-rug

SH5163

▲ **Riverside Camping,** Caer Glyddyn, Pont-rug, Caernarfon, Gwynedd, LL55 2BB
Actual Grid Ref: SH506628
Tel: 01286 672524 / 678781
Fax: 01286 677223
Open: Apr to Oct

Pont-y-Pant

SH7554

▲ **Lledr Valley (Betws-y-Coed) Youth Hostel,** Lledr House, Pont-y-Pant, Dolwyddelan, LL25 0DQ
Actual Grid Ref: SH749534
Tel: 01690 750202
Fax: 01690 750410
Capacity: 61
Under 18: £6.50
Adults: £9.25
Open: Apr to Aug, 5.00pm

Camping
Self-catering facilities • Showers • Shop • Lounge • Dining room • Drying room • Cycle store • Parking • Evening meal available 7.00pm • No smoking • WC • Breakfast available • Credit cards accepted
Former quarry manager's house. The area is rich with slate quarries, copper mines and woollen mills, as well as with forest walks.

Pontllyfni

SH4352

▲ **Llyn-y-Gele Farm Caravan Park,** Pontllyfni, Caernarfon, Gwynedd, LL54 5EL
Actual Grid Ref: SH433525
Tel: 01286 660283
Open: Apr to Sep

▲ **Bryn Cynan Fawr Farm,** Pontllyfni, Caernarfon, LL54 5EE
Tel: 01286 830320
Open: July to Aug

▲ **St Ives Caravan Site,** Lon-y-Wig, Pontllyfni, Caernarfon, Gwynedd, LL54 5EG
Actual Grid Ref: SH432523
Tel: 01286 660347
Open: Mar to Oct

Porthmadog

SH5638

▲ **Tyddyn Llwyn Caravan Park & Camp Site,** Morfa Bychan Road, Porthmadog, Gwynned, LL49 9UR
Actual Grid Ref: SH562383
Tel: 01766 512205 **Fax:** 01766 512205
Open: Easter to Oct

▲ **Tyddyn Adi Touring Caravan & Camping Park,** Morfa Bychan Road, Porthmadog, Gwynedd, LL49 9YW
Actual Grid Ref: SH543379
Tel: 01766 512933
Open: Apr to Oct

▲ **Greenacres Holiday Park,** Black Rock Sands, Porthmadog, Gwynedd, LL49 9YB
Tel: 0845 712 5931
Open: Easter to Oct

Pwllheli

SH3735

▲ **Abererch Sands Holiday Centre,** Pwllheli, Gwynedd, LL53 6PJ
Actual Grid Ref: SH403359
Tel: 01758 612327
Open: Mar to Oct

North West Wales • MAP PAGE 339

▲ **Rhosfawr Nurseries Caravan & Camping Park,** Pwllheli, Gwynedd, LL53 6YA
Actual Grid Ref: SH371397
Tel: 01766 810545
Open: Apr to Oct

Rhos-on-Sea
SH8381

▲ **Dinarth Hall,** Rhos-on-Sea, Colwyn Bay, LL28 4PX
Actual Grid Ref: SH824803
Tel: 01492 548203
Open: May to Sep

Rhos-y-gwaliau
SH9434

▲ **Pen-y-Garth Caravan & Camping Park,** Rhosygwaliau, Bala, Gwynedd, LL23 7ES
Actual Grid Ref: SH941348
Tel: 01678 520485
Open: Mar to Oct

Rhoshirwaun
SH1929

▲ **Brynffynnon,** Rhoshirwaun, Aberdaron, Pwllheli, Gwynedd, LL53 8LF
Actual Grid Ref: SH185302
Tel: 01758 730643 **Open:** Mar to Oct

Rhoslan
SH4841

▲ **Stone Barn Bunkhouse Barn,** Tyddyn Morthwyl, Rhoslan, Criccieth, Gwynedd, LL52 0NF
Tel: 01766 522115
Capacity: 12
Under 18: £5.00 **Adults:** £5.00
Open: All year, any time
Camping for 40 tents: £5.50
Self-catering facilities • Showers • Parking
Sleeping platform for 12, wood burner stove. Shared facilities with campsite.

▲ **Muriau Bach Touring Site,** Rhoslan, Criccieth, Gwynedd, LL52 0NP
Actual Grid Ref: SH484419
Tel: 01766 530642
Open: Mar to Oct

▲ **Tyddyn Morthwyl,** Rhoslan, Criccieth, Gwynedd, LL52 0NF
Actual Grid Ref: SH488402
Tel: 01766 522115
Open: Easter to Oct

Rhoslefain
SH5705

▲ **Llabwst Farm,** Rhoslefain, Tywyn, Gwynedd, LL36 9NE
Tel: 01654 711013
Open: June to Oct

Rhyd-Ddu
SH5652

▲ **Snowdon Ranger Youth Hostel,** Cae'r Orsaf, Rhyd Ddu, Caernarfon, Gwynedd, LL54 7YS
Tel: 01286 650391
Fax: 01286 650093
Capacity: 66
Under 18: £6.90
Adults: £10.00
Open: Feb to Dec (not Xmas/New Year), 5.0pm
Self-catering facilities • Shop • Wet weather shelter • Lounge • Dining room • Games room • Drying room • Cycle store • Parking • Evening meal available • No smoking • WC • Kitchen facilities • Breakfast available • Credit cards accepted
At the foot of the Snowdon Ranger Path. It is possible to swim from a beach on the lake behind the hostel, which is a former inn.

Rhydymain
SH7921

▲ **Broneinion,** Rhydymain, Dolgellau, Gwynedd, LL40 2BU
Actual Grid Ref: SH781213
Tel: 01341 41651
Open: All year

Rowen
SH7571

▲ **Rowen Youth Hostel,** Rhiw Farm, Rowen, Conwy, LL32 8YW
Actual Grid Ref: SH747721
Tel: 01492 650089
Capacity: 24
Under 18: £5.75
Adults: £8.50
Open: All year, 5.00pm
Camping
Self-catering facilities • Showers • Shop • Wet weather shelter • Lounge • Dining room • Cycle store • Parking • No smoking • WC • Kitchen facilities
Simple, remote Welsh hill farmhouse set high above Rowen village with panoramic views of Conwy Valley.

Sarn Bach
SH3026

▲ **Sea View Camping & Caravan Park,** Sarn Bach, Abersoch, Pwllheli, Gwynedd, LL53 7ET
Actual Grid Ref: SH305262
Tel: 01758 712052
Open: Mar to Oct

▲ **Tan-y-Bryn Farm,** Sarn Bach, Abersoch, Pwllheli, Gwynedd, LL53 7UD
Actual Grid Ref: SH305263
Tel: 01758 712093
Open: May to Sep

▲ **Sarn Farm,** Sarn Bach, Abersoch, Pwllheli, Gwynedd, LL53 5BG
Actual Grid Ref: SH305266
Tel: 01758 812144
Open: Apr to Oct

Saron (Llanwnda)
SH4658

▲ **Tyn Rhos Farm Caravan Park,** Saron, Llanwnda, Caernarfon, Gwynedd, LL54 5UH
Actual Grid Ref: SH456581
Tel: 01286 830362
Open: Mar to Oct

Tal-y-Bont (Barmouth)
SH5821

▲ **Bellaport Touring Caravan Site,** Tal-y-Bont, Gwynedd, LL43 2BX
Tel: 01341 247338
Open: Mar to Oct

▲ **Benar Beach Camping & Touring Park,** Tal-y-Bont, Gwynedd, LL43 2AR
Actual Grid Ref: SH574227
Tel: 01341 247571
Open: Mar to Oct

▲ **Dalar Farm,** Tal-y-Bont, Gwynedd, LL43 2AQ
Actual Grid Ref: SH584216
Tel: 01341 247221
Open: Apr to Oct

▲ **Islawrffordd Caravan & Camping Site,** Tal-y-Bont, Gwynedd, LL43 2BQ
Actual Grid Ref: SH590212
Tel: 01341 247269
Open: Apr to Oct

MAP PAGE 339 • **North West Wales**

▲ **Sarnfaen Farm Tourers & Tents,** Tal-y-Bont, Barmouth, Gwynedd, LL43 2AQ
Actual Grid Ref: SH585215
Tel: 01341 247604
Open: Easter to Oct

▲ **Moelfre View Caravan Park,** Tal-y-Bont, Barmouth, Gwynedd, LL43 2AQ
Actual Grid Ref: SH583213
Tel: 01341 247100
Open: Mar to Jan

▲ **Rowen Farm and Benar Isa Farm,** Talybont, LL43 2AD
Actual Grid Ref: SH586219
Tel: 01341 247333
Open: Apr to Oct

Tal-y-Bont (Conwy)

SH7668

▲ **Tyn Terfyn Touring Caravan Park,** Tal-y-Bont, Conway, Conwy, LL32 8YX
Actual Grid Ref: SH768695
Tel: 01492 660525
Open: Mar to Oct

Tal-y-llyn

SH7109

▲ **Dol Elnion,** Tal-y-llyn, Tywyn, Gwynedd, LL36 9AJ
Actual Grid Ref: SH729114
Tel: 01654 761312
Tent pitches: 35
Tent rate: £3.00-£10.00
Open: All year
Dogs allowed • Electric hook-up • Showers • Indoor swimming pool nearby • Riding nearby • Fishing nearby
This flat 3-acre greenfield site nestles into the foot of mighty Cader Idris with direct access to the Minffordd Path to the summit. Within minutes of Tal-y-llyn lake with brown trout fishing facilities. Excellent for walking and birdwatching. Well situated for touring Mid and North Wales.

▲ **Cedris Farm,** Tal-y-llyn, Tywyn, Gwynedd, LL36 9YW
Actual Grid Ref: SH690079
Tel: 01654 782280
Open: Apr to Sep

▲ **Cwmrhwyddfor Campsite,** Tal-y-llyn, Tywyn, Gwynedd, LL36 9AJ
Actual Grid Ref: SH737120
Tel: 01654 761286
Open: Mar to Oct

Talsarnau

SH6135

▲ **Barcdy Caravan & Camping Park,** Talsarnau, Gwynedd, LL47 6YG
Actual Grid Ref: SH622371
Tel: 01766 770736
Open: Easter to Oct

Towyn

SH9779

▲ **Ty Mawr Holiday Park,** Towyn, Abergele, Rhyl, Denbighshire, LL22 9HG
Actual Grid Ref: SH967792
Tel: 01745 832079
Open: Apr to Oct

Trefriw

SH7863

▲ **Glyn Farm Caravan Park,** Trefriw, Betws-y-Coed, LL27 0RZ
Tel: 01492 640442
Open: Easter to Oct

▲ **Plas Meirion Caravan Park,** Gower Road, Trefriw, Betws-y-Coed, LL27 0RZ
Actual Grid Ref: SH783630
Tel: 01492 640247
Open: Easter to Oct

Tudweiliog

SH2336

▲ **Porthysgaden Farm,** Tudweiliog, Nefyn, Pwllheli, Gwynedd, LL53 8PD
Tel: 01758 770206
Open: Apr to Oct

▲ **Towyn Farm,** Tudweiliog, Pwllheli, Gwynedd, LL53 8PD
Actual Grid Ref: SH233374
Tel: 01758 770230
Open: Apr to Nov

▲ **Hirdre Fawr Farm,** Tudweiliog, Pwllheli, Gwynedd, LL53 8YY
Actual Grid Ref: SH249381
Tel: 01758 770278
Open: May to Oct

▲ **Tyddyn Sander,** Tudweiliog, Pwllheli, Gwynedd, LL53 8PB
Actual Grid Ref: SH222364
Tel: 01758 770420
Open: Apr to Sep

Ty-nant (Maerdy)

SH9944

▲ **Glen Ceirw Caravan Park,** Ty-Nant, Corwen, Denbighshire, LL21 0RF
Actual Grid Ref: SH963462
Tel: 01490 420346
Open: Mar to Oct

Tywyn (Aberdovey)

SH5800

▲ **Pall Mall Farm Caravan Park,** Tywyn, Gwynedd, LL36 9RU
Actual Grid Ref: SH595013
Tel: 01654 710384
Open: Mar to Sept

▲ **Ynysymaengwyn Caravan Park,** Tywyn, Gwynedd, LL36 9RY
Actual Grid Ref: SH601021
Tel: 01654 710684
Email: rita@ynysymaengwyn.freeserve.co.uk
Open: Apr to Oct

▲ **Llanllwyda,** Llanfihangel, Tywyn, Gwynedd, LL36 9TW
Actual Grid Ref: SH650077
Tel: 01654 782276
Open: Apr to Oct

▲ **Ty'nymaes,** Talyllyn, Tywyn, Gwynedd, LL36 9AJ
Actual Grid Ref: SH731111
Tel: 01654 761288
Open: May to Oct

▲ **Caethle Farm,** Tywyn, Gwynedd, LL36 9HS
Actual Grid Ref: SN601992
Tel: 01654 710587
Open: Apr to Oct

Uwchmynydd

SH1524

▲ **Ty-Newydd,** Uwchmynydd, Aberdaron, Pwllheli, Gwynedd, LL53 8BY
Actual Grid Ref: SH146257
Tel: 01758 760302
Open: Apr to Oct

You are advised to book in advance for periods of high demand – the Summer months, Half Term holidays and public holidays.

WALES

North West Wales • MAP PAGE 339

Waunfawr
SH5259

▲ **Tyn-yr-Onnen Mountain Farm C & C Park,** *Waunfawr, Caernarfon, Gwynedd, LL55 4AX*
Actual Grid Ref: SH535590
Tourist Board grade: 3 Ticks
AA grade: 3 Pennants
Tel: 01286 650281
Fax: 01286 650043
Tent pitches: 40
Tent rate: £5.00-£12.00
Open: May to Sep **Last arr:** 10.30pm
Facilities for disabled people • Dogs allowed • Electric hook-up • Baths • Calor Gas/Camping Gaz • Children's play area •
Showers • Laundrette on site • Public phone on site • Shop on site • TV room • Games room • Indoor swimming pool nearby • Outdoor swimming pool nearby • Boating/sailing/watersports nearby • Tennis courts nearby • Golf nearby • Riding nearby • Fishing on site
Welcome to a traditional upland farm, secluded and off the beaten track. Freedom to roam our beautiful hills, interesting walks, friendly animals. Immaculate facilities, free showers, toddlers bathroom, games and TV lounge. SAE for brochure.

Ynys
SH5933

▲ **Ynys Graianog,** *Ynys, Criccieth, Gwynedd, LL52 0NT*
Actual Grid Ref: SH467422
Tel: 01766 530234
Open: Apr to Oct

▲ **Gwyndy Mawr,** *Ynys, Harlech, Gwynedd, LL47 6TN*
Actual Grid Ref: SH596353
Tel: 01766 780449
Open: All year

Pembrokeshire

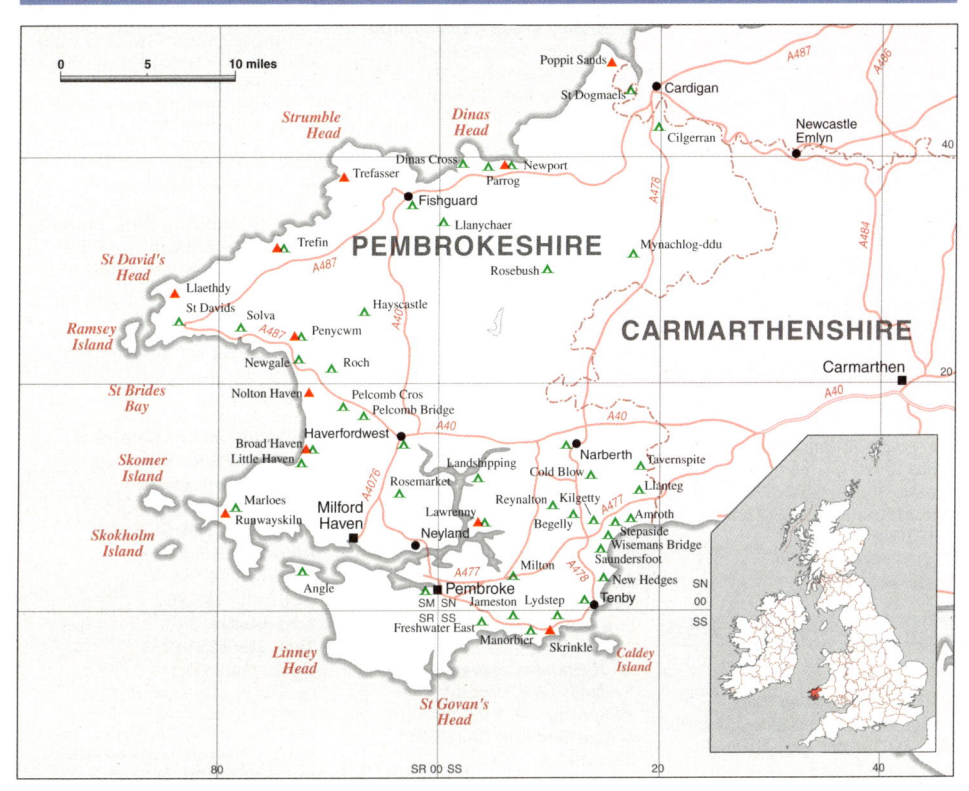

Amroth

SN1607

▲ **Little Kings Park Caravan Park,** Amroth, Narberth, Pembrokeshire, SA67 8PG
Actual Grid Ref: SN145092
Tel: 01834 831330
Open: Mar to Oct

▲ **The Village Touring & Caravan Park,** Summerhill, Amroth, Narberth, Pembrokeshire, SA67 8NS
Actual Grid Ref: SN152072
Tel: 01834 811051
Open: Mar to Oct

Angle

SM8602

▲ **Castle Farm Camping Site,** Angle, Pembroke, SA71 5AR
Tel: 01646 641120
Open: Easter to Oct

Begelly

SN1107

▲ **Stone Pitt Camping Site,** Begelly, Kilgetty, Pembrokeshire, SA68 0XE
Actual Grid Ref: SN116077
Tel: 01834 811086
Open: Mar to Jan

Broad Haven

SM8613

▲ **Broad Haven Youth Hostel,** Broad Haven, Haverfordwest, Pembrokeshire, SA62 3JH
Actual Grid Ref: SM863141
Tel: 01437 781688
Fax: 01437 781100
Email: broadhaven@yha.org.uk
Capacity: 75
Under 18: £7.75 **Adults:** £11.00
Open: Mar to Oct, 1.00pm
Family bunk rooms
Television • Games room • Drying room • Parking • Evening meal available 6.30pm • Facilities for disabled people Category 1 • No smoking • WC • Breakfast available • Credit cards accepted
Award-winning purpose-built hostel close to beach, with fine views of the coastal headlands.

▲ **Broad Haven Holiday Park,** Broad Haven, Haverfordwest, Pembrokeshire, SA62 3JD
Tel: 01437 781277
Open: Apr to Oct

▲ **Creampots Touring Caravan & Camping Park,** Broad Haven, Haverfordwest, Pembrokeshire, SA62 3TU
Actual Grid Ref: SM882131
Tel: 01437 781776
Open: Mar to Oct

Pembrokeshire • MAP PAGE 351

Cilgerran
SN1942

▲ **Penralltllyln Farm,** Cilgerran, Ceredigion, SA43 2PR
Actual Grid Ref: SN213413
Tel: 01239 682350
Open: Mar to Oct

Cold Blow
SN1212

▲ **Wood Office Caravan & Tent Park,** Cold Blow, Narberth, Pembrokeshire, SA67 8RR
Tel: 01834 860565
Open: Easter to Sep

Dinas Cross
SN0039

▲ **Fishguard Bay Caravan Park,** Dinas Cross, Newport, Pembrokeshire, SA42 0YD
Actual Grid Ref: SM984382
Tel: 01348 811415
Fax: 01348 811425
Open: Mar to Dec

Fishguard
SM9537

▲ **Tregroes Touring Park,** Fishguard, Pembrokeshire, SA65 9QF
Actual Grid Ref: SM942632
Tel: 01348 872316
Open: Apr to Oct

Freshwater East
SS0198

▲ **Upper Portclew,** Freshwater East, Pembroke, SA71 5LA
Tel: 01646 672112
Tent pitches: 40
Tent rate: £7.00
Open: May to Sep
Dogs allowed • Electric hook-up • Showers
Walking down sand dunes to beach. Pub and food, boat launch.

Haverfordwest
SM9515

▲ **Pelcomb Cross Farm Caravan Site,** Haverfordwest, Pembrokeshire, SA62 6AB
Actual Grid Ref: SM919179
Tel: 01437 710431
Open: Mar to Jan

Hayscastle
SM8925

▲ **Brandy Brook Caravan Site,** Hayscastle, Haverfordwest, Pembrokeshire, SA62 5PT
Actual Grid Ref: SM884239
Tel: 01348 840272
Open: Mar to Sept

Jameston
SS0598

▲ **Tudor Glen Caravan Park,** Jameston, Tenby, Pembrokeshire, SA70 7SS
Actual Grid Ref: SS063990
Tel: 01834 871417
Fax: 01834 871832
Open: Mar to Oct

Kilgetty
SN1207

▲ **Cross Park Holiday Centre,** Broadmoor, Kilgetty, Pembrokeshire, SA68 0RS
Actual Grid Ref: SN099059
Tel: 01834 811244
Open: Apr to Oct

▲ **Ryelands Caravan Park,** Ryelands Lane, Kilgetty, Pembrokeshire, SA68 0VY
Actual Grid Ref: SN125085
Tel: 01834 812369
Open: Mar to Oct

Landshipping
SN0111

▲ **New Park Caravan Park,** Landshipping, Narberth, Pembrokeshire, SA67 8BG
Actual Grid Ref: SN026111
Tel: 01834 891284
Open: May to Oct

Lawrenny
SN0106

▲ **Lawrenny Youth Hostel,** Lawrenny, Kilgetty, Pembrokeshire, SA68 0PN
Actual Grid Ref: SN018070
Tel: 01646 651270
Fax: 01646 651856

Capacity: 23
Under 18: £5.70
Adults: £8.10
Open: All year
Self-catering facilities • Showers • Lounge • Drying room • Parking • No smoking • Kitchen facilities
Refurbished former Victorian school in village setting with fine Norman church in the southern part of the Pembrokeshire Coast National Park, an area rich in flora and fauna, especially bird life.

▲ **Mountain Park Farm,** Lawrenny, Kilgetty, Pembrokeshire, SA68 0PT
Actual Grid Ref: SN029080
Tel: 01834 891620
Open: All year

Little Haven
SM8512

▲ **South Cockett Caravan & Camping Park,** , Broadway, Little Haven, Haverfordwest, Pembrokeshire, SA62 5PT
Actual Grid Ref: SM878134
AA grade: 3 Pennants
Tel: 01437 781296
Fax: 01437 781296
Tent pitches: 25
Tent rate: £5.65-£8.00
Open: Mar to Oct
Facilities for disabled people • Dogs allowed • Electric hook-up • Calor Gas/Camping Gaz • Showers • Laundrette on site • Public phone on site • Indoor swimming pool nearby • Boating/sailing/watersports nearby • Riding nearby • Fishing nearby
Family-run site, with excellent clean facilities, surrounded with tree lined hedges, site is level and free draining with good access. Situated on the edge of the Pembrokeshire Coast National Park, visitors might take advantage of the proximity of Martin's Haven, where boats leave for Skomer Island.

▲ **Redlands Touring Caravan Park,** Little Haven, Haverfordwest, Pembrokeshire, SA62 3SJ
Actual Grid Ref: SM853109
Tel: 01437 781300
Fax: 01437 781093
Email: nancywhitby@virgin.net
Open: Mar to Oct

▲ **Howelston Caravan Site,** Little Haven, Haverfordwest, Pembrokeshire, SA62 3UU
Actual Grid Ref: SM850120
Tel: 01437 781253
Open: Apr to Sep

MAP PAGE 351 • **Pembrokeshire**

Llaethdy

SM7327

▲ **St David's Youth Hostel,** Llaethdy, St David's, Haverfordwest, Pembrokeshire, SA62 6PR
Actual Grid Ref: SM739276
Tel: 01437 720345 **Fax:** 01437 721283
Capacity: 40
Under 18: £5.75 **Adults:** £8.50
Open: Apr to Oct
Self-catering facilities • Shop • Wet weather shelter • Drying room • Parking • WC • Credit cards accepted
White painted farmhouse, beneath summit of Carn Llidi about 2 miles from St David's. Accommodation is basic, but there is an open fire.

Llancynfelyn

SN6491

▲ **Ty Craig Holiday Park,** Llancynfelyn, Machynlleth, Powys, SY20 8PU
Actual Grid Ref: SN643922
Tel: 01970 832339
Open: Mar to Oct

Llanteg

SN1810

▲ **The Valley,** Amroth Road, Llanteg, Narbeth, Pembrokeshire, SA67 8QJ
Actual Grid Ref: SN161098
Tel: 01834 831226
Open: Mar to Oct

▲ **Rose Park Farm,** Amroth Road, Llanteg, Narberth, SA67 8QJ
Actual Grid Ref: SN164098
Tel: 01834 831203
Open: May to Oct

▲ **Woodview,** Llanteg, Narbeth, Pembrokeshire, SA67 8QJ
Actual Grid Ref: SN178103
Tel: 01834 831207
Open: May to Sep

Llanychaer

SM9835

▲ **Gwaun Vale Touring Park,** Llanychaer, Fishguard, Pembrokeshire, SA65 9TA
Actual Grid Ref: SM973357
Tel: 01348 874698
Open: Mar to Jan

Lydstep

SS0898

▲ **Whitewell Caravan Park,** Lydstep Beach, Lydstep, Tenby, Pembrokeshire, SA70 7RY
Actual Grid Ref: SS095992
Tel: 01834 842200
Open: Mar to Sept

Manorbier

SS0697

▲ **Buttyland Touring Caravan & Tent Park,** Manorbier, Tenby, Pembrokeshire, SA70 7SN
Actual Grid Ref: SS068993
Tel: 01834 871278
Open: Feb to Nov

▲ **Park Farm Caravans,** Manorbier, Tenby, Pembrokeshire, SA70 7SU
Tel: 01646 672583
Open: Easter to Oct

▲ **Manorbier Holiday Park,** Station Road, Manorbier, Tenby, Pembrokeshire, SA70 7SN
Actual Grid Ref: SS068992
Tel: 01834 871952
Open: Mar to Oct

Marloes

SM7908

▲ **East Hook Farm,** Marloes, Haverfordwest, Pembrokeshire, SA62 3BJ
Tel: 01646 636291
Open: All year

▲ **Foxdale,** Glebe Lane, Marloes, Haverfordwest, Pembs, SA62 3AX
Actual Grid Ref: SM796083
Tel: 01646 636243 **Fax:** 01646 636982
Open: All year

▲ **Lower Mullock Farm,** Marloes, Haverfordwest, Pembrokeshire, SA62 3AR
Actual Grid Ref: SM814084
Tel: 01646 636251
Open: All year

Milton

SN0402

▲ **Milton Bridge Caravan Park,** Milton, Tenby, Pembrokeshire, SA70 8PH
Actual Grid Ref: SN039032
Tel: 01646 651204
Open: Mar to Oct

Mynachlog-ddu

SN1430

▲ **Trefach Caravan Park,** Mynachlog-ddu, Clynderwen, Pembrokeshire, SA66 7RU
Actual Grid Ref: SN150290
Tel: 01994 419225
Fax: 01994 419225
Open: Mar to Jan

Narberth

SN1014

▲ **Noble Court Caravan Park,** Redstone Road, Narberth, Pembrokeshire, SA67 7ES
Actual Grid Ref: SN110159
Tel: 01834 861191
Fax: 01834 861484
Open: Mar to Nov

▲ **Dingle Farm Caravan Park,** Jesse Road, Narberth, Pembrokeshire, SA67 7DP
Tel: 01834 860482
Open: Apr to Oct

▲ **Stoneditch Farm,** Narberth, Pembrokeshire, SA67 8BU
Actual Grid Ref: SN104140
Tel: 01834 860693
Open: All year

New Hedges

SN1302

▲ **Wood Park Caravans,** New Hedges, Tenby, Pembrokeshire, SA70 8TL
Actual Grid Ref: SN125028
Tel: 01834 843414
Open: Mar to Sept

▲ **Rowston Holiday Park,** New Hedges, Tenby, Pembrokeshire, SA70 8TL
Actual Grid Ref: SN132028
Tel: 01834 842178 **Open:** Mar to Nov

▲ **Rumbleway Caravan & Tent Park,** New Hedges, Tenby, Pembrokeshire, SA70 8TR
Actual Grid Ref: SN129031
Tel: 01834 3719
Open: Mar to Oct

▲ **The Lodge Farm Caravan & Tent Park,** New Hedges, Tenby, Pembrokeshire, SA70 8TH
Actual Grid Ref: SN130029
Tel: 01834 842468
Open: Apr to Oct

WALES

Pembrokeshire • MAP PAGE 351

▲ **Red House Farm,** New Hedges, Saundersfoot, Pembs, SA69 9DP
Actual Grid Ref: SN128035
Tel: 01834 813918
Open: Apr to Oct

Newgale
SM8422

▲ **Newgale Camping Site,** Newgale, Haverfordwest, Pembrokeshire, SA62 6AS
Actual Grid Ref: SM849222
Tel: 01437 710253
Open: Mar to Oct

▲ **Newgale Farm,** Newgale, Haverfordwest, Pembrokeshire, SA42 6AS
Actual Grid Ref: SM851229
Tel: 01437 710253
Open: All year

Newport
SN0539

▲ **Trefdraeth Youth Hostel,** Newport Youth Hostel, Lower St Mary's Street, Newport, Pembrokeshire, SA42 0TS
Actual Grid Ref: SN058393
Tel: 01239 820080
Fax: 01239 820080
Email: reservations@yha.org.uk
Capacity: 28
Under 18: £6.50
Adults: £9.25
Open: All year, 5.00pm
Family bunk rooms
Self-catering facilities • Showers • Wet weather shelter • Lounge • Cycle store • Parking Limited • Facilities for disabled people Category 2 • No smoking • Kitchen facilities • Credit cards accepted
In the centre of the popular town of Newport on the West Wales coast; a short walk away are shops, pubs, the beach, coastal path, bird sanctuary and estuary. The Preseli Hills have many prehistoric sites to visit.

▲ **Llwyngwair Manor Holiday Park,** Newport, Pembrokeshire, SA42 0LX
Actual Grid Ref: SN072291
Tel: 01239 820498
Open: Mar to Oct

▲ **Tredegar House Caravan Park,** Tredegar House , Newport, Monmouthshire, NP1 9YN
Tel: 01633 815600
Open: Easter to Oct

▲ **Ty Canol Farm,** Newport, Pembrokeshire, SA42 0ST
Actual Grid Ref: SN044396
Tel: 01239 820264
Open: All year

Nolton Haven
SM8618

▲ **Nolton Haven Farmhouse,** Nolton Haven, Haverfordwest, Pembs, SA62 4NH
Tel: 01437 710263
Fax: 01437 710263
Email: stil4@noltonhaven.com
Capacity: 25
Under 18: £7.50
Adults: £15.00
Open: All year (not Xmas), until 10pm
Camping for 30 tents: £5.00
Self-catering facilities • Television • Showers • Central heating • Lounge • Dining room • Grounds available for games • Drying room • Cycle store • Parking
Beside Nolton Haven's sandy beach, the large farmhouse is half way from Marloes to St Davids, sleeping up to 25 in seven bedrooms. Campsite only 100 yards from the beach and inn. Please call for price details, group discounts available.

Parrog
SN0439

▲ **Morawelon,** Parrog, Newport, Pembrokeshire, SA42 0RW
Tel: 01239 820565
Open: Mar to Oct

Pelcomb Bridge
SM9317

▲ **The Rising Sun Caravan Site,** St Davids Road, Pelcomb Bridge, Haverfordwest, SA62 6EA
Actual Grid Ref: SM932171
Tel: 01437 765171
Open: Mar to Oct

Pelcomb Cross
SM9117

▲ **Dunston Hill Farm,** Pelcomb Cross, Haverfordwest, Pembrokeshire, SA62 6ED
Actual Grid Ref: SM919181
Tel: 01437 710525
Open: Mar to Oct

Pembroke
SM9801

▲ **Windmill Hill Farm,** St Daniels Hill, Pembroke, SA71 5BT
Actual Grid Ref: SM979002
Tel: 01646 682392
Open: Apr to Oct

Penycwm
SM8523

▲ **Penycwm (Solva) Youth Hostel,** Whitehouse, Penycwm, Newgale, Haverfordwest, Pembs, SA62 6LA
Tel: 01437 720959
Email: enycwm@yha.org.uk
Capacity: 26
Under 18: £7.75
Adults: £11.00
Open: All year, 4.00pm
Family bunk rooms
Self-catering facilities • Television • Showers • Licensed bar • Lounge • Games room • Cycle store • Parking • Evening meal available 6.30pm • No smoking • WC • Kitchen facilities • Breakfast available • Luggage store
A good base for families, within easy reach a good sandy beach. Ideal also for exploring Pembrokeshire.

▲ **Park Hall Caravan Park,** Penycwm, Haverfordwest, Pembrokeshire, SA62 6LS
Actual Grid Ref: SM842249
Tel: 01437 721606
Open: Mar to Oct

Poppit Sands
SN1548

▲ **Poppit Sands Youth Hostel,** Sea View, Poppit Sands, Cardigan, SA43 3LP
Actual Grid Ref: SN144487
Tel: 01239 612936
Fax: 01239 612936
Email: poppit@yha.org.uk
Capacity: 40
Under 18: £6.50
Adults: £9.25
Open: All year, 5.00pm
Family bunk rooms
Camping
Self-catering facilities • Showers • Shop • Lounge • Drying room • Parking • No smoking • WC • Kitchen facilities • Kitchen facilities • Credit cards accepted
Former inn set in 5 acres reaching down to the estuary and sea, designated a Site of Special Scientific Interest. Occasional dolphins can be seen in the bay.

MAP PAGE 351 • **Pembrokeshire**

Reynalton

SN0908

▲ **Croft Caravan Park,** Reynalton, Kilgetty, Pembrokeshire, SA68 0PE
Actual Grid Ref: SN092092
Tel: 01834 860315 **Fax:** 01834 860315
Open: Mar to Sept

Roch

SM8721

▲ **Rainbolts Hill Farm,** Roch, Haverfordwest, Pembrokeshire, SA62 6AF
Actual Grid Ref: SM874212
Tel: 01437 710208
Open: Mar to Oct

Rosebush

SN0729

▲ **Rosebush Caravan & Camping Park,** Bellevue House, Rosebush, Clynderwen, Pembrokeshire, SA66 7QT
Actual Grid Ref: SN074294
Tel: 01437 532206
Open: Mar to Oct

Rosemarket

SM9508

▲ **Shipping Farm Touring Caravan & Tent Park,** Shipping Farm, Rosemarket, Neyland, Milford Haven, Pembrokeshire, SA73 1JE
Actual Grid Ref: SM958068
Tel: 01646 600286
Open: Apr to Oct

Runwayskiln

SM7707

▲ **Marloes Sands Youth Hostel,** Runwayskiln, Marloes, Haverfordwest, Pembrokeshire, SA62 3BH
Actual Grid Ref: SM778080
Tel: 01646 636667
Capacity: 30
Under 18: £5.25
Adults: £7.50
Open: All year, 5.00pm
Self-catering facilities • Showers • Shop • Wet weather shelter • Lounge • Drying room • Parking 6 cars • No smoking • WC • Kitchen facilities • Credit cards accepted
Small group of farm buildings on NT property, on the Pembrokeshire Coast Path, and with nearby access to Skomer Island. Walking and bird watching are popular.

Saundersfoot

SN1304

▲ **Masterland Farm Touring Caravan & Tent Park,** Broadmoor, Kilgetty, Pembrokeshire, SA68 0RH
Actual Grid Ref: SN097062
Tel: 01834 813298
Fax: 01834 814408
Open: Mar to Oct

▲ **Sunnyvale Holiday Park,** Valley Road, Saundersfoot, Pembrokeshire, SA69 9BT
Tel: 01437 767172
Open: Apr to Oct

▲ **The Leys Camping Park,** Narberth Road, Saundersfoot, Pembrokeshire, SA69 9DS
Tel: 01834 812413
Open: Apr to Sep

▲ **Moysland Farm,** Tenby Road, Saundersfoot, Tenby, Pembrokeshire, SA69 9DS
Actual Grid Ref: SN124037
Tel: 01834 812455
Open: May to Oct

▲ **Trevayne Farm Caravan & Campsite,** Saundersfoot, Tenby, Pembrokeshire, SA69 9DL
Actual Grid Ref: SN142032
Tel: 01834 813402
Open: Mar to Sept

▲ **Moreton Farm Leisure Park,** Moreton, Saundersfoot, Pembs, SA69 9EA
Tel: 01834 812016
Open: Mar to Nov

▲ **Crane Cross,** Devonshire Drive, Saundersfoot, Pembrokeshire, SA68 0RR
Actual Grid Ref: SN118040
Tel: 01834 812708
Open: May to Sep

▲ **Griffithston Farm,** Westfield Road, Saundersfoot, Pembrokeshire, SA69 9ED
Actual Grid Ref: SN125045
Tel: 01834 813370
Open: Apr to Sep

All details shown are as supplied by hostels and campsites in Autumn 2000.

Skrinkle

SS0797

▲ **Manorbier Youth Hostel,** Skrinkle, Manorbier, Tenby, Pembrokeshire, SA70 7TT
Actual Grid Ref: SS081975
Tel: 01834 871803
Fax: 01834 871101
Email: manorbier@yha.org.uk
Capacity: 63
Under 18: £7.75
Adults: £11.00
Open: All year, 5.00pm
Family bunk rooms
Camping
Self-catering facilities • Television • Showers • Licensed bar • Shop • Laundry facilities • Wet weather shelter • Lounge • Dining room • Games room • Drying room • Cycle store • Evening meal available 6.00 to 7.00pm • Facilities for disabled people Category 2 • WC • Kitchen facilities • Breakfast available • Credit cards accepted
Attractively refurbished building, modern & bright, with award-winning sandy beach less than 200 yards away, between Manorbier and Lydstep. In the Pembrokeshire Coast National Park.

Solva

SM8024

▲ **Nine Wells Caravan & Camping Park,** St Brides View, Solva, Haverfordwest, Pembs, SA62 6TB
Tel: 01437 721809
Open: Easter to Oct

▲ **Mount Farm,** Solva, Haverfordwest, Pembrokeshire, SA62 6XL
Actual Grid Ref: SM826245
Tel: 01437 721301
Open: Apr to Oct

St Davids

SM7525

▲ **Caerfai Bay Caravan & Tent Park,** Caerfai Bay, St Davids, Haverfordwest, Pembrokeshire, SA62 6QT
Actual Grid Ref: SM757243
AA grade: 3 Pennants
Tel: 01437 720274 **Fax:** 01437 720274
Email: info@caerfaibay.co.uk
Tent pitches: 92
Tent rate: £5.50-£12.00
Open: Mar to Oct **Last arr:** 10pm
Dogs allowed • Electric hook-up • Calor Gas/Camping Gaz • Showers • Laundrette on site • Public phone on site
Panoramic sea views. Bathing beach and coastal path 300 yards.

Pembrokeshire • MAP PAGE 351

▲ **Camping & Caravanning Club Site,** Dwr Cwmdig, St Davids, Haverfordwest, Pembrokeshire, SA62 6DW
Actual Grid Ref: SM805305
Tel: 01348 831376
Open: Apr to Sep

▲ **Tretio Caravan & Camping Park,** St Davids, Haverfordwest, Pembrokeshire, SA62 6DE
Actual Grid Ref: SM787292
Tel: 01437 781359
Fax: 01437 781600
Open: Mar to Oct

▲ **Hendre Eynon Camp Site,** St Davids, Haverfordwest, Pembrokeshire, SA62 6DB
Actual Grid Ref: SM773280
Tel: 01437 720474
Open: Apr to Oct

▲ **Porth Clais,** St Davids, Haverfordwest, Pembrokeshire, SA62 6RR
Tel: 01437 720256
Open: Mar to Oct

▲ **Rhosson Farm,** St Davids, Haverfordwest, Pembrokeshire, SA62 6PY
Tel: 01437 720335
Open: Easter to Oct

▲ **Glan-y-Mor Tent Park,** Caerfai Bay Road, St Davids, Haverfordwest, SA62 6QT
Actual Grid Ref: SM757247
Tel: 01437 721788
Open: Mar to Dec

▲ **Caerfai Farm Campsite,** St Davids, Haverfordwest, Pembs, SA62 6QT
Actual Grid Ref: SM759244
Tel: 01437 720548
Open: Easter to Oct

▲ **Rhossan Ganol and Rhosson,** Isaf Farm, St Davids, Haverfordwest, Pembrokeshire, SA62 6PY
Actual Grid Ref: SM725250
Tel: 01437 720361
Open: Mar to Oct

▲ **St Davids Farm Park,** Trehenlliw, St Davids, Haverfordwest, Pembrokeshire, SA62 6PH
Actual Grid Ref: SM758264
Tel: 01437 721601
Open: Mar to Oct

▲ **Treginnis Lodge,** St Davids, Haverfordwest, Pembrokeshire, SA62 6RS
Actual Grid Ref: SM731246
Tel: 01437 720524
Open: All year

▲ **Maes-yr-Awel Caravan Park,** The Square and Compass, St Davids, Haverfordwest, Pembrokeshire, SA62 5JJ
Actual Grid Ref: SM845311
Tel: 01348 837893
Open: All year

▲ **Tretio Caravan & Camping Park,** St Davids, Haverfordwest, Pembrokeshire, SA62 6DE
Actual Grid Ref: SM787290
Tel: 01437 720270
Open: Apr to Oct

St Dogmaels
SN1645

▲ **Allty Coed,** St Dogmaels, Cardigan, SA43 3LP
Tel: 01239 612673
Open: All year

Stepaside
SN1307

▲ **Mill House Caravan Park,** Pleasant Valley, Stepaside, Narbeth, Saundersfoot, Pembrokeshire, SA67 8LN
Actual Grid Ref: SN141072
Tel: 01834 812069
Open: Apr to Sep

Tavernspite
SN1812

▲ **South Caravan Park,** Tavernspite, Whitland, Pembrokeshire, SA34 0NL
Actual Grid Ref: SN180127
Tel: 01834 831451
Open: Apr to Oct

▲ **Pantglas Farm,** Tavernspite, Whitland, Carmarthenshire, SA34 0MS
Actual Grid Ref: SN175121
Tel: 01834 831618
Open: Easter to Oct

All details shown are as supplied by hostels and campsites in Autumn 2000.

If you have to cancel your visit to any hostel or campsite, please let them know – it is always possible to make a bed or a pitch available to someone else.

Tenby
SN1300

▲ **Kiln Park Holiday Park,** Marsh Road, Tenby, Pembrokeshire, SA70 7RB
Actual Grid Ref: SN118002
Tel: 01834 844121
Fax: 01834 845159
Open: Mar to Oct

▲ **Trefalun Park,** Devonshire Drive, Florence, Tenby, Pembrokeshire, SA70 8RH
Actual Grid Ref: SN095026
Tel: 01646 651514
Fax: 01646 651514
Open: Apr to Oct

▲ **Well Park Caravans,** Well Park Caravans & Chalets, Tenby, Pembrokeshire, SA70 8TL
Actual Grid Ref: SN127027
Tel: 01834 842179
Open: Apr to Oct

▲ **Meadow Farm Campsite,** North Cliffe, Tenby, Pembs, SA70 8AU
Tel: 01834 844829
Open: Easter to Sep

▲ **Windmills Camping Park,** Lydstep Beach, Lydstep, Tenby, Pembrokeshire, SA70 7RY
Actual Grid Ref: SN128012
Tel: 01834 842200
Open: Apr to Oct

▲ **Hazelbrook Caravan Site,** Sageston Milton, Tenby, Pembrokeshire, SA70 8SY
Actual Grid Ref: SN058033
Tel: 01646 651351
Open: Mar to Jan

To stay in a Youth Hostel affiliated to one of the Youth Hostel associations, you need to be a member. You can join at most hostels – phone in advance to check.

MAP PAGE 351 • **Pembrokeshire**

Trefasser

SM8937

▲ **Pwll Deri Youth Hostel,** Castell Mawr, Trefasser, Goodwick, Pembrokeshire, SA64 0LR
Actual Grid Ref: SM891387
Tel: 01348 891385 **Fax:** 01348 891385
Capacity: 30
Under 18: £5.75 **Adults:** £8.50
Open: Apr to Oct
Self-catering facilities • Showers • Shop • Lounge • Drying room • Cycle store • No smoking • WC • Kitchen facilities • Credit cards accepted
Former private house perched atop 400 ft cliffs next to an ancient hill fort, overlooking Pwll Deri Bay.

Trefin

SM8332

▲ **Trefin Youth Hostel,** Cranog, Trefin, St Davids, Haverfordwest, Pembs, SA62 5AT
Tel: 01348 831414
Email: reservations@yha.org.uk
Capacity: 26
Under 18: £5.75
Adults: £8.50
Open: All year, 5.00pm
Family bunk rooms
Self-catering facilities • Showers • Shop • Lounge • Drying room • Cycle store • Parking • WC • Kitchen facilities • Credit cards accepted
Former village school near Pembs Coast Path. Good area for spotting birds.

▲ **Prendergast Caravan & Camping Park,** Cartlett Lodge, Trefin, Haverfordwest, Pembrokeshire, SA62 5AL
Tel: 01348 831368
Open: Apr to Sep

Wisemans Bridge

SN1406

▲ **Wisemans Bridge Inn,** Wisemans Bridge, Narberth, Pembs, SA69 9AU
Tel: 01834 813236
Open: Apr to New Year

Hostels and campsites may vary rates – be sure to check when booking.

Powys

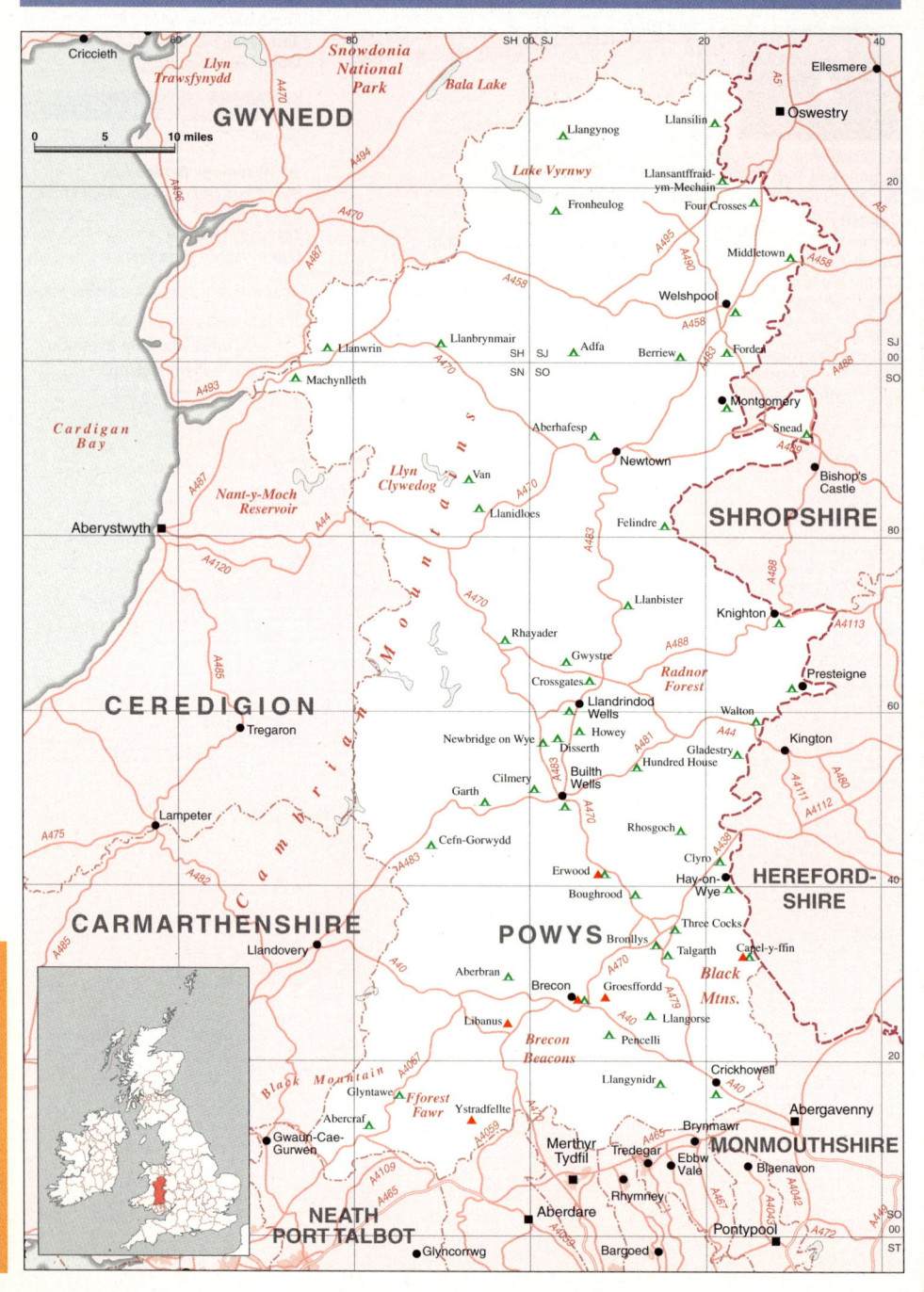

Powys

Aberbran

SN9829

▲ **Aberbran Fawr Farm,** Aberbran, Penpont, Brecon, LD3 9NG
Actual Grid Ref: SN989290
Tel: 01874 623301
Open: Mar to Oct

Abercraf

SN8112

▲ **Dan-yr-Ogof Show Caves,** Abercraf, Glyntawe, Swansea
Actual Grid Ref: SN840158
Tel: 01639 730284
Open: Mar to Oct

Aberhafesp

SO0692

▲ **Tynycwm Camping Site,** Aberhafesp, Newtown, Powys, SY16 3JF
Actual Grid Ref: SO036961
Tel: 01686 688651
Open: May to Oct

Adfa

SJ0501

▲ **Llwyn Celyn Holiday Park,** Adfa, Newtown, Powys, SY16 3DG
Actual Grid Ref: SJ056007
Tel: 01938 810720
Open: Apr to Oct

Berriew

SJ1800

▲ **Maesyrafon Caravan Park,** Berriew, Welshpool, Powys, SY21 8QB
Actual Grid Ref: SJ161022
Tel: 01686 640587
Open: Mar to Oct

Boughrood

SO1339

▲ **New House,** Boughrood, Llyswen, Brecon, Powys, LD3 0BZ
Actual Grid Ref: SO147402
Tel: 01874 754122
Open: All year

Hostels and campsites may vary rates – be sure to check when booking.

Brecon

SO0428

▲ **Canal Barn Bunk House,** Ty Camlas, Canal Bank, Brecon, Powys, LD3 7HH
Tel: 01874 625361
Email: info@canal-barn.co.uk
Capacity: 24
Adults: £8.35
Open: All year, all day
Family bunk rooms
Camping for 3 tents: £4.00
Self-catering facilities • Showers • Central heating • Shop • Laundry facilities • Wet weather shelter • Dining room • Grounds available for games • Drying room • Cycle store • Parking • Facilities for disabled people • No smoking
A great base for outdoor activities in the Brecon Beacons.

▲ **Brynich Caravan Park,** Brecon, Powys, LD3 7SH
Actual Grid Ref: SO068277
AA grade: 4 Pennants
Tel: 01874 623325
Fax: 01874 623325
Email: brynich@aol.com
Tent pitches: 70
Tent rate: £4.00-£10.00
Open: Apr to Oct
Last arr: 11pm
Facilities for disabled people • Dogs allowed • Electric hook-up • Calor Gas/Camping Gaz • Picnic/barbecue area on site • Children's play area • Showers • Launderette on site • Public phone on site • Shop on site • Baby care facilities
Panoramic views of Brecon Beacons, AA Best Campsite Wales 1999.

▲ **Llynfi Holiday Park,** Llangorse Lake, Brecon, Powys, LD3 7TR
Actual Grid Ref: SO128277
Tel: 01874 658283
Fax: 01974 658575
Email: brianstrawford@btinternet.com
Open: Mar to Nov

▲ **Bishops Meadow Caravan Park,** Hay Road, Brecon, Powys, LD3 9SW
Actual Grid Ref: SO056301
Tel: 01874 622051
Open: Mar to Oct

▲ **Neuadd Cantref,** Brecon, Powys
Actual Grid Ref: SO042247
Tel: 01874 665247
Open: All year

Bronllys

SO1435

▲ **Anchorage Caravan Park,** Bronllys, Brecon, Powys, LD3 0LD
Actual Grid Ref: SO144350
Tel: 01874 711246
Open: All year

Builth Wells

SO0350

▲ **Riverside Caravan Park,** Llangammarch Wells, Powys, LD4 4BY
Actual Grid Ref: SN934470
Tel: 01591 620465
Tent pitches: 15
Tent rate: £3.00-£5.00
Open: Apr to Oct
Last arr: 8pm
Dogs allowed • Electric hook-up • Calor Gas/Camping Gaz • Children's play area • Showers • Launderette on site • Public phone on site
Peaceful countryside site surrounded by mountains. Fishing, pony trekking, historic attractions.

Capel-y-ffin

SO2531

▲ **Capel-y-Ffin Youth Hostel,** Capel-y-Ffin, Abergavenny, Monmouthshire, NP7 7NP
Actual Grid Ref: SO250328
Tel: 01873 890650
Capacity: 38
Under 18: £5.75
Adults: £8.50
Open: All year, 5.00pm
Camping
Self-catering facilities • Showers • Shop • Lounge • Drying room • Cycle store • Parking • Evening meal available 7.00pm • No smoking • Kitchen facilities • Breakfast available • Credit cards accepted
Old hill farm set in 40-acre grounds on mountainside in Brecon Beacons National Park.

▲ **The Grange,** Capel-y-Ffin, Abergavenny, NP7 7NP
Tel: 01873 890215
Fax: 01873 890157
Open: All year

All details shown are as supplied by hostels and campsites in Autumn 2000.

WALES

Powys • MAP PAGE 358

Cefn-Gorwydd
SN9045

▲ **Caban Cwmffynon,** Cefn-Gorwydd, Llangammarch Wells, LD4 4DW
Tel: 01591 610638
Open: All year

Cilmery
SO0051

▲ **Prince Llewelyn Inn,** Cilmery, Builth Wells, Powys, LD2 3NU
Tel: 01982 552694
Open: Apr to Oct

▲ **Llewelyn Leisure Park,** Cilmery, Builth Wells, Powys, LD2 3NU
Actual Grid Ref: SO003514
Tel: 01982 552838 **Fax:** 01982 551090
Open: Mar to Oct

Clyro
SO2143

▲ **Ashdale ,** Clyro, Hereford, HR3 5SG
Tel: 01497 821386
Open: Mar to Oct

▲ **Forest Park Caravan Site,** Painscastle Road, Clyro, Hereford, HR3 5SG
Actual Grid Ref: SO201439
Tel: 01497 820156
Email: andy@handycandy.freeserve.co.uk
Open: All year

Crickhowell
SO2118

▲ **Cwmdu Camping Site,** Crickhowell, Powys, NP8 1RU
Actual Grid Ref: SO181232
Tel: 01874 730441
Open: Mar to Oct

▲ **Riverside Caravan & Camping Park,** New Road, Crickhowell, Powys, NP8 1AY
Actual Grid Ref: SO215184
Tel: 01873 810397
Open: Mar to Oct

▲ **Bell Inn,** Glangrwyney, Crickhowell, Powys, NP8 1EH
Actual Grid Ref: SO239163
Tel: 01873 810247
Fax: 01873 812155
Open: Mar to Oct

Crossgates
SO0864

▲ **Park Motel Caravan & Camping Park,** Rhayader Road, Crossgates, Llandrindod Wells, Powys, LD1 6RF
Actual Grid Ref: SO083652
Tel: 01597 851201
Fax: 01597 851201
Open: Mar to Oct

Disserth
SO0358

▲ **Disserth Caravan Park,** Disserth, Howey, Llandrindod Wells, Powys, LD1 6NL
Actual Grid Ref: SO035583
Tel: 01597 860277
Fax: 01597 860277
Open: Mar to Oct

Erwood
SO0942

▲ **Trericket Mill Bunkhouse,** Trericket Mill Vegetarian Guesthouse, Erwood, Builth Wells, Powys, LD2 3TQ
Actual Grid Ref: SO112414
Tel: 01982 560312
Fax: 01982 560768
Email: mail@trericket.co.uk
Capacity: 10
Under 18: £8.50
Adults: £8.50
Open: All year (not Xmas), all day
Family bunk rooms
Self-catering facilities • Television • Showers • Central heating • Drying room • Cycle store • Parking • Evening meal available 7pm
Brilliant location for river and mountains. Twin and family rooms.

▲ **Trericket Mill Vegetarian Guesthouse,** Erwood, Builth Wells, Powys, LD2 3TQ
Actual Grid Ref: SO112414
Tel: 01982 560312
Fax: 01982 560768
Email: mail@trericket.co.uk
Tent pitches: 5
Tent rate: £4.00
Open: All year
Last arr: 10pm
Dogs allowed • Picnic/barbecue area on site • Showers
Small, friendly riverside site in Wye Valley, Mid Wales.

Felindre
SO1681

▲ **Trevland,** Felindre, Knighton, Powys, LD7 1YL
Tel: 01547 510211
Open: All year

Forden
SJ2200

▲ **Severn Caravan Park,** Kilkwydd Farm, Forden, Welshpool, Powys, SY21 8RT
Actual Grid Ref: SJ232044
Tel: 01938 580238
Open: Mar to Oct

Four Crosses (Llansantffraid-ym-Mechain)
SJ2718

▲ **Ty-Coch Bungalow,** Four Crosses, Llanymynech, Powys, SY22 6QZ
Tel: 01691 830361
Open: Mar to Oct

Fronheulog
SJ0418

▲ **Fronheulog Camping Site,** Fronheulog, Llanwddyn, Oswestry, Shropshire, SY10 0LX
Actual Grid Ref: SJ044187
Tel: 01691 870662
Open: Mar to Oct

Garth
SN9549

▲ **Irfon River Caravan Park,** Upper Chapel Road, Garth, Llangammarch Wells, Powys, LD4 4BH
Actual Grid Ref: SN956495
Tel: 01591 620310
Open: Mar to Oct

Gladestry
SO2355

▲ **Offa's Dyke Lodge,** Gladestry, Kington, Herefordshire, HR5 3NR
Tel: 01544 370341
Fax: 01544 370342
Open: All year

MAP PAGE 358 • **Powys**

Glyntawe
SN8416

▲ **Dderi Farm,** Glyntawe, Penycae, Swansea, W Glam, SA9 1GT
Tel: 01639 730458
Open: All year

Groesffordd
SO0727

▼ **Ty'n-y-Caeau Youth Hostel,** Groesffordd, Brecon, Powys, LD3 7SW
Actual Grid Ref: SO074288
Tel: 01874 665270
Fax: 01874 665278
Email: tynycaeau@yha.org.uk
Capacity: 54
Under 18: £6.90
Adults: £10.00
Open: Feb to Oct + Xmas, 5.00pm
Family bunk rooms
Self-catering facilities • Television • Showers • Shop • Dining room • Drying room • Cycle store • Parking • Evening meal available 7pm • No smoking • WC • Kitchen facilities • Breakfast available • Credit cards accepted
An old farmhouse, ideally placed for the Brecon Beacons National Park. Close to reserves, and with easy walking.

Gwystre
SO0665

▲ **Gwystre Inn,** Gwystre, Llandrindod Wells, Powys, LD1 6RN
Actual Grid Ref: SO066656
Tel: 01597 851650
Open: All year

Hay-on-Wye
SO2242

▲ **Hollybush Inn Caravan Site,** Hay-on-Wye, Hereford, HR3 5PG
Tel: 01497 847171
Open: Easter to Oct

▲ **Radnors End Camping,** Hay-on-Wye, Hereford, HR3 5RS
Actual Grid Ref: SO224231
Tel: 01497 820180
Open: Mar to Oct

Howey
SO0558

▲ **Dalmore Caravan Park,** Howey, Llandrindod Wells, Powys, LD1 5RG
Actual Grid Ref: SO045568
Tel: 01597 822483
Open: Mar to Oct

Hundred House
SO1154

▲ **Fforest Fields Caravan & Camping Park,** Hundred House, Llandrindod Wells, Powys, LD1 5RT
Actual Grid Ref: SO098535
Tel: 01982 570406
Fax: 01982 570406
Open: Apr to Dec

Knighton
SO2872

▲ **Cwm Sanaham Farm,** Knighton, Powys, LD7 1TP
Tel: 01547 528431
Open: All year

Libanus
SN9925

▼ **Llwyn-y-Celyn Youth Hostel,** Libanus, Brecon, Powys, LD3 8NH
Actual Grid Ref: SN973225
Tel: 01874 624261
Fax: 01874 625916
Capacity: 40
Under 18: £6.50
Adults: £9.25
Open: Feb to Oct + New Year, 5.00pm
Camping
Self-catering facilities • Showers • Lounge • Dining room • Cycle store • Parking • Evening meal available 7.00pm • No smoking • WC • Kitchen facilities • Breakfast available • Credit cards accepted
Traditional old Welsh farmhouse with some unique wall paintings and a nature trail in its grounds, in a mountain location in the heart of the Brecon Beacons National Park, yet easily accessible.

Llanbister
SO1073

▲ **Brynithon Caravan & Camping Site,** Llanbister, Llandrindod Wells, Powys, LD1 6TR
Tel: 01597 840231
Open: Mar to Oct

▲ **The Lion,** Llanbister, Llandrindod Wells, Powys, LD1 6TN
Tel: 01597 840244
Open: Apr to Oct

Llanbrynmair
SH8902

▲ **Cringoed Caravan and Camping Park,** Llanbrynmair, Powys, SY19 7DR
Actual Grid Ref: SH887015
Tel: 01650 521237
Tent pitches: 10
Tent rate: £6.50
Open: Apr to Oct
Last arr: 11pm
Dogs allowed • Electric hook-up • Calor Gas/Camping Gaz • Showers • Laundrette on site • Public phone on site
Quiet family site, lovely views. Ideal touring, walking exploring mid-Wales.

▲ **Badgers Glade Caravan Park,** Llanbrynmair, Powys, SY19 7DU
Actual Grid Ref: SH891031
Tel: 01650 521622
Open: Apr to Nov

Llandrindod Wells
SO0561

▲ **Builders Arms,** Crossgates, Llandrindod Wells, Powys, LD1 6RB
Tel: 01597 851235
Open: All year

▲ **Bryncrach,** Hundred House, Llandrindod Wells, Powys, LD1 5RD
Actual Grid Ref: SO112549
Tel: 01982 570291
Open: All year

Llangorse
SO1327

▲ **Lakeside Caravan & Camping Park,** Llangorse, Brecon, Powys, LD3 7RR
Actual Grid Ref: SO128272
Tel: 01874 658226
Open: Mar to Oct

Llangynidr
SO1519

▲ **Castle Farm,** Castle Road, Llangynidr, Crickhowell, Powys, NP8 1NG
Tel: 01874 730255
Open: Apr to Oct

WALES

Stilwell's Hostels & Camping 2002   361

Powys • MAP PAGE 358

Llangynog
SJ0526

▲ **Henstent Caravan Park,** Llangynog, Oswestry, SY10 0EP
Tel: 01691 860479
Open: Mar to Oct

Llanidloes
SN9584

▲ **Dol-Llys Farm,** Trefeglwys Road, Llanidloes, Powys, SY18 6JA
Actual Grid Ref: SN963858
Tel: 01686 412694
Tent pitches: 20
Tent rate: £5.00-£6.00
Open: Mar to Oct
Last arr: 11pm
Dogs allowed • Electric hook-up • Picnic/barbecue area on site • Children's play area • Showers • Public phone on site
Dol-Llys touring site is walking distance from the historic town of Llanidloes.

Llansantffraid-ym-Mechain
SJ2120

▲ **Bryn Wyrnwy Caravan Park,** Bryn Wyrnwy, Llansantffraid-ym-Mechain, Powys, SY22 6AY
Actual Grid Ref: SJ233208
Tel: 01691 828852
Open: Apr to Oct

Llansilin
SJ2028

▲ **Lloran Ganol,** Llansilin, Oswestry, Shropshire, SY10 7QX
Tel: 01691 791287
Open: Apr to Oct

Llanwrin
SH7803

▲ **Dyffryn Dyfl,** Brynmeling, Llanwrin, Machynlleth, Powys, SY20 8QJ
Tel: 01650 511252
Open: Easter to Oct

Machynlleth
SH7400

▲ **Llwyngwern Farm,** Machynlleth, Powys, SY20 9RB
Actual Grid Ref: SH754047
Tel: 01654 702492
Open: Mar to Oct

Middletown
SJ3012

▲ **Bank Farm,** Middletown, Welshpool, Powys, SY21 8EJ
Actual Grid Ref: SJ295122
Tel: 01938 570526
Open: Mar to Oct

Montgomery
SO2296

▲ **Bacheldre Watermill,** Churchstoke, Montgomery, Powys, SY15 6TE
Actual Grid Ref: SO243928
Tel: 01588 620489
Open: Apr to Oct

▲ **Mellington Hall Ltd,** Churchstoke, Montgomery, Powys, SY15 6HX
Actual Grid Ref: SO257920
Tel: 01588 620456
Open: All year

Newbridge on Wye
SO0158

▲ **Pont-ar-Ithon,** Newbridge-on-Wye, Builth Wells, Powys, LD2 3SA
Actual Grid Ref: SO019572
Tel: 01597 860203
Open: Apr to Oct

Pencelli
SO0924

▲ **Pencelli Castle Caravan & Camping Site,** Pencelli, Brecon, Powys, LD3 7LX
Actual Grid Ref: SO096248
Tel: 01874 665451
Fax: 01874 665452
Email: pencelli.castle@virgin.net
Open: Mar to Oct

Presteigne
SO3164

▲ **Rockbridge Park,** Presteigne, Powys, LD8 2NT
Actual Grid Ref: SO300654
Tel: 01547 560300
Open: Apr to Sep

Hostels and campsites may vary rates – be sure to check when booking.

Rhayader
SN9768

▲ **Wyeside Caravan & Camping Site,** Llanguris Road, Rhayader, Powys, LD6 5LB
Actual Grid Ref: SN967686
Tel: 01597 810183
Open: Feb to Nov

▲ **Gigrin Farm,** South Street, Rhayader, Powys, LD6 5BL
Actual Grid Ref: SN979677
Tel: 01597 810243
Fax: 01597 810357
Open: All year

Rhosgoch
SO1848

▲ **Goblaen House Farm Caravan & Camping Site,** No 4 Hermon Villas, Rhosgoch, Paincastle, Builth Wells, Powys, LD2 3JY
Tel: 01497 851654
Open: Easter to Oct

Snead
SO3192

▲ **Daisy Bank Touring Caravan Park,** Snead, Bishops Castle, Montgomery, Powys, SY15 6EB
Tel: 01588 620471
Open: All year

Talgarth
SO1533

▲ **Riverside International C & C Site,** Talgarth, Bronllys, Brecon, Powys, LD3 0HL
Actual Grid Ref: SO148347
Tel: 01874 711320
Email: riversideinternatonal@bronllys.freeserve.co.uk
Open: Mar to Oct

▲ **Upper Gefford Farm,** Talgarth, Brecon, Powys, LD3 0EN
Tel: 01874 711360
Open: All year

▲ **Castle Inn,** Pengenffordd, Talgarth, Brecon, Powys, LD3 0EP
Tel: 01874 711353
Open: All year

WALES

MAP PAGE 358 • **Powys**

Three Cocks
SO1737

▲ **Mill Field Caravan Park,** Mill Service Station, Three Cocks, Brecon, Powys, LD3 0SL
Tel: 01497 847381 **Open:** All year

Ty'n-y-Cornel
SN7553

▲ **Ty'n-y-Cornel Youth Hostel,** Ty'n-y-Cornel, Llanddewi Brefi, Tregaron, Powys, SY25 6PH
Actual Grid Ref: SN751534
Tel: 029 2022 2122
Fax: 029 2023 7817 (Wales Regional Office)
Email: reservations@yha.org.uk
Capacity: 16
Under 18: £4.75 **Adults:** £6.75
Open: Apr to Sep
Camping
Self-catering facilities • Showers • Wet weather shelter • Parking • No smoking • WC • Kitchen facilities
Very simple former farmhouse in a very isolated next-to-nature setting at head of Doethie Valley, lit solely by gas and with a log fire.

Van
SN9587

▲ **Esgairmaen,** Van, Llanidloes, Powys, SY18 6NT
Tel: 01686 430272
Open: All year

Walton
SO2559

▲ **Walton Court,** Walton, Presteigne, Powys, LD8 2PH
Actual Grid Ref: SO258598
Tel: 01544 350259
Open: All year

Welshpool
SJ2207

▲ **Hafren Guest House,** 38 Salop Road, Welshpool, Powys, SY21 7EA
Tel: 01938 554112
Open: Apr to Sep

You are advised to book in advance for periods of high demand – the Summer months, Half Term holidays and public holidays.

If you have to cancel your visit to any hostel or campsite, please let them know – it is always possible to make a bed or a pitch available to someone else.

Ystradfellte
SN9213

▲ **Ystradfellte Youth Hostel,** Tai'r Heol, Ystradfellte, Aberdare, Mid Glam, CF44 9JF
Actual Grid Ref: SN925127
Tel: 01639 720301
Fax: 01639 720301
Capacity: 28
Under 18: £5.75
Adults: £8.50
Open: Apr to Oct, 5.00pm
Self-catering facilities • Showers • Wet weather shelter • Lounge • Drying room • Parking • No smoking • Kitchen facilities
Charming mixture of three C17th cottages close to the Nedd and Mellte river systems in the Brecon Beacons National Park.

WALES

Location Index

A

Abbey Wood London	119
Aberaeron Ceredigion	325
Aberbran Powys	359
Abercraf Powys	359
Aberdare Glamorgan	333
Aberdaron N W Wales	339
Aberdeen Aberdeen	257
Aberfeldy Perth	309
Abergavenny Monmouth	336
Abergele N W Wales	340
Abergynolwyn N W Wales	340
Aberhafesp Powys	359
Aberlady Lothian	304
Aberlour Aberdeen	257
Aberporth Ceredigion	325
Abersoch N W Wales	340
Aberystwyth Ceredigion	325
Aboyne Aberdeen	257
Abthorpe Northants	130
Acaster Malbis N Yorks	192
Achalone Highland	286
Acharn Angus	262
Achill Island Mayo	243
Achill Sound, Achill I Mayo	243
Achiltibuie Highland	286
Achininver Highland	286
Acomb Northumb	132
Acton Bridge Cheshire	12
Adderbury Oxon	141
Addlethorpe Lincs	113
Adfa Powys	359
Ainstable Cumb	31
Airlie Angus	262
Airton N Yorks	193
Alcombe Combe Somer	150
Aldeburgh Suffolk	162
Aldeby Norfolk	122
Alderton Gloucs	81
Alford Aberdeen	258
Alfriston E Suss	170
Allerston N Yorks	193
Allerton Park N Yorks	193
Allihies Cork	226
Allonby Cumb	31
Alltsigh Highland	286
Alne N Yorks	193
Alnwick Northumb	132
Alpheton Suffolk	162
Alrewas Staffs	159
Alsop en le Dale Derby	47
Alston Cumb	31
Alstonefield Staffs	159
Altarnun Corn	14
Alves Aberdeen	258
Alveston Warks	181
Alwinton Northumb	132
Alyth Perth	309
Ambergate Derby	47
Amotherby N Yorks	193
Amroth Pembs	351
Ancaster Lincs	113
Anderby Lincs	113
Andover Hants	87
Angle Pembs	351
Annahilt Down	216
Annalong Down	216
Annan D & G	274

Anstruther Fife	280
Antrim Antrim	213
Appleby-in-Westmorland Cumb	31
Applecross Highland	286
Appleton Oxon	141
Appletreewick N Yorks	193
Apse Heath I O W	96
Aran Islands Galway	232
Arbroath Angus	263
Arden Argyll	265
Ardgartan Argyll	265
Ardglass Down	216
Ardmair Highland	286
Arduaine Argyll	265
Ardvasar, Skye Inn Heb	298
Arisaig Highland	286
Arkle Town N Yorks	194
Armagh Armagh	215
Arncliffe N Yorks	194
Arnside Cumb	31
Arran, Isle of Ayrshire	269
Arrochar Argyll	265
Arthog N W Wales	340
Arthurstown Wexford	252
Arundel W Suss	174
Ashbourne Derby	47
Ashburton Devon	55
Ashford Wicklow	254
Ashford-in-the-Water Derby	47
Ashill Somer	150
Ashington Northumb	132
Ashton (Helston) Corn	14
Ashton under Hill Worcs	186
Ashurst Hants	87
Ashurst Kent	100
Ashwell Herts	94
Askam-in-Furness Cumb	31
Aspatria Cumb	31
Assington Suffolk	162
Aston Cantlow Warks	181
Attleborough Norfolk	122
Atwick E Yorks	188
Auchenmalg D & G	274
Auchterarder Perth	309
Aust Gloucs	81
Austwick N Yorks	194
Aviemore Highland	286
Avonwick Devon	55
Axmouth Devon	55
Ayr Ayrshire	269
Aysgarth N Yorks	194
Ayside Cumb	31

B

Badachro Highland	287
Badby Northants	130
Badingham Suffolk	163
Badminton Gloucs	82
Bagby N Yorks	194
Baildon W Yorks	208
Bailey Mill Cumb	31
Bakewell Derby	47
Bala N W Wales	340
Balachroick Highland	287
Balk N Yorks	194
Ballachulish Highland	287
Ballantrae Ayrshire	269
Ballater Aberdeen	258
Ballina Mayo	244

Ballinderry Tipperary	248
Ballinskelligs Kerry	235
Ballintoy Antrim	213
Ballintuim Perth	310
Balloch Glasgow	283
Balloch Perth	310
Ballycasheen Kerry	235
Ballycastle Antrim	213
Ballyconnell Cavan	223
Ballyheigue Kerry	236
Ballykeeran Westmeath	251
Ballylickey Cork	226
Ballymacoda Cork	226
Ballymoney Antrim	213
Ballywalter Down	216
Balmacara Highland	287
Balminnoch D & G	274
Bamburgh Northumb	132
Bamford Derby	47
Banchory Aberdeen	258
Bandon Cork	226
Banff Aberdeen	258
Bangor N W Wales	340
Bangor-is-y-coed Den & Fl.	330
Banham Norfolk	122
Bantry Cork	227
Banwell Somer	151
Barcaldine Argyll	265
Barden (Skipton) N Yorks	194
Bardon Mill Northumb	132
Bardsey W Yorks	209
Barford St Michael Oxon	141
Bargrennan D & G	275
Barmby Moor E Yorks	188
Barmouth N W Wales	340
Barmston E Yorks	188
Barna Galway	232
Barnard Castle Durham	75
Barney Norfolk	122
Barnham W Suss	174
Barnhill Aberdeen	258
Barnstaple Devon	55
Barrasford Northumb	132
Barrow upon Humber Lincs	113
Barrow upon Soar Leics	110
Barrow-in-Furness Cumb	32
Barton Warks	181
Barton-upon-Humber Lincs	113
Bassenthwaite Cumb	32
Baston Lincs	113
Batcombe Somer	151
Bath Somer	151
Bathpool Somer	151
Battlefield Shrops	146
Bawdrip Somer	151
Bay Horse Lancs	106
Beadnell Northumb	132
Beal Northumb	132
Beamish Durham	75
Bearnock Highland	287
Beattock D & G	275
Beaufort Kerry	236
Beauly Highland	287
Beckermet Cumb	32
Beckfoot (Carlisle) Cumb	32
Beddgelert N W Wales	340
Beer Devon	56
Begelly Pembs	351
Belfast Antrim	214

364   Stilwell's Hostels & Camping 2002

Location Index

Belford Northumb 132	Blitterlees Cumb 32	Broadstairs Kent. 100
Bellever Devon 56	Boat of Garten Highland 287	Broadway Worcs. 186
Bellingham Northumb 133	Bodedern Anglesey 318	Brockenhurst Hants. 88
Belton Norfolk. 122	Bodiam E Suss 171	Brodie Aberdeen 258
Belton in Rutland Rutland. 144	Bodinnick Corn. 15	Brokerswood Wilts 184
Ben Lettery Galway 233	Bodmin Corn 15	Brompton-on-Swale N Yorks. 195
Benbecula, Isle of W Isl. 317	Bodorgan Anglesey 318	Bromyard Heref 92
Benderloch Argyll 265	Boggle Hole N Yorks 194	Bronllys Powys. 359
Benhall Suffolk 163	Bolberry Devon. 56	Broome Shrops 146
Benllech Anglesey 318	Bolton le Sands Lancs 106	Broughton Lincs 113
Bennettsbridge Kilkenny 239	Bonchester Bridge Borders 271	Bruntsfield, Edinburgh Lothian 305
Benson Oxon. 141	Bonningate Cumb 32	Bryher Scilly 99
Bere Regis Dorset. 68	Boosbeck Tees 178	Bryncroes N W Wales 341
Berneray, N Uist W Isl 317	Boot Cumb 32	Bryncrug N W Wales. 341
Berrier Cumb 32	Bootle Cumb. 32	Bryngwran Anglesey 319
Berriew Powys. 359	Boroughbridge N Yorks 195	Brynrefail N W Wales 341
Berrynarbor Devon 56	Borrowdale Cumb 33	Brynsiencyn Anglesey 319
Berwick-upon-Tweed Northumb 133	Borth Ceredigion 326	Brynteg Anglesey. 319
Bethania (Nantgwynant) N W Wales 341	Borve, Skye Inn Heb. 298	Buckden N Yorks 195
Bettyhill Highland 287	Boscastle Corn 15	Buckfastleigh Devon. 57
Betws Garmon N W Wales 341	Boston Lincs 113	Buckie (Spey Bay) Aberdeen 258
Betws-y-Coed N W Wales 341	Boswinger Corn 16	Bucknowle Dorset 69
Betws-yn-Rhos N W Wales. 341	Botallack Corn 16	Bude Corn 16
Beverley E Yorks 189	Bothel Cumb. 33	Budleigh Salterton Devon. 57
Bewaldeth Cumb 32	Boughrood Powys 359	Builth Wells Powys 359
Bexhill-on-Sea E Suss 170	Bourton-on-the-Water Gloucs 82	Bunchrew Highland. 287
Bicester Oxon. 141	Bouth Cumb 33	Bungay Suffolk. 163
Bickington (Barnstaple) Devon 56	Bowness (Ennerdale) Cumb 33	Bunmahon Waterford 250
Biddenden Kent 100	Boyle Roscommon 245	Burgh Castle Norfolk 123
Bideford Devon. 56	Bradenham Bucks 8	Burgh le Marsh Lincs 113
Bigbury on Sea Devon 56	Bradfield Essex 78	Burgh St Margaret Norfolk 123
Biggin-by-Hartington Derby 47	Bradwell Bucks 8	Burgh St Peter Norfolk 123
Billingshurst W Suss 174	Bradwell Derby 48	Burghead Aberdeen. 258
Billingsley Shrops 146	Bradwell Norfolk. 123	Burley Hants. 88
Bilton (Harrogate) N Yorks 194	Bradwell-on-Sea Essex 78	Burncourt Tipperary. 248
Binegar Somer 152	Braemar Aberdeen 258	Burnham-on-Crouch Essex 78
Bircher Heref 92	Braithwaite Cumb 33	Burnham-on-Sea Somer 152
Birchington Kent 100	Bramfield Suffolk 163	Burnopfield Durham. 75
Birdham W Suss. 175	Brampton Cambs 10	Burry Port Carmarthen. 322
Birling Northumb. 133	Brampton (Carlisle) Cumb. 33	Burtle Somer. 152
Birnam Perth. 310	Brancaster Norfolk 123	Burton Bradstock Dorset 69
Bishop Monkton N Yorks 194	Brandesburton E Yorks. 189	Burwash E Suss. 171
Bishop Thornton N Yorks 194	Brandon Suffolk 163	Burwell Cambs 10
Bishop's Castle Shrops. 146	Brandy Wharf Lincs 113	Bushmills Antrim. 214
Bishopsteignton Devon 56	Bransgore Hants 88	Bute, Isle of Argyll. 265
Bishopthorpe N Yorks. 194	Braunton Devon. 56	Butley Suffolk 164
Black Sail Cumb 32	Brean Sands Somer 152	Buttermere Cumb 33
Blackawton Devon 56	Brechin Angus 263	Buxton Derby 48
Blackboys E Suss 171	Brecon Powys 359	Bwlchgwyn Den & Fl 330
Blackburn Lothian. 304	Bredfield Suffolk 163	Bwlchtocyn N W Wales. 341
Blackford Cumb 32	Bredons Hardwick Worcs 186	Byrness Northumb. 133
Blackhall Durham. 75	Bremhill Wilts. 184	
Blackpool Lancs 106	Brendon (Lynmouth) Devon 57	**C**
Blackshaw Moor Staffs 159	Bridestowe Devon 57	Caeathro N W Wales. 341
Blackton Durham 75	Bridge of Cally Perth 310	Caergeiliog Anglesey 319
Blackwater Corn 14	Bridgerule Devon 57	Caernarfon N W Wales. 341
Blackwell in the Peak Derby 47	Bridges Shrops 146	Caerwys Den & Fl. 330
Blaencarno Ceredigion 326	Bridgetown Somer 152	Caherciveen Kerry 236
Blaenpennal Ceredigion. 326	Bridgnorth Shrops 146	Caherdaniel Kerry 236
Blair Atholl Perth 310	Bridlington E Yorks 189	Caister-on-Sea Norfolk. 123
Blairlogie Stirling. 313	Bridport Dorset 68	Callander Stirling 313
Blairmore Argyll 265	Brighouse W Yorks 209	Calligarry, Skye Inn Heb 299
Blandford Forum Dorset. 68	Brighstone I O W. 96	Callington Corn 16
Blaney Fermanagh 218	Brightlingsea Essex 78	Calne Wilts 184
Blarney Cork. 227	Brilley Heref 92	Calver Derby 48
Blawith Cumb 32	Bristol Bristol. 6	Calverton Notts 138
Blaxhall Suffolk 163	Brithdir N W Wales 341	Cam Gloucs 82
Bleadon Somer 152	Brixham Devon. 57	Camborne Corn 16
Bleasby Notts 138	Brixton Devon. 57	Cambridge Cambs 10
Blencow Cumb 32	Broad Haven Pembs 351	Camelford Corn 16
Blessington Wicklow. 255	Broad Oak (Heathfield) E Suss 171	Canewdon Essex 78
Bletchingdon Oxon 141	Broadbottom Gtr Manc 85	Canisbay Highland. 287
Blissford Hants 88	Broadford, Skye Inn Heb 298	Cannard's Grave Somer. 152

Stilwell's Hostels & Camping 2002   365

Location Index

Cannich *Highland* 288	Cheltenham *Gloucs* 82	Conwy *N W Wales* 342
Canterbury *Kent* 101	Chertsey *Surrey* 167	Cookstown *Tyrone* 222
Cape Clear Island *Cork* 227	Cheshunt *Herts* 94	Coombe Bissett *Wilts* 184
Capel Curig *N W Wales* 342	Chester *Cheshire* 12	Copt Oak *Leics* 110
Capel Seion *Ceredigion* 326	Chesterfield *Derby* 48	Corfe Castle *Dorset* 70
Capel-le-Ferne *Kent* 101	Chewton Mendip *Somer* 152	Corfe Mullen *Dorset* 70
Capel-y-ffin *Powys* 359	Chichester *W Suss* 175	Cork *Cork* 227
Capernwray *Lancs* 106	Chickerell *Dorset* 70	Corpach *Highland* 288
Capton *Devon* 57	Chingford *London* 119	Corris *N W Wales* 343
Carbis Bay *Corn* 16	Chitts Hills *Essex* 79	Corrour Station *Highland* 288
Cardiff *Glamorgan* 333	Christchurch *Dorset* 70	Corton *Suffolk* 164
Cardigan *Ceredigion* 326	Christleton *Cheshire* 13	Corwen *Den & Fl* 331
Cardington *Shrops* 146	Chudleigh *Devon* 57	Cosham *Hants* 88
Carfraemill *Borders* 271	Church Hill *Fermanagh* 218	Cotes *Leics* 110
Cargill *Perth* 310	Church Stretton *Shrops* 146	Cottonshopeburnfoot *Northumb* 133
Carleen *Corn* 16	Churt *Surrey* 167	Court Hill *Oxon* 141
Carlisle *Cumb* 33	Chwilog *N W Wales* 342	Coverack *Corn* 17
Carloway, Lewis *W Isl* 317	Cilan *N W Wales* 342	Covesea *Aberdeen* 258
Carlton *Suffolk* 164	Cilgerran *Pembs* 352	Cowes *I O W* 96
Carlton Colville *Suffolk* 164	Ciliau Aeron *Ceredigion* 326	Cowgill *Cumb* 34
Carlton Miniott *N Yorks* 195	Cilmery *Powys* 360	Coylton *Ayrshire* 269
Carlton-in-Cleveland *N Yorks* 195	Clacton-on-Sea *Essex* 79	Coylumbridge *Highland* 288
Carlton-on-Trent *Notts* 138	Claddach-Baleshare, N Uist *W Isl* 317	Crackington Haven *Corn* 17
Carlyon Bay *Corn* 16	Claddaghduff *Galway* 233	Cracoe *N Yorks* 195
Carn Dearg *Highland* 288	Clapham *N Yorks* 195	Craig (Glen Carron) *Highland* 288
Carnforth *Lancs* 106	Cleethorpes *Lincs* 113	Craig (Loch Torridon) *Highland* 288
Carnon Downs *Corn* 16	Cleobury Mortimer *Shrops* 146	Craigellachie *Aberdeen* 258
Carnoustie *Angus* 263	Clevedon *Somer* 152	Craignure, Mull *Inn Heb* 298
Carradale *Argyll* 265	Clevelode *Worcs* 186	Crail *Fife* 280
Carrick-on-Suir *Tipperary* 248	Clewer *Somer* 152	Crantock *Corn* 17
Carrickfergus *Antrim* 214	Clifford Bridge *Devon* 57	Craster *Northumb* 133
Carrigtohill *Cork* 227	Clifton *Oxon* 141	Craswall *Heref* 92
Cassington *Oxon* 141	Clippesby *Norfolk* 124	Craven Arms *Shrops* 147
Castel *Guernsey* 1	Clitheroe *Lancs* 106	Crawford *Lanark* 302
Casterton *Cumb* 33	Clogheen *Tipperary* 248	Crawley *Hants* 88
Castle Douglas *D & G* 275	Clogher *Tyrone* 222	Crayke *N Yorks* 195
Castle Hedingham *Essex* 79	Clondalkin, Dublin *Co Dublin* 230	Creacombe *Devon* 58
Castlebar *Mayo* 244	Clonea *Waterford* 250	Creetown *D & G* 275
Castlegregory *Kerry* 236	Clonmany *Donegal* 228	Crianlarich *Stirling* 314
Castlerock *Londonderry* 220	Cloughey *Down* 217	Criccieth *N W Wales* 343
Castleside *Durham* 75	Clumber Park *Notts* 138	Crickhowell *Powys* 360
Castleton *Derby* 48	Clun *Shrops* 146	Crieff *Perth* 310
Castlewellan *Down* 217	Clunton *Shrops* 146	Crockernwell *Devon* 58
Caton *Lancs* 106	Clydach *Monmouth* 336	Crocketford *D & G* 275
Catsfield *E Suss* 171	Clynderwen *Carmarthen* 322	Crockey Hill *N Yorks* 195
Cauldon *Staffs* 159	Clynnog-Fawr *N W Wales* 342	Croft *Lincs* 114
Causewayhead *Cumb* 34	Clyro *Powys* 360	Crolly *Donegal* 228
Cautley *Cumb* 34	Clyst St Mary *Devon* 57	Cromer *Norfolk* 124
Cawood *N Yorks* 195	Coalbrookdale *Shrops* 147	Cromwell *Notts* 138
Cawston *Norfolk* 123	Coalport *Shrops* 147	Crook *Cumb* 34
Cawthorne *S Yorks* 206	Coanwood *Northumb* 133	Crookhaven *Cork* 227
Cayton *N Yorks* 195	Cockburnspath *Borders* 272	Crooklands *Cumb* 34
Cefn-coed-y-cymmer *Glamorgan* 334	Cockerham *Lancs* 106	Cropton *N Yorks* 195
Cefn-ddwysarn *N W Wales* 342	Cockermouth *Cumb* 34	Cross Inn (Nebo) *Ceredigion* 326
Cefn-Gorwydd *Powys* 360	Colby *Cumb* 34	Cross Inn (New Quay) *Ceredigion* 326
Cemaes Bay *Anglesey* 319	Colchester *Essex* 79	Crossgates *Powys* 360
Cenarth *Ceredigion* 326	Cold Blow *Pembs* 352	Crossmolina *Mayo* 244
Cerne Abbas *Dorset* 69	Coldingham *Borders* 272	Crossway Green *Worcs* 187
Cerrigydrudion *N W Wales* 342	Coleford *Gloucs* 82	Crosthwaite *Cumb* 35
Chacewater *Corn* 17	Coleraine *Londonderry* 220	Croston *Lancs* 106
Chadlington *Oxon* 141	Coll, Isle of *Inn Heb* 298	Crowborough *E Suss* 171
Chale *I O W* 96	Colyton *Devon* 57	Crowcombe *Somer* 153
Chapel Hill *Lincs* 113	Combe Martin *Devon* 58	Crowcombe Heathfield *Somer* 153
Charlbury *Oxon* 141	Combe St Nicholas *Somer* 153	Crowden *Derby* 48
Charmouth *Dorset* 69	Comberton *Cambs* 10	Crowhurst *E Suss* 171
Charwelton *Northants* 130	Compton *Devon* 58	Crowland *Lincs* 114
Chatham *Kent* 101	Comrie *Perth* 310	Crowmarsh Gifford *Oxon* 141
Chatteris *Cambs* 10	Conder Green *Lancs* 106	Crows-an-Wra *Corn* 17
Cheadle *Staffs* 159	Coneysthorpe *N Yorks* 195	Croyde *Devon* 58
Cheddar *Somer* 152	Cong *Mayo* 244	Crystal Palace *London* 119
Cheddleton *Staffs* 159	Congresbury *Somer* 153	Cubert *Corn* 17
Chelmarsh *Shrops* 146	Coniston *Cumb* 34	Cullen *Aberdeen* 258
Chelmorton *Derby* 48	Consett *Durham* 76	Culmington *Shrops* 147

366   Stilwell's Hostels & Camping 2002

Location Index

Culrain Highland 289	Dublin Co Dublin 230	Ellingstring N Yorks 196
Cuminestown Aberdeen 258	Dufton Cumb 35	Elmscott Devon 59
Cumnock Ayrshire 269	Dulas Anglesey 319	Elsrick Lincs 114
Cumnor Oxon 142	Dumfries D & G 276	Elterwater Cumb 35
Cumwhitton Cumb 35	Dunbar Lothian 304	Elton Derby 49
Cunninghamhead Ayrshire 269	Dundonnell Highland 289	Elvaston Derby 49
Cushendall Antrim 214	Dungannon Tyrone 222	Elvington N Yorks 196
Cushendun Antrim 214	Dungloe Donegal 229	Ely Cambs 10
Cwmcarn Glamorgan 334	Dunkeld Perth 310	Embo Highland 290
Cwmyoy Monmouth 337	Dunkeswell Devon 58	Emborough Somer 153
Cwmystwyth Ceredigion 327	Dunlewy Donegal 229	Enniskerry Wicklow 255
Cynwyd Den & Fl 331	Dunnet Highland 289	Enniskillen Fermanagh 218
	Dunquin Kerry 236	Erpingham Norfolk 124
D	Dunsford Devon 58	Erwood Powys 360
Daccombe Devon 58	Dunstan Northumb 133	Escrick N Yorks 196
Dalbeattie D & G 276	Dunwich Suffolk 164	Eskdale Cumb 35
Dalchalm Highland 289	Durham Durham 76	Ettrick Valley Borders 272
Dalkeith Lothian 304	Durness Highland 289	Evanton Highland 290
Dalwood Devon 58	Duror Highland 290	Everton Hants 88
Danby Wiske N Yorks 195	Dursley Gloucs 82	Ewhurst E Suss 172
Darley Dale Derby 48	Dyffryn Ardudwy N W Wales 343	Exeter Devon 59
Darsham Suffolk 164	Dymchurch Kent 101	Exford Somer 153
Dartington Devon 58		Exmouth Devon 59
Dartmouth Devon 58	**E**	Eyam Derby 49
Daviot Highland 289	Eamont Bridge Cumb 35	Eynsham Oxon 142
Dawlish Devon 58	Earby Lancs 107	Eype Dorset 71
Deddington Oxon 142	Eardisland Heref 92	Eyton Den & Fl 331
Deeping St James Lincs 114	Earith Cambs 10	
Delabole Corn 17	Earl's Court London 119	**F**
Delph Gtr Manc 85	Earnley W Suss 175	Fakenham Norfolk 124
Denbigh Den & Fl 331	Easingwold N Yorks 195	Falkland Fife 280
Densole Kent 101	Easky Sligo 247	Falmouth Corn 17
Dent Cumb 35	East Allington Devon 59	Falstone Northumb 134
Dent Head Cumb 35	East Barming Kent 101	Fangfoss E Yorks 189
Deri Glamorgan 334	East Bergholt Suffolk 164	Fareham Hants 88
Derwent Water Cumb 35	East Bridgford Notts 138	Farndale N Yorks 196
Devil's Bridge Ceredigion 327	East Calder Lothian 304	Farnham N Yorks 196
Devizes Wilts 184	East Cowes I O W 96	Faversham Kent 101
Dial Post W Suss 175	East Creech Dorset 70	Fazeley Staffs 159
Dimmingsdale Staffs 159	East Harling Norfolk 124	Fearby N Yorks 196
Dinas Cross Pembs 352	East Horsley Surrey 167	Felindre Powys 360
Dinas Dinlle N W Wales 343	East Marton N Yorks 196	Felinfach Ceredigion 327
Dinas-Mawddwy N W Wales 343	East Mersea Essex 79	Felinwynt Ceredigion 327
Dinder Somer 153	East Ord Northumb 133	Felixstowe Suffolk 164
Dingestow Monmouth 337	East Portlemouth Devon 59	Fenny Bentley Derby 49
Dingwall Highland 289	East Prawle Devon 59	Fenstanton Cambs 10
Disserth Powys 360	East Runton Norfolk 124	Ferns Wexford 252
Dochgarroch Highland 289	East Stoke Dorset 70	Fetlar Shetland 312
Dolgellau N W Wales 343	East Winch Norfolk 124	Fetterangus Aberdeen 259
Dolgoch Ceredigion 327	East Wittering W Suss 175	Fiddington Somer 153
Dollar Stirling 314	East Worlington Devon 59	Field Broughton Cumb 36
Dolton Devon 58	Eastbourne E Suss 172	Filey N Yorks 196
Dolwyddelan N W Wales 343	Eastchurch Kent 101	Filham Devon 59
Dolybont Ceredigion 327	Easton Somer 153	Finchampstead Berks 4
Donard Wicklow 255	Ecclefechan D & G 276	Findhorn Aberdeen 259
Donegal Donegal 228	Eckington Worcs 187	Findochty Aberdeen 259
Doogort, Achill I Mayo 243	Edale Derby 49	Fintry Stirling 314
Doolin Clare 224	Eday Orkney 307	Fir Tree Durham 76
Dorchester Dorset 70	Edgerley Shrops 147	Firbank Cumb 36
Dornoch Highland 289	Edinburgh Lothian 305	Fishguard Pembs 352
Dorrington Shrops 147	Edinburgh, Central Lothian 305	Fishnish, Mull Inn Heb 298
Doublebois Corn 17	Edithmead Somer 153	Fiskerton Lincs 114
Douglas I Man 212	Edlingham Northumb 134	Fiunary Highland 290
Douglas Lanark 302	Edmondsham Dorset 70	Fivemiletown Tyrone 222
Dover Kent 101	Edmonton London 119	Flagg Derby 49
Doveridge Derby 48	Edmundbyers Durham 76	Fleet Dorset 71
Downderry Corn 17	Edwinstowe Notts 138	Fleet Hargate Lincs 114
Downings Donegal 229	Edzell Angus 263	Flimwell E Suss 172
Downpatrick Down 217	Egilsay Orkney 307	Flockton W Yorks 209
Drinishader, Harris W Isl 317	Egton N Yorks 196	Flookburgh Cumb 36
Drummore D & G 276	Eigg, Isle of Inn Heb 298	Fochabers Aberdeen 259
Drumnadrochit Highland 289	Elgin Aberdeen 259	Folkestone Kent 101
Drymen Stirling 314	Ellesmere Shrops 147	Folkingham Lincs 114

Location Index

Follifoot *N Yorks* 196
Foolow *Derby* 50
Ford *W Suss* 176
Forden *Powys* 360
Fordoun *Aberdeen* 259
Forest in Teesdale *Durham* 76
Forfar *Angus* 263
Forres *Aberdeen* 259
Fort Augustus *Highland* 290
Fort William *Highland* 290
Forton *Somer* 153
Fossa *Kerry* 236
Four Crosses (Llansantffraid-ym-Mechain) *Powys* 360
Four Lanes *Corn* 18
Four Mile Bridge *Anglesey* 319
Fowey *Corn* 18
Fowlmere *Cambs* 10
Framfield *E Suss* 172
Fraserburgh *Aberdeen* 259
Freshwater *I O W* 97
Freshwater East *Pembs* 352
Fritham *Hants* 88
Frittenden *Kent* 101
Froncysyllte *Den & Fl* 331
Frongoch *N W Wales* 344
Fronheulog *Powys* 360
Furnace *Ceredigion* 327
Furness Vale *Derby* 50
Fylingdales *N Yorks* 196

G

Gairloch *Highland* 290
Galgate *Lancs* 107
Galphay *N Yorks* 196
Galway *Galway* 233
Gamrie *Aberdeen* 259
Ganavan *Argyll* 265
Gargrave *N Yorks* 196
Garsdale *Cumb* 36
Garsdale Head *Cumb* 36
Garstang *Lancs* 107
Garth *Powys* 360
Gartmore *Stirling* 314
Gatehouse of Fleet *D & G* 276
Gedney Broadgate *Lincs* 114
Gilfachreda *Ceredigion* 327
Gillerthwaite *Cumb* 36
Gillingham *Dorset* 71
Gillingham *Kent* 102
Gilwern *Monmouth* 337
Gisburn *Lancs* 107
Gisleham *Suffolk* 164
Gladestry *Powys* 360
Glaisdale *N Yorks* 196
Glandore *Cork* 227
Glasgow, Central *Glasgow* 283
Glassel *Aberdeen* 259
Glasson *Lancs* 107
Glastonbury *Somer* 153
Glen Affric *Highland* 290
Glen Nevis *Highland* 290
Glen of Aherlow *Tipperary* 249
Glenbarr *Argyll* 265
Glenbeigh *Kerry* 236
Glenbrittle, Skye *Inn Heb* 299
Glencoe *Highland* 290
Glendalough *Wicklow* 255
Glendaruel *Argyll* 265
Glendevon *Perth* 310
Glengarriff *Cork* 227
Glenluce *D & G* 276
Glenmore *Highland* 290
Glenridding *Cumb* 36
Glenrosa, Arran *Ayrshire* 269
Glenroy *I Man* 212
Glutton Bridge *Derby* 50
Glyn Ceiriog *Den & Fl* 331
Glyntawe *Powys* 361
Goathland *N Yorks* 196
Godmanchester *Cambs* 10
Godshill *Hants* 89
Golant *Corn* 18
Golden Cross *E Suss* 172
Golden Grove *Carmarthen* 322
Golders Green *London* 120
Goodrington *Devon* 59
Goodwood *W Suss* 176
Goonhavern *Corn* 18
Gorran Haven *Corn* 18
Gorslas *Carmarthen* 323
Gortin *Tyrone* 222
Gosfield *Essex* 79
Gosport *Hants* 89
Goswick *Northumb* 134
Goulceby *Lincs* 114
Gradbach *Staffs* 159
Graffham *W Suss* 176
Grafham *Cambs* 10
Grange-in-Borrowdale *Cumb* 36
Grange-over-Sands *Cumb* 36
Grangemill *Derby* 50
Grangemuir *Fife* 280
Grantown-on-Spey *Highland* 291
Grasmere *Cumb* 36
Greasby *Mersey* 85
Great Ayton *N Yorks* 197
Great Bourton *Oxon* 142
Great Bromley *Essex* 79
Great Broughton *N Yorks* 197
Great Casterton *Rutland* 144
Great Harwood *Lancs* 107
Great Hockham *Norfolk* 124
Great Langdale *Cumb* 37
Great Shelford *Cambs* 10
Great Torrington *Devon* 59
Great Yarmouth *Norfolk* 124
Greenane *Wicklow* 255
Greenbottom *Corn* 18
Greenham *Somer* 153
Greenhead *Northumb* 134
Greenlaw *Borders* 272
Gretna *D & G* 276
Gretna Green *D & G* 276
Greystoke *Cumb* 37
Grinton *N Yorks* 197
Gristhorpe *N Yorks* 197
Groesffordd *Powys* 361
Gronant *Den & Fl* 331
Grosmont *Monmouth* 337
Guestling *E Suss* 172
Guisborough *Tees* 178
Guiting Power *Gloucs* 82
Gulval *Corn* 18
Gunwalloe *Corn* 18
Gwithian *Corn* 19
Gwystre *Powys* 361

H

Haccombe *Devon* 59
Hackney *London* 120
Haddington *Lothian* 306
Haddiscoe *Norfolk* 124
Hailsham *E Suss* 172
Haining *Northumb* 134
Hale *Cumb* 37
Halfway Bridge *N W Wales* 344
Halfway House *Shrops* 147
Halsetown *Corn* 19
Haltcliff Bridge *Cumb* 37
Halton-on-Lune *Lancs* 107
Haltwhistle *Northumb* 134
Hamble *Hants* 89
Hambledon *Surrey* 167
Hambleton *Lancs* 107
Hampton Loade *Shrops* 147
Hamworthy *Dorset* 71
Hanley Swan *Worcs* 187
Happisburgh *Norfolk* 124
Harden *W Yorks* 209
Harlech *N W Wales* 344
Harman's Cross *Dorset* 71
Harome *N Yorks* 197
Harrietsham *Kent* 102
Harris, Isle of *W Isl* 317
Harrogate *N Yorks* 197
Hartington *Derby* 50
Hartland *Devon* 59
Hartlepool *Tees* 178
Hartpury *Gloucs* 82
Haseley Knob *Warks* 181
Hastingleigh *Kent* 102
Hastings *E Suss* 172
Hatfield *S Yorks* 206
Hathersage *Derby* 50
Haverfordwest *Pembs* 352
Hawarden *Den & Fl* 331
Hawes *N Yorks* 197
Hawford *Worcs* 187
Hawick *Borders* 272
Hawkchurch *Devon* 59
Hawkshead *Cumb* 37
Haworth *W Yorks* 210
Hay-on-Wye *Powys* 361
Haybridge *Somer* 154
Haydon Bridge *Northumb* 134
Hayfield *Derby* 50
Hayle *Corn* 19
Hayling Island *Hants* 89
Hayscastle *Pembs* 352
Heacham *Norfolk* 124
Heamoor *Corn* 19
Heathcote *Derby* 50
Hele (Ilfracombe) *Devon* 60
Helensburgh *Argyll* 265
Helmsdale *Highland* 291
Helmsley *N Yorks* 197
Helston *Corn* 19
Hemingford Abbots *Cambs* 10
Hemsby *Norfolk* 124
Hendre *Den & Fl* 331
Hendre *Monmouth* 337
Henfield *W Suss* 176
Henley-on-Thames *Oxon* 142
Heptonstall *W Yorks* 210
Herm *Guernsey* 1
Hersham *Surrey* 167
Hertford *Herts* 94
Hesket Newmarket *Cumb* 37
Hevingham *Norfolk* 125
Hewas Water *Corn* 19
Hexham *Northumb* 134
Heysham *Lancs* 107
High Beach *Essex* 79
High Bentham *N Yorks* 197
High Harrington *Cumb* 37
High Hawsker *N Yorks* 198
Highbridge *Somer* 154
Higher Clovelly *Devon* 60

368 Stilwell's Hostels & Camping 2002

Location Index

Hillberry I Man 212	Inishbofin Island Galway 233	Kilkhampton Corn 20
Hillington Norfolk 125	Inisheer, Aran Is Galway 232	Killaloe Clare 224
Hillway I O W 97	Inishmor, Aran Is Galway 232	Killarney Kerry 236
Hilton Highland 291	Innerleithen Borders 272	Killilan Highland 292
Hinderwell N Yorks 198	Innermessan D & G 276	Killin Stirling 314
Hindhead Surrey 168	Innerwick Lothian 306	Killorglin Kerry 236
Hindshield Northumb 135	Inver (Dunbeath) Highland 291	Kilmacanogue Wicklow 255
Hoath Kent 102	Inveraray Argyll 265	Kilmore, Skye Inn Heb 299
Hoddesdon Herts 95	Inverbeg Argyll 266	Kilmuckridge Wexford 253
Hogsthorpe Lincs 114	Inverbervie Aberdeen 259	Kilmun Argyll 266
Holbeach Hurn Lincs 114	Invercoe Highland 291	Kilninver Argyll 266
Holford Somer 154	Inverey Aberdeen 260	Kilnsey N Yorks 199
Holker Cumb 37	Invergarry Highland 291	Kilrush Clare 224
Hollesley Suffolk 164	Inverness Highland 291	Kiltoom Roscommon 245
Hollingbourne Kent 102	Inverroy Highland 291	Kincraig Highland 292
Hollybush Ayrshire 269	Ipplepen Devon 60	King's Lynn Norfolk 125
Holmbury St Mary Surrey 168	Ipswich Suffolk 164	Kingham Oxon 142
Holme Pierrepont Notts 138	Irongray D & G 276	Kinghorn Fife 281
Holmfirth W Yorks 210	Irvinestown Fermanagh 218	Kings Caple Heref 92
Holmrook Cumb 37	Islandmagee Antrim 214	Kings Cross London 120
Holmsley Hants 89	Islaw'r Dref N W Wales 344	Kingsbridge Devon 60
Holne Devon 60	Islay, Isle of Inn Heb 298	Kingsbury Warks 181
Holsworthy Devon 60	Isle of Whithorn D & G 276	Kingsnorth Kent 102
Holt Fleet Worcs 187	Isley Walton Leics 110	Kingsteignton Devon 61
Holton Heath Dorset 71	Ivinghoe Bucks 8	Kington Heref 92
Holywell Corn 19		Kington Langley Wilts 184
Honeybourne Worcs 187		Kinlochewe Highland 292
Honister Pass Cumb 38	**J**	Kinlochleven Highland 292
Hope Derby 50	Jacobstow Corn 20	Kinnerley Shrops 147
Hopehouse Borders 272	Jameston Pembs 352	Kinninvie Durham 76
Hopeman Aberdeen 259	Janetstown Highland 292	Kinross Perth 310
Horam E Suss 172	Jedburgh Borders 272	Kinsale Cork 227
Horningtops Corn 19	Jenkinstown Kilkenny 239	Kintore Aberdeen 260
Hornsea E Yorks 189	John O' Groats Highland 292	Kinvara Galway 233
Horrabridge Devon 60	Johnshaven Aberdeen 260	Kippford D & G 276
Horseshoe N Yorks 198	Jordans Bucks 8	Kirby Misperton N Yorks 199
Horsey Norfolk 125		Kirk Michael I Man 212
Horsforth W Yorks 210	**K**	Kirk Yetholm Borders 272
Horsley (Newcastle-upon-Tyne) Northumb. . 135	Keel, Achill I Mayo 243	Kirkby N Yorks 199
Horton Dorset 71	Keighley W Yorks 210	Kirkby Lonsdale Cumb 38
Horton Somer 154	Keith Aberdeen 260	Kirkby on Bain Lincs 114
Horton Glamorgan 334	Keld N Yorks 198	Kirkby Stephen Cumb 38
Houghton Cambs 11	Kelsall Cheshire 13	Kirkby Thore Cumb 39
Houghton Cumb 38	Kelso Borders 272	Kirkbymoorside N Yorks 199
Howey Powys 361	Kelvedon Hatch Essex 79	Kirkcaldy Fife 281
Howley Somer 154	Kelynack Corn 20	Kirkcudbright D & G 276
Howmore, S Uist W Isl 317	Kemsing Kent 102	Kirkfieldbank Lanark 302
Howsham Lincs 114	Kendal Cumb 38	Kirkgunzeon D & G 277
Hoy Orkney 307	Kendoon D & G 276	Kirklington Notts 138
Hughley Shrops 147	Kenmore Perth 310	Kirkpatrick Fleming D & G 277
Huna Highland 291	Kenneggy Corn 20	Kirkwall Orkney 308
Hundred House Powys 361	Kennford Devon 60	Knaresborough N Yorks 199
Hunmanby N Yorks 198	Kensington London 120	Knighton Powys 361
Hunstanton Norfolk 125	Kentisbeare Devon 60	Knightstown Kerry 237
Huntley Gloucs 82	Kentmere Cumb 38	Kniveton Derby 50
Huntly Aberdeen 259	Kershader, Lewis W Isl 317	Knock Mayo 244
Hurley Berks 4	Kesh Fermanagh 219	Knockree Wicklow 256
Hurn Dorset 71	Kessingland Suffolk 164	Kyle of Lochalsh Highland 292
Hutton Bonville N Yorks 198	Keswick Cumb 38	Kyleakin, Skye Inn Heb 299
Hutton Roof (Kirkby Lonsdale) Cumb . . . 38	Kettering Northants 130	Kyles Stockinish, Harris W Isl 317
Hutton Sessay N Yorks 198	Kettlewell N Yorks 198	
Hutton-le-Hole N Yorks 198	Kewstoke Somer 154	**L**
	Kidderminster Worcs 187	Lacock Wilts 184
I	Kidlington Oxon 142	Ladram Bay Devon 61
Ilam Staffs 159	Kidwelly Carmarthen 323	Lady's Island Wexford 253
Ilford London 120	Kielder Northumb 135	Lahinch Clare 225
Ilfracombe Devon 60	Kilbarchan Glasgow 284	Laide Highland 292
Ilketshall St Lawrence Suffolk 164	Kilberry Argyll 266	Lairg Highland 292
Illogan Corn 20	Kildonan, Arran Ayrshire 269	Laleham Surrey 168
Indian Queens Corn 20	Kilgetty Pembs 352	Lamlash, Arran Ayrshire 269
Ingleby Cross N Yorks 198	Kilkee Clare 224	Lamorna Corn 20
Ingleton N Yorks 198	Kilkeel Down 217	Lamplugh Cumb 39
Ingoldmells Lincs 114	Kilkenny Kilkenny 239	Lancaster Lancs 107
	Kilkerran Ayrshire 270	

Stilwell's Hostels & Camping 2002 369

Location Index

Landkey Devon 61
Landrake Corn 20
Landshipping Pembs. 352
Langham Rutland 144
Langholm D & G 277
Langport Somer 154
Langsett S Yorks 206
Langthorpe N Yorks 199
Langton Matravers Dorset 71
Langworth Lincs 114
Lanlivery Corn 20
Lanreath Corn 20
Lansallos Corn 20
Larne Antrim 214
Lartington Durham 76
Lauder Borders 272
Laugharne Carmarthen 323
Launcells Corn 20
Launceston Corn 20
Lauragh Kerry 237
Laurencekirk Aberdeen 260
Lawrenny Pembs. 352
Laxdale, Lewis W Isl 317
Lea Derby 51
Lebberston N Yorks 199
Lechlade Gloucs 82
Leeds W Yorks 210
Leedstown Corn 21
Leek Staffs. 160
Leeming Bar N Yorks 199
Legbourne Lincs 114
Legburthwaite Cumb. 39
Leicester Leics 110
Leominster Heref 92
Leoville Jersey. 2
Lerwick Shetland. 312
Letterfrack Galway. 233
Leven Fife 281
Levenhall Lothian 306
Levenwick Shetland 312
Lewis, Isle of W Isl 317
Leyburn N Yorks 199
Leysdown-on-Sea Kent 102
Leysters Heref 92
Leyton London 120
Libanus Powys 361
Liberton, Edinburgh Lothian 306
Lichfield Staffs 160
Limerick Limerick 241
Lincoln Lincs 115
Lingfield Surrey 168
Liniclate, Benbecula W Isl 317
Linlithgow Lothian 306
Linton N Yorks 199
Linton-on-Ouse N Yorks 199
Linwood Hants 89
Lisdoonvarna Clare 225
Lislap Tyrone 222
Lisnarrick Fermanagh 219
Lisnaskea Fermanagh 219
Little Atherfield I O W 97
Little Billing Northants. 130
Little Clacton Essex. 79
Little Cressingham Norfolk. 125
Little Haven Pembs 352
Little Hereford Heref 92
Little Snoring Norfolk 125
Little Stanney Cheshire 13
Little Stretton Shrops 147
Little Thetford Cambs 11
Little Torrington Devon 61
Little Weighton E Yorks 190
Littleborough Gtr Manc. 85

Littlehampton W Suss. 176
Littleport Cambs 11
Litton Cheney Dorset 71
Liverpool, Central Mersey. 85
Liverton Devon. 61
Llaethdy Pembs. 353
Llanaber N W Wales 344
Llanarth Ceredigion 327
Llanbedr N W Wales 344
Llanbedrgoch Anglesey 319
Llanbedrog N W Wales 345
Llanberis N W Wales 345
Llanbister Powys 361
Llanbrynmair Powys 361
Llancynfelyn Pembs 353
Llandanwg N W Wales 345
Llanddarog Carmarthen 323
Llandderfel N W Wales 345
Llanddeusant Carmarthen 323
Llanddulas N W Wales 345
Llandovery Carmarthen 323
Llandow Glamorgan 334
Llandre Ceredigion 327
Llandrillo Den & Fl 331
Llandrindod Wells Powys 361
Llandwrog N W Wales 345
Llandyfaelog Carmarthen 323
Llandysul Ceredigion 327
Llanegryn N W Wales 345
Llaneilian Anglesey 319
Llanellen Monmouth 337
Llanfaes Anglesey 319
Llanfaethlu Anglesey 319
Llanfair N W Wales 345
Llanfairpwllgwyngyll Anglesey 319
Llanfarian Ceredigion 327
Llanfihangel-y-pennant (Abergynolwyn)
 N W Wales. 345
Llanforda Shrops. 147
Llanfwrog Anglesey 320
Llangadog Carmarthen 323
Llangeitho Ceredigion 327
Llangennith Glamorgan. 334
Llangollen Den & Fl 331
Llangorse Powys 361
Llangranog Ceredigion 327
Llangwnnadl N W Wales 345
Llangybi Ceredigion 328
Llangynidr Powys 361
Llangynog Powys 362
Llanidloes Powys 362
Llanon Ceredigion 328
Llanrhystud Ceredigion 328
Llanrug N W Wales 345
Llanrwst N W Wales 346
Llansantffraid Ceredigion 328
Llansantffraid-ym-Mechain Powys . . 362
Llansilin Powys 362
Llansteffan Carmarthen 323
Llanteg Pembs. 353
Llanthony Monmouth 337
Llantilio Crossenny Monmouth 337
Llantwit Major Glamorgan 334
Llanuwchllyn N W Wales 346
Llanwrda Carmarthen 323
Llanwrin Powys 362
Llanychaer Pembs. 353
Llanycil N W Wales 346
Llanystumdwy N W Wales 346
Lloc Den & Fl. 331
Llwyngwril N W Wales 346
Llysfaen N W Wales 346
Loch Eck Argyll 266

Lochearnhead Stirling 314
Lochfoot D & G 277
Lochgilphead Argyll 266
Lochinver Highland. 293
Lochmaben D & G 277
Lochmaddy, N Uist W Isl 317
Lochranza, Arran Ayrshire 269
Lockerbie D & G 277
Locking Somer 154
Lockton N Yorks 199
Lofthouse N Yorks 199
Loftus Tees 178
London Apprentice Corn 21
Londonderry Londonderry 220
Long Lawford Warks 181
Long Sutton Lincs 115
Longhorsley Northumb. 135
Longniddry Lothian 306
Longnor Staffs 160
Longridge Lancs 107
Longstanton Cambs 11
Longthwaite Cumb 39
Longtown Cumb. 39
Longville-in-the-Dale Shrops 148
Looe Corn 21
Lossiemouth Aberdeen 260
Lostwithiel Corn. 21
Lothersdale N Yorks 200
Lough Feeagh Mayo 244
Loughton Essex 79
Louisburgh Mayo 244
Low Bentham N Yorks 200
Low Burnham Lincs. 115
Low Lorton Cumb 39
Low Wray Cumb. 39
Lower Withington Cheshire. 13
Lowestoft Suffolk 165
Lowgill Cumb 39
Luccombe Somer 154
Luddenden W Yorks 210
Luib, Skye Inn Heb 299
Lundy Devon 61
Lupton Cumb 39
Lurgan Armagh 215
Luss Argyll 266
Luxulyan Corn 21
Lydford Devon. 61
Lydstep Pembs 353
Lympsham Somer. 154
Lynbridge Devon. 61
Lyndhurst Hants. 89
Lyneal Shrops 148
Lynton Devon 61
Lytchett Matravers Dorset 71
Lytchett Minster Dorset 71
Lytham St Annes Lancs. 107

M

Mablethorpe Lincs 115
Macduff Aberdeen 260
Machrihanish Argyll 266
Machynlleth Powys 362
Maenporth Corn 21
Maentwrog N W Wales 346
Maesheini Den & Fl 331
Magilligan Londonderry 221
Maidenhead Berks 4
Mainstone Shrops 148
Malborough Devon 61
Malham N Yorks 200
Mallaig Highland 293
Malltraeth Anglesey 320
Malmesbury Wilts 184

Location Index

Location	Page
Malvern *Worcs*	187
Malvern Wells *Worcs*	187
Manby *Lincs*	115
Manchester, Central *Gtr Manc*	86
Mankinholes *W Yorks*	210
Manorbier *Pembs*	353
Mansfield Woodhouse *Notts*	138
Manston *Kent*	102
Marazion *Corn*	21
March *Cambs*	11
Marden *Kent*	102
Margate *Kent*	103
Marian-glas *Anglesey*	320
Mark *Somer*	154
Market Bosworth *Leics*	110
Market Deeping *Lincs*	115
Market Rasen *Lincs*	115
Markethill *Armagh*	215
Markham Moor *Notts*	138
Markinch *Fife*	281
Markington *N Yorks*	200
Marlborough *Wilts*	184
Marldon *Devon*	61
Marlingford *Norfolk*	125
Marloes *Pembs*	353
Marros *Carmarthen*	324
Marsden *T & W*	179
Marston Meysey *Wilts*	184
Martock *Somer*	154
Mary Mount *Cumb*	39
Maryculter *Aberdeen*	260
Mathon *Heref*	92
Matlock *Derby*	51
Matlock Moor *Derby*	51
Mavis Enderby *Lincs*	115
Mawgan *Corn*	21
Mawgan Porth *Corn*	21
Maybole *Ayrshire*	270
Maypool *Devon*	62
Mealsgate *Cumb*	39
Meerbrook *Staffs*	160
Mellwaters *Durham*	76
Melplash *Dorset*	71
Melrose *Borders*	273
Melverley *Shrops*	148
Melvich *Highland*	293
Memus *Angus*	263
Menston *W Yorks*	210
Mere Brow *Lancs*	107
Meriden *W Mids*	182
Meshaw *Devon*	62
Metheringham *Lincs*	115
Michaelchurch Escley *Heref*	92
Middle Rasen *Lincs*	116
Middle Town *Scilly*	99
Middlesbrough *Tees*	178
Middleton *Lancs*	107
Middleton in Teesdale *Durham*	76
Middletown *Powys*	362
Midhurst *W Suss*	176
Midleton *Cork*	227
Milford on Sea *Hants*	89
Millbrook *Corn*	22
Miller's Dale *Derby*	51
Millisle *Down*	217
Millom *Cumb*	40
Milnthorpe *Cumb*	40
Milton *Pembs*	353
Milton Ash *Somer*	154
Minehead *Somer*	154
Minnigaff *D & G*	277
Minster in Sheppey *Kent*	103
Mintlaw *Aberdeen*	260

Location	Page
Mitchel Troy *Monmouth*	337
Mockerkin *Cumb*	40
Modbury *Devon*	62
Moelfre *Anglesey*	320
Moffat *D & G*	277
Molland *Devon*	62
Mollington *Oxon*	142
Moneymore *Londonderry*	221
Monifieth *Angus*	263
Monmouth *Monmouth*	337
Monreith *D & G*	277
Montgomery *Powys*	362
Montrose *Angus*	263
Morcombelake *Dorset*	72
Mordiford *Heref*	92
Morecambe *Lancs*	107
Moreton *Dorset*	72
Moreton *Oxon*	142
Moreton on Lugg *Heref*	92
Moreton Valence *Gloucs*	82
Moreton-in-Marsh *Gloucs*	82
Morfa Bychan *N W Wales*	346
Morpeth *Northumb*	135
Morriston *Glamorgan*	334
Mortehoe *Devon*	62
Morvich (Shiel Bridge) *Highland*	293
Motherwell *Lanark*	302
Mountshannon *Clare*	225
Mountstuart, Bute *Argyll*	265
Mouswald *D & G*	277
Moville *Donegal*	229
Muasdale *Argyll*	266
Much Wenlock *Shrops*	148
Muchelney *Somer*	155
Muker *N Yorks*	200
Mull, Isle of *Inn Heb*	298
Mullion *Corn*	22
Mullion Cove *Corn*	22
Mundesley *Norfolk*	125
Mutford *Suffolk*	165
Mydroilyn *Ceredigion*	328
Mynachlog-ddu *Pembs*	353
Mynytho *N W Wales*	346
Mytchett *Surrey*	168

N

Naburn *N Yorks*	200
Nairn *Highland*	293
Nancegollan *Corn*	22
Nant Peris *N W Wales*	346
Nantgwynant *N W Wales*	346
Nantlle *N W Wales*	346
Nantmawr *Shrops*	148
Nantwich *Cheshire*	13
Narberth *Pembs*	353
Narborough *Norfolk*	125
Nawton *N Yorks*	200
Near Cotton *Staffs*	160
Nefyn *N W Wales*	346
Nentsberry *Cumb*	40
Nether Kellet *Lancs*	108
Nether Westcote *Oxon*	142
Netherhampton *Wilts*	184
New Cumnock *Ayrshire*	270
New Hedges *Pembs*	353
New Lanark *Lanark*	302
New Milton *Hants*	89
New Quay *Ceredigion*	328
New Romney *Kent*	103
New Ross *Wexford*	253
Newark *Notts*	138
Newbawn *Wexford*	253
Newbiggin in Bishopdale *N Yorks*	200

Location	Page
Newbiggin (Stainton) *Cumb*	40
Newbiggin-on-Lune *Cumb*	40
Newborough *Anglesey*	320
Newbourne *Suffolk*	165
Newbridge *I O W*	97
Newbridge on Wye *Powys*	362
Newburgh (Ellon) *Aberdeen*	260
Newbury *Berks*	4
Newby Bridge *Cumb*	40
Newcastle *Down*	217
Newcastle Emlyn *Carmarthen*	324
Newcastle-upon-Tyne *T & W*	179
Newchurch *I O W*	97
Newgale *Pembs*	354
Newhaven *Derby*	51
Newlands *Cumb*	40
Newmarket *Suffolk*	165
Newport *E Yorks*	190
Newport *Monmouth*	337
Newport *Pembs*	354
Newquay *Corn*	22
Newsham *N Yorks*	200
Newton *Northumb*	135
Newton Abbot *Devon*	62
Newton in Bowland *Lancs*	108
Newton Poppleford *Devon*	62
Newton St Loe *Somer*	155
Newton Stewart *D & G*	277
Newtonmore *Highland*	293
Newtownabbey *Antrim*	214
Ninebanks *Northumb*	135
Nolton Haven *Pembs*	354
Nomansland *Devon*	62
Norden *Dorset*	72
Norman's Bay *E Suss*	172
North Berwick *Lothian*	306
North Kessock *Highland*	293
North Kilworth *Leics*	110
North Pickenham *Norfolk*	125
North Runcton *Norfolk*	125
North Shawbost, Lewis *W Isl*	317
North Stainley *N Yorks*	200
North Uist, Isle of *W Isl*	317
North Walsham *Norfolk*	126
North Wootton *Somer*	155
Northam *Devon*	62
Northgate *Lincs*	116
Northrepps *Norfolk*	126
Northwood *I O W*	97
Norton *Gloucs*	82
Norwich *Norfolk*	126
Nostell *W Yorks*	210
Nottage *Glamorgan*	334
Nottingham *Notts*	138
Nutbourne (Horsham) *W Suss*	176

O

O'Brien's Bridge *Clare*	225
Oakdale *Glamorgan*	334
Oare *Somer*	155
Oare *Wilts*	184
Oban *Argyll*	266
Odiham *Hants*	89
Offcote *Derby*	51
Okehampton *Devon*	63
Old Leake *Lincs*	116
Old Scone *Perth*	311
Oldshoremore *Highland*	293
Olney *Bucks*	8
Omeath *Louth*	242
Once Brewed *Northumb*	135
Onich *Highland*	294
Orby *Lincs*	116

Stilwell's Hostels & Camping 2002   371

Location Index

Orcheston Wilts ... 184	Perranwell Corn ... 24	Preesall Lancs ... 108
Ore E Suss ... 172	Perrotts Brook Gloucs ... 82	Prestatyn Den & Fl ... 332
Organford Dorset ... 72	Perth Perth ... 311	Presteigne Powys ... 362
Ormesby St Margaret Norfolk ... 126	Peterborough Cambs ... 11	Preston Dorset ... 72
Ormskirk Lancs ... 108	Peterchurch Heref ... 92	Priddy Somer ... 155
Osmaston (Ashbourne) Derby ... 51	Petham Kent ... 103	Princetown Devon ... 63
Osmington Mills Dorset ... 72	Pett E Suss ... 173	Pulham St Mary Norfolk ... 126
Osmotherley N Yorks ... 200	Pevensey E Suss ... 173	Puncknowle Dorset ... 72
Oswaldkirk N Yorks ... 200	Pevensey Bay E Suss ... 173	Pwllheli N W Wales ... 347
Otterham Corn ... 22	Phibsboro, Dublin Co Dublin ... 230	Pyworthy Devon ... 63
Oulton Broad Suffolk ... 165	Pickering N Yorks ... 201	
Ousby Cumb ... 40	Pinchbeck Lincs ... 116	**Q**
Outgate Cumb ... 40	Pistyll N W Wales ... 347	Quintrell Downs Corn ... 25
Over Haddon Derby ... 51	Pitlochry Perth ... 311	**R**
Overton-on-Dee Den & Fl ... 332	Plwmp Ceredigion ... 328	
Ower Hants ... 90	Plymouth Devon ... 63	Raasay, Isle of Inn Heb ... 298
Owermoigne Dorset ... 72	Plympton Devon ... 63	Rackwick, Hoy Orkney ... 308
Oxenhope W Yorks ... 210	Polegate E Suss ... 173	Radcliffe on Trent Notts ... 139
Oxford Oxon ... 142	Polesden Lacey Surrey ... 168	Radcot Oxon ... 142
Oxwich Glamorgan ... 334	Polladras Corn ... 24	Radwell Herts ... 95
	Polperro Corn ... 24	Raisbeck Cumb ... 41
P	Polruan Corn ... 24	Ramsgate Kent ... 103
Paddock Wood Kent ... 103	Polzeath Corn ... 24	Rathangan Kildare ... 238
Padstow Corn ... 22	Pondwell I O W ... 97	Ratlinghope Shrops ... 148
Paignton Devon ... 63	Ponsongath Corn ... 24	Rattery Devon ... 64
Pakefield Suffolk ... 165	Pont Pen-y-benglog N W Wales ... 347	Rattray Perth ... 311
Palnackie D & G ... 277	Pont-rug N W Wales ... 347	Ravenglass Cumb ... 41
Panborough Somer ... 155	Pont-y-Pant N W Wales ... 347	Ravenscar N Yorks ... 201
Pandy Monmouth ... 337	Ponterwyd Ceredigion ... 328	Ravenstonedale Cumb ... 41
Pant Shrops ... 148	Pontllyfni N W Wales ... 347	Ravenstruther Lanark ... 302
Papa Stour Shetland ... 312	Pontrhydfendigaid Ceredigion ... 328	Reay Highland ... 294
Papa Westray Orkney ... 308	Pontwelly Ceredigion ... 328	Red Wharf Bay Anglesey ... 320
Par Corn ... 22	Poole Dorset ... 72	Redbrook Gloucs ... 83
Parracombe Devon ... 63	Poolewe Highland ... 294	Redcross Wicklow ... 256
Parrog Pembs ... 354	Pooley Bridge Cumb ... 41	Redenhall Norfolk ... 126
Parton D & G ... 278	Poppit Sands Pembs ... 354	Redhill Somer ... 155
Patcham E Suss ... 173	Porlock Somer ... 155	Redruth Corn ... 25
Pateley Bridge N Yorks ... 200	Port Carlisle Cumb ... 41	Reedham Norfolk ... 126
Patterdale Cumb ... 40	Port Charlotte, Islay Inn Heb ... 298	Reen Kerry ... 237
Peak Dale Derby ... 51	Port Ellen, Islay Inn Heb ... 298	Regent's Park London ... 120
Peebles Borders ... 273	Port Eynon Glamorgan ... 334	Reighton N Yorks ... 201
Peel I Man ... 212	Port Talbot Glamorgan ... 335	Rejerrah Corn ... 25
Pelcomb Bridge Pembs ... 354	Port William D & G ... 278	Relubbus Corn ... 25
Pelcomb Cross Pembs ... 354	Portaferry Down ... 217	Renvyle Galway ... 234
Pembroke Pembs ... 354	Portballintrae Antrim ... 214	Repps with Bastwick Norfolk ... 126
Pen-y-Pass N W Wales ... 347	Portesham Dorset ... 72	Resipole Highland ... 294
Penarth Glamorgan ... 334	Portglenone Antrim ... 214	Rewe Devon ... 64
Penbryn Ceredigion ... 328	Porth Corn ... 24	Reynalton Pembs ... 355
Pencelli Powys ... 362	Porthcawl Glamorgan ... 335	Rhandirmwyn Carmarthen ... 324
Pencombe Heref ... 92	Porthmadog N W Wales ... 347	Rhayader Powys ... 362
Pendeen Corn ... 23	Porthtowan Corn ... 24	Rhenigidale, Harris W Isl ... 317
Penhale Corn ... 23	Portland Dorset ... 72	Rhiwderin Monmouth ... 338
Penistone S Yorks ... 206	Portlaoise Laois ... 240	Rhos Lligwy Anglesey ... 320
Penmaen Glamorgan ... 334	Portnablagh Donegal ... 229	Rhos-on-Sea N W Wales ... 348
Penmaenmawr N W Wales ... 347	Portnalong, Skye Inn Heb ... 299	Rhos-y-gwaliau N W Wales ... 348
Penparc Ceredigion ... 328	Portnoo Donegal ... 229	Rhoscolyn Anglesey ... 320
Penpont D & G ... 278	Portpatrick D & G ... 278	Rhosgoch Powys ... 362
Penrhyndeudraeth N W Wales ... 347	Portreath Corn ... 24	Rhoshirwaun N W Wales ... 348
Penrith Cumb ... 40	Portree, Skye Inn Heb ... 299	Rhoslan N W Wales ... 348
Penruddock Cumb ... 41	Portrush Antrim ... 214	Rhoslefain N W Wales ... 348
Penryn Corn ... 23	Portsalon Donegal ... 229	Rhosneigr Anglesey ... 320
Pentewan Corn ... 23	Portscatho Corn ... 24	Rhossili Glamorgan ... 335
Pentraeth Anglesey ... 320	Portskewett Monmouth ... 337	Rhuallt Den & Fl ... 332
Pentre Berw Anglesey ... 320	Portsmouth Hants ... 90	Rhyd-Ddu N W Wales ... 348
Pentre Saron Den & Fl ... 332	Portsoy Aberdeen ... 260	Rhydlewis Ceredigion ... 328
Pentredwr Den & Fl ... 332	Portstewart Londonderry ... 221	Rhydymain N W Wales ... 348
Pentrefelin (Porthmadog) N W Wales ... 347	Potter Heigham Norfolk ... 126	Ribblehead N Yorks ... 201
Penwithick Corn ... 23	Poughill Corn ... 24	Richmond N Yorks ... 201
Penycwm Pembs ... 354	Poulton-le-Fylde Lancs ... 108	Ridge Dorset ... 72
Penysarn Anglesey ... 320	Poundsgate Devon ... 63	Ridgmont Beds ... 3
Penzance Corn ... 23	Poundstock Corn ... 25	Ripon N Yorks ... 201
Perranarworthal Corn ... 23	Powfoot D & G ... 278	Riseley Berks ... 4
Perranporth Corn ... 23	Poynton Cheshire ... 13	Robin Hood's Bay N Yorks ... 201

Location Index

Roch *Pembs* . . . 355
Rochdale *Gtr Manc* . . . 86
Rockcliffe *D & G* . . . 278
Rodney Stoke *Somer* . . . 155
Roecliffe *N Yorks* . . . 202
Romansleigh *Devon* . . . 64
Romsley *Worcs* . . . 187
Rosbeg *Donegal* . . . 229
Rosebush *Pembs* . . . 355
Rosehearty *Aberdeen* . . . 260
Rosemarket *Pembs* . . . 355
Rosemarkie *Highland* . . . 294
Roslin *Lothian* . . . 306
Ross-on-Wye *Heref* . . . 92
Rosses Point *Sligo* . . . 247
Rosslare *Wexford* . . . 253
Rosslare Harbour *Wexford* . . . 253
Rosthwaite (Borrowdale) *Cumb* . . . 41
Rostrevor *Down* . . . 217
Rotherhithe *London* . . . 120
Roundhay, Leeds *W Yorks* . . . 210
Roundwood *Wicklow* . . . 256
Roundyhill *Angus* . . . 263
Rousdon *Devon* . . . 64
Rowardennan *Stirling* . . . 314
Rowde *Wilts* . . . 185
Rowen *N W Wales* . . . 348
Rowlands Gill *T & W* . . . 179
Rowsley *Derby* . . . 52
Roybridge *Highland* . . . 294
Roydon *Essex* . . . 79
Rozel *Jersey* . . . 2
Ruan Minor *Corn* . . . 25
Ruckland *Lincs* . . . 116
Rudston *E Yorks* . . . 190
Rugeley *Staffs* . . . 160
Rumford *Corn* . . . 25
Runswick Bay *N Yorks* . . . 202
Runwayskiln *Pembs* . . . 355
Rush *Co Dublin* . . . 230
Ruthernbridge *Corn* . . . 25
Ruthin *Den & Fl* . . . 332
Ryde *I O W* . . . 97

S

Saffron Walden *Essex* . . . 80
Salcombe Regis *Devon* . . . 64
Salisbury *Wilts* . . . 185
Salmonby *Lincs* . . . 116
Saltash *Corn* . . . 25
Saltburn-by-the-Sea *Tees* . . . 178
Salterforth *Lancs* . . . 108
Sampford Courtenay *Devon* . . . 64
Sampford Peverell *Devon* . . . 64
Sand *Somer* . . . 155
Sandbank *Argyll* . . . 267
Sandend *Aberdeen* . . . 260
Sandhead *D & G* . . . 278
Sandown *I O W* . . . 97
Sandringham *Norfolk* . . . 126
Sandwich *Kent* . . . 103
Sandwith *Cumb* . . . 41
Sandyhills *D & G* . . . 278
Sanquhar *D & G* . . . 278
Saracen's Head *Lincs* . . . 116
Sark *Sark* . . . 2
Sarn Bach *N W Wales* . . . 348
Sarnau *Ceredigion* . . . 328
Saron (Llanwnda) *N W Wales* . . . 348
Saundersfoot *Pembs* . . . 355
Saxmundham *Suffolk* . . . 165
Scalby *N Yorks* . . . 202
Scaniport *Highland* . . . 294
Scarborough *N Yorks* . . . 202
Scarisbrick *Lancs* . . . 108
Scawton *N Yorks* . . . 202
Scole *Norfolk* . . . 126
Scorrier *Corn* . . . 25
Scorton *N Yorks* . . . 202
Scotch Corner *N Yorks* . . . 202
Scourie *Highland* . . . 294
Scratby *Norfolk* . . . 126
Scrooby *Notts* . . . 139
Scunthorpe *Lincs* . . . 116
Sea Palling *Norfolk* . . . 126
Seaford *E Suss* . . . 173
Seahouses *Northumb* . . . 135
Seal *Kent* . . . 103
Seamer (Scarborough) *N Yorks* . . . 202
Seatoller *Cumb* . . . 41
Seaton *Devon* . . . 64
Seatown *Dorset* . . . 72
Sedbergh *Cumb* . . . 41
Sedlescombe *E Suss* . . . 173
Seend *Wilts* . . . 185
Seer Green *Bucks* . . . 8
Selkirk *Borders* . . . 273
Selsey *W Suss* . . . 176
Selstead *Kent* . . . 103
Sennen *Corn* . . . 25
Settle *N Yorks* . . . 202
Severn Beach *Gloucs* . . . 83
Sewerby *E Yorks* . . . 190
Shadingfield *Suffolk* . . . 165
Shadwell *Norfolk* . . . 126
Shaftesbury *Dorset* . . . 73
Shaldon *Devon* . . . 64
Shankill *Co Dublin* . . . 230
Shanklin *I O W* . . . 97
Shardlow *Derby* . . . 52
Sharpitor *Devon* . . . 64
Shaugh Prior *Devon* . . . 64
Sheerness *Kent* . . . 103
Sheffield *S Yorks* . . . 206
Shelford *Notts* . . . 139
Shelve *Shrops* . . . 148
Sherfield English *Hants* . . . 90
Sheriff Hutton *N Yorks* . . . 202
Sheringham *Norfolk* . . . 127
Shevington *Gtr Manc* . . . 86
Shiel Bridge *Highland* . . . 294
Shipham *Somer* . . . 155
Shipley *W Yorks* . . . 211
Shipston on Stour *Warks* . . . 181
Shobdon *Heref* . . . 93
Shoeburyness *Essex* . . . 80
Shoreswood *Northumb* . . . 135
Shortgate *E Suss* . . . 173
Shortlanesend *Corn* . . . 25
Shorwell *I O W* . . . 97
Shotley Bridge *Durham* . . . 76
Shottisham *Suffolk* . . . 165
Shrawley *Worcs* . . . 187
Shrewsbury *Shrops* . . . 148
Sibbertoft *Northants* . . . 130
Sidcot *Somer* . . . 155
Siddington *Cheshire* . . . 13
Sidley *E Suss* . . . 173
Sidmouth *Devon* . . . 64
Silecroft *Cumb* . . . 41
Silloth *Cumb* . . . 41
Silsden *W Yorks* . . . 211
Silverdale *Lancs* . . . 108
Silverknowes, Edinburgh *Lothian* . . . 306
Sinderby *N Yorks* . . . 202
Singleton *Lancs* . . . 108
Sixpenny Handley *Dorset* . . . 73
Skegness *Lincs* . . . 116
Skelmorlie *Ayrshire* . . . 270
Skelsmergh *Cumb* . . . 41
Skiddaw *Cumb* . . . 42
Skipsea *E Yorks* . . . 190
Skrinkle *Pembs* . . . 355
Skye, Isle of *Inn Heb* . . . 298
Slaidburn *Lancs* . . . 108
Slapton *Devon* . . . 64
Sligachan, Skye *Inn Heb* . . . 299
Sligo *Sligo* . . . 247
Slimbridge *Gloucs* . . . 83
Slindon *W Suss* . . . 176
Slingsby *N Yorks* . . . 202
Small Dole *W Suss* . . . 176
Smoo *Highland* . . . 295
Snainton *N Yorks* . . . 202
Snead *Powys* . . . 362
Sneaton *N Yorks* . . . 202
Snettisham *Norfolk* . . . 127
Snitterfield *Warks* . . . 181
Soar *Devon* . . . 64
Soho *London* . . . 121
Solva *Pembs* . . . 355
South Brent *Devon* . . . 65
South Cave *E Yorks* . . . 190
South Cerney *Gloucs* . . . 83
South Kensington *London* . . . 121
South Kilvington *N Yorks* . . . 203
South Laggan *Highland* . . . 295
South Shields *T & W* . . . 179
South Uist, Isle of *W Isl* . . . 317
South Wingfield *Derby* . . . 52
Southam *Warks* . . . 181
Southbourne *W Suss* . . . 176
Southend *Argyll* . . . 267
Southerness *D & G* . . . 278
Southgate *Glamorgan* . . . 335
Southport *Mersey* . . . 86
Southsea *Hants* . . . 90
Southwater *W Suss* . . . 176
Southwold *Suffolk* . . . 165
Sowerby *N Yorks* . . . 203
Spalding *Lincs* . . . 117
Spalford *Notts* . . . 139
Spanish Point *Clare* . . . 225
Sparkford *Somer* . . . 155
Sparsholt *Hants* . . . 90
Spean Bridge *Highland* . . . 295
Spittal *Northumb* . . . 135
Sproatley *E Yorks* . . . 190
St Agnes *Corn* . . . 26
St Agnes *Scilly* . . . 99
St Andrews *Fife* . . . 281
St Audries *Somer* . . . 155
St Austell *Corn* . . . 26
St Bees *Cumb* . . . 42
St Brelade *Jersey* . . . 2
St Briavels *Gloucs* . . . 83
St Buryan *Corn* . . . 26
St Clears *Carmarthen* . . . 324
St Columb Major *Corn* . . . 26
St Cyrus *Aberdeen* . . . 260
St Davids *Pembs* . . . 355
St Day *Corn* . . . 26
St Dogmaels *Pembs* . . . 356
St Eval *Corn* . . . 26
St Ewe *Corn* . . . 26
St Gennys *Corn* . . . 26
St Germans *Corn* . . . 26
St Giles on the Heath *Devon* . . . 65
St Helens *I O W* . . . 97

Stilwell's Hostels & Camping 2002 373

Location Index

St Hilary *Corn* 26
St Issey *Corn* 26
St Ives *Corn* 26
St John's *I Man* 212
St John's Fen End *Norfolk* 127
St Johns-in-the-Vale *Cumb* 42
St Just-in-Penwith *Corn* 27
St Just-in-Roseland *Corn* 27
St Keverne *Corn* 27
St Kew Highway *Corn* 27
St Lawrence *Essex* 80
St Lawrence *I O W* 98
St Leonards *Dorset* 73
St Mabyn *Corn* 27
St Margarets *Heref* 93
St Martin *Jersey* 2
St Martin *Corn* 27
St Mary's *Scilly* 99
St Merryn *Corn* 27
St Minver *Corn* 27
St Monans *Fife* 281
St Neot *Corn* 28
St Neots *Cambs* 11
St Nicholas at Wade *Kent* 103
St Osyth *Essex* 80
St Paul's *London* 121
St Sampson *Guernsey* 1
Staffin, Skye *Inn Heb* 299
Stainforth *N Yorks* 203
Stainsacre *N Yorks* 203
Staintondale *N Yorks* 203
Stalmine *Lancs* 109
Stamford Bridge *E Yorks* 190
Stanbury *W Yorks* 211
Standlake *Oxon* 143
Stanford Bridge *Worcs* 187
Stanhoe *Norfolk* 127
Stanhope *Durham* 76
Stannington, Sheffield *S Yorks* 206
Stansted *Kent* 103
Starcross *Devon* 65
Staxton *N Yorks* 203
Steep *Hants* 90
Steeple *Essex* 80
Stelling Minnis *Kent* 103
Stepaside *Pembs* 356
Stepps *Glasgow* 284
Sternfield *Suffolk* 165
Steventon *Oxon* 143
Steyning *W Suss* 176
Sticklepath *Devon* 65
Stickney *Lincs* 117
Stillingfleet *N Yorks* 203
Stirling *Stirling* 314
Stoborough *Dorset* 73
Stoke Fleming *Devon* 65
Stoke Gabriel *Devon* 65
Stoke St Michael *Somer* 155
Stokenham *Devon* 65
Stonehaven *Aberdeen* 261
Stonehouse *Gloucs* 83
Stonethwaite *Cumb* 42
Stoney Middleton *Derby* 52
Stornoway, Lewis *W Isl* 317
Stourport-on-Severn *Worcs* 187
Stow-on-the-Wold *Gloucs* 83
Stowbridge *Norfolk* 127
Stowupland *Suffolk* 165
Strachan *Aberdeen* 261
Straiton *Ayrshire* 270
Strandhill *Sligo* 247
Strangford *Down* 217
Stranraer *D & G* 278
Stratford-upon-Avon *Warks* 181
Strath (Gairloch) *Highland* 295
Strathpeffer *Highland* 295
Strathyre *Stirling* 315
Streatley *Berks* 4
Street *Somer* 156
Strensall *N Yorks* 203
Stretham *Cambs* 11
Stretton *Derby* 52
Stretton-on-Dunsmore *Warks* 181
Stromness *Orkney* 308
Strontian *Highland* 295
Sudbury *Suffolk* 165
Summerbridge *N Yorks* 203
Summercourt *Corn* 28
Sutton Coldfield *W Mids* 182
Sutton Lane Ends *Cheshire* 13
Sutton on Sea *Lincs* 117
Sutton St Edmund *Lincs* 117
Sutton St James *Lincs* 117
Sutton upon Derwent *E Yorks* 190
Swaffham *Norfolk* 127
Swanage *Dorset* 73
Swansea *Glamorgan* 335
Swinderby *Lincs* 117
Syderstone *Norfolk* 127
Symonds Yat West *Heref* 93
Synod Inn *Ceredigion* 329
Sywell *Northants* 130

T

Tain (Dornoch Firth) *Highland* 295
Tal-y-Bont (Barmouth) *N W Wales* 348
Tal-y-Bont (Conwy) *N W Wales* 349
Tal-y-llyn *N W Wales* 349
Talgarth *Powys* 362
Tallington *Lincs* 117
Talmine *Highland* 295
Talsarnau *N W Wales* 349
Tansley *Derby* 52
Tarbolton *Ayrshire* 270
Tarland *Aberdeen* 261
Tarrington *Heref* 93
Tattershall *Lincs* 117
Tattershall Bridge *Lincs* 117
Taunton *Somer* 156
Tavernspite *Pembs* 356
Tavistock *Devon* 65
Tayinloan *Argyll* 267
Taynuilt *Argyll* 267
Tayport *Fife* 281
Tayvallich *Argyll* 267
Tebay *Cumb* 42
Tedburn St Mary *Devon* 65
Teigngrace *Devon* 65
Telford *Shrops* 148
Telscombe *E Suss* 173
Tenbury Wells *Worcs* 187
Tenby *Pembs* 356
Teversal *Notts* 139
Tewkesbury *Gloucs* 83
The Lizard *Corn* 28
Theberton *Suffolk* 165
Thirsk *N Yorks* 203
Thixendale *N Yorks* 203
Thorn Falcon *Somer* 156
Thornaby-on-Tees *Tees* 178
Thornham Magna *Suffolk* 165
Thornhill *Stirling* 315
Thornthwaite *Cumb* 42
Thornton Cleveleys *Lancs* 109
Thrapston *Northants* 130
Three Cocks *Powys* 363
Three Legged Cross *Dorset* 73
Threshfield *N Yorks* 203
Thrybergh *S Yorks* 207
Thurlby (Bourne) *Lincs* 117
Thurso *Highland* 295
Thurstaston *Mersey* 86
Thurston *Suffolk* 166
Tibenham *Norfolk* 127
Tiddington *Warks* 181
Tighnabruaich *Argyll* 267
Tilford *Surrey* 168
Tilshead *Wilts* 185
Timoleague *Cork* 227
Tintagel *Corn* 28
Tintern *Monmouth* 338
Tiptree *Essex* 80
Tiverton *Devon* 65
Tobermory, Mull *Inn Heb* 298
Tollerton *N Yorks* 203
Tomintoul *Aberdeen* 261
Tongue *Highland* 296
Topsham Bridge *Devon* 65
Tormarton *Gloucs* 83
Torquay *Devon* 66
Torridon *Highland* 296
Torteval *Guernsey* 1
Torver *Cumb* 42
Totland Bay *I O W* 98
Tow Law *Durham* 76
Towednack *Corn* 28
Towyn *N W Wales* 349
Tralee *Kerry* 237
Tramore *Waterford* 250
Trawden *Lancs* 109
Trearddur *Anglesey* 321
Trearddur Bay *Anglesey* 321
Tredegar *Monmouth* 338
Trefasser *Pembs* 357
Trefin *Pembs* 357
Trefriw *N W Wales* 349
Tregaron *Ceredigion* 329
Tregurrian *Corn* 28
Trelawne *Corn* 28
Trematon *Corn* 28
Trentham *Staffs* 160
Tresaith *Ceredigion* 329
Trevellas *Corn* 28
Treverva *Corn* 28
Trevose Head *Corn* 28
Trewellard *Corn* 28
Treyarnon Bay *Corn* 29
Troutbeck (Penrith) *Cumb* 42
Troutbeck (Windermere) *Cumb* 42
Truleigh Hill *W Suss* 176
Truro *Corn* 29
Trusthorpe *Lincs* 117
Tudweiliog *N W Wales* 349
Tummel Bridge *Perth* 311
Tunstall *E Yorks* 190
Tuosist *Kerry* 237
Turriff *Aberdeen* 261
Tuxford *Notts* 139
Ty'n-y-Cornel *Powys* 363
Ty-nant (Maerdy) *N W Wales* 349
Tydd Gote *Lincs* 117
Tyndwr *Den & Fl* 332
Tywyn (Aberdovey) *N W Wales* 349

U

Uffculme *Devon* 66
Ugthorpe *N Yorks* 203
Uig (Uig Bay), Skye *Inn Heb* 300
Uist, North *W Isl* 317

374 Stilwell's Hostels & Camping 2002

Location Index

Entry	Page
Uist, South W Isl	317
Ullapool Highland	296
Ulleskelf N Yorks	203
Ullesthorpe Leics	110
Ulrome E Yorks	190
Ulverston Cumb	43
Ulwell Dorset	73
Umberleigh Devon	66
Under Loughrigg Cumb	43
Underskiddaw Cumb	43
Uploders Dorset	73
Uplyme Devon	66
Upper Broughton Notts	139
Upper Heyford Oxon	143
Upper Largo Fife	281
Uppingham Rutland	144
Upton Somer	156
Urray Highland	296
Uton Devon	66
Uttoxeter Staffs	160
Uwchmynydd N W Wales	349

V

Entry	Page
Vale Guernsey	2
Van Powys	363
Venton (Whiddon Down) Devon	66
Ventry Kerry	237
Verwig Ceredigion	329
Veryan Corn	29

W

Entry	Page
Waddington Lancs	109
Wadebridge Corn	29
Wainfleet Bank Lincs	117
Waldringfield Suffolk	166
Walesby Lincs	117
Walmer Kent	103
Waltham Cross Herts	95
Walton Powys	363
Wandon Staffs	160
Wanlockhead D & G	279
Wareham Dorset	74
Waren Mill Northumb	136
Warmwell Dorset	74
Warningcamp W Suss	177
Warrington Cheshire	13
Warsash Hants	90
Wasdale Head Cumb	43
Wasdale (Nether Wasdale) Cumb	43
Wash Water Berks	5
Washington W Suss	177
Watchet Somer	156
Waterhead Cumb	43
Watermillock Cumb	43
Watermouth Devon	66
Waterville Kerry	237
Watton Norfolk	127
Waunfawr N W Wales	350
Weare Giffard Devon	66
Week St Mary Corn	29
Weeley Essex	80
Weeton Lancs	109
Wellington Cumb	43
Wells Somer	156
Wells-next-the-Sea Norfolk	127
Welsh Bicknor Gloucs	84
Welshpool Powys	363
Wem Shrops	149
Wentnor Shrops	149
West Ashby Lincs	117
West Bay Dorset	74
West Bradford Lancs	109
West Burton N Yorks	204
West Down Devon	66
West Kingsdown Kent	103
West Lulworth Dorset	74
West Mersea Essex	80
West Moors Dorset	74
West Quantoxhead Somer	156
West Runton Norfolk	127
West Wick Somer	156
West Wittering W Suss	177
West Witton N Yorks	204
West Woodlands Somer	156
Westgate in Weardale Durham	76
Westham E Suss	173
Westhay Somer	156
Westhill Aberdeen	261
Weston-super-Mare Somer	156
Westport Mayo	244
Westward Cumb	43
Westwell Kent	103
Wetherby W Yorks	211
Wethersfield Essex	80
Wetton Staffs	160
Wexford Wexford	253
Weybourne Norfolk	127
Weymouth Dorset	74
Whaddon Wilts	185
Whatstandwell Derby	52
Wheathill Shrops	149
Wheddon Cross Somer	156
Whiddon Down Devon	66
Whissendine Rutland	144
Whitby N Yorks	204
Whitchurch Shrops	149
Whitecross (Penzance) Corn	29
Whitecross (Wadebridge) Corn	29
Whitegate Cheshire	13
Whitehills Aberdeen	261
Whiteparish Wilts	185
Whitgift E Yorks	190
Whithorn D & G	279
Whiting Bay, Arran Ayrshire	269
Whitstable Kent	104
Whitstone Corn	29
Whittington Norfolk	127
Whitton Northumb	136
Whixall Shrops	149
Widecombe in the Moor Devon	67
Widemouth Bay Corn	29
Wigan Gtr Manc	86
Wilberfoss E Yorks	190
Willingham Cambs	11
Wilmington Devon	67
Wimborne Minster Dorset	74
Wincanton Somer	156
Winchelsea Beach E Suss	173
Winchester Hants	90
Windermere Cumb	44
Windsor Berks	5
Wing Rutland	144
Winkleigh Devon	67
Winksley N Yorks	204
Winmarleigh Lancs	109
Winsford Somer	157
Winsley Wilts	185
Winston Durham	77
Winterborne Whitechurch Dorset	74
Wirksworth Derby	52
Wisborough Green W Suss	177
Wisemans Bridge Pembs	357
Wiston W Suss	177
Wistow N Yorks	204
Witton-le-Wear Durham	77
Wiveliscombe Somer	157
Wiveton Norfolk	128
Wolverley Worcs	187
Wolvey Warks	181
Woodbridge Suffolk	166
Woodbury Devon	67
Woodbury Salterton Devon	67
Woodhall Spa Lincs	118
Woodland Cumb	44
Woodlands Dorset	74
Woodmancote (Henfield) W Suss	177
Woodthorpe Lincs	118
Wookey Hole Somer	157
Wool Dorset	74
Woolacombe Devon	67
Wooler Northumb	136
Wootton Hants	90
Wootton Bridge I O W	98
Worksop Notts	139
Worle Somer	157
Worsbrough S Yorks	207
Worstead Norfolk	128
Wortham Suffolk	166
Wortwell Norfolk	128
Wotton-under-Edge Gloucs	84
Wrawby Lincs	118
Wrelton N Yorks	204
Wrenbury Cheshire	13
Wrotham Heath Kent	104
Wroxall I O W	98
Wycliffe Durham	77
Wyke Regis Dorset	74
Wykeham (Scarborough) N Yorks	204

Y

Entry	Page
Yarrowford Borders	273
Yettington Devon	67
Ynys N W Wales	350
Ynyslas Ceredigion	329
York N Yorks	204
Youlgreave Derby	52
Ystradfellte Powys	363

Z

Entry	Page
Zennor Corn	29

Order a copy for a friend or colleague

I wish to order the following title(s):

__ **Stilwell's Hostels & Camping 2002** @ £8.95 (inc £1 p&p)
__ **Stilwell's Britain: Bed & Breakfast 2001** @ £11.95 (inc £2 p&p)
__ **Stilwell's Scotland: Bed & Breakfast 2001** @ £7.95 (inc £1 p&p)
__ **Stilwell's Ireland: Bed & Breakfast 2001** @ £7.95 (inc £1 p&p)
__ **Stilwell's National Trail Companion** @ £10.95 (inc £1 p&p)
__ **Stilwell's Cycleway Companion** @ £10.95 (inc £1 p&p)

Please send me my copy within 21 days of receipt of this order.

Name..
Address...
....Postcode................................
Telephone..
Email address..

Send this order form, with a cheque payable to Stilwell Publishing, to:
Copy sales, Stilwell Publishing, 59 Charlotte Road, London EC2A 3QW;
or

Please debit my Visa/Mastercard for the sum of £____.__
Card number: __ __ __ __ __ __ __ __ __ __ __ __ __ __ __ __   Exp __/__
Signature: ....
Please state cardholder name and address here, if different from above:
....